Resources for Teaching

THIRD EDITION

POETRY

An Introduction

21-63

Resources for Teaching

THIRD EDITION

POETRY
An Introduction

Michael Meyer
University of Connecticut, Storrs

Quentin Miller
Gustavus Adolphus College

Kathleen Morgan Drowne
University of North Carolina, Chapel Hill

Christine Francis
Central Connecticut State University

John Repp
Edinboro University of Pennsylvania

Jill McDonough
Boston University

BEDFORD/ST. MARTIN'S   BOSTON ◆ NEW YORK

For information, write: Bedford/St. Martin's, 75 Arlington Street, Boston, MA 02116
(617-399-4000)

ISBN: 0–312–25077–0

Contents

Preface

This instructor's manual is designed to be a resource of commentaries, interpretations, and suggestions for teaching the works included in *Poetry: An Introduction, Third Edition.* The entries offer advice about how to approach individual selections and suggest possible answers to many of the questions raised in the text. No attempt has been made to generate definitive readings of the works; the text selections are rich enough to accommodate multiple approaches and interpretations. Our hope is that instructors will take what they find useful and leave the rest behind. Inevitably, instructors will disagree with some of the commentaries, but perhaps such disagreements will provide starting points for class discussion.

In addition to offering approaches to selections, many of the entries suggest topics for discussion and writing. The format of the entries varies from itemized responses to specific questions to essays that present overviews of individual works. This flexibility allows each entry to be more responsive to the nature of a particular work and the questions asked about it in the text. Any time "Connections to Other Selections" questions are posed in the text at least one is answered in the manual for each selection, and all the entries include suggestions for further connections. The appendix listing selections linked by connections questions serves as a quick reference for instructors who are looking for ideas for pairing selections, and the information also appears with the appropriate individual entries for each selection. The manual includes selected bibliographies for authors treated in depth, and critical readings are mentioned throughout the manual when they are felt to be particularly useful resources for teaching a work. For more general bibliographic guides, see the annotated list of reference sources on pages 558–561of the main text.

The manual also provides instructors with additional resources for teaching the selections in the Album of World Literature and the Album of Contemporary Poems. There is a preface to each of the albums that includes suggestions for teaching this potentially unfamiliar material. In addition, all connections questions posed in the text for selections in these albums, with the exception of questions that explicitly ask students to write an essay, are answered in the manual. An appendix that gives instructors suggestions for teaching thematic units is also included.

The appendix of Film, Video, and Audiocassette Resources for teaching selections in *Poetry: An Introduction* has been updated and expanded for the third edition of the manual. The information contained in this list is incorporated into the appropriate individual manual entries for ease of reference. At the end of the manual, you will find a description of an audio recording of poems from the text, along with information on how to obtain a copy of this recording.

A new feature for this edition is an extensive list of online resources. While this is not meant to be an exhaustive list, it provides great places for students to begin their research. Given the Internet's virtually unlimited potential, these sites should prove to be very helpful.

In addition, there are a number of "Tips from the Field," class-tested teaching suggestions from instructors who have taught from previous editions. If you have a teaching tip that you would like to submit for the next edition of this instructor's manual, please send it to the attention of Aron Keesbury, Editor, at Bedford Books, 75 Arlington Street, Boston, MA 02116. Your teaching suggestion should be approximately fifty words long and suggest ways of teaching a particular author or selection that have been especially effective in your classroom experience. If we use your teaching suggestion, we will be happy to acknowledge you in the manual and pay you an honorarium.

The manual is conveniently arranged to follow the organization of the text. Page references corresponding to the text are included at the top of each right page of the manual and after the title of each entry.

Resources for Teaching

THIRD EDITION

POETRY

An Introduction

THE ELEMENTS OF
POETRY

Brief biographical notes for major poets are included in the first entry for each poet. Check the index for page numbers of first entries. In addition, available resources relating to specific poets and their work are included in the first entry for each poet under the heading "Resources for Teaching." Resources for each of the three poets treated in depth in Chapters 12–14 appear after the final perspective entry for that poet.

1

Reading Poetry

Perhaps the most difficult part of any introductory literature course is convincing the students that they can, in fact, read poetry. Often, students are intimidated by previous experiences, either in high school or other college courses; they have often accepted that they "just don't get it." Thus, it is important to develop students' confidence in themselves as readers. One way to do this is to get the students to articulate what they see actually happening in the poem, to read what is "on the page."

This chapter has several poems that lend themselves to such an application. Robert Hayden's "Those Winter Sundays," John Updike's "Dog's Death," Wole Soyinka's "Telephone Conversation," and Elizabeth Bishop's "The Fish," among others, are poems that have a clear scene or situation that grounds them: they mean what they say in a concrete way. Other meanings and issues can be raised, of course, but Bishop's poem, for instance, is first and foremost about catching a fish. Students will often "get" this level of the poem, but distrust their reading, figuring that it isn't what the poem is "really about." A good reading, however, is grounded in such particulars. You might want to have students offer a one- or two-sentence summary of the action of such poems: "The speaker in Bishop's poem catches an old fish, looks into his eyes, and lets him go." Students can then be encouraged to build on these readings once their "fear of poetry" has been deflated somewhat.

Even such poems as Robert Morgan's "Mountain Graveyard" can become more accessible; what may seem to some as mere wordplay will be more powerful if students slow down and picture the scene evoked by the title.

In some cases, you may be confronted by students who already have all the answers. Such students can easily intimidate a class. A useful exercise can be done with Robert Frost's "The Road Not Taken" (Chapter 13, text p. 338). Many students have encountered this poem in high school; most have "learned" that it is a poem about making a brave choice that leads the speaker to a life of independence, or a poem of regret at lost possibilities. As the text points out, however, close attention to the verb tenses in the final stanza reveals a more ambiguous reading. You may want to distribute a copy of this poem (with no commentary) to the class, and ask them "How old is the speaker in the poem?" Focusing attention on the last two stanzas can prove instructive even to experienced readers, and emphasize the importance of careful attention and multiple readings.

There are two strategies you may find effective in working with students' resistance to poetry and helping them understand the poems they are faced with: reading aloud and short writings. On the surface, this sounds obvious, but having to understand a poem well enough to read it or hearing it spoken can make a difference in students' appreciation of poetry. Tips on encouraging reading aloud can be found in this manual in the introduction to Chapter 7.

Similarly, you might want to assign students short, informal writing to help them think through some of the issues you want to cover in class. These writings can be based on questions in the text, questions of your own, or even student-generated questions based on issues that seem to interest them in discussion. Preparing them before class discussion can help students frame ideas to share. You may want to grade these assignments only on a pass/fail basis, to give students the chance to do experimental thinking in a low-stakes environment. Chapter 20 has a number of questions and strategies you might find useful in these assignments.

MARGE PIERCY, *The Secretary Chant* (p. 9)

This poem provides an opportunity to discuss point of view in poetry. The secretary's view of herself mirrors the way she is treated. She has become a variety of objects, a list of useful items because she is looked at as an object by people outside her. Her attitude toward herself is framed by other people's perceptions of her, although we must assume that she is aware of her ability to write satire. We get an inkling of her "real" self in the last three lines; the misspelled "wonce" mocks misperceptions of her intellect, while "woman" indicates that there is much more to be learned about the speaker.

In a writing assignment, you might ask students to discuss the metaphors in this poem. What assumptions about women and secretaries do the metaphors satirize? How do sound patterns such as "Zing. Tinkle" (line 14) affect the satire?

Possible Connections to Other Selections

E. E. Cummings, "she being Brand" (text p. 57)
Katharyn Howd Machan, "Hazel Tells LaVerne" (text p. 61)

Audiovisual and Online Resources (manual pp. 305, 346)

ROBERT HAYDEN, *Those Winter Sundays* (p. 10)

Useful comparisons can be made between any of the poems in this book that speak of love's transcendence or amplitude and any others, like this one and Theodore Roethke's "My Papa's Waltz" (text p. 217), that speak of its difficulty — the time it sometimes takes to recognize love. Hayden's speaker looks back at his father's unappreciated Sunday labor, at last knowing it for what it was and knowing, too, that the chance for gratitude has long since passed. The poem gives a strong sense, especially in its final two lines, that the speaker has tended to "love's austere and lonely offices" (line 14). The repetition of "What did I know?" seems to be a cry into the silence not only of the past but of the poet's present situation as well. The poem plays the music of the father's furnace work, the hard consonant sounds "splintering, breaking" (6) as the poem unfolds and disappearing entirely by the poem's end.

You might begin discussion by asking students to describe the speaker's father in as much detail as possible based on the speaker's spare description. From the poem's second word, "too," the poem reaches beyond itself to suggest something about the man without naming it. What other details contribute to our impression of him? Following that discussion, you could also ask for a description of the speaker. What does his language reveal about his character? And how does this character contrast with his father's character?

POSSIBLE CONNECTIONS TO OTHER SELECTIONS

Margaret Atwood, "Bored" (text p. 72)
Andrew Hudgins, "Elegy for My Father, Who Is Not Dead" (text p. 242)
Theodore Roethke, "My Papa's Waltz" (text p. 217)

ONLINE RESOURCES (manual p. 334)

JOHN UPDIKE, *Dog's Death* (p. 11)

This narrative poem subtly traces a family's emotional response to the illness and death of their pet dog. Ask students to find the events that lead to the dog's death. How does the speaker relate these events? He tells us the dog's age when he talks about her toilet training and immediately establishes the family's relationship to her by repeating their words: "Good dog! Good dog!" (line 4). Alliteration and assonance soften the story; after they have identified these sound patterns, ask students why the repeated sounds are appropriate to the subject matter. Direct their attention to the enjambment in lines 12–13. Why does the sentence span two stanzas? Might the speaker be reluctant to tell us the dog died?

When he relates his wife's reaction to the death, the speaker describes her voice as "imperious with tears" (14). After they have established a definition of the word *imperious,* ask students to determine why it might be used here. The ambiguous "her" and "she" in the final two lines of the stanza make us puzzle out for a moment the pronouns' referent. Is the speaker talking about his wife or the dog? Are both implied? How does this distortion of identity work in a discussion of death?

The final stanza reads as a eulogy; the consonants become harder — "drawing" (18), "dissolution" (18), "diarrhoea" (19), "dragged" (19) — perhaps because the speaker is working at closing off the experience. In a writing assignment, you might ask students to discuss the three uses of "Good dog." How does the last one differ from the first two? How does the poem prepare us for the change?

POSSIBLE CONNECTIONS TO OTHER SELECTIONS

Seamus Heaney, "Mid-term Break" (text p. 241)
Jane Kenyon, "The Blue Bowl" (text p. 106)
Ronald Wallace, "Dogs" (text p. 685)

ONLINE RESOURCES (manual p. 309)

WILLIAM HATHAWAY, *Oh, Oh* (p. 13)

The reader's delight in the surprise ending of this poem hinges on the mood set up by the language of the first fifteen lines. Which words create this idyllic mood? What happens to the poem if you replace these words with others? For example, what words could replace "amble" (line 1)? How might one wave besides "gaily" (10)? How could the caboose pass other than with a "chuckle" (15)? How does the poem read with your revisions?

Does the poet give any clues as to what lies ahead? What about the "black window" in line 9, the exact center of the poem? A writing activity dealing with denotation and connotation could develop from a study of this poem. Have students consider a picture (one of an old house works well) and describe it first as though it might be used as a setting for *Nightmare on Elm Street*, then for an episode of the *Brady Bunch*. Discuss the word choices that set the different moods.

POSSIBLE CONNECTION TO ANOTHER SELECTION

Robert Frost, "Design" (text p. 356)

AUDIOVISUAL RESOURCES (manual p. 300)

ROBERT FRANCIS, *Catch* (p. 14)

This poem casts metaphor-making as a game of catch between two boys. If you are using the poem to examine metaphor, you might ask students what is missing from the central metaphor that Francis creates: that is, when two boys are playing catch, they are tossing a ball to one another. If we interpret the two players of this game as the poet and the reader, does the game of catch seem one-sided, as though one player is firing a number of balls at the other one? Once you catch the ball in a game of catch, you throw it back. Does the relationship between reader and poet work the same way?

Encourage students to enjoy listening to this poem. Like a good pitcher, Francis finds various ways of throwing strikes. Consider, for example, line 3, with its "attitudes, latitudes, interludes, altitudes," or "prosy" and "posy" later in the poem.

POSSIBLE CONNECTIONS TO OTHER SELECTIONS

Emily Dickinson, "Portraits are to daily faces" (text p. 298)
Robert Francis, "The Pitcher" (text p. 194)
Robert Wallace, "The Double-Play" (text p. 641)

WOLE SOYINKA, *Telephone Conversation* (p. 19)

"Telephone Conversation" is a narrative poem that takes a satiric look at the emotionally charged issue of racism. One way to approach the topic of racism (and race in general) is to begin discussion of this poem by having your students paraphrase the poem. Student paraphrases will undoubtedly focus on the racial dimensions of the conversation and the racial theme of the poem. In comparing prose paraphrases to the language of the poem, students may notice several things about the poet's style that are lost in a paraphrase: the short sentences and sentence fragments, the unusual syntax of many lines, the terse language, and the fast pace. After identifying some of these characteristics, you may wish to ask students what effects these characteristics have on the tone of the poem. It may also be interesting to talk about the effect the poet achieves by printing the words of the landlady in capital letters. What are the political implications of this shift? By the end of the poem, what do readers know about the speakers based solely on the words that have passed between them?

You may want to ask students to do a Marxist reading of this poem. In addition to race, they should consider issues of class, power, and social injustice in Soyinka's poem. Although the poet's deft handling of the account leaves little doubt as to who got in the last word, given the inevitable outcome of the exchange, who seems to have "won," and how?

POSSIBLE CONNECTIONS TO OTHER SELECTIONS

Chitra Banerjee Divakaruni, "Indian Movie, New Jersey" (text p. 162)
Langston Hughes, "Ballad of the Landlord" (text p. 387)
Gary Soto, "Mexicans Begin Jogging" (text p. 271)

ELIZABETH BISHOP, *The Fish* (p. 20)

Born in Worcester, Massachusetts, Elizabeth Bishop knew displacement early: her father died when she was an infant, and her mother was committed to an asylum when she was five. Bishop lived with relatives during her childhood and adolescence in Nova Scotia and New England; after completing a degree at Vassar College, she lived in New York City, Key West, and for sixteen years in Brazil. Travel and exile, as well as the insistent yet alien presence of the "things of the world," figure prominently in her work.

The most arresting feature of "The Fish" is its imagery. Consider, for example, the brown skin that "hung in strips / like ancient wall-paper" (lines 10–11), the ornamentation of "fine rosettes of lime" (17), or the pause to mention and comment again on "the frightening gills" (24). Not only does Bishop have an eye for the particular, even the minute, but in this poem she exhibits an ability to dissect imaginatively flesh, bones, bladder, the interior of the fish's eyes.

After you review the appearance of the fish, it might be a good idea to glance back at the syntax of the poem. Note, for example, the syntactic simplicity and parallelism of lines 5–7, conveying with their flat factuality the fish's implacable "thereness." The syntax becomes a little more complex later on, as Bishop's vision penetrates into the interior of the fish's anatomy and, eventually, into its being. The fish is no longer a mere member of its species but a kind of military hero and a survivor that has escaped at least five attempts on its life.

Bishop's skill transforms the fish into a thing of beauty and an object of admiration, almost without our realizing it. At this point in the discussion, though, it would be a good idea to step back and see what she is looking at. The scene is simply an old fish, brown and battle-scarred, with sullen jaw, staring back at the speaker (Bishop, we assume). Not an ideal setting for the epiphanic moment.

But that is, of course, what occurs — signaled to us by the repetition of the word *rainbow.* In a sense, both fish and poet have transcended themselves — the one by surviving, the other by seeing beyond the ugliness. Victory, indeed, fills up the boat.

PONSSIBLE CONNECTIONS TO OTHER SELECTIONS

Joy Harjo, "Fishing" (text p. 607)
David Solway, "Windsurfing" (text p. 92)

AUDIOVISUAL AND ONLINE RESOURCES (manual pp. 315–316, 324)

PHILIP LARKIN, *A Study of Reading Habits* (p. 22)

This poem about a speaker's developing disillusionment with reading is a clever satire of the speaker's attitude. Note the intricate rhyme pattern in the poem. The poet's use of a complex poetic form while having the poem's speaker use slang and trite phrases provides an excellent opportunity to make students aware of the difference between the poet and the speaker of a poem. Does the slang used in Larkin's poem help to identify the speaker with a particular time period? With what current words would your students replace such words as "cool" (line 4), "lark" (8), "dude" (13)? Is any of the slang used in this poem still current?

After your students have read Larkin's poem, you might ask them to discuss their previous (and present) reading habits or have them write a short essay on this subject. What do they expect to gain from reading? Escape? Pleasure? Knowledge?

POSSIBLE CONNECTIONS TO OTHER SELECTIONS
Anne Bradstreet, "The Author to Her Book" (text p. 117)
Marianne Moore, "Poetry" (text p. 628)

ONLINE RESOURCES (manual p. 339)

ROBERT MORGAN, *Mountain Graveyard* (p. 24)

Ask students if they agree with the assertion that "Mountain Graveyard" is "unmistakably poetry." If they think it is poetry, is it a good poem? Meyer's strong argument in the text may be intimidating, but students should be encouraged to develop their own sense of what poetry is as they work through these chapters. Further, this poem and the next afford opportunities (because of their highly unorthodox forms) to lead students into a discussion of the authority of the printed word: Is a piece of literature good because "the book says so"? Is a story "art" because it is anthologized? It might be useful to return to these questions when your class finishes its consideration of poetry.

As a writing activity, have students choose another setting (college campus, supermarket, playground) and develop a set of anagrams for the new locale. Do different arrangements of the anagrams change the overall meaning of the set? Are any of the arrangements poetry?

POSSIBLE CONNECTIONS TO OTHER SELECTIONS
Helen Chasin, "The Word *Plum*" (text p. 195)
E. E. Cummings "l(a" (below)

E. E. CUMMINGS, *l(a* (p. 25)

E. E. Cummings was born in Cambridge, Massachusetts, the son of a Congregationalist minister. He earned a degree from Harvard University and began writing his iconoclastic poems after coming upon the work of Ezra Pound. His experimentation with syntax and punctuation reflects a seriously playful attitude toward language and meaning and a skepticism about institutional authority.

At first glance, "l(a" seems to be a poem spewed out by a closemouthed computer held in solitary confinement. As with Morgan's "Mountain Graveyard," however, the poem comes into its own as the reader not only deciphers but brings meaning to the text. Implied here is a simile between a falling leaf and loneliness. The use of a natural image to suggest an emotion recalls Japanese haiku (see Chapter 9).

The vertical quality of the poem illustrates the motion of a single leaf falling. Students might also point out the repetition of the digit *one* (indistinguishable in some texts from the letter *l*), along with other "aloneness" words, such as *a* and *one*. If ever a poem's medium enhanced its message, this one surely does.

POSSIBLE CONNECTION TO ANOTHER SELECTION
Robert Morgan, "Mountain Graveyard" (above)

AUDIOVISUAL AND ONLINE RESOURCES (manual pp. 296, 328)

ANONYMOUS, *Western Wind* (p. 26)

Students should be aware that, in England, the coming of the west wind signifies the arrival of spring. How is the longing for spring in this lyric connected to the overall sense of longing or to sexual longing? These brief four lines contain examples of several poetic devices worth noting. Ask students to consider the effects of the apostrophe and the alliteration in the first line. Many modern poets would consider these techniques artificial and overdone, but this poet seems to be interested in making a strong statement in just a few words. Does it work? Also, consider the use of the expletive "Christ" (line 3). This word makes the reader feel the intensity of emotion being conveyed and turns the poem into a kind of prayer — it is both sacred and profane.

For purposes of comparison, consider this poem in conjunction with another lyric that uses the same apostrophe, Percy Bysshe Shelley's "Ode to the West Wind" (text p. 243). Students should note that "Western Wind" is much more personal and less formal in diction than Shelley's poem.

POSSIBLE CONNECTION TO ANOTHER SELECTION

Robert Herrick, "Delight in Disorder" (text p. 211)

REGINA BARRECA, *Nighttime Fires* (p. 26)

This narrative poem has a recurrent theme, indicated by the repetitions of the word *smoke*. Smoke is the end of the father's quest, but what, exactly, is he looking for? His daughter, the speaker, provides a clue when she tells us that her father lost his job, so he had time to pursue fires. Smoke is the father's assurance that there is justice in the world because fires destroy rich and poor people alike. Ask students to look at the images the speaker uses to describe her father: What kind of man is he? How would they characterize the daughter's relationship to him? Does the mother also think of these drives as "festival, carnival" (line 15)? In some respect, the carnival is the father's performance before his family, in which the "wolf whine of the siren" (9) is matched by his "mad" (8) expression.

In a writing assignment, you might ask students to examine the metaphors describing the father. What do these figures tell us about his life? For example, in the final image of the father, his eyes are compared to "hallways filled with smoke" (31). Why is he likened to a house? What might this image tell us about his life?

POSSIBLE CONNECTION TO ANOTHER SELECTION

Robert Hayden, "Those Winter Sundays" (text p. 10)

HELEN FARRIES, *Magic of Love* (p. 30)

Note the ways in which this poem fulfills the greeting-card formula, especially with its "lilting" anapests, internal rhymes, and tried-and-true (and terribly trite) metaphors, all designed to lift the reader's spirits.

You might begin discussion by asking why this poem has withstood the test of time (as greeting-card verse). The pleasure of this specific poem comes not as much from its theme, which is nothing particularly new, as from its elements of sound, especially its internal, and full, end-stopped rhyme. Because poetry evolved, at least partly, from an oral tradition — using rhymes as mnemonic devices — you may even use this poem as a vehicle for discussing the very basic history of poetry. You may ask, for example, *why* strict rhyme and meter serve as such an effective mnemonic device. Does this poem use its devices pleasurably?

POSSIBLE CONNECTION TO ANOTHER SELECTION

Langston Hughes, "Formula" (text p. 382)

JOHN FREDERICK NIMS, *Love Poem* (p. 31)

Greeting cards must speak to the anonymous masses. Nims's poem, while maintaining a simplicity of diction and a directness of sentiment, is far stronger than the greeting-card verse, in part because it is addressing a specific person.

The poem is obviously not a piece to be carved on the pedestal of some faceless ideal; students will probably have at least some curiosity about a poem that begins "My clumsiest dear." After they have become accustomed to this violating of poetic convention, ask them to review the poem for other refreshing and surprising uses of language. They might mention, for example, the use of "shipwreck" as a verb in line 1, the play on "bull in a china shop" (line 3), or the projective quality of "undulant" in line 8 to describe the floor as it appears to the drunk. Again, unlike conventional verse, this poem concludes with an almost paradoxical twist to the most salient feature of this woman who breaks things: her absence would cause "all the toys of the world [to] break."

In a writing assignment, you might ask students to compare this poem with Shakespeare's sonnet "My mistress' eyes . . ." (text p. 229).

POSSIBLE CONNECTION TO ANOTHER SELECTION
William Shakespeare, "My mistress' eyes are nothing like the sun" (text p. 229)

AUDIOVISUAL AND ONLINE RESOURCES (manual pp. 304, 345)

BRUCE SPRINGSTEEN, *Streets of Philadelphia* (p. 32)

Many of your students may be familiar with this song, which was featured in the award-winning film *Philadelphia*. For students who are unfamiliar with the movie, you may want to explain that the movie depicts the true story of a man with AIDS and his landmark court case concerning discrimination against people with AIDS, tried in the city of Philadelphia. Ask your students to consider whether knowing that this song was written to accompany this film influences their reading of the song.

Listening to a recording of the song will undoubtedly provide students with a richer understanding of the tone. It may be helpful to ask students whether their interpretations of the lyrics change when the music is added. You might ask your students to consider how the words and notes interact in this particular song and whether one seems stronger or weaker than the other. To further class discussion comparing the recording of "Streets of Philadelphia" to the printed version, read the work aloud to your students, being careful to pause only for line breaks. Then ask students to consider whether the music contributes more to their understanding of the song. Depending on the response you get, you might ask if the lack of punctuation makes the lyrics more difficult to follow without the music.

POSSIBLE CONNECTION TO ANOTHER SELECTION
Robert Francis, *On "Hard" Poetry* (text p. 35)

AUDIOVISUAL RESOURCES (manual p. 308)

SAUNDRA SHARP, *It's the Law: A Rap Poem* (p. 33)

In a meter and vernacular that will likely be familiar to your students, this poem provides an analysis of what our nation's laws reveal about our collective behavior. This analysis is followed by disgust for the behavior that made the laws necessary. The poem ends with an optimistic response, rendering the laws impotent by presenting "rules." These rules focus on producing positive, creative behavior rather than forbidding negative, destructive behavior.

Sharp states more than once her analysis of what our laws reveal about our cultural behavior: "The rules we break are the laws we make/the things that we fear, we legislate" (lines 3–4); "The laws that we make are what we do to each other/There is no law to make brother love brother" (18–19). This absence of a law enforcing love is the impetus for Sharp's creation of the more positive "rules": the distinction between "rules" and "laws" provides an alternative to the despair of legislation. This is an insistent poem, attacking its point from several angles. The solution Sharp provides for the distressing lessons our laws teach us about ourselves is present in the importance of the rules she presents, beginning with her directive in line 25, "Listen up!" The rules emphasizing education, kindness, and sobriety underscore the need for personal responsibility and self-respect.

You might want to compare other features of rap with more traditional poetic conventions: end rhyme, allusion, alliteration, meter, and clever turns of phrase. Ask students to describe these conventions and to give examples of them from this poem. If you have worked with other twentieth-century poetry, contrast the types of conventions apparent in rap and in other modern poems.

POSSIBLE CONNECTION TO ANOTHER SELECTION

Gwendolyn Brooks, "We Real Cool" (text p. 81)

PERSPECTIVE

ROBERT FRANCIS, *On "Hard" Poetry* (p. 35)

Discussing hard poetry through its opposite, soft poetry, may be the best way into a discussion of this piece. Hard poetry does not use excess words, does not lapse into sentimentality, does not have an undefined or loose form. The hard poem sustains tension between poet and speaker, reader and text. You may want to put Francis's ideas to the test by asking students to find specific lines from "Streets of Philadelphia" that support their argument about whether the lyrics can be characterized as "hard" poetry. Are the speaker's tone and the images used in the song sentimental — or "soft"? Students should be able to point to a number of lines that allow for multiple interpretations — that challenge the reader and create some "resistance." For example, you might ask them to discuss Springsteen's use of the adjective *faithless* in line 21. Why is the kiss of the "brother" who *receives* the speaker described as "faithless"? You might also ask students whether they feel the lyrics are tightly organized. How effective is Springsteen's use of rhyme and repetition?

POSSIBLE CONNECTIONS TO OTHER SELECTIONS

Helen Farries, "Magic of Love" (text p. 30)
Langston Hughes, "Cross" (text p. 382)
Bruce Springsteen, "Streets of Philadelphia" (text p. 32)

RUDYARD KIPLING, *If—* (p. 36)

This poem offers advice from an older man to a younger man; if we take the speaker's use of "son" literally, they are father and son. The meter and rhyme are easy to identify; the advice provided makes for familiar content. The reminder that such advice is dated, by the presence of the final line and its address to a male reader, may provide for more interesting class discussion than the poem itself. Points for discussion could include an examination of the world presented through the advice offered here: do students think this is a realistic or pessimistic world vision? To keep discussion focused, write a list on the board of some of the disasters presented in the poem: examples include getting blamed for something that's not your fault (line 2), being doubted (3), and being lied about (6). The poem refers to being a man; do your students think this refers to masculinity or universality?

In your efforts to encourage student readings, you may want to try a close examination of the last stanza with your class. What do your students make of the "unforgiving minute" (29) and the "sixty seconds' worth of distance run" (30)? A simple rewording might be that one should try to do one's best even when circumstances are against you and time is tight. What are some circumstances in which this analogy might seem fit? What are some unforgiving minutes your students are familiar with? Test taking? Making rent? Cramming lunch in between classes? Juggling school and job?

POSSIBLE CONNECTIONS TO OTHER SELECTIONS

Robert Herrick, "To the Virgins, to Make Much of Time" (text p. 64)
Dylan Thomas, "The Hand That Signed the Paper" (text p. 120)
Alice Walker, "a woman is not a potted plant" (question #1, following)

CONNECTION QUESTION IN TEXT (p. 37) WITH ANSWER

1. Discuss Kipling's treatment of what a man is in contrast to Alice Walker's description of what a woman is not in "a woman is not a potted plant" (below). What significant differences do you find in their definitions?

    Kipling's poem depends on a tradition of advice given to the young and the triumph of will in the face of adversity. Walker's poem provides a new metaphor, a new model for womanhood. While Kipling's poem describes the *behavior* of an adult, Walker's poem describes the *inner* being, the affections, the alliances. Kipling assumes a reader's awareness of the difficulties of dealing in the world: the poorly placed trust and bad decisions, the disappointments in other people, the trying times. With these examples, Kipling emphasizes the need to accept that disappointment and misfortune are a part of adulthood. Walker assumes that the reader is familiar with the idea of a woman being defined by her home and her femininity, "the contours of her sex" (lines 9–10). The freedom expressed in Walker's refusal to allow a woman to be defined by her circumstances is very different from Kipling's decree that a man shouldn't "look too good, nor talk too wise" (8); in contrast, Walker's woman is "wilderness/unbounded" (30–31).

ONLINE RESOURCES (manual p. 339)

ALICE WALKER, *a woman is not a potted plant* (p. 37)

This speaker's definition of womanhood works by contrasting against the metaphor of a potted plant and the confines a potted plant embodies. After the first three stanzas of contrast, the speaker goes on to define woman as "wilderness unbounded" (lines 30–31); even more unbounded than a flying wild animal such as a bee. The effect of describing what womanhood is *not* is a strong rhetorical device, evident in poetry dating back at least as far as the English Renaissance (as in the opening line of Ben Jonson's "To Penshurst," "Thou art *not*, Penshurst, built to envious show . . ."). Students may be interested not only in the effect of this rhetoric but in its power — as though the speaker is arguing with someone before he or she has even asserted anything. This speaker's strong voice allows her to make her point in such a way that her opinion comes across loud and clear, so her rhetorical stance is appropriate to the topic of the poem: the need to redefine womanhood.

This is truly a polemical poem, then; but students may be interested in discussing the contrast between the message — which might be described as political, or which can be said to be historical in the sense that Walker is redefining woman *against* the more "traditional" definition — and the imagery, which is completely natural. Why does she select a natural metaphor rather than a metaphor from history or politics to communicate her message? Ask students to describe any hierarchies they see in nature as a way of unpacking the hierarchy inherent in the poem's structure: the progression from a potted plant to a bee. You may want to pause at each of the steps of the hierarchy to discuss how each represents a stereotypical view of womanhood. In addition to Marge Piercy's "The Secretary Chant" (text p. 9), the title poem from Walker's collection *Her Blue Body Everything We Know* can enhance students' understanding of Walker's use of woman as a metaphor for nature.

POSSIBLE CONNECTIONS TO OTHER SELECTIONS

Marge Piercy, "The Secretary Chant" (question #1, following)

William Shakespeare, "My mistress' eyes are nothing like the sun" (text p. 229)

CONNECTION QUESTION IN TEXT (p. 38) WITH ANSWER

1. Compare Walker's take on female identity in this poem with Marge Piercy's in "The Secretary Chant" (p. 9). How are their conceptions similar? Different?

   In both cases, women have been dehumanized, yet Walker describes women in terms of nature, whereas Piercy's speaker considers herself in mechanical terms. In one sense, Walker's poem responds to the situation presented in Piercy's, arguing that women should be considered boundless. Walker's speaker is distant from her subject, though, whereas Piercy's is immersed. Consequently, Walker's speaker is much stronger, taking a firm position on how women should be regarded.

AUDIOVISUAL AND ONLINE RESOURCES (manual pp. 309, 353)

LISA PARKER, *Snapping Beans* (p. 38)

This poem, in the voice of a college student returning home to Grandma's, contrasts the familiarity of family with new knowledge of the outside world. "Snapping Beans" is a kind of shorthand for the tenuous middle ground the speaker and grandmother share, with Grandma's home still comforting and beautiful to the speaker. Students will probably be able to relax with Parker's straightforward narrative, simple vocabulary, accessible imagery, and earnest tone. The sudden violent dispatch of the leaf from the tree and Grandma's observation of it provide a parallel to the speaker's separation from the grandmother's world.

Students are likely to be familiar with the distance between loved ones and the shifts that occur when we grow up and move away from our families. Consider asking them to spend ten or fifteen minutes engaged in a journal writing exercise that examines how their own relationships with family members have changed since they left for college. Asking them to read aloud selections from their writing could establish a sense of community in the classroom.

POSSIBLE CONNECTIONS TO OTHER SELECTIONS

Margaret Atwood, "Bored" (text p. 72)

Robert Frost, "Birches" (text p. 347)

Gary Soto, "Behind Grandma's House" (question #1, following)

CONNECTION QUESTION IN TEXT (p. 39) WITH ANSWER

1. Discuss the treatment of the grandmother in "Snapping Beans" and in "Behind Grandma's House" by Gary Soto (p. 167).

   The tough wisdom of Soto's grandmother is in possible contrast to the uncertain level of self-awareness of Parker's: Soto's grandmother is certainly aware of the connection between her words and her action. Parker's grandmother may or may not be aware of the comparison her observation of the "hickory leaf, still summer green" (41) provides, illuminating the speaker's predicament.

WYATT PRUNTY, *Elderly Lady Crossing on Green* (p. 39)

"Elderly Lady Crossing on Green" undercuts the reader's expectations; although unlike William Hathaway's "Oh, Oh" (text p. 13), this poem's surprise comes early on in the poem. The reader's expectations that an elderly woman crossing a street will be feeble, helpless, and aged, are blown away first by her rejection of all of the nice gestures young people offer, then by the vision that she was not only once young, but also vicious. The poem becomes a vision of a younger version of the woman behind the wheel, driving like a maniac, disregarding all pedestrians in her path.

That the poem begins *in medias res* adds to an invisible litany of the reader's expectations, set up by the title. Having students write a list of images that come to mind when they see or think about old women, then listing these images on the board may lead to an interesting discussion of stereotypes and expectations. Why is it relatively acceptable to harbor stereotypes about the elderly in our culture while it is taboo to harbor stereotypes about race, ethnicity, gender, etc.? The speaker begins by assuming that we all know (and perhaps share) these stereotypes, and the vision of his menacing subject as a young woman points up our prejudice. We are even denied the opportunity to romanticize her past, to dwell on the fact that she was once a "widow, wife, mother, or a bride" (line 14).

Is this poem meant to be funny, as "Oh, Oh" is? Does it play up our pity even as it confounds our expectations? Much of the interpretation hinges on the last two stanzas, and you may have to work hard to get students to transfer their attention from the relatively simple fantasy about the past to the somewhat philosophical ending. Is the poem entirely a fantasy based on a woman's anger? Is she feeling alienated, "a small tug on the tidal swell" (19)? Is her rejection of nice gestures in the first stanza motivated by fear rather than cantankerousness? While exploring these questions, you might want to ask students to examine the references to death in the poem, for example: "run you flat as paint" (6), "jaywalked to eternity" (12), "the other side" (16). Why do we sometimes treat death in such a cartoonish, ostensibly humorous way?

POSSIBLE CONNECTIONS TO OTHER SELECTIONS

William Hathaway, "Oh, Oh" (question #1, following)
Aron Keesbury, "Song to a Waitress" (text p. 218)

CONNECTION QUESTION IN TEXT (p. 40) WITH ANSWER

1. Write an essay comparing the humor in this poem with that of William Hathaway's "Oh, Oh" (p. 13).

    The humor in this poem depends on the image of an elderly woman acting against our expectations: young, uncaring, and aggressive. In Hathaway's poem, the Hell's Angels act exactly as we expect them to, so the humor hinges on the speaker's perception of them as they present an element of danger in his bucolic scene. Another significant difference is that the humor in "Oh, Oh" occurs at the end of the poem, causing us to rethink the rest of the poem from the title on. In Prunty's poem, much of the humor occurs at the beginning; by the end, we feel pity for the elderly lady rather than mirth.

ONLINE RESOURCES (manual p. 347)

ALBERTO RÍOS, *Seniors* (p. 40)

You might begin your discussion of this poem by asking students to talk about its use of slang, particularly in the first stanza. The slang establishes the speaker's environment as well as his conversational tone. As the poem progresses, it focuses on the speaker, and the tone becomes more meditative. Although they modify his relationship to other people, the images of cavities, flat walls, and water (particularly in stanza III) distance the speaker from the social realm, until he is left "on the desert" in the last stanza.

Students might write an essay on these images. How does their evocation of sexual experience prepare us for the last line of the poem? What is the speaker trying to say about sex, about life? How does the language of the final stanza compare with that of the first stanza? What might this changed diction indicate in the speaker's attitude toward himself and the world?

POSSIBLE CONNECTIONS TO OTHER SELECTIONS

T. S. Eliot, "The Love Song of J. Alfred Prufrock" (question #2, following)
Sharon Olds, "Sex without Love" (question #1, following)

CONNECTIONS QUESTIONS IN TEXT (p. 41) WITH ANSWERS

1. Compare the treatment of sex in this poem with that in Sharon Olds's "Sex without Love" (p. 76).

    Olds talks about sex as a sport, noting how lovers who have sex without love treat their bodies as separate from "truth." The images Olds uses to make her point are unlike Ríos's imagery. Ríos talks about bodies as continually fading away. His speaker calls the body of the woman he first kissed almost "nonexistent" (line 18), comparing all sexual experiences to a "flagstone wall" (22), vacationing in Bermuda, swimming ("all water," 27). For Ríos's speaker, sex provides a vehicle for capturing the past; for Olds's speaker, sex is the subject for a lesson about love.

2. Think about "Seniors" as a kind of love poem and compare the speaker's voice here with the one in T. S. Eliot's "The Love Song of J. Alfred Prufrock" (p. 405). How are these two voices used to evoke different cultures? Of what value is love in these cultures?

    J. Alfred Prufrock's voice bespeaks an empty culture, characterized by "sawdust restaurants" and "yellow smoke" as well as by empty conversations and rituals. "Prufrock" is a love poem that never comes to be because the speaker is too fearful to act: "Do I dare / Disturb the universe?" Ríos's speaker also describes a lost culture, particularly in his use of slang and his references to materialism in the first two stanzas. In fact, many of the images in "Seniors" are complemented by similar, though starker, images in "Prufrock." In each poem, love symbolizes the speaker's individual feelings of loss and the collective emptiness of the culture.

AUDIOVISUAL AND ONLINE RESOURCES (manual pp. 306, 348)

JOHN DONNE, *The Sun Rising* (p. 42)

John Donne was born Roman Catholic when England was staunchly anti-Catholic, a circumstance that made his pursuit of worldly success significantly more difficult than it might otherwise have been for one with his intelligence, energy, and wit. Donne attended Oxford and Cambridge Universities and trained in the law for a time. After a youth and young manhood full of worldly pleasure, Donne became an Anglican preacher in 1615.

This aubade uses a typical metaphysical conceit transforming two lovers in bed into a universal microcosm. The speaker entreats the sun to leave him and his lover alone and to bother others who need to get out of bed. The dialogue is ostensibly between the speaker and the sun, but students will probably wish to discuss the relationship between the speaker and his lover. What is implied by the metaphor, "She is all states, and all princes I" (line 21)? Does the speaker seem more preoccupied with his wordplay or with his lover?

The speaker's blunt message is to leave the lovers alone and bother other people who need waking to get on with the work of their ordinary lives. The tone softens in the second stanza, as Donne thinks more of his beloved. When he is with her, the world seems to be concentered in their presence. If the sun were to shine only on their room, it would be everywhere.

In the final stanza the speaker continues to expound on how, when you are in love, your heaven, earth, and kingdom are contained in your beloved. As he writes in the opening of this stanza, "She is all states, and all princes I" (21), and later, "All honor's mimic, all wealth alchemy" (24). Some students might point out that the idea that true love is a treasure worth far more than any amount of money still persists.

POSSIBLE CONNECTIONS TO OTHER SELECTIONS

John Donne, "The Flea" (text p. 604)
Andrew Marvell, "To His Coy Mistress" (text p. 65)
Richard Wilbur, "A Late Aubade" (question #1, following)

CONNECTION QUESTION IN TEXT (p. 42) WITH ANSWER

1. Compare this lyric poem with Richard Wilbur's "A Late Aubade" (p. 68). What similarities do you find in the ideas and emotions expressed in each?

   Both speakers have in common the desire to linger in bed with their lovers, but Donne's speaker blames the sun for trying to separate them. He is implicated in the impending parting because he, too, must rise and leave. By contrast, Wilbur's speaker blames his lover, who seems to have more tasks or obligations than he does. Another difference is the scope of the rhetoric they use. Typical of "metaphysical" conceits, Donne's speaker presents the situation in grand terms, making his lover "all states" (line 21) and their bedroom the entire universe. Wilbur's speaker does not make such grand pronouncements; he simply states that it is nicer to linger in bed and kiss than to busy oneself with routine occurrences.

AUDIOVISUAL AND ONLINE RESOURCES (manual pp. 297, 329–330)

LI HO, *A Beautiful Girl Combs Her Hair* (p. 43)

Like his predecessor Li Po, Li Ho did not serve as a civil servant, an unusual choice for poets of the T'ang Dynasty in China. He wrote poems while riding on a donkey and revised them at the end of each day.

Juxtaposition, one of the most important techniques in Chinese poetry, is amply evident in this poem, as is one of Li Ho's characteristic touches: supernatural mystery appearing alongside unvarnished description ("singing jade"; "her mirror / two phoenixes / a pool of autumn light"). The poet deftly brings the senses into play; the girl's "spilling hair" has a precise fragrance; it is not simply black but the "color of raven feathers / shining blue-black stuff"; and it defeats her "jade comb," which in the middle of the poem falls without sound.

You might ask students to think about where the speaker is in relation to this scene and what significance his location might have for his exasperation. Reading the poem without the speaker's outburst in lines 23–26 might lead to a productive discussion of the effects of metaphor and connotation. What sort of girl is this "wild goose" with blackest hair so carefully attended? How much does the speaker know of her? How much does he wish to know?

POSSIBLE CONNECTIONS TO OTHER SELECTIONS

Sylvia Plath, "Mirror" (text p. 126)

David Solway, "Windsurfing" (text p. 92)

Cathy Song, "The White Porch" (question #1, following)

CONNECTION QUESTION IN TEXT (p. 44) WITH ANSWER

1. Compare the description of hair in this poem with that in Cathy Song's "The White Porch" (p. 111). What significant similarities do you find?

    Song's "The White Porch" has a tone similar to that of this poem, with alluring, almost seductive images of a woman's hair. Both women's hair is thick and unmanageable. Each woman gathers vegetation from the garden, again pointing to her ripe sexuality. In both poems hair serves as a way of knowing the women, a means of access to their restlessness and self-consciousness. You might ask students to comment on differences in the poems resulting from the difference in speakers. Li Ho's speaker watches the woman dress her hair and is upset by her "slovenly beauty" (line 24). The speaker in Song's poem is the possessor of the hair and of the erotic power it symbolizes and releases.

ONLINE RESOURCES (manual p. 335)

ROBERT HASS, *Happiness* (p. 44)

The speaker of this poem builds up to a definition of "happiness" that is based on his and his lover's appreciation of a natural scene of foxes eating windfall apples. After seeing this scene, they each write. These events, coupled with other details from their cozy life, cause the speaker to reflect on his mood.

Students, of course, have access to a huge genre of "Happiness is . . ." clichés in the form of greeting cards, coffee mugs, and bathroom wall hangings. It is important to get them to see how complex and specific Hass's definition of happiness is by emphasizing what's contained within the dashes of this poem. Students might find themselves eliminating those sections to get the gist of the speaker's happiness; yet these are crucial descriptions. The speaker sees something of the beauty and mystery of nature, and he twice tries to speculate about what creatures might "symbolize." The symbolic value of foxes ("the wakefulness of living things" [line 5]), of mist ("the luminous and indefinite aspect of intention" [13]), and of swans ("mystery" [16]) gives the poem a dimension that students might initially resist in an attempt to glean the bottom line about happiness. The figurative meaning of natural creatures has a nice inversion in the final line, in which the speaker and his lover are compared to bats. Encourage students to explore the relationship between the speaker's attempt to situate himself and his wife or lover in nature and the process of their writing. Happiness seems to emerge from these two acts, which together amount to interpreting nature, a prominent *poetic* motif.

POSSIBLE CONNECTIONS TO OTHER SELECTIONS

James Dickey, "Deer Among Cattle" (text p. 104)

Emily Dickinson, "I like a look of Agony," (question #1, following)

1. Write an essay that compares and contrasts "Happiness" with Emily Dickinson's "I like a look of Agony," (p. 300). Do they both succeed in capturing an emotion? What message do you take away from each?

    Students may see "Happiness" as a poem that explores emotion and Dickinson's poem as one that suppresses emotion. We have a good sense of the personality of Hass's speaker, but Dickinson's speaker seems eccentric and unfamiliar. Hass's imagery churns up a genuine feeling in the speaker and in the reader, whereas Dickinson's speaker describes death in very cold, matter-of-fact terms. Yet both poems value genuine emotion, and in both cases people have little control over genuine emotion, which originates in something outside themselves.

2

Writing about Poetry

Comments often overheard in introductory literature classes suggest that many students believe that they are simply incapable of understanding poetry. Thus, their attempts to find meaning in poems are often hindered by their feelings of intimidation and ineptness. The Questions for Responsive Reading and Writing in Chapter 2 may prove to be particularly useful to these insecure students because they break down general poetry analysis into smaller components, which students may feel better able to manage. These questions, however, can also aid more confident and capable students in their analysis and interpretation of poetry by offering specific places for them to begin their literary investigations.

You might also use these questions in class to teach your students how to approach writing about poetry. Have your students work individually or in small groups, exploring possible answers to these questions using assigned poems. Brief written responses to these questions might lead to longer, more detailed interpretations at a later time. Of course, not every question will relate meaningfully to every poem. To help students learn to apply a certain type of question in their analysis, you might devise an exercise in which your students decide which questions are best suited to which particular poems in a set. You might also remind them that these questions about poetry are open-ended and often require more than a one-word or one-sentence response. Ask your students to provide evidence for their answers by quoting directly from the poems they have chosen to analyze. Also, it is important for students to feel comfortable using the terminology that describes particular elements of poetry; be sure to refer them to the Glossary of Literary Terms included in the anthology (text p. 687) if they are having trouble understanding any of these terms.

Chapter 2 includes a brief sample student paper analyzing Elizabeth Bishop's poem "Manners" (text p. 48). Ask your students to read the poem and then discuss how they might approach the assignment that was given to this student writer. What specific aspects of the poem might they choose to explore? What would they do differently from the writer of the sample? You may consider assigning your class a writing task similar to the one described in this chapter, using any poem your students have studied. The sample paper, while not necessarily a blueprint for effective poetry analysis, may offer your students a useful model of strong student writing that they may try to emulate. At the same time, you might ask your students to treat the sample student paper as an unfinished draft of an essay and have them suggest ways to revise this paper that would make it an even more effective piece.

3

Word Choice, Word Order, and Tone

Since poetry depends for its effects on the concentrated use of language, word choice can play a pivotal role in determining the meaning of a poem. For instance, in Martín Espada's "Latin Night at the Pawnshop," the choice of the word *apparition* as the first noun in the poem echoes Pound's "In a Station of the Metro." One word sets up an allusion to a key imagist poem, and thus puts Espada's poem in the context of that tradition. Still, students may remain unconvinced that word choice is all that important to a poem.

As an exercise to emphasize the importance of word choice, you might have students type up a short poem or section of a poem on a word processor. Most word processors now come with a thesaurus function that allows the user to replace a word with a synonym provided from a list. Have students replace either a couple of key words in the poem or a word in each line with the synonyms offered, and then read their new poems to the class. After a few examples, it should become clear how important word choice is to the overall effect of the poem.

You might try a similar exercise for word order with some of the selections. Having students think hypothetically about other options for a poem can help them develop an appreciation for the reasons a poem is the way it is. In general, counterfactuals help sharpen critical thinking skills.

The reasons a poem conveys a certain tone are sometimes hard to pin down, and can initially prove frustrating for students. You might find it helpful to encourage students to look not only at word choice but also other features of the poem in their discussions of tone.

The pairing of Hardy's and Slavitt's poems about the *Titanic* can very effectively show students the workings of diction. The popularity of the James Cameron movie *Titanic* will ensure that students know something about the event itself. A similar pairing that can prove interesting is Keats's "Ode on a Grecian Urn" and Olds's "Sex without Love." Both poems describe a beautiful aesthetic object but differ greatly in their ultimate conclusions, a difference that has much to do with tone. It may be a challenge, but having students articulate this difference in class discussion or a short writing can prove useful to their understanding of how tone and theme are related.

RANDALL JARRELL, *The Death of the Ball Turret Gunner* (p. 56)

Randall Jarrell attended Vanderbilt University and so became influenced by the Agrarian literary movement, an anti-industrial movement that sought to reinstate the values of an agricultural society. Jarrell's poem probably reflects on personal experience, as he was an air force pilot from 1942 until the end of World War II. However, like most of his poems, it evokes universal human pain and anguish, regardless of its specific circumstances.

The textual discussion of this poem calls attention to Jarrell's intentional use of ambiguity in some of his word choices, but is the overall tone of the poem ambiguous? How would you describe the speaker's attitude toward his subject? Have students look at Alfred, Lord Tennyson's "The Charge of the Light Brigade" (text p. 216) for another depiction of death in war. What are the word choices Tennyson makes in order to create the tone he wants? How does the tone of Tennyson's poem compare to that of Jarrell's?

The scene depicted in Jarrell's poem might almost be a synopsis of one of the major story lines in Joseph Heller's novel *Catch-22*. Compare Jarrell's word choices and the mood created by them to Heller's depiction of the gunner in Chapter 5 of *Catch-22*:

> That was where he wanted to be [atop the escape hatch, ready to parachute to safety] if he had to be there at all, instead of hung out there in front like some goddam cantilevered goldfish in some goddam cantilevered goldfish bowl while the goddam foul black tiers of flak were bursting and billowing and booming all around and above and below him in a climbing, cracking, staggered, banging, phantasmagorical, cosmological wickedness that jarred and tossed and shivered, clattered and pierced, and threatened to annihilate them all in one splinter of a second in one vast flash of fire. (New York: Dell, 1974, p. 50)

POSSIBLE CONNECTIONS TO OTHER SELECTIONS

Wilfred Owen, "Dulce et Decorum Est" (text p. 102)

Alfred, Lord Tennyson, "The Charge of the Light Brigade" (text p. 216)

AUDIOVISUAL AND ONLINE RESOURCES (manual pp. 301, 337)

E. E. CUMMINGS, *she being Brand* (p. 57)

This poem is a naughtily playful allegory of a young man's attempt to initiate a sexual experience with his girlfriend. Language accommodates the situation of the poem nicely, since some men seem to respond to cars and women with equal measures of affection and caretaking and refer to both cars and women as "she." Cummings drops innuendos of his witty double entendres early on. Listen, for example, to the opening eight lines, in which the poet seems to pause over words like "stiff" (line 4), "universal" (6), and even "springs" (8), which could suggest springs of affection. Knowing the "secret" of the poem, the class should enjoy lines such as "next / minute i was back in neutral tried and / again slo-wly;bare,ly nudg. ing (my" (lines 13–15). This work also offers good opportunities to discuss the function of punctuation in poetry.

POSSIBLE CONNECTIONS TO OTHER SELECTIONS

Sharon Olds, "Sex without Love" (text p. 76)

Marge Piercy, "The Secretary Chant" (text p. 9)

JUDITH ORTIZ COFER, *Common Ground* (p. 59)

This poem examines a shared heritage through the genetic legacy that is the body. The broad homily of the first stanza becomes more pointed and personal in the second, as the speaker confides in the reader about her awareness of her own aging face and hands. She uses the changes in her body to examine the ways in which her consciousness is evolving to contain the perspectives of her family members, lives shared and "pain and deprivation / I have never known" (lines 12–13). Students might benefit from a discussion of what Cofer might mean by "the stuff of your origin" (7) rising up through your pores. To help focus discussion, five minutes of freewriting on students' individual family traits might be helpful. In the poem, the arrows that point downward also point inward at the common ground of the title, the new understanding of a shared heritage. Through a shared appearance, the speaker discovers other things she has in common with her family members. How do shared physical traits help your students identify with family members? Do they imagine these connections might become more pronounced with age?

POSSIBLE CONNECTIONS TO OTHER SELECTIONS

Elizabeth Bishop, "Manners" (text p. 48)

Theodore Roethke, "My Papa's Waltz" (text p. 217)

AUDIOVISUAL AND ONLINE RESOURCES (manual pp. 295, 327)

ROBIN MORGAN, *Invocation* (p. 60)

This poem examines the relation between a public tragedy, reported in a newspaper, and the personal response of the speaker. The *Oxford English Dictionary* tells us that *invoke* is from the Latin *invocare*, "to call upon," especially as a witness or for aid. An invocation, then, is the act of calling upon God or a deity in prayer or supplication, asking for help or protection. Morgan's nontraditional invocation is a denouncement of the "insane, sadistic gods" (line 1) she calls upon, and these adjectives reflect her helplessness before the tragedy in the paper. While she insults the gods, she still makes a request: she explicitly asks that the gods let her be "worthy of such children" (9), let her be equal to her pain (11), and let her, in the "broken teeth of horror, sing" (12).

The effects of these lines are many: the reader may be surprised that this is Morgan's request. Rather than demand that these acts of injustice and cruelty stop, Morgan presents a more personal prayer: that she be allowed to retain her humanity and compassion in the face of them. A class discussion could benefit from the question raised here: Is that a sufficient request? Is Morgan being selfish, realistic, or compassionate? What do students make of her tone and of her beliefs?

POSSIBLE CONNECTION TO ANOTHER SELECTION

James Merrill, "Casual Wear" (question #1, following)

CONNECTION QUESTION IN TEXT (p. 61) WITH ANSWER

1. How is the strategy used in the final line of this poem similar to that of the final line in James Merrill's "Casual Wear" (p. 159)? Though the strategy is similar, how is the tone different at the end of each poem?

   Both Merrill and Morgan depend on a small detail to focus the gaze of their poems on their haunting last lines. However, the source of those details and their resulting tones sharply contrast with one another. The designer jeans provides a concrete detail, while the "broken teeth" of Morgan's last line are metaphoric. The hope present in her request for the ability to sing in the face of this tragedy is not present in the cold statistics offered in Merrill's poem.

KATHARYN HOWD MACHAN, *Hazel Tells LaVerne* (p. 61)

You might begin discussing this poem by talking about names and how they too have connotative value. Would our expectations be the same if the poem were titled "Sybil Speaks with Jacqueline"? By and large this poem does a good job at getting across its meaning through denotative language. But the fact that Hazel does use language almost exclusively in denotative terms is in itself a sign of her personality. As in a dramatic monologue by Robert Browning, Hazel tells more about herself, her social class, and her impenetrably matter-of-fact outlook on life than she does about her encounter with the frog. We as readers then fill in the gaps of the speaker's perceptions as well as piece together her outlook and attitude.

You might ask students to respond to Hazel's personality. She is likable; her matter-of-factness cuts through any of the fairy tales the world might try to sell her, and she's funny. Students can probably provide examples of characters from TV shows who are like Hazel and whose humor derives from their plain-spoken concreteness. We all admire the survivor who cannot be duped.

POSSIBLE CONNECTIONS TO OTHER SELECTIONS

Robert Browning, "My Last Duchess" (question #1, following)

Marge Piercy, "The Secretary Chant" (text p. 9)

CONNECTION QUESTION IN TEXT (p. 62) WITH ANSWER

1. Although Robert Browning's "My Last Duchess" (p. 164) is a more complex poem than Machan's, both use dramatic monologues to reveal character. How are the strategies in each poem similar?

    The speakers of each poem reveal something about themselves as they try to narrate a story. The speaker of this poem repeats the line "me a princess," indicating that her bravado is just a front for her dreams. The speaker of Browning's poem uses more sophisticated language, and he believes that he is in control of the narrative situation, but the more he talks the more he reveals about his true desires and motives. His asides are what give him away; as he pauses to consider how he should express something, he gives us the opportunity to analyze not only the content of his speech but his expression of it as well.

MARTÍN ESPADA, *Latin Night at the Pawnshop* (p. 62)

This imagist poem describes a scene of a man looking into the window of a pawnshop. In the instruments suspended there, he sees the apparition of a salsa band. The poet compares the instruments to a dead man with a toe tag.

There is nothing apparently "difficult" about this poem, so students may be quick to dismiss it, feeling that they "get the point" instantly. The challenge for discussion then becomes to fill in the considerable space around the poem. The liveliness of a salsa band coupled with the fact that the poem takes place on Christmas, a day of celebration, contribute to the blunt emotional overtones of the poem. What does the speaker's presence at a pawnshop on Christmas suggest? The speaker is implicitly mourning the passage of something vital. Unlike the Christmas ghosts of a character students are familiar with, Dickens's Scrooge, this apparition does not seem to provide any comfort or hope for the future. The apparition is the *absence* of the band, with its instruments apparently sold cheaply. As a way of pointing out what exactly has been lost, emphasize all of the economic allusions in the poem (pawnshop, Liberty Loan, golden, silver, price tags). Does the poem seek to make a broad point about class and culture in contemporary America? Consider the title as a follow-up to this question. Students may think of other examples of the various ways in which immigrants in America must "sell out" their culture for more fundamental survival needs (i.e., money).

POSSIBLE CONNECTION TO ANOTHER SELECTION

Cornelius Eady, "The Supremes" (text p. 670)

SARAH LINDSAY, *Aluminum Chlorohydrate* (p. 63)

This poem begins with an elaborate description of the movement of aluminum chlorohydrate molecules through the body, from the armpit rubbed with deodorant to the brain's synapses. At the time Lindsay wrote this poem, some theorized that

Alzheimer's disease may be caused by excess levels of aluminum in the brain, possibly deposited there through the use of deodorants that use the metal. The speaker is either coming to grips with this possible risk or merely overreacting to a medical hypothesis. For discussion, you could consider what the poem gains or loses if the theory proves to be false and the speaker's fears unwarranted.

This is a complex poem, combining a quiet scene of modern terror with clear delight in vocabulary. Students will come gradually to different levels of understanding it as they discern the different themes and vocabularies — both chemical and anatomical — Lindsay uses. Your students might enjoy focusing on the words in the poem; consider asking them to come up with synonyms that would change the tone. Another writing assignment could take a cue from Lindsay's use of a medical vocabulary: Students could try writing poems of their own that take advantage of the lexicons they are familiar with, such as slang or the jargon of the Internet.

POSSIBLE CONNECTIONS TO OTHER SELECTIONS

Alice Jones, "The Foot" (question #1, following)
Adrienne Rich, "Living in Sin" (text p. 633)

CONNECTION QUESTION IN TEXT (p. 63) WITH ANSWER

1. Discuss the ways in which diction helps to create tone in "Aluminum Chlorohydrate" and in "The Foot" by Alice Jones (p. 208). What does each poem have to say about what it means to be a human being?

    Both Lindsay and Jones react to the body with a vocabulary that revels in the smallest detail; the synapse and the capillary become vessels worthy of larger ambition, symbolic of history and future, holding a vast capacity for cumulative experience, bearing proof of a long, linear ancestry. These elaborate vocabularies react to the body with thought, with the full measure of medicine's calculated inventory; everything deserves a name, and every name deserves to be learned, repeated, and enjoyed. The wonder of our humanity, the miracle of each tiny cog in our elaborate mechanisms, is celebrated in the intellectual tone these poems offer.

ROBERT HERRICK, *To the Virgins, to Make Much of Time* (p. 64)

Robert Herrick, son of a well-to-do London goldsmith, rather halfheartedly became an Anglican clergyman assigned to Dean Prior in Devonshire, in the west of England. He wrote poems secretly, making up for many of them alluring, exotic, phantom mistresses. After losing his position when the Puritans rose to power, Herrick published his only book, containing some 1,200 poems, in 1648.

This is one of the better-known poems of the *carpe diem* (seize the day) tradition. Here, Herrick is advising young women in a tone of straightforward urging to make the most of their opportunities for pleasure while they are in the prime of youth and beauty. These "virgins," Herrick implies, are like the sun at its zenith or a flower in full bloom; they will soon begin to decline and may never have the same opportunities for marriage again. The word *virgins,* rather than *women,* accommodates the advice in the last stanza to "go marry" and carries with it as well the connotation of sought-for sexual fulfillment. Some of your students might point out how a young woman's situation is much more complex today than it apparently was in Herrick's time, since "seizing the day" can and often does mean pursuing opportunities for career over those for marriage.

One possible way to enter a discussion of the poem is to consider the arrangement of the argument. The speaker has a definite intent: to communicate bits of wisdom to the "virgins" of the title. What effect does the order of his points of argument have on the way the poem reads? What would happen if we were to rearrange the first three stanzas: Would the message of the poem remain exactly the same?

POSSIBLE CONNECTIONS TO OTHER SELECTIONS

Robert Frost, "Nothing Gold Can Stay" (text p. 354)
Richard Wilbur, "A Late Aubade" (text p. 68)

AUDIOVISUAL AND ONLINE RESOURCES (manual pp. 300, 335)

ANDREW MARVELL, *To His Coy Mistress* (p. 65)

After graduating from Cambridge University in 1639, Andrew Marvell left England to travel in Europe. Almost nothing is known of his life from this time until he became the tutor of the daughter of a powerful Yorkshire nobleman in 1650. Most of his poems seem to have been written during the next seven years. He served for a short time as John Milton's assistant when Milton was Latin secretary for the Commonwealth, and he represented Hull, his hometown, in Parliament from 1659 until he died.

This seduction poem is structured with a flawless logic. Marvell begins with a hypothetical conjecture, "Had we but world enough, and time," which he then disproves with hyperbole, promising his "mistress" that he would devote "an age at least" to praising her every part. Time is, of course, far more limited, and the second section of the poem makes clear time's ravages on beauty. The third section expounds the *carpe diem* theme: if time is limited, then seize the day and triumph over life's difficulties with love.

From his initial tone of teasing hyperbole, the poet modulates to a much more somber tone, employing the metaphysically startling imagery of the grave to underscore human mortality. Lines 31–32 are an example of understatement, calculated to make the listener react and acknowledge this world as the time and place for embracing.

Some classes may need help in recognizing that the verbs in the first part of the poem are in the subjunctive mood, while those in the last are often in the imperative. At any rate, students should easily recognize that the last section contains verbs that all imply a physical vigor that would seize time, mold it to the lovers' uses, and thus "make [time] run" (46) according to the clock of their own desires.

The poem seems far more than a simple celebration of the flesh. It confronts human mortality and suggests a psychological stance that would seize life (and face death) so that fulfilling of one's time would be a strategy of confronting time's passing.

As a writing topic you might ask students to explain the radical and somewhat abrupt change in tone between the opening twenty lines and the rest of the poem. Marvell offers more than one reason to temper his initial levity.

Refer students to Bernard Duyfhuizen's " 'To His Coy Mistress': On How a Female Might Respond" (text p. 67) for a contemporary perspective on the poem.

TIP FROM THE FIELD

I use point-of-view writing assignments that ask students to assume a persona in a poem or story and respond to the other characters or situations in the selection accordingly. For example, I have students read Andrew Marvell's "To His Coy Mistress" and then write an essay from the point of view of the wooer or the wooee.

— SANDRA ADICKES, *Winona State University*

POSSIBLE CONNECTIONS TO OTHER SELECTIONS

Diane Ackerman, "A Fine, a Private Place" (text p. 69)

John Keats, "Ode on a Grecian Urn" (text p. 79)

Richard Wilbur, "A Late Aubade" (text p. 68)

AUDIOVISUAL AND ONLINE RESOURCES (manual pp. 303, 341)

PERSPECTIVE

BERNARD DUYFHUIZEN, *"To His Coy Mistress": On How a Female Might Respond* (p. 67)

You might ask your students in a writing assignment to use Duyfhuizen's analysis as a model in writing their own description of a female's response to a male poet's address. They could use the poems in this section (Robert Herrick's "To the Virgins, to Make Much of Time" [text p. 64] and Richard Wilbur's "A Late Aubade" [text p. 68]), or they might choose a poem like Shakespeare's "Shall I compare thee to a summer's day?" (text p. 228). Students could also choose an address by a female poet to a male — Margaret Atwood's "you fit into me" (text p. 116), for example — or a poem by a woman about a relationship with a man — Adrienne Rich's "Living in Sin" (text p. 633) — and analyze the male's response.

RICHARD WILBUR, *A Late Aubade* (p. 68)

A prolific poet, critic, translator, and editor, Richard Wilbur (b. 1921) studied at Amherst and Harvard and was awarded the Pulitzer Prize and the National Book Award in 1957 for *Things of This World*. Influenced by the works of the Metaphysical Poets and Wallace Stevens, Wilbur's poetry has been described by poet and critic John Ciardi as often concerned with "the central driving intention of finding that artifice which will most include the most of life."

It is difficult to translate the forms of Renaissance charm and wit into the more hurried, less mannered tones of the twentieth century. So Wilbur seems to find as he writes his "late" aubade ("late," one supposes, as in "late Corinthian," as well as late in the day), in which going means staying and seizing the day dictates staying in bed. Despite the turnabout in manners and customs, this poem achieves its own special charm. You might begin discussion, though, by asking the class to evaluate the speaker here as rhetorician or persuader. Does he keep to the rules of logic, or does he beg some questions and employ loaded language in other instances? Obviously, he has no admiration for women who spend hours in either libraries or shopping malls, and with dead-pan doggerel he sets up a rhyme in stanza 1 between "carrel" (line 1) and "Ladies' Apparel" (4) that devalues both activities. Likewise, he colors the attitude of the person being addressed by talking of planting a "raucous" (5) bed of salvia (which yield bright blue or red flowers) or lunching through a "screed" (7) (the archaism is deliberate here) of someone's loves.

The poem is an appeal to the assumed and presumed sensuality of both the speaker and the woman he addresses. Thus the Matisselike still life of chilled white wine, blue cheese, and ruddy-skinned pears with which Wilbur concludes the poem is a fitting tri-color tribute to the senses, even though the woman here is still the one who serves and waits.

A writing assignment could be organized around a comparison of Herrick's "To the Virgins, to Make Much of Time" (text p. 64), Marvell's "To His Coy Mistress" (text p. 65), and this poem. Wilbur's poem is more conversational and relaxed, reflecting a commonality of spirit between the lovers. The speaker here dwells more on the prolonged moment than on the bleak foreknowledge of death.

POSSIBLE CONNECTIONS TO OTHER SELECTIONS

John Donne, "The Sun Rising" (text p. 42)
Robert Herrick, "To the Virgins, to Make Much of Time" (questions #1 and #2, following)
Andrew Marvell, "To His Coy Mistress" (questions #1 and #2, following)
Sharon Olds, "Sex without Love" (text p. 76)

CONNECTIONS QUESTIONS IN TEXT (p. 69) WITH ANSWERS

1. How does the man's argument in "A Late Aubade" differ from the speakers' in Herrick's and Marvell's poems? Which of the three arguments do you find most convincing?

    Unlike the other two writers, Wilbur's speaker is not immediately concerned with the passing of his youth. Herrick's and Marvell's poems try to convince their listeners to seize the moment because they feel the pressure of old age and mortality. Consequently, their rhetoric is loftier than Wilbur's, encompassing history and popular mythology. Wilbur's speaker tries to convince his lover in relatively simple language — "Isn't this better?" (line 12) — that the morning is more pleasantly spent in bed with him than elsewhere. Students are likely to find Wilbur's speaker the most convincing; his rhetoric is influenced by the "give the people what they want" philosophy of the twentieth century, whereas the other two poets are influenced by models of classical rhetoric of the English Renaissance. If the consensus tends this way, you might want to consider how rhetoric changes over time.

2. Explain how the tone of each poem is suited to its theme.

    Herrick's speaker argues from a position of wisdom, even condescension, which is fitting since the theme urges young women to live the moment of their youth. Marvell's poem seems more desperate; the speaker feels the pressure of "Time's wingéd chariot" (line 22) because he, along with his lover, senses his own passing youth. Wilbur's speaker is not as young — this is a *late* aubade — so his tone, his language, and his argument are all more leisurely, as though he is not worried about losing the moment of his youth as much as he would simply like his lover to remain in bed with him.

AUDIOVISUAL AND ONLINE RESOURCES (manual pp. 310, 354)

DIANE ACKERMAN, *A Fine, a Private Place* (p. 69)

Ackerman's poem might serve as sequel to Marvell's "To His Coy Mistress" (text p. 65) because it focuses less on the man's pursuit of his love (the subject of the speaker's rhetorical assault in Marvell's poem) than on the actual act of intercourse. The title of this poem is an allusion to the following lines from "To His Coy Mistress": "The grave's a fine and private place, / But none, I think, do there embrace" (lines 31–32). Ackerman depicts a grave of sorts — below the surface of the ocean — where the lovers in her poem, referred to at different times as "a pirate vessel" (48) and "a Spanish Galleon" (60), do embrace. Underwater, the man can phrase his desire only in physical gestures. Beginning with the description of his erection, when the woman notices "the octopus / in his swimsuit / stretch one tentacle / and ripple its silky bag" (15–18), Ackerman constructs an elaborate extended metaphor in which the lovers' bodies and their actions are construed in the highly specific imagery of the underwater world.

While Ackerman devotes significant and elaborate description to the couple and their lovemaking, enacting Marvell's speaker's plea to "tear our pleasures with rough strife" (43), there are instances in the poem in which, like Marvell, she seems to regard the woman as a commodity, as a "sea-geisha" (24). The lovers return to the surface only after the male is satisfied, and after he gives the signal. We are told that he leads the woman to safety (80). Throughout this process, even the ocean pets the woman, "cell by cell, murmuring / along her legs and neck, / caressing her / with pale, endless arms" (85–88). How does she seem to regard this?

It is only at the end of the poem that Ackerman delves into the woman's response to her experience. Whereas Marvell focuses solely on the male's perspective, Ackerman remedies this in the final lines of her poem, in which the woman continues to envision the surface world in marine terminology. She sees the snowflakes as "minnows" (109) and savors "holding a sponge / idly under tap-gush" (111–112) as it reminds her of her underwater tryst. The final stanza would seem to suggest that the woman treasures her experience underwater. Ask students to identify the poem's tone. Are we to regard the relationship portrayed in the poem as an ideal encounter?

POSSIBLE CONNECTIONS TO OTHER SELECTIONS

Emily Dickinson, " 'Heaven' — is what I cannot reach!" (text p. 299)

Andrew Marvell, "To His Coy Mistress" (question #1, following)

CONNECTION QUESTION IN TEXT (p. 72) WITH ANSWER

1. Write an essay comparing the tone of Ackerman's poem with that of Marvell's "To His Coy Mistress" (p. 65). To what extent are the central ideas in the poems similar?

   Both poems value passionate sex, but Marvell's poem anticipates the sexual encounter, whereas Ackerman's poem recalls it. As a result, Marvell's poem is more rushed, hurried on by "Time's wingéd chariot" (line 22) and Ackerman's poem is more leisurely, both in terms of its tone and its length. In a sense, their messages are opposite: Marvell's speaker argues that his youth is passing away quickly and that he is hurtling toward death, so he must enjoy passion when he is young. The subject of Ackerman's poem recalls her sexual encounter during the mundane moments of her daily routine, intimating that the moment of youth lives on in memory instead of passing away forever — the fear of Marvell's speaker.

ONLINE RESOURCES (manual p. 321)

MARGARET ATWOOD, *Bored* (p. 72)

This adult speaker reflects on her boredom as a young girl spending time with her father. She recounts their activities together, and ultimately realizes that her mature perceptions differ greatly from her childhood perceptions. She ends with the wistful realization, "Now I would know." Careful readers will notice that the relationship between the speaker and the "he" of the poem is likely that of a daughter and father; she sits in the back seat, helps him to build a garden, and learns about nature from him. It might be interesting to discuss why no one else exists in the poem. Is it primarily about him or about her? If the daughter is sitting in the back seat, it is likely that her mother is sitting in the front seat; why is her mother never mentioned?

The poem's single stanza doesn't help to identify points at which the speaker's attitude, point of view, or definition of boredom shift. It may be productive to have students identify and discuss these points: when boredom transmutes into "looking hard and up close at the small / details" (lines 13–14), or when her activity merges with "what / the animals spend most of their time at" (24–25). How does the meaning of the word "bored" change from the title through line 37? Students might be more likely to recognize the pun with "board" (4) — an object that almost seems an extension of the speaker in the early lines. However, the more elusive pun on boring as digging or burrowing represents a crucial turn in the speaker's perspective, as it allows the speaker to connect her activities with those of the animals her father "pointed . . . out" (27–28). "Boring" — a negative word to any child — becomes a positive word from the speaker's adult perspective since it connotes digging deeper in order to find meaning, resulting in a mature appreciation of her father.

POSSIBLE CONNECTION TO ANOTHER SELECTION

Robert Hayden, "Those Winter Sundays" (question #1, following)

CONNECTION QUESTION IN TEXT (p. 73) WITH ANSWER

1. Write an essay on the speaker's attitude toward the father in this poem and in Hayden's "Those Winter Sundays" (p. 10).

   The two poems end with strikingly similar sentiments: the penultimate line of Hayden's poem is, "What did I know, what did I know," and the final line of Atwood's is "Now I would know." Both speakers look back on their youthful relationship with their fathers from the point of view of a relatively wise and experienced adult. Yet a much greater gulf exists between the speaker of "Those Winter Sundays" and his father, who is associated with "the chronic angers of that house" (line 9). Atwood's speaker has a more intimate relationship with her father, who whistles, boats, and drives a car. Hayden's speaker's father works too hard and is alienated from his family. The bond of love between them is apparent, but it is an intense kind of "tough love."

AUDIOVISUAL AND ONLINE RESOURCES (manual pp. 292, 323)

THOMAS HARDY, *The Convergence of the Twain* (p. 73)

Between the ages of fifteen and twenty-one, Thomas Hardy was apprenticed to an architect in his native Dorchester, an area in southwest England that he was to transform into the "Wessex" of his novels. He went to London in 1862 to practice as an architect and pursue a growing interest in writing. Though he enjoyed a successful career as a novelist, Hardy stopped writing fiction after publishing *Jude the Obscure* in 1895, concentrating instead on the poetry that ranks him among the major English poets.

This poem ushers in an event that some consider to be the beginning of the modern era: the sinking of the *Titanic*. The final two stanzas support this idea. What is the true significance of the event, according to the speaker? What are the implications of a God who is described as both "The Immanent Will that stirs and urges everything" (line 18) and "the Spinner of the Years" (31)? On a superficial level, the "twain" of the title signifies the ship and the iceberg; what are some of the connotative meanings of the word?

The *Titanic* as described in this poem is "gaily great" (20) in its luxurious opulence, but Hardy also stresses the ship's "vaingloriousness" (15), planned by the "Pride of Life" (3). It is as though in this dramatic gesture of invention and design humanity became the tragic overreacher. In a writing assignment, you might ask the class to compare the tones of the speakers in this poem and in Percy Bysshe Shelley's "Ozymandias" (text p. 636).

The "marriage" between ship and iceberg is suggested through the use of several words and phrases, such as "sinister mate," (19), "intimate welding," as in "wedding" (27), and "consummation" in the final line.

Hardy, the master celebrator of "Hap" (see text p. 606), assigns the disaster to Fate, or as he allegorizes it, the "Immanent Will" (18) that directs all things and the "Spinner of the Years" (31), who decides when time has run out.

Stephen Crane, "A Man Said to the Universe" (text p. 146)

David R. Slavitt, "Titanic" (text p. 75)

Wallace Stevens, "The Emperor of Ice-Cream" (text p. 638)

AUDIOVISUAL AND ONLINE RESOURCES (manual pp. 299, 333)

DAVID R. SLAVITT, *Titanic* (p. 75)

Although Slavitt's poem acknowledges the power of fate, it focuses on human attitudes rather than cosmic forces. The first stanza, for example, calls attention to our gullibility; its weary, yet affectionate tone originating in the "this is how we are" shrug of the two *who* clauses. The speaker ponders death, deciding that since "we all go down" (line 4), it would be better to do so with some company and some notice from the rest of the world. But the speaker's gentle urging that it wouldn't be "so bad, after all" (11) to go "first-class" (14) includes some simple, unambiguous descriptions of what such a mass loss of life would actually be like: "The cold water" (11–12), which would be "anesthetic and very quick" (12); the "cries on all sides" (13). Death always wins, "we all go down, mostly / alone" (4–5), so wouldn't it be fine to die "with crowds of people, friends, servants, / well fed, with music" (4–5)?

You might ask students to compare in a short paper the attitudes toward fate in "Titanic" and Hardy's "The Convergence of the Twain" (text p. 73) and how each poem's diction and tone contribute to the communication of these attitudes.

POSSIBLE CONNECTION TO ANOTHER SELECTION

Thomas Hardy, "The Convergence of the Twain" (questions #1 and #3, following)

CONNECTIONS QUESTIONS IN TEXT (p. 75) WITH ANSWERS

1. How does "Titanic" differ in its attitude toward opulence from "The Convergence of the Twain" (p. 73)?

    In Hardy's poem, the opulence of the passengers on board the *Titanic* is emblematic of their lack of humility, and it seems partially responsible for the crash. Slavitt's poem, at least on the surface, celebrates the style with which the same passengers exited the world, arguing that, as long as we have to die, we might as well be having fun while we do it.

3. Compare the speakers' tones in "Titanic" and "The Convergence of the Twain."

    Hardy's poem is serious, formal in its use of language, form, and rhyme. "Titanic" is much more colloquial, less brooding in its tone and its language. Both poems could be described as philosophical, but Slavitt's brand of philosophy is more home-spun and optimistic.

ONLINE RESOURCES (manual p. 351)

LIONEL JOHNSON, *A Decadent's Lyric* (p. 76)

This poem celebrates the intimacy and union the speaker and his beloved find in bed together. Students are likely to enjoy this portrayal of sexual love from a nineteenth-century poet's perspective. The contrast between what they may have assumed such a poet would write about love and the provocative celebration of these lines may surprise them. The title serves as a sort of apology to those who are likely to be offended by the overt sexual content. This apology allows Johnson the freedom to write about sex with impunity: He has already acknowledged the decadence of his speaker.

The title provides a bold introduction to the poem's celebratory tone and explorations of desire and sexual fulfillment. Students may enjoy a discussion of these and other effects of the title on the poem. Questions to ask in generating discussion could include the distinction this title provides between the speaker and the poem: Does Johnson distance himself from his verse through this title? Does it take away from the delight the poem conveys? Or does it convey a sense of pride?

POSSIBLE CONNECTIONS TO OTHER SELECTIONS

Robert Herrick, "Delight in Disorder" (text p. 211)
Robert Herrick, "Upon Julia's Clothes" (text p. 225)
Sharon Olds, "Sex without Love" (question #1, following)

CONNECTION QUESTION IN TEXT (p. 76) WITH ANSWER

1. Discuss the view of sexuality presented in this poem and in "Sex without Love" by Sharon Olds (below).

   Both Johnson and Olds use creative and original metaphors to offer portraits of sexual activity. Johnson includes visions of "one living flame" (line 2); "ardour and agony unite" (5); "she and I / Play on live limbs love's opera!"(11–12). Olds's images focus less on the unity of two lovers and more on the individual's experience: ice skaters and runners, not musicians in concert. Unlike Johnson's poem, which illustrates a nearly spiritual experience, Olds's poem features lovers who are focused on the physical satisfaction sex brings.

SHARON OLDS, *Sex without Love* (p. 76)

The word *beautiful*, which begins the second sentence of this poem, may puzzle students at first. Coupled with the ambiguity of the initial question (which may indicate either the speaker's envy or her disdain), the appeal of the lovers as performing artists may signal a positive view of them. But students will soon recognize that the beautiful images of the poem are surface images only; they are also empty and somewhat violent. The textural imagery — "ice" (line 3), "hooked" (4), and even "red as steak" (6) — suggests an undertone of danger in this act. As an artist, the poet must show the lovers as beautiful forms, but as an artist with a social consciousness, she must also explore the vacuum beneath the forms.

A discussion of the poem's imagery may begin with an exploration of all the possible meanings of its initial question. The speaker examines not only the moral implications of this self-centered experience but also the mechanics of the physical act: *how* as well as *why* they do it. Discuss the shift in tone from the portrayal of the lovers as ice skaters and dancers in the initial lines to their likeness to great runners. This last metaphor solidifies the coldness of the speaker's assessment. Like great runners, the lovers concentrate only on the movement of their bodies, surrendering their mental and emotional health to the physical act. Students will see that the energy and concentration of runners are essential to a track event but not to an act of mutual communication. It is essential for the couple to think of themselves as athletes in order to escape the negative moral and potentially painful emotional implications of their act.

The religious images of the poem contrast with its athletic metaphors. Beginning with "God" (line 9) and moving into "light / rising slowly as steam off their joined / skin" (11–13), the speaker subtly distinguishes between the false, body-bound vision of the lovers and the "true religion" that is implied through their negation. Ask students to identify the speaker's tone in these lines: is she really talking about a religious experience, or is she pointing out the lovers' self-absorption? The mathematical language with which the speaker imagines her subjects talking about themselves, "just factors" (21), is undercut by her derogatory tone. Although *they* may act as if they are God, if we are searching for truth, we know that we can never really be single bodies alone in the universe. The implied "truth" here is a communal one, just the opposite of what is described.

In a writing assignment, you might ask students to explore what is not said in the poem. What is the alternative? Why would the speaker not state her idea of truth directly?

POSSIBLE CONNECTIONS TO OTHER SELECTIONS

E. E. Cummings, "she being Brand" (question #1, following)

Alberto Ríos, "Seniors" (text p. 40)

Richard Wilbur, "A Late Aubade" (question #2, following)

CONNECTIONS QUESTIONS IN TEXT (p. 77) WITH ANSWERS

1. How does the treatment of sex and love in Olds's poem compare with that in Cummings's "she being Brand" (p. 57)?

   Cummings and Olds do not share a similar notion of sex in these poems. Cummings's speaker is flippant, implying in his language that having sex is like driving a new car. Olds also talks about sex as mechanistic, but her disdain for that attitude is obvious. Cummings's speaker is less interested in the "truth" of the sexual relationship than he is in making the experience live on the page. Olds's speaker implies with regret that "truth" and love are ignored by those who have sex without love. One of the ways to reveal the different attitudes of these speakers is to compare their poems' very different images and sounds.

2. Just as Olds describes sex without love, she implies a definition of love in this poem. Consider whether the lovers in Wilbur's "A Late Aubade" (p. 68) fall within Olds's definition.

   The lovers in Wilbur's poem may well fall under Olds's definition of sex without love. The speaker in "A Late Aubade" clearly cares for their physical relationship, urging his beloved to forget worldly business and get them some wine and cheese. However, Wilbur's speaker's deliberate persuasive appeal to his lover establishes verbal communication, which is not even present in Olds's poem.

AUDIOVISUAL AND ONLINE RESOURCES (manual pp. 305, 345)

CATHY SONG, *The Youngest Daughter* (p. 77)

This poem describes the experience of a grown woman who has stayed at home to take care of her aging parents. The speaker is bound by duty to stay in the family home until her parents die. The long-standing nature of her situation is presented early on in images: "the sky has been dark / for many years" (lines 1–2). The escape planned at the end of the poem is symbolized by the thousand paper cranes in the window, flying up in a sudden breeze. The speaker suggests ambivalence about the mother through the "sour taste" in her mouth in line 26 and the "almost tender" (30) way the speaker soaps the blue bruises of her mother's body. The toast to the mother's health following an acknowledgment that the speaker is not to be trusted demonstrates the ambivalence further: once the mother dies, the youngest daughter can leave home; the sour taste and tenderness for her circumstances, the familiar silence and the migraines, will all change for both better and worse.

Asking students to analyze their own ambivalence about their parents in journal entries could help them establish a connection with Song's narrative. Spend a little time before the writing period suggesting circumstances that could provide context for their writing. Their departures for college may provide illustration of their changing relationships with their parents.

POSSIBLE CONNECTION TO ANOTHER SELECTION

Wyatt Prunty, "Elderly Lady Crossing on Green" (text p. 39)

ONLINE RESOURCES (manual p. 351)

JOHN KEATS, *Ode on a Grecian Urn* (p. 79)

The speaker's attitude toward this object of beauty is a rapt expression of awe at its evocative and truth-bearing power and presence. Life portrayed on the urn is forever in suspended animation: no one gets old; the "wild ecstasy" goes undiminished; the love, never consummated, is yet never consumed and wearied of. Keats seems to admire this portrait of the sensuous ideal, which exists unmarred by mortality or the vagrancy of human passion.

The significant question about this ode (beyond the meaning of the closing two lines and whether the speaker or the urn pronounces all or a part of them) appears to rest with "Cold Pastoral!" (line 45) and the ambivalence these words imply. Earlier, in stanza III, Keats had admired the love "for ever warm and still to be enjoyed" (26) that was portrayed on the urn. Has the temperature of the urn changed by stanza V? Has the speaker discovered, in essence, that even though the urn portrays a sensuous ideal of courtship and pursuit, it is still merely a cold form that, because it is deathless, can never feel the warmth of human life?

Still one of the best studies on this ode is the essay (bearing the same title as the ode) by Earl R. Wasserman in *The Finer Tone: Keats's Major Poems* (Baltimore: Johns Hopkins UP, 1953, 1967, 11–63). For the record, Wasserman argues that the closing lines are spoken by the poet to the reader; as Wasserman explains, the ode is *on* a Grecian Urn, not *to* the urn. Hence, "it is Keats who must make the commentary on the drama" (59).

POSSIBLE CONNECTIONS TO OTHER SELECTIONS

Emily Dickinson, "Success is counted sweetest" (text p. 294)

John Keats, "To Autumn" (question #3, following)

Andrew Marvell, "To His Coy Mistress" (question #1, following)

Richard Wilbur, "Love Calls Us to the Things of This World" (question #2, following)

CONNECTIONS QUESTIONS IN TEXT (p. 80) **WITH ANSWERS**

1. Write an essay comparing the view of time in this ode with that in Marvell's "To His Coy Mistress" (p. 65). Pay particular attention to the connotative language in each poem.

   In Keats's ode, time wastes human beings but does not affect art. Art provides hope, friendliness, and beauty to human beings, making their misery more understandable in its "truth." In Marvell's poem, which dwells much more in the physicality of human experience, the speaker urges his listener to "make [the sun] run" (line 46), because time will destroy her anyway. The difference in the poems' treatments of time results from their different subjects. Whereas Keats's ode discusses art *vs.* human existence, Marvell's work claims that human existence is all we have.

2. Discuss the treatment and meaning of love in this ode and in Richard Wilbur's "Love Calls Us to the Things of This World" (p. 643).

Keats presents the moment before the kiss as the peak of a relationship because this moment is full of anticipation and ripeness, but Wilbur makes the very earthly lovers into heavenly angels. The value of anticipation over experience in Keats's mind is ambiguous, however. After all, he describes his vision as a "Cold Pastoral" in stanza V. Perhaps he thinks that loving is more important than art, but it is hard to tell. Unlike Keats's speaker, the speaker in Wilbur's poem traces the moment after the epiphany, when souls descend from fresh laundry into the living bodies of lovers waking to ordinary day.

3. Compare the tone and attitude toward life in this ode with those in Keats's "To Autumn" (p. 109).

In "To Autumn" Keats celebrates a moment at the end of fall, asking us to appreciate the passage of time in his timeless work of art. In a sense the Grecian urn, a celebration of timeless beauty in art, competes with the ephemeral season of autumn. The poems are perfectly juxtaposed; one celebrates finitude, the other immortality. "To Autumn" appeals directly to the senses, whereas in "Ode on a Grecian Urn," the urn stands between the speaker and his audience, and between the audience and the ephemeral experience frozen forever on the urn. "Ode on a Grecian Urn" creates a sense of aesthetic distance and self-consciously questions the meaning and value of art in a way that "To Autumn" does not.

AUDIOVISUAL AND ONLINE RESOURCES (manual pp. 301, 338)

GWENDOLYN BROOKS, *We Real Cool* (p. 81)

Gwendolyn Brooks, who grew up in Chicago and who won the Pulitzer Prize in 1950, has been a deeply respected and influential poet for more than forty years.

In this poem, Brooks sets forth a tableau in a montage of street language. The poetic conventions she uses include alliteration, assonance, and internal rhyme. Students may be so taken with the sounds of the poem that they will be surprised that it has a decidedly somber focal point. How does the rest of the poem prepare us for the final line? Is there a "message" implicit in the poem? If so, how is the message affected by the spare yet stunning language of the poem?

The repeated "we" sounds the menacing note of the communal pack, its members secure perhaps only when they are together. The truncated syntax reflects both a lack of and a disdain for education, yet the poem celebrates the music of its vernacular, a quality that would be mostly lost were the pronouns to appear at the beginnings of lines.

Brooks's attitude toward this chorus that finds strength in numbers is a measured anger against its self-destructiveness. The absence of "we" in the final line is a silent prophecy of their future, moving us toward an understanding of the theme of the poem: death (burial/shovel) at an early age and the corruption of a golden opportunity to spend youth more wisely. The "Golden Shovel" also bespeaks an ironic promise that the events of the last line sadly belie.

POSSIBLE CONNECTION TO ANOTHER SELECTION

Langston Hughes, "Jazzonia" (text p. 379)

AUDIOVISUAL AND ONLINE RESOURCES (manual pp. 294, 325–326)

ERIC ORMSBY, *Nose* (p. 81)

This curious poem, stiff and formal in tone, provides a scholarly examination of a part of the body rendered silly by comics like Jimmy Durante and Groucho Marx. The complex nature of the nose is present in Ormsby's assertion that the nose both "snuffles" (line 2), a decidedly ignoble activity, and "recoils / in Roman nobility" (2–3). The poem moves from the role the nose has played in classical sculpture to an exploration of its bulbous qualities in comparing the nose to corms and rhizomes. In the third stanza the poem touches on how the nose divides the face, creates the symmetry we have agreed is beautiful, and plays with the idea of exulting, rising up from the horizontal surfaces of the sleeping face.

Exult comes from the Latin *ex-*, "out," and *salire*, "to leap." Its original meaning in English is to spring or leap up for joy; this definition is now obsolete. The current meaning of *exult* is to rejoice exceedingly, to be elated or glad. You might find it helpful to make two lists of words on the board: words that Ormsby uses to evoke the noble lines of the nose, and words he employs to stress its earthy function.

POSSIBLE CONNECTIONS TO OTHER SELECTIONS

Alice Jones, "The Larynx" (question #1, following)
Theodore Roethke, "Root Cellar" (text p. 94)

CONNECTION QUESTION IN TEXT (p. 82) WITH ANSWER

1. Compare the central idea of the "Nose" with "The Larynx" by Alice Jones (below). Which poem do you prefer? Why?

   Although both Jones and Ormsby examine a familiar part of our anatomy with vivid vocabulary and imagery, Jones focuses more on medical language. Students may take pleasure in the numerous contrasts in Ormsby's poem, or prefer the pleasure of phrases like "puzzle box / of gristle" (lines 14–15) in Jones's lines.

ALICE JONES, *The Larynx* (p. 82)

The long breathy sentence of this poem focuses attention on the reader's own larynx when the poem is read aloud. Having a student read the poem to the class could help students see the function the long sentence structure serves. The complex mechanisms involved in creating a single tone are described in both scientific terms and poetic phrases. The scientific language, like "transparent sacs knit / with small vessels into a mesh" (lines 7–8) progresses into the more poetic phrases of the final third of the poem: "they flutter, / bend like birds' wings finding just the right angle to stay / airborne" (23–26).

Ask students how their understanding of the poem would be different if Jones had left out the explicit mention of song. The long breathy explication of how the voice works comes to a clear culmination; without it, students might have gotten lost in reading the poem. Asking which lines provide hints that the poem is leading toward song could help direct discussion.

POSSIBLE CONNECTIONS TO OTHER SELECTIONS

Helen Chasin, "The Word *Plum*" (text p. 195)
Alice Jones, "The Foot" (question #1, following)
Eric Ormsby, "Nose" (text p. 81)

CONNECTION QUESTION IN TEXT (p. 83) WITH ANSWER

1. Compare the diction and ending that Jones writes in "The Larynx" with those of "The Foot" (p. 208), another poem by Jones.

   Jones takes advantage of rich anatomical vocabulary in both poems. "The Larynx" uses phrases such as "epiglottic flap" (line 1) and "bronchial / fork" (3–4) to introduce an instructive tone before departing for more figurative language. "The Foot" makes a litany of "calcaneus, talus, cuboid, / navicular, cuneiforms, metatarsals, / pha-langes" (3–5) to introduce the oblique evolution that produced this miraculous sup-port. While "The Larynx" examines the process by which the larynx produces sounds, "The Foot" takes a journey of discovery through the anatomy of the foot to arrive at "the distal nail" (22), the reminder of our cave-dwelling ancestors and their claws.

OLIVER RICE, *The Doll House* (p. 83)

Rice's poem, an examination of a doll house, employs the childish diction of its adjectives — "itsy" (line 3), "bitsy" (4), "teeny" (5), and "weeny" (6) — to press the point of its cuteness until it becomes its antithesis. The poem contrasts this association of doll-houses with childish things and the associations raised by the reference to Ibsen. This stark contrast is established within the first stanza. The tensions of the home, examined in miniature, become a threatening thing to learn about in "this little milieu" (8); the reference to Ibsen, and the contrast between childish and adult language, establish a new reading of the lessons a doll house teaches. The explicit reference to the playwright in the poem and the implicit reference to his play *A Doll House* have imbued the title and subject of this poem with a tension not present merely in the miniature furniture and apparent absence of dolls. The rules that may discover the game, in line 14, may refer to the social constructs that rule family life and the ways in which children learn about adulthood and its unpleasantries through play.

It is possible to catch the off-putting tone of this poem without knowing anything about Ibsen; asking students who are familiar with the play to summarize it could help direct discussion. Also consider asking students unfamiliar with the play to identify pas-sages that prevent this from being a cheerful and innocent examination of a child's toy.

POSSIBLE CONNECTIONS TO OTHER SELECTIONS

Margaret Atwood, "you fit into me" (text p. 116)
Alice Walker, "a woman is not a potted plant" (text p. 37)

LOUIS SIMPSON, *In the Suburbs* (p. 84)

Students may resist this spare poem's desolate presentation of the fate of the American suburbanite. The suburban phenomenon began a dozen years before Simpson published his poem, but the poem is as relevant as ever since Americans continue to move to the suburbs. At least some of your students are likely to be from suburban households. A discussion of the American Dream may be a productive place to begin, perhaps even before students have read the poem. It might also be useful to have them define "middle class," in terms of both yearly income and lifestyle choices. Once you have established (and perhaps complicated) their sense of the middle class in America, you can work your way into the poem: where does the speaker of this poem get off equat-ing a middle-class existence with a "waste" (line 2) of life? Does "middleclass" (3) neces-sarily mean suburban or vice versa? Is the situation as fatalistic as the poet suggests it is? (Half of the poem's six lines contain the phrase "were born to" (lines 2, 3, 5), and the first line is "There's no way out").

This apparently simple poem is complicated considerably by the final two lines. The poet connects a suburban lifestyle with one of religious devotion. Because of the nega-tive diction ("no way out" in line 1, "waste" in line 2, for example) the comparison invites a discussion not only of the worst aspects of middle-class existence, but of religion, too. But what alternatives are there? Consider, too, the positive aspects of suburbia and reli-gion. What connotations does the poem's last word, "singing," carry? At the end of the discussion, you might point out how powerful word choice can be in a simple, spare poem like this one for generating ideas.

Comparisons of this poem to John Ciardi's "Suburban" (text p. 161) are likely to yield observations of a stark difference in tone. Ciardi's poem is funny, Simpson's is quite serious. Yet do the poems share a similar attitude about what is important in life? Does the speaker of "Suburban" lead a typical middle-class life? Does the speaker in "In the Suburbs"? How do the differences in speaker and point of view affect the reader's reception of each poem?

POSSIBLE CONNECTIONS TO OTHER SELECTIONS

John Ciardi, "Suburban" (question #1, following)

Florence Cassen Mayers, "All-American Sestina" (text p. 236)

CONNECTION QUESTION IN TEXT (p. 84) WITH ANSWER

1. Write an essay on suburban life based on this poem and John Ciardi's "Suburban" (p. 161).

   Based on the speakers' attitudes in these two poems, the suburbs are, ostensibly, devoid of life, or repressed. Mrs. Friar, the neighbor in Ciardi's poem, fails, out of an overdeveloped sense of propriety, to value the "organic gold" (line 11) of the dog's "repulsive object" (5). The speaker in Simpson's poem regards suburban, middle-class life as a "waste [of] life" (2). Yet each poem concludes on a hopeful note, stressing the life that is beneath an otherwise sterile-seeming appearance: Simpson's poem concludes with the hopeful last word, "singing" (6); and Ciardi's hints at the "resurrection" (20) into plant life of even the foul "repulsive object."

AUDIOVISUAL AND ONLINE RESOURCES (manual pp. 307, 351)

A NOTE ON READING TRANSLATIONS

SAPPHO, *Hymn to Aphrodite* with four translations by HENRY T. WHARTON, T. W. HIGGINSON, RICHARD LATTIMORE, and JIM POWELL (pp. 85–88)

In this appeal to Aphrodite, Sappho asks that the lover who has spurned her be afflicted with yearning and filled with desire for Sappho. All four of these versions of this poem, Sappho's most famous, try to conform to the original's stanzaic form — a form that has come to be known as the sapphic. A sapphic is three eleven-syllable lines followed by one five-syllable line; or two eleven-syllable lines followed by one sixteen-syllable line. The Greeks used a metrical system based on syllable length rather than stress: thus a Greek metric foot would consist of a combination of short and long syllables rather than unstressed and stressed syllables. This metric system, called quantitative, is difficult in English, where it is usually replaced — as in these versions — with a more familiar accentual-syllabic approximation.

In spite of their common formal aims and their dedication to accurately rendering the original, each of these poems is unique. Both Wharton's and Higginson's versions sound high-flown and a bit archaic — almost biblical — to our ears, and they wouldn't have sounded like ordinary speech to nineteenth-century readers, either. Compare, for instance, Higginson's elaborate image "the most lovely / Consecrated birds" (lines 10–11) with Lattimore's simple "sparrows" (9). Where Higginson's version is grandiose, full of ornate phrasing and imagery, Lattimore's is both stately and intimate. Lattimore stresses this intimacy in his closing, where Aphrodite acts as a guardian, almost maternal, where in other versions she is cast in a less consoling role: as military ally (in Wharton and Powell), as venerated deity,

"Sacred protector" (34) in Higginson. Though Jim Powell's version is most faithful to the meter of the classical Greek, clearly his diction is the most up-to-date: his use of contractions and of italics to add emphasis makes his version sound almost casual at times.

Studying this poem makes clear how much of translation is interpretation, how much a translator is limited or informed by the context in which he or she is writing. You might want to discuss Higginson's editorial decision to change the pronoun for Sappho's lover from "she" to "he" in the sixth stanza, though the lover was certainly a woman in the original (25–30). The practice of editing poems in such a way was not uncommon in previous centuries — even Shakespeare was not immune. Although students may find this sort of obvious editing troubling, it is interesting to note the extent to which decisions these translators make in choosing a style or a level of diction change the poem in equally — or more — profound ways.

4

Images

Students are already very familiar with imagery through advertising. You may find it an interesting exercise to have students compare ads and poems dealing with similar subject matter: a recruitment commercial and Owen's "Dulce et Decorum Est," for instance. This may prove to be a controversial exercise — be prepared for students' resistance. You may instead (or additionally) want to have students focus on several advertisements or television shows and write a short response to the imagery they find there. This exercise can be beneficial because it will show students they already know how to read imagery, and will also help sharpen their critical thinking skills by applying analysis in an area they are unused to.

Still, students can sometimes have trouble with very imagistic poems: such poems may require more effort on the part of students than they suspect. Often, it may help to ask students to consider why it is that a poet focuses so closely on a given scene or object. Whitman's "Cavalry Crossing a Ford" can seem like just a pretty scene unless one puts it in the context of the Civil War and realizes the possible fate in store for these men — a fate of which Whitman was all too aware from his work in a hospital. If students can be helped to see that poets often use images to emphasize significance or preserve a fleeting moment, they may appreciate the poems more.

Another important point in this chapter is that images need not be exclusively visual. Croft's "Home-Baked Bread" and Song's "The White Porch" both employ a variety of imagery to enhance the sensual themes of the poems. Blake's "London" is full of auditory images, while Roethke's "The Root Cellar" and Baca's "Green Chile" use smell and taste, respectively. Baca's poem raises an interesting point about the cultural specificity of imagery, particularly when compared to a poem such as Wilbur's "A Late Aubade." Some students may, in fact, be more familiar with the taste of green chile con carne than bleu cheese and wine.

You may find that it helps to have students experiment with their own writing in this chapter: they could be asked to write a descriptive paragraph or poem concretely rendering an object, scene, or activity. This can serve to emphasize ideas raised in class about the significance of detail.

The paragraph from Hulme at the end of the chapter can also be useful in this regard, as it highlights some of these ideas. It can also provide a good starting place for discussions either now or later in the class about the distinction between poetry and prose.

WILLIAM CARLOS WILLIAMS, *Poem* (p. 90)

William Carlos Williams was born and lived most of his life in Rutherford, New Jersey, a town near Paterson, the city that provided the title and much of the subject matter of his "modern epic" poem *Paterson*. He had a thriving medical practice for fifty years, delivering more than 2,000 babies and writing his poems, novels, short stories, and essays at night and in the moments he could snatch between patient visits during the day.

This poem is an imaged motion, but the verse has a certain slant music too. Notice the *t*-sounds that align themselves in the second tercet, the consonance in "hind" (line 8) and "down" (9), the repetitions in "pit of" (10), "empty" (11), and "flowerpot" (12). Sound also helps convey the poem's sense of agility and smoothness.

Students may initially resist this poem because, being apparently simple, it may not conform to their expectations. If this situation arises, or perhaps even if it doesn't, you can use this opportunity to ask the question, "what should poetry do or be?" In all likelihood, you can convince skeptics that Williams's poem does what they don't think it does. In any case, it is an opportunity to refine a definition of poetry while exploring its power to appeal to our imagination.

Possible Connections to Other Selections

Matsuo Bashō, "Under cherry trees" (text p. 240)
Ezra Pound, "In a Station of the Metro" (text p. 110)

Audiovisual and Online Resources (manual pp. 310–311, 355)

JEANNETTE BARNES, *Battle-Piece* (p. 90)

This poem provides an attentive examination of a battlefield that is now used for picnic grounds. Few who visit, according to the speaker, recognize the tragic history of the war monument. Barnes contrasts the fleeting engagement of picnickers at the peaceful site with the "sharp surprise" (lines 30–31) of the soldiers who died there, using vivid images to reconstruct the past. Barnes's tone could be construed as judgment passed on those who frequent the area without taking the time, as she does, to reconstruct the events that made it monumental. The picknickers "get gone" (2) and the "prize of plastic daisies" (13) is belittled with the acknowledgment that "nobody calls this lazy" (14).

You might ask your students to assign a chronology to the poem; what kinds of transitions does Barnes provide between her discussion of current events and her imagining of the events of 1864 at this site? In the first stanza, the "sting, snap, / grit in clenched teeth" convey a sense of immediacy. Barnes suggests that these horrible images of war are still available for understanding even though the public is indifferent.

Through her use of the words "shock" and "surprise," Barnes also compares the "shock" (18) of her own vision of this battle with the "sharp / surprise" (30-31) of death's scythe arriving, until the fallen soldiers are "astonished by the sky" (33). The past overshadows the present in this poem, and the shock of the deaths of the soldiers is more genuine than the plastic daisies used to honor their sacrifices. You might want to ask students how Barnes conveys this primacy of past over present: her techniques include the picknickers' lack of names, while the soldiers are identified as "Clem, Eustace, Willy" (9). Further, the soldiers filch apples and chew spruce gum, while the picnic baskets remain unimagined in this poem.

Possible Connections to Other Selections

Wilfred Owen, "Dulce et Decorum Est" (text p. 102)
Henry Reed, "Naming of Parts" (text p. 160)

WALT WHITMAN, *Cavalry Crossing a Ford* (p. 92)

Walt Whitman is, with Emily Dickinson, one of the two poetic giants of the American nineteenth century. Born in Huntington, Long Island, he grew up in Brooklyn, leaving school at age eleven for a job as an office boy in a law firm. His poetry grew out of his experiences as a reporter, teacher, laborer, and Civil War nurse. He self-published the first edition of his book — his life's work, really — *Leaves of Grass* in 1855.

Whitman's descriptive words lend a colorful, paradelike quality to this scene. The flashing arms with their musical clank along with the guidon flags fluttering gaily create an image that suggests liveliness and energy. Yet, "Behold" in lines 3 and 4, with its biblical overtones and its arresting sense of absorbing the sight ("be-hold"), is more stately than *look* or *see* and, with its long vowels, is almost ministerial. How does Whitman manage these two apparently contrasting tones?

The speaker in this poem (we can assume Whitman himself) seems to be fairly distant from the scene and possibly slightly elevated to see the entire picture. He scans the troops with a panning gaze that is, nonetheless, able to come in for some close-ups as he looks at the brown-faced men, "each group, each person, a picture" (4).

A productive discussion of this poem might take into account Whitman's lines and how their rhythm contributes to the description in the poem. Does the momentum of the lines have anything to do with the movement of the troops? To what degree is the description "arranged," and to what degree does it mirror the speaker's perception of the scene as it impresses itself upon him?

POSSIBLE CONNECTIONS TO OTHER SELECTIONS

Faiz Ahmed Faiz, "If You Look at the City from Here" (text p. 658)

William Carlos Williams, "Poem" (text p. 90)

AUDIOVISUAL AND ONLINE RESOURCES (manual pp. 309–310, 354)

DAVID SOLWAY, *Windsurfing* (p. 92)

"Windsurfing" is a poem full of action and motion. The poem begins with "It"; the poet does not pause long enough to even explain exactly what "it" is, but instead allows the motion of the poem to mirror the motion of the windsurfer. The man who is windsurfing is referred to directly only twice; the man and the windsurfer move so forcefully together that the two share a single identity. The intensity of the motion of the windsurfer as it careens across the water is suggested through the carefully chosen verbs ("plunge" [line 20], "snapping" [37], "lashing" [38], "shearing" [39], "lunging" [27], etc.), which reveal the violence, grace, and beauty of the scene.

Because "Windsurfing" conveys one particular scene vividly, you may wish to ask students to compare the water imagery, the fluidity of motion between the man and his windsurfer, and the sensual imagery to those of other poems with similar settings (such as Matthew Arnold's "Dover Beach" [text p. 95] and Diane Ackerman's "A Fine, a Private Place" [text p. 69]).

POSSIBLE CONNECTIONS TO OTHER SELECTIONS

Elizabeth Bishop, "The Fish" (question #2, following)

Li Ho, "A Beautiful Girl Combs Her Hair" (question #1, following)

CONNECTIONS QUESTIONS IN TEXT (p. 94) WITH ANSWERS

1. Consider the effects of the images in "Windsurfing" and Li Ho's "A Beautiful Girl Combs Her Hair" (p. 43). In an essay, explain how these images produce emotional responses in you.

    Solway's imagery moves fluidly, one metaphor leading into another with active verbs. Li Ho's imagery is somewhat more startling, juxtaposing images that seem to have less to do with one another but that create an overall impression that ultimately coheres.

2. Compare the descriptions in "Windsurfing" and Elizabeth Bishop's "The Fish" (p. 20). How does each poet appeal to your senses to describe windsurfing and fishing?

The fish in Bishop's poem is not in motion the way the windsurfer is. Bishop's speaker regards the fish, then looks more closely and more closely still, describing details as they impress themselves upon her and relying on simile and details to convey an impression of the fish as though she is slowly zooming in with a camera. Solway's windsurfer is moving much more quickly, and he provides us with metaphors that change at rapid-fire pace, mimicking the movement of his subject.

THEODORE ROETHKE, *Root Cellar* (p. 94)

The theme of this brief lyric with its powerful images is stated in the penultimate line: "Nothing would give up life." In the darkness of the root cellar, dank with a perpetual humidity, nothing sleeps; the atmosphere is ideal for engendering life. Normally we associate the underground with death and decay, but here decay is shown to be a source of life.

Some of the imagery in this poem is aimed at the olfactory sense, particularly when Roethke summons up the "congress of stinks" (line 6). "Congress" is an especially appropriate word choice here, for it can mean not only a political body but sexual intercourse as well. Coming together, as all these odoriferous bodies do, brings forth life out of putrefaction, mold, slime, and bulbous decay.

The sense of sight, however, also operates in the poem, and we are asked to use our imaginative powers to see shoots "lolling obscenely" (4) or hanging down "like tropical snakes" (5). Even our sense of touch is called upon to apprehend the "leaf-mold, manure, lime, piled against slippery planks" (9). Note too the consonance of *ms* and *ps* in this carefully constructed line. As ugly and odoriferous as some of these images are, the poem ends on a small cry of victory — "Even the dirt kept breathing a small breath" (11) — and this closing line recapitulates the tone of admiration, even wonder, that Roethke seems to feel as he enters the root cellar.

POSSIBLE CONNECTION TO ANOTHER SELECTION

John Keats, "To Autumn" (text p. 109)

AUDIOVISUAL AND ONLINE RESOURCES (manual pp. 306–307, 348–349)

MATTHEW ARNOLD, *Dover Beach* (p. 95)

Matthew Arnold was born in the English village of Laleham, in the Thames valley. His father was a clergyman and a reformist educator, a powerful personality against whom the young Arnold rebelled in a number of ways, including nearly flunking out of Oxford. After several years as private secretary to a nobleman, in 1851 Arnold became an inspector of schools, a post he held for thirty-five years. For the characteristic jauntiness of his prose style, Walt Whitman once referred to him as "one of the dudes of literature."

Many of us have had the experience of looking out on a landscape and registering its beauty (and possibly its tranquillity) and its undercurrent of something lost or awry. Such is the case for the speaker of "Dover Beach" as he looks out at the shore awash in moonlight. The private moment has its wholeness, for he stands in the "sweetness" of the night air with his beloved. But all the security and peace he could expect to feel are shaken by his concerns beyond the moment and his awareness of the ravages that history brings to bear on the present. We are not fragments of our time alone, the poem seems to say; we are caught in the "turbid ebb and flow / Of human misery" (lines 17–18) that Sophocles heard so long ago.

In the third stanza, Arnold goes beyond commenting on the sadness that seems an inevitable part of the human condition, as his thoughts turn to the malaise of his own time. Faith, which once encircled humanity, is now only the overheard roar of its waters withdrawing to the rock-strewn edges of the world. In short, for whatever happens there is no solace, no consolation or reason to hope for any restoration, justice, or change. Humankind is beyond the tragic condition of Sophocles, and in this poem, Arnold seems to be tipping the balance toward a modernist existential worldview. The tone of the poem barely improves by the final stanza, for the image Arnold leaves us with is that of "ignorant armies" clashing in the night — the sound and fury once again signifying nothing.

The images of Dover Beach or some other imagined seascape work well to evoke the tone that Arnold is trying to convey. In discussion, or perhaps as a writing topic, you might ask the class to review the poem for natural details and images (in lines 9–14 or most of the third stanza, for example) that suggest the dreary, stark, and ominous portrait Arnold is painting here.

General essays on this poem appear in A. Dwight Culler's *Imaginative Reason: The Poetry of Matthew Arnold* (New Haven: Yale UP, 1966) and James Dickey's *Babel to Byzantium* (New York: Farrar, 1968).

POSSIBLE CONNECTIONS TO OTHER SELECTIONS

Anthony Hecht, "The Dover Bitch" (question #2, following)
Wilfred Owen, "Dulce et Decorum Est" (question #1, following)

CONNECTIONS QUESTIONS IN TEXT (p. 95) WITH ANSWERS

1. Explain how the images in Wilfred Owen's "Dulce et Decorum Est" (p. 102) develop further the ideas and sentiments suggested by Arnold's final line concerning "ignorant armies clash[ing] by night."

    The crippled soldiers in Owen's poem illustrate the final line of Arnold's, their decrepitude confirming what Arnold only hinted at. The gruesome images — "coughing like hags" (line 2), "blood-shod" (6), "choking, drowning" (16) — graphically demonstrate the consequences of those "ignorant armies clash[ing] by night."

2. Contrast Arnold's images with those of Anthony Hecht in his parody "The Dover Bitch" (p. 609). How do Hecht's images create a very different mood from that of "Dover Beach"?

    In a conversational style and lighthearted tone, Hecht's speaker refers to the immediate pleasures of a more bawdy reality while defending the implied listener in Arnold's poem. Hecht's images evoke the daily life of the woman, contrasting sharply with Arnold's interest in the more philosophical issues of his day. Although we cannot assume much about the listener in Arnold's poem (is she even real?), we might presume that she would be far more respectful toward the speaker than Hecht's images imply. Indeed, Hecht intimates that the listener is a "loose woman": "I give her a good time" (26).

AUDIOVISUAL AND ONLINE RESOURCES (manual pp. 292, 323)

JIMMY SANTIAGO BACA, *Green Chile* (p. 96)

You might begin a discussion of this poem by focusing on the way the differences between the red and green chiles reflect the differences between the speaker and his grandmother. Students may note that in the poem the red chiles function as decoration while the green chiles symbolize passion and tradition. For example, the speaker likes to have "red chile" (line 1) with his "eggs and potatoes for breakfast" (1, 2) and also uses them as decoration throughout his house (3, 4).

The speaker's use of red peppers could be seen as signs of the speaker's assimilation into mainstream United States culture, for the speaker eats a traditional breakfast of "eggs and potatoes" (1–2), whereas the grandmother prepares "green chile con carne / between soft warm leaves of corn tortillas / with beans and rice" (32–34). In contrast to the speaker, who uses red chile peppers as decoration, the grandmother views the green chile peppers as a "gentleman" (19) — more than a decoration, green chile peppers represent "passion" (31) and "ritual" (45). Considering the contrast in the function of the red and green chile peppers, ask your students to discuss what the speaker could be implying about the differences between his generation and his grandmother's generation. Is it possible that the speaker finds himself separated from the passion and intensity of the Hispanic community in which his grandmother lives? How does the image of the chile peppers work to reconcile the life-style of the speaker with the life-style of the grandmother? What could the speaker hope to convey in the sexual description of his grandmother's relationship with the green chile?

Because of the implicit and explicit connections between food and sexuality, you might ask students to further explore those links through other poems in which food and eating are framed in sexual terms — the vegetables in Roethke's "Root Cellar" (text p. 94), for example, or the food metaphors in Sally Croft's "Home-Baked Bread" (text p. 107), and Elaine Magarrell's "The Joy of Cooking" (text p. 134).

POSSIBLE CONNECTIONS TO OTHER SELECTIONS

Carolynn Hoy, "In the Summer Kitchen" (text p. 267)
Lisa Parker, "Snapping Beans" (text p. 38)

AUDIOVISUAL AND ONLINE RESOURCES (manual pp. 292, 323)

H. D. [HILDA DOOLITTLE], *Heat* (p. 98)

Hilda Doolittle was born in Bethlehem, Pennsylvania, and educated at private schools in Philadelphia. In 1911 she moved to London, where she married English poet Richard Aldington. Although an American poet and novelist, H. D. was involved with the Bloomsbury group for a time and was an important figure in the Imagist movement as well. Ezra Pound, who encouraged her poetic aspirations and submitted her work to *Poetry* magazine under the name "H. D., Imagiste," was probably the most influential of a group of friends that included T. S. Eliot, William Carlos Williams, and D. H. Lawrence. In 1933, Freud agreed, at the request of the poet, to accept her as a subject of study, and H. D.'s later poems, such as "The Walls Do Not Fall" (1944), are markedly influenced by her own and her mentor's interests in psychoanalysis, religion, and mythology.

One way to open up discussion is to examine the nature of the heat, the wind, and the fruit as they are described in the poem. In what sense are these things abstract? What qualities are associated with each of them? Do students all have the same impression of the type of heat the speaker is describing? Heat becomes a living force in these lines, capable of occupying space and offering resistance to seemingly denser objects: "Fruit cannot drop / through this thick air —" (lines 4–5). The ripeness and fullness implied in the images of the fruit in the second stanza are somewhat threatened by the relentless heat. We can almost feel the fruit shriveling in response, deprived of oxygen, unable to participate in the natural cycle that will make them fall to the ground. A heat that is able to blunt the points of pears and round grapes (8–9) acquires the power of an elemental force.

The image of the cutting plow in lines 10 through 13 builds on the personification of the wind in the first line. The wind becomes a creative agent, a matching elemental force called up to cut through the heat and restore order in the natural world. However, the plow is also a domestic tool at the service of human beings. The poet's words conjure and direct the wind. By framing the poem as an invocation, the poet calls attention to her own ability to control this natural scene.

POSSIBLE CONNECTIONS TO OTHER SELECTIONS

Ezra Pound, "In a Station of the Metro" (text p. 110)
William Carlos Williams, "Poem" (text p. 90)

AUDIOVISUAL AND ONLINE RESOURCES (manual pp. 297, 330)

MICHAEL COLLIER, *The Barber* (p. 98)

The barber in this poem is introduced through a vicious lawn-mowing technique and a violent, burning scent that reminds the speaker of "the hot shoe of the shaver" (line 8). The barber is portrayed as "Fat, inconsolable" (15), "gruff when he wasn't silent" (24), "a neighbor to fear" (25), "a father we could hate" (26–27). Getting out of the barber shop seems to have been an escape from a brush with death. The images of the barbershop — "the violet light of the scissors" (21–22), "the pinkish darkness" (30) — combine with the characterization of the barber to create a serious force to be feared and reviled in the mythology of a boy's awareness of community. While the poem provides many vivid images and concrete details about the poet's memories of the barber and the barbershop, all reflect on the speaker himself, and on the importance of his experience, rather than on some imagined view of the barber. The images of the boys in the mirrors "hung below / his license in its cheap black frame" (20–21) and above the pickled combs in glass jars; their images, stolen, exposed, "vulnerable" (18), were a departure from the world. A loss of childlike innocence is apparent: "He sent us back / into the world burning and itching, alive with the horror" (28–29).

You might want to draw students' attention to the way the poem subverts their expectations. Collier's speaker's distrust of adults and his frustration that he cannot hate his father are revealed in the description of the barber as "a father we could hate" (26–27). Images from childhood are often thought to be rosy, very different from the "pinkish darkness" presented here.

POSSIBLE CONNECTIONS TO OTHER SELECTIONS

Margaret Atwood, "Bored" (text p. 72)
Stephen Perry, "Blue Spruce" (question #1, following)

CONNECTION QUESTION IN TEXT (p. 99) WITH ANSWER

1. Compare the treatment of the barber and the barbershop in this poem with that of Stephen Perry's "Blue Spruce" (p. 135).

   The barbershop in this poem is a dark and threatening place, with the barber's "huge stomach" (11) and "flat hand" (12) bullying the speaker. The speaker in Perry's poem remembers a grandfather barber who was overly generous with his love and attention. He was eager to celebrate life and raised the speaker "as if I were a note / he'd play into light —" (44–45). Perry's barbershop is remembered as "smelling of lotions he'd slap on your face" (2); Collier's is embalmed in germicide, inactive, to be endured, not celebrated.

ONLINE RESOURCES (manual p. 327)

MARY ROBINSON, *London's Summer Morning* (p. 99)

This poem, set in eighteenth-century London, refers to the act of listening to "the busy sounds / of summer's morning" (lines 1–2). Aural details convey the sounds of the street: shouting "chimney-boy" (4), rattling "milk-pail," "tinkling bell" (7), and "the din of hackney-coaches" (10). Robinson moves on to visual details, listing the "neat girl" (19) walking with a hat box, the sunlight "on the glitt'ring pane" (21), and "pastry dainties" (27). The sounds have roused the speaker, who now watches the street. The opening line invites the reader to acknowledge the familiarity of these sights and sounds, then pulls the focus from the street to the bedroom, where "the poor poet wakes from busy dreams" (41) to write the poem, and concludes with an image of the poet in the act of writing.

When your students try to work on their own listings of the morning's events, draw their attention to the use of aural and visual detail; Robinson's poem does not get tangled in narrative but focuses on sight and sound. What are some of the ways in which other senses could enter this litany? As a preparatory writing exercise, you might want to ask your students to move through the poem, expanding it to include other details such as the taste of the vegetables the vendors offer, the smells of the horses pulling the hackney coaches, and the weight of the "busy mop" (18) in the hands of the housemaid.

POSSIBLE CONNECTIONS TO OTHER SELECTIONS

William Blake, "London" (question #1, following)
Ezra Pound, "In a Station of the Metro" (text p. 110)
William Wordsworth, "London, 1802"(text p. 128)

CONNECTION QUESTION IN TEXT (p. 100) WITH ANSWER

1. How does Robinson's description of London differ from William Blake's "London" (below)? What would you say is the essential difference in purpose between the two poems?

   Blake opens his vision of London with "I wander" (1); Robinson constructs her poem around the sounds and visions available through a bedroom window. Robinson's poem is a cheerful list of images accompanied by the music of a busy street on a summer morning, while Blake sets his poem in "midnight streets" (13). Blake's vision of London is essentially a negative view of a corrupt city; Robinson's vision is positive and innocent of Blake's bleak account.

WILLIAM BLAKE, *London* (p. 101)

William Blake's only formal schooling was in art, and he learned engraving as an apprentice to a prominent London engraver. After his seven years' service, Blake made his living as a printer and engraver, writing poetry on the side. The private mythology that came to dominate his poems was worked out in almost total obscurity: at the time of his death Blake had acquired some notice for his art but almost none for his writing.

This poem may seem pessimistic, but is it entirely so? If students would go so far as to call it "apocalyptic," does their knowledge of history help them to discern where the speaker's attitude comes from? The use of "chartered" (line 1) to describe streets and the River Thames makes all the boundaries in the poem seem unnatural and rigid; the cries heard are cries of pain and sadness. Like the rigidities of the chartered streets, the legislation of the "mind-forged manacles" (8) does nothing to promote civil liberty and happiness. Blake implies here that the "manacles" of religion and government that should protect individuals fail miserably to ensure good lives. Children are sold into near slavery as chimney sweeps, their own dark and stunted faces casting a pall (appall) on the benevolent state and the Christian tradition. Soldiers sent off to war die or kill other soldiers. Sexual restrictions invite prostitution and thus promote disease, which may, in turn, afflict marriages and resulting births. Social regulations ("manacles") thus induce societal ills.

The image of the soldier dying for the state, for example, (11–12), is described in a condensed and effective manner that suggests not only his lucklessness (or helplessness) but also the indifference of a government removed from the individual by class ("Palace" [12]), its insularity ("walls" [12]), and the imperturbable security of law.

Comparison of the two versions of the final stanza provides an excellent writing topic. Notice, though, how much more endemic the societal failings and wrongdoings appear in the second (revised) version. Instead of "midnight harlot's curse," the phrase becomes the "midnight streets" (13) (evil as pervasive) and "the youthful Harlot's curse" (14) (a blighting of innocence at an early age). By reversing "marriage hearse" and "infant's tear," Blake suggests not a mere (and societally sanctioned) cause-effect relation between marriage and the birth of afflicted infants but the presence of syphilis in even the youngest members of society and the conditions that would sustain its presence.

How do the urban ills of contemporary society compare with those of Blake's time? It might be an interesting exercise to ask students to write a poem about contemporary social ills, either urban or rural, in Blake's style. What has changed?

POSSIBLE CONNECTIONS TO OTHER SELECTIONS

Claribel Alegría, "I Am Mirror" (text p. 656)
George Eliot, "In a London Drawingroom" (text p. 606)
Faiz Ahmed Faiz, "If You Look at the City from Here" (text p. 659)

AUDIOVISUAL AND ONLINE RESOURCES (manual pp. 293, 325)

WILFRED OWEN, *Dulce et Decorum Est* (p. 102)

This poem is an argument against war, not against a country. So often war is an act surrounded by image-making words of glory and honor and flanked by the "nobility" of slogan sentiments. Here Owen has presented the actuality of battle and death by a particularly dehumanizing and agonizing weapon: poison gas. He wants his audience to know a little more exactly what war entails.

The famous indictment of war centers around the experiences and emotions of a disillusioned World War I soldier. It might be necessary to provide a little background about the nature of warfare during "the war to end all wars." The ground war was fought mostly in trenches, where not only did close and relentless combat last much longer than anyone initially expected, but the threat of illness from decomposing bodies and diseases that bred in the mud of the trenches was very real. You are likely to push some buttons by doing so, but you may want to try to discuss the final lines first.

Owen seems to want to collar and talk to each reader directly. After the vividness of his description, some of which is in the present tense, Owen's attitude toward the "lie" (line 28) that his "friend" (26) might tell is disdainful, and understandably so.

You may want to ask students where the notion that it is noble to fight for one's country comes from. Under what circumstances does such a notion break down? Is war still glamorized by way of songs, films, and poetry? (If students respond quickly, "No; all that ended with Vietnam," push the question a little further: what about movies that take on an abstract enemy, like the popular patriotic alien-fighting thriller *Independence Day*?)

Matthew Arnold, "Dover Beach" (text p. 95)

Sharon Olds, "Rite of Passage" (text p. 265)

AUDIOVISUAL AND ONLINE RESOURCES (manual pp. 305, 345)

SANDRA M. GILBERT, *Mafioso* (p. 103)

Gilbert's poem focuses on stereotypes of Italian American men to examine the Italian ethnic heritage and finds that those images leave her needing more information. The stereotypes of Italians are conveyed primarily through violence and food. The "half dozen Puritan millionaires" (line 23), who arrived ahead of the Italians, are in contrast with the public images of the "bad uncles" (9) who are represented by the violent and imprisoned gangsters.

The conclusion of the poem contains multiple meanings in the readiness of the Puritans "to grind the organs out of you" (26). Gilbert invokes stereotypical images of Italians to protest the legacy they have left for her speaker. It is, presumably, the "Puritan millionaires," those earlier arrivals who had already established control over the country, who stood ready to stereotype the Italians.

You might want to spend some time with your students establishing how these stereotypes have entered into our communal consciousness. How do they know what they know about Italian American culture? Is their knowledge derived from movies featuring the Mafia? Gilbert wrote this poem in 1979; how are the stereotypes she employs perpetuated or defied by a television series like "The Sopranos"?

POSSIBLE CONNECTIONS TO OTHER SELECTIONS

Jimmy Santiago Baca, "Green Chile" (question #1, following)

Saundra Sharp, "It's the Law: A Rap Poem" (text p. 33)

CONNECTION QUESTION IN TEXT (p. 103) WITH ANSWER

1. Discuss the ways in which ethnicity is used to create meaning in "Mafioso" and in Jimmy Santiago Baca's "Green Chile" (p. 96).

   The bitterness of Gilbert's borrowed stereotypes of mafia members as "bad uncles" (line 9) is in contrast with the deliberate examination of an actual grandmother in Baca's poem. The fondness Baca's speaker conveys for his grandmother and the "old, beautiful ritual" (45) is viewed tenderly from firsthand experience. In contrast, Gilbert is unable to locate an authentic image of her Italian ancestors and bitterly regards those "Puritan millionaires" (23) who were ready to destroy the Italian immigrants she imagines arriving at Ellis Island. Ethnicity is a borrowed construct of externally established, insufficient stereotypes in Gilbert's poem; it shapes a home in Baca's.

ONLINE RESOURCES (manual p. 332)

PATRICIA SMITH, *What It's Like to Be a Black Girl (For Those of You Who Aren't)* (p. 104)

Using vernacular with a matter-of-fact tone, this poem defines race and gender in very personal terms, examining, simultaneously, how the speaker's race shapes her sexuality and how her gender and sexuality affect her understanding of her race. The poem uses a second-person perspective to establish an immediate connection with the reader; it conveys a sense that "you're not finished" (line 2). There are forces that make "something, / everything, wrong" (3–4), your own physical appearance is insufficient, and blue food coloring and "a bleached / white mophead" (6–7) would be preferable to your own eyes and hair. This is also a coming-of-age poem, moving from "being 9 years old" (1) to "finally having a man reach out for you" (18). Sexuality, physicality, athleticism, and profanity are all present and fiercely accounted for. The final image, caving in around a man's fingers, presents a good opportunity for discussion: is the speaker responding to the man's touch in relief or in defeat? Ask students to defend their opinion with reference to other lines in the poem.

You might want to ask students to attempt a freewriting exercise that defines them in terms of their gender and ethnicity; what's it like being a White Boy? An Asian Girl? How do gender and ethnicity work to define us all?

POSSIBLE CONNECTIONS TO OTHER SELECTIONS

Margaret Atwood, "you fit into me" (text p. 116)
Gwendolyn Brooks, "We Real Cool" (text p. 81)

JAMES DICKEY, *Deer Among Cattle* (p. 104)

The speaker of this poem, who observes a nighttime meadow scene with a flashlight, considers the contrasts between the herd of cattle grazing there and the lone deer who has joined them. He contemplates not only the differences between the "wild one" (line 5) and those "bred- / for-slaughter" (8–9), but also their subtle similarities: the deer is also "domesticated" (7) but "by darkness" (8) rather than by humankind. However, the differences far outweigh the similarities, and at the end of the poem the speaker is compelled to acknowledge the different way the "sparks from [his] hand" (19) reflect in the eyes of the deer as opposed to the cattle.

This relationship between the speaker and all of the animals together becomes more interesting than the relationship between the deer and the cattle as the poem concludes. The words "human" (4) and "inhuman" (16) set up a dichotomy in the poem that is not as easily recognizable as it might at first appear to be. The speaker's hand holds a "searing beam" (1) and "sparks" (19) — images of destruction — and he observes the scene behind a "paralyzed fence" (10) which contains "human grass" (6) and a wild animal "domesticated / by darkness" (7–8). The night becomes "the night of the hammer" in the penultimate line. Ask students to try to make sense of the speaker's attitude toward this scene by situating him within it: does he feel more part of the human realm or the animal realm? (Recall that the grass and the light in the cows' eyes are described as "human" [4] and that the grass enclosed by the fence is "a green frosted table" [12]). The speaker seems detached from the scene, but the poem begins and ends with the illumination from his flashlight, seen through his eyes.

POSSIBLE CONNECTIONS TO OTHER SELECTIONS

William Blake, "The Tyger" (text p. 214)
Rainer Maria Rilke, "The Panther" (question #1, following)

CONNECTION QUESTION IN TEXT (p . 105) WITH ANSWER

1. Discuss the idea of confinement in "Deer Among Cattle" and Rainer Maria Rilke's "The Panther" (below).

    Rilke's "The Panther" involves no such speaker, no explicit "I/eye" observing the scene. Rilke's poem feels more confined than Dickey's does; there doesn't seem to be any world "behind the bars" (line 4) in "The Panther," but there is a forest beyond the field in "Deer Among Cattle." Still, it is complicated, since the deer has entered the world within the "paralyzed fence" (10), the field contained therein is described as "wide-open country" (18).

AUDIOVISUAL AND ONLINE RESOURCES (manual pp. 296, 329)

RAINER MARIA RILKE, *The Panther* (p. 105)

Born in Austria-Hungary (now the Czech Republic), Rainer Maria Rilke was educated in Catholic schools but later rebelled against his faith. He migrated to Munich after studying philosophy at Prague. In 1909 he went to Paris, a gathering place for many artists at the time. Rilke's images have been described as having classical plasticity: precise, chiseled, and visual. His mixture of squalor and art may have come from the time he spent in Paris.

The form and content of "The Panther" unite to indicate increasing confinement. In each of the stanzas, Rilke moves from exterior to interior and from action to inaction, leaving the reader with something more finite to consider each time — paralleling the confinement experienced by the panther. The first line of the first stanza refers to the world beyond the bars: by the end of the stanza, there are only "a thousand bars; and behind the bars, no world" (line 4). In the first line of the second stanza, the panther is moving in "cramped circles, over and over" (5); at the end of the stanza, we find "a mighty will [which] stands paralyzed" (8). The third stanza traces the path of an image as it penetrates "the curtain of the pupils" (9) until it "plunges into the heart and is gone" (12). This final image is so far within the panther that it remains unidentifiable. As a result, like the panther, we are forced by the form of the poem into a stillness and a recognition of our inability to control the situation. In a sense, Rilke is dropping the curtain over our own pupils.

POSSIBLE CONNECTION TO ANOTHER SELECTION

Emily Dickinson, "A Bird came down the Walk —" (question #1, following)

CONNECTION QUESTION IN TEXT (p. 106) WITH ANSWER

1. Write an essay explaining how a sense of movement is achieved by the images and rhythms in this poem and in Dickinson's "A Bird came down the Walk —" (p. 173).

    Dickinson's bird moves with jerky movements, reflected in her brief, restless lines, until the end of the poem when the bird's movements are compared to rowing. Rilke's panther is at once more graceful and more cramped. His "ritual dance around a center / in which a mighty will stands paralyzed" (lines 7–8) is almost hypnotic so that we are especially surprised by the unexplained rushing image in the final stanza.

AUDIOVISUAL AND ONLINE RESOURCES (manual pp. 306, 348)

JANE KENYON, *The Blue Bowl* (p. 106)

The speaker of this poem recounts how she and someone else (presumably a husband or lover) buried their dead cat the day before the poem is written. The burial is ritualistic; the speaker compares herself and her fellow undertaker to "primitives." Though they go about the burial rather methodically, the event has affected them deeply. They are "silent" (line 12) the rest of the day and seemingly empty: "we worked, / ate, stared, and slept" (12–13).

The title of this poem provides its most challenging point of interpretation. In addition to asking about the blueness of the bowl, ask students why the title focuses on the seemingly inconsequential bowl at all; why not entitle the poem "The Burial"? The bowl's blueness calls attention to other colors in the poem that may have otherwise been overlooked: the cat's "long red fur" (7) and the incongruous "white feathers / between his toes" (7–8). There is something *off*, something unsettling about the entire poem. Note how the first line, read alone, raises fundamental questions about meaning: do primitives bury cats with bowls? The speaker has difficulty communicating; she interrupts her description ("long, not to say aquiline, nose" [9]) in the same way that the robin or the neighbor of the final simile say "the wrong thing" (17).

Burial is meant to be a neat, finalizing procedure, but death is a messy business, both physically and emotionally. Nothing about it can be satisfying. In discussing the psychological implications of burial and comparing this poem to Updike's "Dog's Death" (text p. 11), students may be reluctant to leap over the next level of taboo into a comparison of human burial to pet burial. How might the nature of "The Blue Bowl" have changed if the speaker were burying a person rather than a pet? How might it have remained the same?

POSSIBLE CONNECTIONS TO OTHER SELECTIONS

Rachel Hadas, "The Red Hat" (text p. 210)
John Updike, "Dog's Death" (question #1, following)

CONNECTION QUESTION IN TEXT (p. 107) WITH ANSWER

1. Write an essay comparing the death of this cat with the death of the dog of Updike's "Dog's Death" (p. 11). Which poem draws a more powerful response from you? Explain why.

    One difference is that the cat of Kenyon's poem is never described as it was when it was alive. We do not see it die, whereas we witness the death of the dog in Updike's poem firsthand. Kenyon's speaker states that "There are sorrows keener than these" (line 11) as she buries the cat, but Updike's speaker shows us the grief of the family. It is likely that students will find Kenyon's poem unsettling and will find Updike's poem viscerally upsetting or pathetic.

AUDIOVISUAL AND ONLINE RESOURCES (manual pp. 302, 338)

SALLY CROFT, *Home-Baked Bread* (p. 107)

This poem describes a seduction by way of cooking, cleverly departing from the title of the source of the epigraph, *The Joy of Cooking*, into another popular text from the 1970s, *The Joy of Sex*. The great-aunt of the second stanza is an interesting inroad. Great-aunts are generally associated more with cooking than with seduction; is this one figured into the poem as a contrast to the amorous speaker, or does she reinforce the idea that all women have their "cunning triumphs" (line 2), which are sometimes hidden or only suggested?

"Cunning triumphs," appearing amid the measured dryness of a cookbook text, certainly has the potential to arrest someone's poetic sensibilities. *Cunning* seems more appropriately applied to the feats of Odysseus than to the food in *The Joy of Cooking*. At any rate, "cunning triumphs" rises, as it were, beyond the limits of technical discourse. It shines, it sparkles, it almost titillates the kitchen soul.

"Insinuation" (3), too, is a pivotal word in the poem. It looks back on the questioning attitude of the opening lines and points toward the wily, winding seductiveness of what will follow.

At first we hear the speaker reading and questioning the cookbook. Then we hear the speaker transformed into a new identity — of Lady Who Works Cunning Triumphs. She is addressing someone she would charm and seduce.

The poem achieves a unity through the repetition of certain images, such as the room that recalls the great-aunt's bedroom as well as the other reiterated images, of honey, sweet seductiveness, warmth, and open air.

POSSIBLE CONNECTIONS TO OTHER SELECTIONS

Elaine Magarrell, "The Joy of Cooking" (text p. 134)
Cathy Song, "The White Porch" (text p. 111)

ANN CHOI, *The Shower* (p. 108)

This poem at first appears to be an occasional poem written to celebrate the impending marriage of the speaker's childhood friend; it could be read at a bridal shower. The details that describe the friend, the "you" of the poem, are loving in their careful attention. However, upon close reading these three stanzas provide an example of a poem with many readings, one whose meaning depends on the opinions and beliefs of its readers.

A poem that celebrates marriage might be expected to leave out the dishes and weight gain of pregnancy and mention love or intimacy. Some readers will decide that Choi's choice of images to represent married life are realistic and tender, while others may think they signal a kind of disappointment. A clearer passage looks back on childhood to foreshadow not happy marriages but "things expiring / without our knowledge" (lines 11–12). This conveys uncertainty and sadness about the changes adulthood brings. The speaker and her friend are "caught by the permanence of the ring" (15), an especially revealing image about the importance of this marriage's effects on the friendship of the speaker and the "you" of the poem.

The friend is defined by her limitations and her grace in accepting them in the first stanza. Choi does not employ traditional ideas of marriage as a mark of womanhood and positive change; this stanza does not end with the small, uncomplaining hands growing into the graceful hands of an adult woman. Rather, her hands then "were not much smaller / than they are now" (2–3). The shortcomings represented by these small hands are overcome through "diligence" (18). This characterization depends more on the reader than the writer for its weight; some may view diligence as an admirable trait, while others would prefer to overcome their difficulties with inspiration or joy; Choi does not state her speaker's preference.

The poem moves from adolescence to adulthood, from sixth graders discussing time and their own development into "women in bright clothes" (14) to an anticipation of the effects of the marriage. The tone is ambivalent and subdued; students may find it touching and loving or quietly bitter. Passages that could be interpreted to support a sad reading could shift between the sounds associated with the music that was awarded a "house full of trophies" (10) to the "sounds of dishes / and of children" (20–21). Students who think these domestic details are positive and tender will find it celebratory; the speaker does not say whether she herself enjoys the sounds of dishes and children. The conclusion, children "whose small fingers will separate/to play staccato" (23–24) may be read as a hopeful vision of a future filled with talented children, or the sadness of a friend who gives up her musical talent to marry. Choi leaves this open to the reader's interpretation as well.

POSSIBLE CONNECTIONS TO OTHER SELECTIONS

Katharyn Howd Machan, "Hazel Tells LaVerne" (text p. 61)
Helen Farries, "Magic of Love" (text p. 30)

JOHN KEATS, *To Autumn* (p. 109)

"To Autumn" was the last major lyric Keats wrote. But despite its tone and imagery, particularly in the last stanza, there is no indication that Keats had an exact foreknowledge of his impending death.

Personification is a major device in this poem. In stanza I, which suggests the early part of the day, autumn is the "bosom-friend" (line 2) of the sun and a ripener of growing things. In stanza II, which has a midday cast, autumn is a storekeeper and a harvester or gleaner. In the final stanza, which reflects "the soft-dying day" (25), the image of autumn is less directly named, but the idea of the contemplative is suggested. One sees things ripening in the opening stanza; in stanza II, autumn feels the wind and drowses in the "fume" (17) of poppies; in the final stanza, autumn and the reader both are invited to listen to the special music of the close of the day and of the year.

In his brief poetic career, Keats seems to have grown into a more serene acceptance of death, preferring the organic ebb and flow of life over the cool, unchanging fixity of the artifact.

Possible Connections to Other Selections

Robert Frost, "After Apple-Picking" (question #1, following)

John Keats, "Ode on a Grecian Urn" (text p. 79)

Theodore Roethke, "Root Cellar" (question #2, following)

Connections Questions in Text (p. 110) with Answers

1. Compare this poem's tone and its perspective on death with those of Robert Frost's "After Apple-Picking" (p. 346).

    More metaphoric, perhaps, than literal, the apple picker's description of the recent harvest in "After Apple-Picking" could be a summary of his life. Already drowsy, he allows the time of day and the season to ease him into a reverie. The harvest he contemplates is a personal one — the apples he picked or let fall. This musing might occasion more brooding than is found in "To Autumn," in which the poet surveys more impersonally the season's reign and the year's end. "To Autumn" captures the last moments before winter, preserving them in all their ripeness and sensuality. Although both poems imply that death is near, Keats's speaker is far less willing to yield to it before appreciating the last moments of life as fully as he can.

2. Write an essay comparing the significance of the images of "mellow fruitfulness" (line 1) in "To Autumn" with that of the images of ripeness in Roethke's "Root Cellar" (text p. 94). Explain how the images in each poem lead to very different feelings about the same phenomenon.

    The images in "To Autumn" provide a sharp contrast to those in "Root Cellar." The root cellar is "a congress of stinks" (6), a place where ripeness is dank and almost obscene. Keats's images of fruitfulness are, in his word, "mellow" (1). One reason for the difference could be that Keats describes the end of a harvest, the cessation of growth, whereas Roethke traces the undying process that will begin growth all over again.

CHARLES SIMIC, *Filthy Landscape* (p. 110)

This poem describes a landscape in terms one might use to describe a bordello or sex club. As we read, we see that Simic is playing in the title "Filthy Landscape" with the double sense of *filthy* as "physically unclean" and "smutty." With its playful tone, this poem does not achieve a portrait of its subject, but develops a game based on its perception of it. Students will probably be surprised by this poem: the title leads one to expect an urban scene, not a sexualized pastoral. Filth in a landscape is usually described with physical images such as bottlecaps, cigarette cellophane, and newspaper. The filth here is not these objective, quantifiable pieces of litter; rather, it is a judgment passed on the poem's use of sexualized comparisons. By using such sexually charged adjectives, Simic plays on the euphemism for sex, "the birds and the bees."

In an interview with the *Cortland Review*, Charles Simic was once asked when he was first inspired to write poetry. His response: "When I noticed in high school that one of my friends was attracting the best looking girls by writing them sappy love poems." You might want to ask your students to take five minutes at the beginning of class to organize their thoughts on Simic's intent: Is the poem a love poem to the landscape? A commentary on the eye of the beholder? An exercise in perspective? A portrait of a landscape? A joke? Consider collecting the results on the board; over the course of your class discussion, one reading may fall out of favor with the group, while another may become more popular. A discussion of the word *filthy* might be appropriate here as well; what makes something *filthy*? What did students expect, given the title?

POSSIBLE CONNECTIONS TO OTHER SELECTIONS

Sophie Cabot Black, "August" (question #1, following)

Timothy Steele, "An Aubade" (text p. 439)

Henry Reed, "Naming of Parts" (text p. 160)

CONNECTION QUESTION IN TEXT (p. 110) **WITH ANSWER**

1. Discuss the use of images to evoke summer in "Filthy Landscape" and in "August" by Sophie Cabot Black (p. 125). How do the poems' images create very different perceptions of a summer landscape?

   The landscape in "August" reflects the exhausted mindset of "a man" (line 3); the ominous uncertainty of his "faulty predictions" (7) are present in "tired" (10) pastures, a hoarding well, "guessing rains" (9), and "reckless leaves" (13). Simic's poem is a reflection of judgment. The adjective *filthy*, which makes sense to us when used to describe overtly sexual material, becomes absurd when it's applied to meadows and hilltops rather than human bodies. The "lurid wildflowers" (1) of Simic's summer have only the weight of the judgment passed upon them; Black's "tired" pastures are seeped in the pressures that summer places on farmers.

ONLINE RESOURCES (manual p. 350)

EZRA POUND, *In a Station of the Metro* (p. 110)

Ezra Pound was born in Idaho and grew up in Philadelphia, eventually attending the University of Pennsylvania. There he befriended William Carlos Williams and H. D. (Hilda Doolittle) and concentrated on his image as a poet (affecting capes, canes, and rakish hats) as well as on his studies. He later attended Hamilton College and returned to UPenn for graduate work in languages, completing a master of arts in 1906. Two years later he moved to London, beginning a lifelong voluntary exile during which he worked as secretary to William Butler Yeats; began and abandoned numerous literary movements; started his "epic including history," *The Cantos*; lived in Paris, Venice, and Rapallo (Italy); furthered the literary careers of Hemingway, Joyce, Eliot, Frost, and Marianne Moore, among others; broadcast for Mussolini and ended up under arrest for treason. Declared insane at his trial, Pound spent twelve years in a Washington, D.C., hospital. Freed through the efforts of his writer friends, Pound spent the rest of his life in Italy. Despite his glaring shortcomings, Pound is seen by many as the most technically accomplished poet and one of the most gifted critics of his generation.

Pound helped articulate the ideas of imagism, one of his early efforts to "make it new." Although the halves of this poem work as if the second half were describing the first, each of the two lines possesses its own integrity as well as a capacity to make us see those faces.

POSSIBLE CONNECTION TO ANOTHER SELECTION

Matsuo Bashō, "Under Cherry Trees" (text p. 240)

AUDIOVISUAL AND ONLINE RESOURCES (manual pp. 306, 347)

CATHY SONG, *The White Porch* (p. 111)

The speaker in this poem establishes a conversation with her listener in the first stanza: "your" (line 10), "think" (12). She projects her listener into the future even as she captures the present moment through the description of her newly washed hair. The second stanza moves the conversation toward sexual innuendo, comparing the speaker's arousal to a flower, a flock of birds, and a sponge cake with peaches. Ask students to determine how these images give us a sense of what the speaker is like. What is her relationship to the listener? The final stanza returns us to the initial image of hair, but whereas the first stanza moves toward the future, the third plunges us back into the past. Students will enjoy comparing the images describing the mother to those describing the lover in the final lines. Like the rope ladder (an allusion to Rapunzel?), the poem is column-shaped, inviting its listener into the experience of reading it as it talks about a sexual relationship.

In a writing assignment, ask students to examine the concrete nouns and participial verbs in the poem. How do they evoke the speaker's message? How do images of domestic life summon the speaker's more "philosophical" side?

POSSIBLE CONNECTIONS TO OTHER SELECTIONS

Sally Croft, "Home-Baked Bread" (question #1, following)
Li Ho, "A Beautiful Girl Combs Her Hair" (text p. 43)

CONNECTION QUESTION IN TEXT (p. 112) WITH ANSWER

1. Compare the images used to describe the speaker's "slow arousal" in this poem with Croft's images in "Home-Baked Bread" (p. 107). What similarities do you see? What makes each description so effective?

   Croft also uses domestic images to talk about sexual intimacy and poetry writing. Both "Home-Baked Bread" and "The White Porch" invite the listener into the experience, promising food and warmth; each poem, for example, uses peaches to seduce its listener. The imagery is full of anticipation and ripeness. There is an element of danger, too, in each poem, enticing the audiences into delicious but forbidden experiences.

PERSPECTIVE

T. E. HULME, *On the Differences between Poetry and Prose* (p. 113)

As a class exercise, you might ask students to bring in examples of prose that contradict Hulme's claims. Students might want to bring in examples of prose they read elsewhere. In another writing assignment, you might ask students to flesh out Hulme's theory with especially vivid examples of poems that "hand over sensations bodily."

5

Figures of Speech

The material in this chapter can build on issues raised in the previous two: considerations of word choice, tone, and images both influence and reflect choices in figurative speech. You might have your students draw these connections explicitly by having them select a poem from this chapter and analyze it both in terms of its figurative language and also in terms of concepts discussed earlier. Doing so will help them understand how various elements make up the total effect of a poem.

Another possible exercise for this chapter would be to have students think about and list instances of figurative language used in their everyday speech, working either alone or in small groups. You might have them do this at the beginning of the chapter (after a brief discussion of figurative language) and again at the end: the difference in the number of instances they derive should be encouraging.

It is likely that students are already aware of the difference between simile and metaphor; the distinction will become important to them only if they can understand that it has some significance. Similes tend to call attention to the comparison itself, as in Atwood's "you fit into me" or Wordsworth's "London, 1802": the comparison becomes an important feature of the poems, foregrounding the "you and me" in Atwood's case, or Milton in Wordsworth's. Conversely, metaphors tend to focus on the *content* of the comparison, shifting the focus from the separate entities being compared to the nature of those entities, as in Dickinson's "Presentiment — is that long Shadow — on the lawn — ."

Metonymy and synecdoche can be difficult for students to grasp; for some reason, they find it more difficult to remember "metonymy" than "metaphor." You might find it useful to point out (or to have students point out) uses of metonymy in everyday language: "The White House confirms" or "University A beat University B" or "The Chancellor's office responded." This can help students get a grasp of the concepts involved and defuse their anticipation of being unable to understand these terms.

Paradox and oxymoron can be useful tools to encourage students' critical thinking skills. Puzzling out paradoxes and explaining oxymorons often require students to think in unusual ways. Poems that lend themselves to this are Donne's "Batter My Heart" and "Death Be Not Proud," as well as nearly any poem by Emily Dickinson.

WILLIAM SHAKESPEARE, *From* Macbeth *(Act V, Scene v)* (p. 115)

After asking students to identify each of the things to which Shakespeare's Macbeth compares life, and to consider how life is like each of them, have them decide which of these figures of speech is the most effective. Does one overpower the others, or does the overall effect depend on the conjunction of all of them?

Have students recall other things to which they have heard life compared. Are these common images examples of strong figurative language, or merely clichés? For example,

"Life is a bed of roses" conveys the idea that life is easy and beautiful, but it is such a well-worn phrase that it now lacks the impact it might once have had. As a writing assignment, students could come up with their own similes and metaphors and explain how life is like the image they have created.

See Robert Frost's " 'Out, Out —' " (text p. 350) for one example of how a modern poet has made use of Shakespeare's famous passage. Students familiar with William Faulkner's *The Sound and the Fury* might be able to comment on how another twentieth-century writer has used the reprinted passage from *Macbeth*.

POSSIBLE CONNECTION TO ANOTHER SELECTION

Robert Frost, " 'Out, Out —' " (text p. 350)

AUDIOVISUAL AND ONLINE RESOURCES (manual pp. 307, 349–350)

MARGARET ATWOOD, *you fit into me* (p. 116)

Students may need help with the allusions called up by the first two lines of this poem: the hook and eye that fasten a door shut; the buttonhook used to fasten women's shoes in the early twentieth century. You might ask students to compose a poem in which a figure of speech produces first pleasant associations and later unpleasant or, as in Atwood's poem, lurid ones. You might also ask the class in a brief writing assignment to determine how the simile and its expansion work. Would the poem be as successful, for example, if "eye" were not a part of the human anatomy?

POSSIBLE CONNECTION TO ANOTHER SELECTION

Emily Dickinson, "Wild Nights — Wild Nights!" (text p. 300)

AUDIOVISUAL AND ONLINE RESOURCES (manual pp. 292, 323)

EMILY DICKINSON, *Presentiment — is that long Shadow — on the lawn —* (p. 116)

As noted in the text, Dickinson uses richly connotative words such as *shadow* and *darkness* in order to express in a few words the sense of fear and danger inherent in her "Presentiment." You might explore with your students other connotations of the word *presentiment*. Are all premonitions warnings about negative occurrences? Have any of your students had premonitions about good things? What kinds of words might one want to use in order to express — economically — the possibility of pleasant surprise? You could have students, individually or in groups, try to identify specific words and then a controlling metaphor that would be appropriate to express this alternative kind of surprise.

POSSIBLE CONNECTION TO ANOTHER SELECTION

Emily Dickinson, "Success is counted sweetest" (text p. 294)

ANNE BRADSTREET, *The Author to Her Book* (p. 117)

This speaker regards her collection of poetry as though it were her child, considering both its penchant for brattiness and her mother's affection for it. Ask students to trace the extended metaphor in this poem, pointing out the way diction influences tone. What, for example, do the words *ill-formed* and *feeble* (line 1) tell us about the speaker's attitude toward her work? Does this attitude change at all as the poem progresses? Although her initial attitude toward the book is disdain, the speaker's reluctance to part with her creation in the final lines could be the result of both modesty and affection.

Sound patterns and meter are also good topics for discussion of this poem. The meter is iambic pentameter, but there are variations in rhythm that are linked to meaning. Line 15 presents the problem of metrical arrangement, providing an example in line 16: "Yet still thou run'st more hobbling than is meet."

In a writing assignment, you might ask students to discuss the way this poem talks about the writing process. How does Bradstreet suggest a book is written?

POSSIBLE CONNECTION TO ANOTHER SELECTION

William Shakespeare, "Not marble, nor the gilded monuments" (text p. 435)

AUDIOVISUAL AND ONLINE RESOURCES (manual pp. 294, 325)

ROSARIO CASTELLANOS, *Chess* (p. 118)

You might begin by asking students what associations they have with the game of chess. Traditionally, chess is thought of as an intellectual game — a game that relies on intricate moves and countermoves, with players anticipating one another's strategies as they plan their own. Considering the emphasis on strategy, chess could be called a "mind game" that two people agree to play. Thus, in lines 2 and 3, the reader learns that in adding chess as "one more tie / to the many that already bind . . ." the players have very deliberately set up and engaged in the "mind game" of chess. Encourage students to notice the confrontational terms the poet uses to describe the competition — the board was "between" the players, they "divided" the pieces, they "swore to respect" the rules, and the "match" began (lines 5–9).

Ask students to discuss why two people might choose to add another "tie" (2) to a relationship, for although there are hints in the first stanza that what's been set up is more than a simple chess game, the final stanza leaves little doubt about the metaphoric scope of the contest. By using the hyperbolic "centuries" in line 10, the poet intensifies the sense that the players have reached a stalemate. That they are meditating "ferociously" (11) for a way to deal "the one last blow" (12) that will "annihilate the other one forever" (13) underscores the hostile nature of the contest.

While the features of the competition revealed in the second and third stanza will probably provide students with much to discuss, perhaps the most interesting feature of this poem occurs in the first stanza, where the speaker characterizes the relationship between the players with these words: "Because we were friends and sometimes loved each other" (1). There are no clues in the poem as to the gender of either player or to the nature of the "love" referred to in the opening line. Obviously, there is already some relationship between the players, since they decided to "add one more tie / to the many that already bound [them]" (2–3). Likewise, the plural word "games" implies that other interactions have taken place or exist as possibilities. While it may prove interesting for students to debate their own perceptions of the gender of the players in this poem, it may be helpful at some point to acknowledge that the real key is not the gender of the players but the nature of the relationship — are these lovers in the romantic and sexual sense, or are they friends that love? Students' understanding of the last two lines may vary depending on their understanding of the "love" relationship. Is the last blow a competitive personal rivalry, a way of ending the relationship, or something even stronger and more violent?

POSSIBLE CONNECTION TO ANOTHER SELECTION

Sylvia Plath, "Daddy" (text p. 630)

ONLINE RESOURCES (manual p. 327)

EDMUND CONTI, *Pragmatist* (p. 119)

As a writing assignment, you might ask the class to discuss whether the mixed tone of this poem is successful. Is, for example, "coming our way" (line 2) too liltingly conversational for the idea of apocalypse?

Samuel Taylor Coleridge, "What Is an Epigram?" (text p. 237)
William Hathaway, "Oh, Oh" (text p. 13)

DYLAN THOMAS, *The Hand That Signed the Paper* (p. 120)

Dylan Thomas's *Eighteen Poems,* published in 1934, when he was twenty, began his career as a poet with a flourish: here, it seemed, was an answer to T. S. Eliot, a return to rhapsody and unembarrassed music. Thomas's poems became more craftsmanlike as he matured, but they never lost their ambition for the grand gesture, the all-embracing, bittersweet melancholy for which the Romantics strove. Thomas lived the role of the poet to the hilt: he was an alcoholic, a philanderer, a wonderful storyteller, a boor, and a justly celebrated reader of his own poems and those of others. Although he never learned to speak Welsh (he was born and grew up in Swansea, Wales), it is said that his poems carry the sounds of that language over into English. He died of alcohol poisoning during his third reading tour of the United States.

Although Thomas seems to be referring to no specific incident in this poem, the date of the poem (1936) indicates a possible concern with the political machinations leading up to the outbreak of World War II. The "five kings [who] did a king to death" (line 4) may even recall the five major powers who signed the Treaty of Versailles to end World War I but in their severe dismantling of Germany set the stage for another war. Some critics suggest that the poem, especially in the last two stanzas, refers to a wrathful God. Which words or phrases would lend credence to this reading? Students may suggest other situations in which a person in power can, by performing a seemingly simple act, adversely affect people at long range.

Discuss the title's allusion to the saying "The hand that rocks the cradle rules the world." Both phrases make observations about the power inherent in the acts of a single person. How are the acts to which they refer alike and different? How does the allusion to motherhood create irony in the poem? (Students familiar with the 1992 horror film *The Hand That Rocks the Cradle,* which deals with a deranged babysitter, may have their own associations with this poem.)

Alice Jones, "The Foot" (text p. 208)
Wole Soyinka, "Future Plans" (text p. 664)

JANICE TOWNLEY MOORE, *To a Wasp* (p. 121)

Discuss with students how an awareness of the intensity and seriousness of purpose that usually accompany the use of apostrophe affect their reading of this poem, which is, after all, about a common insect. In what way is the fist in the last line being waved at both the speaker and the wasp? Whose fist is it? How does the word *chortled* in the first line help us understand the speaker's view of the wasp? Discuss the paradox inherent in the notion of "delicious death" (line 11).

POSSIBLE CONNECTIONS TO OTHER SELECTIONS

John Donne, "The Flea" (text p. 604)

David McCord, "Epitaph on a Waiter" (text p. 238)

J. PATRICK LEWIS, *The Unkindest Cut* (p. 123)

Students will enjoy this humorous quatrain that is a play on the saying "the pen is mightier than the sword." To open discussion, ask students to point out the paradox inherent in this simple poem. Discuss also the title of the poem, pointing out that the title is an allusion to Shakespeare's *Julius Caesar* (III.ii.188).

POSSIBLE CONNECTION TO ANOTHER SELECTION

Sylvia Plath, "Daddy" (text p. 631)

ONLINE RESOURCES (manual p. 340)

SUE OWEN, *Zero* (p. 123)

This poem's controlling metaphor is its characterization of zero as a person. Owen creates a biography of "zero," a lonely character, an "only child" (lines 3–4), "a sad case" (19) with a "cold, missing heart" (24). Owen takes advantage of our understanding of zero's absence, zero's mathematical separation from the other numbers, zero's existence as a demilitarized zone between the two sides of the number line. Using these defining characteristics, she establishes a fictional persona for a nonperson, a nonthing. Its sad fate, divided life, and inability to interact with others form the hollow center of this story, which depends on our understanding of zero's physical appearance (round as a mouth or eye) and our knowledge of mathematics (zero has no effect on other digits when added or subtracted).

Metaphors and similes that may be especially effective for students include the mysterious presence of winter, the reference to negative and positive degrees building up to and away from the center of the number line, and the division between positive and negative. The poem relies on our understanding of their differences and "how they mimic each other" (10) as well as the parallels that are created with those digits and "the past and future" (9), "emotion and silence" (20–21).

As an exercise, consider asking students how other numbers could be characterized by considering familiar phrases such as "three's a crowd," "sweet sixteen," "one for the road," and "dressed to the nines." Examining the possibilities of numbers as symbols may help them connect with more complex symbols down the road.

POSSIBLE CONNECTIONS TO OTHER SELECTIONS

H. D. [Hilda Doolittle], "Heat" (text p. 98)

Andrew Hudgins, "Seventeen" (text p. 156)

MARGARET ATWOOD, *February* (p. 124)

"February," on the surface, comprises the ruminations of a speaker whose cat wakes her up in the morning. The feeling it evokes is familiar to everyone, particularly those who live in northern climes: "time to get this depressing season over with." The speaker initially rejects sex (suggesting that people should spay and neuter not only their animals but themselves!) and embraces the human version of hibernation ("Time to eat fat / and watch hockey" [lines 1–2]). The cat seems to be responsible for her attitude, and by the end, she entreats it to "get going / on a little optimism around here" (32–33).

Though the speaker's tone is generally humorous, it might be productive to begin by encouraging students to locate all of the death imagery in the poem, obvious or otherwise. The cat's breath is "of burped-up meat and musty sofas" (10) for instance, and "famine / crouches in the bedsheets" (20–21) along with the speaker. Our efforts to propagate life seem to lead to death in the speaker's mind: "love . . . does us in" (19), heating our bodies produces pollution, etc. How does the speaker's humorous tone interact with the apparently serious subject matter and imagery? Ask students to try to figure out why she suddenly rejects this "month of despair / with a skewered heart in the centre" in lines 26 and 27, how the cat is converted into "the life principle, / more or less" (31–32). Is she shaking off the despair of the season by rejecting the cat? Is the cat somehow an emblem of winter, or is it an envoy of nature in general?

Possible Connections to Other Selections

Stephen Crane, "A Man Said to the Universe" (text p. 146)

Richard Wilbur, "A Late Aubade" (text p. 68)

SOPHIE CABOT BLACK, *August* (p. 125)

This poem, a description of an impending change from summer into autumn, is unusual for one so contemporary in that it seems so unbothered by the horrors of the modern world. It depicts both natural and human reactions to the passing of summer and anticipations of the coming of a killing season. It is a nature poem that approaches the pastoral; the human subject within it is nearly part of the landscape. Yet the theme is not typically pastoral. The world described is not idyllic; it is a world that seems to be running down toward its own destruction, brought about by the impending fall.

The language of the poem subtly reinforces this mood. The man, presumably a farmer, knows the "*tilt* and *decline* of each field, / his own *faulty* predictions" (lines 6–7). Nature seems old and sloppy, characterized by words like "tired," "loose," "unguarded," and "reckless" (10–13). It might be productive to have students draw their own associations of August or of harvest-time: what are some typical harvest rituals? As we celebrate harvest, do we seem, like the leaves at the end of this poem, "unaware" that things are about to die? This awareness contrasts nicely with the speaker of Atwood's poem "February," who is trapped by the despair of her gray month, but who knows at the end that there is hope for the coming spring.

Possible Connections to Other Selections

Margaret Atwood, "February" (question #1, following)

James Dickey, "Deer Among Cattle" (text p. 104)

Jane Kenyon, "Surprise" (text p. 147)

Connection Question in Text (p. 126) with Answer

1. Discuss the moods created in "August" and Atwood's "February." To what extent do you think each poem is successful in capturing the essence of the title's subject?

   The mood of Atwood's poem is at least partially humorous, as though the speaker has resigned herself to the desperateness of the month and given up on the depression it engenders. She creates her mood obliquely, through objects such as her cat, french fries, and hockey, which would seem to have little to do with one another. Black's poem is concerned head-on with its topic; all the creatures and plants together seem attuned to the impending change of season, and it unsettles them, or makes them behave recklessly.

ERNEST SLYMAN, *Lightning Bugs* (p. 126)

This three-line poem casts lightning bugs (also called "fireflies") as spies who invade the speaker's backyard. It might be difficult to sustain a discussion about such a short poem, but you could begin by asking students to describe the speaker, the conditions under which he might make this observation, and the sights and sounds that surround him. Does his paranoia come from his sense that he is alone or from his sense that he is all too crowded?

Without the title, we would think this poem is about people. The title frames the experience by identifying the image to be captured in the lines that follow. Then, the image of the "peepholes" (line 2), coming as it does before the "snapshots" (3), makes us first imagine the bugs as human beings, who require peepholes to see who is outside. When mention of snapshots is added to this image, the bugs become like tourists, waiting for someone to come out of the house so they can take a picture. This is ironic, for it is really the bugs who are the celebrities, fascinating the speaker, who watches them.

POSSIBLE CONNECTION TO ANOTHER SELECTION

Ezra Pound, "In a Station of the Metro" (text p. 110)

ONLINE RESOURCES (manual p. 351)

SYLVIA PLATH, *Mirror* (p. 126)

Sylvia Plath grew up with an invalid father (he refused to seek treatment for what he thought was cancer but was actually diabetes) who died when she was eight. Her mother was a teacher, who by example and instruction encouraged her daughter's precocious literary ambitions (Plath published her first poem before she was nine). Plath attended Smith College on scholarship, won a Fulbright to study in England, received a number of awards for her writing, and eventually married the English poet Ted Hughes. In the last few harrowing months of her life (which she spent alone because Hughes was having an affair), she wrote most of her finest poems, sometimes at the rate of two or three a day. She killed herself on February 11, 1963.

This poem speaks from the point of view of a mirror reflecting an aging woman. The poem's brilliant use of personification may mask some other concerns in the poem; you might begin discussion by asking students to consider why the poet chooses this device. Is it possible to speak from an inhuman point of view? This speaker claims to "have no preconceptions" (line 1) and to be "unmisted by love or dislike" (3). These are decidedly inhuman characteristics, yet the speaker has a human voice and a human consciousness. Does the use of personification express some desire, in this case, to shed what can be painful human emotions? How does that desire in the poet reflect the persona of the aging woman who is the subject (or object) of the second stanza?

Without the use of personification, the poem would simply be another flat statement on a woman watching herself grow old. But that action of watching is enlivened by the mirror taking on some organic attributes. The pink wall it reflects becomes part of its heart, for example, and despite the truth it gives back to the woman, it feels important and necessary. Without the responsive quality of the mirror, it is unlikely that the last images would be quite so startling. But the personified mirror literally acquires a depth it probably would not have otherwise, and it figures in the poem as a lake, a drowning pool, and the source of the "terrible fish" (18). In the final simile, the image is no longer a mere reflection but a figure of assault coming up out of the depths of self to frighten her.

Possible Connections to Other Selections

Li Ho, "A Beautiful Girl Combs Her Hair" (text p. 43)
Sylvia Plath, "Mushrooms" (text p. 187)

Audiovisual and Online Resources (manual pp. 305–306, 346)

SHARON OLDS, *Poem for the Breasts* (p. 127)

This poem first establishes separate identities for the breasts of the speaker, remarking on one's "quick intelligence" (line 4), then assigning attributes, such as "wise, generous" (8), and eventually, "dumb" (38) and "mortal" (39). The second half of the poem tells the story of the separation of the speaker and her husband through the double perspective of the speaker and her breasts. The humor and grace that this strategy allows make for a poignant analysis of loss, one that is more effective because of the distance created through the development of this other entity, the personae of the breasts.

Lines 1–18 establish a mock-serious tone, examining and personifying the breasts, celebrating their positive attributes, comparing them to "someone one deeply loves" (13). The second half of the poem shifts to a more complex tone with an undercurrent of bitterness, "heavy with grief" (27) as the speaker marks the first anniversary of her husband's departure. The speaker compares the "excitement and plenty" (29) her breasts represented in the marriage to the "long nothing" (36) she imagines enduring without her husband. The conclusion lightens, acknowledging that although her breasts are "dumb" (38), "do not know language" (36–37), and "are waiting for him" (37), their company is "sweet" (39) and "refreshing" (40). Rather than continuing with a development of the "long nothing" that could be her solitude, the speaker anticipates some small measure of happiness in the company of her breasts, however dumb.

Lines 33–36 establish a connection between "goodbye" and "god be with you" and "god by"; these are earlier and more formal forms of "goodbye" in English. Olds manages to establish the departure of the husband without using the phrase "goodbye," as if the speaker stubbornly refuses to hear or repeat it.

Possible Connections to Other Selections

Anne Bradstreet, "The Author to Her Book" (question #1, following)
Sharon Olds, "Sex without Love" (question #2, following)
Eric Ormsby, "Nose" (text p. 81)

Connections Questions in Text (p. 128) with Answer

1. Compare and contrast the use of extended metaphor in "Poem for the Breasts" and in Anne Bradstreet's "The Author to Her Book" (p. 117).

These poems by Bradstreet and Olds establish connections between the speaker and what she has to offer: the breasts and book take on human characteristics, become like children in relation to the speakers in the poems. Bradstreet and Olds assign attributes to these entities that may not be shared with the speaker but are closely connected to her own sense of self. Bradstreet sends her book out into the world, fatherless, acknowledging her own flaws by establishing that she cannot outfit and perfect the book-child as she would like. Olds's poem concludes with an antithetical arrangement; the speaker's husband departs, and the speaker is left to live alone with her breasts. Both poems establish the speaker's identity through the personification of their subjects.

2.   Discuss Olds's strategies for using extended metaphors in "Poem for the Breasts" and in two other poems by her: "Sex without Love" (p. 76) and "Rite of Passage" (p. 265).

In these poems, breasts become companions, the self engaged in sexual activity is seen as a "single body alone in the universe / against its own best time" (lines 23–24), and a birthday party full of children is recognized as a ritual, a sort of battleground where the young establish a brutal, theoretical hierarchy. All three poems depend on the establishment of complex connections between rather simple, mundane entities — breasts, sex, and birthday parties — to a new and strange clarity in understanding and analyzing them.

WILLIAM WORDSWORTH, *London, 1802* (p. 128)

William Wordsworth was born in the English Lake District, in Cockermouth, West Cumberland, and grew up roaming the countryside. He completed his undergraduate degree at Cambridge University in 1791 and spent a year in revolutionary France. By the age of 27, he had settled in Somersetshire to be near Samuel Taylor Coleridge, with whom, in 1798, he published one of the most influential volumes in the history of English poetry, *Lyrical Ballads*. Wordsworth enjoyed increasing public reward as a poet (becoming poet laureate in 1843) even as his private life suffered from frequent tragedy and disappointment.

The metonymic nouns following the colon in line 3 of "London, 1802" all point to areas within British culture and civilization that Wordsworth thinks have declined since Milton's day. All things have suffered loss — from the strength of the church, the army, or the accomplishment of writers to the more immediate and individual quality of home life — in particular an "inward happiness," along with a sense of strength and security.

Milton seems to have represented for Wordsworth an epitome of the heroic, a kind of guiding star apart from other human beings, with a voice that was expansive, at one with the sublime in nature, and morally incorruptible.

POSSIBLE CONNECTIONS TO OTHER SELECTIONS

William Blake, "London" (text p. 101)
George Eliot, "In a London Drawingroom" (text p. 606)

AUDIOVISUAL AND ONLINE RESOURCES (manual pp. 311, 355)

JIM STEVENS, *Schizophrenia* (p. 129)

The ways in which personification, stanzaic form, and title combine to create meaning in this poem can be a fruitful approach to discussion. Stevens personifies the house as a victim suffering from the turmoil of its inhabitants. You might ask students to find examples of ways in which the house is physically "hurt" by their activities (see especially lines 2–5 and 17–20). The sequencing and relative lengths of the stanzas draw the reader to important statements of meaning in the poem. The poem is framed by two identical statements that "it was the house that suffered most." Moving toward the center from these identical lines, 2–5 and 17–20 deal specifically with physical things happening to the house. The next two stanzas toward the center, lines 6–9 and 13–16, depict the people doing things to the house, using it as a means of carrying out their aggressions toward one another. The very center of the poem, set off by a three-line stanza when the ones surrounding it have contained four lines, specifies what has been going on between the people themselves.

It is the title, however, that brings the poem together as a whole and allows us to relate the suffering *of* the house to the suffering *in* the house. *Schizophrenia* literally means a split mind; it is a psychosis characterized by radical changes in behavior. Have the students notice the change in behavior and its effects on the house between the beginning and end of the poem. In the first nine lines, the house is being violently abused: doors and dishes are slammed around, the carpets are intentionally scuffed, and grease, much harder to deal with than plain dirt, is ground into the tablecloth. In lines 5–9, the pattern moderates slightly: the slammed doors get locked, the dishes remain dirty instead of being slammed around, the feet stand still instead of scuffing. The third long stanza provides a transition into a mode of behavior radically opposite to what has come before. It casts the turmoil in terms of the inhabitants' violence toward one another, but also indicates that this violence is no longer occurring. Instead, what we see in lines 12–16 is the people dividing the house between them, splitting it between them to stay out of one another's way and put an end to the fighting. Note the ominous tone of line 15, an allusion to the biblical warning that "a house divided against itself cannot stand." Indeed, the effects on the house of this new kind of warfare are all seen in terms of things splitting apart — the paint coming away from the wood, the windows breaking into pieces, the front door coming loose from its hinges, and the roof tiles coming off the roof. The last word (*madhouse*) of the poem proper, before the refrain of the last line, brings the reader back to the title. You might discuss with your students whether the word refers to the house itself, which the speaker contends is suffering, or whether it means a house that contains mad people, or both. Is the idea of "home," the combination of house and people, the real victim of the madness? Would "Madhouse" have been a better title than "Schizophrenia"?

POSSIBLE CONNECTIONS TO OTHER SELECTIONS

Emily Dickinson, "One need not be a Chamber — to be Haunted —" (text p. 308)
Langston Hughes, "doorknobs" (text p. 393)
Edgar Allan Poe, "The Haunted Palace" (text p. 141)

WALT WHITMAN, *A Noiseless Patient Spider* (p. 130)

In this poem, Whitman participates in a fairly long and distinguished tradition, starting with the homely tropes of Edward Taylor or Anne Bradstreet, that explores analogies between lower forms of natural life and the human condition. In this instance, the analogy is effective since both soul and spider are isolated — and are trying to reach across vast space to forge connections between themselves and the rest of the world. The emphasis within the soul seems to be a reflective activity (musing, venturing, throwing, seeking), while the activity of the spider seems more a physical compulsion, especially with the repetition of "filament."

POSSIBLE CONNECTION TO ANOTHER SELECTION

Emily Dickinson, "I heard a Fly buzz — when I died —" (text p. 307)

JOHN DONNE, *A Valediction: Forbidding Mourning* (p. 130)

The questions in the text show how richly metaphorical this metaphysical poem in fact is. Virtually every statement here is made through a comparison. The lovers should tolerate their separation with the same grace with which "virtuous men" leave this earth. They are not like the "Dull sublunary" lovers who need physical presence to sustain each other; they represent something finer. This sense of refinement is picked up and developed further in the simile in line 24, when the strength of the love between Donne and his wife is compared to gold, which does not shatter when beaten but expands to delicate, fine plate. Donne concludes his poem with the well-known compass metaphor. You might have to explain at this point what sort of compass

Donne is describing, since we live in an age of computer graphics, not drafting skills. Because the compass here is used to draw circles, it is a most appropriate simile to describe unity and perfection.

POSSIBLE CONNECTIONS TO OTHER SELECTIONS

Anne Bradstreet, "To My Dear and Loving Husband" (text p. 436)
John Donne, "The Flea" (text p. 605)
William Shakespeare, "Shall I compare thee to a summer's day?" (text p. 228)

AUDIOVISUAL AND ONLINE RESOURCES (manual pp. 297, 329)

LINDA PASTAN, *Marks* (p. 132)

In teaching this poem, it would probably be a good idea to discuss the social expectations of motherhood and those of being a student. The latter relationship, in which the person is constantly being judged and is answerable to an authority figure, is not always ego enhancing, a point that Eugène Ionesco carried to absurd limits in *The Lesson*. The situation of the mother in Pastan's poem seems not much better; although anyone in any job or academic setting is frequently under review, is not a mother's "job" more an act of ongoing generosity than a fulfilling of job or course requirements? Class discussion could challenge the appropriateness of the metaphor here.

The speaker's increasingly bitter, ironic tone serves (as irony often does) as a weapon against the "marks" (the hurt and disillusionment) inflicted on her by her family. Can she easily leave school; leave her responsibilities?

As a writing assignment, ask students to analyze how this poem challenges and mocks its central metaphor.

POSSIBLE CONNECTION TO ANOTHER SELECTION

Indira Sant, "Household Fires" (text p. 663)

AUDIOVISUAL AND ONLINE RESOURCES (manual pp. 305, 346)

THOMAS LYNCH, *Liberty* (p. 132)

This poem acknowledges the limitations suburban life places on man's wild nature by claiming one small holdover from the romantic "fierce bloodline" (line 6) of the past: the freedom to "piss on the front lawn" (1). The speaker defines not "liberty" but what he seeks liberty from: "porcelain and plumbing and the Great Beyond" (3). The speaker uses a humorous tone and claims his own silliness as well as his own right to "do it anywhere" (14). The presence of the ex-wife serves to allow the reader to take sides; is the reader suffering from the "gentility or envy" (13) that plagued the wife, or is the reader aligned with the speaker, tied genetically to "the hedgerow of whitethorn" (19) and the "vast firmament" (30)? "Crowns," "crappers," and "ex-wives" (32), representing figures of authority and the suffocating nature of domestic life, are what Lynch's speaker seeks to escape.

Students may find the poem foolish and trifling, or they may enjoy its humorous perspective. Lynch's speaker is rebelling against home life and suburbia; how do your students rebel? What are they rebelling against? In a freewrite, ask them to consider what acts of rebellion they engage in, and why they are pleasurable or necessary.

POSSIBLE CONNECTIONS TO OTHER SELECTIONS

John Ciardi, "Suburban" (question #1, following)
Robert Frost, "Acquainted with the Night" (text p. 139)

1. Discuss Lynch's treatment of suburban life and compare it with John Ciardi's in "Suburban" (p. 161). What similarities are there in the themes and metaphoric strategies of these two poems?

   Both speakers use humor to portray themselves as separate from the suburban culture they hope to subvert. Ciardi's feigned indictment of the mystery dog's act when he says, "The animal of it" (line 16), parallels the speaker in "Liberty," who at times refuses to "pee / in concert with the most of humankind / who do their business tidily indoors" (10–12). The "animal" in Ciardi's poem is connected to the "fierce bloodline" in line 6 of Lynch's in a refusal to be tamed or fenced in by the stultifying surroundings of the suburbs.

STEPHEN DUNN, *John & Mary* (p. 133)

The launching pad for this humorous poem is an excerpt from a student's short story. The speaker extends the student's example by creating several absurd similes — John & Mary as gazelles, postal workers, religious devotees, dolphins, and trains. As the poem progresses, so too does our sense that any meeting is as improbable as the freshman says it is.

CONSIDERATIONS FOR CRITICAL THINKING AND WRITING

1. Because we know that the epigraph is written by a freshman, we understand that he or she is still a beginning writer, learning the rules of clarity and accuracy. By creating a catalogue of similar absurdities, the speaker reveals his own imagination and sense of humor as a writing teacher and poet.

2. The freshman's simile doesn't work because it compares two unlike things. The unintentional humor of the lines inspires Dunn to force other unlike things together throughout the rest of the poem.

3. Give students some time to see the epigraph's humor and its importance to the rest of the poem. It might take students a couple of readings before they can relax and enjoy Dunn's associative leaps from one improbable meeting to the next. If they think that the speaker is making fun of his student, remind them that the freshman's short story excerpt has inspired a whole poem.

4. A certain sadness exists in lines 20–23 for which the previous lines do not prepare us. Physical laws can never be violated, even in "another world." Two parallel lines can never intersect; stars appear cool and distant, not kindred and close, as the speaker claims they might. The final lines of the poem confirm the literal meaning of lines 14–15.

POSSIBLE CONNECTION TO ANOTHER SELECTION

Mark Halliday, "Graded Paper" (text p. 445)

ONLINE RESOURCES (manual p. 330)

ELAINE MAGARRELL, *The Joy of Cooking* (p. 134)

This grisly poem is from the point of view of a disgruntled sibling who has, on a literal level, cooked parts of her sister and brother. On a metaphorical level, she is attacking their attributes which have injured her. Ask students whether they think the poem is humorous or horrifying. They are bound to recall some news story or horror movie featuring cannibalism, even of one's family members. Is the speaker's fantasy tempered by these incidents, or does her tone and her reliance on the discourse of cookbooks make it impossible to accept the poem as anything but a metaphor with humorous intent?

The tongue and heart are extended metaphors for the siblings. The sister is described as needing spices to make her more interesting. We can imagine that hers is not an effervescent personality. The brother, characterized as a heart, seems heartless. Whereas most hearts feed six, his "barely feeds two" (line 16). He is "rather dry" (10), requiring stuffing to make him palatable. Neither sibling is complete enough when left alone to warrant the speaker's unadorning description; she must "doctor them up" to make them palatable to her audience and herself.

POSSIBLE CONNECTIONS TO OTHER SELECTIONS

Sally Croft, "Home-Baked Bread" (question #1, following)

Maxine Hong Kingston, "Restaurant" (text p. 193)

CONNECTION QUESTION IN TEXT (p. 135) WITH ANSWER

1. Write an essay that explains how cooking becomes a way of talking about something else in this poem and in Croft's "Home-Baked Bread" (p. 107).

   Croft at first questions *The Joy of Cooking,* wondering why it should treat its subject as one would a human mystery. Carried away by the language, she moves into the role of seductress, luring her listener into the erotic sensuality of her poem. Magarrell's adaptation from the same book takes an entirely different form. Her tone is bitter. Rather than seducing her listeners, she startles and perhaps alienates them through her arresting images.

STEPHEN PERRY, *Blue Spruce* (p. 135)

Perry's poem is very visual, moving back and forth between metaphors and weaving images together on several levels. Some of the references in this poem may seem a little foreign to contemporary students — few students have had first-hand experience with a barber shop, a razor strop, horses and carriages, or even a bandstand. However, these images are central to the charm of the piece, and a good starting place may be to point out that the title, "Blue Spruce," works on many levels — it not only signifies a type of evergreen tree (and thus a connection to winter), but also was the name of a scent of aftershave lotion. Consequently, the title "Blue Spruce" points to the connection between the metaphors that help characterize the grandfather — the barber shop, the winter images of snow and ice, and the bandstand and instruments that appear beneath the evergreens. It may be helpful to ask students to trace each of these metaphors in order to see how the images are interwoven in the poem. You may also wish to discuss which aspect of the grandfather each of the images signifies (for example, the barber shop as his identity, the winter images as his age, the bandstand as his love). Students will undoubtedly have their own understandings of the symbolic value of these images, and it may be useful to have students write a short explanation of how they interpret the images in Perry's poem.

You may wish to point out that from the opening lines of the poem, the speaker establishes a connection between shaving and sexuality: "the black razor strop hung like the penis of an ox" (lines 3–4). This connection is explored throughout the poem, since it is the grandfather's sexual behavior that gets him in trouble with the town and with his family. Some students may see the grandfather's behavior as irresponsible; others may see him as irrepressible and extravagant — a man who lived life with a flourish and with a great deal of show. When asking students to determine whether the speaker wishes for readers to admire or to scorn the grandfather, you might ask them to identify where in the poem their own reaction to the grandfather begins to take shape. The speaker first mentions the possibility of hating the grandfather in lines 32–34, and many students might find it hard to admire a man who flirts with nurses at his wife's "last death" (36). An interesting related question is whether the speaker even intends to influence the reader either way. Although he pretends not to hate the grandfather (he asks, "How could you hate him?" and he does not list himself among the family members that do [32–34]) there seem to be some underlying resentments that rise to the surface with observations of his grandfather's "oompah love," his "bandstand love," his "brassy love" (26–27) and with the acknowledgment that the grandfather has acted in ways that have harmed the speaker's family (30–32; 34).

Perhaps the final analysis of the speaker's reaction to his grandfather's activities occurs in the final memory he re-creates: the moment where the grandfather, "a deep lather / of laughter" (40–41), takes the speaker from his mother and raises him into the bell of his instrument, as if he were "a note / he'd play into light —" (44–45). Have your students consider whether the speaker is saying that he feels connected to the grandfather, and that he will be the child that carries the grandfather forward into the future, or that this is simply one more example of the grandfather grandstanding his love, viewing the child as his own private hope.

POSSIBLE CONNECTIONS TO OTHER SELECTIONS

Regina Barreca, "Nighttime Fires" (text p. 26)
Theodore Roethke, "My Papa's Waltz" (text p. 217)

PERSPECTIVE

JOHN R. SEARLE, *Figuring Out Metaphors* (p. 136)

In a writing assignment, ask students to find two poems in which the metaphors work and two in which they don't. The students' essays should explain their choices, that is, define the metaphors in the poems and explain why they work (or why they don't). If possible, the students should speculate about the characteristics of a successful metaphor based on the evidence of the poems they have chosen.

A class exercise or another writing assignment might involve students finding metaphors in sources other than poems — in the newspaper, for example, or in popular songs or television programs. Once found, these examples could also be analyzed as successful or unsuccessful metaphors.

6

Symbol, Allegory, and Irony

The discussion on symbol and allegory can follow naturally from the discussion of figurative language. In a sense, symbols are metaphors with one term left open, and it is up to the reader to complete them. Many of the poems in the previous chapter lend themselves well to symbolic readings — a good transition between the chapters might have students select a previously covered poem and examine its symbols.

Another exercise that can be useful is to have students brainstorm a list of symbols found in popular culture and articulate the connotations that surround them: what the American flag means, for instance. (This exercise can also illustrate how symbols can have different meanings for different groups.) This can help give students a sense of how symbols work, and how they can be simultaneously specific and general.

Students often seem to believe that every poem is immediately symbolic, which can be simultaneously encouraging and frustrating in their zeal to leap to the "real" meaning of the poem. Alternately, they may be committed to a kind of relativism, in which they believe that some poems can be symbolic of anything. While it is true that some symbols are more loosely focused than others, one of the challenges of discussion in this chapter is to encourage students to offer well-thought-out readings. It is a difficult line to walk between putting pressure on students to read critically and shutting down all discussion because the students come to believe that the teacher has "the right answer," and unless they can provide this they are better off keeping quiet. In fact, students may use silence as a tactic to bring out "the right answer" from the teacher. In this chapter, it is perhaps better to err on the side of caution and try to draw out students' own interpretations, even if these interpretations are initially somewhat off track. You may find it useful to avoid giving your own interpretations at all, relying instead on student input shaped by questions from you and from other students. Students may find this frustrating at first, particularly when they are used to being given answers by authorities, but ultimately it will sharpen their abilities as readers.

Irony can be difficult to explain directly — in this case, examples are a great help. Irony often depends on an understanding of the context, as Janice Mirikitani's "Recipe" illustrates. Without some idea of the "beauty myth," the irony in this poem will not be evident. It may be useful to compare some kinds of irony to an inside joke in that they depend on a shared bit of information before the audience can "get it." Students may in fact be quite familiar with situational irony, as in Jane Kenyon's "Surprise." They may be able to readily call incidents to mind in which all was not as it initially seemed. For an interesting take on irony, you might look at Linda Hutcheon's book *Irony's Edge: The Theory and Politics of Irony*, which is an occasionally dense but well-supported argument about the place of irony in contemporary society.

ROBERT FROST, *Acquainted with the Night* (p. 139)

This poem investigates the mind of a speaker who has seen a part of humanity and of nature that he cannot overlook. His experience has led him to see things that other people have not necessarily seen. The poem invites us to read it on more than one level, as is the case with many of Frost's poems. You might ask the students to discuss in a two-page essay the function of the clock in this poem. How does its presence modify the tone of the poem? Do we read it literally, symbolically, or as a mixture of both?

Possible Connections to Other Selections

T. S. Eliot, "The Love Song of J. Alfred Prufrock" (text p. 405)
Robert Frost, "Stopping by Woods on a Snowy Evening" (text p. 353)
Octavio Paz, "The Street" (text p. 662)

EDGAR ALLAN POE, *The Haunted Palace* (p. 141)

Edgar Allan Poe was born in Boston, the son of itinerant actors. He lived an often harrowing life marked by alcoholism, disease, and misfortune, managing to eke out a rather precarious existence primarily as an editor for a number of newspapers and periodicals in Philadelphia, New York, and Baltimore. Although he was renowned in his lifetime as the author of "The Raven," his most abiding ambition was to be a respected critic. He died after collapsing in a Baltimore street.

Students may have had little exposure to allegory, since it is not frequently used by modern writers. Thus it might be useful to explicate at least one stanza of the poem, discussing how a particular part of the palace corresponds to a particular part of the human body or mind. Notice the two "characters" actually personified by Poe in the poem: Thought (line 5) and Echoes (29). Does there seem to be a particular reason for singling out these two?

What is the purpose of using such archaic expressions as "Porphyrogene" (22) and "red-litten" (42)? What other words in the poem seem especially well chosen for their connotative meanings?

As a short writing assignment or subject for further class discussion, ask your students to contrast the depictions of the "windows" and the "door" of the palace when they first appear in the poem (stanzas III and IV) with their portrayal in the last stanza, after the coming of the "evil things" (33). How do they seem to change?

Possible Connections to other Selections

Emily Dickinson, "One need not be a Chamber — to be Haunted — " (text p. 308)
Jim Stevens, "Schizophrenia" (text p. 129)

Audiovisual and Online Resources (manual pp. 306, 347)

EDWIN ARLINGTON ROBINSON, *Richard Cory* (p. 143)

Edwin Arlington Robinson became a professional poet in the grimmest of circumstances: his father's businesses went bankrupt in 1893, one brother became a drug addict and another an alcoholic, and Robinson could afford to attend Harvard University for just two years. He eked out a livelihood from the contributions of friends and patrons, finally moving to New York City, where his work received more critical attention and public acceptance. He won three Pulitzer Prizes for his gloomy, musical verse narratives.

As a writing assignment, you might ask students to analyze how Robinson achieves the power of the final line of "Richard Cory," paying special attention to the regal language that describes Cory as well as the strong contrasts in the couplets of the final stanza.

Possible Connections to Other Selections

M. Carl Holman, "Mr. Z" (text p. 612)

Percy Bysshe Shelley, "Ozymandias" (text p. 636)

Online Resources (manual p. 348)

KENNETH FEARING, *AD* (p. 144)

How does the double meaning inherent in the title of the poem — "AD" is an abbreviation for "advertisement" as well as for "in the year of the Lord" — prepare the reader for the satire that follows? Notice how even the type used for this poem contributes to its meaning. The italicized words and phrases might occur in any high-powered advertising campaign. How is the effect of the advertising words undercut by the words in standard type? What is the effect of the reversal of type patterns in the last line?

Students should be aware that the poem alludes, in part, to the Uncle Sam "I want you" army recruiting posters. Discuss whether the purpose of the satire in "AD" is to expose a situation that exists, to correct it, or both. Is the situation to which the poem refers — the attempt to draw people into a horrifying occupation by making the work sound exciting and rewarding — confined to the pre–World War II era?

Possible Connections to Other Selections

Janice Mirikitani, "Recipe" (below)

Wole Soyinka, "Future Plans" (text p. 664)

Online Resources (manual p. 331)

JANICE MIRIKITANI, *Recipe* (p. 144)

Before discussing this poem, be sure students understand the literal message of the poem — this is a recipe for "Round Eyes" (that is, caucasian eyes) written by a Japanese American poet. The poem is fairly straightforward, outlining the necessary equipment and the step-by-step process involved in making eyes that are not round into round eyes. However, a close examination shows that the poem is loaded with double meanings. For example, examine the final instruction of the recipe: "Do not cry" (line 16). Ask your students to consider the tone and stance of the speaker in light of line 16. What do the round eyes represent, and why does this speaker imply that round eyes might be desirable? Discuss what the poem implies about cultural standards of beauty and the price individuals — particularly women and women of color — are required to pay to meet these standards.

This poem also serves as an excellent example of irony. Ask students how irony functions in the poem. In order to help students appreciate the difficulty of employing a successful ironic strategy, and in order to help them examine some cultural assumptions that are often taken for granted, you might ask students to write a similar cultural critique — to choose a cultural standard of beauty or success and to write an ironic piece describing how this cultural standard may be obtained or maintained, and at what cost.

Possible Connection to Another Selection

Kenneth Fearing, "AD" (question #1, following)

1. Why are the formulas for an advertisement and a recipe especially suited for
   Fearing's and Mirikitani's respective purposes? To what extent do the ironic strategies lead to a similar tone and theme?

   Generally speaking, advertisements and recipes regard something potentially positive — either something the reader (or viewer) would *want* to buy or to make. In
   these two poems, the conceits of an advertisement and recipe try to convince men
   to die and women (Asian women in particular) to tape their eyelids up, respectively.
   The irony becomes apparent not only through the use of each conceit for its apparently opposite purpose, but also through the diction of each poem. Fearing's "horror" (line 4) and "dying in flames" (7) play against our ideas of an advertisement
   selling something; Mirikitani's "false" (line 4) and her final word — "cry" — do the
   same with the recipe formula.

ONLINE RESOURCES (manual p. 343)

E. E. CUMMINGS, *next to of course god america i* (p. 146)

The speaker of this poem is trapped by jingoistic clichés that render his speech
almost meaningless. His intent is to manipulate his audience, convincing them that the
men who have sacrificed their lives in war are "heroic" and "happy" (line 10). As a writing assignment, you might ask students to analyze how Cummings portrays character
without employing direct description.

POSSIBLE CONNECTIONS TO OTHER SELECTIONS

Langston Hughes, "Un-American Investigators" (text p. 392)

Florence Cassen Mayers, "All-American Sestina" (text p. 236)

STEPHEN CRANE, *A Man Said to the Universe* (p. 146)

What sort of answer does the man in the poem expect to get from the universe?
What does that say about the man? What other emotions, besides amusement, does this
poem evoke? How does a reader's own perception of how the universe operates affect his
or her response to the poem? Students are likely to concur that the more distance they
feel between themselves and the man, the more amusing they find the poem.

POSSIBLE CONNECTIONS TO OTHER SELECTIONS

Robert Frost, "'Out, Out' — " (text p. 350)

Langston Hughes, "Lenox Avenue: Midnight" (text p. 383)

ONLINE RESOURCES (manual p. 328)

JANE KENYON, *Surprise* (p. 147)

From the perspective of the woman "surprised," this poem encompasses many of
the conflicting emotions of a surprise party in spare, deliberate imagery. Distracted by
the unnamed male, and oblivious to the gathering elsewhere, the speaker notes all of the
changes around her as a result of the onset of spring. The last three lines of the poem
reverse the mood, suggesting that the speaker's surprise comes at the ease with which
her husband/lover has deceived her, opening up the possibility that there is something
wrong with their relationship.

It might be useful to begin by asking students if they have ever been involved in a
surprise party — either as the victim or as the scheming organizer. A discussion of what
a surprise party intends to do leads naturally into a discussion of what it often actually
does. Similarly, the poem leads us from the mundane — "pancakes at the local diner"

(line 1), "casseroles" (4) — to the surprising renewal of nature in springtime, to the woman's astounding realization that the man has had such an easy time lying to her. The word "astound," with its connotations of bewilderment, directs our attention away from the surprise party and into speculation about the relationship between them. The irony centers around the renewal of the spring birthday juxtaposed against some almost funereal undertones (consider "spectral" in line 8, and "ash" in line 9, for example). The tension between images enables us to interpret their relationship in a novel, surprising way.

POSSIBLE CONNECTIONS TO OTHER SELECTIONS

William Hathaway, "Oh, Oh" (question #1, following)

Sharon Olds, "Rite of Passage" (question #2, following)

CONNECTIONS QUESTIONS IN TEXT (p. 147) WITH ANSWERS

1. Write an essay on the nature of the surprises in Kenyon's poem and in Hathaway's "Oh, Oh" (p. 13). Include in your discussion a comparison of the tone and irony in each poem.

    "Oh, Oh" is much more humorous than this poem, but the effects are similar. In both cases, the final line tells us something that we didn't know, something that causes us to rethink the rest of the poem, especially the title. In Hathaway's poem, we know that something is coming, though, since the title clues us in. In this poem, we may at first take the "surprise" to be simply the surprise party, so we are especially surprised to learn that there is something amiss between this couple who seem to have enjoyed their breakfast and spring walk.

2. Compare and contrast in an essay the irony associated with the birthday parties in "Surprise" and Sharon Olds's "Rite of Passage" (p. 265).

    The irony in Olds's poem comes partially from the speaker's sense that her son and his friends are treating life so lightly at a birthday party. He is transformed from a frail, innocent thing to a general plotting the death of a weaker being. The young partygoers are not any more aware of this irony than the guests at the party in Kenyon's poem are. In both cases, the irony is something shared only between the poet and the reader, although any adult at Olds's party would be likely to notice something vaguely disturbing in the boys' comments.

LAURE-ANNE BOSSELAAR, *The Bumper-Sticker* (p. 148)

The central theme of this poem is the need to repair the past, a need so dire that it insists on following every lead, even the advice of a bumper sticker. The symbols present here take the reader on a journey; the use of second person insists on company. The absurdity of the poem provides humor, but there are serious aspects to it as well; the reference to your mother as an old jalopy "that nearly killed you and broke your back every day" (line 16) is hardly a sentimental portrait of Mom. Buicks and bumper stickers are funny, prosaic American artifacts that serve as clues in this poem's search for a new childhood, "happy" as advertised. Bosselaar takes advantage of automotive vocabulary to consider changing the past "like tires with a bad grip" (7) or old motor oil, "murky and dark" (8). These new uses for familiar language provide a funny conjunction between pop psychology and the love of the open road, both part of the American experience.

The narrative is structured like a stream of consciousness; ideas of past, childhood, and memory get tangled with left-hand turns and smooth riding. The sudden conclusion, when the near-hypnotic state is broken, is signified by a line break, a stanza break, and a near-miss of an accident. Students might enjoy trying their hand at the symbolic journey: What kind of philosophical questions could be answered on a long drive through the prairies to the Rocky Mountains, along the Pacific coast, or down a crowded street? Try creating a list of possible forms of locomotion that could be used as symbols with your class, writing their ideas on the board before they begin attacking the assignment.

POSSIBLE CONNECTIONS TO OTHER SELECTIONS

Jane Kenyon, "Surprise" (question #1, following)
Philip Larkin, "This Be the Verse" (text p. 621)

CONNECTION QUESTION IN TEXT (p. 148) WITH ANSWER

1. Discuss the use of irony in this poem and in Jane Kenyon's "Surprise." How does irony reveal the sensibilities of the speaker in each poem?

    In one clear example of Bosselaar's irony, a truck labeled "Safeway" (25) shatters an imaginative quest for a fresh childhood by nearly sideswiping the "you" of the poem. The dreams of establishing a safe and secure base for the new life, made possible by imagining a perfect childhood, are harshly dispelled. Kenyon's poem establishes the speaker as someone who is not simply grateful and excited for the party and the planning that created it but who also sees the event as evidence of the beloved's skill at lying. Both poems reveal thoughtful, analytic speakers with eyes for detail who are ready to believe the worst.

RENNIE McQUILKIN, *The Lighters* (p. 149)

This poem examines the possible importance of what we choose to keep in later life. The voice is not that of the eighty-nine-year-old woman who is the subject of the poem, but one of an imaginative observer. The initials of the best man on one of the lighters indicates that they were favors distributed at the unnamed woman's wedding; while she is casting aside most of her other sentimental possessions, these remain valuable. The speaker suggests that they provide a symbolic entrance to the world of memory and nostalgia. Like the lighters, the "antique gap-toothed keys" (line 9) are also seen as possible connections to the world of the dead and a means by which she can remember those who left behind the cherished objects.

While the physical appearance of the woman is not directly mentioned, attributes of the things she keeps include "square-shouldered" (4), "gap-toothed" (9), and "high-backed" (11). The poem's mood is mildly mournful but conscious of the many ways in which this woman has been loved: children are present, and the word "boudoir" (3) conveys echoes of a nostalgic sensuality. The poem employs other resonant words as keys to its almost supernatural concluding image: the lighters are lined up "gravely" (8), the keys are thought to open a sunken chamber. This conclusion indicates the separation between the living and the dead; in this poem, it is the dead who gather to remember the living, while the living remember the dead by accumulating their goods.

Consider asking students to write for a few minutes imagining the importance of a family treasure or personal memento. Why has the object been kept? What role could it play in connecting the keeper to another time or place?

POSSIBLE CONNECTIONS TO OTHER SELECTIONS

Wyatt Prunty, "Elderly Lady Crossing on Green" (question #1, following)
Andrew Hudgins, "Seventeen" (text p. 156)

CONNECTION QUESTION IN TEXT (p. 149) WITH ANSWER

1. Compare the treatment of this elderly woman with that of Wyatt Prunty's "Elderly Lady Crossing on Green" (p. 39). How is aging depicted in each poem?

Both poems rely on a definition of old age that is rich with events past. In these poems the dead are remembered, our relationships with them are present, and the feats of our youth still define us. These old women are not merely old women, but the summation of the events, actions, and relationships that gave their whole lives shape.

ONLINE RESOURCES (manual p. 342)

KATHY MANGAN, *An Arithmetic* (p. 149)

The first half of this poem provides a sensual memory of the language and process by which we learn arithmetic as children. Through careful attention, Mangan establishes the pleasures of math in school: "the fat green pencil" (line 4), "rounded / threes, looping eights" (5–6), "the speckled / yellow newsprint" (6–7). But these pleasures are linked exclusively to addition; in the second half, subtraction provides less pleasurable lessons, teaching us to *"take away"* (13) and "settle" (14). The pleasures of addition are natural in childhood, Mangan's speaker suggests, because "the world insists on still giving and giving at six" (1). Subtraction is a longer, more painful lesson; the sensual pleasure of the first stanza gives way to the philosophical concerns of the second. Addition becomes the pleasures we take from the world, while subtraction teaches us the hard lesson of the difference "between what I have wanted / and what I got" (21–22).

Students approaching the writing assignment can take pleasure in the novelty of the language of math when placed in these new contexts; Mangan employs this diction to great effect. It could prove useful to take a moment before the class attempts this assignment to make a list on the board of the language associated with math class: *positive, negative, remainder, lowest common denominator, exponential, table, root* — all these words contain multiple meanings within and outside their mathematical context. Students, who may actually be enrolled in a math class, are likely to have other helpful suggestions.

POSSIBLE CONNECTIONS TO OTHER SELECTIONS

Judy Page Heitzman, "The Schoolroom on the Second Floor of the Knitting Mill" (question #1, following)
Margaret Avison, "Tennis" (text p. 592)
Sue Owen, "Zero" (text p. 123)

CONNECTION QUESTION IN TEXT (p. 150) WITH ANSWER

1. Compare this memory of childhood and school with that of Judy Page Heitzman's "The Schoolroom on the Second Floor of the Knitting Mill" (p. 446). What significant similarities do you find in the two poems?

    Both poems present the pleasure of the classroom and the quiet, mundane horror of what we learn there. Heitzman represents that pleasure in the sun streaming into her memory and "the tether ball, its towering height, the swings" (line 11); Mangan refers us to the pleasures of "shedding graphite" (5) and arriving at "plump sums" (10). The horrors both poets expose in their second stanza hinge on the longevity of lessons we learn in our childhoods. Even as an adult, Heitzman's speaker is haunted by her teacher's words, she says in the last line, "every time I fail." Mangan's speaker sees subtraction not as a continuation of the pleasures of addition but as a loss, a gradual understanding that she hasn't gotten what she has wanted.

ROBERT BLY, *Snowbanks North of the House* (p. 150)

This is a series poem — a poem that presents a list of observations that may seem disconnected but that have some internal coherence. You might ask students to try to identify the link between all of the images and lines in this poem, although it may be difficult for them to put the relationship into concrete language.

This poem focuses on the idea of things that end, and the great sense of loss and loneliness that accompanies certain kinds of endings. This theme is apparent in lines that describe the high school boy who stops reading (line 3), the son who stops calling home (4), the mother who no longer makes bread (5), the woman who ceases to love her husband (6), and the minister who falls leaving the church (7); however, it is less apparent in lines like "It will not come closer — the one inside moves back, and the hands touch nothing, and are safe" (9) or in the final lines that describe the man in the black coat. Ask students to attempt to interpret these lines: What will not come closer? Who is the man in the black coat, and why is he portrayed the way he is? You might also ask students to explore the connections between the images in the poem that seem to defy our general expectations. Why might the poet have included lines that appear to be unrelated to the rest of the poem?

POSSIBLE CONNECTIONS TO OTHER SELECTIONS

William Blake, "London" (text p. 101)

Robert Bly, "Snowfall in the Afternoon" (text p. 593)

Robert Frost, "Stopping by Woods on a Snowy Evening" (question #1, following)

William Butler Yeats, "The Second Coming" (text p. 653)

CONNECTION QUESTION IN TEXT (p. 151) WITH ANSWER

2. Compare and contrast the symbolic images in "Snowbanks North of the House" and Robert Frost's "Stopping by Woods on a Snowy Evening" (p. 353).

    In each poem the snow is a metaphor for a sadness underlying the speakers' ruminations. Whereas Frost's snowy setting contributes to the overall weary sadness, Bly is more direct, linking the "drift[s]" (line 1) with the "thoughts that go so far" (2).

AUDIOVISUAL AND ONLINE RESOURCES (manual pp. 293–294, 325)

PERSPECTIVE

ROBERT BLY, *On "Snowbanks North of the House"* (p. 151)

Bly's generous perspective walks the reader through the poem line by line, explaining the emotional origin of each line as he goes. There are a couple of ways to use this perspective — both for this poem in particular, and for poetry in general. You may want to have students read the perspective after a substantial discussion of the poem. Certainly many students will view the poem differently than Bly, which will pave the way for a discussion of how author-intent and reader response can differ. Similarly, Bly's understanding of the emotional impact of the poem will, at times, coincide with that of your students. In order for students to relate to the poem, is it necessary for them to have the same specific experience that caused Bly to write each line? Consider Bly's own, more general metaphor for poetry: a "nourishing mud pond in which partly developed tadpoles can live for a while."

You may also wish to use this perspective for discussions of other poems. Bly begins by quoting William Stafford's opinion regarding assertions in a poem. This seemingly "over-analytical" approach to a poem may initially turn off some students. But it also provides an interesting inroad to the process of writing poetry and how that process, in turn, affects the reader. Perhaps a more accessible poem (because of its immediate and overt appeal to the reader) is Marianne Moore's "Poetry." How does Moore control the use of assertions to guide readers through her poem? Can your students think of other poems that use assertions similarly? Consider how Bly himself begins with a discussion of his assertions and ends by asserting that a poem is a "mud pond."

CARL SANDBURG, *Buttons* (p. 154)

This poem examines a topic that continues to be present whenever the media examine the costs of war; televised coverage of the wars in Vietnam and the Persian Gulf instigated similar commentary since this poem was written in 1915. Sandburg's poem hinges on the "laughing young man, sunny with freckles" (line 5), seemingly unaware of the meaning of his actions as he marks the day's casualties on the map "slammed up for advertising" (1) in a newspaper office. The map itself is a symbol for the war losses; the absence of gravity in the actions of the man who works to update that symbol is the inconsistency that drives the poem. The parenthetical examination of the "buttons" of the poem's title demonstrates the distance between the thoughtlessness of the young man and the tragic events played out on the actual battlefield.

Students are likely to be familiar with other media and their relation to tragedy: how do television and radio announcers convey the gravity of the deaths they report? How do doctors and police officers on television series vary their emotional responses to crime and death depending on context?

POSSIBLE CONNECTIONS TO OTHER SELECTIONS

Jeannette Barnes, "Battle-Piece" (text p. 90)

Kenneth Fearing, "AD" (question #1, following)

Henry Reed, "Naming of Parts" (question #1, following)

CONNECTION QUESTION IN TEXT (p. 155) WITH ANSWER

1. Discuss the symbolic treatment of war in this poem, Kenneth Fearing's "AD" (p. 144), and Henry Reed's "Naming of Parts" (p. 160).

   Sandburg's poem establishes the symbol of buttons for the losses of wartime, with a parenthetical examination that imagines the actual deaths and wounds beyond the map and its markers of victory and loss. Fearing's poem symbolizes the burgeoning Nazi movement by imagining the absurdity of a help-wanted ad detailing the attributes required of would-be Nazis. Reed's poem focuses on a small task, part of a soldier's training; this task is explicitly nonviolent, an exercise in vocabulary and mechanics, not related to death and wounds. All three authors focus on some small detail of wartime, real or imagined, that allows the reader to grasp the actual horror of war.

ONLINE RESOURCES (manual p. 349)

WILLIAM STAFFORD, *Traveling through the Dark* (p. 155)

This poem is a gut-wrenching narrative of a man who finds a deer by the side of the road who has been struck dead but whose unborn fawn is still alive. After hesitating a moment, he decides to pursue his original course of action and throw her over the edge of the road. Students might be taken aback by the speaker's reaction to this incident, especially the language he uses to describe the occurrence: "It is usually best to roll them into the canyon" (line 3). Do we believe that he is emotionless or simply that he must suspend his emotions in order to accomplish his task? What is the effect of the truncated final stanza?

One of the surprising qualities about this poem is just how much time Stafford takes to describe his car. Given this description, with its glowing light, its "warm exhaust," the "steady" engine that "purred," the car acquires a stronger lifelike sense than anything else in this poem, which laments the death of something beautiful in the natural world. The car, "aimed ahead," seems symbolically to foreshadow a darker, more inhuman future, in which mechanization replaces old-fashioned Fate.

Providing every physical detail of his encounter with the deer, the speaker sounds like a news reporter, calmly telling his story to his listeners. But the final stanza suggests that he is meditative and brooding, that this incident means much more to him than its details imply, that his thinking involves the fate of the deer as well as that of the human race.

The short final stanza emphasizes its contemplative tone, setting it against the previous stanzas, moving the focus away from the deer, toward the speaker and his fellow human beings. It also suggests the finality of his decision.

POSSIBLE CONNECTIONS TO OTHER SELECTIONS

Andrew Hudgins, "Seventeen" (below)
Langston Hughes, "Dream Variations" (text p. 380)
Alden Nowlan, "The Bull Moose" (text p. 157)
John Updike, "Dog's Death" (text p. 11)

AUDIOVISUAL AND ONLINE RESOURCES (manual pp. 308, 352)

ANDREW HUDGINS, *Seventeen* (p. 156)

This brutal poem describes the experience of a teenaged speaker who watches a dog nearly die as it spills out of a pick-up truck ahead of him. After a brief confrontation with the truck driver, it is up to the speaker to put the dog out of its misery. He does so, methodically, and indicates that some time has passed between the event and the present, during which he has been able to contemplate the meaning of it.

Seventeen is not that long ago for many college students, and it may be productive to begin by asking them to describe any defining moments or events that they experienced at or around that age. The speaker cusses at an adult for the first time in his life and expects "a beating" (line 18) in return, which is the punishment a child would have received. What he undergoes is much more painful; you might want to ask students to describe the psychological or social differences between being beaten up and having to do away with a suffering animal.

The poem relies on verbs to communicate the scene; you might want to isolate some of these verbs and discuss why the speaker chose them to paint the picture. It is interesting to note how the speaker begins to rely on adjectives — consider "blue" (33), "loose" (35), and "orange and purple" (36) — in the final six lines of the poem. Does this event somehow change the way he thinks about the world? How does the preponderance of adjectives vs. verbs reflect the speaker's emotional or mental state? Why is it significant that he didn't know the words for "butterfly weed and vetch" at the time, but now, when he writes about the scene, he both uses these words and emphasizes that he didn't know the words before?

POSSIBLE CONNECTIONS TO OTHER SELECTIONS

Jane Kenyon, "The Blue Bowl" (text p. 106)
William Stafford, "Traveling through the Dark" (question #1, following)

CONNECTION QUESTION IN TEXT (p. 157) WITH ANSWER

1. Write an essay that compares the speakers and themes of "Seventeen" and "Traveling through the Dark."

   In both "Seventeen" and "Traveling through the Dark" the speakers come across animals in the road. Each speaker is presented with a moral dilemma: whether and how to kill the animal. Yet William Stafford's speaker seems more detached and ruminative — less emotional; and his moral dilemma is more complex. Hudgins's speaker, though it is clear that he must kill the dog, is also undergoing a certain rite of passage that we can assume has already happened to Stafford's. "Traveling through the Dark" is, perhaps, about complicated choices, "Seventeen" is about growing up.

ONLINE RESOURCES (manual p. 336)

ALDEN NOWLAN, *The Bull Moose* (p. 157)

This poem describes a conflict between man and nature, one in which man, through his actions, futilely attempts to make nature (that is, the moose) look ridiculous, but is rewarded only by appearing cowardly and cruel. The speaker, observing the interactions of a lost bull moose and the townspeople, succeeds in making the townspeople and not the moose look ridiculous. The people demonstrate a complete misunderstanding of the moose; they lack respect for creatures of the wild in general and this trapped moose in particular. They condescend to the moose, treating it like a sideshow freak by feeding it beer, opening its mouth, planting "a little purple cap / of thistles on his head." Their affection for the animal is utterly skewed; they don't realize the moral problems inherent in so amiably agreeing that "it was a shame / to shoot anything so shaggy and cuddlesome." The moose's last act was one of power, strength, and dignity — it refused to die with bottles in its mouth or thistles on its head. As "the bull moose gathered his strength / like a scaffolded king, straightened and lifted its horns," it terrified the onlookers, even the wardens. But the final act of the young men, the honking of the car horns as the moose is executed, serves as both a way to mask their guilt by drowning out the sounds of the screaming moose, and as a sort of victory cry upon winning a cruel, unfair, and dishonorable battle.

POSSIBLE CONNECTION TO ANOTHER SELECTION

William Stafford, "Traveling through the Dark" (question #1, following)

CONNECTION QUESTION IN TEXT (p. 158) WITH ANSWER

1. In an essay compare and contrast how the animals portrayed in "The Bull Moose" and in Stafford's "Traveling through the Dark" (p. 155) are used as symbols.

    In both poems there is a violent clash between humanity and the animal world. In Nowlan's poem, the bull moose symbolizes the reluctant power of nature, which man has abused but which continues to be fearsome. Stafford's speaker thinks deeply and quickly about his ability to influence nature, and though his action is painful, he is ultimately humane in letting the unborn fawn expire.

ONLINE RESOURCES (manual p. 345)

JULIO MARZÁN, *Ethnic Poetry* (p. 158)

The phrase "The ethnic poet said" begins each of the poem's five stanzas, followed by a quotation and the response of the ethnic audience. In each case, the poet speaks in language or imagery that isn't "conventional" — it seems to disrupt conventions of typical Western poetry or thought. In each case, the audience responds by eating ethnic food or playing on ethnic instruments. In the final stanza, though, the poet quotes from Robert Frost's "Mending Wall," and the audience's response is to "deeply [understand] humanity" (line 20).

The poem invites us to consider the "proper" response to poetry as it satirizes the notion that poetry is a philosophical venture, that it is supposed to evoke in its listeners a deep understanding of human nature. The irony (and subtle humor) is made thicker by the fact that Frost's poem is about divisions between neighbors and that this poem begins with the assumption that there are differences between ethnic and other poetry.

It might be interesting to apply the notion that poetry is meant to evoke a deep understanding about human nature to the poems excerpted within each stanza of "Ethnic Poetry." Is it possible to do so? Why does the "ethnic audience" choose to respond differently? What assumptions are made about the ethnicity of the poet and the audience in each stanza?

This poem may tend to touch off discussions of the "proper" response to poetry and the proper way to construct a poem. Langston Hughes's poem "Formula" (text p. 382) can deepen this discussion since it suggests that poetry is frequently elitist. Is it implicitly so? Has our perception of poetry made it an elitist form as much as the poet's conception that, as Hughes says, it "should treat / Of lofty things"? This is a good opportunity to get students to consider the nature of the barriers between "high" and "low" culture: where do they experience poetry in their lives besides in college courses? And what is their response to it? Do they ever *read* poetry "for fun," or do they know anyone who does? Have they ever been to a poetry reading? Is the emphasis in contemporary music on lyrics or on melody, instrumentation, etc.? Would their response to the lyrics of their favorite band be altered if those lyrics were presented in a classroom? (The general question: does our understanding of poetry depend more on the context in which we read it or on the nature of the poetry itself?)

POSSIBLE CONNECTIONS TO OTHER SELECTIONS

Robert Frost, "Mending Wall" (text p. 342)

Langston Hughes, "Formula" (question #1, following)

CONNECTION QUESTION IN TEXT (p. 159) WITH ANSWER

1. Write an essay that discusses the speaker's ideas about what poetry should be in "Ethnic Poetry" and in Langston Hughes's "Formula" (p. 382).

    Both poems ironically consider the notion that poetry "should treat / Of lofty things." In Hughes's poem, lofty poetry is not separated from poetry about everyday occurrences specifically by ethnicity; his concern is that poetry overlooks the pain of human existence. Marzán's concern is that listeners might tend to privilege poetry that seems deeply philosophical rather than culturally resonant.

JAMES MERRILL, *Casual Wear* (p. 159)

Merrill has been called a conversational poet. His familiarity with the lives of American aristocrats may result from his wealthy background, which especially influenced his earlier poetry.

Jeans, of course, are "casual wear," and by implication, this act of random terrorism appears to be a casual flourish of some unseen hand. That relation in sum seems to be the import of this poem. Because of the enjambment of lines between stanzas, students may not at first observe that the stanzas rhyme with an *abba* pattern — except the middle two lines of the first stanza. But then, what would rhyme with "Ferdi Plinthbower"? Rhyme, however, along with odd lengthy names, precise statistics, and descriptions of human beings as proper demographic models, detracts from our ability to feel the weight of this crime against humankind and our intuitive understanding of the moral workings of the universe. The inverse parallels between "tourist" and "terrorist" seem just too chillingly neat.

So what might Merrill actually be saying in this poem? Perhaps he is not so much speaking out against terrorist activity as talking about the media, with its formulaic scenarios, and the number-plotting social scientists, who surround such an event with their own dehumanizing mist of facts and figures. In the final irony of the poem, we know the name of the clothing designer but not that of the terrorist's victim.

Comments on Merrill's poetry include *James Merrill: Essays in Criticism,* edited by David Lehman and Charles Berger (Ithaca: Cornell UP, 1983) and Judith Moffet's *James Merrill: An Introduction to the Poetry* (New York: Columbia UP, 1984).

POSSIBLE CONNECTIONS TO OTHER SELECTIONS

W. H. Auden, "The Unknown Citizen" (text p. 591)
Peter Meinke, "The ABC of Aerobics" (question #1, following)

CONNECTION QUESTION IN TEXT (p. 160) WITH ANSWER

1. Compare the satire in this poem with that in Peter Meinke's "The ABC of Aerobics" (p. 270). What is satirized in each poem? Which satire is more pointed from your perspective?

   Meinke's satire directs itself at the frantic health-conscious exercising that has become a part of our culture. Merrill's addresses a different aspect of the same culture, the materialism and media hype that eradicate the individual, leaving us with facts, figures, and wardrobe reports. Merrill's poem has a sobering life-and-death message, whereas Meinke's seems to have more hope for immediate change. Merrill's speaker is bitter; Meinke's satire is comical.

AUDIOVISUAL AND ONLINE RESOURCES (manual pp. 303, 342)

HENRY REED, *Naming of Parts* (p. 160)

The irony of this poem is situational. The instructor (no doubt an army sergeant addressing a group of raw recruits) is filled with self-importance as he drones on about naming the rifle parts, wholly oblivious to the silent beauty of the spring day. The season, though, arouses in the young recruit's thoughts reminders of a world far more vibrant than that of weaponry. Students should be able to distinguish between sergeant and recruit in the exchange of voices. The recruit's musings begin in the second half of the fourth line of each stanza, and the final line works to deflect the authoritative tone of the earlier part of the stanza. Discussion of rifle parts summons up with ironic aptness physical allusions, which the young recruit inevitably thinks of as he looks at the beautiful gardens in spring, assaulted by the vigorous bees.

POSSIBLE CONNECTIONS TO OTHER SELECTIONS

E. E. Cummings, "she being Brand" (text p. 57)
Linda Pastan, "Marks" (text p. 132)

JOHN CIARDI, *Suburban* (p. 161)

In "Suburban," Ciardi satirizes the artificial behavior of those who live in the suburbs. Note that Mrs. Friar seems unable to look at or refer to by name the object that incites her to phone the poet — the word *turd* does not occur until the final stanza, when the poet is returning to his own property. Ask students to compare Ciardi's perception of the turd — "organic gold" (line 11) — to Mrs. Friar's — "a large repulsive object" (5). What does the difference indicate about their contrasting worldviews?

How do the poet's tone and behavior alter when he crosses the property line? His attitude when Mrs. Friar first asks him to come over and remove the offending object — a humorous observation that his dog is in another state — is contrasted with his behavior in Mrs. Friar's yard, as he scoops and bows (16). How would Mrs. Friar have responded if Ciardi had shared his vision of what his dog, his son, and his son's girl-friend were doing in Vermont? How would she have responded if he had refused to come over? If Ciardi lacks any respect for the pseudodelicate sensibilities of his sub-urban neighbors, why does he humor them and conform to their accepted behavior in this instance?

Suburban neighborhoods are noted for being well-organized and highly developed; like them, the first four stanzas of the poem conform to a single pattern (note the per-fect, standard indentation of the second and fourth lines in each). Yet the final line of the poem stands alone, beyond the conformity of the preceding stanzas. As Ciardi seems to be alone in his ability to accept the "turd" as an aspect of "real life," so this final line presents a different aspect of the suburbs. Ask students to assess the tonal shift and meaning of this final, isolated line, which provides a key to much of the pre-ceding material.

POSSIBLE CONNECTIONS TO OTHER SELECTIONS

Louis Simpson, "In the Suburbs" (text p. 84)
John Updike, "Dog's Death" (question #1, following)

CONNECTION QUESTION IN TEXT (p. 162) WITH ANSWER

1. Compare the speakers' voices in "Suburban" and in Updike's "Dog's Death" (p. 11).

   The speaker of Ciardi's poem is much more satirical than Updike's speaker, which is consistent with the subject matter of each. There is something raw and honest about the way Updike's speaker approaches his topic, but Ciardi's speaker has his tongue in his cheek throughout the poem, emphasizing the "I said" and "she said" of his story to comic effect. The settings of the poems are similar, but the comic presence of Mrs. Friar in this poem and the tragic death of the dog in Updike's poem alter the tones of each considerably.

AUDIOVISUAL RESOURCES (manual p. 295)

CHITRA BANERJEE DIVAKARUNI, *Indian Movie, New Jersey* (p. 162)

The speaker in "Indian Movie, New Jersey" contrasts the safety and hope of the world inside the movie theater with the threats and disappointments of the world out-side. The irony of the poem is that the movie theater itself underscores the thwarted pos-sibilities and expectations that America represents — "the America that was supposed to be" (line 51).

You might begin a discussion of this poem by asking students to identify and describe a "world" they participate in, such as a university or college, that is different from the "real world" they know. One way to further the discussion is to focus on the idea of the "American Dream." Ask students to read Louis Simpson's "In the Suburbs" (text p. 84). After they read the poem, begin a discussion as to why these poets seem dis-illusioned by this concept. (Or do they?)

POSSIBLE CONNECTIONS TO OTHER SELECTIONS

Langston Hughes, "Theme for English B" (text p. 442)
Tato Laviera, "AmeRícan" (text p. 269)

ONLINE RESOURCES (manual p. 329)

PAUL MULDOON, *Symposium* (p. 163)

This poem takes pleasure in the connections between aphorisms and clichés in English, establishing fresh meanings by splicing traditional sayings together. Students may want to spend some time plucking out the original clichés from the new creations in this poem. On a first reading the meaning of the poem may be smothered by the mind's efforts to establish order, to fill out the whole cliché in each partial one; subsequent readings, especially after the actual aphorisms and their meanings have been established, are likely to give more pleasure and meaning. *Symposium* has its roots in the Greek term for drinking party, a meeting for drinking and intellectual entertainment. A more contemporary meaning of *symposium* leaves out the drinking, but the author playfully uses this root to give intention to the mix-ups in the slurred speech of the speaker.

POSSIBLE CONNECTIONS TO OTHER SELECTIONS

E. E. Cummings, "next to of course god america i" (question #1, following)
Kathy Mangan, "An Arithmetic" (text p. 149)

CONNECTION QUESTION IN TEXT (p. 164) WITH ANSWER

1. Discuss the use of irony in this poem and in E. E. Cumming's "next to of course god america i" (p. 146).

   Both poems distort familiar phrases to establish a larger meaning, while conveying humor and providing a pleasurable game for the reader. While Muldoon's poem employs aphorisms and clichés and creates new meaning by twisting their structure, Cummings exposes the emptiness of nationalistic rhetoric.

ROBERT BROWNING, *My Last Duchess* (p. 164)

Robert Browning lived with his parents in a London suburb until he married Elizabeth Barrett at age thirty four; he had previously left home only to attend boarding school and for short trips abroad. He and his wife lived in Italy for fifteen years, a period in which he produced some of his first memorable poems. *Men and Women,* published in 1855, gained Browning the initial intimations of his later fame. The poet returned to England after his wife died in 1861. His work continued to elicit increasing public (if not always critical) acclaim.

Ironically, the speaker is talking about the portrait of his last duchess (how many went before?) to the marriage broker, who is handling the current arrangement between the duke and the broker's "master," father of the bride-to-be.

The last wife's principal fault was that she was too democratic in her smiles; she did not reserve them for the duke alone. The duke holds no regard for kindness and thoughtfulness; he thinks only of money, rank, and name. He treats women as objects and possessions.

The visitor seems to want to leave early, perhaps to warn his master of the unfeeling tyrant who would marry the master's daughter at a cut rate (cf. lines 47–54).

Students may have already read this dramatic monologue in high school. The second time around they should appreciate the irony even more as the duke reveals so much of his own character while ostensibly controlling the situation.

POSSIBLE CONNECTIONS TO OTHER SELECTIONS

Mark Halliday, "Graded Paper" (text p. 445)
Katharyn Howd Machan, "Hazel Tells LaVerne" (question #1, following)

CONNECTION QUESTION IN TEXT (p. 165) WITH ANSWER

1. Write an essay describing the ways in which the speakers of "My Last Duchess" and "Hazel Tells LaVerne" (p. 61) by Katharyn Howd Machan inadvertently reveal themselves.

In both cases, the speaker has a story to tell, and both speakers are trying to paint a favorable picture of themselves as they do so. The speaker of Browning's poem gets himself in trouble as he continues to talk, indicating the fate of his last duchess through unsuppressed expressions of his own unfulfilled desire. As he describes the portrait, he eventually gets away from art and into the character of the duchess, wondering all the while how he should express himself. The speaker of "Hazel Tells LaVerne" reveals her unconscious desire to be taken away from her situation as she repeats the line "me a princess," focusing (without meaning to do so) on herself rather than on the frog whose story she is narrating. Students with a background in psychology might be able to flesh out the motivations behind these speakers' tales even more.

AUDIOVISUAL AND ONLINE RESOURCES (manual pp. 294, 326)

WILLIAM BLAKE, *The Chimney Sweeper* (p. 166)

There is an ironic distance in this poem between the speaker, who seems to be too young to make judgments, and Blake, who through his ironic perspective underscores the harm that comes from too meekly doing one's duty, not to mention the evil of a society indifferent to the plight of "thousands of sweepers" whose only pleasure is in dreams. Needless to say, sacrificing one's hair for the sake of on-the-job cleanliness is not a principle Blake would endorse.

On the surface the poem could be interpreted as a dream of desire for some beneficent angel to release the boys from their "coffins of black" (the chimneys). More likely, the dream expresses a desire for release through death from the tortuous and life-threatening trials of sweeping soot from chimneys. Here again, irony operates, in that a dream of death makes it easier for the boy to face his life the next morning.

POSSIBLE CONNECTION TO ANOTHER SELECTION

Langston Hughes, "Negro" (text p. 377)

DIANE THIEL, *The Minefield* (p. 166)

The brief and blunt sentences of this poem focus attention on the horror of the speaker's father's experience. This attention is framed by the stanza breaks, which pause to provide chilling context after the initial stanza. The couplet that follows indicates that the father told this horror story at dinner and then "continued eating" (line 11). The absence of grief expressed over this incident is present in the minefield of anger the father's life represents, in his sudden outbursts of violence, and in the way he taught his children how "anything might explode at any time" (21). The minefield of the title can be read symbolically as the vision of life this father conveys to his children and as a vivid parallel to the experience of living with the father's explosive anger. The horrible death of his friend in the minefield is presented as a cause of the father's violence and, in turn, is the source of the expectant dread the children experience even as adults.

It might be effective to establish room for discussion in class about what is forgivable in this poem, and under what circumstances allowances can be made. The speaker forgives the father his violent outbreaks; do your students forgive him, as well? How much violence is permissible, given an experience like the father's? A few minutes of freewriting at the beginning of class could help focus discussion.

POSSIBLE CONNECTIONS TO OTHER SELECTIONS

Regina Barreca, "Nighttime Fires" (question #1, following)

Philip Larkin, "This Be the Verse" (text p. 621)

CONNECTION QUESTION IN TEXT (p. 167) **WITH ANSWER**

1. Discuss the treatment of fathers in "The Minefield" and in Regina Barreca's "Nighttime Fires" (p. 26). Compare how the memory of the father affects the speaker in each poem.

    The father in "The Minefield" is viewed with eyes open to both his shortcomings as a parent and the horrors that induced these flaws. The "secret, brittle heart" (line 18) of the father in Barreca's poem is not as justified, although the speaker does imagine what it was like for the father after he "lost his job" (5). This father, "who never held us" (22), does not beat his children, but the aggravating circumstances do not appear to be sufficient, to the speaker, to explain the decay of his spirit.

GARY SOTO, *Behind Grandma's House* (p. 167)

In this poem, Soto captures a moment that almost every individual experiences in growing up — the trying on of different identities to discover one that "fits." Ultimately, the grandma in the poem helps the speaker along in the process by showing him how the identity he is trying cannot work. Students may connect the episode described in this poem to times in their own lives when they've searched for an identity or tried too hard to prove something to themselves or others.

You might begin the class discussion by suggesting that the real "happening" of the poem is the arrival of the grandma, who, with total nonchalance, sets the speaker straight on what it means to be tough. Ask students why Soto limited his description of the grandma to simply "her apron flapping in a breeze, / her hair mussed" (lines 19–20). She seems a fairly "typical" grandma in appearance — clearly she's not looking for a fight — yet her simple "Let me help you" followed by a well-aimed punch teaches the speaker more about toughness than he learned through an entire alley's worth of vandalism.

POSSIBLE CONNECTION TO ANOTHER SELECTION

Sharon Olds, "Rite of Passage" (question #1, following)

CONNECTION QUESTION IN TEXT (p. 168) **WITH ANSWER**

1. Write an essay comparing the themes of "Behind Grandma's House" and Sharon Olds's "Rite of Passage" (p. 265).

    Both poems suggest that boys will be boys; in this poem we get the sense that some boys, like this speaker who "wanted fame" (line 1), will cross the boundaries of acceptable behavior to be accepted. In Olds's poem, it seems that all boys are capable of doing so, but for them the notion of acceptable behavior changes with context. The boy in Soto's poem is not going to achieve fame by behaving this way in front of his grandmother, or even behind her house. The boys at the birthday party in Olds's poem will only achieve fame if they conform because they are at a party. The speaker in Olds's poem is unlike the grandmother in Soto's poem because she is outnumbered; her son is bound to go through his rite of passage with his peers. Soto's speaker also grows and learns something, but it is through the discipline of an elder rather than through the coaxing of friends.

AUDIOVISUAL AND ONLINE RESOURCES (manual pp. 307–308, 351)

ROBERT BLY, *The Man Who Didn't Know What Was His* (p. 168)

This poem considers the personality of a man who, as a child, was given mixed signals as to what was truly his. The gist of the argument is that a child who is told to finish what is on *his* plate or to go to *his* room will begin to feel as though nothing is truly his. Since he has no freedom as a child, he has no imagination as an adult, and as a result, becomes "helpful and hostile at the same time" (line 11). This person both "leans toward you and leans away"; the speaker concludes by asking the reader, "Do you feel me leaning?"

Some students may relish the opportunity to complain about how they were brought up. Bly describes too much control as a "demon" in line 2; could too much freedom also be considered a "demon"? Which is worse? Ask students to consider the symbolism of dinner, the assumption that a child's parents are commanding him to finish what's on his plate or sit on his chair. This rhetoric is no doubt familiar to students, and they might offer other examples of it from their own childhood. Be prepared, if you go this route, to monitor a debate about the proper means of child rearing: how much freedom can children handle? Where is the line between parental guidance and excessive control? Or, in connection with Heitzman's poem (see "Possible Connections," below), when does an adult's need for order interfere with or damage a child's sense of self?

A more difficult concept is the idea behind line 1: "There was a man who didn't know what was his." How do students interpret that line? What, as an adult, belongs to you? Students are likely to recognize that Bly is speaking in terms beyond material possession, but they might find it difficult to articulate exactly what he means. It might help to have them write about what they think is theirs, excluding material possessions, before discussing the poem, and to extrapolate by asking them how they think such things could be lost.

Possible Connections to Other Selections

Robert Frost, "Birches" (text p. 347)

Judy Page Heitzman, "The Schoolroom on the Second Floor of the Knitting Mill" (question #1, following)

Connection Question in Text (p. 169) with Answer

1. In an essay consider how early childhood experiences affect adult identities in "The Man Who Didn't Know What Was His" and in Judy Page Heitzman's "The Schoolroom on the Second Floor of the Knitting Mill" (p. 446).

   In Bly's poem, children are not allowed any volition or sense of possession; a child is told to finish "his" plate or go to "his" room even though neither one is truly his. The effect of such an upbringing is to raise an adult who has no "foundation" (line 10) and who must consequently rely on others. The situation is slightly different in Heitzman's poem, in which an adult teacher blames a child for failing to control other children. By being told that she is not a good leader, the young girl is set up for a pattern of self-blame for failure that lasts for the rest of her life. Her shame comes from the fact that her peers hear the teacher's scorn. It is not as though she is dispossessed, as is the case in Bly's poem, but rather that she is singled out and ridiculed.

PERSPECTIVE

EZRA POUND, *On Symbols* (p. 169)

Consider Pound's use of the word *natural* in the first line of the passage. Does he mean that a symbol should be drawn from an object in nature or that a symbol should have a natural, easy relationship to the idea it is meant to symbolize? Students might suggest other interpretations. Does Pound's example of the hawk at the end of the passage help to clarify his meaning? Ask students what a hawk might symbolize. Using other Pound poems in this anthology, identify the symbols the poet employs and discuss whether they are "natural" in either sense of the word. Look at Poe's "The Haunted Palace" (text p. 141), wherein the human mind and head are compared to a house, or Millay's "I will put Chaos into fourteen lines" (text p. 229), in which writing poetry is compared to rape, as examples to discuss which method of using symbols they think conveys meaning most effectively.

7

Sounds

In this chapter, encouraging students to read aloud is vital. You may find that you have to lead by example, initially. However, you will probably want to shift the focus onto student readers at some point. In some cases, you may find yourself confronting a considerable degree of resistance, particularly if there has not been much reading aloud previously. Much of this resistance stems from fear of embarrassment, and dealing with it requires either the creation of a "safe space" in which students can read without fear of others snickering, or a slightly raucous classroom environment in which students don't feel as much pressure to be "cool."

If you have a group of particularly shy students, you might find it helpful to assign students poems in advance, so that they have a chance to read the poem through a couple of times before being called on to speak out before the class. If you have a mix of extraverts and introverts, you might schedule the class so that the extraverts read "cold," and announce at the end of class the poems the introverts will read in the next session, to give them fair warning.

In most cases, the addition of student voices to the classroom will help increase involvement and raise the energy level. If the class has not featured student reading much so far, this chapter would be an appropriate time to introduce this feature of the class.

In addition to including student voices in the classroom, this chapter affords an opportunity to include the voices of the poets as well: Kinnell, Hopkins, Carroll, Pope, and Kingston each have recordings available that will allow students to hear either the voice of the poet or a skilled reader reciting the poems. It is perhaps a judgment call as to whether you should introduce these readings before students have done much reading on their own, in order to provide models of reading for them, or to wait until after students have some experience, to keep from intimidating them into silence. If you have included recordings in previous chapters, this may not be an issue here. In any event, recordings can be very useful in giving students a sense of the reality of the people "behind the page," as it were. You may find it appropriate to do readings or bring in recordings of poems that have been popular with students earlier in the class, and evaluate the poets' use of sound in relation to the students' own preference of these poems.

Thematically, there are some interesting poems in this chapter. If you do not want the focus on reading to overwhelm a discussion of these poems, you could use the reading as a springboard to raise the class's interest and energy, and to give them specific features to discuss when they make connections between the sound of a poem and its "message."

ANONYMOUS, *Scarborough Fair* (p. 171)

Your students may or may not be acquainted with the Simon and Garfunkel version of this ballad that was used in the 1960s as an antiwar song, and the use of this traditional ballad in that context may lead to some interesting discussion about the difference between the oral and written tradition.

As a ballad, "Scarborough Fair" follows a clear pattern: four feet to a line with an *abab* rhyme scheme and repeated second and fourth lines. In addition, in all but the first stanza, the first words of the stanza are "Tell her to" followed by the introduction of an impossible task that, if performed, will reconcile the speaker of the poem to the "bonny lass" who was once his true lover. The impossible nature of these tasks is perhaps a clue as to how much hope the speaker in the poem has of reconciliation.

The effect of the refrain is soothing — readers and listeners come to expect the repeated lines, and the rhythm of these lines is peaceful. The herbs that are mentioned in the refrain are associated with female power (parsley was used to decorate tombs, sage represents wisdom, rosemary is for memory, and thyme is thought to enhance courage). In addition, both sage and rosemary had the connotation of growing in gardens where women ruled the households. Why might the poet have chosen these herbs as repeated symbols in this ballad? What message might the poet have been trying to convey?

POSSIBLE CONNECTIONS TO OTHER SELECTIONS

Anonymous, "Bonny Barbara Allan" (text p. 589)

John Donne, "A Valediction: Forbidding Mourning" (text p. 130)

JOHN UPDIKE, *Player Piano* (p. 172)

This poem is a listening exercise in how to translate the sounds poetry can produce to musical analogues we have already heard. From light ditties through more somber 1920s chase-scene music, perhaps, to a medley of chords and light cadences, this poem explores a player piano's repertoire. In doing so, does the poem do anything *besides* impress us with its sounds? Does reading the poem allow us anything beyond the sheer joy of the sounds of words and the way they can be manipulated?

MAY SWENSON, *A Nosty Fright* (p. 172)

Since "A Nosty Fright" is much more about sound than sense, be sure to read it, or have students read it, aloud (this may be more difficult than one might anticipate, for the transposed consonants often have the effect of creating tongue-twisters). Does the fractured diction have any purpose other than humor? Remind students that people who are upset or frightened often find it difficult to speak clearly.

Notice that sometimes the poetic technique used here results in transpositions that are actual words. Do any of these seem appropriate in this poem, for instance, "Bat" in line 24, or "fright" in line 25? Do any of them seem out of place, like "mitten" (20)? Have students suggest definitions for some of the nonsense words and phrases, based on their sounds. Compare the poem to Lewis Carroll's "Jabberwocky" (text p. 186). Are the techniques for creating new words the same in both poems?

POSSIBLE CONNECTION TO ANOTHER SELECTION

Lewis Carroll [Charles Lutwidge Dodgson], "Jabberwocky" (text p. 186)

AUDIOVISUAL AND ONLINE RESOURCES (manual pp. 308, 352)

EMILY DICKINSON, *A Bird came down the Walk* — (p. 173)

Silent reading of this poem, followed by reading it aloud, will reinforce the connection between sound and sense. In particular, students should hear the difference between the irregular movement of the first three stanzas and the smoothness of the last six lines, a difference created visually by punctuation but even more obvious when the poem is heard.

One of the poetic techniques that characterizes Emily Dickinson's poetry is her use of unexpected words and images. Consider her depiction of the bird's eyes and of his flight. How can eyes be "rapid" (line 9)? How can they hurry (10)? How can feathers "unroll" (15)? How is flight like rowing (16)? What is the effect created by the use of unusual language to describe an ordinary creature?

Compare the way the sounds of poetry are used to create a sense of an animal's movement in this poem and in Rilke's "The Panther" (text p. 105). Are the panther's movements in any way like the bird's?

POSSIBLE CONNECTION TO ANOTHER SELECTION

Rainer Maria Rilke, "The Panther" (text p. 105)

GALWAY KINNELL, *Blackberry Eating* (p. 176)

Some poems are memorable for their themes, while others are enjoyed not for what they say but for how they say it. This poem seems to fall into this second category, as Kinnell tries in lieu of the blackberries themselves to offer us a blackberry language. It would probably be a good idea to read this poem aloud in class. Kinnell plays with the kinesthesia of the sound in words such as *strengths* or *squinched,* which by their compacted consonance physically suggest to him the pressure of the tongue bursting open the berry's mysterious ("black art") icy sweetness. What other words are there (you might ask) that seem to touch the inside of the body before they are spoken? Look at some of the heavily consonantal words in lines 12 and 13, marking especially words like *splurge* and *language.* Lines 4–6, besides containing good examples of consonance patterns, also express a pathetic fallacy, with Kinnell's imaginative supposition that blackberry bushes are punished with nettles for knowing the art of blackberry making. You might ask what, if anything, this image adds to the poem. Probably it underscores Kinnell's whimsical sense of the black artistry of blackberry making.

The sound then moves from the hard *b* of *blackberry* to the softer *ss* of the final lines. Many assonant *o*s occur in the first lines, *e*s and *a*s in the middle of the poem. The sounds attempt to capture the delectable berries, making the experience of reading the poem as sensuous as eating a berry.

More than providing a message of "truth" for its reader, this poem invites us into an experience of sound and image. The poem is about language in that it considers the difficulty of capturing an idea in words and communicating it effectively. Attempting to write a poem can be as much a learning experience about poetry as attempting to write about a poem. Perhaps some members of the class would like to try writing their own lyric beginning with the words *I love to.*

POSSIBLE CONNECTIONS TO OTHER SELECTIONS

Helen Chasin, "The Word *Plum*" (text p. 195)
Pablo Neruda, "Sweetness, Always" (text p. 660)

AUDIOVISUAL AND ONLINE RESOURCES (manual pp. 302, 338)

RICHARD ARMOUR, *Going to Extremes* (p. 177)

What are the "extremes" to which this poem goes? How does the poet connect the two words that describe the extremes?

Even if students are unfamiliar with scansion, they should be able to detect a difference in the way words are emphasized in lines 1 and 3 as opposed to lines 2 and 4. Ask them to describe how the sound shifts coincide with the action of the poem. In speaking lines 1 and 3 aloud, one can almost feel the sharp movements of the bottle. In lines 2 and 4, it is as though the bottle is at rest, with the person who has been shaking it now waiting to see whether or not the catsup will come. Having students actually "shake" an imaginary catsup bottle as they recite the poem might be an effective way to connect sound to sense.

POSSIBLE CONNECTION TO ANOTHER SELECTION

Margaret Atwood, "you fit into me" (text p. 116)

ROBERT SOUTHEY, From *The Cataract of Lodore* (p. 177)

Although Robert Southey is now known chiefly for his association with some of the great poets of the Romantic period, such as Wordsworth and Coleridge, he was very popular in his own time and became the poet laureate of England in 1813. He is also credited with the first published version of the children's story *The Three Bears.*

In a twenty-three-line introductory stanza that is not excerpted here, the poet reveals that his son and daughter had requested him to tell them — in verse — about the water at Lodore. He also introduces himself as the poet laureate. Does having this information in any way change your students' response to the poem that follows?

Are any lines in the poem especially memorable? Why is it appropriate that line 69, with its thirteen syllables, is metrically the longest line of the poem?

TIP FROM THE FIELD

One tip I've found helpful in teaching sound in poetry, is to have students stand in a tight circle and recite the excerpt from "The Cataract of Lodore" in round-robin fashion, one after another. Each student reads a line in the order of the poem, repeating the poem several times, faster each time. The results, in terms of student response, are remarkable.

— NANCY VEIGA, *Modesto Junior College*

POSSIBLE CONNECTION TO ANOTHER SELECTION

A. E. Housman, "Loveliest of trees, the cherry now" (text p. 224)

ONLINE RESOURCES (manual p. 351)

PERSPECTIVE

DAVID LENSON, *On the Contemporary Use of Rhyme* (p. 180)

You might ask students to find contemporary poems that make subtle use of rhyme. Philip Larkin's poems are good examples of the effective use of slant rhyme and enjambment to camouflage the rhymes in a poem. Conversely, you might ask students to look for songs that don't use rhyme. Bruce Springsteen's "Streets of Philadelphia" (text p. 32) uses some rhyme, but not in every line. What is the effect of the sporadic rhyme in his song?

Students might be interested in speculating on why writers are returning to rhyme. Is more formal poetry appropriate for our time and culture? Or is it simply a question of rebelling against the norm (in our time, unrhymed poetry)?

GERARD MANLEY HOPKINS, *God's Grandeur* (p. 181)

Gerard Manley Hopkins was a deeply religious man, a Jesuit ordained in 1877. He had previously graduated from Oxford University and joined the Roman Catholic

Church in 1866. He served a number of parishes before being appointed a professor of classics at University College, Dublin. Although he tried to keep his poetic vocation from interfering with his spiritual one, he wasn't successful, and he suffered greatly because of this conflict, once burning all his finished work and another time forsaking poetry for seven years.

Although this poem follows sonnet form and an exact rhyme scheme, the first eight lines still read very roughly. How does the poet achieve this effect? Note the disruptions in rhythm as well as the use of cacophonic sounds. Have students try reading line 4 aloud to better appreciate its difficulty. Is there any change in the level of disruption or the level of cacophony in the last six lines? What is the effect of the inserted "ah!" in the last line?

Compare the halting beginning and smooth ending of this poem to the similar transition that occurs in Emily Dickinson's "A Bird came down the Walk — " (text p. 173). How does Dickinson's bird compare to the bird image Hopkins evokes in the last two lines?

POSSIBLE CONNECTION TO ANOTHER SELECTION

William Wordsworth, "The World Is Too Much with Us" (text p. 227)

AUDIOVISUAL AND ONLINE RESOURCES (manual pp. 300, 336)

EDGAR ALLAN POE, *The Bells* (p. 182)

Divided into four sections, each corresponding to a type of bell (sleigh bells, wedding bells, alarm bells, and death-knells), this poem relies heavily on onomatopoeia. As the poem's stanzas grow increasingly longer and the subject becomes increasingly heavier, the reader moves through a series of psychological adjustments, exploited by the sonorous qualities of language.

The sound of the bells also becomes increasingly heavy as the poem progresses, from tinkling to tolling. Any discussion of this poem will depend largely on the way it is read aloud in class. You might have to coax students to read the poem as it calls to be read. Take, for example, the repetition of the word *bells* at the end of each stanza. How do we know how long to pause between each utterance of this word based on the rest of the words in that stanza? You may want to ask your students to try to quantify the pauses in the poem. Is it productive to treat each pause the same in a reading? Poe's poem can be thought of as an argument for why poetry should always be read aloud; much of its effect comes from the ways its sounds fall upon the ear.

In addition to the effect of repetition and onomatopoeia, "The Bells" also serves as a model for other poetic conventions, notably alliteration and assonance, and end-stopped rhyme. Students may become so caught up in Poe's sound-play that they overlook the meaning of the words or the effect of the poem's structure. You can prompt them to elucidate the theme by having them compare parts of speech in each of the four stanzas; what does the progression of the adjectives in the four stanzas tell us (from crystalline to liquid to mad to melancholy)? The same effect can be achieved with nouns, verbs, or adverbs. Would the poem's theme change if the order of the stanzas were mixed up? Have them compare the phrases "keeping time, time, time" and "Runic rhyme" in the first and last stanzas; has the rest of the poem changed the import of these phrases? Is it ironic that the "Runic rhyme" as described in the final stanza is "happy" when the mood seems to have changed from happy to melancholy? The poem's trajectory seems to be important to its theme. A comparison to Southey's "The Cataract of Lodore" (p. 177) might highlight this difference since Southey's poem seems more driven by momentum than by a thematic focal point.

POSSIBLE CONNECTIONS TO OTHER SELECTIONS

Anonymous, "Bonny Barbara Allan" (text p. 589)

Robert Southey, "The Cataract of Lodore" (question #1, following)

CONNECTION QUESTION IN TEXT (p. 185) WITH ANSWER

1. Compare Poe's sound effects with Robert Southey's in "The Cataract of Lodore" (p. 177). Which poem do you find more effective in its use of sound? Explain why.

    The poets use different methods to create their sound effects. Poe relies more on repetition than Southey does. "The Cataract of Lodore" strings together words that rhyme — "And rushing and flushing and brushing and gushing" (line 63) — rarely returning to a word that has already been used. Poe also combines rhyming words in quick succession — "By the twanging / And the clanging" (58–59), but the refrain always returns to bells. Southey's poem thus conveys the sense of something rushing endlessly onward, whereas Poe's poem conveys the sense of something that resounds. Each is appropriate to its subject.

PAULA GUNN ALLEN, *Hoop Dancer* (p. 185)

The sound of this single sentence mirrors the hoop of its title and the movements of a dancer. Its syntax, the blurred boundaries of its grammar, and its absent punctuation mimic the fluid grace of a dancer in a circle. The completion of a line like "together Sky and Water one dancing one" (line 11) demonstrates the marriage of form and content. The repetition at the conclusion, "out of time, out of / time, out / of time" (13–15) is rendered more complex by the line breaks. The repetition also provides for a slowing down, a completion in sound and sense, as the poem ends.

The circular sound of this run-on sentence and its repetitions begins with "It's hard to enter" (1) and ends with "out / of time" (14–15), creating a narrative of the dance it describes. Images of circling include the references to clocks and to turning clockwise and counterclockwise, mirroring the hoop of the title.

POSSIBLE CONNECTIONS TO OTHER SELECTIONS

Maxine Hong Kingston, "Restaurant" (text p. 193)

Anna Laetitia Barbauld, "On a Lady's Writing" (text p. 215)

ONLINE RESOURCES (manual p. 322)

LEWIS CARROLL [CHARLES LUTWIDGE DODGSON], *Jabberwocky* (p. 186)

" 'Jabberwocky' is no mere piece of sound experimentation but a serious short narrative poem describing a young man's coming of age as he seeks out and kills the tribal terror." Test that description on your students, and they will, one hopes, turn around and tell you that the fun of this poem and the justification for its being reside in its sound and word creations.

Carroll kept his own glossary for some of the words in this poem, which Alice read through her looking glass. The glossary entries and copious notes about the poem are provided by Martin Gardner in *The Annotated Alice* (New York: Bramhall House, 1960), pp. 191–197. The notes are too extensive to include here — but as a sampling, here is the first stanza "translated":

'Twas time for making dinner (bryllyg — to broil),
        and the "smooth and active" (slimy + lithe) badgers

Did scratch like a dog (gyre — giaour)
>   and drill holes (gimble) in the side of the hill:

All unhappy were the Parrots (now extinct; they lived on veal and
>   under sundials),

And the grave turtles (who lived on swallows and oysters) squeaked.

Reality bores its head through the hills and holes of "Jabberwocky," and certain words in the poem have their place in the *OED*. These include *rath*, an Irish word for a circular earthen wall; *Manx*, a Celtic name for the Isle of Man; *whiffling*, smoking, drinking, or blowing short puffs; *Caloo*, the sound and name of an arctic duck; *beamish*, old form of *beaming*; *chortled*, Carroll's own coinage, meaning "laughed"; and *gallumphing*, another of Carroll's creations, which according to him is a cross between *gallop* and *triumphant* and means "to march on exultantly with irregular bounding movements."

POSSIBLE CONNECTION TO ANOTHER SELECTION

May Swenson, "A Nosty Fright" (question #1, following)

CONNECTION QUESTION IN TEXT (p. 187) WITH ANSWER

1. Compare Carroll's strategies for creating sound and meaning with those used by Swenson in "A Nosty Fright" (p. 172).

   Whereas Swenson transposes letters to create amusing sound patterns and effects, Carroll combines and alters words to invent a new language for his speaker. Carroll's technique is harder to translate word for word; it requires more of his audience's imaginative effort.

AUDIOVISUAL AND ONLINE RESOURCES (manual pp. 295, 327)

SYLVIA PLATH, *Mushrooms* (p. 187)

Ostensibly, the speaker of this poem is a mushroom speaking on behalf of other mushrooms pushing their way into the world and gaining strength through their ever-increasing number. Despite their unobtrusiveness and the fact that they are "meek" (line 26) and "bland-mannered" (21), the mushrooms claim that they "shall by morning / Inherit the earth" (31–32).

It may be a natural impulse to take "mushrooms" metaphorically; readers are more likely to squeeze out some truth about "human nature" than to accept the possibility that this poem might be simply an imaginative projection into the point of view of a fungus. These two readings are made possible through the noncommittal title: do students take "mushrooms" to be a metaphor for a certain type of people: "Our kind" (30)? How does the poem allow us to read mushrooms as such a metaphor? Does it essentially matter whether or not we take mushrooms literally or metaphorically? Isn't the poem more about the mushrooms (whatever we take them to be) in relationship to the rest of the earth that they threaten to "inherit" (32)?

The mushrooms are personified, but they are also specifically mushrooms, growing in "loam" (5) and so forth. Students must read the poem closely, highlighting what they feel to be its key poetic conventions, in order to support their interpretation of the poem's theme and tone. Are these mushrooms threatening or sinister in any way? Do we feel pity for them, do we respect them? Are we as readers meant to side with the mushrooms or with the rest of the world? You may want to consider Plath's pervasive use of assonance and alliteration. How do the sounds — "soft fists insist on" (10), for example

— contribute to our understanding of tone? How do they work with the content? Is this poem humorous?

WILLIAM HEYEN, *The Trains* (p. 188)

For students who don't know, explain that Treblinka is the name of a Nazi concentration camp located near Warsaw, Poland. To illustrate Heyen's use of sound, you may want to open discussion by reading the poem aloud to your class. By repeating the word *Treblinka*, and by relying on choppy words with sharp, hard consonant sounds, Heyen creates the sound and rhythm of the wheels of a train — a rhythm that is intensified with the repetition of *Treblinka* until it resonates within the reader. In this way the poet uses sound and rhythm to affect the reader. Ask students to provide specific examples from the poem of how sound is used to intensify the horror of Treblinka.

At first, Heyen tells the facts of the story — listing with detachment and distance the statistics of what was removed from Treblinka on freight trains. However, as the poem continues, the statistics gain strength and the reader's horror mounts with each new revelation: clothing became paper (line 7), watches were saved and kept (8), and women's hair was used for mattresses and dolls (9).

In the fourth stanza, Heyen implies that many people are indirectly linked to the atrocities of Treblinka through the legacy of the material goods culled from the Holocaust. He suggests that the words of his poem might "like to use some of that same paper" (10); "One of those watches may pulse in your own wrist" (11), much like the rhythm of breathing or a pulse; and that someone the reader *knows* may "collect dolls, or sleep on human hair" (12). Ask students to consider the effect of this stanza. Is the poet implying a collective guilt for the Holocaust? Or is he implying that the horror of Treblinka lives on through the material legacy of the dead? In the end, no one escapes Heyen's indictment, and although Commandant Stangl of Treblinka may be dead at last, his legacy lives on in word and sound within anyone who hears the story.

ONLINE RESOURCES (manual p. 335)

VIRGINIA HAMILTON ADAIR, *Dirty Old Man* (p. 189)

Using persistent rhyme to establish a humorous tone, this poem examines the gradual drunkenness of the old man of the title and the resulting request of Saint Ignatius. Patron of archers, athletes, and soldiers, Ignatius seems unlikely to respond to this prayer, but perhaps the agility of the rhyme scheme will help. The first seven lines end with an adjective that could be used to describe the old man himself; while this is only a caricature of a person, the details Adair uses are effective and playful. In order to fully appreciate the humor in the poem, it may be helpful to discuss the meanings of these adjectives with the class. Along with the bawdy tone, the poem's use of rhyme seems related to limericks in its sly development and resolution in the almost exact rhyme of the final line.

POSSIBLE CONNECTIONS TO OTHER SELECTIONS

Anonymous, "There was a young lady named Bright" (text p. 239)
David McCord, "Epitaph on a Waiter" (text p. 238)

ONLINE RESOURCES (manual p. 321)

JOHN DONNE, *Song* (p. 189)

This poem explores a number of supposed impossibilities, ending with "a woman true, and fair" (line 18). The poem is at once bawdy and cynical; women are promiscuous, but the speaker also feels that they cannot be otherwise. Once students have discerned the speaker's attitude and his tone, take some time to investigate the way the speaker builds his argument. What types of mysteries does he use for comparison in the first stanza?

Donne manages to mix cynicism and lightheartedness here as he verbally throws up his hands at the possibility of finding an honest mind or a woman who is both true and fair. You might spend some time in class discussion exploring how he holds at bay the darker tones of his cynicism. Can we identify with Donne's dilemma today, or have attitudes toward women changed too much? What does the humor in the poem tell us about his fundamental attitude toward women? Students will probably appreciate the hyperbole in the poem. It is as though Donne were saying, "You might as well get with child a mandrake root, as find an honest mind."

The last stanza is especially humorous. Donne claims he would not even go next door to see this reputedly loyal woman. Her reputation for loyalty might hold long enough for his friend to write a letter describing her, but by the time the speaker arrived, she would have been false to two or three other lovers.

As a writing assignment, you might ask the students to discuss the humor in this song, humor that would definitely include Donne's use of hyperbole. The students should then try to anticipate a listener's reaction to the speaker and decide whether the speaker is perfectly "straight" in his observations.

POSSIBLE CONNECTIONS TO OTHER SELECTIONS

Anonymous, "Scarborough Fair" (text p. 171)
John Donne, "The Flea" (text p. 604)

MONA VAN DUYN, *What the Motorcycle Said* (p. 190)

The bravado of the motorcycle and its role as symbol of youthful rebellion in America is present in this poem. Written with clear attention to sound, the poem should be read aloud in order to fully appreciate the sounds of the motorcycle. The introductory stanza and various lines throughout the poem depend on onomatopoeia to establish the sound of the motorcycle's voice, and the jerky, abrupt punctuation instructs the reader on how to imitate the intended rhythms. The poem draws on brief soundbites to sketch a portrait of various eras the motorcycle has affected: "Freud's path" (line 11) and the "middle-class moneymakers" (17) are those the motorcycle passes by; the "Nowsville" (19) of the motorcycle's consciousness consists of Whitman, and "how to get VD, stoned" (24).

Students may find some passages of the poem dated or difficult to decipher. It's hard to know if phrases like "VD" are conscious markers of a bygone era or an earnest attempt at representing the motorcycle's interests in 1973. Consider taking some time to translate the dated or symbolic passages into terms your students can understand. In doing so, you may want to ask your students how a motorcycle speaks for the early seventies and have them relate their understanding of this tumultuous time in American history.

POSSIBLE CONNECTIONS TO OTHER SELECTIONS

E. E. Cummings, "she being Brand" (text p. 57)
Walt Whitman, From "Song of the Open Road" (question #1, following)

CONNECTION QUESTION IN TEXT (p. 191) WITH ANSWER

1. Compare the theme and tone of "What the Motorcycle Said" with the excerpt from Walt Whitman's "Song of the Open Road" (p. 202).

The masculine swagger of "What the Motorcycle Said" embraces a history of rebellion and adolescent likes and dislikes. The pleasure, camaraderie, joy, and insistence of "Song of the Open Road" displays more openness and less ego. Whitman's speaker takes pleasure in language and the freedom of travel; the motorcycle seems less interested in movement and more interested in making noise.

ONLINE RESOURCES (manual p. 330)

ALEXANDER POPE, From *An Essay on Criticism* (p. 191)

Alexander Pope was born in London and, after age twelve, grew up in Windsor Forest. Because his family was Catholic, and because he had been afflicted with tuberculosis of the spine, most of his education was completed at home. Catholics couldn't attend university or hold office, chief routes to patronage in those days, so Pope became by necessity as well as by desire and talent the first writer to show that literature could be one's sole support. His work, beginning with translations of the *Iliad* and the *Odyssey*, was both critically approved and financially profitable.

You might begin discussion of this selection by reminding students that the debate over which should take precedence, sound or sense, has been of greater concern to poets than many of us realize or recall.

Pope enjoys a little self-reflective mockery in these lines, like the bumper sticker that reads "Eschew Obfuscation." What he says, he does: the iambs march with strict, tuneful regularity in line 4. The word *do* in line 10 is an expletive, or meter filler. Line 11 presents a parade of monosyllables. "Chimes" in line 12 sets up the anticipated "rhymes" in line 13, and line 21 exceeds its bounds, albeit slowly, with the long alexandrine. Line 20 ("A needless Alexandrine") is also a clever play on Pope's name and on himself.

Line 23 uses assonance and some alliteration to suggest what it means; line 24 is a fine example of "easy vigor," straightforward and brief enough; lines 32 and 33 imitate the thought through the manipulation of sounds, in particular the sibilance of the *s*-sound, the growling of the *r*s, and the forcefulness of the blocks of heavy-stressed words, as in "when loud surges lash."

In line 34 the sounds get stuck in one's throat ("rock's vast weight") and reflect this resisting struggle. Accents in line 35 on "líne tóo lábors," and on "wórds móve slów" create an almost plodding rhythm that imitates the sense of the words. These lines contrast with lines 36 and 37, which contain far more light-stressed words and employ a much more direct and smooth syntax.

Careful reading of much contemporary poetry will reveal the continuing validity of Pope's observations. In any case, the power of words fashioned into lines with close attention to sound can be amply demonstrated by observing the structure of popular songs and advertisements.

POSSIBLE CONNECTION TO ANOTHER SELECTION

Langston Hughes, "Formula" (text p. 382)

AUDIOVISUAL AND ONLINE RESOURCES (manual pp. 306, 347)

GWENDOLYN BROOKS, *Sadie and Maud* (p. 192)

This poem recalls Miss Mary Mack, with shiny buttons all down her back; and Miss Lucy, who called the doctor, the nurse, and finally the lady with the alligator purse. Employing these traditional rhythms, Brooks's poem takes its two title characters from early adulthood to very different ends. The distinction between the two women is present primarily in the absence of narration about Maud: the reader knows only that she went to college, was shocked by Sadie's unmarried pregnancies, and "is living all alone / in this old house" (lines 19–20). The "fine-tooth comb" (4) with which Sadie achieves her education and takes pleasure out of life, as one of the "livingest chits" (7) around, is passed on to her daughters in the fourth stanza. The brief gloss over both lives does not state explicitly the happiness or unhappiness each character finds, but Sadie's insistence on living life to the fullest is clearly a decision that is supported, tonally, by the poet.

This poem begins with two simple lines that define the characters in contrast to one another; Sadie's action in this first line is merely inaction, but the ramifications of this decision are multiple and far-reaching. You might ask your students to examine other choices that they have made or are aware of that, while they may not be the most socially acceptable or profitable, offer future benefits difficult to imagine now.

POSSIBLE CONNECTIONS TO OTHER SELECTIONS

Robert Frost, "The Road Not Taken" (text p. 338)

Elaine Magarrell, "The Joy of Cooking" (text p. 134)

MAXINE HONG KINGSTON, *Restaurant* (p. 193)

You may wish to begin a discussion of this poem by noting the way Kingston has structured the lines — they are rhymed couplets (though often the rhymes are slant), and they have no regular rhythm or meter. Because there is no particular meter, the rhymes are subtle and unpredictable, and the line breaks take the reader by surprise. This irregular rhythm lends a sense of breathlessness to the poem — readers rarely get to relax as they move from one line to the next, since many of the lines are heavily enjambed as they adhere to the poem's rhyme scheme. To demonstrate this breathless pacing, you might ask students to read aloud the first eight lines, where only lines five and eight are end-stopped, and where all the rest of the lines create a strong sense of tension and resolution in the reader. The breathless quality of the poem captures the breathlessness of the scene the speaker is describing — the frantic pace of a restaurant kitchen.

Have your students consider lines 15–16, when the speaker admits, "In this basement / I lose my size." Students may have different interpretations of these lines. One possible interpretation is that the speaker loses her individual identity in the basement as she slaves away. Other students might interpret these lines to mean that the speaker had imagined herself to be "too big" for this job — above it somehow — and as a result is diminished by the reality of her situation. Although the speaker may lose size, she still demonstrates a remarkable strength, lifting "a pot as big as a tub with both hands" (18).

The final lines of the poem contain a powerful image — one that students are not likely to miss for its unavoidable irony. After the exhausting ordeal in which so many workers expend so much energy to create a meal, the "clean diners" dine in luxury — "behind glass in candlelight" (25), blissfully unaware of the effort it took to create the meal they are enjoying. This is the first moment in the poem where the speaker moves from description into something more reflective, as the frantic pace of the kitchen slows to allow the workers to observe the fruits of their labor.

Student readings of this poem may be enriched by some understanding of Marxist literary theory (text p. 493), since Kingston presents a startling picture of difference based on privilege and wealth.

POSSIBLE CONNECTIONS TO OTHER SELECTIONS

Langston Hughes, "Dinner Guest: Me" (text p. 394)

Elaine Magarrell, "The Joy of Cooking" (question #1, following)

1. Write an essay analyzing how the kitchen activities described in "Restaurant" and Magarrell's "The Joy of Cooking" (p. 134) are used to convey the themes of these poems.

   The kitchen in "Restaurant" is a metaphorical site in which working people must ultimately work together, and their frenetic activity stands in stark contrast to the diners who are gently illuminated in candlelight. The other poem applies the discourse of cooking to the culinary preparation of people, which acts as a metaphor for revenge. In both cases, the preparation of food represents a fundamental human interaction, whether it divides or unites people. Both also cast the preparation of food as a cruel yet tender activity; you might ask students how dining can be considered both a cruel and tender experience.

AUDIOVISUAL AND ONLINE RESOURCES (manual pp. 302, 338)

PAUL HUMPHREY, *Blow* (p. 194)

The class may not be familiar with the term *luffed,* which is a nautical word meaning "to turn the head of the ship into the wind." The woman here is metaphorically transformed into a sailing ship — appropriately enough since both would be spoken of as "she." The marvelous final line gives a blow to the gesture of the speaker trying to quell the woman's wind-filled skirt. Here the alliteration creates a kind of humor, and the quick end-stopped monosyllables with their *t*-sounds emphasize the deftness that marks the woman's movements. Point out to the class how these short, light sounds are used, almost as a verbal photograph, to capture the moment.

POSSIBLE CONNECTION TO ANOTHER SELECTION

Robert Herrick, "Upon Julia's Clothes" (text p. 225)

ROBERT FRANCIS, *The Pitcher* (p. 194)

This poem ostensibly describes a baseball pitcher's art, but the poet seems also to be describing the art of poetry. When poems discuss poetry, it is always important to consider whether their claims are meant to be universal or whether they are meant to apply only to a specific type of poetry, usually the poetry that the poet favors. You might also consider how the poem functions on a literal level: does the metaphor ever break down? In what sense is a reader analogous to a batter?

If a pitcher is too obvious, the batter will easily figure out how to hit the balls he throws. The pitcher and batter play a cat-and-mouse game in which the pitcher must stay within the boundaries but not pitch directly to the hitter. While the other players throw directly to one another, he must seem to throw a fast ball only to throw a curve and vice versa. But he cannot throw wildly, or he has failed to do his job. In a similar way, the poet's play with language must "avoid the obvious" and "vary the avoidance." Line 4, almost (but not quite) a repetition of line 3, does what it says by avoiding the repetition.

Like the pitcher's task of avoidance within bounds, the rhymes in the poem are not quite but almost there. We have the sense of a potential never actualized. The final lines illustrate the perfect rhyme that is avoided in the previous lines, indicating the completed pitch and the finished poem.

The poet, like the pitcher, chooses his words and delivers them as he feels he must, making the reader wait patiently. Ironically, the pitcher is on the defensive side, although he appears to be on the offensive as he aims at his target. This fact may lead us to question the real relationship between poet and audience suggested in this analogy.

POSSIBLE CONNECTIONS TO OTHER SELECTIONS

Robert Francis, "Catch" (text p. 14)

Robert Wallace, "The Double-Play" (question #1, following)

CONNECTION QUESTION IN TEXT (p. 194) WITH ANSWER

1. Compare this poem with Robert Wallace's "The Double-Play" (p. 641), another poem that explores the relation of baseball to poetry.

    Wallace's analogy discusses the importance of agility and skill in the writing of poetry, whereas Francis's concentration on the pitcher reveals his belief that poetry is more involved with moderate deception than with speed or skillful movement.

HELEN CHASIN, *The Word* Plum (p. 195)

The title of this poem suggests that it is about words. The relationship of the word *plum* to the object plum will generate an interesting discussion of the nature of language. Do words correspond to objects? Does poetry do more than point dimly to the sensuous realm?

The alliteration and assonance make our lips move the way they might when eating a plum. They also call attention to the sound of the poem, so that it is also about writing poetry.

POSSIBLE CONNECTIONS TO OTHER SELECTIONS

Galway Kinnell, "Blackberry Eating" (question #1, following)

Pablo Neruda, "Sweetness, Always" (text p. 660)

CONNECTION QUESTION IN TEXT (p. 196) WITH ANSWER

1. How is Kinnell's "Blackberry Eating" (p. 176) similar in technique to Chasin's poem? Try writing such a poem yourself: choose a food to describe that allows you to evoke its sensuousness in sounds.

    Both poets draw a direct comparison between the sound of the words associated with eating fruit and the experience of eating the fruit itself. It is perhaps no accident that they both use such sensuous language to describe fruits, the sexual organs of plants. Both poets anthropomorphize the fruit, to a degree; Chasin emphasizes the skin and flesh of plums, and Kinnell's blackberries, who know "the black art / of blackberry-making" (lines 5–6), fairly lower themselves into his mouth. If students choose foods besides fruit to write about, do those foods share any of the sensual qualities of fruit? (If you have covered T. S. Eliot's "The Love Song of J. Alfred Prufrock" [text p. 405], you might use these poems to make sense of Prufrock's deliberation over whether to "eat a peach.")

JOHN KEATS, *Ode to a Nightingale* (p. 196)

Earl R. Wasserman in *The Finer Tone: Keats's Major Poems* (Baltimore: Johns Hopkins UP, 1953, 1967) discusses this ode at length and places it in context with other Keats poems, including "Ode on a Grecian Urn" and "La Belle Dame sans Merci." He finds here a set of impossible contradictions, for it appears that happiness or ecstasy can be achieved only by an annihilation of self. As Wasserman writes, "By attempting to gain 'happiness,' one is brought beyond his proper bound, and yet, being mortal, he is still confined to the earthly; and thus he is left with no standards to which to refer, or rather, with two conflicting sets of standards" (183).

As a result of his complete empathic entrance into the bird's state, the poet finds himself "too happy in thine happiness." The poet has exceeded his own mortal bounds. In stanza II he longs for escape from this world — through an inebriation from the waters of poetic inspiration. Such a fading or leave-taking would be a means of fleeing from the strain of mortality (stanza III). The bird, which at first had signified beauty and oneness with nature, is now becoming identified with immortality and the ability to transcend the mortal state. The speaker admits his fascination with "easeful Death," but at the close of stanza VI, he realizes the ultimate dilemma: if he did die, the bird would go on singing but the speaker would be as responsive as "sod."

The introduction of Ruth is interesting, because she symbolizes life, family, and generational continuity. Having lost her husband, she stayed with her mother-in-law in an alien land, remarried, and bore a son.

The word *forlorn* recalls the speaker to his senses in stanza VIII, for he realizes that in this world of death, spirit, and the imagination — this ethereal world of transcendent essences — he is as nothing, and the word *forlorn*, like a bell, not only recalls him to himself but could also serve as his death summons. Note how many of the attractive sensuous details in the poem exalt physical, mortal life. At the close of stanza V, for example, Keats rescues even the flies for our poetic appreciation.

POSSIBLE CONNECTION TO ANOTHER SELECTION

Percy Bysshe Shelley, "Ode to the West Wind" (text p. 243)

PERSPECTIVE

DYLAN THOMAS, *On the Words in Poetry* (p. 198)

As Thomas emphasizes, the power of words often lies in their sound. Encourage students to read poetry aloud; in performance, the rhyme, rhythm, and character of a poem become more apparent. Thomas's own words on the subject of language and poetry are filled with character: "Out of them came the gusts and grunts and hiccups and heehaws of the common fun of the earth" (paragraph 2). Ask students to assess the effect of such words, identifying their denotations and connotations. Words, according to Thomas, clearly convey emotions. Thomas personifies words at the end of this excerpt, when he writes about their "forms and moods, their ups and downs, their chops and changes, their needs and demands" (2). Ask students to create a list of words that have obvious "moods" or "demands." They might also be interested in hearing some of Thomas's own poetry in connection with this perspective.

8

Patterns of Rhythm

As in Chapter 7, reading aloud can be of great benefit here. Abstract discussions of prosody will almost certainly turn students off. However, if students can understand how rhythm contributes to the overall impression a poem makes, they will be more likely to show interest in questions of meter. One way to emphasize this impression is to have students read these poems out loud.

These readings will also show that even the strictest metrical forms are not absolute — no one really reads iambic meter da-dum da-dum da-dum, and students will find attempts to do so unnatural (and perhaps humorous). There are variations in rhythm built into the language, and often into the meter of the poems themselves. Once students understand this, they can approach prosody as a descriptive rather than prescriptive activity, and can see scansion as a way of understanding effects rather than as an end in itself.

You may want to encourage this perception in the kinds of writing you have students do in this chapter. Critics almost never use exclusively prosody-based arguments about poems; students would be well advised to do the same. You might craft the writing assignments to have students talk about prosody among other features of a poem that contribute to its overall effect or meaning. This kind of assignment has the added advantage of keeping skills students have developed in previous chapters alive by continued use.

This chapter also lends itself well to the inclusion of popular culture — rap music, for instance, can be very sophisticated metrically. Students will probably immediately understand the difference in feeling between songs with a heavy beat (for instance, L. L. Cool J's "Momma Said Knock You Out") and ones where the rhythms are lighter and more trippingly phrased (the Fresh Prince's "Summertime"). Depending on the tastes of your class, the students themselves may be able to provide better and more current examples.

Another exercise you might try would be to have students look for patterns of rhythm in other kinds of language — Martin Luther King, Jr.'s "I Have a Dream" speech lends itself particularly well to this application, and can be compared in structure to the selection from Whitman's "Song of the Open Road."

From the Collection of Poems, Philip Larkin's "This Be the Verse" is a particularly good example of the use of rhythm to help the overall impact of the poem. The rhythms Larkin employs create a cadence that emphasizes certain words and brings out a certain tone, at once flippant and cynical. In fact, in this poem the rhythms and the content work somewhat at cross purposes to produce this effect: the rhythms are light and almost singsong in places, the content dark and ultimately despairing about the human project.

WALT WHITMAN, From *Song of the Open Road* (p. 202)

Walt Whitman's poem proclaims the glorious freedom of the open road, but its form is not completely "free." The stanzas are nontraditional, rather than totally anarchic. Ask students to look for links within and between the two stanzas, for patterns that hold them together. The first stanza, after beginning with the foreign word *allons,* employs several exclamatory phrases, many of which begin with the word *let.* The second stanza also begins with a foreign word — *camerado* — and after one transitional exclamation proceeds with three phrases that repeat the word *give.* In addition, the second stanza mentions several items that are supposedly left behind in the first and replaces these old values with new ones: "my love" is offered as a replacement for money (lines 4 and 8), "myself" for preaching and law (6 and 9).

Ask students to recall other places where they have seen repetition used as a rhetorical device. They might mention speechmaking, legal documents, or the Bible. Discuss the implications of Whitman's use of a technique that characterizes the very things he wishes to abandon.

Ask students whether they find the narrator's attitude attractive or repulsive. Does he seem naive or insightful? Are they drawn to the idea of leaving books, laws, and religion behind for the "Open Road"?

POSSIBLE CONNECTIONS TO OTHER SELECTIONS

Alfred, Lord Tennyson, "The Charge of the Light Brigade" (text p. 216)
Walt Whitman, From *I Sing the Body Electric* (text p. 252)

WILLIAM WORDSWORTH, *My Heart Leaps Up* (p. 205)

The text discusses the enjambment in lines 8–9. What is the effect of the enjambment in the first two lines? Note that all the lines between are end-stopped. Is there a thematic connection between the pairs of enjambed lines? Between the end-stopped lines?

Ask students to discuss what they think Wordsworth means by "the child is father of the Man" (line 7). Do any current songs or other elements of popular culture reflect this same sentiment, or is it dismissable as a nineteenth-century Romantic impulse?

POSSIBLE CONNECTION TO ANOTHER SELECTION

William Blake, "The Lamb" (text p. 214)

TIMOTHY STEELE, *Waiting for the Storm* (p. 206)

The text thoroughly discusses the poem's metrics and how they contribute to its meaning. In addition, you may wish to discuss word choices in the poem. How can darkness be "wrinkling," as stated in line 1? Why do you suppose Steele uses such a prosaic title for a poem so full of poetic images? You might have students examine the individual images and discuss the senses to which they appeal. Is the poem mostly auditory, visual, tactile, or does it touch all of the senses? Why does Steele start and end with the images he does? Can your students suggest other prestorm sensations the poet might have included? Would their inclusion alter the mood of the poem? You might have students decide on a topic for description and brainstorm to produce images that draw on each of the senses. Are some senses harder to utilize than others?

POSSIBLE CONNECTION TO ANOTHER SELECTION

Sylvia Plath, "Mushrooms" (text p. 187)

ONLINE RESOURCES (manual p. 352)

WILLIAM BUTLER YEATS, *That the Night Come* (p. 207)

William Butler Yeats was born in Dublin and spent his youth in Dublin, London, and Sligo (his mother's family's home) in the west of Ireland. After graduating from high school, Yeats decided to attend art school (his father, J. B. Yeats, was a painter) and made poetry an avocation. He dropped out soon after and published his first poems at age twenty in the *Dublin University Review*. His poetic influences include Spenser, Shelley, Blake, and the pre-Raphaelite poets of 1890s London, but a perhaps equally important shaping force was his religious temperament. Never satisfied with Christian doctrine, he invented, piecemeal, a mythology that informs his poetry in often obscure ways. For range and power, no twentieth-century poet equals Yeats.

Discuss the central metaphor of the poem: that the woman's longing for death is like a king's longing for the consummation of his marriage. Note especially the word *desire* (line 2). How can the desire for death possibly be equated with the desire for sex? Compare this poem to one of the *carpe diem* poems students have read. In the *carpe diem* tradition, sexuality is opposed to death; in this poem, is sexuality equated with death? Why does the speaker call death "proud" (3)? Does the speaker see death as a proud bridegroom awaiting his bride? Is this an allusion to Donne's "Death Be Not Proud" (text p. 276)?

POSSIBLE CONNECTION TO ANOTHER SELECTION

Emily Dickinson, "I read my sentence — steadily — " (text p. 306)

AUDIOVISUAL AND ONLINE RESOURCES (manual pp. 311, 355)

ALICE JONES, *The Foot* (p. 208)

The anatomical terms make "The Foot" scholarly and intellectually precise. The speaker of the poem clearly knows a great deal about the foot — the scientific terminology communicates much more than most people know about their feet. Given that poems are scanned in metrical feet, you might suggest to your students that this poem can be read as a pun; the metrical feet of a poem, such as iambs, support the poem just as human feet support people. The scholarly and foreign terms used to describe the subject of the poem obscure the function of the foot, just as overly scholarly terminology about scansion can obscure the function (and enjoyment) of a poem.

Certainly, the poem can be read not only as a pun. The first line of the poem does reveal the speaker's surprise about the human foot — that it is our "improbable" support — and the ending of the poem returns to this sense of mystery when it alludes to our connection to "an ancestor" (line 23) with a "wild / and necessary claw" (24–25). It might be interesting to have students explore one or more of the following questions in writing: What effect does the poet achieve by using language the common reader does not understand? Likewise, why would a poet write about a familiar object and make it seem foreign? Does the poet intend to humble readers by suggesting that despite all our learning we still are rooted in a past that contains ancestors with claws rather than feet?

A. E. HOUSMAN, *When I was one-and-twenty* (p. 209)

The basic metrical pattern here is iambic trimeter. The first stanza is tightly rhymed, with only two rhyming sounds. The second stanza picks up on the first rhyming word of stanza I (*twenty*), but Housman in this stanza uses more rhyming words (four sounds in the eight lines), as though he were opening up to experience. Appropriately, given his unhappy romance, "rue," "two," and "true" echo one another in rhyme. Love in both stanzas is metaphorically treated with marketplace terminology. In the first stanza the wise man advises the speaker to keep his fancy free. In the second stanza the wise man observes that the heart "was never given in vain," and moreover, the cost of buying or selling this seat of affection is immeasurable. The repetition of " 'tis true" is like a shaking of the head, of one in a state of endless "rue."

You might enter a discussion of this poem by asking students about their reactions to advice from elders. They will probably have stories about how they had to learn through experience, not advice. If that is the case, what is our relationship to the speaker of the poem? Are we meant to reject his advice, too, in favor of learning on our own? Is the speaker somewhat foppish, because he believes he has aged so much in just one year?

POSSIBLE CONNECTIONS TO OTHER SELECTIONS

Margaret Atwood, "Bored" (text p. 72)
Robert Frost, "Birches" (text p. 347)

NIKKI GIOVANNI, *Clouds* (p. 210)

Giovanni's poem employs repetition to imagine a life lived to the fullest, one in which each activity is accompanied by its experts, one in which the company is at one with its task. The richness of each activity is suggested by the idea of mimicking the hippos in their pleasure in the water, or establishing one's own hunger as on a par with that of lions, one's sense of style as natural and sharp as a penguin's. Students may want to use their imagination to think of other examples Giovanni could have used.

The rhythms of the lines render punctuation unnecessary because we are immediately familiar with the formula; the line breaks signify each different activity, in the company of animals known to have perfected it. The longer lines at the conclusion allow the poem to become slightly more complex, extending its reach beyond that of a children's rhyme. The conclusion, in slangy, comfortable speech, suggests a cowboy riding on off into the sunset at the end of a western.

POSSIBLE CONNECTIONS TO OTHER SELECTIONS

Gerard Manley Hopkins, "God's Grandeur" (text p. 181)
Edward Hirsch, "Fast Break" (text p. 219)

ONLINE RESOURCES (manual p. 332)

RACHEL HADAS, *The Red Hat* (p. 210)

The child of the speaker of this poem has recently begun to walk to school alone. The speaker and her husband take turns secretly following the boy most of the way toward school. She finds this change toward maturity unsettling; rather than feeling joy at her child's newfound independence, she and her husband feel "empty, unanchored, perilously light" (line 21). The title of the poem, and its post-Christmas setting, emphasize the youth of the boy and the irrevocable loss of childlike innocence that is the basis for the poem's core emotion.

The poem is written in heroic couplets, but the poet prevents the rhythm from sounding singsongy with enjambment, punctuating the lines unevenly, ending a sentence midline; or often by altering the meter with a semicolon or colon. Ask students how this rhythm affects the poem's tone: Would it have been as poignant if the poet hadn't interrupted the rhythm with punctuation? If the rhymes had been end-stopped and full? Does the uneven meter have something to do with the theme of the poem? This theme is obviously related to the sometimes painful passage from childhood into adulthood, the "pull / of something more powerful than school" (lines 15–16), less commonly presented from the parent's point of view than from a child's. Who do students sympathize with? Do they better understand the child's need to be independent, or the parent's need to follow him at a distance?

POSSIBLE CONNECTIONS TO OTHER SELECTIONS

Robert Bly, "The Man Who Didn't Know What Was His" (question #1, following)
Sharon Olds, "Rite of Passage" (text p. 265)

CONNECTION QUESTION IN TEXT (p. 211) WITH ANSWER

1. In an essay discuss the themes of "The Red Hat" and Bly's "The Man Who Didn't Know What Was His" (p. 168). Pay particular attention to the way parents are presented in each poem.

    In Robert Bly's "The Man Who Didn't Know What Was His," the speaker is definitely sympathetic to children rather than to their parents. Both poems will inspire discussions about the proper mix of guidance and "letting go," but also compare them as poetry. Bly seems to have an axe to grind, Hadas does not; does that observation affect how students view the form of each poem as well as the tone? Do students have different emotional responses to the two poems?

ONLINE RESOURCES (manual p. 333)

ROBERT HERRICK, *Delight in Disorder* (p. 211)

The speaker of this poem prefers in women a slightly disheveled appearance to one that presents the wearer as though she is perfect. Not coincidentally, the poem's strength is not only in its artfulness, its reliance on poetic conventions like end-rhyme and alliteration, but on the slight disorderliness of his rhythm. Vague impressions of court life in seventeenth-century England may be sufficient to initiate a discussion of the importance of dress at the time. If you are also discussing Ben Jonson's "Still to Be Neat," the next poem in this section, you might be able to get some mileage out of a discussion on the relationship between the two arts of fashion and poetry and the way they interact.

You might begin discussion of this poem by asking students what connotations the word *neat* holds for them. Then explore Herrick's use of *disorder,* as contrasted with our word *disorderly,* along with *wantonness.* Clearly, disorder and wantonness arouse in the speaker here a "fine distraction" and exercise a certain appeal that would not be present if the person addressed were prim and proper.

The speaker is bewitched but not bothered by his lady's "sweet disorder." Words are chosen to indicate a tantalizing of the passions by "erring" lace, "tempestuous" petticoats, and shoestrings tied with a "wild civility."

Herrick subtly illustrates his theme by working changes in the basic iambic tetrameter rhythm. Iambs change to trochees (cf. lines 2 and 4, for example), and in line 10 dactyls appear.

Ask students to turn back to the second question in the text and in a writing assignment analyze how patterns of rhyme and consonance work to create a subtle and pleasing artistic order.

POSSIBLE CONNECTION TO ANOTHER SELECTION

Ben Jonson, "Still to Be Neat" (text p. 212)

BEN JONSON, *Still to Be Neat* (p. 212)

Stepson of a bricklayer, Jonson was one of the first English writers to make his living by his pen. Admired for his lyrical poetry and literary criticism, Jonson is perhaps best known for his satiric comedies — including *Volpone* (1605), *The Alchemist* (1610), and *Bartholomew Fair* (1614) — and for the elaborate masques he created with designer Inigo Jones for the court of James I.

It may seem odd then that Jonson would choose to reject the elaborate fashions of the time, yet that is what Jonson is doing in this poem. The speaker dislikes the artful manners and dress of the woman. "Sweet" refers both to her smell, which is sweet, and their relationship, which presumably has some difficulties, perhaps because of her preoccupation with her own appearance. The speaker is suspicious about the reason for this preoccupation.

He asks the woman to be more sincere in her attentions to him, to pay less attention to her appearance. Neglecting herself is "sweet" to him because it is more natural, less deceptive. Words such as *adulteries* (line 11) and *face* play with the relationship between art and nature, intimating that the woman's efforts to make herself into a beautiful object only mar her natural beauty.

The disruptions in the rhythms reinforce Jonson's point until the final line. In line 6 the rhythm and the caesura in the middle of the line force the reader to slow down, emphasizing the speaker's insistence that the woman stop her artful motion and remove the mask. In the final line, the iambic tetrameter brings the speaker's point home in a succinct statement of his case.

POSSIBLE CONNECTION TO ANOTHER SELECTION

Robert Herrick, "Delight in Disorder" (questions #1 and #2, following)

CONNECTIONS QUESTIONS IN TEXT (p. 212) WITH ANSWERS

1. Write an essay comparing the themes of "Still to Be Neat" and Herrick's preceding poem, "Delight in Disorder" (p. 211). How do the speakers make similar points but from different perspectives?

   Herrick's speaker asks for a similar absence of artistry and emphasis on irregularity. But the poems seem to treat the art-nature dichotomy differently. For Herrick, a "sweet disorder" may be part of the art, whereas for Jonson the relationship between art and nature is more troubled. Jonson's speaker does not want his beloved to be artful; Herrick's simply asks that the art not be "too precise in every part."

2. How does the rhythm of "Still to Be Neat" compare with that of "Delight in Disorder"? Which do you find more effective? Explain why.

   With trochees interrupting the iambic rhythm throughout, Jonson's poem is more insistent than Herrick's. The speaker in "Still to Be Neat" is calling for an end to false art. Herrick's smoother rhythm and more easily flowing syllables suggest the speaker's delight in observing the disorder of his lady's dress. The differences in meter are in keeping with the different relationship between art and nature in the two poems.

AUDIOVISUAL AND ONLINE RESOURCES (manual pp. 301, 337)

DIANE BURNS, *Sure You Can Ask Me a Personal Question* (p. 213)

Using one side of a well-worn conversation, this poem uses repetition to demonstrate the exasperation that comes from enduring the same questions again and again.

The speaker is addressing a well-intentioned person, possibly an amalgam of all the people who have acted out the unheard portion of similar conversations. We know that the other participant in this conversation claims to have an "Indian Princess" great-grand-mother (line 14), claims to have Indian friends, lovers, or servants, apologizes for the treatment of Native Americans by the United States Government, and talks at length about Native American "Spirituality" (32). The serious theme beneath the numerous repetitions and the absence of the, easy-to-imagine other participant provide a quick gloss of the stereotypes many people have of Native Americans. Burns's speaker addresses these images with humor, but it is humor that bites, is frustrated, and finally refuses to go along; the conversation about spirituality is a nodding, absentminded one with lots of "Uh-huh"s; the last three lines give away the frustration and annoyance of the speaker and provide a terse ending for anyone who thought she was just kidding around. You may want to ask your students if they were surprised by this last line. What does she mean by this short declaration?

POSSIBLE CONNECTIONS TO OTHER SELECTIONS

Robert Browning, "My Last Duchess" (text p. 164)

Patricia Smith, "What It's Like to Be a Black Girl (For Those of You Who Aren't)" (text p. 104)

WILLIAM BLAKE, *The Lamb* and *The Tyger* (p. 214)

These two poems when paired make excellent examples of diction, rhythm, and sound and how these elements enhance tone. Ostensibly, each poem employs a four-stress pattern of trochaic feet, but the gliding *l*-sounds of the opening of "The Lamb" make the first stress on "Little" seem much lighter than the emphasis "Tyger" receives. The rhyme in the opening two lines of "The Lamb" is feminine, again unlike the stressed rhyme in "The Tyger." Only one question ("Who made Thee?") is asked of the lamb, and that question is repeated several times, giving the poem a sense of childlike simplicity and innocence. In this poem, moreover, there is a figural pattern of exchangeable identities between Lamb and Creator (Lamb of God), and speaker as child and Christ as God's child. Unlike the fearful symmetry of "The Tyger," this poem reflects a wholeness and innocence by the cohesiveness of these identities.

"The Tyger" poses far more questions about the creation of this powerful, regal beast, including the question in line 20: "Did he who made the Lamb make thee?" Ways of reading that question include the debate over the presence of evil in a God-created universe and the possibility of a second creator from whom darkness, evil, and fierce energy emanate. Could not the tiger stand for positive expressions of power? By and large, though, the questions in "The Tyger" go unanswered. Notice, for example, the substitution of *dare* in the final line for *could* in line 4.

As a writing assignment, you might ask students to examine several elements in each poem, including rhythm, patterns of consonance and assonance, pace, tone, even levels of ambiguity so that they are able on a fairly sophisticated level to articulate the differences between the two lyrics.

POSSIBLE CONNECTION TO ANOTHER SELECTION

William Wordsworth, "I Wandered Lonely as a Cloud" (text p. 646)

ANNA LAETITIA BARBAULD, *On a Lady's Writing* (p. 215)

This poem provides an example of tidy, ladylike writing to make its point: the verse of a lady should be as contained and elegant as its author. The even meter, as exemplified by the iambic pentameter in "Her even lines her steady temper show," mirrors the point the poem makes about a woman's worth being present in her poetic skill. It might be a good idea to review metrical terms with students to make sure they can recognize the stresses in Barbauld's lines.

Duke University has a Web site on Barbauld that you might find helpful: **http://duke.usask.ca/~vargo/barbauld/**. The site includes some of her poems and essays, as well as commentary, a timeline of her life, and a file of articles written around the same time as "On a Lady's Writing." The historical context provided by these supplementary articles might help your students to see the poem as part of a dialogue about women's writing in the late 1700s: perhaps students could write summaries of these articles and present the varying perspectives to the class.

You might ask students to consider the assumptions Barbauld makes about the relationship between a person and his or her work. How do the topics writers choose reflect their personalities? How could a review of someone's prose act as an indictment of his or her character?

POSSIBLE CONNECTIONS TO OTHER SELECTIONS

Robert Herrick, "Delight in Disorder" (question #1, following)
——, "Upon Julia's Clothes" (text p. 225)
Ben Jonson, "Still to Be Neat" (text p. 212)

CONNECTION QUESTION IN TEXT (p. 216) WITH ANSWER

1. Discuss the idea of order in "On a Lady's Writing" and in Robert Herrick's "Delight in Disorder" (p. 211). How does each poem implicitly — though coincidentally — comment on the other?

   Both Barbauld and Herrick use regular meter and comparisons between feminine qualities and the accomplishments of good art. While Barbauld's poem admires the qualities of a lady and her writing, Herrick focuses first on the imperfections that make the woman charming. He then uses his conclusion to suggest that the same comparisons can be made with respect to art.

ALFRED, LORD TENNYSON, *The Charge of the Light Brigade* (p. 216)

This poem praises and honors the light brigade, those "noble six hundred" men who charge "into the valley of Death" even though they know that they will die. The poem raises questions about the nature of bravery during wartime; the soldiers are praised for their glory, their honor, their nobility, but there is a nagging sense that their deaths could have been avoided. They knew that "some one had blundered" (line 12) but this logic is tempered by the sentiment behind the famous lines "Their's not to make reply, / Their's not to reason why, / Their's but to do and die" (13–15).

The rhyme and meter make the poem sound like a typical poem celebrating the heroes of war. The phrase "six hundred" is rhymed repeatedly, with "thundered" (21), "wondered" (31), and "sundered" (36); the word "blundered," which sounds a discordant note in the second stanza, is nearly buried by what appears to be the poem's laudatory tone. Students may debate about whether the poem focuses on praising the brigade for its courage or on criticizing the brigade for its blind obedience, which leads many of them to death. The effect would certainly be different if the sentiment of the second stanza were to come at the end of the poem. Since it doesn't, questions about the poem's tone and the speaker's attitude must take into consideration both the poem as a whole and the second stanza in particular. The "honor" that is proposed for the "noble six hundred" in the final stanza is altered not only by the second stanza but by the fact that the six hundred are less than six hundred in the stanzas IV and V.

POSSIBLE CONNECTIONS TO OTHER SELECTIONS

Wilfred Owen, "Dulce et Decorum Est" (question #1, following)
Walt Whitman, "Cavalry Crossing a Ford" (text p. 92)

CONNECTION QUESTION IN TEXT (p. 217) WITH ANSWER

1. Compare the theme of "The Charge of the Light Brigade" with Owen's "Dulce et Decorum Est" (p. 102).

    The tone of "Dulce et Decorum Est" makes its theme much more obvious; would students go so far as to say that the speakers of the two poems share the same attitude but that they simply differ in their degrees of subtlety? Is there a certain nobility associated with the warfare Tennyson describes, with its charges on horseback and sabers, as opposed to Owen's description of World War I with its invisible enemy, its lethal gas, and the horrors of trench warfare?

AUDIOVISUAL AND ONLINE RESOURCES (manual pp. 308, 353)

THEODORE ROETHKE, *My Papa's Waltz* (p. 217)

From the perspective of a man looking back at his childhood, the speaker recollects the drunken lurchings of his working-class father as he waltzed around the room. The remembrance is one of those strong early memories that, years later, one sifts through. The rhythm of the poem reflects well those moments the speaker recalls with some pain. Notice the spondees, for example, in "My right ear scraped a buckle" (line 12) or in "You beat time on my head / With a palm caked hard by dirt" (13–14). The title, with its use of *Papa*, seems to indicate a memory from early childhood — as does line 12. It also connotes a certain gentle affection for "Papa," despite all the other memories.

POSSIBLE CONNECTIONS TO OTHER SELECTIONS

Regina Barreca, "Nighttime Fires" (text p. 26)
Dylan Thomas, "Do not go gentle into that good night" (text p. 233)

ARON KEESBURY, *Song to a Waitress* (p. 218)

The speaker of this poem is a somewhat belligerent diner patron whose repeated demands for "hot" coffee in a "big fat mug" add to the depiction of a gruff man who appears to know what he wants. The scene, reminiscent of the famous Jack Nicholson routine from *Five Easy Pieces*, evokes a nearly mythical American landscape, a kind of diner frontier in which "big," "hot," "fat," and "full" are the values that matter, in which "pink, pansy / sugar packets in dainty little cups" (lines 7 and 8) represent a rejected set of values.

The central irony of the poem is that it is a poem at all. Its title, "Song to a Waitress," conjures up a centuries-long tradition of a poetic form, and it is composed of three four-line stanzas completed with a rhymed couplet, reminiscent of a Shakespearean sonnet (traditionally, a love poem). Yet the poem resists these conventions, too, just as it rejects the "pink, pansy / sugar packets." The speaker's tone clashes with the very notion of poetry and with the idea that his attitude toward the waitress could be construed as a song. If you choose to have students write a response to the speaker, they will also be participating in a poetic tradition that was common during the English Renaissance, that of response to a love song, and they may reject the speaker's values from the point of view of the waitress just as the Nymph rejects those of the Shepherd. In doing so, do they choose to make use of any of the various repetitions in this poem? Do they make use of all of them?

Katharyn Howd Machan, "Hazel Tells LaVerne" (question #1, following)

CONNECTION QUESTION IN TEXT (p. 219) WITH ANSWER

1. Write a reply to the speaker in "Song to a Waitress" from the point of view of the waitress. You might begin by writing a prose paragraph and then try organizing it into lines of poetry. Read Machan's "Hazel Tells LaVerne" (p. 61) for a source of inspiration.

    Students should strive to get the voice of the waitress right, for which they can use Machan's poem as a source of inspiration, but they also should not ignore the metrical principles of Keesbury's poem. They should attempt to make the reply similar to the original, just as the Nymph's reply to the Shepherd undoes the Shepherd's rhetoric. In other words, you may have to remind students that they are not only creating a speaker, but that she is replying to a specific outburst by the speaker of Keesbury's poem.

EDWARD HIRSCH, *Fast Break* (p. 219)

This poem, a description of a fast break in basketball, takes the reader through the action at a frenzied pace. Like the play it describes, the poem seems chaotic or random, but the end result is a vision of perfection. The poem is one long sentence, punctuated sparingly, divided into two-line stanzas. How would the effect of the poem change if it were punctuated or divided more conventionally?

Run-ons make us feel that we are watching the basketball game as we read the poem. The one long sentence is an appropriate choice because the poem describes a few seconds of activity on a basketball court; we feel both the urgency and the rapidity of the play. In keeping with the spirit of the game, in which quick moves, sudden reversals, and surges of power are of the essence, the meter is irregular.

The tribute to the dead friend attempts to sing the praises of a short but successful life. The image of the power-forward exploding past other players in a fury (lines 25, 26) suggests someone burning through life radiant with energy and resolve. The player scores the point in the final lines. We sense both a resolution to the play and a resolution to the life.

In its attempt to capture a single moment on the court, to encircle the actions of all of the players in that moment, and to make the audience feel as if they are a part of it, this poem can be called "a momentary stay against confusion." The poem freezes a moment in time, seeming to simplify a life's journey in a single play. The poem shows us the player's life making sense.

Alfred, Lord Tennyson, "The Charge of the Light Brigade" (text p. 216)

DAVID BARBER, *A Colonial Epitaph Annotated* (p. 220)

This poem's speaker imagines the personality of a woman who died in 1771, taking the clues her epitaph provides and reconstructing a life for her. He describes her as "no flower" (line 19), a quick thinker who didn't put up with people she didn't admire, who said what she thought about politics and religion, and who "revelled in repartee" (24). The tone is one of admiration, fleshing out a portrait of a woman with pluck and persistence in a time that did not appreciate "the sting in her tongue" (28).

While the poem employs the stanza format and rhyme scheme of the original epitaph, the third and fourth stanzas contain slant rhymes. Students may appreciate a quick examination of the success of these rhymes before they attempt to write their own rhyming stanzas; slant rhyme can be very forgiving.

POSSIBLE CONNECTIONS TO OTHER SELECTIONS

Anna Laetitia Barbauld, "On a Lady's Writing" (question #1, following)
Linda Pastan, "Marks" (text p. 132)

CONNECTION QUESTION IN TEXT (p. 221) WITH ANSWER

1. Compare the rhythms and themes of this poem with those of "On a Lady's Writing" by Anna Laetitia Barbauld (text p. 215).

    The occasional loose rhymes and pleasure in a woman's imagined rebellion are the most obvious indicators of difference between Barber's poem and "On a Lady's Writing." While Barbauld's verse claims that women who write are still capable of ladylike behavior, Barber's poem questions these values by celebrating the ways in which one woman violated the norms Barbauld's speaker embraces.

ONLINE RESOURCES (manual p. 324)

PERSPECTIVE

LOUISE BOGAN, *On Formal Poetry* (p. 221)

You might ask students to compare Bogan's questions about form as repression with Whitman's assertion that "the rhyme and uniformity of perfect poems show the free growth of metrical laws and bud from them as unerringly and loosely as lilacs or roses on a bush, and take shapes as compact as the shapes of chestnuts and oranges and melons and pears, and shed the perfume impalpable to form" (p. 254). Students could write an essay about these perspectives on "form" in poetry, using two or three examples from the Collection of Poems.

9

Poetic Forms

There is some degree of controversy over the role of form in poetry. The movement calling itself New Formalism advocates a widespread return to form, and criticizes what it calls the status quo of open form. (A possible introduction to this position is in Dana Gioia's "Notes on the New Formalism" in the Autumn 1987 *Hudson Review*, reprinted in *Can Poetry Matter?* Also, see Timothy Steele's *Missing Measures*.) There are also, however, several defenses of open form (perhaps the best of which is Stanley Plumly's "Chapter and Verse" in the January/February and May/June issues of *American Poetry Review*). You might find it interesting to introduce your students to this controversy and have them find their own positions on the matter. This exercise can help students understand that there are reasons for the choice to write in or out of traditional forms, and that traditional forms are not always or necessarily conservative. In addition, it emphasizes the idea that poetry is a dynamic genre, full of conflict and contradiction.

As in previous chapters, this material will likely be most appealing to students in terms of its relation to the overall impact of a poem — form only takes on meaning when married to content and presented in context. Quizzes that ask students to give the structure of a Petrarchan sonnet tend not to work as well as those that ask students to explain how the form of a particular sonnet contributes to its overall effect. (Some historical notes might be useful in this chapter, since the importance of traditional forms has as much to do with the history of those forms as with each current instance of the form.)

The section on sonnets is particularly good at emphasizing the different uses to which the form was put; each use, however, draws on the structure of the sonnet to help create meaning and coherence in the poem. Mark Jarman's "Unholy Sonnet," in conjunction with the sonnets from Donne found in the Collection of Poems, make good test cases. Students can see how the sonnet form allows Jarman to engage in a cross-century and cross-faith debate with Donne; the sonnet ensures that despite the historical and religious differences, the discussion takes place on the same terrain.

Another example that can help students understand the union of form and content can be found in the section on the villanelle — the kinds of repetition this form requires can be used for emphatic statement, as both Dylan Thomas's and Robin Sarah's poems demonstrate.

A. E. HOUSMAN, *Loveliest of trees, the cherry now* (p. 224)

The speaker in this poem greets life with a warmhearted *joie de vivre*. Although he is young, he already has a sense of life's limits. He means to enjoy the beauty of life every minute he is alive. Even then, he claims, he could not absorb all the beauties of life. The connotations of rebirth and spring are reinforced by the mention of Eastertide in line 4.

Yet behind the gaiety and cheerful resolve is an awareness of the imminence of death. You might explore, either in class discussion or as a writing assignment, the question of whether this could be considered a *carpe diem* poem.

POSSIBLE CONNECTIONS TO OTHER SELECTIONS

Robert Frost, "The Road Not Taken" (text p. 338)

Robert Herrick, "To the Virgins, to Make Much of Time" (text p. 64)

AUDIOVISUAL AND ONLINE RESOURCES (manual pp. 300, 336)

ROBERT HERRICK, *Upon Julia's Clothes* (p. 225)

Herrick uses so many of the elements of poetry — rhyme, rhythm, the sound and choice of words — so well in this brief lyric that it is worth taking some class time to analyze. The first tercet of iambic tetrameter is absolutely regular and thus suggests the sweetly flowing liquefaction of Julia's clothes. In the second tercet, trochees interrupt the established pattern to capture in rhythmic terms "that brave vibration." *Brave* is used here in the sense of "making a fine show or display," as in a banner waving.

POSSIBLE CONNECTION TO ANOTHER SELECTION

Paul Humphrey, "Blow" (question #1, following)

CONNECTION QUESTION IN TEXT (p. 225) WITH ANSWER

1. Compare the tone of this poem with that of Humphrey's "Blow" (p. 194). Are the situations and speakers similar? Is there any difference in tone between these two poems?

   The situations are dissimilar in that Herrick's subject is "my Julia" (line 1) but the speaker of Humphrey's poem has no relationship with his subject. He is more self-deprecating than Herrick's speaker is; when the woman laughs and leaves in the final lines, we sense that she is laughing at him rather than at her situation. His gallantry becomes buffoonery. Herrick's emphasis is on the speaker's reverie; he is ecstatic rather than ridiculous.

SONNET

JOHN KEATS, *On First Looking into Chapman's Homer* (p. 226)

The principal theme of Keats's sonnet is discovery; he uses the sudden and unexpected discovery of the Pacific Ocean by early explorers of the Americas as a metaphor for those moments in life when we feel that a previously held view has been radically shaken.

You might ask students whether they have experienced a moment of discovery similar to that which Keats describes. After they have read Keats's poem, give them a few minutes to write about a moment when they felt a sense of revelation similar to that felt by "stout Cortez" and his men, and then discuss the results.

A comparison of Keats's sonnets provides ample evidence of the poet's continual experimentation with form during his brief career. In "Chapman's Homer," Keats utilizes the characteristic division of the Italian sonnet into octave and sestet, with the opening eight lines setting up a situation or argument and the remaining six resolving it. You may wish to compare Keats's use of the sonnet form in "Chapman's Homer" with his use of the form in other poems in the chapter. In some sonnets Keats favors the Italian or Petrarchan form, but in "When I have fears" (text p. 618) he uses the English or Shakespearean rhyme scheme (three quatrains and a couplet).

POSSIBLE CONNECTION TO ANOTHER SELECTION

Robert Hass, "Happiness" (text p. 44)

WILLIAM WORDSWORTH, *The World Is Too Much with Us* (p. 227)

Like Hopkins in "God's Grandeur" (text p. 181), Wordsworth is protesting here the preoccupation with worldliness — banking, buying, getting, spending — that makes it increasingly difficult to feel the mystery and power in the natural world. Proteus (a god of the sea) and Triton (another sea god, who stirred up storms) lie dormant, their power to kindle in the human soul a spirit of awe suppressed in the commercialized world, where people have bartered their hearts away. "Great God!" is the speaker's spontaneous and ironic response to the decline of spirituality, for it appears that the pagan world possessed a stronger sense of godliness.

POSSIBLE CONNECTIONS TO OTHER SELECTIONS

Matthew Arnold, "Dover Beach" (text p. 95)
Gerard Manley Hopkins, "God's Grandeur" (question #1, following)

CONNECTION QUESTION IN TEXT (p. 228) WITH ANSWER

1. Compare the theme of this sonnet with that of Hopkins's "God's Grandeur" (p. 181).

   Both Wordsworth's sonnet and "God's Grandeur" draw from the social and industrial worlds to discuss the greatness of creation and the human threat to that greatness. The speaker in Hopkins's sonnet places his faith in the creator, who can overcome the destructive actions of human beings. Wordsworth's sonnet returns to pagan myths for comfort, although the speaker has little hope of overcoming the bleakness of the world that is "too much with us." Hopkins dwells on bleak images of all "seared with trade," but he is convinced that nature is still available to us and that even humanity can be redeemed.

WILLIAM SHAKESPEARE, *Shall I compare thee to a summer's day?* (p. 228)

The speaker in this sonnet praises his beloved not only for her loveliness but also for her temperateness of manner. Unlike nature, which is forever changing, she shows a steady devotion. Moreover, the speaker tells us that this love will extend well into the future, even beyond the grave. Such love, like the art that celebrates it, confers a measure of immortality on the lovers and, self-reflexively, on the sonnet. Notice, for example, how the stressed words in the couplet reinforce this idea. *Long* is stressed in both lines of the couplet, along with other significant words that link continued "life" with "this," the sonnet that confers immortality, and "thee," the object the sonnet addresses.

POSSIBLE CONNECTIONS TO OTHER SELECTIONS

John Frederick Nims, "Love Poem" (text p. 31)
William Shakespeare, "My mistress' eyes are nothing like the sun" (text p. 229)

AUDIOVISUAL AND ONLINE RESOURCES (manual pp. 307, 349)

WILLIAM SHAKESPEARE, *My mistress' eyes are nothing like the sun* (p. 229)

Students may have read this sonnet in high school, and you might begin by asking them what they think the mistress looks like. Some clarification of Shakespeare's use of the term *mistress* (beloved or chosen one) may be in order. This sonnet plays with the conventions and clichés of the Petrarchan sonnet, which elaborated on the extraordinary qualities of the maiden's eyes as compared to the splendor of the sun. But Shakespeare refuses to do this and thus argues for a poetry that avoids cliché and the excess metaphor that tries to outdo reality. He is, in fact, asserting the beauty of his beloved in the last line. She is as attractive as any other woman who has been "belied" (made to seem more beautiful) by false comparison.

POSSIBLE CONNECTION TO ANOTHER SELECTION

William Shakespeare, "Shall I compare thee to a summer's day?" (text p. 228)

EDNA ST. VINCENT MILLAY, *I will put Chaos into fourteen lines* (p. 229)

In structure, Millay's list of paradoxes and resolutions adheres strictly to the verse form of the Italian, or Petrarchan, sonnet: it consists of fourteen lines of iambic pentameter with a rhyme scheme based upon an octave and a sestet. The octave is a single sentence describing the poet's efforts to force Chaos to unite with Order; the sestet recounts the happy results of such a union.

The poem accomplishes the apparently impossible feat of "containing" both Chaos "himself" and his various manifestations. The poet literally "puts Chaos into" the poem through personification, by portraying the abstract idea of Chaos as a character in a sonnet. The highly ordered verse form controls the disorderly, negative power of Chaos — "Flood, fire, and demon" (line 4) — by the physical act of shaping the words into the iambic pentameter line. One might expect that such restrictions would humble, even emasculate such a powerful figure, but according to the poet, the "sweet" sonnet form does not deprive Chaos of his energy; it concentrates the energy in a pattern of beauty and harmony — it "make[s] him good" (14).

The poet's use of figurative language reinforces the paradox inherent in the poem's structure. The image of "pious rape" in line 6 may seem irresolvably paradoxical in the 1990s, when a rape is such a highly charged negative issue. However, this is an excellent opportunity to encourage students to go beyond themselves in order to examine the poem on its own terms. The "rape" here is rape in a mythic sense; the dramatic situation in lines 3–8 recalls the creation myths of Hesiod or Genesis, with the poet herself as the agent who brings Order to Chaos and calls it "good." The poet insists that the forcible control exercised does not hurt Chaos, but actually benefits him by adding sweetness and goodness to his formidable power.

The personification of Chaos as a male entity produces another paradox in addition to the contradiction created by juxtaposing the orderly sonnet form with a disorderly central character. Because we know that the poet is female, we have a highly unusual role reversal here — the male is raped by the female in the poem. The female poet forces Chaos into the "strict confines" (5) of the sonnet until he "mingles and combines" (8) with Order.

POSSIBLE CONNECTION TO ANOTHER SELECTION

Robert Frost, "Design" (question #1, following)

CONNECTION QUESTION IN TEXT (p. 230) WITH ANSWER

1. Compare the theme of this poem with that of Robert Frost's "Design" (p. 356).

    Frost's "Design," like "I will put Chaos," is structured as an Italian sonnet, but in contrast to Millay's poem, which begins with an abstract concept and uses imagery to make it more concrete, "Design" begins with a small, concrete image and extrapolates it to a larger, more abstract one. In general, Frost tends to affirm the power of poetic form to harness the chaos of life, to create a momentary stay against confusion, much as Millay does in "I will put Chaos." However, Frost's images of death and terror in "Design" suggest that if there is a controlling order in the universe, it is largely a force of evil. In contrast to Millay's theme, Frost suggests that Chaos can force Order to become a channel for his negative energy.

MARK DOTY, *Golden Retrievals* (p. 230)

This poem, in the voice of a golden retriever, describes the relationship between dog and master as that of a canine "Zen master" (line 13) and a human novice. In a sonnet, with the satisfactions of some rich internal slant rhyme (fetch, catch; wind, again), the dog illustrates the differences between his own antics and his human companion's during the course of a walk. The dog is constantly in the present; even Fetch and Catch are beyond his short attention span. The shape of his desire is much more present and fleeting. Singular, simple nouns — "muck, pond, ditch, residue" (5) — serve to satisfy his constantly shifting interest. The human accompanying the canine speaker is unable to experience the present without help: he or she is "sunk in the past" (7) or "in some fog concerning — tomorrow" (9–10). The true retrieval here is of the human master; the dog works to pull the human into the present.

Your students might enjoy some time spent attempting sonnets of their own from another animal's perspective. Examples include a family pet when a new baby is brought home, a possum on the highway as a pickup truck approaches, or a cardinal looking in a kitchen window. Pointing them toward the third and fifth lines of this poem, with their fractured, scattered focus, could help them imagine how to create an animal's consciousness.

POSSIBLE CONNECTIONS TO OTHER SELECTIONS

Robert Frost, "Stopping by Woods on a Snowy Evening" (question #1, following)
Walt Whitman, "A Noiseless Patient Spider" (text p. 130)

CONNECTION QUESTION IN TEXT (p. 231) WITH ANSWER

1. Compare the relationship between dog and master in this poem and horse and owner in Robert Frost's "Stopping by Woods on a Snowy Evening" (p. 353). Though these poems are quite different in tone, what similarities do you find in their themes?

    While Doty's poem is written in a dog's voice, imagining his human master's thoughts, Frost's poem is written in a human's voice, imagining how his brown study must appear to his "little horse" (5). The depth of Frost's speaker's pleasure in being present in the woods mirrors Doty's dog's pleasure in the moment; Doty's master and Frost's horse are the ones concerned with the future.

ONLINE RESOURCES (manual p. 330)

MOLLY PEACOCK, *Desire* (p. 231)

This somewhat complex treatment of desire reads almost like a riddle, and students may productively spend time trying to figure out exactly what the speaker is describing. The answer to the riddle is contained both in the title and in the final phrase: "Desire . . . the drive to feel" (line 14). But the metaphors and similes throughout the body of the poem present its chief interpretive problem: what exactly is the poet's point about desire, and why is it useful to define it the way she does?

The best way to reorganize the poem initially may be to list all of the metaphors for desire and to consider them individually; for instance, in what sense is desire "blunt" (10), "like a paw" (9)? Once you have done so, consider the metaphors together. Do they have anything in common? Students should notice that these metaphors often have to do with something animal and youthful, something wild and unsophisticated. The intimation is that socialization and civilization bring us farther away from our instinctive "drive to feel" (14), which is why desire is "what babies bring to kings" (5) as opposed to the material gifts that the three wise men brought to the infant Jesus.

POSSIBLE CONNECTIONS TO OTHER SELECTIONS

Diane Ackerman, "A Fine, a Private Place" (question #1, following)
Walt Whitman, From *I Sing the Body Electric* (text p. 252)

CONNECTION QUESTION IN TEXT (p. 231) WITH ANSWER

1. Compare the treatment of desire in this poem with that of Ackerman's "A Fine, a Private Place" (p. 69). In an essay, identify the theme of each poem and compare their conceptions of desire. How alike are these two poems?

    A comparison of this poem to Ackerman's "A Fine, a Private Place" should yield some interesting results since this poem is much more abstract. If students take the themes of the two poems to be similar, they can illustrate Peacock's ideas with Ackerman's poem, demonstrating how the lovers in "A Fine, a Private Place" enact "the blind instinct for life unruled." If they consider the themes dissimilar, you might ask them how the form of each poem underscores this difference.

ONLINE RESOURCES (manual p. 346)

MARK JARMAN, *Unholy Sonnet* (p. 232)

This poem is an example of an Italian, or Petrarchan, sonnet. You may wish to begin discussion by having students read the poem aloud, since the lines are so heavily enjambed that the rhythm and rhyme occur subtly. In dealing with this piece as a sonnet, you might point out that Italian sonnets are characterized by the usual fourteen lines of iambic pentameter, but unlike other sonnet forms, this type usually contains a shift in content between the octave and the sestet — a movement from suggestion to resolution.

This shift occurs in terms of both style and content in this poem. In the opening octave, many of the lines begin with a dactylic rather than an iambic foot (lines 1–4 each begin this way), and all of the lines in the octave have feminine endings. By contrast, the sestet lines each begin with a standard iambic foot and conclude with a masculine ending. In content, the repeated use of the word "after" — which occurs five times in the octave — sets up a sense of suspense in the first part of the poem that is then resolved through the repeated "there is" in the concluding sestet. In addition, the octave uses the pronouns "us" and "our," while the answering sestet uses the pronouns "you" and "your." Ask students to consider whether this shift in pronouns affects the reading of the poem. Does it strengthen or detract from the sense of resolution contained in the poem's concluding sestet?

POSSIBLE CONNECTIONS TO OTHER SELECTIONS

John Donne, "Batter My Heart" (question #1, following)
——, "Death Be Not Proud" (question #1, following)

ONLINE RESOURCES (manual p. 337)

CONNECTION QUESTION IN TEXT (p. 232) WITH ANSWER

1. Jarman has said that his "Unholy Sonnets" (there are about twenty of them) are modeled after John Donne's *Holy Sonnets* but that he does not share the same Christian assumptions about faith and mercy that inform Donne's sonnets. Instead, Jarman says, he "work[s] against any assumption or shared expression of

faith, to write a devotional poetry against the grain." Keeping this statement in mind, write an essay comparing and contrasting the tone and theme of Jarman's sonnet with John Donne's "Batter My Heart" (p. 604) or "Death Be Not Proud" (p. 276).

Jarman's sonnet considers the disparity between what we are trying to do through practicing religion and what we actually do. He believes that the rituals of church-going do nothing to eradicate our basic (and base) human nature. The two sonnets by Donne describe a much more personal faith on the part of the speaker. Human activity does not interfere with his relationship with God or with his belief in eternal life through faith. The subject in Jarman's poem is collective first person and second person; in Donne's poems, the subject is first-person singular. In writing "a devotional poetry against the grain," Jarman is responding not only to Donne but to modern views of religion. Yet in terms of form, Jarman's sonnet does work as a kind of inversion of Donne's logic; all three poems end with a bold sentiment in the final couplet.

VILLANELLE

DYLAN THOMAS, *Do not go gentle into that good night* (p. 233)

This poem is a villanelle, a French verse form ordinarily treating light topics, whose five tercets and concluding quatrain employ only two end rhymes. The first and third lines of the poem must alternatively conclude the tercets and form a couplet for the quatrain. Despite these formal restrictions, Thomas's poem sounds remarkably unforced and reflects quite adequately the feeling of a man who does not want his father to die.

Just as remarkable is the poem's rich figurative language; this villanelle could be used as a summary example of almost all the points outlined in this chapter. Variety is achieved through the metonymies for death, such as "close of day" (line 2), "dark" (4), "dying of the light" (9). The overall effect is to describe death metaphorically as the end of a day and thus, in some sense, to familiarize death and lessen its threat. Even to describe death as "that good night" (1) reduces it to a gesture of good-bye. Other figures of speech include a pun on "grave" men (13) (both solemn and mortal), an oxymoron in "who see with blinding sight" (13), various similes, such as "blaze like meteors" (14), and the overall form of the apostrophe.

Thomas introduces several examples of people who might be expected to acquiesce to death gently but who, nonetheless, resist it. "Wise men" (philosophers, perhaps) want more time because so far their wisdom has not created any radical change ("forked no lightning"). Men who do good works (theologians, possibly) look back and realize that the sum total of their efforts was "frail" and if they had devoted more time to a fertile field ("green bay"), their deeds might have been more effective. "Wild men" (inspired artists, writers) know their words have caught and held time, but they know too how in various ways — with their relations with others or perhaps with alcohol and drugs — they have "grieved" the sun. Grave men at the end of their lives realize too late that joy is one means of transcending time. All these groups experience some form of knowledge that makes them wish they could prolong life and live it according to their new insights.

As a writing assignment you might ask students to analyze a character or group of people that they have read about in a short story who seem to fit into one of the categories Thomas describes. What advice would he give them? How otherwise could they lead their lives?

POSSIBLE CONNECTION TO ANOTHER SELECTION

Sylvia Plath, "Daddy" (question #1, following)

1. In Thomas's poem we experience "rage against the dying of the light." Contrast this with the rage you find in Sylvia Plath's "Daddy" (p. 631). What produces the emotion in Plath's poem?

   For Thomas, rage is an outpouring of passion, a summoning of strength that will preserve the speaker's father's vitality. In the final stanza, cursing and blessing amount to the same thing because they connote this same sense of vitality. The rage in Plath's poem is a reaction to injustice. This rage, too, gives the speaker a sense of power: the power to use language as a way of condemning her oppressor. Both poets value rage as a fundamental element of our humanity, but in each poem it springs from different sources. Plath's speaker is uncorking a pent-up emotion, whereas the father in Thomas's poem is being asked to reach into himself to squeeze out whatever emotion is left in him.

ROBYN SARAH, *Villanelle for a Cool April* (p. 234)

This villanelle uses the repetition of its form to slow the poem down, to make its pace mirror the one being championed. The speaker compares a cool April with a gradually developing love relationship; the "present tense" (line 3) of "pleasures slow and one by one" (8) can be found in both the green buds of a cool April and the "feathered touch, a button just undone" (14) of deferred desire.

The poem veers from being a pure villanelle in its fourth stanza, in which "I like a leafing-out by increments" (1, 6) becomes "a leafing-out to love in increments" (12); this departure clarifies the focus of the comparison, and the variation on the repeated line might make the poem's diction seem more natural. Ask your students what they think; if it says it's a villanelle, should it stick firmly to its form? Is Sarah cheating?

Students might enjoy drawing comparisons between different kinds of love relationships and months; what are the virtues of a relationship that could be more easily compared to a hot July? December in Miami? The descending chill of October? February in a coldwater flat?

POSSIBLE CONNECTIONS TO OTHER SELECTIONS

Margaret Atwood, "February" (question #1, following)
Sophie Cabot Black, "August" (question #1, following)

CONNECTION QUESTION IN TEXT (p. 234) WITH ANSWER

1. Compare this description of April with Margaret Atwood's "February" (p. 124) and Sophie Cabot Black's "August" (p. 125). Which poem did you find to be the most effective description of a month? Explain why.

   Students will differ in their opinions of which poem provides the most effective description. The desperation and humor in Atwood's sedentary observations of the "small pink bumhole" (29), Black's elegant portrait of the "loose, unguarded" (12) gold that threatens farmers, and Sarah's clear presentation of the virtues of "the cool of swooning sense" (13) all have their virtues.

SESTINA

ELIZABETH BISHOP, *Sestina* (p. 235)

This poem strikes the ear as particularly sad because it portrays unexpressed emotion in an intimate domestic setting. There seems to be no shared awareness between grandmother and child, although one suspects they are sad for similar reasons. To make matters even worse, that sadness seems as foreordained as the rain showers that the almanac predicts. Here the almanac functions for the grandmother as a soothsayer, fore-telling sadness and loss. For the child, the Marvel Stove operates in the same way (line 25), its cast-iron blackness serving as a kind of mute doomsayer. Note, for example, the repetition of "tears" and "rain" in stanzas II and III and how they are connected with "grandmother," "almanac," "child," and "stove."

Bishop's father died of Bright's disease at age thirty-nine, when the poet was only eight months old. Her mother subsequently suffered several nervous breakdowns, and Bishop was sent from her home in Worcester, Massachusetts, to live with her maternal grandmother in Nova Scotia. The grandmother had lost her own father in a sailing acci-dent when she was a child. A good summary of Bishop's childhood is offered by Robert Giroux in his introduction to *Elizabeth Bishop: The Collected Prose* (New York: Farrar, 1984). If your students enjoy Bishop's poetry, they might also enjoy the fiction and descriptive pieces offered in this collection.

POSSIBLE CONNECTIONS TO OTHER SELECTIONS

Elizabeth Bishop, "Manners" (text p. 48)
Adrienne Rich, "Living in Sin" (text p. 633)

FLORENCE CASSEN MAYERS, *All-American Sestina* (p. 236)

In a sense, this poem is an inverted sestina since the first words of each line (rather than the end words) conform to the conventions of a sestina. The poem runs through a series of American clichés involving the numbers one through six and fits them into this difficult poetic form. Mayers departs from her own scheme a few times, though: what should be "six" in the third stanza is "sixty-" (line 14) and it wraps around to the next line, "four-dollar question"; and "hole in one" (27) in stanza five, and "high five" (34) in stanza six break the pattern of having the number begin the line.

Students might debate about whether this poem raises important themes or whether it's just a clever exercise. You may want to gear discussion toward a considera-tion of what is particularly "All-American" about the clichés in the poem. (Is the fact that they are clichés all-American?) It might help to try to classify the images; the categories may vary, but most seem to have something to do with a kind of consumer hucksterism: "one-day sale" (8), "five-year warranty" (9), "sixty-four-dollar question" (14–15); or with nostalgia: "five-cent cigar" (5), "one-room schoolhouse" (36); or with excess: "six-pack Bud" (7), "two-pound lobster" (17), "four-wheel drive" (25). Students may come up with entirely different categories. Encourage them to be flexible when creating these cate-gories. Do they see an emerging pattern that might help to define "All-American"? Do any of the phrases not fit neatly into any category? A comparison to Cummings's "next to of course god america i" (text p. 146) may highlight these themes. But does Mayers critique America in the same way that Cummings does? Is it possible to read the poem as a celebration rather than a critique? Or is it simply a neutral portrait? In any case, why does she choose this form to represent it?

POSSIBLE CONNECTIONS TO OTHER SELECTIONS

E. E. Cummings, "next to of course god america i" (question #1, following)
Tato Laviera, "AmeRícan" (text p. 269)

CONNECTION QUESTION IN TEXT (p. 237) WITH ANSWER

1. Describe and compare the strategy used to create meaning in "All-American Sestina" with that used by Cummings in "next to of course god america i" (p. 146).

Both poems rely on the distance between relatively meaningless American cultural clichés and real ideas to create meaning, but the speaker of Cummings's poem builds toward a definite point. In Mayers's sestina there is little progress. The poem's meaning wouldn't change much if the stanzas were rearranged; meaning comes primarily from the building panorama of clichés. Cummings's speaker begins with hollow phrases and departs from there to try to convince his audience that the war dead performed their duties cheerfully.

EPIGRAM

SAMUEL TAYLOR COLERIDGE, *What Is an Epigram?* (p. 237)

A. R. AMMONS, *Coward* (p. 238)

DAVID McCORD, *Epitaph on a Waiter* (p. 238)

PAUL LAURENCE DUNBAR, *Theology* (p. 238)

Note how crucial the technique of word selection becomes in poems that use as few words as these. Have students write in prose the ideas conveyed in each of the first three epigrams. These summaries will probably be considerably more verbose and less witty than the poems from which they stem. Which specific words in each epigram are used to condense meanings that might normally be expressed by means of longer words or phrases?

Also consider how important titles become in the epigrams by Ammons, McCord, and Dunbar. Have the students discuss how each epigram would be different if it were presented without its title. Ammons's could be a statement of family pride. McCord's title informs the reader of his subject's occupation and his decease, whereas the poem might refer to anyone who had gone through life exceedingly preoccupied. What does McCord's poem imply about the waiter without saying it specifically? For how much of Dunbar's poem does the title "Theology" seem appropriate? Which words contribute to the serious tone implied by the title? Where does the meaning seem to shift?

Note: For a list of resources for teaching Coleridge, see manual pages 295–296.

LIMERICK

ANONYMOUS, *There was a young lady named Bright* (p. 239)

LAURENCE PERRINE, *The limerick's never averse* (p. 239)

The name "limerick" derives from a form of extemporaneous nonsense verse that always ends with the refrain, "Will you come up to Limerick?" The five-line anapestic verses we now call limericks evolved during the nineteenth century at the hands of humorous versifiers like Edward Lear (1812–1888), as well as numerous anonymous writers.

The extemporaneous nature of limericks is an indication of the ease with which they can be composed. After reviewing the examples in the book, ask the students to compose some limericks, either individually or in small groups.

In addition to overtly bawdy situations, the limerick often relies upon puns and other wordplay for its humor. "There was a young lady named Bright" plays on the term *relative* to draw attention to the possibility, implicit in certain theories of modern physics, that you can arrive in a place before you leave it. "*She Don't Bop*" plays on our familiarity with the phrase "rooty toot," related to "rootin' tootin'" as an onomatopoet-ic term indicating the sound of a trumpet, and used to mean something noisy or riotous. The joke of Laurence Perrine's "The limerick's never averse" depends upon a simple pun. You might draw students' attention to Perrine's departures from pure anapestic meter in the poem's first, fourth, and fifth lines. Do these variations in meter contribute anything to the poem?

You may wish to use a discussion of limericks to reinforce the point that anapestic meter — like the dactylic meter of "Hickory, dickory, dock" (text p. 202) — is used almost exclusively in light, humorous, or children's verse.

KEITH CASTO, *She Don't Bop* (p. 239)

HAIKU

MATSUO BASHŌ, *Under cherry trees* (p. 240)

Bashō is usually considered the greatest of the haiku poets. He was born near Kyoto, growing up as the companion of a local nobleman's son. He moved to Edo (now called Tokyo) when he was twenty-three and eventually became a recluse, living outside the city in a hut. He made several long journeys, always relying for food and shelter on the gen-erosity of local Buddhist temples and on other poets. *The Narrow Road to the Deep North*, a collection of interlocked prose and haiku chronicling one of these journeys, is perhaps his best-known work in the West.

CAROLYN KIZER, *After Basho* (p. 240)

This poem demonstrates the importance Bashō still has, in many languages, for poets who write haiku. The reference to the "famous" (3) moon indicates the writer's familiarity with the moon as a constant trope in nature poetry in general and haiku in particular. Some Bashō poems that examine the moon include these:

Felling a tree
and seeing the cut end —
tonight's moon.

Harvest moon —
walking around the pond
all night long.

Bashō himself, writing more than a thousand years before Kizer, indicated his awareness of the familiarity of the moon as trope:

It's not like anything
they compare it to —
the summer moon.

ONLINE RESOURCES (manual p. 324)

ELEGY

SEAMUS HEANEY, *Mid-term Break* (p. 241)

This elegy commemorates the death of the speaker's brother at the age of four. It is written in poignant, terse flashes of memory. It might be considered a narrative poem as well as an elegy. How does the story unfold? Do the events of the child's death matter more or less than the emotions of the speaker or the reactions of the adults around him?

The starkness of the images in this poem tells us a lot about the speaker. He observes the scenes as if from a distance, trying to control his own reactions to the tragedy. The simple details of the baby cooing and laughing (unaware of the tragedy) and the old men greeting the speaker awkwardly make the young boy's death even more somber and haunting.

The last line tells us more about the boy than we know until this point. He is four years old. Standing apart, the line suggests that the poem is another kind of vessel for the young boy's life. As the coffin holds his body, the poem remembers him long after death.

POSSIBLE CONNECTIONS TO OTHER SELECTIONS

A. E. Housman, "To an Athlete Dying Young" (question #1, following)

John Updike, "Dog's Death" (text p. 11)

CONNECTION QUESTION IN TEXT (p. 241) WITH ANSWER

1. Compare Heaney's elegy with A. E. Housman's "To an Athlete Dying Young" (text p. 614). Which do you find more moving? Explain why.

   The rhymes and regular meter in "To an Athlete Dying Young" give that poem a more formal, more public tone than the stark, conversational tone of Heaney's elegy. Heaney's little brother is not mythologized the way Housman's hero is. The athlete is an older boy who has presumably accomplished more than the young child. Heaney's poem reads as both elegy and catharsis for the speaker, whereas Housman's speaker is at some distance from the dead boy he commemorates.

AUDIOVISUAL AND ONLINE RESOURCES (manual pp. 300, 334)

ANDREW HUDGINS, *Elegy for My Father, Who Is Not Dead* (p. 242)

The speaker of this poem, unlike his father who is "ready" (line 2) to die, is not convinced "about the world beyond this world" (4). His father seems ready to die, happy "in the sureness of his faith" (3) that his journey into the afterlife will be like a vacation to a place where he will wait for his son to join him. The speaker is skeptical; he "can't / just say good-bye as cheerfully / as if he were embarking on a trip" (14–16). The difference in their attitudes is represented in terms of a ship; the speaker is convinced only that his father's "ship's gone down" (19) while the father is convinced that he will eventually wave and shout "welcome back" (21) to his son when his son's time comes.

The poem raises a crucial question: will the son adopt his father's attitude when he himself is closer to death, or is he simply more skeptical than his father? Both options are raised; the speaker acknowledges, "He's ready. I am not" (14), but he also says "I do not think he's right" (13). Does our attitude toward death change as we get older because we have accepted our mortality, or is belief in the afterlife a defense mechanism? This question is central to the poem's interpretation, as is the speaker's focus: is he more concerned about his father's death or his own? The poem is rather self-involved for an "elegy." Is the poet playing with two senses of the term "elegy" — a poem of mourning and a meditation on death?

POSSIBLE CONNECTIONS TO OTHER SELECTIONS

Donald Hall, "Letter with No Address" (text p. 673)

Dylan Thomas, "Do not go gentle into that good night" (question #1, following)

1. Write an essay comparing attitudes toward death in this poem and in Thomas's "Do not go gentle into that good night" (p. 233). Both speakers invoke their fathers, nearer death than they are: what impact does this have?

   Thomas's "Do not go gentle into that good night" brings the speaker and his father into direct contact, which is a good starting point for contrasting these two poems. Would the speaker of Hudgins's poem express his sentiments differently if he were speaking to his father? Is there any trace of doubt or cynicism apparent in Thomas's speaker?

ODE

PERCY BYSSHE SHELLEY, *Ode to the West Wind* (p. 243)

Percy Bysshe Shelley was born to wealth in Horsham, Sussex. Educated in conventional privileges, he was taunted by his schoolmates for his unconventionality and lack of physical prowess. His rebellion against this environment helped make him both a nonconformist and a democrat. He was expelled from Oxford in 1811 for coauthoring a pamphlet called *The Necessity of Atheism.* He eventually married Mary Wollstonecraft Godwin and in 1818 settled in Italy, where he wrote his most highly regarded work, including "Prometheus Unbound" and "Ode to the West Wind." Shelley drowned while sailing with a friend, and his ashes were buried in a cemetery in Rome near the graves of his son, William Shelley, and John Keats.

The west wind in England is hailed as the harbinger of spring. As an introduction to this ode, you might have the students read the anonymous "Western Wind" (text p. 26).

The tercets and couplets that form each section of this ode should pose no problems; basically, the tercets interweave (*aba, bcb, cdc, ded, ee*). Since Shelley is describing wind, the ethereal element, it is appropriate that the sounds of the couplet (*ee*), which appear at the end of every twelfth line in the first three sections, should have an airy, wind-rushed quality, as in "hear," "atmosphere," "fear."

The first three sections describe the powers the wind has in nature – on land in autumn, in the clouds in "the dying year" (winter), and on the bay (a mixture of land and sea) in the summer. When Shelley turns to his own problems, including his sense of despair and his need for inspiration (sections IV and V), the rhyme of the couplet (*ee*) is changed and a more mournful, weighted sound ("bowed," "proud") is substituted. The rhyme scheme almost makes the poem generalize in the final section, when "Wind" and the promises of spring are bestowed upon "mankind."

For a close reading of this ode, see S. C. Wilcox's, "Imagery, Ideas, and Design in Shelley's 'Ode to the West Wind,' " *Studies in Philosophy* 47 (October 1950): 634–649.

As a three-page writing assignment, ask students to analyze the symbolic meaning of the west wind.

POSSIBLE CONNECTIONS TO OTHER SELECTIONS

Sophie Cabot Black, "August" (text p. 125)
Henry Wadsworth Longfellow, "Snow-Flakes" (text p. 622)

AUDIOVISUAL AND ONLINE RESOURCES (manual pp. 307, 350)

PICTURE POEM

MICHAEL McFEE, *In Medias Res* (p. 245)

Students will probably have fun identifying the puns in this portly poem. A handful for consideration: "His waist / like the plot / thickens" (lines 1–3) — just as in a murder mystery, his increasing girth is out to get him, as the darker tone of the second half of this poem implies. "Wedding / pants" (3–4) — do we read this as the pants from the suit he wore at his wedding, no doubt a smaller size, or as the waist "wedding," or uniting, with the waistband of the pants? "Breathtaking" (4) no longer means spellbinding but rather a kind of choking. The "cinch" (5) can be read either as a girth or belt, or a snap, an easy thing to do.

ONLINE RESOURCES (manual p. 342)

PARODY

PETER DE VRIES, *To His Importunate Mistress* (p. 246)

Money is at the root of the distress in this work. In contrast, Marvell's main complaint was lack of time (text p. 65). "Picaresque" (line 7) is used in the sense of "our roguish affair." De Vries imitates Marvell's idiom quite closely. He picks up on the middle to high level of diction, the long sentences with verbs separated from their objects, and Marvell's rather Latinate style with the verbs coming at the ends of the sentences.

POSSIBLE CONNECTION TO ANOTHER SELECTION

Anthony Hecht, "The Dover Bitch" (question #1, following)

CONNECTION QUESTION IN TEXT (p. 247) WITH ANSWER

1. Read Anthony Hecht's "The Dover Bitch" (p. 609), a parody of Arnold's "Dover Beach" (p. 95). Write an essay comparing the effectiveness of Hecht's parody with that of De Vries's "To His Importunate Mistress." Which parody do you prefer? Explain why.

   The parodies have different aims: Hecht's parody goes at Arnold's poem directly, faulting the speaker for his effete lack of attunement to his lover's sexual desires, whereas De Vries's parody satirizes our culture, which seems to demand that we spend our time making money, not making love. De Vries's parody is also closer to the original in terms of its tone. Hecht's parody is more colloquial than the original, countering Arnold's measured lines with phrases like "etc. etc." (line 5) and "Anyway" (20). Students should articulate what makes a parody effective rather than simply stating their preference for one or the other.

X. J. KENNEDY, *A Visit from St. Sigmund* (p. 247)

You might begin a discussion of "A Visit from St. Sigmund" by brainstorming in class about what students already know about Freud. Many students will undoubtedly have some prior knowledge of psychoanalytic theory, and because Freudian psychology has become part of our cultural literacy, even students with minimal knowledge of Freud's theories can enjoy this parody of Moore's "A Visit from St. Nicholas." Kennedy's tone in this poem is humorously satirical; at every opportunity he gives psychoanalysis a jab as he plays with the central tenets of Freud's theories. Mead's opening quotation provides Kennedy with a springboard into the poem. Her comparison between Santa and Freud is appropriate since both have become cultural icons — paternal figures concerned with the behavior (both good and bad) of girls and boys.

You might have students identify specific passages from the poem where the poet uses humor to gently poke fun at psychoanalytic humor. Responses might include the substitution of Freud's "baggage" (hangups, psychoses, a couch, symbols, subliminal meanings, the unconscious, phallic jokes) for the "baggage" of St. Nicholas in the original poem (stockings, reindeer, a sack, a sleigh, a jolly laugh, and so on).

You may want to read the original poem in conjunction with the parody to show how the poet manipulates Moore's famous poem. Students will see that Kennedy merely uses the original poem as the scaffold for "A Visit from St. Sigmund." The real joke here is on Freud, and the Christmas references simply add depth and richness to the humor Kennedy employs.

POSSIBLE CONNECTION TO ANOTHER SELECTION

Blanche Farley, "The Lover Not Taken" (text p. 365)

PERSPECTIVE

ROBERT MORGAN, *On the Shape of a Poem* (p. 249)

Students might enjoy analyzing Morgan's own "Mountain Graveyard" (text p. 24) in light of his idea that "all language is both mental and sacramental, is not 'real' but is the working of lip and tongue to subvert the 'real.' " How does his anagrammatic, spare prose "subvert the 'real' "?

Elizabeth Bishop's "Sestina" in this chapter (text p. 235) or Dylan Thomas's villanelle "Do not go gentle into that good night" (text p. 233) are good examples to use when discussing Morgan's statement that "poems empearl irritating facts until they become opalescent spheres of moment, not so much résumés of history as of human faculties working with pain."

Ask students to think about form in other aspects of their lives — the formal behavior at a funeral, for example, as a way of dealing with painful emotion.

ELAINE MITCHELL, *Form* (p. 249)

By comparing form to a corset, Mitchell develops the idea that there is a time and a place to use form in poetry and a time and a place not to use it. Ask students to identify in the poem the various moments when the poet suggests that form can be helpful. Responses might include that it can "shape and deceive" (line 5), "It / 's an ace up your sleeve" (7–8), "it / might be a resource" (12–13), or "your grateful slave" (14). Then ask them to identify places where the poet warns that form can prove too confining, such as "Don't try to force it" (3), "Ouch, too tight a corset" (6), "No need to force it" (9), and "sometimes divorce it" (16). Ultimately, Mitchell seems to be suggesting that poets need to recognize when form works to their advantage and when it is forced. When form is forced, poets need to be willing to abandon it rather than continue to impose form where it doesn't work.

By adhering to poetic form herself (three-line stanzas — except the final stanza — constructed with an *aba* rhyme scheme throughout) the poet forces her own poem to conform to the restrictions of form she's set up. Indeed, she creates a very controlled rhythm (dactylic dimeter) and rhyme scheme to provide the poem with structure. Some students may recognize that, ironically, Mitchell forces words together and pulls them apart in totally outrageous ways in order to maintain the form she's established. Ask students to consider whether this effect is intentional.

10

Open Form

Whereas traditional forms depend on the interplay of the poet's current speech and an established form, open form hinges on the poet's (and the reader's) ability to discover a form that works toward the overall effect the poet wishes to produce. Just as in the previous chapter, each of the poems here can form the basis of a rewarding discussion about how form relates to content. With open form, the poet theoretically has absolute control over the form chosen, although some may choose a fairly constraining pattern to guide the poem — witness Peter Meinke's "ABC of Aerobics." As a result of this freedom, the poem must actually withstand closer and more critical reading, as each formal choice takes on greater significance.

Poems like E. E. Cummings's "in Just-" obviously foreground the layout of the poem on the page as a formal technique. In fact, some of Cummings's poems cannot to be read aloud because of their formal experimentation. Cummings's poems, like those of William Carlos Williams, tend toward spareness and intense focus on the medium of language. By contrast, a poet like Whitman uses repetition, catalog, and long rhythmic units to create a sense of plenitude and richness, a spilling over of language onto the page.

For some students, a poem like Galway Kinnell's "After Making Love We Hear Footsteps" may seem to be formless. This results from Kinnell's "plain speech" style and the seeming randomness of the line breaks. You may find it productive to push students to examine the breaks and rhythms in the poem more closely. The breaks serve to create units of meaning and to insert very slight pauses in the reading, which help create rhythms that add to the overall mood of the poem. You might ask students why Kinnell chooses to put a stanza break between lines 18 and 19. Why not run the whole poem together? In both traditional and open forms, stanza breaks create a pause in which ideas can shift, focuses can change, or previous statements can be reassessed. Line breaks can do this on a much smaller scale. In either event, the white space on the page can be as telling as what is said in words.

Similarly, the absence of regular metrics or stanzas does not mean the absence of structure. Tato Laviera's "AmeRícan" demonstrates a use of repetition that is reminiscent of Whitman and serves to create a similar sense of flow and plenitude.

As an exercise, you might have your students experiment with line breaks by taking a poem from the book and redoing the breaks. They might then give that poem to another student and have that student evaluate the new poem, asking themselves "Has the meaning of the poem (or parts of the poem) changed?" This exercise may help to emphasize felicitous or infelicitous choices in poetic structure. A related exercise might have students create found poems by taking a piece of prose and inserting line breaks. Students could again evaluate the results, looking for meanings that have been altered or significances that have been added by the change in form.

E. E. CUMMINGS, *in Just-* (p. 251)

Exactly how poems operate as a graphic medium on our visual sense is not well understood by critics. The open-endedness of the question provides a good occasion for students to make their own guesses. Notice, for example, that the most important thematic word in this poem, *spring,* either is set off from the line (as in line 2) or appears by itself, as in lines 9 and 18. In fact, the placement of *spring* at approximately the beginning, middle, and end of the poem is almost an organizational motif. Another repeated phrase, "whistles far and wee," also is placed first on one line (5) with "whistles" later receiving separational emphasis, over two lines (12 and 13), with "far and wee" receiving space — like long pulses on the whistle — and, at the close of the poem, on separate lines, as though the sound of the whistle were still present but moving away.

The whistle is, of course, united with spring as a modern rendition of Pan's pipes drawing Persephone from the underworld and awakening the calls of birds and the sounds of wildlife. In response to the "goat-footed" (Pan) balloon man's pipes, "bettyand-isbel" come running — the elision of their names mimicking the pronunciation, the swift movement, even the perception patterns of children.

Many other word patterns offer themselves for discussion in this poem. These comments are only a beginning, and an enthusiastic class can discover much more.

POSSIBLE CONNECTION TO ANOTHER SELECTION

Robert Frost, "The Pasture" (text p. 340)

WALT WHITMAN, From *I Sing the Body Electric* (p. 252)

Whitman's outpouring is an homage to the body, the soul, and poetry all at once. In a word, Whitman offers here an anatomy of wonder.

The rhythm of this portion of the poem is striking. Notice how many of the lines begin with a trochee or a spondee. The initial heavy stresses lend a kind of relentless thoroughness to Whitman's catalog of the human body. You might have the class scan a portion of the poem, say from line 25 to line 30. The lines change from heavily accented to a lighter, roughly iambic rhythm that suggests "the continual changes of the flex of the mouth."

The chief difficulty is, of course, discerning the exact relationship between these things. We tend to think of them as separate from each other. Does Whitman's poem help us to unify them in our minds? The poem lists a number of body parts: do any of them tend to stand out or to form any sort of unexpected patterns?

POSSIBLE CONNECTION TO ANOTHER SELECTION

Jane Hirschfield, "The Lives of the Heart" (text p. 676)

PERSPECTIVE

WALT WHITMAN, *On Rhyme and Meter* (p. 253)

In addition to assigning Consideration 3 as a writing topic, you might ask students to write a few paragraphs about Whitman's use of catalogs or lists as an element of the organic form he espouses. The excerpt from *I Sing the Body Electric* (text p. 252) is especially useful for this exercise. Why is Whitman's tactic of listing appropriate to his subject?

JAY MEEK, *Swimmers* (p. 254)

This prose poem creates a series of images to describe the distance the speaker feels in his or her associations with other people. The "some-thing" (lines 1–2) the speaker describes, like "light" (3), "like grease" (5), is a "film over our / lives" (6–7). This film "is slippery" (6) and prevents real contact between people, making it seem "as if / nothing has happened" (7–8). The theme is a mysterious, sourceless distance, which "doesn't go away" (4). Some of the poetic images resonate with this mystery: the "some-thing" (1–2) is described in terms of what it is not: "not sensual, not exciting" (6). The film described is over "clothing" (2) and "hands" (2), but it quickly grows to cover "our / lives" (6–7). You may want to ask your students to discuss the ways in which the speaker's feeling of alienation is a shared human experience.

One effect of the prosy appearance of this poem is to underline the mystery of the shadowy theme by presenting it not in lines but in what appears to be a straightforward paragraph. Very little about this poem is straightforward, however; the contrast between what is expected of a paragraph and what is barely contained in these lines creates a tension of strange images and prosaic form that establishes the work as poetic.

POSSIBLE CONNECTIONS TO OTHER SELECTIONS

Sharon Olds, "Sex without Love" (p. 76)
Robert Hass, "A Story about the Body" (p. 264)

GALWAY KINNELL, *After Making Love We Hear Footsteps* (p. 255)

Kinnell's poetry is known for its directness, precision, and carefully controlled idiom. In his *Book of Nightmares,* from which this poem is taken, he explores the difficult project of explaining human mortality to our children. Love is his answer in many of the poems, but it requires confronting physical as well as emotional issues.

This is a popular poem with students because it vividly presents a scene that is familiar to many of them. Ask them to describe the speaker. What does his language tell us about his character?

In an essay, you might ask students to explore the poem's auditory appeal. How do the various sounds create a mood for the speaker's discussion of his relationship to his child and his wife?

POSSIBLE CONNECTIONS TO OTHER SELECTIONS

Robert Frost, "Home Burial" (question #1, following)
Peter Meinke, "The ABC of Aerobics" (text p. 270)

CONNECTION QUESTION IN TEXT (p. 256) WITH ANSWER

1. Discuss how this poem helps to bring into focus the sense of loss Frost evokes in "Home Burial" (p. 343).

   In concrete images such as the baseball pajamas and the expression "loving and snuggling," Kinnell's speaker establishes a sense of what his child is like. The boy's presence fills the poem as it fills the space between the speaker and his wife. Frost's poem explores what it would be like to have this space suddenly emptied, how he would talk to his wife about their loss, how it would affect their relationship. Frost's speaker's relationship to his wife is painfully awkward, just the opposite of Kinnell's. As Kinnell's poem overflows with affection and love, Frost's echoes in emptiness, silence, grief, and loss.

KELLY CHERRY, *Alzheimer's* (p. 256)

This narrative poem illustrates the personal and emotional resonance within the clinical name of the title. The story centers on the moment at which the "crazy old man" (line 1) returns from the hospital and stands at his doorstep. What he remembers, from the far past, and what he doesn't recall, including the identity of his wife, establishes the scattered reality he is able to construct. Seeing the house triggers memories, but he is uncertain who the "white-haired woman" (27) is who greets him.

The man is characterized through careful examinations of everything he touches: the contents of his suitcase and the vision of the house he remembers "as his" (15) both paint a portrait of this nameless man's identity. The flowers around the house "slug it out for space, claw the mortar" (7), presenting a violent desperation not usually associated with "Roses and columbine" (7). The sun doesn't simply shine on the house, it "hardens the house, reifies it" (10): the scrappy verbs used to shape the reader's perception reflect on the "crazy old man" (1) as well. This dismissive label, a stereotype of someone with Alzheimer's, is undermined by the rich details associated with the house, the suitcase, and his memories of being younger. This detail, and the obsessive repetition and confusion surrounding his inability to recognize the "white-haired woman" (27), develop a character far richer than "Alzheimer's" or "crazy old man" indicates.

Your students may benefit from some discussion of the different ways in which this man is characterized: How could they employ a detailed description of a thing to describe a person? Ask students to write descriptions of a grandmother's purse, a sister's toolbox, a father's car, a friend's bookshelf: how do details of these objects help construct three-dimensional portraits of their owners?

POSSIBLE CONNECTIONS TO OTHER SELECTIONS

Sarah Lindsay, "Aluminum Chlorohydrate" (question #1, following)
Sharon Olds, "Poem for the Breasts" (p. 127)
Anne Bradstreet, "The Author to Her Book" (p. 117)

CONNECTION QUESTION IN TEXT (p. 257) WITH ANSWER

1. Compare the treatment of remembering and forgetting in "Alzheimer's" and in Sarah Lindsay's "Aluminum Chlorohydrate" (p. 63). How does the final image of an old woman in each poem affect your understanding of the poem's thematics?

   The terror of the "old unfamiliar woman's face" (line 25) in the mirror in Lindsay's poem is in contrast with the gentle task of deciding "who / This woman is, this old, white haired woman" (26–27) at the end of Cherry's poem. The inability to recognize the self is imagined, in "Aluminum Chlorohydrate," as a terrible future for the speaker, while the speaker's inability to recognize his wife at the end of "Alzheimer's" provides very little threat; she is, after all, "welcoming" (29). While Lindsay's poem presents a horror story of an envisioned future, Cherry's poem examines a more mundane aspect of the same illness.

ONLINE RESOURCES (manual p. 327)

WILLIAM CARLOS WILLIAMS, *The Red Wheelbarrow* (p. 257)

This poem has a syllabically structured form, like a haiku, of four and two, three and two, three and two, and four and two syllables in each couplet. Also like a haiku, this poem is imagistic and suggestive rather than directly representational. Each couplet contains two stresses in its first line and one in its second.

X. J. Kennedy, in a footnote to the poem that appears in his *Introduction to Poetry,* Sixth Edition, notes that according to a librarian's account, Williams was "gazing from the window of the house where one of his patients, a small girl, lay suspended between life and death" (Boston: Little, 1986, p. 32). This information does enrich the first phrase, "so much depends," which seems to speak of a sympathetic vitality exchanged between ourselves and the objects of our landscape. Without this biographical detail, the poem is usually described as an example of Imagism, in which the image is made to speak for itself.

Does the poem "improve" with the librarian's recollection? This question might be taken up in a writing assignment.

TIP FROM THE FIELD

To help students see the value in pure imagery, try connecting and comparing the importance of images in poetry to those in visual art. Students are often biased by their expectation that poems must have deep meanings. Conversely, they expect art to simply present them with something pleasing to look at and are intimidated if visual art expresses deep meaning. You might discuss the Imagism movement, in which poets embraced the use of imagery alone to convey a poem's emotion and message, and then show slides of modern art in which the image is everything (i.e., Charles Demuth's "I Saw the Figure 5 in Gold" or anything by Andy Warhol). Then have your students write their own version of a poem like William Carlos Williams's "The Red Wheelbarrow" purely for the enjoyment of their own images.

— ROBIN CALITRI, *Merced College*

POSSIBLE CONNECTION TO ANOTHER SELECTION

William Carlos Williams, "Poem" (text p. 90)

KATE RUSHIN, *The Black Back-Ups* (p. 257)

This poem catalogs stereotypes — including those endured by the women in the speaker's family, "Aunt Jemima on the Pancake Box" (77), and Lou Reed's "colored girls" (11) — of black women. Rushin examines the ways in which black women have been "Back-Ups" not only in American music but as housekeepers, "who listened and understood" (50), who care for the speaker, wipe her forehead, and make her "a cup of tea" (91). The poem examines the fact that these women, of primary importance, have been relegated to "Back-Up" status.

Rushin mirrors this phenomenon in her own poem: the experiences of the women named in the first stanza frequently take a back seat to the speaker's own "real pain" (92). The families who hired the speaker's family members as domestic helpers got new clothes and whole days with the women she loves. The speaker presents her side of the story, the effects of living with women who were depended upon elsewhere, in her resentment of the "Perfectly Good Clothes" in lines 35–43.

The poem takes much of its rhythm and form from popular music, including frequent repetition of the chorus from Lou Reed's "Take a Walk on the Wild Side." This repetition, and the long list of names and examples Rushin provides, indicate the persistence of the injustice she describes.

POSSIBLE CONNECTIONS TO OTHER SELECTIONS

Patricia Smith, "What It's Like to Be a Black Girl" (For Those of You Who Aren't) (text p. 104)

Walt Whitman, From "I Sing the Body Electric" (question #1, following)

CONNECTION QUESTION IN TEXT (p. 260) WITH ANSWER

1. Compare Rushin's strategy for creating lists in this poem with Walt Whitman's in the excerpt from "I Sing the Body Electric" (p. 252). How do you respond to the lists in each poem?

   Students will have different responses to the lists in each poem, perhaps preferring the broad sweeps of Whitman's universalist rhetoric or the personal tabulations Rushin makes in her analysis of ways black women back others up.

JONATHAN HOLDEN, *Cutting Loose on an August Night* (p. 260)

The single sentence of this poem illustrates the freedom of driving at night and the importance of speed. The rush of language presents a breathless litany, imitating in form the fast-driving content of the poem. Depictions of speed include the "packed earth / being unpacked and shredded / up with speed" (lines 6–8) and "you" "weightless / in the thick of speed" (31–32). Speed is flexible here, able to be both a violent actor and a static fluid that suspends you, all at once. Speed is also conveyed through the rapid shifts between subjects: the poem moves from fields to "bug-spattered windshield" (10) to sports and weather on the radio to the conclusion, the "you" of the poem "fixed firmly" (26) at the center of the drive.

The title provides an external view of the events unfolding in this poem, but the poem itself provides a rich parsing of the stream of consciousness, the view from the inside that propels the "August Night" forward. Asking students to focus on the ways in which speed is conveyed in this poem could help them direct a discussion toward the effects of that speed: Why is speed important to us? What does it provide? The speaker of this poem uses the second-person perspective to draw the reader in, to demonstrate that we share a need for speed, a desire to cut loose "and keep it / floored" (2–3). A discussion of the ways speed effects us, coupled with an examination of the ways speed is presented in this poem, could provide for a lively discussion.

POSSIBLE CONNECTIONS TO OTHER SELECTIONS

Sophie Cabot Black, "August" (text p. 125)
Thomas Lynch, "Liberty" (question #1, following)

CONNECTION QUESTION IN TEXT (p. 261) WITH ANSWER

1. Compare the sense of freedom expressed in this poem with that offered by Thomas Lynch in "Liberty" (p. 132). What significant similarities and differences do you find in the poems' themes and the manner in which they are presented?

   The speaker in Lynch's poem cites tradition as his defense for his rebellion against society; Holden's speaker uses the contemporary symbol of the car as a means of escape. While both poems examine the urge to step outside the confines of our normal lives, Holden's poem, in its imagery and use of the second-person perspective, reaches for communion with the reader and a shared love of the open road.

MARILYN NELSON WANIEK, *Emily Dickinson's Defunct* (p. 261)

You might begin discussion of this poem by asking what associations students have with Emily Dickinson. For some background information, it might be interesting to read the text's introduction to Dickinson on page 289 and the Perspectives by Dickinson, Higginson, and Todd that follow the collection of Dickinson's poems on pages 313–315. Dickinson is thought to have been somewhat of a recluse, a woman isolated in her home and in her room, writing her life away in solitude and silence.

Waniek's poem presents a Dickinson that is radically different; this Dickinson is a tough woman, earthy, and bold. Ask students to provide specific examples from the poem that redefine Dickinson in this light. Responses might include references to Dickinson being "dressed for action" (7), smelling human (12), and being a "two-fisted woman" (25). In this way, Waniek's poem effectively revises (or at least plays with) the image of Dickinson we've become accustomed to, imagining that underneath her reclusive exterior and "gray old lady / clothes" (5–6) there was a wilder and more adventuresome woman — an idea that is borne out in Dickinson's poetry.

The title of Waniek's poem functions in several ways, and it may be interesting to ask students to discuss or write briefly about the title. *Defunct* means extinct, or no longer living. Having died in 1886, Emily Dickinson is of course literally defunct. But the title may also suggest that the Emily Dickinson we've known in the past is defunct, for a revised image of the New England poet is being suggested by the poem.

After studying the poem, you may wish to ask students to read some Dickinson poems in order to identify connections between Dickinson's poems and the allusions contained in Waniek's poem.

POSSIBLE CONNECTIONS TO OTHER SELECTIONS

E. E. Cummings, "Buffalo Bill 's" (question #1, following)
Emily Dickinson, "I heard a Fly buzz — when I died —" (question #1, following)

CONNECTION QUESTION IN TEXT (p. 262) WITH ANSWER

1. Waniek alludes to at least two other poems in "Emily Dickinson's Defunct." The title refers to E. E. Cummings's "Buffalo Bill 's" (p. 602) and the final lines (27–30) refer to "I heard a Fly buzz — when I died — " (p. 307). Read those poems and write an essay discussing how they affect your reading of Waniek's poem.

    All three poems take on the topic of death, and on the surface all three seem to equate being dead with being "defunct," as the titles of Waniek's and Cummings's poem indicate and as the final line of Dickinson's poem emphasizes: "I could not see to see — ." Yet there is the sense that death is not final, that it does not render us "defunct." Waniek's and Cummings's poems celebrate the vitality of their subjects after their deaths, and Dickinson's poem posits a life after death, even after the speaker loses her sight in the final line. Death is staved off through the lack of decisive end punctuation in Cummings's and Dickinson's poems, and the buzzing of the flies in Waniek's poem suggests an ongoing celebration of the life of this poet.

JEFFREY HARRISON, *Horseshoe Contest* (p. 262)

This narrative poem paints a portrait of a Fourth of July observance, complete with all the requisite images of a small town celebration. The "parade / of tractors and fire trucks" (lines 1–2) and the "cakewalk and hayrides" (6) place the reader at the scene to watch, with Harrison, the "old guys" (19), high stakes, and graceful movements of the contest of the title. The tournament is important to the players because their skill in this field defines them as "their whole idea / of who they are" (25–26). The tournament also enables them to reclaim the glory the participants experienced during their youth while competing in high school athletics.

The speaker stays to the sidelines during the development of this comfortable scene. It is only at the end that the first person "I" is used, a development that establishes a totally new tone for the whole of the poem. The importance of the grace these "heroes, / becoming young again" (54–55) exhibit is not fully realized until the speaker admits that this expertise, in any field or endeavor, is worth "almost anything" (68).

Students may be struck by the prosiness of this narrative. This might be a good time to work together on defining, as a class, what makes something poetry. Who gets to determine what's poetry and what isn't? Are Harrison's line breaks and imagery sufficient to make this a poem, rather than a story broken into lines? Is this a poem because Harrison says so? Is Bruce Springsteen's "Streets of Philadelphia" (text p. 32) a poem? Is Robert Hass's "A Story about the Body" (text p. 264) a poem? Is something a poem because it appears in a poetry textbook? Opening class discussion so students can define poetry for themselves may help make poetry less threatening and more enjoyable.

POSSIBLE CONNECTIONS TO OTHER SELECTIONS

David Barber, "A Colonial Epitaph Annotated" (text p. 220)

Edward Hirsch, "Fast Break" (question #1, following)

CONNECTION QUESTION IN TEXT (p. 264) WITH ANSWER

1. Consider the contest described by Harrison along with Edward Hirsch's "Fast Break" (p. 219). What similarities and differences are there in the theme?

   While paying tribute to the participants, both Harrison and Hirsch describe moments of athletic accomplishment and importance. For Harrison, the context of this moment — men reaching back to ideas held "since high school" (line 27) and cherished in adulthood "as dairymen and farmers" (62) — is central to the theme of the poem. Hirsch's poem is focused more on the actual movement, the event, the game itself, the grace of the players, and a sharp description of their movements. While Harrison's poem describes explicitly the meaning this moment has for those present, Hirsch's poem presents the moment and allows its importance to the players and the speaker to remain implicit.

ONLINE RESOURCES (manual p. 334)

ROBERT HASS, *A Story about the Body* (p. 264)

This prose poem turns on a relationship that fails before it starts. A young man, a composer, decides not to act on his interest in an older woman, a painter, when he discovers that both her breasts have been removed. The conclusion of this poem provides a powerful metaphor: a bowl of dead bees covered with rose petals. It's a rich symbol, mingling the potential of bee stings, the impotence of dead bees, and the delicate beauty of rose petals.

Students may disagree on what this bowl symbolizes: the painter's unseen physical flaws? The superficial nature of the composer's attraction to the painter? Discussing the possibilities could create some interesting tension in your class. Students are likely to see one reading immediately. To initiate discussion, you might want to ask them to write down what they think the petal-covered bowl of bees describes, and then ask them to compare their answers for an enlightening discussion of the power of metaphor.

POSSIBLE CONNECTIONS TO OTHER SELECTIONS

Walt Whitman, From *I Sing the Body Electric* (text p. 252)

Jay Meek, "Swimmers" (text p. 254)

AUDIOVISUAL AND ONLINE RESOURCES (manual pp. 300, 334)

SHARON OLDS, *Rite of Passage* (p. 265)

Olds's work is often focused on gender distinctions and characteristics. In "Rite of Passage," Olds emphasizes the highly masculine qualities inherent in males of any age.

The title refers not only to the birthday party — a ritual by which we celebrate milestones in the maturation process — but also the boys' transition from child to adult behavior. Even six- and seven-year-olds demonstrate adult male characteristics: "Hands in pockets, they stand around / jostling, jockeying for place, small fights / breaking out and calming" (lines 5–7). They also emulate adult male behavior by comparing themselves to each other and by valuing power, force, assertiveness: "They eye each other, seeing themselves / tiny in the other's pupils. They clear their / throats a lot, a room of small bankers, / they fold their arms and frown" (9–12). The final lines, in which "they clear their throats / like Generals, they relax and get down to / playing war" (24–26), provide an overt context for much of the preceding covert activity. Socializing is akin to war: at this party, even the cake — "round and heavy as a / turret" (14–15) — is evocative of combat.

The power in Olds's poem lies in her insistence in the final lines, where the birthday boy assures his guests, *"We could easily kill a two-year-old"* (22), that this transition occurs much earlier than we might commonly expect. The "clear voice" of this child contrasts sharply with the thoughts he expresses, indicating dissonance between the image of a child and the reality of that image. Ultimately, the "rite of passage" refers less to the son's celebrating a birthday than to our own recognition that these children contain and manifest even at this early age the energy and the desire for brutality.

POSSIBLE CONNECTIONS TO OTHER SELECTIONS

Wilfred Owen, "Dulce et Decorum Est" (question #2, following)
Gary Soto, "Behind Grandma's House" (text p. 167)

CONNECTION QUESTION IN TEXT (p. 267) WITH ANSWER

1. Discuss the use of irony in "Rite of Passage" and Owen's "Dulce et Decorum Est" (p. 102). Which do you think is a more effective antiwar poem? Explain why.

    In both cases, young boys participate in warfare, somewhat unwillingly at first. The images of actual warfare and death in Owen's poem are likely to make it the popular choice for a more effective antiwar poem. Students are likely to see Olds's poem as nothing more than a birthday party, which is its central irony. The boys at the birthday party might turn into bankers rather than soldiers, so the critique of war is somewhat dispersed.

AUDIOVISUAL AND ONLINE RESOURCES (manual pp. 305, 345)

JULIO MARZÁN, *The Translator at the Reception for Latin American Writers* (p. 266)

This poem examines the sudden end of a conversation: Once the origins of the speaker are known, the new acquaintance loses interest. The imaginative center of the poem is the comparison of the acquaintance to a director. The speaker imagines the man is disappointed in the "lurid script" (line 19) he sees as the only possible potential for "Puerto Rico and the Bronx" (5). Marzán assumes that readers will recognize the separation between the mundane nature of domestic issues — "dreary streets" (21), "pathetic human interest" (22) — summoned by mention of "Puerto Rico and the Bronx" (1) and the exotic "Mayan pyramid grandeur" (14) associated with other Latin American locales.

The setting helps establish this tension: the reception is "high culture" (23), while "Puerto Rico and the Bronx" (5) represent areas with few economic advantages. This friction sees its result in the abrupt ending of the conversation as the acquaintance seeks other company. The speaker's tone remains amused and detached, however, demonstrating the real separation: readers would likely choose the company of the speaker over the rude, unimaginative man who prefers cheese.

POSSIBLE CONNECTIONS TO OTHER SELECTIONS

Mark Halliday, "Graded Paper" (text p. 443)

Tato Laviera, "AmeRícan" (text p. 269)

Wyatt Prunty, "Elderly Lady Crossing on Green" (text p. 39)

CAROLYNN HOY, *In the Summer Kitchen* (p. 267)

The simple details of this poem offer a vivid impression of a poignant moment that the speaker experiences while doing the wash with her grandmother. Though only the briefest mention is made of the infant Harry's death, the depth of her grandmother's loss is made evident to the granddaughter. This moment provides an intimate emotional context for the spearing, "churning and scooping" that goes on in the first stanza. The speaker takes in the significance of the grandmother's loss as quickly as the grandmother turns away from it to continue with the wash. Apparently the speaker knows enough about her grandmother and her grandmother knows enough about grief so that each refuses to dwell on the loss. Instead, the granddaughter takes her grandmother's cue to snap to the attention required by the immediate moment of doing the laundry — and by life itself. Even so, "as straight and squared" as the grandmother launders the moment, something does pass "from her hand to mine" in addition to the wash. The speaker understands the intense self-control of her grandmother and recognizes "The dignity of it all," a dignity that is passed on in the speaker's tribute to her grandmother in the form of a tightly controlled poem that might serve as the epitaph for her "chiseled headstone." Students who read carefully will find the diction and images in this poem perfectly aligned with its meanings.

POSSIBLE CONNECTION TO ANOTHER SELECTION

Emily Dickinson, "The Bustle in a House" (question #1, following)

CONNECTION QUESTION IN TEXT (p. 267) WITH ANSWER

1. Compare the tone of this poem with that of Emily Dickinson's "The Bustle in a House" (p. 312).

    Both poems are characterized by silence and solemnity. The "bustle" in each case takes a back seat to the silence with which it is undertaken. The poets achieve this effect in different ways, though: Hoy builds toward the sharp, spare language of the final two stanzas, whereas Dickinson's form is evenly eerie throughout her short poem.

ALLEN GINSBERG, *First Party at Ken Kesey's with Hell's Angels* (p. 267)

This poem describes a disorderly if not chaotic late-night party scene and concludes with the image of four police cars arriving on the scene, presumably to put an end to the revelry. Students will most likely be familiar with the type of scene Ginsberg describes, and a few will probably be familiar with both Kesey and Ginsberg, counterculture icons of the '50s and '60s. As with many "Beat" poems, this one demands to be read aloud, allowing the lines to create their own rhythm in conjunction with one's breathing, like an improvised riff on a saxophone. Would a poem like this one have a different effect if it were written in a stricter poetic form?

"Hell's Angels" in the title helps to set the scene and tone for this poem. You may want to begin discussion by asking students whether they would find this scene inviting. Though the party is with the notorious motorcycle gang, Ginsberg paints a fairly bucolic scene by using words like "cool" (line 1), "shade" (2), and "stars dim" (3), for example. It isn't until "blast" in line 8 that the speaker introduces any rowdiness. With this setup, what effect do the "red lights" of the police cars have, "revolving in the leaves" (19)? Is the image threatening? Or do the police cars fit in as another part of the scene? Are there "good guys" or "bad guys" in this police intervention?

POSSIBLE CONNECTION TO ANOTHER SELECTION

William Hathaway, "Oh, Oh" (question #1, following)

CONNECTION QUESTION IN TEXT (p. 268) WITH ANSWER

1. Write an essay that compares the impact of this poem's ending with that of Hathaway's "Oh, Oh" (p. 13).

   A comparison between this poem and Hathaway's "Oh, Oh" is especially interesting because Hell's Angels are the source of anxiety in "Oh, Oh," but the police are that source of anxiety in "First Party . . ." Furthermore, Hell's Angels are good guys, or at least neutral figures, in Ginsberg's poem. Yet students might not interpret the police as altogether negative in Ginsberg's poem. Are they simply part of the tableau he creates?

AUDIOVISUAL AND ONLINE RESOURCES (manual pp. 299, 332)

ANONYMOUS, *The Frog* (p. 268)

Although a number of violations of grammatical rules appear in this poem, such as lack of agreement between subject and verb: "bird . . . are" (line 1), or "he hop" (3), or double negatives: "He ain't go no" (4), there is a certain structure to its content. Following the odd assertion that the frog is "a wonderful bird" (1), the poet catalogs the frog's characteristics and follows them up with a list of what the frog lacks. The final line is a sort of culmination of both approaches: "When he sit, he sit on what he ain't got almost" (6). And although the literal meaning of the poem and its ungrammatical sentences might seem confusing, the poet provides a clear image of the frog, almost in spite of the language. The repetition of words such as *almost* and *hardly* and the reliance on many one-syllable words contribute to the overall rhythmic pattern of the work. You might ask students what the effect of comparing a frog to a bird is in this poem.

POSSIBLE CONNECTION TO ANOTHER SELECTION

William Carlos Williams, "The Red Wheelbarrow" (text p. 257)

TATO LAVIERA, *AmeRícan* (p. 269)

"AmeRícan" relies on a complex structure and innovative use of language for its power. Encourage students to examine the components and the physical layout of each section of this ever-changing, ever-moving poem. Each of the first three stanzas begins with the phrase "we gave birth to a new generation." The new generation is composed of those AmeRícans who will gather the elements of their culture and move into the mainstream American culture represented by New York. The seventh stanza (lines 21–24) highlights the poem's narrative development and the poet's creative use of language. Marking the transition between native and American culture, the poet embodies the literal movement, the disorientation, and the character of the new environment through the rearrangement and repetition of *across, forth,* and *back.* Appropriately, residence in New York (an island connected by bridges) is indicated by the line "our trips are walking bridges" (24). What other meaning is indicated by this line?

The eighth stanza breaks from the form established by the preceding stanzas. Ask students why it is appropriate to omit the beginning word "AmeRícan" here. In what way is this physical detail a response to the "marginality that gobbled us up abruptly!" (31)? In what other ways do the content and tone of this stanza contrast with the rest of the poem?

The poem is infused with the poet's sense of both Puerto Rican and American cultures. Encourage students to note the comparisons between the first and second halves of this poem, in which the poet touches on the music, spirit, and language of each culture. Also, students might notice instances (particularly toward the end of this poem) in which the cultures seem fused — for example, in words such as *spanglish* (41).

What is the tone of the final two stanzas? Literally, there is a celebration of the myth of America — "home of the brave, the land of the free." The penultimate stanza alludes to the understanding fostered by our Puritan forefathers that America is God's chosen country, "a city on a hill" that should be an example to all nations. The lines in which the poet refers to "our energies / collectively invested to find other civil- / izations" (52–54) also touch on our history of Manifest Destiny. The final stanza conveys the joy experienced by an assimilated AmeRícan, yet there is also considerable loss of identity in the speaker's "dream to take the accent from / the altercation, and be proud to call / myself american" (57–59).

POSSIBLE CONNECTIONS TO OTHER SELECTIONS

Chitra Banerjee Divakaruni, "Indian Movie, New Jersey" (question #1, following)
Julio Marzán, "The Translator at the Reception for Latin American Writers" (text p. 266)

CONNECTION QUESTION IN TEXT (p. 270) WITH ANSWER

1. In an essay consider the themes, styles, and tones of "AmeRícan" and Divakaruni's "Indian Movie, New Jersey" (p. 162).

   Both poems consider the plight of immigrants in America who live a kind of liminal existence between their native culture and mainstream American culture. Laveria's poem is more of a celebration of this liminal state than Divakaruni's is, though; both poets sense a blending of the two cultures, but the Indian immigrants and their families in Divakaruni's poem are alienated and discriminated against. Laveria's poem uses a hybrid language and a new poetic form to celebrate the new, hybrid culture that is the subject of his poem. It is ultimately a more hopeful rendition of the immigrant experience.

ONLINE RESOURCES (manual p. 339)

PETER MEINKE, *The ABC of Aerobics* (p. 270)

Born in Brooklyn, Peter Meinke often experiments with form, preferring to let the poem dictate its own form. Works whose titles begin "The ABC of ..." usually are primers designed to teach the basic elements of a subject. You might start discussion of this poem by asking whether it fulfills the expectations its title sets up. In a kind of playful, semisatiric thumbing of the nose at cholesterol-level and heart-rate calculators, the poem at least acknowledges the obligations of its title. The speaker, apparently, has tried to ward off the effects of aging by jogging, but he expends all this effort with a despairing sense of his past sins and the dark forebodings of his genetic history manifested in the portrait of Uncle George. Small wonder, then, that his thoughts turn to Shirley Clark, and the poem concludes with the speaker "breathing hard" and gasping for his lost flame at his own "maximal heart rate."

At least two aspects of this poem merit some consideration. One is the carefully controlled use of consonance and alliteration, often for humorous effect. Notice, for example, the alternating *l-* and *b-*sounds in line 12 followed by the nasal hiss of "my / medical history a noxious marsh." Later, in a spoofing of health and fitness fads, Meinke shows the direction of his true inclinations by exchanging "zen and zucchini" for "drinking and dreaming."

The second aspect of this poem that students should feel comfortable enough to enjoy is the humor, which derives in part from the poem's dip into the vernacular. "Probably I shall keel off the john like / queer Uncle George," Meinke unabashedly tells us in line 16, while he describes the lucky lover who married the fabled Shirley as a "turkey" who lacks all aesthetic appreciation for her wondrous earlobes. We are inclined to like the speaker in this poem, and both his personality and the radiated humor act as rhetorical devices, helping us to feel the way he feels about "The ABC of Aerobics," which, by the way, takes us to the end of the alphabet with "zen and zucchini."

Critical studies of Meinke's work include Philip Jason's "Speaking to Us All" in *Poet Lore* (Washington, D.C.: Heldref Publications, 1982), and Eric Nelson's "Trying to Surprise God" in *Mickle Street Review* (Camden: Walt Whitman House Association, 1983).

Possible Connections to Other Selections

Galway Kinnell, "After Making Love We Hear Footsteps" (question #2, following)
James Merrill, "Casual Wear" (text p. 159)
Sharon Olds, "Sex without Love" (question #1, following)

Connections Questions in Text (p. 271) with Answers

1. Write an essay comparing the way Olds connects sex and exercise in "Sex without Love" (p. 76) with Meinke's treatment here.

   Olds's subject is really not exercise and its obsessions, but sex. Her analogy to exercise explores the absence of mutual experience or feeling in sex without love. Meinke's concern *is* exercise. Like Olds, he sees exercise as a desperate attempt to fight off the inevitable process of aging. The difference in the poems' attitudes toward exercise is a matter of diction and theme. Whereas Olds thinks that exercise involves a competition with oneself, Meinke reveals that it is really a struggle against "death and fatty tissue." Meinke's images of exercise are darker and more colloquial.

2. Compare the voices in this poem with those in Kinnell's "After Making Love We Hear Footsteps" (p. 255). Which do you find more appealing? Why?

   Kinnell's poem celebrates a child as a sign of life and love, whereas Meinke's criticizes our culture's inability to accept death. Kinnell's poem will probably appeal to your more optimistic students; the more cynical will be comfortable with Meinke's view.

GARY SOTO, *Mexicans Begin Jogging* (p. 271)

Born in America but mistaken for a Mexican, the speaker of this poem is encouraged by his factory boss to run out the back door and across the Mexican border when the border patrol arrives. Rather than protest, the speaker runs along with a number of Mexicans, yelling *vivas* to the land of "baseball, milkshakes, and those sociologists" (line 18) who are apparently keeping track of demographics.

It is noteworthy that the speaker doesn't protest his boss's orders but joins the throng of jogging Mexicans because he is "on [the boss's] time" (11). Why wouldn't he simply stand his ground and show proof that he is a U.S. citizen? The key may lie in the word "wag" (12), which describes a comic person or wit in addition to its familiar associations with movement: to move from side to side (as in "tail"), or even to depart. The speaker's parting gesture, after all, is "a great silly grin" (21). The joke is on the boss, or the border patrol, or on America in general with its paranoid sociologists. Although the tone is somewhat comic, the subject is serious, whether students take it to be the exploitation of workers from developing nations, or prejudice based on appearance (i.e., the speaker is taken to be Mexican because he looks like he is). What effect does the tone have on a consideration of these subjects? Is there a "point" to his irony?

POSSIBLE CONNECTIONS TO OTHER SELECTIONS

Julio Marzàn, "The Translator at the Reception for Latin American Writers" (text p. 266)
Peter Meinke, "The ABC of Aerobics" (question #1, following)

CONNECTION QUESTION IN TEXT (p. 272) **WITH ANSWER**

1. Compare the speakers' ironic attitudes toward exercise in this poem and in Meinke's "The ABC of Aerobics" (p. 270).

   Whereas each poem uses running as a vehicle for meditation, Gary Soto's speaker runs to avoid the border patrol, and the speaker of "The ABC of Aerobics" exercises for exercise's sake. For each speaker, exercise is somewhat futile: Soto's speaker doesn't really need to be running, as he is an American, and Meinke's speaker comes to realize that if he had love, it would replace the exercise. (Meinke's speaker spends lines 1–16 discussing how, regardless of exercise, the city's air is still filthy, and how it does him little good anyway because of "tobacco, lard and bourbon" [12].)

FOUND POEM

DONALD JUSTICE, *Order in the Streets* (p. 272)

The poem outlines a process, with each step in a separate stanza. As we read the poem, we observe the process with the speaker. The word *jeep,* without an article, is repeated at the beginnings of three stanzas, lending an air of impersonality to its actions, as if there were no driver. The poem is itself impersonal, reducing "Order in the Streets" to a series of mechanized steps, devoid of human presence.

POSSIBLE CONNECTION TO ANOTHER SELECTION

Sharon Olds, "Rite of Passage" (text p. 265)

AUDIOVISUAL AND ONLINE RESOURCES (manual pp. 301, 338)

11

Combining the Elements of Poetry

Once students have grasped some of the individual elements of a poem, there remains the task of combining these separate insights into a coherent whole. Class discussion in introductory courses often takes up this challenge. While students make specific observations about a poem, the instructor attempts to connect the observations, in order to give students a bigger picture. But this isn't always easy. The Questions about Elements in Chapter 11 may help students who need to add more component elements to their understanding of the poem or those who have a grasp of the components but still need a way of integrating them in discussion or in written assignments. The questions may also help more advanced students. Even if these students have a good understanding of a poem's structure, the questions could suggest ways of structuring their own papers on the poem.

You might also want to use these questions to facilitate class discussion. After determining which questions are particularly useful for a given poem, have separate groups of students explore separate questions. Then have the groups report to the class as a whole. Ask them to support their responses with citations from the poem. In the discussion following, try to engage the groups in dialogue with one another. How do their insights overlap? How might they combine their observations in a paper? This type of exercise should be valuable since it enacts the very task of the chapter.

Chapter 11 includes a sample student paper explicating John Donne's "Death Be Not Proud." Have your students read Donne's poem, and then discuss how they might approach the assignment given to the student writer. You might want to ask them how they would write a similar paper, but with a different combination of elements. How would they write such a paper about a different poem? What can they learn about combining elements from this sample paper? You might even ask them to critique the paper, and suggest revisions.

APPROACHES
TO POETRY

12

Emily Dickinson: A Body of Work

There are several difficulties in teaching Dickinson. One lies in having students unlearn previous assumptions about her, assumptions dealt with wonderfully in Marilyn Nelson Waniek's "Emily Dickinson's Defunct." Emily Dickinson was, in fact, a real person, and did, from time to time, get out of the house. Dickinson can be read as a poet of passion and exuberance, as well as irony and playfulness. The popular image of her as an agoraphobic introvert has done a disservice to such readings. Emphasizing that she was an actual human being can help students find a juncture between the erotic Dickinson, the death-obsessed Dickinson, the religious Dickinson, the playful Dickinson, and so on.

In addition, students may find many of her poems to be extremely challenging, though some may seem deceptively simple. When you ask students to "get their hands dirty" with these poems, they may find that they can dig much deeper than they initially thought. The challenging poems are often difficult because of Dickinson's use of occasionally unfamiliar vocabulary, wordplay, understatement, and gaps in her poetry. You may find it useful to encourage students to bring to bear all the skills they have developed in previous chapters, including reading the poems aloud and writing about them.

EMILY DICKINSON

If I can stop one Heart from breaking and If I shouldn't be alive (p. 291)

You might wish to impress on your class the difference in quality between these two poems by means of a prereading experiment. Before your students have read the introductory text for this section, show them copies of the two poems with key words removed, and have them attempt to fill in the blanks. They will probably have no trouble with phrases like "in vain," "Robin," or "his Nest again" in the first poem, but do any of them anticipate "Granite lip" in the second?

You might begin discussion of "If I can stop" by asking students to consider the comments on sentimentality and the greeting-card tradition in the text (pp. 29–30). Dickinson's relation to such popular occasional verse is, after all, not so far-fetched, since she is reputed to have honored birthdays and other social occasions by composing poems. Ask students to speculate on why this poem was so popularly successful and then to explore its limitations. The poem's simplicity and the extent to which it recounts what we *think* it should are among its popular virtues. If students have trouble seeing the poem's limitations, ask them if it is possible to live life with only one rule of conduct. Would they consider their entire lives successful if they saved one robin? You might also speculate with students on why the least common denominator of a poet's work is so often what the popular mind accepts. Recall as a parallel Walt Whitman's poem on Lincoln, "O Captain! My Captain!" — a rhymed lyric that has found its way into many high-school anthologies and may be even more popular since its use in the film *Dead Poets Society*.

"If I shouldn't be alive" is much more in keeping with Dickinson's usual ironic mode. In what ways does this poem seem to be like the previous one? What emotions are evoked by the use of the Robin in each poem? Where does "If I shouldn't be alive" break away from the world of sentimentality evoked by "If I can stop one Heart . . ."? What does the speaker's concern that she might be thought ungrateful, suggested by the second stanza, say about her? How do the speakers of these two poems differ?

As a way of enabling students to appreciate the master stroke of the "Granite lip" in the last line, you might have them rewrite the line so that it steers the poem back toward a more conventional expression.

POSSIBLE CONNECTION TO ANOTHER SELECTION ("If I shouldn't be alive)

Emily Dickinson, "Because I could not stop for Death —" (text p. 308)

The Thought beneath so slight a film — (p. 293)

Just as laces and mists (both light, partial coverings) reveal the wearer or the mountain range, so a veiled expression reveals the inner thought or opinion. Dickinson is here implying that the delicate covering makes the eye work harder to see the form behind the veil; therefore, misted objects appear in sharper outline.

Ask students to suggest other metaphors Dickinson might have used to describe the distinctness of things that are partially hidden. Depending on your class, you might be able to discuss one of the more obvious examples: whether or not seminudity is more erotic than complete nakedness. Why does Dickinson use such totally different metaphors — women's clothing and a mountain range — to make her point here? Is there any connection between the two? Do your students agree with Dickinson's premise? Are things more distinct, or simply more intriguing, when the imagination must become involved? Does one see another person's thoughts more clearly when a "film" necessitates working harder to understand, or is it just as likely that the "understanding" that results is a hybrid of two persons' thoughts?

POSSIBLE CONNECTIONS TO OTHER SELECTIONS

Emily Dickinson, "Portraits are to daily faces" (text p. 298)

——, "Tell all the Truth but tell it slant —" (text p. 312)

To make a prairie it takes a clover and one bee (p. 293)

"To make a prairie" reads like a recipe — add this to that and you will get the desired result. But it could just as well be a call for props in a theater production: take these items and add a little reflective imagination and the result will be a prairie, itself a symbol of open-endedness and freedom of spirit.

To enable students to understand the poem more clearly, you might ask them to explore the idea of essential ingredients by writing their own "recipe" poem: How do you make a family? A term paper? A painting? What happens to each of these entities as various ingredients are removed? What cannot be removed without destroying the entity or changing its character completely?

POSSIBLE CONNECTIONS TO OTHER SELECTIONS

Emily Dickinson, "I felt a Cleaving in my Mind —" (text p. 309)

Robert Frost, "Mending Wall" (text p. 342)

Success is counted sweetest (p. 294)

The power of this poem, to some degree, is its intangibility. We puzzle over how desire enables those who will never succeed to know success better than those who actually achieve it. Ask students to talk about the comparison of success to "a nectar" (line 3). It is odd that the verb *comprehend* should be paired with nectar; what does it mean to comprehend? When they begin to talk about the pairing of understanding and physical images, ask students to think about "need" (4) as both a physical and an intellectual desire for success.

You might also have students discuss the word *burst* in the final line. Are the failures the true achievers? If so, what is it they achieve?

POSSIBLE CONNECTIONS TO OTHER SELECTIONS

Emily Dickinson, "I like a look of Agony," (text p. 300)

———, "Water, is taught by thirst" (text p. 296)

John Keats, "Ode on a Grecian Urn" (question #1, following)

CONNECTION QUESTION IN TEXT (p. 295) WITH ANSWER

1. In an essay compare the themes of this poem with those of John Keats's "Ode on a Grecian Urn" (p. 79).

   The themes of both "Success is counted sweetest" and "Ode on a Grecian Urn" have to do with wanting. Dickinson holds that success, or as she later calls it, "victory" (line 8), is "counted sweetest / by those who ne'er succeed" (1–2). In other words, the want of success makes success itself seem better. To use a cliché, the grass is always greener. . . . Similarly, Keats's image of the lovers forever chasing one another recalls the agony of the unsuccessful listener in Dickinson's poem. Yet the agony is not entirely negative. Consider how sweetly the success in Keats's poem is counted.

These are the days when Birds come back— (p. 295)

This poem examines Indian summer through images that evoke summer and autumn simultaneously. The co-existence of "a Bird or two" (line 2) and "blue and gold" (6) June-like skies with seeds and "a timid leaf" (12) suggest Indian summer. The former, unauthorized title could help students to identify the paradox of summery conditions when summer has past.

The "fraud" (7) being perpetrated by these aspects of summer is in the suggestion of true summer they establish, when winter is on the way. Still, the "plausibility" (8) of these summer signs makes the speaker long to pledge allegiance to the perception, to place her faith in the "sacred emblems" (16) of the season. The symbolic death of nature in late fall recalls the death of Christ in the line "Oh Last Communion" (14).

It may help students to consider the "sacred emblems" of other seasons. Are winter, spring, and autumn as deserving of the belief the speaker claims? What would the emblems of those seasons look like? Writing imitations of Dickinson's work could help students focus on her technique while considering these questions for themselves.

Sophie Cabot Black, "August" (p. 125)

Emily Dickinson, "Some keep the Sabbath going to Church —" (p. 298)

Water, is taught by thirst (p. 296)

Thematically, this poem reiterates the contention in previous Dickinson poems, such as "Success is counted sweetest" (text p. 294) and "The Thought beneath so slight a film —" (text p. 293), that the inability to grasp something physically brings its essential qualities into sharper focus. It might be interesting to have students suggest what Dickinson's pattern is in this poem. The first four lines appear to work by oppositions: water is defined by its lack, land is defined by the oceans surrounding it, transport (ecstasy) by agony, and peace by war. But how is "Memorial Mold" related to love (line 5), and how can a bird be defined in relation to snow? The images in the poem seem to move from the concrete to the abstract (although the last line seems to subvert this reading). Perhaps the reader is meant to consider the more abstract connotations of the words in the last line. What are some of the ideas or feelings that birds and snow call to mind? Are any of these ideas opposites?

POSSIBLE CONNECTIONS TO OTHER SELECTIONS

Emily Dickinson, " 'Heaven' — is what I cannot reach!" (text p. 299)

——, "I like a look of Agony," (text p. 300)

——, "Success is counted sweetest" (question #1, following)

CONNECTION QUESTION IN TEXT (p. 296) WITH ANSWER

1. What does this poem have in common with the preceding poem, "Success is counted sweetest"? Which poem do you think is more effective? Explain why.

    Both poems argue that we learn through deprivation. We gain not just through necessity, but through experiencing desperate circumstances. Students are likely to argue that this poem is more effective because it emphasizes its theme through repetition and variation. But "Success is counted sweetest" is at once more specific and broader in scope. It might be interesting to revisit this question after you have covered more of Dickinson's poetry or to have students try to isolate what they believe her most effective (or affecting) poem is.

Safe in their Alabaster Chambers — (1859 version) (p. 296) **and** *Safe in their Alabaster Chambers* — (1861 version) (p. 296)

Probably the most physically obvious change Dickinson made in revising this poem was the combining of the last two lines in the first stanza into one line. The latter poem seems more regular because its line and rhyme schemes are the same in both stanzas. The change also has the effect of de-emphasizing the more pleasant image of the original last two lines — the satin rafters — and emphasizing the colder, harder image of the stone. The emphasis becomes even more pronounced with the addition of the strong punctuation at the end of line 5 in the 1861 version.

The physical changes in the first stanza, coupled with a complete change of imagery for the second stanza, result in a different tone for the two versions of the poem. In the 1859 version, the dead are lamented, but life goes on around their tombs in anticipation of their eventual resurrection at the end of the world (note that in line 4 they only "sleep"). In the 1861 version of the poem, the dead "lie" in their graves and the larger universe continues in its course as though human deaths are of little importance. The second poem's mention of "Diadems" and "Doges" (9) serves to emphasize that even the fall of the earth's most powerful people makes little impact on the universe. The human relationship to nature here is more like that in Stephen Crane's "A Man Said to the Universe" (text p. 146).

You might have students note at this point Dickinson's emphasis on white, translucent things in her imagery. Have students recall such images from earlier poems. They might mention film, lace, mountain mists, or snow. Note the contrast between Dickinson's conviction that we comprehend life more clearly through the mists and Emerson's idea that we should ideally become like a "transparent eyeball" in order to know Nature.

POSSIBLE CONNECTION TO ANOTHER SELECTION (1859 version)

Emily Dickinson, "Apparently with no surprise" (text p. 328)

POSSIBLE CONNECTIONS TO OTHER SELECTIONS (1861 version)

Emily Dickinson, "Apparently with no surprise" (text p. 328)
Robert Frost, "Design" (question #1, following)

CONNECTION QUESTION IN TEXT (p. 297) WITH ANSWER

1. Compare the theme in the 1861 version with the theme of Robert Frost's "Design" (p. 356).

    Both poems have to do with perspective and proportion, focusing first on something small and then pulling back to examine how those smaller things fit into a larger scheme. Frost's spider and moth retain their significance despite the ironic final line, "If design govern in a thing so small." Dickinson's "meek members of the Resurrection" (line 4), by contrast, are rendered insignificant by the entire second stanza. They are faceless and unimportant; the poet does not bother to pause and observe them, unlike Frost's speaker who concentrates on the spider, moth, and flower in detail before dismissing them.

How many times these low feet staggered — (p. 297)

This poem mourns the death of this "Indolent Housewife" (line 12) by remarking on her "cool forehead" (5), usually hot with work, stony fingers used to wearing a thimble, her "low feet" accustomed to housework. This understated elegy remarks on the labors the housewife endured in life and considers the work that will lie undone without her.

In death she is "indolent"; the current meaning of this word is slothful or lazy, but its Latin roots suggest the absence of grief. The pathological sense of this word reflects these roots: an indolent tumor is one that is painless. The housewife's indolence can be seen to reflect both aspects of this word: in death she is lazy, and the flies and spiders need not fear her hand. She is also indolent, without pain, no longer having to stagger under the grief of housework

Images of death in this poem center on the stillness of a corpse: they include "the soldered mouth" (2), fixed with "awful rivet" (3) and "hasps of steel" (4); "the cool forehead" (5); "the listless hair" (6); and "the adamantine fingers" (7). All of these images are in contrast to the constant movement and work of her life.

POSSIBLE CONNECTIONS TO OTHER SELECTIONS

Emily Dickinson, "I heard a Fly buzz — when I died —" (question #1, following)
——, "What Soft — Cherubic Creatures" (p. 302)

1. Discuss Dickinson's treatment of the fly in this poem and in "I heard a Fly buzz — when I died—" (p. 307). How is the fly in each poem a significant element of the poem's themes?

   The presence of the fly in each poem establishes a kind of victory for mundanity over the life ending in each poem. In "How many times these low feet staggered," the "dull flies" (9) are triumphant in the final quatrain: in the absence of the house-wife, there is no danger that they'll be swatted down. In "I heard a Fly buzz — when I died —," the speaker and those around the deathbed are silent, waiting for the moment "when the King / Be witnessed — in the Room —" (7–8); the fly steals the spotlight, sending the expectations of the speaker and reader stumbling, "uncertain" (13) as the fly itself in the absence of the expected King.

Portraits are to daily faces (p. 298)

Before asking students to discuss the analogy presented in "Portraits," you might want to remind them of the analogy sections on their SAT or ACT tests. They probably were at some point taught the strategy of making a connection between one pair of words and trying to apply it to a second pair. What happens when your students try to apply this strategy to Dickinson's poem? One difficulty is that it is hard to determine whether the comparison in the first line is meant to be taken in a positive or a negative manner. Is a portrait a daily face that is perfected and idealized, captured so that it never grows old? Or is it a static, posed rendering of something that was meant to be alive and constantly changing? The word *pedantic* in line 3 suggests a negative connotation for the second term in each analogy. The sunshine is ostentatious in its glory — in its "satin Vest." Do your students object to the characterization of bright sun as "pedantic"? After all, there is nothing inherently inferior about sunshine — or about living human faces, for that matter.

POSSIBLE CONNECTIONS TO OTHER SELECTIONS

Emily Dickinson, " 'Faith' is a fine invention" (text p. 327)
——, "Tell all the Truth but tell it slant —" (text p. 312)
——, "The Thought beneath so slight a film —" (question #3, following)
Robert Francis, "Catch" (question #1, following)
Robert Frost, "Birches" (text p. 347)
——, "Mending Wall" (text p. 342)

CONNECTIONS QUESTIONS IN TEXT (p. 298) WITH ANSWERS

1. Compare Dickinson's view of poetry in this poem with Francis's perspective in "Catch" (p. 14). What important similarities and differences do you find?

   In both poems the reader must work hard to understand the meaning. Dickinson's poem embodies this circumstance, whereas Francis's illustrates it. But we have the impression that Francis believes in authorial intention, that there is a single "point" that the reader can "get," even if that point is obscure. Dickinson's poem (and her poetry in general), presents wide gaps between the reader and poet; we are not sure if we are meant to understand exactly what one of her poems means, nor if that meaning can remain stable over multiple readings.

3. How is the theme of this poem related to the central idea in "The Thought beneath so slight a film —" (p. 293)?

   Portraits are held to be superior to daily faces presumably because they allow the viewer to interpret them and to regard them with a sense of wonder. The thought beneath a slight film also allows for interpretation and awe. In both cases, art is preferred to quotidian existence.

Some keep the Sabbath going to Church — (p. 298)

One way to help students grasp more concretely the ideas Dickinson posits here is to have them draw up a chart comparing the practices of the "I" and the "Some" in this poem. How does the level of comparison shift between the first two stanzas and the third? The most important comparisons come in the last stanza; like the Puritans, the speaker claims that his or her religious practices result in a direct relationship to God, with no middleman. While the earlier lines may suggest a "to each his own" approach to religion, stanza three leaves little room for doubting which experience the speaker considers to be "real" religion. Discuss the distinction made in the last two lines between focusing on the goal one is journeying toward and focusing on the journey itself. Which attitude do your students feel reflects their own outlook?

POSSIBLE CONNECTIONS TO OTHER SELECTIONS

Gerard Manley Hopkins, "Pied Beauty" (text p. 613)
Walt Whitman, "When I Heard the Learn'd Astronomer" (question #1, following)

CONNECTION QUESTION IN TEXT (p. 299) WITH ANSWER

1. Write an essay that discusses nature in this poem and in Walt Whitman's "When I Heard the Learn'd Astronomer" (p. 642).

   For both poets, nature is sacred and should be approached through direct experience rather than through the filter of other human perspectives. Although both speakers value their direct experience of nature, they contextualize it differently: for Whitman's speaker it is an alternative to science and for Dickinson's speaker it is an alternative to religion. These contexts give very different meanings to "nature." Science, especially astronomy, is a way of explaining natural phenomena, but religion is a way of providing moral instruction, a human phenomenon. Both speakers demonstrate the same impulse, but their quests differ in specific ways.

"Heaven" — is what I cannot reach! (p. 299)

You might begin discussion of this poem by having students recall other stories they have encountered that deal with the attraction of "forbidden fruit." The first stanza may allude to the story of Adam and Eve and/or to the myth of Tantalus, who was punished for trying to deceive and humiliate the gods by being placed in a pool in Hades, where the water at his feet receded every time he tried to take a drink, and the luscious fruits growing above his head moved away whenever he tried to pluck them to assuage his hunger. Can your students think of other tales that emphasize the same idea? Does this affirm or contradict their own experiences? Why does this speaker consider the unattainable to represent heaven? What does this say about him or her?

Besides the apple that is out of reach, what other images of the unattainable does Dickinson employ in this poem? The last stanza is particularly difficult in its syntax as well as its diction. How, for example, can "afternoons" (line 9) be a "decoy" (10)?

As a further topic for discussion, or as a writing assignment, you might wish to have students consider other Dickinson poems that posit a thesis similar to or different from this one.

POSSIBLE CONNECTIONS TO OTHER SELECTIONS

Diane Ackerman, "A Fine, a Private Place" (question #2, following)
Emily Dickinson, "I like a look of Agony," (text p. 300)

———, "Water, is taught by thirst" (text p. 296)

Linda Hogan, "Hunger" (text p. 677)

CONNECTION QUESTION IN TEXT (p. 300) WITH ANSWER

2. Discuss the speakers' attitudes toward pleasure in this poem and in Ackerman's "A Fine, a Private Place" (p. 69).

    For the speaker of this poem, pleasure is always just out of reach. She can presumably *see* the objects of her pleasure, but the experience is frustrating nonetheless, as the allusion to Tantalus makes clear. Whereas Dickinson's speaker cannot reach the apple on the tree, Ackerman's speaker is fully able to grab the peach at the end of her poem and sink her teeth into it; she is, of course, also able to experience her unusual sexual tryst and to relive it through memory. Hers is a much less inhibited attitude toward pleasure; she can and does experience it and enjoy it. Dickinson's speaker can neither experience nor enjoy the things she desires.

I like a look of Agony, (p. 300)

You might want to ask your class whether the speaker in this poem has an outlook similar to or different from those of the speakers in other Dickinson poems they have read. Whereas many of the previous speakers have professed a love of things half seen, this one seems obsessed with certainty. Ask students to point out words that have to do with truth or falsehood; they will be able to find several in this short verse. Is death the only certainty for human beings? Are there any other times when it is possible to be certain that the image a person projects is an accurate one? Note also the words *I like* in line 1 and the characterization of Anguish as "homely" in the last line. Does this speaker actually find pleasure in people's death throes?

Flannery O'Connor once wrote, in justifying her use of violent encounters in her fiction, that "it is the extreme situation that best reveals what we are essentially." What would the speaker of this poem say to such a statement?

POSSIBLE CONNECTIONS TO OTHER SELECTIONS

Emily Dickinson, "The Bustle in a House" (text p. 312)

———, " 'Heaven' — is what I cannot reach!" (question #1, following)

———, "Success is counted sweetest" (question #1, following)

———, "Water, is taught by thirst" (text p. 296)

CONNECTION QUESTION IN TEXT (p. 300) WITH ANSWER

1. Write an essay on Dickinson's attitudes toward pain and deprivation, using this poem, " 'Heaven' — is what I cannot reach!" (p. 299), and "Success is counted sweetest" (p. 294) as the basis for your discussion.

    According to these poems, it would seem that Dickinson is something of an ascetic, if not a masochist. Each poem describes a blissful state that the speaker cannot achieve. Yet each poem also describes a yearning; that is, in each poem the speaker is not content with her state of deprivation and pain so much as she uses that state to gauge her emotions. In this poem, the desired condition is not necessarily death but rather honest purity. The same could be said for the other two poems as well: on the surface, the speaker inclines toward death, but unadulterated honesty — so rare in our daily lives — is at the heart of her quest.

Wild Nights — Wild Nights! (p. 300)

A class discussion of this poem could focus on a few well-chosen words. Researching the etymology of *luxury* (line 4) will leave no room for doubt as to the intended eroticism of the poem; it comes from the Latin *luxuria,* which was used to express lust as well as extravagant pleasures of a more general sort, which it has now come to mean. You might also discuss the use of natural imagery in the second and third stanzas. The heart in stanza two has no more need of compass or chart. Ask your students what these images mean to them. They seem to imply attention to order, rules, and laws. These images are set aside in the third stanza in favor of Eden and the sea.

A study of "Wild Nights" provides an excellent opportunity to discuss the possibility of disparity between the author of a work and the created narrator who speaks within the work. Students may wish to dismiss the eroticism of this poem if they have stereotyped Dickinson as a pure spinster in a white dress. However, the speaker of this poem cannot be specifically identified as Dickinson. Indeed, it is debatable whether the speaker is male or female.

POSSIBLE CONNECTION TO ANOTHER SELECTION

Margaret Atwood, "you fit into me" (question #1, following)

CONNECTION QUESTION IN TEXT (p. 301) WITH ANSWER

1. Write an essay that compares the voice, figures of speech, and theme of this poem with those of Atwood's "you fit into me" (p. 116).

    Atwood's poem is characterized by sarcasm and irony, as though the speaker is trying to flatter her addressee only to deflate him with a wry insult. The speaker of Dickinson's poem is much more sincere, desiring sexual union without anticipating the pain that Atwood's speaker focuses on. The imagery of this poem suggests security, whereas Atwood's imagery upends such security and replaces it with a disturbing image of pain: a fish hook in a human eye.

Nature — sometimes sears a Sapling — (p. 301)

This poem establishes a distinction between the losses suffered by trees and those suffered by people. Nature is, Dickinson suggests through her repetition of "sometimes" in the first two lines, capricious: it is impossible to predict what setbacks must be endured. While the trees die, leaving "Fainter Leaves — to Further Seasons" (line 5), people "do not die" (4). While Nature's acts may sear and scalp trees, human nature suffers a different consequence: "We — who have the Souls — / Die oftener" (7–8). These small deaths may be what make us human, what distinguishes those with souls from trees, which "die" (8) less often but more permanently.

POSSIBLE CONNECTIONS TO OTHER SELECTIONS

Emily Dickinson, "Apparently with no surprise" (question #1, following)

——, "The wind begun to knead the grass" (text p. 310)

CONNECTION QUESTION IN TEXT (p. 301) WITH ANSWER

1. Discuss the treatment of nature in this poem and in "Apparently with no surprise" (p. 328), paying particular attention to the verbs associated with nature in each poem.

    In this poem, nature "sears" (1) and "scalps" (2); in "Apparently with no surprise," nature is personified as an assassin who "beheads" (3). Both poems characterize nature as an unwitting force, whose actions contain a cruelty that has no intention or motivation. The violent forces of nature are random and unexpected but always present.

I would not paint — a picture — (p. 301)

This poem provides three different views and examples of art and the speaker's hesitancy to attempt it. In the first stanza, the speaker would not be a painter, claiming to prefer art appreciation. She would rather "wonder how the fingers feel" (line 5) that created the "bright impossibility" (3). The second stanza features the speaker choosing to be the notes "Raised softly to the Ceilings" (11) rather than the one who plays the cornet. The final stanza considers the "dower" that would have to be paid for the ability to create poetry, and decides the privilege would be too dear.

Each stanza conveys a high respect for art, supported with the doubt that the speaker can, herself, achieve it. While all three examples are accorded high regard, poetry is distinct from the other art forms for the speaker. Painting and music are considered "rare — celestial" (6), notes "raised softly" (11); these are delicate, refined images. On the other hand, poetry stuns "With Bolts of Melody" (24). This opinion of the power of poetry is repeated in the comments attributed to Dickinson by Thomas Wentworth Higginson in "On Meeting Dickinson for the First Time" (p. 314): "If I feel physically as if the top of my head were taken off, I know *that* is poetry." A helpful writing assignment might include asking students to write imitations of these stanzas in which another art form — sculpture or dance, for example — were discussed with similar respect.

POSSIBLE CONNECTIONS TO OTHER SELECTIONS

Emily Dickinson, "I dwell in Possibility —" (question #1, following)
———, "This was a Poet — It is That" (question #1, following)
John Keats, "Ode on a Grecian Urn" (text p. 79)

CONNECTION QUESTION IN TEXT (p. 302) WITH ANSWER

1. Discuss Dickinson's attitude toward poetry in this poem, "I dwell in Possibility —" (p. 304), and "This was a Poet — It is That" (p. 305).

   This poem presents an awe of poetry, the "License" (20) and "privilege" (21) to write poetry being out of the speaker's reach. "I dwell in Possibility —" conveys a sense of the limitlessness of poetry, the speaker "spreading wide my narrow Hands / To gather Paradise —" (11–12). "This was a Poet — It is That" presents the figure of the poet as one who "Distills amazing sense / From ordinary Meanings" (2–3). All three poems convey a profound respect for the art.

What Soft — Cherubic Creatures — (p. 302)

A brief discussion of societal expectations for women in the mid–nineteenth century may help students to appreciate Dickinson's satirical intent in this poem. A woman was expected to be "the Angel in the House" who exerted a spiritual influence on those around her and made family life harmonious. In her book *Dimity Convictions: The American Woman in the Nineteenth Century* (Athens: Ohio UP, 1976), which draws its title from this poem, Barbara Welter notes that "religion or piety was the core of woman's virtue, the source of her strength," and that "religion belonged to woman by divine right, a gift of God and nature." Further, woman was to use her "purifying passionless love [to bring] erring man back to Christ." Among other evidence from mid–nineteenth-century women's magazines, Welter cites a poem that appeared in an 1847 *Ladies' Companion*. The title alone — "The Triumph of the Spiritual over the Sensual" (*Dimity Convictions*

21–22) — is enough to convey the sense of disembodied spirituality Dickinson attacks in the poem.

Ask students to notice the particular adjectives the poet uses to describe the "Gentlewomen." They are "Soft," "Cherubic" (line 1), and "refined" (6), but by the end of the poem they are "Brittle" (11). The crucial lines 7–8, which divide the positive from the negative attributes, are especially important. Not only are the women disconnected from both the human and the divine, but their attitudes would seem, by extension, to dissociate them from the central tenet of Christianity, that God became man. The last two lines make it clear that the first stanza is intended to be read satirically. How might the comparisons to "Plush" (3) and to a "Star" (4) be construed negatively? Notice the two uses of the word *ashamed,* in lines 8 and 12. Who is ashamed in each case? What is the effect of the repetition of this word?

POSSIBLE CONNECTIONS TO OTHER SELECTIONS

Emily Dickinson, " 'Faith' is a fine invention" (question #1, following)
Christina Georgina Rossetti, "Some Ladies Dress in Muslin Full and White" (text p. 634)

CONNECTION QUESTION IN TEXT (p. 303) WITH ANSWER

1. How are the "Gentlewomen" in this poem similar to the "Gentlemen" in " 'Faith' is a fine invention" (p. 327)?

    Dickinson attacks the false faith of "gentlemen" and "gentlewomen" in these poems. Both groups pretend to be pious, but Dickinson characterizes them as hypocritical and superficial, with no clear sense of redemption and no knowledge of their souls.

The Soul selects her own Society — (p. 303)

You might begin a discussion of this poem by asking students to consider whether the image projected here matches the image of a female who spends her life in near solitude. They are likely to notice that one stereotypically assumes that a woman remains alone because she has no other choice (more so when this poem was written than today), whereas the "Soul" described here operates from a position of power. The verbs associated with the soul are all active: she "selects" (line 1), "shuts" (2), chooses (10), and closes off her attention (11), unmoved by chariots (5) or even emperors (7).

How does the meter in lines 10 and 12 reinforce what is happening in the poem at this point? What seems to be the purpose of the soul's restrictions on her society? You might have the students discuss both the limitations and the benefits of such exclusiveness. Do they think the advantages outweigh the disadvantages, or vice versa? What does the speaker of the poem think? How do you know?

POSSIBLE CONNECTIONS TO OTHER SELECTIONS

Emily Dickinson, "I dwell in Possibility —" (text p. 304)
——, "Much Madness is divinest Sense —" (text p. 304)

Much Madness is divinest Sense — (p. 304)

This poem could be the epigram of the radical or the artist. For all its endorsement of "madness," however, its structure is extremely controlled — from the mirror-imaged paradoxes that open the poem to the balancing of "Assent" and "Demur" and the consonance of "Demur" and "dangerous." Try to explore with the class some applications of the paradoxes. One might think, for example, of the "divine sense" shown by the Shakespearean fool.

POSSIBLE CONNECTION TO ANOTHER SELECTION

Emily Dickinson, "The Soul selects her own Society —" (question #1, following)

CONNECTION QUESTION IN TEXT (p. 304) WITH ANSWER

1. Discuss the theme of self-reliance in this poem and "The Soul selects her own Society —" (p. 303).

   In this poem Dickinson scorns conformity, specifically in terms of the often wrong-headed attempt to separate sense from insanity. The theme is that we must try to see beyond the notion that consensus necessarily equals what is right. (You might highlight the fact that the poem was written in 1862, at the start of the Civil War; before this period, slavery was accepted in America because it reflected a majority opinion.) Dickinson focuses on the individual in "The Soul selects her own Society —," turning the focus away from the majority and to the individual who decides for oneself what is right, good, or just by aligning oneself only with others who share the same beliefs, even if those others represent a minority.

I dwell in Possibility — (p. 304)

In the first two lines of the poem, the speaker sets up the general premise that poetry is superior to prose. The imagery employed in the next ten lines specifies the reason that the speaker values poetry. One possible strategy for teaching the poem is to explore the metaphor of the house and then return to the original premise and ask students whether they find it convincing.

The imagery in this poem moves outward from man-made, earthly examples to examples from nature to a final image of the supernatural. In lines 3 and 4, the speaker compares poetry to prose as though they were both houses. Why is it important that the comparison focuses specifically on the windows and doors of the house? The second stanza draws the metaphor outward to compare the rooms and roof of the house of poetry to entities in nature. The chambers in the house are likened to cedar trees (line 5), trees known for the durability of their wood and for their longevity. The cedars of Lebanon are also a familiar biblical allusion. According to the first book of Kings, the house of Solomon was built "of the forest of Lebanon . . . upon four rows of cedar pillars, with cedar beams upon the pillars" (vii.2); the lover in the Song of Solomon sings, "The beams of our house are cedar" (i.17). The roof of the house of poetry is compared to the sky (7–8), but again the speaker adds a qualifier — the word *everlasting* (7) — to raise this roof to an even higher level. The final word of the poem — *paradise* — ends the comparison at the farthest possible reaches of expansiveness.

Returning to the comparison made in the opening lines, students will probably see that the speaker considers poetry to be the "fairer House" on the basis of its capacity to expand, to open up to ever wider capacities. A fruitful discussion might result from the question of whether or not students agree with the speaker of this poem. Can they think of examples of prose that are expansive, or poetry that is narrow? How does the example of Dickinson's own prose — her letter to Higginson (text p. 313) — fit into this argument?

POSSIBLE CONNECTIONS TO OTHER SELECTIONS

Emily Dickinson, "The Soul selects her own Society —" (text p. 303)
T. E. Hulme, "On the Differences between Poetry and Prose" (question #1, following)

CONNECTION QUESTION IN TEXT (p. 304) WITH ANSWER

1. Compare what this poem says about poetry and prose with Hulme's comments in the perspective "On the Differences between Poetry and Prose" (p. 113).

Hulme contrasts the symbolic nature of prose with the metaphorical and imagistic properties of poetry. For him, poetry employs a "visual concrete" language. Dickinson argues that poetry is less confined than prose, which is a different point altogether. For her, poetic language is about the endless possibilities for signification in poetry. Her version of poetry is ethereal, taking us through the "Everlasting Roof" of "The Gambrels of the Sky" (lines 7–8), whereas Hulme sees poetry as "a pedestrian taking you over the ground." Of course, for him prose is no more ethereal, but simply more direct, like "a train which delivers you at a destination." Prose for Dickinson is simply more constrained than poetry is, a house with fewer windows, inferior doors, and an actual roof.

This was a Poet — It is That (p. 305)

In this poem the speaker defines poetry by contrasting it to ordinary experience and perception. The poet distills extraordinary perfumes from ordinary flowers, and discloses a picture that we had not seen before. The speaker endows the poet with "a Fortune — / Exterior — to Time" (lines 15–16) and depicts the rest of the world as living in "ceaseless Poverty" (12).

This poem is complicated by its first line, which sounds like a eulogy: "This was a poet." Why does the speaker use the past tense here? The tense never stays still for long — ironic given that the poem's final gesture is to declare the poet's "Fortune — / Exterior — to Time" (15–16). Is the speaker's intent to define the role of a poet or to make some philosophical statement about art and time? You can deepen this discussion even further by pointing out that "Attar" (4), in addition to being a perfume derived from flowers, is also the name of a thirteenth-century Persian poet. The timeless fortune of a poet also contrasts nicely with "the familiar species / That perished by the Door" (5–6), which can signify something ordinary that simply lives and dies, unlike the poet, who is extraordinary and who lives on through verse.

POSSIBLE CONNECTIONS TO OTHER SELECTIONS

Emily Dickinson, "A Bird came down the Walk —" (question #2, following)
———, "I dwell in Possibility" (question #1, following)
John Keats, "When I have fears that I may cease to be" (text p. 618)
William Shakespeare, "Not marble, nor the gilded monuments" (text p. 435)

CONNECTION QUESTION IN TEXT (p. 305) WITH ANSWER

1. Write an essay about a life lived in imagination as depicted in this poem and in "I dwell in Possibility —" (p. 304).

The first line of this poem again presents difficulty. The poet does not truly seem "exterior to time" if he or she is dead. "I dwell in Possibility —" seems much more eternal, with its final gesture of gathering Paradise.

2. Discuss "A Bird came down the Walk —" (p. 173) as an example of a poem that "Distills amazing sense / From ordinary Meanings —" (lines 2–3).

The contrast between the first and last stanzas of "A Bird came down the Walk —" demonstrates this definition well. The sense of a mundane occurrence is expanded through the poet's transformation. A bird hopping and eating becomes the source of wonderment at the vast mysteries of nature and a metaphor of humanity's humble relationship to the universe.

I read my sentence — steadily — (p. 306)

The speaker of this poem is handed a death sentence, which she reads carefully in order to ensure that she has understood it accurately. She prepares her soul to meet death, only to learn that they are already "acquainted" (line 11), even "friends" (12). In other words, the sentence is inevitable and predestined; the speaker really has no role of which to speak.

The metaphor of death as a "sentence" is also a pun, made evident by the fact that the speaker reads it, inspecting "its extremest clause" (4). Students might begin to interpret the first line to mean "I reviewed my life," or even "I revised my writing." Do either of these readings hold up throughout the poem? As a way of explaining line 7, it might help to point out that it was common for judges in nineteenth- and early twentieth-century America to follow a death sentence with the phrase "May God have mercy on your soul."

The speaker's attitude toward death will probably yield the most fruitful discussion. Her *soul* is nonchalant toward death, but where is the speaker in relation to her soul? If the soul has foreknowledge of death, what is it that causes us to fear death? Is it our bodies, frightened of decay? Is it our rational selves? Perhaps students won't think that the speaker is sincere in the final line, "And there, the Matter ends," in that she is acting blasé about the business of death as a defense mechanism against the horror of it. Point out that "Matter" could also be taken as a pun, in the sense of being both an "encounter" and matter as bodily existence (in contrast to the soul).

POSSIBLE CONNECTIONS TO OTHER SELECTIONS

Emily Dickinson, "Because I could not stop for Death" (question #1, following)
——, "I heard a Fly buzz — when I died —" (text p. 307)
——, "I like a look of Agony" (question #2, following)
Andrew Hudgins, "Elegy for My Father, Who Is Not Dead" (text p. 242)
Dylan Thomas, "Do not go gentle into that good night" (text p. 233)
Miller Williams, "Thinking About Bill, Dead of AIDS" (text p. 644)

CONNECTIONS QUESTIONS IN TEXT (p. 306) WITH ANSWERS

1. Compare the treatment of death in this poem and in "Because I could not stop for Death —" (p. 308).

   Death is a mannered thing in both poems. There is a formality about it, like a polite but grim gentleman. Death seems to deliver the speaker somewhere in "Because I could not stop for Death —", though not in some eternal place as she had surmised. Here death is not only final, but instant; "the Matter ends" just as abruptly as the poem ends.

2. In an essay discuss the "Agony" in this poem and in "I like a look of Agony," (p. 300).

   Agony in both cases comes with death, and it seems to happen only once. You can't rehearse this agony, in other words. Yet does it really seem like agony in this poem? The final four lines indicate that what may appear to others as "a look of agony" is actually less painful than it might appear.

After great pain, a formal feeling comes — (p. 306)

In an interesting inversion of her often-used technique of using metaphors from life to explore the territory of death and beyond, Dickinson in this poem uses a metaphor of death — the ceremony of a funeral — to evoke an image of one who has dealt with great pain in life. It is interesting that psychologists consider the funeral ritual to be generally more valuable for the survivors than for the deceased, because this poem is about survivors and how they are able eventually to get past their pain. In addition to the controlling image of a funeral, the poet uses two other strategies to convey the idea of a place that is past pain. Dickinson's choices of words here abound in objects and adjectives that permeate the poem with a sense of numbed feelings. If you ask your students to point out some of these words, they might mention "formal" (line 1), "tombs" (2), "stiff" (3), "mechanical" (5), "wooden" (7), "Quartz" and "stone" (9), "Lead" (10), and "Snow" (12), among others.

The entire poem deals with life after the initial sharp pain of loss has subsided. Lines 12–13 concern the movement from palpable discomfort, to apathetic stupor, to true release. Ask your students if their own experiences with pain confirm or repudiate this scenario. Does the speaker hedge a bit in line 11? Are there other human rituals besides funerals by which we formally let go of pain?

Possible Connections to Other Selections

Emily Dickinson, "The Bustle in a House" (question #1, following)
Robert Frost, "Home Burial" (text p. 343)
Donald Hall, "Letter with No Address" (text p. 673)

Connection Question in Text (p. 307) with Answer

1. How might this poem be read as a kind of sequel to "The Bustle in a House" (p. 312)?

   The poems might be looked at as stages one goes through when coping with loss. "The Bustle in a House" describes an immediate return to daily routine following death, almost a denial about the gravity of the situation even though this bustle is the "solemnest of industries / Enacted upon Earth" (lines 3–4). This poem describes the emotions that might follow the immediate need to return to the relative order of everyday life, the gradual process that allows us to let go of our grief.

I heard a Fly buzz — when I died — (p. 307)

This poem is typical of Dickinson's work as a willed act of imagination fathoming life after death and realizing the dark void and limitation of mortal knowledge. David Porter in *Dickinson: The Modern Idiom* (Cambridge: Harvard UP, 1981) observes:

> At a stroke, Dickinson brilliantly extracted the apt metonymical emblem of the essential modern condition: her intrusive housefly.... The fly takes the place of the savior; irreverence and doubt have taken the place of revelation. Her fly, then, "With Blue — uncertain stumbling Buzz" is uncomprehension, derangement itself. It is noise breaking the silence, not the world's true speech but, externalized, the buzz of ceaseless consciousness. (239)

You might introduce this idea and then, either in discussion or in a writing assignment, ask the class to explore the tone of this poem and its accordance with Porter's comment.

POSSIBLE CONNECTIONS TO OTHER SELECTIONS

Marilyn Nelson Waniek, "Emily Dickinson's Defunct" (text p. 261)

Walt Whitman, "A Noiseless Patient Spider" (question #1, following)

CONNECTION QUESTION IN TEXT (p. 307) WITH ANSWER

1. Contrast the symbolic significance of the fly with the spider in Whitman's "A Noiseless Patient Spider" (p. 130).

    The fly in Dickinson's poem is a kind of otherworldly messenger that fills up the space between death and life. Still, there is no connection between the fly and the speaker, nor does the fly seem to belong to the other world, unlike Whitman's spider, whose job is to connect the soul with the world of the living.

One need not be a Chamber — to be Haunted — (p. 308)

This poem, in gothic fashion, describes the psychological terrors of the brain and how it can be haunted by partially repressed, horrifying memories more frightening than real horrors. The first stanza devalues external horrors in comparison to internal ones and explains that "The Brain has Corridors" (line 3) that have the potential to be far scarier than corridors in any haunted house.

You might begin discussion of this poem by asking students to explain Dickinson's comparisons between external and internal "hauntings." What words or lines most effectively characterize the speaker's fear of himself or herself? Ask your class to consider how each stanza is divided into an examination of both external and internal terrors. Each stanza concludes that the inner horrors are much harder to face than the outer ones. For example, the fourth stanza asserts that it is easier to protect oneself from an external "Assassin" (15) than it is to close the door on one's memory. You might ask your class to discuss why one's own personal "hauntings" might be scarier than facing any "External Ghost" (6).

You might also ask your students to consider the tone of this poem. Could it be read as a sort of warning? To whom and from whom? Consider also the poem as an eerie message from an insane mind. Still another vantage point would be to read the poem as a relatively objective discussion of psychological terror. Ask students what words and phrases contribute to their perception of the tone of the poem.

POSSIBLE CONNECTIONS TO OTHER SELECTIONS

Edgar Allan Poe, "The Haunted Palace" (question #1, following)

Jim Stevens, "Schizophrenia" (question #1, following)

CONNECTION QUESTION IN TEXT (p. 308) WITH ANSWER

1. Compare and contrast this poem with Poe's "The Haunted Palace" (p. 141) and Stevens's "Schizophrenia" (p. 129). In an essay explain which poem you find the most frightening.

    All three poems advance the idea that minds are more likely to be haunted than structures are. All three poems also use haunted structures as metaphors for some sort of mental disorder, yet they do so in different ways. Dickinson's poem is the most direct in terms of this metaphor since it explicitly links the mind and a haunted chamber in the first stanza. Stevens's poem only intimates the connection between mind and building in the title, and Poe never explicitly makes the connection, although it is apparent to the careful reader.

Because I could not stop for Death — (p. 308)

Here is one Dickinson poem in which the speaker manages to go beyond the moment of death. The tone changes in the exact center of the poem, from the carefree attitude of a person on a day's leisurely ride through town and out into the country, to the chill of the realization that he or she is heading for the grave. However, the final images are not those of horror but of interest in the passage from time to eternity, and its ramifications.

The first line of the poem makes the reader aware of the speaker's lack of control over the situation; Death is clearly in charge. Still, as Death is described as kind (line 2) and civil (8), and as Immortality is along for the ride, the situation is not immediately threatening. In the third stanza, the carriage takes the speaker metaphorically through three stages of life: youth, represented by the school children; maturity, represented by the fields of grain; and old age, pictured as the setting sun.

Lines 13 and 14, which describe the chill felt as the sun goes down, constitute the turning point of the poem. Both the figurative language and the rhythm pattern signal a change. Dickinson abruptly reverses the alternating four-foot, three-foot metrical pattern of the first twelve lines so that line 13 contains the same number of feet as the line that immediately precedes it. The caesura after "Or rather" serves to emphasize the speaker's double take. You might wish to discuss the speaker's tone as the poem concludes.

POSSIBLE CONNECTIONS TO OTHER SELECTIONS

Emily Dickinson, "Apparently with no surprise" (question #1, following)

——, "If I shouldn't be alive" (text p. 291)

——, "I read my sentence — steadily —" (text p. 306)

CONNECTION QUESTION IN TEXT (p. 309) WITH ANSWER

1. Compare the tone of this poem with that of Dickinson's "Apparently with no surprise" (p. 328).

   Both poems cast the process of death as something methodical and mannerly. Yet this poem sounds more philosophical than "Apparently with no surprise," perhaps because its subject is human death as opposed to the cycles of nature. There are also a multitude of dashes in this poem, whereas the other one ends with a period, making it sound more like a clever observation than a deep meditation.

I felt a Cleaving in my Mind — (p. 309)

This poem describes an experience of mental disintegration or serious psychological strain. The speaker relates the feeling that his or her "Brain had split" (line 2), and that as a result, the speaker's thoughts become increasingly disjointed. Eventually they seem to unravel, like balls of yarn rolling across the floor. You might discuss with your students this likening of the unraveling balls of yarn (7–8) to a mental breakdown. Ask them what is so effective about connecting the homely, domestic image of yarn with the anguish of psychological decay.

Structured in perfect iambic pentameter and incorporating full rhymes, this Dickinson poem is unusual in its regularity. Much of the power of "I felt a Cleaving" lies in its sharp contrast between form and content. Discuss with your students the disparity between its smooth patterns of rhythm and rhyme and its disturbing theme. Point out that the first stanza reads almost like a jingle — how do the soothing musical qualities of the poem increase the horror of the experience? Poetically, the speaker's thoughts are joined together seamlessly, in perfect sequence. Yet this is precisely what the speaker claims is impossible for him or her to do. Ask your students to speculate why Dickinson would write such a smooth poem to describe such a jarring experience.

You might also consider asking your students to investigate the dictionary meanings of several words in this poem. Interestingly, "cleave" is defined as both "to separate" and "to adhere," and "ravel," which is actually a synonym for "unravel," means both "to entangle" and "to disentangle." You might ask your students to consider some of the possible implications of these double meanings.

POSSIBLE CONNECTIONS TO OTHER SELECTIONS

Emily Dickinson, "To make a prairie it takes a clover and one bee" (question #1, following)
John Keats, "Ode to a Nightingale" (text p. 196)

CONNECTION QUESTION IN TEXT (p. 310) WITH ANSWER

1. Compare the power of the speaker's mind described here with the power of imagination described in "To make a prairie it takes a clover and one bee" (p. 293).

   The speaker in this poem is relatively powerless. The cleaving of her mind is beyond her control, and she is not able to mend it, as when one wakes from a dream and tries to fall asleep again to see how it will turn out. In "To make a prairie" the mind has the power to create even without the things of the earth, but it is unclear whether the mind has the power to consciously create in itself a state of reverie.

The Wind begun to knead the Grass — (p. 310)

The details of this vivid litany convey all the parts of a satisfying thunderstorm. The poem establishes a development of a storm, moving through the wind to the grass, leaves, and road, to the rush of people on the streets, to the thunder and lightning, to the hurrying home of animals, and then satisfying expectations with the full rush of water. The personification of the storm in its many different parts demonstrates the busy-ness of the endeavor, all the factors that combine to create such a storm.

The broad expanse of the damage done is limited to the sphere outside the speaker's "Father's House" (line 19), although it succeeds in "Quartering a Tree" (20). The "Just" (20) preceding that lucky exclusion of the father's house from all that was "Wrecked" (18) in the storm is an understatement that establishes some friction with the whole of the poem. The rest of the poem is earnest in its depictions of the storm's violent potential, but the conclusion offers this sudden dismissal of the storm's actions.

POSSIBLE CONNECTIONS TO OTHER SELECTIONS

Emily Dickinson, "Nature — sometimes sears a sapling —" (question #1, following)
——, "Wild Nights — Wild Nights!" (p. 300)

CONNECTION QUESTION IN TEXT (p. 310) WITH ANSWER

1. Discuss the themes of this poem and "Nature — sometimes sears a sapling —" (p. 301).

   Both poems focus on the awe nature's force can inspire. This poem focuses more on the mercy that can be experienced at random: the storm "overlooked" the speaker's "Father's House" (19). "Nature — sometimes sears a sapling —" focuses more on the suffering nature can "sometimes" (1) dish out, drawing a comparison to the sufferings of "We — who have the Souls" (7).

A loss of something ever felt I —" (p. 311)

This poem examines the speaker's consistent sense of grief, present all her life. It is impossible to know for certain what is being grieved: the speaker herself says she grieved "of what I knew not" (line 3). The sense of loss has affected the speaker's life since childhood, although as an adult she is no longer "bemoaning" her lost "Dominion" (7). Her seeming despair has been tempered slightly: she is now "softly searching / For" (11-12) the "Delinquent Palaces" (12) she feels she lacks. This search leads her, she fears, to look "oppositely" (15) for the "Kingdom of Heaven" (16). This final stanza provides an example used in the *Oxford English Dictionary* to define the word *oppositely*. While the speaker's view of her eternal grief seems despairing, the presence of the "Finger" (13) that "Touches my Forehead now and then" (14) could be seen as divine intervention that may provide clarity.

While the speaker characterizes herself in adulthood as "a session wiser" (9), she recognizes she is "fainter, too" (10); the new version of her search is less impassioned but still important. The "Suspicion" (13), however, seems to be associated only with adulthood. Many of Dickinson's poems center on an unspecified topic. Asking your students to imagine what the speaker is grieving in this poem could help develop their interest in reading more of Dickinson's work.

POSSIBLE CONNECTIONS TO OTHER SELECTIONS

Emily Dickinson, "After great pain, a formal feeling comes" (text p. 306)

——, "I felt a Cleaving in my Mind—" (question #1, following)

CONNECTION QUESTION IN TEXT (p. 311) WITH ANSWER

1. To what extent are the "Delinquent Palaces" in this poem present in "I felt a Cleaving in my Mind —" (p. 309). How are the themes in each poem related?

   In this poem, the inability to find the "Delinquent Palaces" (line 12) presents a larger problem, one that must be wrestled with throughout life. In "I felt a Cleaving in my Mind —" the difficulty the speaker has wrapping her mind around a new thought is a problem, but not one that she will struggle with for long. While the "Cleaving in my Mind" may be impossible to "match" (3), it does not present the lifelong problem that the loss "of what I knew not" (3) offers in "A loss of something ever felt I —."

Oh Sumptuous moment (p. 311)

This poem begs a long-awaited, delightful moment to go by more slowly, to allow the speaker to savor it. However, the poem itself moves away from the specific glories of the "Sumptuous moment" (line 1) to anticipate how much more difficult moments after this one will be. The future, aware of pleasures like those at hand but bereft of them, is compared to someone led to "the Gallows" (8) while it is morning, knowing that the full day will unfold in his absence.

The sounds of the first stanza create an even rhythm and rhyme that makes the reading move more slowly, just as the speaker begs the moment to stay. Reading this poem out loud will likely increase your students' pleasure in it. Consider asking your students to freewrite, imagining what might qualify as a "Sumptuous moment" worthy of this comparison. Considering what students have learned about Dickinson's life, they may be able to anticipate what kind of rarity she's celebrating here.

POSSIBLE CONNECTIONS TO OTHER SELECTIONS

Emily Dickinson, " 'Heaven' — is what I cannot reach!" (question #1, following)

——, "Water, is taught by thirst" (question #1, following)

——, "Wild Nights — Wild Nights!" (text p. 300)

CONNECTION QUESTION IN TEXT (p. 312) WITH ANSWER

1. Compare and contrast the themes of this poem, "Water, is taught by thirst" (p. 296) and " 'Heaven' — is what I cannot reach!" (p. 299).

   All three of these poems define something positive in terms of its absence: a thing is more valuable if it is difficult to do without. "Oh Sumptuous moment" skips over the sumptuous moment itself to stress the agony of living without it, in the knowledge of its possibility. "Water, is taught by thirst" demonstrates how we learn to understand and love something only when we are forced to do without it. " 'Heaven' — is what I cannot reach!" demonstrates that the very notion of "Heaven" is predicated on the impossibility of reaching it in this life: therefore, for the speaker, everything out of reach takes on the sheen of paradise.

The Bustle in a House (p. 312)

The images in this poem suggest that getting on with mundane, everyday activities helps us to move beyond the pain of death. In contrast, the use of the funeral metaphor in "After great pain" (text p. 306) promotes the idea that a formal ritual helps us to accomplish this purpose. You might ask students which method strikes them as being more effective. Look closely at the diction in line 7. The phrase "We shall not want" echoes the Twenty-third Psalm, a hymn of comfort and confidence in God's support at the time of death. But does the expression also imply that even though we don't want to deal with any thought other than being reunited with the loved one in eternity, the reality may not be so simple?

In *Literary Women* (Garden City: Doubleday, 1976), Ellen Moers claims that "Emily Dickinson was self-consciously female in poetic voice, and more boldly so than is often recognized" (61). Does the imagery in this poem confirm or repudiate Moers's assertion? Ask your students to consider the many speakers they have encountered in Dickinson's poems. Is her poetic voice generally identifiable as female? If so, how? If not, how would you characterize her poetic voice(s)?

POSSIBLE CONNECTIONS TO OTHER SELECTIONS

Emily Dickinson, "After great pain, a formal feeling comes —" (text p. 306)

——, "I like a look of Agony," (question #2, following)

Donald Hall, "Letter with No Address" (text p. 673)

Carolynn Hoy, "In the Summer Kitchen" (text p. 267)

CONNECTION QUESTION IN TEXT (p. 312) WITH ANSWER

2. How does this poem qualify "I like a look of Agony," (p. 300)? Does it contradict the latter poem? Explain why or why not.

   The focus of the two poems is slightly different since there is no "I" in this poem. "I like a look of Agony," raises questions about the speaker, whereas this poem states a more objective truth. Yet both poems treat the subject of death and its effects, and in that respect there is a slight contradiction between them since this one ends with the notion of eternity, whereas "I like a look of Agony," concentrates on the physical death of a person without alluding to the state of the soul afterward.

Tell all the Truth but tell it slant — (p. 312)

You might open consideration of "Tell all the Truth" by having students discuss how the speaker characterizes "Truth." The imagery used here centers around the idea of light; in only eight lines, the poet uses "slant" (line 1), "bright" (3), "Lightning" (5), "dazzle" (7), and "blind" (8), besides the punning reference in the word *delight* (3). The speaker considers direct truth to be a light so powerful that it is capable of blinding. Students may suggest other contexts in which they have seen this idea expressed. Biblical stories often recount appearances of God as a light too blinding to be looked at directly. What is it about Truth, which after all only allows us to see things as they really are, that is potentially so destructive?

Don't let your students miss the exquisite word choices in lines 3 and 4 as Dickinson contrasts human fallibility — "our infirm Delight" (De-light?) — with the perfection of "Truth's superb surprise."

How does poetry in general affirm this poem's thesis? Would you expect a writer who believed this premise to prefer writing poetry to writing prose?

POSSIBLE CONNECTIONS TO OTHER SELECTIONS

Emily Dickinson, "I know that He exists" (question #1, following)

———, "Portraits are to daily faces" (text p. 298)

———, "The Thought beneath so slight a film —" (text p. 293)

CONNECTION QUESTION IN TEXT (p. 313) WITH ANSWER

1. How does the first stanza of "I know that He exists" (p. 327) suggest an idea similar to this poem's? Why do you think the last eight lines of the former aren't similar in theme to this poem?

   Both poems argue that the truth is not necessarily obvious or that the deepest truths are cloaked in mystery. The difference in theme between the two poems has to do with the difference of the subjects: the implications of "truth" are not as grave as the implications of God's existence.

PERSPECTIVES ON DICKINSON

Dickinson's Description of Herself (p. 313)

Probably the most immediately evident characteristic of Dickinson's personal correspondence is that, as in her poetry, the language comes in spurts interspersed with an abundance of dashes. Also, as in her poetry, she uses numerous metaphors. Have your students explore some of these metaphors, such as Dickinson's reference to criticism of her poetry as "surgery" (paragraph 2) and her discussion of "undressed thought" (3). Do such metaphors hide or clarify her meaning?

Dickinson's comment that she had written only "one or two" poems before that winter, when in fact she had written nearly three hundred, could lead to a discussion of the constructed self that appears even in personal correspondence. Have your students consider how they might write about last weekend's party in a letter to their parents as opposed to a letter to their best friend from high school. Without necessarily being dishonest, we generally shape any presentation of self depending on how we wish to appear to a particular audience. How do you suppose Dickinson appeared to Higginson when he first read this letter?

THOMAS WENTWORTH HIGGINSON, *On Meeting Dickinson for the First Time* (p. 314)

The first part of Higginson's letter to his wife reports his encounter with Emily Dickinson at her home in Amherst in a fairly straightforward fashion. If your students have read the poet's letter describing herself to Higginson, you might ask them to consider how closely the poet's description of herself matches his observations. Although Higginson refers to the poet's manner and appearance as childlike three times in a short space, he is also struck by her wisdom when she begins to speak to him.

Dickinson's definition of poetry would be an interesting topic for class discussion. Students might be encouraged to talk about the aptness and/or the limitations of her definition. Should all poetry produce the violent reaction in a reader that she describes? Would Dickinson's own works qualify as poetry according to her definition? The last comments of Dickinson that Higginson records, concerning her relation to the outside world, also merit consideration. Why would she have such an extreme reaction to the thought of mixing in society? Which of her comments might Mrs. Higginson have considered foolish?

MABEL LOOMIS TODD, *The* Character *of Amherst* (p. 315)

While Todd refers to Emily Dickinson both as a character and as a myth, her examples in this letter tend to cast Dickinson more as a ghost; several times she notes that no one ever sees the poet. None of her characterizations of Dickinson is particularly positive. Referring to someone as a "character" usually denotes unusual, even amusing behavior, and portraying that person as a ghost suggests that that person has no substance. Todd does not even use the term *myth* in its powerful, archetypal sense, but more to connote something unreal or not to be believed. The comments in this letter would seem to negate Dickinson's thesis, often stated in her poetry, that things seen half-veiled are more clearly seen than things in plain view. You might ask students what Todd's observations about Dickinson reveal about Todd herself and about the way Dickinson may have been perceived by her Amherst neighbors. As a topic for writing or for class discussion, you may wish to have your students piece together information from this letter and the previous two in order to produce a composite "portrait" of Emily Dickinson. However, what may emerge from these pieces is the enigmatic quality of her character.

RICHARD WILBUR, *On Dickinson's Sense of Privation* (p. 315)

According to Wilbur, Dickinson's fascination with the concept of want, both human and personal, emerges in her poetry in two ways. Her apprehension of God as a distant, unresponsive deity compels her to write satirical poetry protesting this situation on behalf of other human beings. However, the poet who rages against an uncaring creator on behalf of her fellow creatures also tolerates such privations and emulates such aloofness on a personal level. For Dickinson, "less is more" is merely another Christian paradox to be savored, such as the paradoxes of dying to live or freeing oneself by becoming a slave. In fact, depriving herself of everything possible, especially human companionship, seems to have been Dickinson's technique for achieving that appreciation for and knowledge of what she and other humans were missing that inspired her poetry. You may wish to have your students discuss this second premise more thoroughly; it may be a difficult concept for those not accustomed to dealing with paradox. Do they see any parallels in their own lives or in the culture at large to the idea that, as Wilbur says, "privation is more plentiful than plenty"? Can they think of times when deprivation has produced positive results, or do they feel that Dickinson uses this highly contradictory premise as a rationalization for her own eccentricities?

SANDRA M. GILBERT AND SUSAN GUBAR, *On Dickinson's White Dress* (p. 316)

You might wish to preface your discussion of this piece with a freewriting exercise in which your students explore their own associations with whiteness. Do their connotations mostly involve positive qualities, negative qualities, or nothingness? Gilbert and Gubar contrast William Sherwood's assertion that Dickinson's white dress was a sign of her commitment to the Christian mystery of death and resurrection with Melville's suggestion that whiteness may be the "all-color of atheism." They go on to suggest that whiteness may have been, for Dickinson, the perfect expression of a fascination with paradox and irony, that she was drawn to the color precisely because it was capable of representing opposite ends of any spectrum. You might ask your students whether they find any of the above theories convincing before having them propose their own theories as to why Dickinson wore only white (see question #3 in the text, p. 317).

You might caution your students that Gilbert and Gubar's characterization of the dress on display at the Dickinson homestead as "larger than most readers would have expected" is not shared by all who have seen it. Given the feminist perspective of Gilbert and Gubar's work, why might they emphasize the size of Dickinson's dress in this manner?

KARL KELLER, *Robert Frost on Dickinson* (p. 317)

Using Frost's words about Dickinson, Keller suggests that Frost had mixed feelings about his predecessor's deviations from regular rhyme and meter. On the one hand, two of Keller's quotes from Frost specifically mention that Frost feels Dickinson's strength in these situations, as though her urgency to communicate truth clashed with the limitations of form and she was determined that truth emerge the winner. On the other hand, another Frost quote attributes Dickinson's variations to her haste to move along to the next poem, a sign of weakness rather than strength. You might wish to have your students discuss whether or not these comments are necessarily inconsistent. Could Frost have found Dickinson's battles with form appropriate in some poems and careless in others? Could he have found her flouting the principles of rhyme and meter generally inappropriate, but admirable in some respects? What is Keller trying to prove by using these particular quotes? Does he suggest that they are contradictory?

Frost's comments about poetry give us another definition to think about. Do your students agree that "Poetry is play. . . . Poetry is fooling"? Does Frost seem to be talking about writing poetry, reading poetry, or both?

As a writing or a discussion topic, you might have your students respond to Frost's assertion, "I deny in a good poem or a good life that there is compromise."

CYNTHIA GRIFFIN WOLFF, *On the Many Voices in Dickinson's Poetry* (p. 319)

Wolff acknowledges the multiplicity of voices represented by the speakers in Dickinson's poems, from child to housewife to passionate woman to New England Puritan. However, she insists that the presence of these different voices affirms cohesion rather than indicates a fragmentation of the poet's psyche. According to Wolff, what the voices have in common is a concern with specific human problems, particularly those problems that threaten "the coherence of the self." Thus, the many voices become not a difficulty to be overcome but a tool by which the poet seeks to overcome difficulties. Wolff is especially adamant in her assertion that the voice selected for any particular poem does not represent the poet's particular mood of the moment, but is a "calculated tactic," a part of her artistic technique, an aspect of an individual poem that is as carefully chosen as any of the poem's words might be.

In discussing this passage, you might ask your students to consider whether they have different "voices" for different occasions and what determines how they speak at any given time. Do they get a sense of unity in reading Dickinson's poetry? If it is true that Dickinson again and again returns to the idea of encounters that threaten "the coherence of the self," what are some of these encounters, and in what ways are they threatening?

PAULA BENNETT, *On "I heard a Fly buzz — when I died —"* (p. 320)

According to Bennett, the fly in Dickinson's poem represents humankind's ignorance of what awaits us after death. This ignorance is dramatically emphasized in Dickinson's poem by the dying speaker, who, anticipating a divine experience at her death, is shocked when she is assailed by the buzzing of a fly instead. Ask students if they agree with Bennett's assertion that Dickinson's conclusion about death and the afterlife in this poem is that "we don't know much." Are there other ways to interpret Dickinson's depiction of the dying moment? Is Dickinson's poem necessarily, as Bennett puts it, a "grim joke" about the fate of human corpses — to be devoured by flies?

GALWAY KINNELL, *The Deconstruction of Emily Dickinson* (p. 321)

The speaker of this poem arrives at a public lecture on Dickinson late. He tries to contribute to the conversation about Dickinson and publication by reciting one of her poems, but he is interrupted by the professor. He would like to retort with some snappy witticism when the professor allows him to continue, but he finds himself weakly reciting the poem, "like a schoolboy called upon in class" (line 53). His final gesture is to return to his private dialogue with Dickinson, one which he keeps up in his mind, "But she was silent" (66).

The speaker feels that the professor's approach to Dickinson's poetry and/or her life overlooks the poetry in favor of the critical method, by seeking to unearth meaning by digging into the etymology of words and revealing their ambiguity. The speaker criticizes the professor for failing to listen to Dickinson (30), for wanting to hear himself speak rather than to hear the words of the author (34–35), and for misunderstanding the context of Dickinson's words as he delves into etymology (46). The irony is that the speaker never *says* any of this in public. Like Dickinson, he is trapped by his own shyness, or his reluctance to be a public spectacle, and his one public gesture of reciting the poem fails because he is unable to speak with forcefulness after the professor's spiel. It is also ironic that the speaker arrives after the lecture takes place, indicating that he did not care to hear it, but still feels the need to contribute. Perhaps this line of inquiry might help students respond to the question about the difference between a poet's response and a critic's response to poetry: where do their differing senses of authority come from? (Note that "authority" begins with the word "author," and recall the professor's etymological reading.) Have students witnessed people at lectures, or even in classes, who always feel the need to voice their opinion or to argue with the point that is being presented?

At some point during this discussion, you might want to bring your discussion of the theme of the poem back to Dickinson: why is this type of critique-in-poetry particularly useful when applied to a poet like Dickinson? Is she a poet whose words are meant to be "uprooted" (29), or is it best just to "listen" (30) to her? Which other poets might be equally appropriate for such a discussion, and why? And what of Dickinson's silence at the end of the poem: has she failed the speaker, or has he failed her? Is his connection to her superficial, or is her presence in the poem meant to tell us something deep about the speaker's experience? One final point to consider is the striking difference between Kinnell's poem and Dickinson's poetry in terms of form, language, and rhythm. Can students discern any similarities between Kinnell's poetics and Dickinson's? Would it have been appropriate, or even possible, to write this poem in Dickinson's style, with elliptical dashes, irregular capitalization, and steady rhythm?

POSSIBLE CONNECTION TO ANOTHER SELECTION

Marilyn Nelson Waniek, "Emily Dickinson's Defunct" (text p. 261)

TWO COMPLEMENTARY CRITICAL READINGS

CHARLES R. ANDERSON, *Eroticism in "Wild Nights — Wild Nights!"* (p. 323)

Anderson finds, in the declaration "Wild Nights should be / Our luxury" (lines 3–4), the image that contains all the other images in Dickinson's poem. According to Anderson, Dickinson's theme is that love is intense but temporal. He discusses the poem's other images, such as those of Eden and storms, in terms of how they emphasize these qualities of love. Each figure the poet uses, from Anderson's perspective, contains a double reference to ecstasy and brevity, and the phrase "Wild Nights" refers to the tumult outside and inside the lovers' paradise. Anderson's argument is consistent and brings all the major figurative language of the poem together in support of a common theme. What he does not deal with in depth is the "frank eroticism" of the poem that he mentions at the beginning of his discussion. You might ask your students how erotic they find the poem to be. Is it truly sensual, or does it just upset our expectations of this particular poet? Another possible topic for discussion is the relationship of this poem to themes found in Dickinson's other work. Is her frequent emphasis on how the narrowness of an experience intensifies our response to it connected with the qualities of love she foregrounds here?

DAVID S. REYNOLDS, *Popular Literature and "Wild Nights — Wild Nights!"* (p. 324)

Reynolds contrasts the rhetoric of Dickinson's poem with that of the sensational literature of her day to support his thesis that the greatness of Dickinson's "Wild Nights" lies in its being erotic and distinct from the lesser literature of the genre. He argues that in the first stanza, the yoking of the sensational adjective "wild" to the natural image of the "Night" serves to "purify" sexual desire (note that Reynolds ignores Dickinson's use of the word *luxury*, which Anderson focused on in the previous piece in order to highlight the poem's eroticism). In the next stanza, the more abstract natural images of sea and harbor further distance the passion expressed in the poem from crude sensationalism. The reference to "Eden," in the last stanza, adds a religious quality to the images that precede it. The cumulative effect, according to Reynolds, is the expression of intense but unconsummated sexual longing without the accompanying connotations of prurience. One question for students to consider, assuming they find Reynolds's argument convincing, is whether or not sexual passion abstracted in this way remains erotic.

ADDITIONAL DICKINSON POEMS ACCOMPANYING QUESTIONS FOR WRITING ABOUT AN AUTHOR IN DEPTH

"Faith" is a fine invention (p. 327)

This poem highlights a witty, even satirical side of Dickinson. Have students note the words that define each of the alternative ways of seeing. "Faith" is an "invention" (line 1), and microscopes are "prudent" (3). When examining Dickinson's diction, it is helpful to note the variety of possible definitions for ordinary words used in an unusual manner. *Invention* not only means a created or fabricated thing; it also carries the more archaic sense of an unusual discovery or a find. Likewise, while *prudence* has a rather stilted, utilitarian ring to it in the twentieth century, it once meant having the capacity to see divine truth. You might want to ask your class whether they feel the speaker favors religion or science. Since both faith and microscopes are meant to help people perceive directly rather than through a mist, is it possible that the poet favors neither side in this argument?

Ask your students what they think of Charles R. Anderson's comment on this poem in *Emily Dickinson's Poetry* (New York: Holt, 1960): "This is a word game, not a poem" (35).

<small>POSSIBLE CONNECTIONS TO OTHER SELECTIONS</small>

Emily Dickinson, "Portraits are to daily faces" (text p. 298)

———, "What Soft — Cherubic Creatures —" (text p. 302)

I know that He exists (p. 327)

Dickinson here seems to be at the cutting edge of modern sensibility and its dare-seeking fascination with death. The poem begins as a testimony of faith in the existence of a God who is clearly an Old Testament figure. If you ask students how the poem's speaker characterizes this deity, they may note the attributes of refinement, hiddenness, and removal from the gross affairs of earthly life. With this in mind, the tone of the next stanza, in which God seems to be the orchestrator of a cosmic game of hide-and-seek between Himself and whichever of His creatures will play, and in which the reward is "Bliss" (line 7), may be puzzling to students. The word *fond* in line 6 begins to sow a seed of doubt about the rules of this game. Does it mean "affectionate" or is it being used in its older sense of "foolish"?

In the third stanza, the speaker more fully comprehends the meaning of the game: finding God can mean finding oneself in God at the moment of death. Instead of death being a discovery that begins a condition of everlasting bliss, one may be confronted with an abrupt and everlasting ending. "Death's — stiff — stare" (12) caps three lines of halting verse, further emphasized by the hardness of the alliteration (you may wish to read these lines aloud so that students will appreciate their impact). By the third stanza, the ironic barb pierces through the texture of ordinary language. Instead of saying that the joke has gone too far, the speaker substitutes the verb *crawled*, which summons up the image of the serpent in the Garden of Eden in addition to bringing the lofty language of the first stanza down to earth.

This poem receives a brief but adequate discussion in Karl Keller's *The Only Kangaroo among the Beauty* (Baltimore: Johns Hopkins UP, 1979, p. 63). Keller observes that the "tone of voice moves from mouthed platitude to personal complaint." Ask your students if they agree with this assessment.

<small>POSSIBLE CONNECTIONS TO OTHER SELECTIONS</small>

Emily Dickinson, "Tell all the Truth but tell it slant —" (text p. 312)

Robert Frost, "Design" (text p. 356)

I never saw a Moor — (p. 328)

This straightforward profession of faith follows a pattern of expansion of imagery from the natural to the supernatural. Despite its simplicity, it reflects sound theology;

one of the basic theological proofs of the existence of God is the existence of the universe. Ask your students if the poem would be as effective if the first stanza relied on images of man-made things such as the Pyramids. Why or why not? How would it change the impact of the poem if the stanzas were reversed?

POSSIBLE CONNECTION TO ANOTHER SELECTION

Emily Dickinson, " 'Heaven' — is what I cannot reach!" (text p. 299)

Apparently with no surprise (p. 328)

While a first reading of "Apparently with no surprise" seems to present the reader with a picture of death in an uncaring, mechanistic universe overseen by a callous God, a closer look reveals a more ambiguous attitude on the part of the speaker. Most of the poem deals with an ordinary natural process, an early-morning frost that kills a flower. Framing this event is the viewpoint of the speaker, who acknowledges by means of the word *apparently* that his or her perspective may not be correct. According to the speaker, God is not involved in the event, other than to observe and to approve, as the speaker apparently does not. An examination of the adjectives and adverbs used in the poem reinforces the uncertainty of tone for which we have been prepared by the opening word. "No surprise" (line 1), "accidental power" (4), and the Sun proceeding "unmoved" (6) suggest a vision of nature as devoid of feeling. However, how can anything proceed and at the same time be *un*moved? How can power be used forcefully, as "beheads" (3) and "Assassin" (5) imply, and yet be accidental? The description of the frost as a "blond Assassin" in line 5 is particularly worth class discussion. Does the noun *Assassin* suggest that the frost is consciously evil? What about the adjective *blond*? You may wish to have your students recall other images of whiteness in Dickinson's poetry. Can they come to any conclusions as to the connotations this color has for her?

POSSIBLE CONNECTIONS TO OTHER SELECTIONS

Emily Dickinson, "Because I could not stop for Death —" (text p. 308)
——, "Safe in their Alabaster Chambers —" (1859 version) (text p. 296)

ADDITIONAL RESOURCES FOR TEACHING DICKINSON

SELECTED BIBLIOGRAPHY
Anderson, Charles R. *Emily Dickinson's Poetry.* New York: Holt, 1960.
Bennett, Paula. *Emily Dickinson: Woman Poet.* Iowa City: U of Iowa P, 1990.
Bloom, Harold, ed. *Emily Dickinson.* New York: Chelsea, 1985.
Chase, Richard. *Emily Dickinson.* New York: William Sloane Assocs., 1951.
Dickinson, Emily. *The Complete Poems of Emily Dickinson.* Ed. Thomas H. Johnson. Boston: Little, 1955.
——. *The Letters of Emily Dickinson.* Ed. Thomas H. Johnson and Theodora Ward. Cambridge: Belknap Press of Harvard UP, 1958.
——. *The Master Letters of Emily Dickinson.* Ed. Ralph W. Franklin. Amherst: Amherst College P, 1986.
Diehl, Joanne Feit. *Dickinson and the Romantic Imagination.* Princeton: Princeton UP, 1981.
Farr, Judith. *The Passion of Emily Dickinson.* Cambridge: Harvard UP, 1992.
Ferlazzo, Paul J., ed. *Critical Essays on Emily Dickinson.* Boston: Hall, 1984.
Johnson, Thomas H. *Emily Dickinson: An Interpretive Biography.* New York: Atheneum, 1955.
Juhasz, Suzanne, ed. *Feminist Critics Read Emily Dickinson.* Bloomington: Indiana UP, 1983.

Leyda, Jay. *The Years and Hours of Emily Dickinson*. New Haven: Yale UP, 1960.

Orzeck, Martin and Robert Weisbuch, eds. *Dickinson and Audience*. Ann Arbor: U of Michigan P, 1996.

Patterson, Rebecca. *Emily Dickinson's Imagery*. Amherst: U of Massachusetts P, 1979.

Porter, David. *Dickinson, the Modern Idiom*. Cambridge: Harvard UP, 1981.

Smith, Martha Nell. *Rowing in Eden: Rereading Emily Dickinson*. Austin: U of Texas P, 1992.

Stocks, Kenneth. *Emily Dickinson and the Modern Consciousness: A Poet of Our Time*. New York: St. Martin's, 1988.

Stonum, Gary Lee. *The Dickinson Sublime*. Madison: U of Wisconsin P, 1990.

Wardrop, Daneen. *Emily Dickinson's Gothic: Goblin with a Gauge*. Iowa City: U of Iowa P, 1996.

AUDIOVISUAL AND ONLINE RESOURCES (manual pp. 296, 329)

TIP FROM THE FIELD

I have my students become "experts" on one of the poets treated in depth in the anthology. The students then work in pairs and "team-teach" their poet to two other students who are experts on another poet.

— KARLA WALTERS, *University of New Mexico*

13

Robert Frost: A Life and Work

Like Dickinson, Frost may have a somewhat sanitized image in the minds of some students. The introduction addresses this point, and the section from Trilling helps greatly to break down these preconceptions. If students remain unconvinced, "Home Burial" and "Out, Out — " should provide ample evidence of the dark side of Frost.

Many of Frost's poems change on a second or third close reading — the text offers "The Road Not Taken" as an example of this. "Mending Wall" and "Nothing Gold Can Stay" also exhibit this behavior. Frost can provide a good opportunity for students to pay attention to their own reading habits. You might assign short writings that ask students to not only interpret the poems, but also to notice how their interpretations might change between readings.

ROBERT FROST

The Road Not Taken (p. 338)

This poem has traditionally been read as the poet's embracing of the "less traveled" road of Emersonian self-reliance, but the middle two stanzas complicate such a reading. Ask students to read the first and last stanzas alone and then to notice that in the middle two stanzas, the speaker actually seems to equivocate as to whether or not the roads were actually different. After reading those two stanzas, do they trust the assertion that "I took the one less traveled by" (line 19)? In "The Figure a Poem Makes" (text p. 359), Frost states that a poem can provide "a momentary stay against confusion." Against what kind of "confusion" is the poet working? How do the uses of rhyme, meter, and stanza form work against confusion? Is there a "clarification of life" (another of Frost's claims for poetry) in this poem?

At least three times in this poem (2, 4, and 15), the word *I* disrupts the iambic rhythm. Why would the poet do this? What is the effect of the dash at the end of line 18?

Richard Poirier, in *Robert Frost: The Work of Knowing* (New York: Oxford UP, 1977), claims that Frost's poems are often about the making of poetry. Is there any sense in which this poem could refer to writing poetry? For instance, do a poet's choices of rhyme, meter, or metaphor at the beginning of a poem dictate how the rest of the poem will proceed? Do poets try to choose roads not taken by their predecessors in order to be original? Are they sometimes unable to return to standard forms later, once they have launched out on a new poetic path?

As a writing assignment, you might ask your students to discuss or write about decisions they have made that closed off other choices for them.

POSSIBLE CONNECTION TO ANOTHER SELECTION

George Herbert, "The Collar" (text p. 610)

The Pasture (p. 340)

Ask students to suggest reasons why Frost chose to place "The Pasture" at the beginning of several volumes of his poetry. What might readers of this poem infer about the poems that followed? Could the references to raking the leaves away and watching the water clear in lines 2 and 3 suggest something more than the performance of spring chores?

Notice that the speaker twice informs the reader that "I shan't be gone long" (lines 4 and 8). The need to return to stable ground after going out and making discoveries is a recurring theme in Frost's poetry, as is evident in "Birches" and "Stopping by Woods on a Snowy Evening." Poems wherein the return is not assured — "Acquainted with the Night," for example — tend to be much more negative in tone. They often foreground what Lionel Trilling called the "terrifying" side of Robert Frost. How does Frost's practice of using a fixed form, such as blank verse or sonnet, yet altering the form by varying the meter or rhyme schemes (something he frequently does through the use of dialogue) demonstrate a similar desire to return to stable ground? Does this put the poet's often-quoted comment that writing free verse is like "playing tennis with the net down" in a different light? Is writing free verse, for Frost, more like casting loose from all one's moorings without an anchor?

POSSIBLE CONNECTIONS TO OTHER SELECTIONS

Robert Frost, "After Apple-Picking" (text p. 346)

Walt Whitman, "One's-Self I Sing" (text p. 642)

Mowing (p. 341)

This poem offers an amiable meditation on "the sweetest dream that labour knows" (line 13). The "long scythe" (2), so often a symbol of time or death, here establishes the power and pleasure of work. That symbolic resonance combines with references to fairy tales to establish the edge of a forest as a mysterious place where one might receive "the gift of idle hours, / or easy gold at the hand of fay or elf" (7–8). But the speaker discounts these ephemeral notions: "Anything more than the truth would have seemed too weak" (9). These allusions are secondary to the productive and happy relationship between the speaker and the right tool for the job.

The narrative of the poem is more clearly conveyed when it is read aloud: The first six lines examine the "whispering" (2) voice of the scythe, the last eight resist the tradition of fairy tales that prefer "idle hours" (7) or "easy gold" to the satisfactions of work well done. The speaker is alone, in "the heat of the sun" (4), but these circumstances are not presented in a negative light; the laboring speaker does not complain but revels in his work.

POSSIBLE CONNECTIONS TO OTHER SELECTIONS

Sophie Cabot Black, "August" (text p. 125)

Robert Frost, "The Pasture" (text p. 340)

Jeffrey Harrison, "Horseshoe Contest" (text p. 262)

Mending Wall (p. 342)

Students may already be familiar with this work from their high-school reading. Although the poem is often considered an indictment of walls and barriers of any sort, Frost probably did not have such a liberal point of view in mind. After all, the speaker initiates the mending, and he repeats the line "Something there is that doesn't love a wall." For him, mending the wall is a spring ritual — a kind of counteraction to spirits or elves or the nameless "Something" that tears down walls over the winter. It is gesture, ritual, and a reestablishment of old lines, this business of mending walls. The speaker teases his neighbor with the idea that the apple trees won't invade the pines, but to some measure he grants his conservative neighbor his due.

POSSIBLE CONNECTIONS TO OTHER SELECTIONS

Emily Dickinson, "Portraits are to daily faces" (text p. 298)

——, "To make a prairie it takes a clover and one bee" (question #1, following)

Robert Frost, "Neither Out Far nor In Deep" (question #2, following)

CONNECTIONS QUESTIONS IN TEXT (p. 343) WITH ANSWERS

1. How do you think the neighbor in this poem would respond to Dickinson's idea of imagination in "To make a prairie it takes a clover and one bee" (p. 293)?

    The neighbor in "Mending Wall" might accuse the speaker in Dickinson's poem of being foolish and impractical. Dickinson's speaker does not seem to think that boundaries make people happier, but the neighbor's experience has proved to him that "Good fences make good neighbors." The speaker in Frost's poem, more open to the kind of imagination Dickinson celebrates, wants his neighbor to imagine that elves have brought the wall down — but the neighbor probably won't.

2. What similarities and differences does the neighbor have with the people Frost describes in "Neither Out Far nor In Deep" (p. 356)?

    In both poems Frost presents people who seem to be content with a single point of view, resisting new or even alternative views of the world. The neighbor, "like an old-stone savage armed," appears to be part of some primeval mystery that fascinates the speaker in "Mending Wall." In contrast, the people in "Neither Out Far nor In Deep" are the ones transfixed by a mystery — that of the vast ocean.

Home Burial (p. 343)

"Home Burial" is a dialogue in blank verse between a husband and wife who have recently lost their child and who have different ways of coping with loss. One way to begin discussion is to consider the form of the poem: does it seem more like a poem or a miniature play? How does the rhythm of the poem affect its theme? The haunting repetition of the word "don't" in line 32, for example, is realistic dialogue when we consider the tension behind the situation, but it also serves to mark a turning point in the poem. At what other points in the poem do similar repetitions occur, and do they also mark turning points in the dramatic situation, or do they reveal something about the psychological state of the characters?

Biographical criticism is beginning to come back into fashion, and you might remind the class of some of the introductory notes on Frost in this chapter before discussing the poem. Clearly the speaker is more matter-of-fact than his wife, and there is decidedly a communication problem between them. Note how Frost splits their dialogue in the interrupted iambic lines. But doesn't the husband deserve some special commendation for possessing the courage and integrity to initiate a confrontation with his wife? Discussion of the poem might also consider the value that ancients and moderns alike ascribe to a catharsis of emotions.

You might, if the class seems at all responsive, examine the speaker's claim that "a man must partly give up being a man / With women-folk" (lines 52–53). What does this statement mean? Has feminism done anything to challenge what are uniquely man's and uniquely woman's provinces of concern?

POSSIBLE CONNECTIONS TO OTHER SELECTIONS

Emily Dickinson, "After great pain, a formal feeling comes —" (text p. 306)

Robert Frost, " 'Out, Out—' " (text p. 350)

Jane Kenyon, "The Blue Bowl" (text p. 106)

After Apple-Picking (p. 346)

The sense of things undone and the approach of "winter sleep" seem to betoken a symbolic use of apple picking in this poem. Moreover, the speaker has already had an experience this day — seeing the world through a skim of ice — that predisposes him to view things strangely or aslant. At any rate, he dreams, appropriately enough, of apple harvesting. Apples take on connotations of golden opportunity and inspire fear lest one should fall. As harvest, they represent a rich, fruitful life, but as the speaker admits, "I am overtired / Of the great harvest I myself desired" (lines 28–29).

Apples are symbolically rich, suggesting everything from temptation in the garden of Eden, with overtones of knowledge and desire, to the idea of a prize difficult to attain, as in the golden apples of Hesperides that Hercules had to obtain as his eleventh labor. Here they can be read as representing the fruit of experience.

POSSIBLE CONNECTION TO ANOTHER SELECTION

John Keats, "To Autumn" (text p. 109)

Birches (p. 347)

This poem is a meditative recollection of being a boyhood swinger of birches. In the last third of the poem, the speaker thinks about reliving that experience as a way of escaping from his life, which sometimes seems "weary of considerations." Swinging on birches represents a limber freedom, the elation of conquest, and the physical pleasure of the free-fall swish groundward. Note, in contrast, Frost's description of what ice storms do to birches. Images like "shattering and avalanching on the snow-crust" suggest a harsh brittleness. The speaker in the end opts for Earth over Heaven because he (like Keats, to some extent) has learned that "Earth's the right place for love."

Frost's blank verse lends a conversational ease to this piece, with its digressions for observation or for memory. A more rigid form, such as rhymed couplets, would work against this ease.

In a writing assignment, students might analyze the different forms of knowing in "Birches," contrasting Truth's matter-of-factness (lines 21–22) and the pull of life's "considerations" (43) with boyhood assurance and the continuing powers of dream and imagination.

POSSIBLE CONNECTIONS TO OTHER SELECTIONS

Emily Dickinson, "Portraits are to daily faces" (text p. 298)

Pablo Neruda, "Sweetness, Always" (text p. 660)

A Girl's Garden (p. 349)

Through the re-telling of a neighbor's childhood story, this poem provides Frost's perspective on his neighbor, on childhood, on the stories we choose to tell of our lives, and on the lessons gardening can teach us. This poem can serve many disparate readings: It works as a parable about how everything works out regardless of our intent or ability, a pleasant story from childhood without much larger significance, proof of the long-lasting effects of our thoughtless "childlike" activities, or an acknowledgment of the sublime results of simple activities. Examining each reading and discussing the ways they can co-exist can help students see the rich potential of poetry.

The central comparison in this poem will provide different readings depending on what students think Frost intends when he refers to "village things" (line 42). It may be a good idea to spend some time at the beginning of class reading the poem out loud — very helpful in demonstrating the subtle effect of the enjambed rhymes — and then making a list of possibilities. The levels of comparison are many and complex; asking students to look carefully at the actions of the little girl in the narrative for clues about the nature of "village things" could help focus the discussion.

POSSIBLE CONNECTIONS TO OTHER SELECTIONS

Robert Frost, "Mending Wall" (question #2, following)
——, "Stopping by the Woods on a Snowy Evening" (question #1, following)

CONNECTIONS QUESTIONS IN TEXT (p. 350) WITH ANSWERS

1. Compare the narrator in this poem to the narrator in "Stopping by Woods on a Snowy Evening" (p. 353). How, in each poem, do simple activities reveal something about the narrator?

    Both the narrative from the neighbor's childhood and the episode described in "Stopping by Woods" demonstrate an appreciation of the ordinary moments in life. The narrator has considered the events described by the neighbor and noticed that the story is repeated when "it seems to come in right" (line 43). The act of noticing connections and beauty invests these simple activities and observations with the larger meaning.

2. Discuss the narrator's treatment of the neighbor in this poem and in "Mending Wall" (p. 342).

    The speaker's implication of his neighbor in "Mending Wall" is a little more forceful than it is in "A Girl's Garden." The quiet nudges the speaker provides to demonstrate his thoughts on the neighbor's fond use of the story seem more like a smirk than the impatient characterizations of the neighbor as "old-stone savage armed" (line 40) or moving "in darkness" (41).

"Out, Out —" (p. 350)

Often when disaster strikes, we tend to notice the timing of events. Frost implies here that "they" might have given the boy an extra half-hour and thereby averted the disaster. This perspective, coupled with the final line, in which the family seems to go on with life and ordinary tasks, can appear callous. But compare the wife's chastisement of her husband in "Home Burial" (text p. 343). Is the attitude callousness, or is it, rather, the impulse of an earth-rooted sensibility that refuses pain its custom of breaking the routine of life-sustaining chores and rituals? Very little in this poem seems to be a criticism of the survivors; rather, like *Macbeth* and the famous speech that proclaims life's shadowy nature (text p. 115), it seems to acknowledge the tenuous hold we have on life.

POSSIBLE CONNECTIONS TO OTHER SELECTIONS

Stephen Crane, "A Man Said to the Universe" (question #3, following)
Emily Dickinson, "From all the Jails the Boys and Girls" (text p. 442)
Robert Frost, "Home Burial" (question #2, following)
——, "Nothing Gold Can Stay" (question #1, following)

CONNECTIONS QUESTIONS IN TEXT (p. 351) WITH ANSWERS

1. What are the similarities and differences in theme between this poem and Frost's "Nothing Gold Can Stay" (p. 354)?

    In this poem the speaker presents a tragic experience involving human beings or property and then sets it in the larger context of the natural world. In "Nothing Gold Can Stay," the focus is on the natural world and the feeling of an Edenic spring.

2. Write an essay comparing how grief is handled by the boy's family in this poem and the couple in "Home Burial" (p. 343).

    Grief separates the couple in "Home Burial," as the wife accuses the husband of being unfeeling when the husband suggests that they must go on living despite their child's death. Miscommunication lingers in the split lines as well as in the situation of the couple, separated by the length of a staircase. In " 'Out, Out —' " the bereaved "turned to their affairs," choosing the response of the man in "Home Burial." Death unites them in that it reaffirms their commitment to the duty of living.

3. Compare the tone and theme of " 'Out, Out —' " and those of Crane's "A Man Said to the Universe" (p. 146).

    " 'Out, Out —' " and Crane's poem share a moral view that there is little ground on which humanity and the universe might meet. Crane's tone is slightly humorous, whereas Frost's approach is more poignant, but both rely heavily on dialogue to make their opinions known. Frost's borrowing from *Macbeth*, as well as the subject of the dead boy, gives his poem a more tragic quality than is present in Crane's sobering message.

A Boundless Moment (p. 352)

This poem is the playful speaker's retelling of a practical joke played on a gullible friend, "too ready to believe the most" (line 4). The friend sees a "young beech" (12) through the March maples, "fair enough for flowers" (6), and doesn't recognize it. The windy chill of March makes many eager for the approach of true spring, and the speaker's friend is no exception. The "Boundless Moment" of the title is not merely a gentle prod at the friend's gullibility but a celebration of his willingness to believe that some portent of spring has arrived.

The speaker himself is willing to believe the "Paradise-in-Bloom" (5) fiction he's created, describing himself as "one his own pretense deceives" (10). The "strange world" (9) of the last stanza is one created out of the speaker's imagination and his friend's will to believe, a moment boundless in possibility and wonder, until the speaker "said the truth" (11) and the pair moved on. The tone of the last line, in which the fantastic "Paradise-in-Bloom" (5) is revealed as "A young beech clinging to its last year's leaves" (12), does not disappoint: Even this modest figure provides a catalyst for the wonder the two men create so quickly. You may want to ask your students if this simple image of a beech tree surprised them. Were they expecting something more extraordinary to make such an impression?

POSSIBLE CONNECTIONS TO OTHER SELECTIONS

Robert Frost, "Birches" (text p. 347)

———, "Nothing Gold Can Stay" (question #1, following)

CONNECTION QUESTION IN TEXT (p. 352) WITH ANSWER

1. Discuss the tone and theme of "A Boundless Moment" and "Nothing Gold Can Stay" (p. 354).

In "Nothing Gold Can Stay," the speaker is resigned to the inevitable changing of the seasons. The tone is matter-of-fact, tinged with a weight of sad certainty. "A Boundless Moment" provides some resistance to this certainty, establishing a fresh reality with humor and imagination, although it, too, accepts the inevitable change of seasons.

The Investment (p. 352)

This Italian, or Petrarchan, sonnet depicts a speaker questioning his neighbor's decision to invest in a piano and new paint for "an old, old house" (line 3). The context is important: The neighborhood Frost's speaker sees is a depressed one, where "winter dinners" (7) are counted out in sections of a potato patch. "Over back where" (1) and "back there" (9) provide more than a physical location for these people: The speaker uses these phrases to distance himself from them, establishing class difference through their speech and in his understanding of the lives they lead. Still, these impoverished people have chosen to shun despair. Their decision prompts the speaker to consider that the household may have come into some money, or that new love has encouraged this "extravagance" (11). His final consideration is the defiant couplet that concludes the poem, deciding that "color and life" (14) are fine returns on any investment.

POSSIBLE CONNECTIONS TO OTHER SELECTIONS

Robert Frost, "Home Burial" (question #1, following)
Adrienne Rich, "Living in Sin" (text p. 633)

CONNECTION QUESTION IN TEXT (p. 353) WITH ANSWER

1. Compare the relationship of the man and wife in "The Investment" with that of "Home Burial" (p. 343).

   "Home Burial" presents a couple struggling with the death of a child and their difficulty communicating with one another about it. It reveals specific detail and dialogue to provide an intimate view of their life together. "The Investment" is not in the voice of the "man and wife" (line 13) it describes, but it uses the curiosity of an unnamed observer to establish a possible sketch of a married couple. The final assumption in "The Investment" is of a married pair determined to be joyful. The effect of the dialogue in "Home Burial" leaves the reader uncertain about the health of the marriage depicted.

Fire and Ice (p. 353)

With a kind of diabolic irony, the theories for the way the world might end grow as our knowledge and technology increase. Students can probably supply a number of earth-ending disaster theories: overheating of the earth because we are moving sunward; the greenhouse effect with the chemical destruction of the ozone layer; war, apocalypse, or "nuclear winter"; a change in the earth's orbit away from the sun; the return of the ice age; and so on. Frost here also speaks of the metaphoric powers of hatred (ice) and desire (fire) as destroyers of the earth. To say that ice would "suffice" to end the world is a prime example of understatement.

POSSIBLE CONNECTION TO ANOTHER SELECTION

William Butler Yeats, "The Second Coming" (text p. 652)

Stopping by Woods on a Snowy Evening (p. 353)

With very few words, Frost here creates a sense of brooding mystery as the speaker stops his horse in a desolate landscape between wood and frozen lake. The attraction of the woods is their darkness, the intimation they offer of losing oneself in them. The speaker gazes into them with a kind of wishfulness, while his horse shakes his bells, a reminder to get on with the business of living. The repetition in the last lines denotes a literal recognition that the speaker must move on and connotes that there is much to be done before life ends.

You might use the final question in the text as a brief writing assignment to show how rhyme relates and interlocks the stanzas and offers in the final stanza (*dddd*) a strong sense of closure.

POSSIBLE CONNECTION TO ANOTHER SELECTION

Henry Wadsworth Longfellow, "Snow-Flakes" (text p. 622)

Nothing Gold Can Stay (p. 354)

Students often misread the first image in this poem as the brilliant golds of fall fading into winter. Caution them to read carefully; the poem describes the early days of *spring*, when the leaf buds (in New England, at least) emerge in a brief burst of yellowish-green before turning their deeper summer green. The other images in the poem, dawn losing its colors and becoming the brighter but less colorful day and the ideal of Eden becoming the reality of life after the Fall, reinforce the sense of loss. You might ask your students to consider the ambiguous nature of the images used in this poem. The speaker certainly takes a negative viewpoint: the leaf "subsides," Eden "sank," and the dawn "goes down." But isn't it true that what early spring gives way to is the glory of summer, and dawn to the fullness of the day? Also, the loss of Eden is often referred to as a "fortunate fall." Why do you suppose there is no indication of the other side of these images? Why would Frost use such ambiguous images, when the gold of autumn fading into winter would fit so much better with the tone of the poem? Do your students agree with the speaker's negative appraisal of the passing of time?

POSSIBLE CONNECTIONS TO OTHER SELECTIONS

Robert Frost, " 'Out, Out —' " (text p. 350)
Robert Herrick, "To the Virgins, to Make Much of Time" (question #1, following)

CONNECTION QUESTION IN TEXT (p. 354) WITH ANSWER

1. Write an essay comparing the tone and theme of "Nothing Gold Can Stay" with Herrick's "To the Virgins, to Make Much of Time" (p. 64).

   Both poems have as their basis the idea that youth is ephemeral and that life passes quickly and inevitably. Herrick's poem offers advice regarding this condition, while Frost's presents it as a universal truth. The tone of Herrick's poem is somewhat lighter (without explicit reference, for instance, to "grief") since it keeps its young audience in mind. His purpose is ultimately rhetorical; Frost's is philosophical.

The Armful (p. 354)

This poem provides an examination of the speaker's difficulty holding onto all the things he cares about. The simplest reading, of a man walking down a road struggling with an armload of parcels, gives way to a broader portrait of someone trying to live a balanced life, refusing to cast anything or anyone aside. He makes a vow in the center of the poem that belies the simplicity of the original reading: "With all I have to hold with, hand and mind / And heart, if need be, I will do my best / To keep their building balanced at my breast" (lines 6–8).

The rhyme and meter of this poem establish a formal model of the successful juggling the content strives to achieve. A looser free verse poem might leave the reader in greater doubt of the success of the speaker's venture. Asking students to consider what parcels they are holding onto in their own lives might help them see the effectiveness of Frost's metaphor.

POSSIBLE CONNECTIONS TO OTHER SELECTIONS

Emily Dickinson, "I felt a Cleaving in my Mind" (question #1, following)
Robert Herrick, "Delight in Disorder" (text p. 211)

CONNECTION QUESTION IN TEXT (p. 355) WITH ANSWER

1. Compare the central metaphor and theme of "The Armful" with those of Emily Dickinson's "I felt a Cleaving in my Mind —" (p. 309).

    Both poems establish familiar, concrete examples — a scattering of rolling balls, juggling of an armful of parcels — to illustrate feelings about life. While Dickinson's speaker struggles with two thoughts, difficult to connect, Frost is working with a "whole pile" (line 3). Both provide, with similar good-natured effort, clear, brief depictions of complex abstractions.

Spring Pools (p. 355)

This poem paints a portrait of pools that "chill and shiver" (line 3), lovely in springtime. They "reflect / The total sky" (1–2) before the green foliage of summer expands to interrupt their views. The speaker sees their loveliness, "the flowers beside them" (3), and knows their fate: they will not spill "out by any brook or river" (5); the trees will drink them up and "blot out" (10) the pools' clear reflections. The speaker knows this is the way of seasons: the snow melts, the pools form, flowers bloom and fade, and trees' "pent-up buds" (7) give way to "summer woods" (8) and drain the spring pools. But he would have them stay a while, "think twice" (9) about the effects of their actions, and realize that their ascendancy means the fading of another.

This poem, like many of Frost's, provides a detailed picture of nature that can serve as a poignant parallel with other realms. Students may want to think of other examples that can be derived from the poem's lesson. The conclusion reminds the reader that the pools themselves were once snow, which likely had its own virtues. This establishes a series of connections: the trees, too, will fade in time, adding to the lessons extrapolated from the portrait. The careful rhyme and meter are remarkably natural to the ear; this effect is achieved in part through the slant rhyme in lines 7 and 8, as well as the enjambment in the second stanza.

POSSIBLE CONNECTIONS TO OTHER SELECTIONS

Robert Frost, "Design" (question #1, following)
——, "Nothing Gold Can Stay" (text p. 354)

CONNECTION QUESTION IN TEXT (p. 356) WITH ANSWER

1. Compare the speaker's reaction to nature in this poem and in "Design" (p. 356).

    Both poems use rhyme and meter to establish order: while "Spring Pools" incorporates slant rhyme, "Design" depends on a strict rhyme scheme. In both poems the speaker wonders at the will that orders nature. He cautions the trees to "think twice before they use their powers" (line 9) in "Spring Pools," knowing what changes those powers will bring. In "Design" the speaker asks how the spider, flower, and moth came together, and determines it is the "design of darkness to appall" (13). A relentless movement toward cyclical change, which includes death, is at the center of both poems.

Design (p. 356)

The opening octave of this sonnet is highly descriptive and imagistic in its presentation of spider, flower, and moth, all white. The sestet asks the question of design: who assembled all these elements in just such a way as to ensure that the moth would end up where the spider was — inside a "heal-all" (ironic name for this flower), its "dead wings carried like a paper kite"? Frost has in mind the old argument of design to prove the existence of God. There must be a prime mover and creator; otherwise, the world would not be as magnificent as it is. But what of the existence of evil in this design, Frost asks. The final two lines posit choices: either there is a malevolent mover (the "design of darkness to appall") or, on this small scale of moth and spider, evil occurs merely by chance ("If design govern . . ."). The rhyme scheme is *abba, abba, acaa, cc,* and its control provides a tight interlocking of ideas and the strong closure of the couplet.

Randall Jarrell's remarks on the imagery and ideas here are superb; he appreciates this poem with a poet's admiration (see his *Poetry and the Age* [New York: Farrar, 1953, 1972], pp. 45–49). He notes, for example, the babylike qualities of "dimpled . . . fat and white" (not pink) as applied to the spider. Note, too, how appropriate the word *appall* is since it indicates both the terror and the funereal darkness in this malevolently white trinity of images.

A comparison with the original version of this poem, "In White" (text p. 358), should prove that "Design" is much stronger. The title of the revised version, the closing two lines, and several changes in image and diction make for a more effective and thematically focused poem.

As a writing assignment, you might ask students either to compare this poem with its original version or to analyze the use of whiteness in "Design" and show how the associations with the idea of whiteness contrast with the usual suggestions of innocence and purity.

Possible Connections to Other Selections

Emily Dickinson, "I know that He exists" (question #2, following)
——, "Safe in their Alabaster Chambers —" (1861 version, text p. 296)
Robert Frost, "In White" (text p. 358)
William Hathaway, "Oh, Oh" (question #1, following)
Edna St. Vincent Millay, "I will put Chaos into fourteen lines" (text p. 229)

Connections Questions in Text (p. 356) with Answer

1. Compare the ironic tone of "Design" with the tone of Hathaway's "Oh, Oh" (p. 13). What would you have to change in Hathaway's poem to make it more like Frost's?

    Hathaway's "Oh, Oh" has a far less serious tone than Frost's poem, as the poet plays a joke on his audience, beginning the poem in a slaphappy, conversational tone, only to change it to a note of impending doom. To be more like Frost's poem, "Oh, Oh" would have to make its audience aware of the entire situation from the beginning.

2. In an essay discuss Frost's view of God in this poem and Dickinson's perspective in "I know that He exists" (p. 327).

In "Design" the speaker questions the existence of God by suggesting that only a malevolent deity could preside over the relentless mechanisms of nature, whereby one species destroys another to survive. In "I know that He exists," Dickinson's speaker speculates not on the nature of God, but just on the hiddenness — the absence against which she must assert her belief. Frost is less comfortable with a God who must be malevolent than with no God at all. God's absence is what troubles Dickinson.

Neither Out Far nor In Deep (p. 356)

This poem, particularly in its last stanza, comments on humanity's limitations in comprehending the infinite, the unknown, the inhuman and vast. Again, Randall Jarrell's comment is useful. He writes, "It would be hard to find anything more unpleasant to say about people than that last stanza; but Frost doesn't say it unpleasantly — he says it with flat ease" (*Poetry and the Age* 42–43). You might organize a writing assignment around the tone of this poem.

POSSIBLE CONNECTION TO ANOTHER SELECTION

Robert Frost, "Mending Wall" (text p. 342)

The Silken Tent (p. 357)

This Shakespearean sonnet uses an extended conceit to compare one woman's equipoise to the silken tent that remains erect on a summer's day. The center-positioned cedar pole, we are told, points "heavenward," and this detail, as well as the silken substance of the tent, suggests the spiritual centeredness of the person. She seems serenely balanced but not aloof from human affairs, since the ties that connect her soul to their groundward stakes are those of "love and thought." Only by slight changes ("the capriciousness of summer air") is she made to feel these ties, which are more connection than bondage. Overall, the tone of the poem, enhanced by the sounds of the words, suggests serenity.

Since the poem is a Shakespearean sonnet, you can begin discussion by considering that form: does the final couplet of the poem change the meaning of the three quatrains before it? Do the quatrains suggest a development of the argument in three distinct points? To what end does Frost use other poetic devices in the poem, such as alliteration? The sonnet was originally titled "In Praise of Your Poise" and was written for Frost's secretary, Kay Morrison.

POSSIBLE CONNECTIONS TO OTHER SELECTIONS

Robert Herrick, "Delight in Disorder" (text p. 211)
William Shakespeare, "Shall I compare thee to a summer's day?" (text p. 228)

PERSPECTIVES ON FROST

"In White": Frost's Early Version of "Design" (p. 358)

Many of the alterations Frost made in changing "In White" to "Design" have the effect of shifting the poem's focus from an individual occurrence to a more generalized one, from the questioning of a single death to the questioning of the force that caused, or allowed, the death to occur.

Students could begin by noting as many differences as they can find between the two poems. Probably the most obvious is the change in title. Whereas the title of the earlier poem announces a concern with the color white, which seems to represent death, the later title suggests a larger concern: the question of order (or the lack of it) in the universe.

Frost retained the sonnet form when he revised, but the rhyme scheme for the sestet changes from six lines with the same rhyme to the much more complex *abaabb*. This throws a sharper emphasis on the last two lines of "Design," the lines in which the poet suggests that events are shaped either by forces of evil or not at all.

Ask students to discuss how changes in individual word choices affect the poem. Some of the most striking of these are the change from "dented" to "dimpled" in line 1 and from "lifeless" to "rigid" in line 3 (i.e., even more dead, as though rigor mortis has set in). Another interesting change is that whereas the poem once *began* with a general observation and *ended* with the very personal "I," it now *begins* with "I" and moves outward to *end* with a general statement. Also note the use of the word *if* in the last line of the final version of "Design." This is one of Frost's favorite ways of injecting ambivalence and uncertainty into his poems.

Possible Connection to Another Selection

Robert Frost, "Design" (text p. 356)

Frost on the Living Part of a Poem (p. 358)

Intonation in musicians' parlance refers to pitch and the idea of playing in tune. Does Frost use the word in that sense here? If not, what does he mean later on by the "accent of sense" and how the word *come* can appear in different passages as a third, fourth, fifth, and sixth note?

In introducing this prose passage, you might point out that poets construct poetry out of fairly near-at-hand vocabularies, words we have already tasted on our tongues. One of the appeals of poetry is the physical way we intone its sounds, even when we read silently, so that we become in a sense a resonating chamber for the poem. It might be well to recall too that poetry originally was a spoken, not a written medium, and those things that were regarded as important enough to be remembered were put in verse.

Frost makes several unqualified statements here. Students, by and large, receive as part of their first-year college training the advice to be chary of the committed word. You might spend some of the class discussion exploring when and where rhetoric must be unequivocating.

AMY LOWELL, *On Frost's Realistic Technique* (p. 359)

Elsewhere in her review, Lowell describes Frost's vision as "grimly ironic." She goes on: "Mr. Frost's book reveals a disease which is eating into the vitals of our New England life, at least in its rural communities." In discussing the characters in Frost's poems she calls them "the leftovers of old stock, morbid, pursued by phantoms, slowly sinking to insanity." You might ask students to find evidence for Lowell's observations in the Frost poems in this chapter. Are there opposite tendencies in these characters that save them from what Lowell describes as a "disease eating into the vitals"?

Frost on the Figure a Poem Makes (p. 359)

In this introduction to his *Collected Poems*, Frost calls the sounds of a poem "the gold in the ore." Perhaps the best way to discuss Frost's assertion is to put it to the test. How do Frost's own poems stand up? How does he use sound? His more conversational poems, such as "Home Burial," provide insight into individual characters through an imitation of their speech patterns. The contemplative poem, exemplified by "Birches" or

"After Apple-Picking," can be analyzed both for the speaker's character as it is revealed in his diction and for the way sounds both reaffirm and undermine the speaker's point.

Poems are, according to Frost, spontaneous in that they are derived from the poet's imagination as it interacts with his surroundings. But the imagination is not groundless because poets take many of their ideas from what they've read, often unconsciously: "They stick to nothing deliberately, but let what will stick to them like burrs where they walk in the fields." Frost's belief in the predestination of poetry involves the idea that the poem is an act of belief, of faith: "It must be a revelation, or a series of revelations, as much for the poet as for the reader." Not entirely the product of either spontaneity or predestination, the poem takes on a life of its own: "Like a piece of ice on a hot stove the poem must ride on its own melting."

In giving up claims to democracy and political freedom, Frost resists the process of naming something that supposedly is without limitation. Once defined as "free," whatever we call free ceases to be just that. Frost uses as an example our "free" school system, which forces students to remain in it until a certain age; it is, therefore, not free. Resisting confining labels, Frost as an artist is more able to reach a world audience; once he states a political bias, his art is one of exclusion. You might ask students to examine Frost's statements in the context of the more political poems in the Album of World Literature.

Frost on the Way to Read a Poem (p. 362)

Experience with one or two poems by an author often eases the way for reading other poems by him or her. But will reading "Birches," for example, prepare the way for understanding "Fire and Ice"? Not necessarily. Beyond our literary experience, some of our "life learning" enters into the reading of poems as well.

The image of reader as "revolving dog" also seems a little discomforting, no matter what one's feelings about dogs. Poetry reading requires a certain point of stability, like the cedar pole in "The Silken Tent." Without it, one might be at a loss to distinguish sentiment from the sentimental, the power of the image from the fascination of the ornament.

You might ask students to try Frost's advice with two or three of his own poems. They can read one in the light of another and then write about the experience.

LIONEL TRILLING, *On Frost as a Terrifying Poet* (p. 362)

With a take your students may find surprising, Trilling objects to the Frost of readers who use the poet to promote their causes: Frost as simple American, Frost as simple poet, Frost as modernist with a twist. He argues, using D. H. Lawrence's conception of the American writer, that Frost is a truly radical poet, in a tradition of radical American thinkers whose poetic work "is carried out by the representation of the terrible actualities of life in a new way."

To introduce them to Frost's biography (and how it affects his world-view and poetry) you might refer students to Lawrance Thompson's three-volume biography of Frost: *Robert Frost: The Early Years, 1874–1915; Robert Frost: The Years of Triumph, 1915–1938,* and Lawrance Thompson and R. H. Winnick, *Robert Frost: The Later Years, 1938–1963* (New York: Holt, 1966, 1970, 1976). For a more contemporary and controversial biography, consult William H. Pritchard's *Frost: A Literary Life Reconsidered* (New York: Oxford UP, 1984).

HERBERT R. COURSEN JR., *A Parodic Interpretation of "Stopping by Woods on a Snowy Evening"* (p. 364)

This critical spoof offers a fine opportunity to articulate just what we seek from literary criticism and why we accept one writer's word and reject another's. One important factor in the Frost poem that is not considered here is tone and the speaker's own fascination with the woods, which are "lovely, dark, and deep."

If we were to isolate factors that mark good literary criticism, we might speak of (1) completeness (Are there any significant details omitted?); (2) coherence (Coursen advertises the simplicity of his theory but then talks at length about veiled allusions and obfuscation); and (3) fidelity to experience (No, Virginia, a horse is never a reindeer, not even on Christmas Eve). Good criticism avoids the overly ingenious.

This spoof also lends itself to a review of principles of good writing, which students have probably already acquired in a composition course. You might ask, too, what it was that inspired Coursen to write this essay. What, in other words, is he objecting to in the practice of literary criticism?

BLANCHE FARLEY, *The Lover Not Taken* (p. 365)

The fun of parodies derives in part from recognition of their sources — in this instance "The Road Not Taken." In Farley's parody, we see again the distressed speaker who wants to have it both ways. As is usually the case with Frost's deliberators, the woman in this poem seems to have many hours to devote to "mulling." Farley mimics Frost's faint archaisms with the line (present in both poems) "Somewhere ages and ages hence." She also plays with and lightly satirizes the rigors of Frost's blank-verse line. Notice, for example, how she carries over the key word that would round out the sense of the line between lines 8 and 9, only to accommodate the pentameter scansion. At the close of her poem, Farley plays down the need for choosing and asserts that there was no difference between the lovers. Appropriately for this parody, she closes with a heroic couplet.

DEREK WALCOTT, *The Road Taken* (p. 366)

Pay careful attention to Walcott's definition of an uncle as students respond to Walcott's description of Frost as "avuncular" rather than "paternal." Students may tend to read their impressions of their *own* uncles into Frost's character. This might not be a bad thing, in terms of extending Walcott's analogy — in what *other* ways can Frost be said to be avuncular? — but Walcott qualifies his analogy in specific ways. Also, note that Walcott seems to answer his own rhetorical question in the second paragraph, but the answer may not satisfy. What is it about the American character that craves an uncle? "Because uncles are wiser than fathers" seems ironic in its simplicity, and students may want to offer other responses.

If students select a poem demonstrating that Frost is a "master ironist," they have a number to select from; but what about those students who don't think that Frost is a master ironist? Can they find opposite evidence? Much depends on a careful definition of "mastery" rather than of irony; for instance, if mastery denotes subtlety, " 'Out, Out! —' " could be used to illustrate that Frost is decidedly *not* a master ironist!

If you are working with either of the other two poets which the anthology covers in depth — Dickinson or Hughes — you might want to try to apply Walcott's terms "democratic" and "autocratic" to these other poets as a way of comparing them with Frost. Do these terms mean as much when applied to the other writers, or are the terms only useful insofar as they compare Whitman and Frost? There are also ample examples of

Whitman's poetry in the anthology, which students can use to test Walcott's observations.

TWO COMPLEMENTARY CRITICAL READINGS

RICHARD POIRIER, *On Emotional Suffocation in "Home Burial"* (p. 367)

You could begin class discussion of this perspective by asking students to find particular moments in Frost's poem that suggest that the couple's home has become, as Poirier suggests, a "mental hospital." What is it about this couple that reveals both their profound suffering and their perceived inability to escape their circumstances? You might ask your students to compare and contrast the anguish of the husband and the wife. In what ways are both of them emotionally suffocating in the house and in their relationship?

Poirier argues that "Home Burial" suggests "alienation, secretiveness, [and] male intimidation" (paragraph 3); where in the poem do your students find examples of these qualities? Do they agree with Poirier's interpretation? Does your class wholly identify with one character rather than the other? If not, you might explore the reasons class sympathy is divided between the husband and wife. Why might one elicit more sympathy from the reader than the other?

KATHERINE KEARNS, *On the Symbolic Setting of "Home Burial"* (p. 368)

Kearns asserts that "the woman can 'see' through the window and into the grave in a way her husband cannot." You might open class discussion by asking students to describe these different ways of "seeing." Why do they see differently, and what does each of them see? Kearns also states that the husband and wife in "Home Burial" are "in profound imbalance." Ask your students to explain how they might be considered imbalanced. Responses might include not only the physical but the emotional reactions of the two to their young son's death and the fact that their marriage is in great danger of being permanently "unbalanced" by the woman's escape. Class discussion might also encompass Kearns's idea that this poem is caught up not only in the issues surrounding the death of a child, but also in those surrounding the institution of marriage itself and the "rights and privileges" that are associated with marriage. You might ask your students which issue they believe to be the primary one, and why.

ADDITIONAL RESOURCES FOR TEACHING FROST

SELECTED BIBLIOGRAPHY
Bagby, George F. *Frost and the Book of Nature.* Knoxville: U of Tennessee P, 1993.
Bloom, Harold, ed. *Robert Frost.* New York: Chelsea, 1986.
Brodsky, Joseph. *Homage to Robert Frost.* New York: Farrar, Straus & Giroux, 1996.
Cox, James Melville, ed. *Robert Frost: A Collection of Critical Essays.* Englewood Cliffs: Prentice, 1962.
Frost, Robert. *Interviews with Robert Frost.* Ed. Edward Connery Lathem. New York: Holt, 1966.
——. *The Poetry of Robert Frost.* Ed. Edward Connery Lathem. New York: Holt, 1979.
——. *Robert Frost: A Time to Talk.* Ed. Robert Francis. Amherst: U of Massachusetts P, 1972.
——. *Robert Frost on Writing.* Ed. Elaine Barry. New Brunswick: Rutgers UP, 1973.
——. *Selected Letters.* Ed. Lawrance Thompson. New York: Holt, 1964.
——. *Selected Prose.* Ed. Hyde Cox and Edward Connery Lathem. New York: Holt, 1966.
Gerber, Philip L. *Critical Essays on Robert Frost.* Boston: Hall, 1982.

Kearns, Katherine. *Robert Frost and a Poetics of Appetite*. Cambridge, Eng.: Cambridge UP, 1994.

Marcus, Mordecai. *The Poems of Robert Frost: An Explication*. Boston: Hall, 1991.

Meyers, Jeffrey, ed. *Early Frost: The First Three Books*. Hopewell: Ecco Press, 1996.

Monteiro, George. *Robert Frost and the New England Renaissance*. Lexington: UP of Kentucky, 1988.

Oster, Judith. *Toward Robert Frost: The Reader and the Poet*. Athens: U of Georgia P, 1992.

Poirier, Richard. *Robert Frost: The Work of Knowing*. New York: Oxford UP, 1977.

Pritchard, William H. *Frost: A Literary Life Reconsidered*. New York: Oxford UP, 1984.

Squires, James Radcliffe. *The Major Themes of Robert Frost*. Ann Arbor: U of Michigan P, 1969.

Thompson, Lawrance. *Fire and Ice: The Art and Thought of Robert Frost*. New York: Russell, 1970.

——. *Robert Frost: The Early Years, 1874–1915*. New York: Holt, 1966.

——. *Robert Frost: The Years of Triumph, 1915–1938*. New York: Holt, 1970.

Thompson, Lawrance, and R. H. Winnick. *Robert Frost: The Later Years, 1938–1963*. New York: Holt, 1982.

AUDIOVISUAL AND ONLINE RESOURCES (manual pp. 298, 331)

14

Langston Hughes: Culture and Work

Of the three poets covered in depth, Hughes perhaps demands most to be read aloud: his use of blues and jazz in the structuring of his poems rewards such reading. Additionally, this section may be enriched by the inclusion of audiovisual material dealing with the Harlem Renaissance and jazz. Hughes self-consciously puts himself at the juncture of popular culture and the intellectual and political questions of his time, and you might find it useful to provide some of this background for students, or to have students do their own research and presentations on it. These presentations might be done singly or as group projects, focusing on such topics as jazz and blues music, the situation of African Americans and the struggle for civil rights during Hughes's lifetime, the history of the Harlem Renaissance, labor and radicalism in the 1930s, and so forth. Such presentations have the advantage of making a great deal of information available to the class with relatively little work on the part of any individual, and encouraging students to be active contributors of knowledge to the classroom environment.

Students' attitudes about race will be inescapable in this section. Nearly every poem in this section could be the focal point of a controversial discussion in class. You might want to foreground these issues early in the discussion, asking students to write about whether or not Hughes has any relevance to current racial issues. This will help students verbalize their own assumptions about race in a space that is not directly confrontational.

LANGSTON HUGHES

The Negro Speaks of Rivers (p. 372)

Since rivers are clearly the central image in this poem, you might begin discussion of "The Negro Speaks of Rivers" by asking students what ideas they commonly associate with rivers. How do associations such as fertility, life, timelessness, and exploration add to the poem's meaning? Also note that the Euphrates River is one of the legendary rivers that bordered the Garden of Eden. How does this association with the Christian myth of creation add to the meaning of the poem? It may be helpful for your students to recognize the geographic locations of these rivers and the fact that they flow in different directions. The Nile and the Congo are African rivers, the Euphrates flows through Turkey and Iraq, and the Mississippi splits the United States. You might ask your students what these diverse locations and directions suggest about the speaker's history.

Another important dimension of this poem is Hughes's use of time. Notice how the speaker stands outside of historical time; the narrative "I" has experienced these times and places over the course of human existence. You might ask students to explore the connection between the timeless narrator and the endurance and timelessness of rivers.

Consider the serious tone of this poem. Ask your students if they think this poem can be interpreted as a celebration. If so, what is the speaker celebrating, and what details contribute to this interpretation? Ask students to consider how the speaker has taken an active role in the history described in the poem ("I bathed . . ." [line 5], "I built my hut near the Congo . . ." [6], "I looked upon the Nile and raised the pyramids . . ." [7], etc.). What do these actions suggest about the history of the "Negro" in the title?

POSSIBLE CONNECTIONS TO OTHER SELECTIONS

Maya Angelou, "Africa" (text p. 589)

Langston Hughes, "Negro" (text p. 377)

I, Too (p. 375)

This poem reveals the speaker's optimism about the future of race relations in America despite the overwhelming discrimination that he must endure daily. The speaker's acknowledgment that "I am the darker brother" (line 2) indicates the brotherhood between blacks and whites that he feels. In the final line the speaker asserts, "I, too, am America" (18), demonstrating his unwavering belief in his rightful national identity and equal standing in society.

In class discussion, consider how this poem incorporates images of racial injustice yet still manages to suggest a hopeful outlook for the future. Ask students to examine the image of the "darker brother" (2) sent to the kitchen to eat. Segregation was still firmly in place when this poem was written; how does the image of eating in the kitchen expose the racial injustices the speaker is forced to endure? You might ask your students to examine the reaction of the speaker to his "banishment" to the kitchen (5–7). What do they think this reaction to discrimination reveals about the speaker?

Ask students to discuss or write about the attitude of the speaker toward his current situation and toward America. Is his optimistic vision of the future clouded by his present predicament? The speaker's pride and confidence in the future are evident in his declaration that "Tomorrow / I'll be at the table / When company comes" (8–10). Discuss how this conviction helps him sustain his vision of a racially unified nation. You might raise the issue of why the speaker longs for acceptance in America, a country that has denied him his freedom for so long. Examine the speaker's prediction that race relations will improve owing to both the strength of black Americans and the shame of white Americans. How has this prophecy of 1925 been realized or not realized?

POSSIBLE CONNECTIONS TO OTHER SELECTIONS

Countee Cullen, "Yet Do I Marvel" (text p. 601)

Langston Hughes, "Dinner Guest: Me" (text p. 394)

Negro (p. 377)

This poem chronicles the history of exploitation that black people have endured through the ages. The speaker acknowledges the broad history of the black experience, including slavery, the unappreciated role that blacks have had in the building of civilizations, the positive contributions blacks have made as artists, and the extent to which blacks have been victimized around the world.

Notice that the role of the speaker shifts throughout the poem; the speaker has been a slave, a worker, a singer, and a victim. Yet the self-definition of the speaker does not vary; the poem begins and ends with the line "I am a Negro" (lines 1, 17). Ask students to consider how this change in verb tense (from the present to the past and then back to the present) contributes to the speaker's personal and collective sense of identity. You might ask students to consider why the speaker, presumably an American "Negro," nevertheless identifies so closely with "my Africa" (3, 19).

Ask students to discuss, in terms of space and time, the scope of the racial exploitation this poem addresses. In the second stanza, the speaker offers two examples of his enslavement: to Caesar and to Washington (5-6). Ask your students how this image adds to their historical understanding of Caesar. Ask them also to consider the contrasting images of Washington as a revolutionary freedom fighter and as a colonial slave owner. Students might discuss or write about how this poem forces the reader to reconsider and reevaluate particular details of history.

The repetition of the first and last stanza brings this poem full circle; what words or phrases suggest the speaker's ability to endure hardships and victimization? You may want to ask students if they can see other ways in which the experiences of the speaker may be considered "cyclical." Do your students think that this poetic "cycle" suggests that the speaker recognizes no improvement in the living conditions of blacks in America?

POSSIBLE CONNECTIONS TO OTHER SELECTIONS

William Blake, "The Chimney Sweeper" (question #2, following)

Langston Hughes, "Dream Variations" (text p. 380)

——, "The Negro Speaks of Rivers" (text p. 372)

CONNECTION QUESTION IN TEXT (p. 378) WITH ANSWER

2. Write an essay comparing the treatment of oppression in "Negro" with that in Blake's "The Chimney Sweeper" (p. 166).

   Both Blake and Hughes point to specific rather than general oppression. Blake speaks of the experience of the two chimney sweepers (while incidentally mentioning the other "thousands of sweepers"), and indicting, by association, the system that forces them into the job. Hughes's speaker, on the other hand, reaches further, assuming the archetypal personality of Negro "slaves" (line 4), "workers" (7), "singers" (10), and "victims" (14) throughout history. Whereas (ironically, or not) Blake's characters have a chance, through death, of redemption, Hughes seems to indicate, in the first and last stanzas, some redemption in being "black like the depths of [his] Africa."

Danse Africaine (p. 378)

This poetic rendition of an African dance relies heavily on the sound-value of the repetition of words like "low," "slow," "beat," and "tom-toms." The effect of these sounds is that the music "Stirs your blood" (lines 5, 15). In attempting to link the sounds with meaning students may respond that the poem has no meaning, that it is "simply" designed to create a mood. If they respond this way, you may have to back up a bit and talk about poetic meaning: who creates it, for whom does it exist, and so on. The "meaning" of this poem might lie in the relationship between the speaker and the addressee, if not the poet and the reader. Why the startling command to "Dance!" in line 6? What is the effect of the repeated line "Stirs your blood"? What is the meaning of that phrase? It connotes some kind of passion, or the exercise of vitality; what might be the manifestations of that stirring?

POSSIBLE CONNECTIONS TO OTHER SELECTIONS

Martín Espada, "Latin Night at the Pawnshop" (text p. 62)

Langston Hughes, "Formula" (question #1, following)

Edgar Allan Poe, "The Bells" (text p. 182)

1. Try rewriting this poem based on the prescription for poetry in "Formula" (p. 382).

   Students may have different responses to this question; on one hand, "Danse Africaine" does not "treat / Of lofty things" (lines 1–2) in the sense that it is about something human and primal rather than about something ethereal. At the same time, this poem describes a beautiful moment of a girl whirling softly in a circle of light, but it does not account for the "earthly pain [which] / Is everywhere" (12–13). "Formula" describes not only the content of poetry, but also the method that should be used in treating this content. Is it possible to argue that this poem doesn't need to be rewritten in order to conform to the definition of poetry in "Formula"?

Mother to Son (p. 378)

This poem uses dialect and a matter-of-fact tone to establish a mother's voice. The description of the difficulties she has suffered, through the metaphor of a "crystal stair" (line 2), provides encouragement to a troubled son. This central metaphor is lavishly established, providing an ample basis for new metaphors for different difficulties. The speaker's path has been rough, with "tacks in it, / And splinters" (3–4); sometimes it's been difficult to see the way clearly, when "there ain't been no light" (13).

The overly luxurious notion of a crystal stair makes it clear that the mother would frown on the son giving up simply because it's "kinder hard" (16). Carpeted stairs would not be sufficiently grand to draw the son's attention to the difficulties the mother has experienced. Her use of the metaphor allows her to address her son without resorting to lecturing. The tone is not angry or resentful, but tender; the speaker calls her son "honey" (18) and remains focused on encouragement rather than accusation.

Students might enjoy continuing with this metaphor or establishing a new one to describe their own lives: What kind of stairways have their lives been? What kind of roads or rivers?

POSSIBLE CONNECTIONS TO OTHER SELECTIONS

Gwendolyn Brooks, "Sadie and Maude" (text p. 192)

Katharyn Howd Machan, "Hazel Tells LaVerne" (text p. 61)

Jazzonia (p. 379)

This poem creates both a visual and an aural effect, something like viewing a modernist painting while listening to jazz. On one level the poem serves as a vivid description of a Harlem nightclub in which "Six long-headed jazzers play" (lines 4, 17), but the sense of the poem extends outward with allusions to Eve and Cleopatra and with glimpses of "rivers of the soul" (2, 8, 15).

The repeated and varied lines about the tree ("silver" in line 1, "singing" in line 7, "shining" in line 14) and the lines about the rivers of the soul that follow them are a good way into the poem. What is the relationship between this tree and the rivers of the soul? How do students interpret the tree? What kind of mind might describe a tree as either silver, singing, or shining? The variations within these and other lines in the poem make sense when we consider the title; if you have access to a jazz recording from the 1920s, especially a live recording in which performers allow themselves a good deal of improvisation and variations on a theme, it would be helpful to play it when discussing Hughes's poetry, and especially appropriate when discussing this poem.

The fourth stanza is likely to provide some difficulties, especially when taken along with the rest of the poem. It stands apart, first because of its odd number of lines, but also because its words seem unconnected to the rest of the poem. Point out that these musings about Eve and Cleopatra are initiated in lines 5 and 6 when the speaker describes a dancing girl. Students may be baffled as to why he would choose such archetypal female figures to describe this dancing girl, but he has, after all, been describing the soul in terms of rivers and trees. If you work with the two complementary readings by Countee Cullen and Onwuchekwa Jemie at the end of this chapter, "Jazzonia" might be a good place to apply them. Does this poem address universal themes, or is it limited by its setting in a Harlem cabaret?

POSSIBLE CONNECTIONS TO OTHER SELECTIONS

Allen Ginsberg, "First Party at Ken Kesey's with Hell's Angels" (text p. 267)

Langston Hughes, "Danse Africaine" (question #1, following)

——, "Rent-Party Shout: For a Lady Dancer" (text p. 386)

CONNECTION QUESTION IN TEXT (p. 380) WITH ANSWER

1. Compare in an essay the rhythms of "Jazzonia" and "Danse Africaine" (p. 378).

    The rhythms of "Jazzonia" are more even than those in "Danse Africaine," in which the expected rhythms shift because of lines like "Dance!" (line 6). Despite the repetition of lines and phrases, "Danse Africaine" employs an irregular scheme; "Jazzonia" is smoother. Each is consistent with the types of music it describes.

Dream Variations (p. 380)

The dreamlike qualities of this poem seem to surface more easily when read aloud; you may wish to ask a student, or several students, to read this poem to the class. Notice how the natural rhythms of the lines speed up or slow down to reflect the natural rhythms of the daytime or the nighttime.

Have your students consider the "dream" in this poem as a description of an idyllic experience without boundaries or inhibitions. How do vibrant, energetic words like "whirl" (line 3), "dance" (3), and "fling" (10) suggest the speaker's desire to transcend conventional restrictions? Ask students to connect this abstract dream of freedom with the social and political climate of the 1920s, in which African Americans could not generally enjoy uninhibited freedom. Overall, how does this dream motif reflect the black experience in America?

Ask your students to consider the way that active images and words (such as "To fling my arms wide" [1] and "To whirl and to dance" [3]) are associated with the "white day" (4), and calmer, more subdued words (such as "cool" [5], "gently" [7], and "tenderly" [16]) are linked to the nighttime. Compare the speaker's vision of day and night. Ask your students how they can be different and yet both be incorporated into the "dream." You might also point out that there are an equal number of lines describing the day and the night. Yet the speaker directly identifies with the nighttime ("Dark like me" [8], "Black like me" [17]). Ask your class how these details influence the reader's understanding of the speaker.

POSSIBLE CONNECTIONS TO OTHER SELECTIONS

Langston Hughes, "Dream Boogie" (question #2, following)

——, "Negro" (text p. 377)

CONNECTION QUESTION IN TEXT (p. 380) WITH ANSWER

2. Discuss the significance of the dream in this poem and in "Dream Boogie" (p. 390).

The dream in this poem connotes an American dream, a hope for a better future; but this dream is also like a literal dream with surreal imagery. As the title indicates, there are slight variations between the two stanzas: the "white day" (line 4) becomes the "quick day" (13) for instance, and "Dark like me" (8) becomes "Black like me" (17). The dream in "Dream Boogie" is the "dream deferred" that is a recognizable hallmark of Hughes's poetry. It is not dreamlike in a literal sense, but rather the dream of a future of equality. The dream is deferred in this poem to the point that it is forgotten.

The Weary Blues (p. 380)

The rhythmical, rhyming lines of "The Weary Blues" suggest that this poem is like the lyrics to a blues song. Singing the blues is depicted as an emotional release — an outlet that is necessary in order to survive one's painful, lonely life. The blues are intensely personal, "Coming from a black man's soul" (line 15). The "drowsy syncopated tune" (1), the "melancholy tone" (17) of the singer's voice, and the "lazy sway" (6) of his body all combine to reveal that the subject of his song may be the weariness of both body and soul. To begin class discussion ask students what the theme of this poem might be and what details in "The Weary Blues" make the theme evident.

The turbulent emotions of the singer are reflected in the lyrics of his song; first he resolves to put aside his troubles and live on (20–21), but then he feels like giving up and wishes that he were dead (27–30). Yet in spite of the admission that "I ain't happy no mo' / And I wish that I had died" (29–30), "The Weary Blues" may be interpreted as a life-affirming experience. Through the melancholy song, the singer is purged of his personal pain long enough to sleep deeply and enjoy at least a temporary respite from his troubles. Thus the blues may be seen as cathartic, changing pain into peace. You might ask your students to discuss which elements of the poem contribute to this catharsis and what the relationship might be between the singer and the speaker. Has the speaker undergone any sort of catharsis as well?

Ask students to think about certain details of this scene, such as the "old gas light" (5) and the "rickety stool" (12). How do these details and others contribute to the overall effect of the poem? This poem employs many sensual images; ask students to consider which details the poet uses to make the reader "see" or "feel" this scene.

POSSIBLE CONNECTION TO ANOTHER SELECTION

Langston Hughes, "Lenox Avenue: Midnight" (question #1, following)

CONNECTION QUESTION IN TEXT (p. 381) WITH ANSWER

1. Discuss "The Weary Blues" and "Lenox Avenue: Midnight" (p. 383) as vignettes of urban life in America. Do you think that, although written more than seventy years ago, they are still credible descriptions of city life? Explain why or why not.

    Some details of urban life have changed since Hughes's time. In these poems specifically, urban life is characterized by jazz and blues rhythms, gas lights, and the rumble of streetcars. The new urban rhythms belong to rap and hip-hop; gas lights seem romantic and quaint compared to today's streetlights, and the rumble of streetcars is also obsolete and, most likely, less deafening than the street noises of today. Students might argue that the weariness that weighs on these two poems has been replaced by a frenetic vitality and the danger that goes along with it. Rage has replaced feelings of weariness and pain. It might be interesting to have students write a contemporary update of Hughes's poems with these changes in mind.

Cross (p. 382)

This brief poem, using stark and simple language, deals with the complicated and often painful issue of biracial identity. There is also the hint of a slave-master relationship between the speaker's father and mother, based on the father's dying in a "fine big house" (line 9) and the mother dying "in a shack" (10). In this poem Hughes suggests some of the implications of miscegenation, including the emotional stress and insecurity of children born of forced interracial relationships. Ask your students to discuss some of the difficulties they may recognize as inherent in trying to forge a biracial identity in America, both when Hughes was writing and today.

Ask your students how the title of the poem, "Cross," may be interpreted on several levels. Possible responses might include the facts that the speaker's identity is a "cross" between races, that the cross is a religious symbol of suffering and persecution, and that "cross" may refer to the anger the speaker feels toward his or her parents for making the speaker "neither white nor black" (12). You might ask your students which interpretation of the title seems to add the most meaning to the poem.

Since the speaker's parents are both dead, the speaker no longer has anyone to curse for his or her racial in-betweenness. The speaker must now begin a personal journey toward some sense of racial identity. Interestingly, the speaker's preoccupation seems to be not where to live, but where to die. Ask your students why this is so and how the speaker's insecurity about where he or she will die adds meaning to the issue of acceptance into a society that devalues biracial people.

POSSIBLE CONNECTIONS TO OTHER SELECTIONS

Robert Francis, "On 'Hard' Poetry" (question #1, following)
Langston Hughes, "Red Silk Stockings" (text p. 384)

CONNECTION QUESTION IN TEXT (p. 382) WITH ANSWER

1. Read the perspective by Francis, "On 'Hard' Poetry" (p. 35), and write an essay explaining why you would characterize "Cross" as "hard" or "soft" poetry.

   This poem is neither soft in form, since it follows a strict scheme of rhyme and meter, nor soft in thought and feeling, since it addresses its tough subject head-on. There is no excess verbiage, nothing to "water down" the ideas, imagery, or direct language. It would be difficult to argue that this poem is anything but "hard," according to Francis's perspective. In the second half of his perspective, he implies that there are degrees of hardness, and students may debate the relative hardness of this poem. As a way of addressing this point even further, it might help to have students compare this poem to another poem by Hughes that they believe is softer than this one, and to yet another poem which is harder.

Formula (p. 382)

"Formula" parodies romantic misunderstandings about poetry which suggest that good poems have only idyllic, extravagantly elegant subjects. The speaker mocks this attitude, particularly in his repeated suggestion that poetry ought to be about "birds with wings" (lines 4, 16). This poem itself does not adhere to its own "formula." While it ostensibly suggests that poetry should be restricted to "lofty things" (2, 14), "Formula" is clearly not a poem about such idealized images.

By denying that poetry should be "dirty," the speaker actually manages to establish the facts "That roses / In manure grow" (7–8) and "That earthly pain / Is everywhere" (11–12). You may want to ask your students how the poem seems to contradict itself and what effect these apparent contradictions might have on the reader.

You may wish to explain to students that "The Muse of Poetry" (5, 9) is a mythical goddess who was called upon by ancient poets for inspiration. Ask your students how the Muse is treated in this poem. Can certain information be withheld from the Muse of Poetry?

Langston Hughes's poetry, in general, deals with the "earthly pain" (11) of life; clearly he as a poet does not subscribe to the ideas put forth in this poem. You may wish to open class discussion by asking students why they think Hughes wrote such a mocking poem about lofty, idealistic poetry. What could he have been trying to accomplish? Possible responses might include the idea that through satirizing "lofty" poetry, Hughes may be suggesting that one cannot separate the pain of life from one's art, or that poetry that ignores earthly pain cannot be very real or valuable.

POSSIBLE CONNECTIONS TO OTHER SELECTIONS

Helen Farries, "Magic of Love" (question #2, following)
Archibald MacLeish, "Ars Poetica" (text p. 624)

CONNECTION QUESTION IN TEXT (p. 383) WITH ANSWER

2. Write an essay that explains how Farries's "Magic of Love" (p. 30) conforms to the ideas about poetry presented in "Formula."

   This question should give students plenty of room to explore the parodic intent of Hughes's poem. There is no trace of earthly pain or of the manure that fertilizes roses in Farries's greeting-card verse. Her poem attempts to emphasize that it is lofty and soaring by ending each stanza with an exclamation point. Moreover, it is formulaic verse, which aligns it with the title of Hughes's poem. It might be fun to have students rewrite "Magic of Love" with an awareness of earthly pain or of the manure in which roses grow. Is it possible to do so while maintaining the poem's tone or theme?

Lenox Avenue: Midnight (p. 383)

You might begin discussion of this poem by closely examining the first two lines: "The rhythm of life / Is a jazz rhythm." Ask students why jazz and life are so closely connected. Possible responses might include the ideas that jazz, like life, includes solos, improvisations, varied tempos, and melodies that can range from the joyful to the melancholy. Jazz (and life) is unpredictable and often unrehearsed; therein lies much of its beauty and appeal. Ask students to think also about how the word "Honey" (lines 3, 12) in the poem functions in several different ways. For example, "Honey" could be the person the speaker is addressing, or "Honey" could be the sweet heaviness that characterizes both jazz rhythms and life.

You might continue the discussion by asking students why the poet believes that "The gods are laughing at us" (4, 14). The poet seems to be describing the vast distance between human and godly experience; gods are so far away, or perhaps are so cruel, that they laugh instead of weep for the pain they see on Lenox Avenue.

Ask students to consider how the setting of this poem, midnight on Lenox Avenue in Harlem, contributes to its meaning. Lenox Avenue is the backdrop for the speaker's (and Hughes's) life — it is the place where his life is "located." Our own "Lenox Avenues" are the places where we see our own lives, where we see ourselves reflected in our surroundings. You might ask students to explore, in discussion or in a writing assignment, the places that best characterize their own life experiences.

Stephen Crane, "A Man Said to the Universe" (text p. 146)

Emily Dickinson, "I know that He exists" (question #1, following)

Thomas Hardy, "Hap" (question #2, following)

Langston Hughes, "Jazzonia" (text p. 379)

Octavio Paz, "The Street" (text p. 662)

Connections Questions in Text (p. 383) with Answers

1. In an essay compare the theme of this poem with that of Emily Dickinson's "I know that He exists" (p. 327).

    The supreme being in each poem, whether it be God or gods, is distant from humanity and playful at our expense. Hughes's poem implies that the gods are laughing at the way we live our lives. The poem is vital, beginning with "the rhythm of life." Dickinson's poem meditates on the relationship between death and life. For her, the game that God plays with us has a deadly serious element that has to do with the relationship between life and the afterlife, a relationship that Hughes does not address specifically.

2. Compare and contrast the speaker's tone in this poem with the tone of the speaker in Thomas Hardy's "Hap" (p. 606).

    Hardy's speaker, like Hughes's, imagines gods that are laughing at him, but they are laughing because they take pleasure in his pain and suffering. He realizes that this scenario is not accurate, that the pain we must suffer is a product of chance or fate, the wills only of Time or Casualty. The gods in Hughes's poem do not depress the speaker in the same way that they depress Hardy's speaker. He does not seem to change his behavior as a result of the laughter of the gods, but rather to describe the scene as he sees it. He is in this sense more detached than Hardy's speaker is.

Song for a Dark Girl (p. 384)

This poem mourns in the voice of a girl whose "black young lover" (line 3) has been lynched. The bitterly ironic references to "Way Down South in Dixie" (1, 5, 9) allude to the Confederate anthem that swears allegiance to the South, pledging "to live and die in Dixie." The culture that made lynching possible also made seeking justice for those murdered impossible: the "white Lord Jesus" (7) is a symbol of the helplessness the speaker feels in a culture dominated by hatred and racial injustice.

The contrast of this cultural hatred and the speaker's mournful love provides tension and weight to this poem. The impossibility of love in such a place is highlighted by the final sentence: in Dixie, "Love is a naked shadow / On a gnarled and naked tree" (11–12). The vulnerability of that love is apparent in the death of the beloved and in the repetition of "naked" (11, 12).

If students are not familiar with the historical fact of lynchings in the American South, perhaps a small group of students could be assigned to present some information to the class. Web sites that could prove helpful include **www.journale.com/withoutsanctuary/main.html**, which provides photographs from souvenir postcards of lynchings. A book of these same photographs, *Without Sanctuary: Lynching Photography in America*, by Hilton Als and James Allen, is available from Twin Palms Publishers. While the post office outlawed these postcards in 1908, the most recent image in the book is from 1961. Another Web site, **http://ccharity.com/lynched/lynch.htm**, provides a partial listing of the names of individuals lynched since 1859 and links to other sites.

POSSIBLE CONNECTIONS TO OTHER SELECTIONS

Emily Dickinson, "If I can stop one Heart from breaking" (question #1, following)
Patricia Smith, "What It's Like to Be a Black Girl (For Those of You Who Aren't)" (text p. 104)

CONNECTION QUESTION IN TEXT (p. 384) WITH ANSWER

1. Compare the speaker's sensibilities in this poem and in Emily Dickinson's "If I can stop one Heart from breaking" (p. 291). What kinds of cultural assumptions are implicit in each speaker's voice?

   The plucky sentimentalism of "If I can stop one Heart from breaking" is not unusual for its time, relying on a Christian ethic of cheerful helpfulness to propel its speaker. The speaker in Hughes's poem would be less familiar a figure to contemporary readers. The broken heart of the speaker in "Song for a Dark Girl" addresses an injustice not yet universally condemned when Hughes wrote his poem and indicts the southern Christian culture that permitted lynchings to continue.

Red Silk Stockings (p. 384)

The speaker of this poem urges his addressee, a black woman, to wear red silk stockings so that "de white boys" (line 3) will admire her. The speaker implies that the white boys will do more than admire her, though, since he predicts that "tomorrow's chile'll / Be a high yaller" (8–9): that is, a mixed-race child. The speaker is contemptuous toward the addressee, who evidently thinks that she's "too pretty" (7) for him and for the rest of the black boys. His advice to her is motivated by his scorn rather than by his concern for her best interests.

Students might jump to the conclusion that Hughes is the speaker. You can contrast this poem with almost any other by him to point out the difference between the language this speaker uses and Hughes's typical poetic voice. ("Rent-Party Shout..." may be the exception.) Do they feel that Hughes is making a broad statement about race relations, or is he just allowing a voice he has heard to speak in his poetry? Like many of Hughes's other poems, this one relies on repetition for emphasis, but the meter of the lines and the length of the three stanzas are irregular. What is the effect of repeating the last two lines from the first stanza as the third stanza? How would the poem read differently if the third stanza were omitted? In general, why is repetition such a prevalent device in Hughes's poetry?

POSSIBLE CONNECTIONS TO OTHER SELECTIONS

Gwendolyn Brooks, "We Real Cool" (text p. 81)
M. Carl Holman, "Mr. Z" (text p. 612)
Langston Hughes, "Dinner Guest: Me" (question #1, following)
———, "Rent-Party Shout: For a Lady Dancer" (text p. 386)

CONNECTION QUESTION IN TEXT (p. 385) WITH ANSWER

1. Write an essay that compares relations between whites and blacks in this poem and in "Dinner Guest: Me" (p. 394).

   The connection to "Dinner Guest: Me" must take into consideration the publication dates of the poem ("Red Silk Stockings" was published nearly forty years earlier). If students feel that Hughes's depiction of race relations has changed based on these two poems, can they account for that change in terms of history?

Bad Man (p. 385)

This poem takes its form from traditional blues lyrics, depending on repetition and wit to move it forward. While the speaker is unquestionably "bad," students may find the audacity and self-awareness of the speaker redeeming; the poem's musicality may also win over some readers.

POSSIBLE CONNECTIONS TO OTHER SELECTIONS

Michael Collier, "The Barber" (text p. 98)
Diane Thiel, "The Minefield" (text p. 166)

Rent-Party Shout: For a Lady Dancer (p. 386)

This poem sounds as much like a song lyric as it does a poem; the short lines make the tempo fast and sharp, like the words themselves. You may wish to ask students to consider this "shout" as a story; ask them to describe the speaker's situation and her feelings toward her "man." Ask your students if they see any humor in this "shout." Responses might include the speaker's declaration that "I knows I can find him / When he's in de ground —" (15–16) — her jealousy is taken to a bitingly satirical extreme.

Ask students to describe the setting of this poem. Point out that the backdrop to this piece is desperate poverty, where friends and neighbors have to help raise a person's rent money. So the music played at such a party would need to be energetic, entertaining, and cathartic enough to distract the partyers from their own personal troubles. In this way, "Rent-Party Shout" can be interpreted simultaneously as a threat to the wayward man and as a necessary release for the singer herself. Ask students to discuss what might be considered "therapeutic" about this woman's singing about her troubles.

You might also consider asking your students, in discussion or in writing, to draw comparisons between "Rent-Party Shout" and other poems in which Hughes incorporates song lyrics, such as "The Weary Blues" (text p. 380). Ask them to describe how the lyrics contribute to the meanings of the poems.

POSSIBLE CONNECTION TO ANOTHER SELECTION

Langston Hughes, "Dream Boogie" (text p. 390)

Drum (p. 386)

This poem employs a steady rhythm to insist upon the inevitability of death. The speaker presses forward, imagining not only "death" (line 2) and "forever" (3) but also the "last worms" (4), "last stars" (6), and "last atom" (7). Finally the speaker points to the fate of "space itself" (11): "nothing nowhere" (12). The indiscriminate nature of death and fate is not portrayed in a particularly negative light. The conclusion demonstrates the allure of death, the way it calls to everything, "Come! / Come!" (17–18). The use of a drum as a metaphor and drumbeats as a model for the rhythm of the poem establishes continuity, a parallel to the universality of the death described.

POSSIBLE CONNECTIONS TO OTHER SELECTIONS

Emily Dickinson, "If I shouldn't be alive" (question #1, following)
Robert Frost, "Nothing Gold Can Stay" (text p. 354)

CONNECTION QUESTION IN TEXT (p. 387) WITH ANSWER

1. Discuss the definition of death in "Drum" and in Emily Dickinson's "If I shouldn't be alive" (p. 291).

While both poems employ a lighthearted, eerie tone, Dickinson's speaker imagines her own death, while Hughes's speaker focuses on Death's "signal drum" (line 14), calling to every living creature, star, and atom, even "space itself" (11). In both poems death is always present in life.

Ballad of the Landlord (p. 387)

In his poetry Hughes was often concerned with incorporating the rhythms and feeling of blues and jazz. It's not difficult to imagine "Ballad of the Landlord" as a slow blues. Whereas the results of the protagonist's rebellion are anything but unfamiliar, his willingness to fight for what little is his — and the verve with which he speaks of that struggle — affords him a certain nobility even though the landlord undeniably "wins." The poem also shows in derisive terms the idiocy of the landlord's and authorities' overreaction to reasonable and modest concerns about safety (even the landlord's) and comfort.

Ask your students how this poem might be interpreted as political and social commentary. You might point out to them that the tenant is not jailed for his legitimate complaints about the condition of his home, but because the landlord unfairly accuses him of being a political radical. As a background for this poem, you might discuss with your students the influence of Senator McCarthy's anticommunist initiatives in 1950s' America and how this poem reflects the rampant political paranoia of that era. Students might also consider manifestations today of a social system that tends to victimize the powerless and defend the privileged.

Possible Connections to Other Selections

Aron Keesbury, "Song to a Waitress" (text p. 218)

Wole Soyinka, "Telephone Conversation" (question #1, following)

Connection Question in Text (p. 388) with Answer

1. Write an essay on landlords based on this poem and Soyinka's "Telephone Conversation" (p. 19).

    Landlords are either indifferent toward their tenants, discriminatory, or both based on these two poems. Both landlords seem complicit in a larger pattern of societal discrimination. It could be argued that they are more than complicit in this pattern, that they represent the worst aspects of the societal divisions fostered by modern capitalist society.

Uncle Tom (p. 388)

This poem offers a compassionate portrayal of the oft-criticized figure of "Uncle Tom." Students may or may not be familiar with the character who originated in Harriet Beecher Stowe's 1852 book, *Uncle Tom's Cabin*. This term continues to refer to a black person who is overly subservient to whites. While today the phrase is pejorative, Hughes's speaker acknowledges the humanity of his subject, referring first to his "beated pride" (line 2). The exterior appearance of this figure is far easier to calculate than his inner life: having been "Taught well" (10), he is unlikely to risk honesty. The speaker withholds judgment of Uncle Tom: adjectives like "low, obsequious" (5), "sly and servile" (7) are tempered with an awareness of the difficulties that produced these characteristics.

Possible Connections to Other Selections

Robert Frost, "A Girl's Garden" (text p. 349)

Langston Hughes, "Frederick Douglass: 1817–1895" (question #1, following)

CONNECTION QUESTION IN TEXT (p. 389) WITH ANSWER

1. Compare this Uncle Tom here with that of "Frederick Douglass: 1817–1895" (p. 395). How do these two figures represent polar opposites in the culture of African American manhood?

    "Frederick Douglass: 1817–1895" focuses on the determination of Douglass and the force of will that is articulated in the lines "Who would be free / Themselves must strike / The first blow" (lines 18–20). The "frightened tread" (3) that, according to the speaker, would have threatened his life and soul, comprises the chosen path of Uncle Tom. As Douglass, fierce, and "bold" (7), spurns fear and shouts out his beliefs, Uncle Tom remains silent, his interior well guarded and his exterior "low, obsequious" (5). The two poems present polar opposites in choices made by African American men in a racist culture.

Madam and the Census Man (p. 389)

This poem captures an exchange between an officious census man and the stubborn resistance to disrespect personified by Madam Alberta K. Johnson. Cues that may help students create physical descriptions of these two characters include the formal tone and exclamation points in Johnson's speech (lines 20, 26, 32) and the parenthetical "snort" (22) of the census man. While the conflict is presented with a humorous tone, your students are likely familiar with the historical injustices the census has in recent years attempted to avoid: minorities may be underrepresented in part because of stereotyping on the part of those who create and collect census materials.

POSSIBLE CONNECTIONS TO OTHER SELECTIONS

Langston Hughes, "Un-American Investigators" (text p. 392)
———, "Uncle Tom" (question #1, following)

CONNECTION QUESTION IN TEXT (p. 390) WITH ANSWER

1. Contrast Madam's demeanor with that of the subject of "Uncle Tom" (p. 388). How might the poems be read as companion pieces?

    These two poems present character portraits of two very different individuals: Uncle Tom is a broken man, servile to those in power. Alberta K. Johnson, on the other hand, insists on being given her due.

Dream Boogie (p. 390)

This poem, like many of Hughes's others, relies heavily on musical influences. You might ask your students what makes this poem so closely resemble a song. Responses might include the fast-paced rhymes of the first stanza and the final four lines, which sound more like lyrics than the conclusion of a poem.

You might also ask your students about the voices in this poem, which seem to interrupt each other. The voice in line 7 is interrupted by a new voice that poses the question: *"You think / It's a happy beat?"* (lines 8–9). This question seems to refer back to "The boogie-woogie rumble / Of a dream deferred" (3–4) in the first stanza. Ask students to examine the meaning of this "rumble" — to what or to whom is the speaker referring? Students might mention that the "rumble" could allude to the lives of those black Americans who cannot achieve their dreams in this country, and that the beat, or rhythm, of their lives is not necessarily a happy one. Students might connect this poem to blues music, which can appear to be uplifting but in fact may be deeply melancholy and troubled.

Ask students to comment on the final four lines of this poem. Have them speculate on why Hughes ended his poem this way. Who might this poem be specifically addressing? You might also ask your students to discuss "The boogie-woogie rumble / of a dream deferred" (3–4) in the context of the next Hughes poem in this collection: "Harlem" (text p. 391).

POSSIBLE CONNECTIONS TO OTHER SELECTIONS

Langston Hughes, "Dream Variations" (question #2, following)
———, "Harlem" (text p. 391)

CONNECTION QUESTION IN TEXT (p. 390) WITH ANSWER

2. How are the "dreams" different in "Dream Boogie" and "Dream Variations" (p. 380)?

   Both dreams connote hope for the future, but the dream in this poem does not seem to connote a literal dream as well, as it does in "Dream Variations." In other words, this poem's sensibility is wide awake. "Dream Variations" has an impressionistic quality, making its dream both literal and figurative.

Harlem (p. 391)

Discussion of this poem might be couched in a discussion of how your students define "the American Dream." You might ask your class to discuss or to compile a list of their associations with the American Dream. Their responses might include education, financial security, hopeful prospects for their children, social status, respect, justice, and so on. You might then ask your students how people might be affected if they found their "dreams" to be unattainable for social, political, economic, or racial reasons. This discussion leads into a discussion of the poetic similes that Hughes uses to describe the results of the dreams themselves, when they are "deferred" (line 1).

Ask your students to consider the words that Hughes uses to describe the possible results of "a dream deferred." Words such as "dry up" (2), "fester" (4), "stink" (6), "crust and sugar over" (7), and "sag" (9) offer very diverse images of decay and deterioration. Ask them if they recognize any sort of progression in these images, from the raisin that dries up fairly harmlessly, to a sore that causes pain to an individual, to rotten meat and sweets gone bad, which can poison several, to a heavy load that can burden many. The final alternative that Hughes offers is that a deferred dream might "explode" (11). Ask students how this final possibility is different from the previous ones and how this violent image of explosion might be related to the social and political realities in the United States at the time Hughes wrote this poem. Although this poem predates the civil rights movement, the 1950s were a time of great social upheaval and tense race relations in America. You might ask your students to discuss whether or not this poem may be interpreted as a threat to white Americans who contribute to "deferring" the dreams of minority Americans.

POSSIBLE CONNECTIONS TO OTHER SELECTIONS

Langston Hughes, "Dream Boogie" (text p. 390)
———, "Frederick Douglass: 1817–1895" (text p. 395)
James Merrill, "Casual Wear" (question #1, following)

CONNECTION QUESTION IN TEXT (p. 391) WITH ANSWER

1. Write an essay on the themes of "Harlem" and Merrill's "Casual Wear" (p. 159).

The theme of "Casual Wear" is that the lives of strangers can meet randomly and result in tragedy. The theme of "Harlem" also ends in tragedy, but it is not so specific or individualized. It is the direct result of a "dream deferred," whereas the terrorist in Merrill's poem is not necessarily a disillusioned dreamer, although he may be disillusioned in general.

Democracy (p. 391)

This poem employs rhyme, meter, and precise line placement to indicate a careful diction, moved to convince the reader. Some students, basing their opinion on the repetition, may find the tone too strong; some may feel that Hughes made his point in the first stanza and the rest is unnecessary. Others may feel that the last line weakens the tone by establishing common ground with the intended audience. The impatience of Hughes's speaker is illustrated by the images of necessity and urgency: "I do not need my freedom when I'm dead. / I cannot live on tomorrow's bread" (lines 13–14). The speaker does not want to wait for freedom and criticizes the passivity of others.

POSSIBLE CONNECTIONS TO OTHER SELECTIONS

Langston Hughes, "Frederick Douglass: 1817–1895" (text p. 395)

——, "Un-American Investigators" (text p. 392)

Un-American Investigators (p. 392)

To appreciate this poem, it is important for your students to have some understanding of the political climate of the 1950s and the operations of the congressional Special Committee on Un-American Activities. You might begin class discussion by asking students what they know about McCarthyism and the influence of the Special Committee. This background information may assist students in recognizing that the members of this committee are, according to the tone of the poem and the vision of the speaker, as "un-American" as the activities they are supposedly investigating.

You might ask your students to examine carefully the words the poet uses to describe the investigators on this committee. The "fat" (line 1) and "smug" (2) investigators are sharply contrasted with the "brave" (7) victims of their interrogation. Furthermore, the repeated fact that the "committee shivers / With delight in / Its manure" (21–23) clearly condemns their actions for being arbitrary, intrusive, and corrupt.

Given the radical political background of Langston Hughes and the communist sympathies he held for many years, you might ask students to discuss the risks the poet might have been taking in satirizing this very powerful committee in 1953. In discussion or in a writing assignment, you might ask students to compare and contrast this poem with some of Hughes's earlier, more hopeful poems about America such as "I, Too" (p. 375). You might also ask your class how the "victim" in this poem differs from the "victims" in other poems by Hughes. In this case, the person summoned before the Committee is named Lipshitz, a Jewish name. Students might recognize that there are no specific racial issues addressed in this poem; the speaker is attacking a committee that scapegoats unfortunate individuals from many different backgrounds.

POSSIBLE CONNECTION TO ANOTHER SELECTION

E. E. Cummings, "next to of course god america i" (question #1, following)

CONNECTION QUESTION IN TEXT (p. 393) WITH ANSWER

1. Write an essay that connects the committee described in this poem with the speaker in E. E. Cummings's "next to of course god america i" (p. 146). What do they have in common?

The committee in this poem and the speaker in Cummings's are both smug and filled with empty patriotism and a false sense of religion. Both try to manipulate and influence others while preserving their own polished self-image.

Old Walt (p. 393)

This poem has been interpreted as a celebration of the poetry of Walt Whitman (1819–1892). To begin class discussion, you might ask your students what they already know about Whitman. Important details might include the fact that Whitman considered himself to be a poet of the people and that he tried to include the common man in his poetry by using common language. Given this fact, you might ask your students to make some comparisons between Hughes and Whitman. How might the two poets be considered "poets of the people"? Ask your students to give examples of Hughes's poems that are particularly directed toward the "common man." You might also mention to your students that Whitman's poetry has been noted for its long lists of people or details, intended to include many different kinds of people and situations.

It might also be useful to have students characterize the tone of this poem. The speaker refers to Whitman as "Old Walt" (lines 1, 10); ask your students what this familiarity reveals about the speaker's attitude toward Whitman. What other details do they believe might contribute to the tone of the poem?

POSSIBLE CONNECTIONS TO OTHER SELECTIONS

Langston Hughes, "Frederick Douglass: 1817–1895" (question #1, following)
Walt Whitman, "One's-Self I Sing" (text p. 642)

CONNECTION QUESTION IN TEXT (p. 393) WITH ANSWER

1. How does Hughes's tribute to Whitman compare with his tribute to Frederick Douglass (p. 395)?

   Hughes's respect for Douglass as a person is more evident than his respect for Whitman. He admires what Whitman did — his endless pleasure in seeking and finding truth through his poetry — but he admires Douglass both for what he did and for who he was. Even the titles of the poems indicate the difference in tone between them: Hughes's respect for "Old Walt" is fondness, as opposed to the unmitigated admiration and formal tribute he shows Douglass.

doorknobs (p. 393)

You might begin discussion of this poem by offering some historical context to your students. Ask them what they know about the social and political climate of the early 1960s in America. The civil rights movement was gaining momentum when this poem was published, and the nation was facing an important turning point. In this context, ask your students what the "doorknob on a door / that turns to let in life" (lines 2–3) might represent. Ask them to explain what might be so terrifying about a metaphorical doorknob turning and opening the door to "life."

Students might also consider the uncertainty and fear that the speaker feels toward whoever might be behind that door, waiting to enter. Ask them to examine the implications of the description that the "life / on two feet standing" (3–4) may be male or female, drunk or sober, happy or terrified. Ask your students to characterize the speaker in this poem. What details in the poem contribute to the readers' understanding of the speaker's persona?

Stylistically, this poem is very different from the other Hughes poems in this collection. One unusual detail is that "doorknobs" is one long sentence that may be read both literally and symbolically. You might ask students to examine the final three lines. Why might the "yesterday" (24) that is "not of our own doing" (25) be so terrifying to the speaker?

POSSIBLE CONNECTION TO ANOTHER SELECTION

Jim Stevens, "Schizophrenia" (question #1, following)

CONNECTION QUESTION IN TEXT (p. 394) WITH ANSWER

1. Write an essay comparing the theme of this poem with that of Stevens's "Schizophrenia" (p. 129).

   Both poems play with the psychological tension between physical places and the people who inhabit them. Both imply that the terror associated with doorknobs or other elements of houses symbolizes the terror of the people who are shut up in those houses. Yet the two poems differ subtly in their treatment of the subject: Stevens's poem uses his house as a metaphor for a troubled mind whereas Hughes's doorknob is symbolic.

Dinner Guest: Me (p. 394)

It is important for students to know that "the Negro Problem" was at one time a common term used by whites to refer to the complicated issues of civil rights and the social treatment of blacks in America. The speaker's immediate announcement that "I know I am / The Negro Problem" (lines 1–2) reveals both the speaker's understanding of this term and his keen sense of the irony of his situation, in which white guests at an elegant dinner party inquire of their single black companion the details of the black American experience. This scenario ridicules the white "quasi-liberalism" of the 1960s.

Ask your students to consider the white diners' statement, "I'm so ashamed of being white" (14), in the context of this luxurious lobster dinner on Park Avenue. Do they see humor in this remark? Empathy? Sarcasm? You might ask your students to discuss the speaker's impression of the white diners. Do they believe the speaker when he says "To be a Problem on / Park Avenue at eight / Is not so bad" (19–21)? What does it cost the speaker to partake of this lavish dinner?

You might also ask your students to consider the way Langston Hughes uses setting in his poems, particularly his tendency to name actual streets in New York in order to set the scene for his readers. Ask your class to compare Hughes's mention of Park Avenue (20) in this poem with his reference to Lenox Avenue — in "The Weary Blues" (text p. 380) and "Lenox Avenue: Midnight" (text p. 383). You might ask your students how Hughes incorporates these specific streets into his poetry so that even someone who has never been to New York understands these points of reference.

POSSIBLE CONNECTIONS TO OTHER SELECTIONS

M. Carl Holman, "Mr. Z" (text p. 612)
Maxine Hong Kingston, "Restaurant" (question #1, following)

CONNECTION QUESTION IN TEXT (p. 395) WITH ANSWER

1. Write an essay on the speaker's treatment of the diners in this poem and in Kingston's "Restaurant" (p. 193).

The diners in both poems are complacent about their country's problems. In Kingston's poem, though, the diners seem oblivious to the problems. There is no connection between the speaker and the diners once the former has prepared dinner for the latter. The speaker in Hughes's poem is aware of the problems; he even describes himself as "the Problem" in lines 19 and 22. His complacency stems not from ignorance but from the fact that he has been wooed by the white diners who seek solace from him, if not solutions.

Frederick Douglass: 1817–1895 (p. 395)

You might begin class discussion by asking your students to share what they already know about Frederick Douglass. Important points that may arise might include the facts that Douglass was born a slave, escaped from his master, and became a well-known and well-respected abolitionist, writer, orator, and freedom fighter for all oppressed people in America. In this poem, Hughes seems to be celebrating Douglass's personal courage, spirit, and dedication to his beliefs. Douglass overcame seemingly insurmountable odds to become the mouthpiece for all those Americans who were not free and could not speak for themselves.

You might ask your students to consider the second stanza: *"Who would be free / Themselves must strike / The first blow*, he said" (lines 18–20). Hughes attributes these lines to Douglass addressing the slaves. Ask your students how those words might have been interpreted more broadly in 1966 and if this poem can be interpreted as an incitement to violence. You might further this idea by asking your class to debate whether or not using violence to gain freedom is justifiable.

You might ask your students, in discussion or in writing, to examine the seemingly contradictory final two lines of this poem: "He died in 1895. / *He is not dead*" (21–22). Ask your students to explain in what sense Douglass is not dead. If his spirit lives on, in what form does it endure?

Possible Connection to Another Selection

Galway Kinnell, "The Deconstruction of Emily Dickinson" (text p. 321)

Connection Question in Text (p. 396) with Answer

1. How is the speaker's attitude toward violence in this poem similar to that of the speaker in Hughes's "Harlem" (p. 391)?

    Violence is not construed as negative in either poem. In this poem, it is necessary for Douglass to employ violence in order to realize his life's goal. In "Harlem," violence is an inevitable outcome, or at least a possibility. It is not necessarily positive, but given the choice of other possibilities Hughes presents for a dream deferred, it is the best option.

PERSPECTIVES ON HUGHES

Hughes on Racial Shame and Pride (p. 396)

Ask your students to discuss the possible reasons why Hughes feels that "it is the duty of the younger Negro artist" to make black people realize "I am a Negro — and beautiful." Ask your students how Hughes performs this "duty," citing specific examples from his poetry that celebrate the black American identity. In this perspective, Hughes describes the black Philadelphia clubwoman who is ashamed of her heritage and denies a "true picture of herself" as "near white in soul." Ask your students how Hughes seems to be characterizing "whiteness" and "blackness." What aspects of this clubwoman's character seem particularly offensive to Hughes? Do your students sense any sympathy that Hughes might feel for her?

Hughes on Harlem Rent Parties (p. 397)

Hughes describes rent parties in a deeply nostalgic tone; ask your students what details in the Perspective suggest that he longs to reexperience these evenings of "dancing and singing and impromptu entertaining." You might also open discussion about this Perspective by asking your students to identify details of these rent parties that Hughes does not include in this description. For instance, Hughes makes no mention of the impoverished, desperate conditions that forced people to throw rent parties in the first place. He eliminates any mention of human suffering in his celebration of the warm, compassionate community spirit that these social gatherings fostered.

You might ask your students to look closely at the invitation card. Have them consider the language used. Nowadays would they consider these cards to be offensive in any way? This might lead into a class discussion about the nature of "labels" to define people in terms of their color; ask them to articulate some of the reasons the term "yellow girls" might not be as acceptable now as it was in the 1930s.

DONALD B. GIBSON, The Essential Optimism of Hughes and Whitman (p. 398)

One way to open discussion about this Perspective is to ask your students how many agree with Gibson's description of Hughes and how many do not. Using evidence from Hughes's poetry, ask your class to debate whether or not Hughes had any genuine sense of racial injustice as evil. They might pay particular attention to the ways in which Hughes's poetry changed and developed over the years. You could ask them, in discussion or in writing, to compare Hughes's social vision of America in the 1920s with his vision in the 1960s.

Gibson maintains that Hughes could not have written "The Negro Speaks of Rivers" or "I, Too" in the 1960s; ask your students if they agree with this statement. In the 1920s, Hughes was a young man full of hope for his country; in the 1960s, he was an adult who had witnessed the disintegration of the civil rights movement and had perceived little actual improvement in race relations in America. You might ask your students to discuss whether or not they think Hughes might have developed a more threatening, real sense of evil over the years.

JAMES A. EMANUEL, Hughes's Attitudes toward Religion (p. 399)

In this Perspective, Emanuel cites Hughes's comment that he (Hughes) is against "the misuse of religion." Ask your students to reread some of Hughes's poems, looking for religious images and symbols. If they can identify the influence of religion in one or more poems, have them discuss whether Hughes "misuses" Christianity, as he was accused of doing. If he seems to dismiss or embrace Christianity, is he also dismissing or embracing Christians?

You might also ask your students to comment on Hughes's statement that "we live in a world . . . of solid earth and vegetables and a need for jobs and a need for housing." How and where do they recognize Hughes's practical understanding of worldly needs in his poetry? You might also discuss with your students Hughes's acknowledgment that his formative religious experiences related more to music than to preaching. How does this musical influence surface in his poetry?

RICHARD K. BARKSDALE, *On Censoring "Ballad of the Landlord"*
(p. 399)

You might approach this Perspective by asking students to discuss current social tensions between the "haves" and "have-nots" in our society or between whites and blacks. Would a poem or story written today about social inequality and oppression have the same incendiary potential that it did in the 1960s? Ask them to articulate why they do or do not think so. You might help students to understand the social climate at the time of the poem's censoring by reminding your class about the Rodney King beating and subsequent riots in Los Angeles in 1992. Ask them to consider how a poem about police brutality written in the 1970s might take on "new meanings reflecting the times" in the 1990s. Ask students to think of other examples of texts acquiring new meanings as time passes.

Hughes's "Ballad of the Landlord" was censored ostensibly to avoid exacerbating racial tensions between whites and blacks. This plan obviously backfired, resulting in a great deal of unanticipated attention to this particular poem. This might lead into a class discussion about the nature of censorship and whether or not censoring inflammatory literature can be a useful way of soothing social tensions.

DAVID CHINITZ, *The Romanticization of Africa in the 1920s* (p. 400)

Students may find this passage tough going, but it is worthwhile to spend some time reading it closely. Part of the difficulty may come from the discourse (words like "atavism"), part from their potential lack of understanding of the historical context for such a discussion. It is important not only that they understand the tenets of primitivism, but also to understand Chinitz's take on this development (he refers to "clichés" at one point, indicating that he thinks this primitivist strain is a little hokey). Is there any such romanticization of African culture today? If not, do students find post–World War I disillusionment to be a valid explanation of why this romanticization took place in the 1920s?

Many of Hughes's poems from the 1920s can be productively examined through Chinitz's lens. As far as some later poems that show Hughes rejecting this mind-set, "Note on Commercial Theatre," "Harlem," and "Dinner Guest: Me" work well.

TWO COMPLEMENTARY CRITICAL READINGS

COUNTEE CULLEN, *On Racial Poetry* (p. 401)

It is interesting to note that Countee Cullen, a black poet, quarrels with Hughes's insistence on writing about what Cullen calls "strictly Negro themes." He says that he admires the "jazz poems" that are included in *The Weary Blues*, but regards them merely as "interlopers in the company of the truly beautiful poems in other sections of the book," which do not deal so specifically with the black experience in America.

It is important for your students to take into consideration the era in which Cullen was writing. In 1926, black American artists were only beginning to be recognized by white mainstream audiences, and Cullen might have feared that Hughes would be marginalized or dismissed entirely for becoming a "racial artist" as opposed to an artist "pure and simple." Ask your students to discuss what Cullen may have meant by the term "racial artist." Is that term at all relevant today? Or may all contemporary artists be considered "artists pure and simple"?

ONWUCHEKWA JEMIE, *On Universal Poetry* (p. 402)

Onwuchekwa Jemie's Perspective, written a half-century later than Countee Cullen's, takes issue with Cullen's conviction that an artist's work will be considered more universally relevant and important if that artist avoids dealing with "racial material." Jemie accuses Cullen of equating "universal" with "white" or "Western," thereby denying the universal qualities of all human experience regardless of racial background. Jemie challenges the notion that black experiences are less appropriate than white experiences when comparing artistic merit and extends Hughes's own argument about the value and universality of the African American experience.

Ask your students to notice how Cullen discounts precisely the qualities in Hughes's writing that Jemie so ardently celebrates. How might your students account for this difference, based on the time periods that produced these two perspectives? One might argue that Jemie's defense of the black experience as universal might extend to other minority experiences, such as those of women, Hispanics, Jews, and homosexuals. Ask your students to discuss this possibility, and then ask them what makes a particular experience "universally" meaningful. You might also discuss with your class the possibility that describing the specific experiences of particular groups as universally relevant might detract from the meaning of that experience in some way. Ask your students whether they agree or disagree with that possibility, and why.

ADDITIONAL RESOURCES FOR TEACHING HUGHES

SELECTED BIBLIOGRAPHY

Bloom, Harold. *Langston Hughes*. New York: Chelsea, 1988.

Bonner, Pat E. *Sassy Jazz and Slo' Draggin' Blues: Music in the Poetry of Langston Hughes*. New York: Lang, 1992.

Emanuel, James A. *Langston Hughes*. New York: Twayne, 1967.

Gates, Henry Louis Jr., ed. *Langston Hughes: Critical Perspectives Past and Present*. New York: Penguin USA, 1993.

Hughes, Langston. *The Collected Poetry of Langston Hughes*. Ed. Arnold Rampersad. New York: Knopf, 1994.

Jemie, Onwuchekwa. *Langston Hughes: An Introduction to the Poetry*. New York: Columbia UP, 1976.

Miller, R. Baxter. *The Art and Imagination of Langston Hughes*. Lexington: UP of Kentucky, 1989.

Mullen, Edward J., ed. *Critical Essays on Langston Hughes*. Boston: Hall, 1986.

O'Daniel, Therman B., ed. *Langston Hughes, Black Genius: A Critical Evaluation*. New York: Morrow, 1971.

Tracy, Steven C. *Langston Hughes and the Blues*. Urbana: U of Illinois P, 1988.

15

Critical Case Study: T. S. Eliot's "The Love Song of J. Alfred Prufrock"

One of the problems you may encounter with this chapter is that the presence of material by professional critics may intimidate students into silence about their own readings. You may find it appropriate to have students articulate their own approaches to the poem before they turn to critical sources. On the other hand, critical sources can help in students' understandings of a poem, particularly one as complex as this. If students seem to be having trouble with the poem, you might direct them to one or more of the critical selections.

Another difficulty students may have with this chapter lies in their ability to deal with competing critical attitudes toward the same poem. Students tend to fall into an easy relativism, claiming that each approach highlights a different aspect of the poem and that each is equally valid. While this is true, it would be fair to put a bit of pressure on this attitude. The critical perspectives provided here are incommensurable in many ways. You might recognize this in class, and assign an informal writing or hold a class discussion centered around the question "Which of these readings are better and why?" This discussion should lead into considerations of evidence and argumentation, as well as situation or context: why certain readings are better for certain purposes, or more interesting to certain audiences. This will help students when it comes time for them to write using outside sources, as it will give them valuable experience with thinking critically about other positions.

T. S. ELIOT, *The Love Song of J. Alfred Prufrock* (p. 405)

This dramatic monologue is difficult but well worth the time spent analyzing the speaker, imagery, tone, and setting. Begin with the title — is the poem actually a love song? Is Eliot undercutting the promise of a love song with the name J. Alfred Prufrock? Names carry connotations and images; what does this name project?

The epigraph from Dante seems to ensure both the culpability and the sincerity of the speaker. After reading the poem, are we, too, to be counted among those who will never reveal what we know?

The organization of this monologue is easy enough to describe. Up until line 83, Prufrock tries to ask the overwhelming question. In lines 84–86, we learn that he has been afraid to ask it. From line 87 to the end, Prufrock tries to explain his failure by citing the likelihood that he would be misunderstood or by making the disclaimer that he is a minor character, certainly no Prince Hamlet. Notice how the idea of "dare" charts Prufrock's growing submissiveness in the poem from "Do I dare / Disturb the universe?" to "Have I the strength to force the moment to its crisis?" (which rhymes lamely with "tea and cakes and ices") and, finally, "Do I dare to eat a peach?"

You might ask students to select images they enjoy. Consider, for example, Prufrock's assertion that he has measured out his life in the shallowness of the ladies Prufrock associates with: "In the room the women come and go / Talking of Michelangelo" (lines 13–14). The poem offers many opportunities to explore the nuances of language and the suggestive power of image as a means of drawing a character portrait and suggesting something about a particular social milieu at a particular time in modern history.

Grover Smith, in his *T. S. Eliot's Poetry and Plays* (Chicago: U of Chicago P, 1960), provides extensive background and critical comment on this poem.

As a writing assignment, you might ask the class to explore a pattern of images in the poem — those of crustaceans near the end, for example — and how that pattern adds to the theme. You might also ask the class to give a close reading of a particular passage — the final three lines come to mind — for explication.

POSSIBLE CONNECTIONS TO OTHER SELECTIONS

John Keats, "La Belle Dame sans Merci" (text p. 619)
Alberto Ríos, "Seniors" (text p. 40)
Wallace Stevens, "The Emperor of Ice-Cream" (text p. 638)
Walt Whitman, "One's-Self I Sing" (question #1, following)

CONNECTION QUESTION IN TEXT (p. 409) WITH ANSWER

1. Write an essay comparing Prufrock's sense of himself as an individual with that of Walt Whitman's speaker in "One's-Self I Sing" (p. 642).

These two songs have very different melodies as well as harmonies. Eliot's "love song" is really a dirge for an individual whose isolation from society far outweighs his connection to it. Prufrock never manages to connect himself with any other figure in his poem, except for the "eternal Footman" who snickers at him. His tone is morbid, self-pitying at best, as opposed to Whitman's speaker, who celebrates all aspects of both the individual and of the society he or she belongs to. The "Life immense in passion, pulse, and power" (6) that he celebrates has drained out of Prufrock "like a patient etherized upon a table" (3). Whitman's speaker is eternally awakening to life, Eliot's is eternally dying.

AUDIOVISUAL AND ONLINE RESOURCES (manual pp. 297, 331)

ELISABETH SCHNEIDER, *Hints of Eliot in Prufrock* (p. 409)

Schneider acknowledges that literal details of Eliot's life do not match those of Prufrock, yet asserts that "Prufrock was Eliot, though Eliot was much more than Prufrock." Her essay suggests that readers look at the internal workings of the mind of Prufrock, rather than the details of his life, for links to the poet who created him. What kind of "character profile" of Eliot could students create by using Prufrock's personality as a model? What does Schneider mean by her statement that "Eliot was much more than Prufrock?" Does Schneider's comment that "friends who knew the young Eliot almost all describe him, *retrospectively* but convincingly, in Prufrockian terms" (emphasis added) strengthen or weaken her argument? Does the fact that Eliot was in his early twenties when he wrote the poem (around 1910–1911) argue for or against a biographical interpretation?

BARBARA EVERETT, *The Problem of Tone in Prufrock* (p. 410)

Everett asserts that it is difficult to describe tone in Eliot's poetry because the voice in his poems "seems disinterested in what opinions it may happen to be expressing." That is, the distance that Eliot establishes between the speaker and the scene is so great that the tone of the voice becomes unrecognizable and, to some extent, undefinable. You might ask students to locate particular moments in the poem when this detachment becomes especially noticeable. What might this suggest about Prufrock's character? Everett quotes from the poem: "I have known them all already, known them all." You might ask your class to discuss how this retrospective moment in the poem complements Everett's argument for the speaker's detachment from the action.

MICHAEL L. BAUMANN, *The "Overwhelming Question" for Prufrock* (p. 411)

Baumann's formalist approach cites specific passages in the text of "Prufrock" to argue that the "overwhelming question" facing Eliot's character is whether or not to commit suicide. In particular, he mentions the allusion to John the Baptist (lines 81–83) and the references to drowning in the closing lines of the poem to substantiate his thesis. You might ask your students why he does not also use the reference to Lazarus. Are there other passages regarding death that Baumann does not choose to discuss? In concentrating on a few examples and developing them thoroughly in order to make his point, does he ignore details that would weaken his theory? Do your students agree with Baumann that the "overwhelming question" concerns suicide? What else might it be?

FREDERIK L. RUSCH, *Society and Character in "The Love Song of J. Alfred Prufrock"* (p. 413)

Rusch utilizes the socio-psychological theories of Erich Fromm to pose yet another possible interpretation of Prufrock's "overwhelming question." Fromm contends that because human beings are separated by their self-consciousness from nature, they turn to human society for a sense of belonging. Prufrock's dilemma is that he is alienated by the depersonalizing structure of modern life. Rusch argues that Prufrock understands his alienation but does not know what to do about it. He concludes that Prufrock's solution is an imaginary return to the animal state, suggested by the image of the "ragged claws" in the sea at the end of the poem. The significance of water as an archetypal symbol of the unconscious or of rebirth lends further credence to Rusch's conclusion. The essay ties in nicely with Baumann's argument by supporting the depiction of Prufrock as a hopelessly depressed man, although its conclusion differs.

It might be interesting to discuss with your students whether Fromm's work and Rusch's analysis of Prufrock's dilemma are gender-based. That is, do women, who historically have grown up knowing they are separate from the power structures of society, suffer the same shock of alienation Fromm describes? Do women feel the same disconnectedness from other human beings that men do?

ROBERT SWARD, *A Personal Analysis of "The Love Song of J. Alfred Prufrock"* (p. 415)

If students do not think that this dialogue approach to criticism is serious, point out that it has been used since Plato, if not before, and revived by modern critics such as Oscar Wilde. This dialogue between a sailor and a ranking officer is highly stylized, although it seems to rely on earthy sailor-talk (like how the T. S. of Eliot's name stands for "Tough Shit"), it seems like a fictionalized portrait, if not a fictional one. You might ask students to select passages of the essay that indicate that Sward's narrative couldn't really have happened that way; is the essay truly "personal"? Why is this setting, on a ship en route to Korea with sailors drinking rum out of coffee cups, crucial to this particular reading of the poem? Although it seems radically different from the other critical selections in terms of tone, point out that this reading has many elements in common with the other readings, such as the need to sort through Eliot's biography, the analysis both of Prufrock's character and Eliot's method in conjunction with one another, and the will to construct Prufrock as a kind of "everyman" at the end of the essay. If students attempt to analyze another poem using Sward's method, do they embellish their account at all by relying on some device like a dialogue? If not, will the reading suffer, or will it be that much fresher for its honesty?

AUDIOVISUAL AND ONLINE RESOURCES (manual pp. 300, 337)

16

Cultural Case Study:
Julia Alvarez's "Queens, 1963"

This chapter presents a poem along with various materials that will aid students in understanding the historical and cultural context of the poem. This may seem a great departure to students if the class has previously taken a more formalist approach, or even to students who have dealt with the poems more thematically, as it grounds discussion in a consideration of a specific historical moment. The poem could stand on its own, even based on the limited knowledge that most students have of recent history. However, the other materials can show students what can be added to the understanding of a poem by a careful investigation of its cultural context.

The poem "Queens, 1963" deals with issues of neighborliness, immigration, and racism. It is followed by an excerpt from an interview with Alvarez (the full text of which is available online — see Additional Resources for Teaching). The interview presents in a concise form many of the pressures that Alvarez felt as an immigrant and that have informed her poetry. It puts a human face on some of the events listed in the chronology, and can be useful to students in that capacity.

The other resources deal more with the wider cultural context of New York and America at the time. The ad for Gibson's Homes may initially be puzzling to the students. However, the picture in the ad can give them a sense of the physical environment in which the events of the poem took place. Students' experiences with "neighborhoods" can vary widely, from rural to suburban to urban, and this may help them more clearly understand the setting. The newspaper article provides a complementary picture of life in Queens. Students may or may not be cynical about such obvious public relations rhetoric; considering this article in relation to the poem may provide for an interesting discussion.

In stark contrast to these sanitized views of life in Queens, the photograph of the demonstrator and police reveals a hidden underside that is not all light and air. You might find it appropriate to point out that the picture was taken the same year as the events in the poem and the newspaper article; dissent was contemporaneous with images of the "good life," a fact that the poem also acknowledges, in its portrayal of the darker side of the "good neighborhood."

As an interesting exercise for this unit, you might have students do a similar cultural case study for one of the other poems in the text, or a cultural portfolio of a place familiar to them: either their hometown or where they are going to school. You may find that it is easier on students if you make this an assignment for small groups, which will enable them to cover more ground with less work.

Queens, 1963 (p. 423)

This poem deals with the childhood experience of an immigrant girl in Queens who discovers open racism for the first time. It contains an interesting meditation on immigration, assimilation into a culture, and racism.

When a black family moves into the neighborhood that the immigrants have only recently joined, the speaker sees racism covered over by a variety of guises: the

Haralambides's desire to avoid trouble, Mr. Scott's separatism, Mrs. Bernstein's seemingly enlightened position undercut by her worry over property values. These are counterpointed by the presence of the police, which shows even official involvement in trying to maintain barriers between the races. The speaker tries for a connection, a welcoming wave, but fails to bridge the gap, one that she can bridge only through sympathy and imagination. The final image of the poem retreats to an idyllic moment before any immigration. This final affirmation of a land before immigrants of any sort serves to undercut the self-righteousness of the immigrants in the poem, and points out that all the property owners were, at one point, immigrants themselves.

The connections between immigrants wanting to assimilate themselves into America and the racism perpetrated against African Americans makes this a particularly fascinating poem. You might ask your students if they believe that the black family will be integrated into the neighborhood in a year, just like the Alvarez family, or if they believe the dynamic will be fundamentally different this time. Lorraine Hansberry's play *A Raisin in the Sun* would be a particularly interesting parallel text to consider in this case.

Students may misunderstand the presence of the police car in line 68, and believe that the family is being arrested for some reason. A close reading provides no evidence of this however: merely that the police are performing a subtle kind of intimidation on the family, making them feel like criminals despite the fact that they have committed no crime. This may be a touchy point for students who have accepted the current police-heavy answers being offered for social problems.

This poem can be read as indicting American culture on many levels, from personal reactions to civil servants to supposedly impersonal property values. Students, however, may be uncomfortable with this kind of reading. You might want to take this into account in the class discussion, and use the analyses of the later cultural materials to present this idea in a less threatening manner, one that will enable productive discussion and disagreement.

If you have been following the previous chapters and dealing with formal issues in the course, you may find it interesting to have students apply their skills in these areas to this poem, particularly noting the use of significant detail and irony.

MARNY REQUA, *From an Interview with Julia Alvarez* (p. 426)

The interview raises several themes that are important to a consideration of the poem: immigration, cultural identity, and belonging. Alvarez speaks of the old "model for the immigrant," which meant buying into the American melting-pot ideology, an ideology that has since come under fire from a variety of sources. She also speaks of being caught between two worlds, American and Caribbean. It is precisely this sense of not-quite-belonging that enables the sympathetic identification between Alvarez and the black girl across the street.

An Advertisement for Tudor Row Houses (p. 427)

As mentioned above, this ad can be puzzling to students, who may be unsure why it was included. In addition to giving them a better sense of the scene of the poem, it can give insight into the rhetoric of American identity in the first part of the century. You might encourage students to examine the selling points: driveways, low pricing, ideal for children, sewers, and so on. What do these selling points say about the promise of "the good life" in America? It is no coincidence that the development is billed as "The Perfect Low Priced American Home," particularly given the immigrant populations that came to occupy it. It is also interesting that the establishments mentioned are schools, churches, stores, and amusements. You might ask students how these institutions relate to ideas about "the American Dream" and the idealized versions of America popular throughout the century.

Additionally, you might encourage students to make connections between this ad and the interview, to articulate how it might appeal to the kinds of immigrants Alvarez describes, people all too eager to become American. You might also draw some connections in terms of style and rhetoric to the newspaper article that follows: in forty-three years, the perceptions of "the good life" in Queens appear to have remained largely unchanged. Another approach would be to ask students to evaluate this ad for irony, particularly in light of the poem and the photograph of the demonstrator.

Queens: "The 'Fair' Borough" (p. 428)

The questions given in the text can help anchor a discussion of this article, focusing on the ironies revealed by its juxtaposition with the poem and photograph. You might find it helpful to ask students why the brochure was produced in the first place. Why is there a need to "'reacquaint our residents' with the borough's history and present stature?" What sort of function is this brochure actually performing? Another interesting detail worth comment is the historical note at the end of the article: how does this fact about religious freedom mesh with the story America tells about itself, and how does the poem call this story into question?

NORMAN LEAR, "Talkin' about Prejudice" in Queens (From Meet the Bunkers) (p. 429)

Though presumably taking place in Queens in 1971, eight years after Julia Alvarez's "Queens, 1963," this episode of the popular *All in the Family* sitcom highlights similar racial tensions that existed for Alvarez's speaker. For one thing, even before Lionel's entrance, the conversation focuses largely on race. In the scene presented here, the issue remains in the forefront of the characters' consciousness — and as the centerpiece of conversation. You may want to have students look for specific lingual clues that present each character's view on race. When the class has characterized the overall racial climate of Queens in 1971 that Lear shows us, have them do the same thing with "Queens, 1963." What climate changes seem to have taken place in the eight years between these selections? How would your students characterize these changes? Is one view more hopeful? More cynical?

A Civil Rights Demonstration (photograph) (p. 432)

This photograph stands in stark contrast to the happy pictures of Queens life offered in the previous two entries. You might have students note the visual composition of the photograph: the dark wall of police cutting off the protestors, and the one protestor's face clearly visible in the center of the photo, staring at the camera. You might want to talk as a class about the power of such images, and similar images of demonstrations in civil rights protests and at Kent State. You might also have the class draw connections between the presence and function of police in this photograph and in the poem.

ADDITIONAL RESOURCES FOR TEACHING

SELECTED BIBLIOGRAPHY
Alvarez, Julia. *The Other Side/El Otro Lado: Poems.* New York: Dutton, 1995. The collection from which this poem is taken.

——. *Something to Declare: Essays.* Chapel Hill: Algonquin, 1998.

Requa, Marny. "The Politics of Fiction." *Frontera* 5 (29 Jan. 1997). **http://www.fronteramag.com/issue5/Alvarez**. The magazine itself might be an interesting resource for students to explore.

ONLINE RESOURCES (manual p. 322)

17

Two Thematic Case Studies

POEMS ABOUT LOVE

Students of poetry are usually good at brainstorming. When they get past whatever initial fear of poetry they've had, they often excel at making observations about the poem and connections between those observations. But once they've done this, they need to use their observations and connections to address the central theme of the poem. The questions in Chapter 17, which follow the poems in the two thematic case studies, encourage students to focus on theme and to back up their statements about theme with specific evidence. These questions should be useful to students who need to make the jump from analyzing specifics to understanding the whole. The questions, however, might also have a reverse application. Sometimes, when discussing themes, students can get a little too abstract. These questions encourage students to ground their abstractions in specifics.

You might decide to use the questions during class time. Try having the class spend a few minutes jotting down their responses to the questions about a given poem. Then have them read their responses to the class. In the discussion that follows, try isolating their thematic observations from the more formal observations. Then try integrating the two in a way that would suggest the kind of movement between abstractions and specifics that you'd like to see in a cogent paper. You could even ask them to write their own creative response to the issues of the poem (see question 3 for "The Passionate Shepherd to His Love"). By sparking their interest in the theme, this exercise should get students to relate the poem to the world they inhabit.

The questions in Chapter 17 should also help students prepare to write essays on a given poem. You might want to choose specific questions for a paper assignment. Or you might ask the students to write a paper that addresses two questions of their choice. Try making connections between the way you've discussed theme in class and the way you'd like to see them do it in a paper. Class discussion can be a good primer for essay writing.

CHRISTOPHER MARLOWE, *The Passionate Shepherd to His Love* (p. 434)

Marlowe was the first English dramatist to use blank verse in his plays. He completed a master of arts at Cambridge in 1587 and was stabbed to death six years later, having lived an eventful, though somewhat mysterious, life.

Anyone with an ounce of romance will respond favorably to this pastoral lyric, whose speaker pledges to do the impossible (yet how inviting to entertain the vision of "a thousand fragrant posies" on demand!) if only his beloved will be his love. What lovers have not believed, for a time at least, that they could "all the pleasures prove," that all the pleasure the world offered was there for the taking?

It's significant, of course, that his song is sung in May, the month when spring takes firm hold (in England, at least) and when the end of winter was (and still is) celebrated with great exuberance.

Possible Connections to Other Selections

John Donne, "The Sun Rising" (text p. 42)
Sir Walter Ralegh, "The Nymph's Reply to the Shepherd" (question #1, following)

Connection Question in Text (p. 435) with Answer

1. Read Sir Walter Ralegh's "The Nymph's Reply to the Shepherd" (p. 632). How does the nymph's response compare with your imagined reply?

    Students will likely enjoy writing their own more contemporary versions of this love poem: the pastoral lyric employed in a more modern setting is likely to produce humorous results. Ralegh's response presents a pragmatic nymph with very real concerns: "rocks grow cold" (line 6). The idealized world Marlowe evokes is lovely in May, but winters as a shepherd's wife are unlikely to hold "a thousand fragrant posies" (10).

Audiovisual and Online Resources (manual pp. 303, 341)

WILLIAM SHAKESPEARE, *Not marble, nor the gilded monuments* (p. 435)

The central point of this poem, that poetry, more than any monument, possesses the power to immortalize its subject, was a common one in the Petrarchan love sonnets of Shakespeare's day. This same conceit appears in Shakespeare's "Shall I compare thee to a summer's day?" (text p. 228). Have students find conventional images of permanence in the poem. With what destructive forces are these images juxtaposed? Even marble, the most durable of building materials, becomes "unswept stone" when it is "besmeared with sluttish time" (line 4), the most destructive force of all. Yet according to the poet, his lover will live until judgment day in "this powerful rhyme" (2). How do your students respond to this conceit? Can a poem immortalize a person? Do poems last forever? Can students suggest other things that might last longer, other ways of achieving immortality?

Possible Connections to Other Selections

Emily Dickinson, "This was a Poet—It is That" (text p. 305)
Christopher Marlowe, "The Passionate Shepherd to His Love" (question #2, following)
Andrew Marvell, "To His Coy Mistress" (question #1, following)

Connections Questions in Text (p. 436) with Anwers

1. Compare the theme of this poem with that of Andrew Marvell's "To His Coy Mistress" (p. 65), paying particular attention to the speaker's beliefs about how time affects love.

    While both poets acknowledge the eternal worth of the beloved, Marvell employs "Deserts of vast eternity" (line 24) to convince her to "sport us while we may" (37). Shakespeare's pledges do not have such obvious ulterior motives.

2. Discuss whether you find this love poem more or less appealing than Christopher Marlowe's "The Passionate Shepherd to His Love" (p. 434). As you make this comparison, consider what the criteria for an appealing love poem should be.

    Students will have to choose between the lush detail of Marlowe's shepherd's ephemeral "ivy buds" (17) or Shakespeare's speaker's confident pledge that the beloved shall be praised "in the eyes of all posterity" (11). Both have their charms.

ANNE BRADSTREET, *To My Dear and Loving Husband* (p. 436)

Anne Bradstreet, Anglo-America's first female poet, is noted for her Puritan devotion, her belief that all worldly delights are meaningless when placed in the context of the afterlife. Yet there is an ambiguous strain within her poetry that complicates this position; she is human, and thus drawn to worldly things. Note how she describes not only love but heaven in terms of material wealth. With this ambiguity in mind, ask students to assess whether Bradstreet's devotion is directed more toward her husband here on earth or toward the eternal rewards of heaven. The final two lines are themselves ambiguous; she does indicate that she believes in eternal life, but she also declares that at some point she and her husband will "live no more" (line 12). You might also point out that the final two lines comprise the only part of the poem not written in heroic couplets (they are eleven syllables each), a fact that adds to their ambiguity. Students might also enjoy discussing the tone of the poem as a dedication to one's husband: does the speaker seem warm? Rational? Self-absorbed or self-effacing?

POSSIBLE CONNECTIONS TO OTHER SELECTIONS

Anne Bradstreet, "Before the Birth of One of Her Children" (question #1, following)
Donald Hall, "Letter with No Address" (question #2, following)

CONNECTIONS QUESTIONS IN TEXT (p. 437) WITH ANSWERS

1. How does the theme of this poem compare with that of Bradstreet's "Before the Birth of One of Her Children" (p. 594)? Explain why you find the poems consistent or contradictory.

    "To My Dear and Loving Husband" closes with the hope that "we may live ever" (line 12); "Before the Birth of One of Her Children" concedes, in the first line, "All things within this fading world hath end" (1). Students may find the fear of death contradictory to the faith in eternal life, or they may see both as different facets of a very human and vivid love.

2. Discuss the relationship between love and the contemplation of death in this poem and the relationship between love and the reality of death in Donald Hall's "Letter with No Address" (p. 673).

    While the body of Bradstreet's poem focuses on a living couple, Hall's poem reveals the death of the beloved in the first stanza. Bradstreet concludes her love poem, a celebration of her relationship with her husband, with a reference to an imagined hereafter that only serves to extend the reach of the love she praises. Hall's poem accepts the real death of the beloved, lives within its scope, and has none of the certain hope that Bradstreet's conclusion urges. Bradstreet looks happily to the future, advising her husband, "in love let's so persevere / That when we live no more, we may live ever" (11–12), establishing hope for a shared eternity. In contrast, Hall recalls, "We never dared / to speak of Paradise" (59–60).

ELIZABETH BARRETT BROWNING, *How Do I Love Thee? Let Me Count the Ways* (p. 437)

The wide scope and specific reach of this poem's depiction of love remains, for many readers, timeless. The extremes of the speaker's devotion, the confident tone established by the simple declarative sentences, and the employment of human nature and the speaker's own "childhood's faith" (line 10) and "lost saints" (12) establish a familiar fulfillment. While the poem acknowledges God's power, it establishes a hierarchy in which love retains the superlative position until the penultimate line, when God is invoked only to permit the love to extend "after death" (14).

POSSIBLE CONNECTIONS TO OTHER SELECTIONS

William Shakespeare, "Not marble, nor the gilded monuments" (text p. 435)
Christina Georgina Rossetti, "Promises like Pie-Crust" (question #1, following)

CONNECTION QUESTION IN TEXT (p. 437) WITH ANSWER

1. Compare and contrast the images, tone, and theme of this poem with those of Rossetti's "Promises Like Pie-Crust" (p. 634). Explain why you find one poem more promising than the other.

   Students will have different preferences here: Rossetti's poem provides an open-eyed account of the possibilities of love's disappointment that will strike some readers as honest and accurate, while Browning's presents a heartfelt, earnest declaration of undying love that may be convincing for others. Browning's speaker focuses on the thorough penetration of the "breath, / Smiles, tears" (lines 12–13) attained by the beloved, employing an earnest tone and a wide array of comparisons. Rossetti uses a matter-of-fact tone, while she acknowledges previous relationships, scrutinizes her current love and its possibilities, and then chooses "frugal fare" (23). Browning declares her love with the extravagance of "all my life" (13) and proposes to continue "after death" (14).

AUDIOVISUAL AND ONLINE RESOURCES (manual pp. 294, 326)

E. E. CUMMINGS, *since feeling is first* (p. 438)

Once again in the head-heart debate, the heart comes out the winner in this poem. The eliding of the syntax supports the value of feeling over rational thought. Students will probably enjoy the syntactical turn of line 3, which can either complete line 2 or be the subject of line 4. Considering the mention of death and its prominent position in the poem, you might explore with the class — or use as a writing assignment — a defense of this as a *carpe diem* poem.

POSSIBLE CONNECTIONS TO OTHER SELECTIONS

John Donne, "The Flea" (text p. 604)
Christopher Marlowe, "The Passionate Shepherd to his Love" (question #1, following)
Molly Peacock, "Desire" (question #2, following)

CONNECTIONS QUESTIONS IN TEXT (p. 438) WITH ANSWERS

1. Contrast the theme of this poem with that of Marlowe's "The Passionate Shepherd to His Love" (p. 434). How do you account for the differences, in both style and in content, between the two love poems?

   While Marlowe's theme revolves around convincing the beloved by means of physical offerings — "beds of roses" (line 9), "A gown made of the finest wool" (13) — Cummings's poem focuses on the primacy of the intangible: "feeling" (1), "Spring" (6), "kisses" (8), and "your eyelids' flutter" (12). The style of Marlowe's poem, with its formal accomplishments, concise stanzas, and clean rhymes, makes sense of his love in the same concrete fashion as his gifts. Cummings, on the other hand, employs loose stanzas, absent punctuation, and lowercase letters to defy the conventions that drive more traditional verse and more traditional notions of love.

2. Discuss attitudes toward "feeling" in this poem and in Molly Peacock's "Desire" (p. 231).

Cummings presents "feeling" as an entity unfettered by syntax and rules, briefly glimpsed in images of eyelids, "blood" (7), and laughter. Although these images serve to shape the primacy of feeling, their reach is beyond even images, untouchable, immune to rules and description. Peacock's speaker also stresses the importance of "the drive to feel" (14), but she is not bothered by the difficulty of trying to capture it in language. Instead, she constructs a series of images, metaphors, and definitions to provide boundaries for understanding desire: it "doesn't speak and it isn't schooled" (1), it has "wettened fur" (2), "smells and touches" (7), like "a paw" (9) or "a pet" (10). These descriptions conjure up a strange creature, but it dwells in a much more concrete place than that evoked by Cummings.

JANE KENYON, *The Shirt* (p. 438)

Students might be interested to know about the relationship Jane Kenyon had with Donald Hall, who wrote "Letter with No Address" (p. 673), included in this volume. The couple were married from 1972 until her death in 1995.

The sly, sensual wit of this poem provides a rapid departure from the chaste visions offered by the title in only six lines. The last words of each line — "neck" (line 1), "back" (2), "sides" (3), "belt" (4), "pants" (5), and "shirt" (6) — do little to demonstrate how Kenyon moves from a description of a garment on a man to an expression of desire. An obvious title like "Below His Belt" would prepare readers too quickly and thoroughly for the poem's ultimate direction.

POSSIBLE CONNECTIONS TO OTHER SELECTIONS

Anne Bradstreet, "To My Dear and Loving Husband" (question #1, following)

Elizabeth Barrett Browning, "How Do I Love Thee? Let Me Count the Ways" (question #1, following)

CONNECTION QUESTION IN TEXT (p. 439) WITH ANSWER

1. What does a comparison of "The Shirt" with Bradstreet's "To My Dear and Loving Husband" (p. 436) and Browning's "How Do I Love Thee? Let Me Count the Ways" (p. 437) suggest to you about the history of women writing love poems?

Bradstreet's poem, published in 1678, directs the powerful love she feels for her husband toward a religious devotion: "Thy love is such I can no way repay, / The heavens reward thee manifold, I pray" (9–10). Browning's 1850 poem also incorporates the spiritual, but only to request of a higher power an extension, a place in the afterlife so her speaker can "love thee better after death" (14). Kenyon's poem does not concern itself with an afterlife at all, nor does it focus on declarations of love. While Bradstreet propels her poem through love toward faith, and Browning uses faith to expand the reach of her love, Kenyon keeps her rhetoric subtle, just remarking obliquely on the body of the beloved.

TIMOTHY STEELE, *An Aubade* (p. 439)

As the title implies, this poem partakes in the centuries-old tradition of a morning song from one lover to another. The speaker surveys the room as his lover showers, recalls her body, and spends the rest of the poem shifting between his perceptions of the bedroom and his recollections of his lover. He plans to lounge in bed doing so until she appears in the room, bringing together in the final line these two poles: his naked lover and the contents of the room.

The title tips us off to the poet's consciousness that he is partaking in a poetic tradition. Students should notice this self-awareness when they characterize the speaker. If they don't immediately describe him as a poet, have them list the poetic conventions that the poem utilizes: the alliteration of "she," "showering," and "shine" in the first two lines; the strict scheme of end-rhyme; the poem's even pentameter, ten or tropes such as personification (the "face" of the flashlight [line 15]). The speaker emphasizes his awareness of his place in an old tradition at the end of the first stanza, comparing the folds of his sheet to "paintings from some fine old master's hand" (5).

Yet this is a contemporary poem: Does it feel like one? Do modern details such as showers and flashlights root us firmly in the twentieth century? What is the effect of mixing timeless and contemporary details as the poet does?

POSSIBLE CONNECTIONS TO OTHER SELECTIONS

Robert Herrick, "To the Virgins, to Make Much of Time" (text p. 64)

Richard Wilbur, "A Late Aubade" (question #1, following)

CONNECTION QUESTION IN TEXT (p. 440) WITH ANSWER

1. How does the tone of Steele's poem compare with Richard Wilbur's "A Late Aubade" (p. 68)? Explain why you prefer one over the other.

    Wilbur's "A Late Aubade," another aubade in which the speaker punctuates "the rosebuds-theme of centuries of verse" (line 23) also includes details from contemporary life, such as elevator cages. The tone is slightly different, though, and this difference pertains to the question of categorizing Steele's poem as a *carpe diem* poem: Wilbur's speaker is trying to lure his lover back into bed, Steele's speaker is content with the knowledge that pleasure is "brief and fugitive" (19). A close examination of this difference will challenge students to consider the ways in which both poets play with time — how they see the present as a function of both the past (memory) and the future (imagination).

RON KOERTGE, *1989* (p. 440)

In a matter-of-fact voice, the speaker describes the mood at "a lot of memorial services" (line 2) at a time when "AIDS was slaughtering people left and right" (1). The atmosphere at these events is slightly numbed, resigned, made "tolerable" (5) by "the funny stories people / got up and told about the deceased" (5–6). The poem has a straightforward, amiable narrative, amplified by conversational phrases like "The other thing" (4) and "That was more like it" (29). The first two stanzas establish this light tone: the speaker prefers the relief of humor to the steady solemnity traditionally associated with memorial services. The conclusion offers a more poignant center to this casually described grief; the last two lines offer "a roomful of people laughing and crying, taking off / their sunglasses to blot their inconsolable eyes" (30–31). The use of the word "inconsolable" and the heightened diction of the last two lines shift the tone beyond the limited reach of a funny story.

Because of its speaking of love for the dead, its attachment to the ways in which we express our love for the deceased, this can be considered a love poem. Students may decide it's not; there is no specific beloved, the poem is not addressed to an individual, and the humor in the face of death does not provide the serious answer to the death of a loved one that most expect.

POSSIBLE CONNECTIONS TO OTHER SELECTIONS

Donald Hall, "Letter with No Address" (text p. 673)

Miller Williams, "Thinking about Bill, Dead of AIDS" (question #1, following)

CONNECTION QUESTION IN TEXT (p. 441) WITH ANSWER

1. Discuss the connection between love and death in "1989" and in "Thinking about Bill, Dead of AIDS" (p. 645), by Miller Williams.

    Koertge's poem establishes a connection between love and death by examining the behavior of the living in the face of the death of the beloved. He stresses the relief of humor, acknowledging the small comfort it provides those with "inconsolable eyes" (line 31). While Koertge's speaker focuses on the mourners, Williams's poem centers on an individual victim of AIDS and the difficulties presented by the widespread ignorance, in 1989, of the dangers AIDS presented. Williams's speaker addresses the bravery necessary, in the center of that ignorance, to be loving toward the dying, uncertain of the risks associated with shaking hands or kissing, uncertain of the ways AIDS was attacking Bill's body, and uncertain of his needs as he approached death.

POEMS ABOUT TEACHING AND LEARNING

EMILY DICKINSON, *From all the Jails the Boys and Girls* (p. 442)

Here is a perfect poem for the last day of the semester! Dickinson captures the joy and energy of children released from school by playing trios of images against one another. The "Jails" of the first line and the "Prison" and "keep" — a pun that evokes both a sense of being held and the medieval image of a castle dungeon — in the fourth express the confinement the children endure during the school day. The released prisoners "leap" (line 2), and "storm" and "stun" (5) the world into which they escape. The sense of attacking life to demand everything it has to give is unmistakable, especially when one considers the use of transcendent words such as "ecstatically" (2), "beloved" (3), and "bliss" (6). The triple alliteration of *F*s in the last two lines attempts to bring things back down to earth. You might ask your students whether or not the last two lines have the tempering effect that the bearers of the frowns hope to convey. With which feeling does the end of the poem leave students?

POSSIBLE CONNECTIONS TO OTHER SELECTIONS

William Blake, "The Garden of Love" (text p. 592)
Cornelius Eady, "The Supremes" (text p. 670)
Robert Frost, " 'Out, Out —' " (question #2, following)
Judy Page Heitzman, "The Schoolroom on the Second Floor of the Knitting Mill" (text p. 446)

CONNECTION QUESTION IN TEXT (p. 442) WITH ANSWER

2. In an essay discuss the treatment of childhood in this poem and in Robert Frost's " 'Out, Out —' " (p. 350).

    Both poems — particularly Frost's bleak allusion to *Macbeth* — paint a fairly depressing portrait of childhood. Frost's picture indicates, not only by the more obvious "child at heart," "doing a man's work" (line 24), but also the apron-clad sister, that the children in this poem work, and work hard. Furthermore, the parents, after their extremely brief horror, return to work. Childhood is hard in " 'Out, Out —.' " Similarly, Dickinson's children of "solid Bliss" (6) come out of the "Jails" (1) (presumably of their homes), and have fun, only to return in the end to their parents, who are their "foes" (8) and wear predatory "Frowns" (7).

The difference between the two poems, however, is that in Frost's poem, life seems hard for everybody. Perhaps it is so for the "Frowns" in "From all the Jails the Boys and Girls," but it is never stated. One last note: the children in Dickinson's poem actually do have a little fun. Frost doesn't indicate any such thing in " 'Out, Out —'."

LANGSTON HUGHES, *Theme for English B* (p. 442)

This poem reads like a personal narrative, and indeed it does embody certain elements of Hughes's life. For example, "the college on the hill above Harlem" (line 9) is a reference to Columbia University, where Hughes was (briefly) a student. Therefore, asking a student to read this narrative to the class might make the speaker's story appear more poignant than if it were read in silence. You might ask students to pay particular attention to lines 21–26. The speaker defines himself in terms of the things he likes, which are nearly universal in their appeal, and recognizes that "being colored doesn't make [him] *not* like / the same things other folks like who are other races" (25–26). Ask students how this observation complicates the speaker's understanding of his relationship with the white college instructor and with whites in general.

You might also ask students how the double meaning of "theme" adds to the meaning of the poem. The speaker's assignment is to write a one-page "theme," that is, a brief composition. But the subject, or "theme," of that "theme" is far broader and more complicated: race relations and personal experiences. You might ask students if they noticed any other words with more than one interpretation in the context of this poem. One example might be the word *colored,* which means both that the writer is black and that he has been "colored," that is, affected, by the racial conditions into which he was born.

Ask your class to consider, in discussion or in a brief writing assignment, the importance of lines 31–33. How does the speaker understand himself and the white instructor to be part of each other? Why does he consider this to be particularly "American" (33)? You might also ask your students to think about this poem in the context of other poems in which Hughes attempts to define what is "American," such as "I, Too" (text p. 375). How would your students describe Hughes's vision of America?

POSSIBLE CONNECTIONS TO OTHER SELECTIONS

Chitra Banerjee Divakaruni, "Indian Movie, New Jersey" (question #2, following)
Mark Halliday, "Graded Paper" (text p. 445)

CONNECTION QUESTION IN TEXT (p. 444) WITH ANSWER

2. Discuss the attitudes expressed toward the United States in this poem and in Divakaruni's "Indian Movie, New Jersey" (p. 162).

   Both poems express the uneasiness of being a minority in white America. There is a grudging relationship between the minority and majority cultures, expressed in Hughes's poem as "You are white — / yet a part of me, as I am part of you. / That's American" (lines 31–33). The Indians in Divakaruni's poem do not even have that much of a connection to white America. They can only dream their version of the American dream while they are in the dim foyer of a movie theater, isolated from the rest of the culture. You might introduce the phrase "melting pot" when students address this question: has that metaphor ever accurately described our nation? How would the speakers of each of these poems respond to it?

MARILYN HACKER, *Groves of Academe* (p. 444)

From the point of view of a weary poetry professor, this poem encompasses the various responses she receives when she asks, "Tell me about the poetry you're reading." All of the responses dodge the question, focusing instead on the budding poets themselves rather than on the seemingly nonexistent poetry they are reading.

As students of poetry themselves, your students may feel uncomfortable as the subjects of this poem. They may also tend to distance themselves from the student voices in the poem. They may characterize the speaker as cynical: why doesn't she include any of the brilliant responses from students who *do* take the initiative to read poetry that isn't required in class? You might ask them if it is necessary to read poetry if you are to be a poet. If so, how does one find the time to do so in college? This may spark a lively discussion about the undergraduate experience — how valuable a commodity time is, how professors have no sense that students are taking more than one course, and so forth.

Having flushed out the attitudes of the speaker and students in the poem, you may return the discussion to the topic of "Groves of Academe" as a poem. It has an elaborate rhyme scheme, for instance, which addresses the student's question in lines 12–13. How else do Hacker's techniques play with the content of the poem? While characterizing the speaker, it is also useful to characterize the poem: is it a satire? Is the poet exaggerating the voices that she represents? (She has fit them into a rhyme scheme, so it isn't likely that she's copied them verbatim from students.) Is the humor biting — the speaker wants to foster "perversity" in herself, after all — or is it light? Point out how each of the students emphasizes themselves in their responses. Is the speaker arguing that all young poets are egotistical?

Possible Connections to Other Selections
Robert Browning, "My Last Duchess" (text p. 164)
Mark Halliday, "Graded Paper" (question #1, following)

Connection Question in Text (p. 444) with Answer
1. Write an essay that compares the teachers in "Groves of Academe" and in Halliday's "GradedPaper" (p. 445). Which teacher would you rather have for a course? Explain why.

   Although both professors are cynical, Halliday's professor is much more pointed in his critique, which has more to do with the student's writing ability than with students' general attitude. Hacker's speaker doesn't really offer any optimism for her students, but Halliday's speaker realizes that students are not the same person that he is. They are younger, for starters, and that fact may be more valuable than he has acknowledged. Students might not be able to separate the "A-" from the rest of the comment on the paper in Halliday's poem, just as they are often blind to our own comments when a grade is attached. If it is possible, you might want to level the playing field a bit by asking students to disregard that grade and to focus on the comment only, or, if that is not possible, to imagine what kind of grader Hacker's speaker is. What students probably want is a professor who will criticize them but give them a good grade anyway. How do they feel about cynicism? Do they understand where it comes from, or do they consider it a professional flaw?

MARK HALLIDAY, *Graded Paper* (p. 445)

This poem takes the theme of a professor's written comments on a paper and examines them for poetic content. Using humor and taking advantage of the diction employed in academic contexts, the poem establishes a connection between professor and student, examining the ways in which the graded paper serves as a communiqué between generations, a kind of love note shuffled back and forth. In its conclusion, the speaker acknowledges that, in spite of the student's difficulty with semicolons, the real problem is that "You are not / me, finally" (lines 34–35). The "delightful provocation" (38) this presents is the crux of the poem.

The grader of the paper is characterized as intelligent and familiar with academic culture but ultimately willing to allow room for honesty in the teacher-student relationship, opening the way for examination of a larger possibility. The final lines, beginning with "And yet" (29), offer an excuse for the fine grade awarded: anyone who is having trouble with semicolons, opaque thinking, and confused syntax shouldn't be getting an A-, but the "impressive, . . . cheeky" (33) confidence of the student overrides the professor's initial "cranky" reaction.

POSSIBLE CONNECTIONS TO OTHER SELECTIONS

Robert Browning, "My Last Duchess" (question #1, following)

Linda Pastan, "Marks" (text p. 132)

CONNECTION QUESTION IN TEXT (p. 446) WITH ANSWER

1. Compare the ways in which Halliday reveals the speaker's character in this poem with the strategies used by Browning in "My Last Duchess" (p. 164).

    Halliday and Browning both use formal speech in the first lines of their poems and then settle into a more honest, revealing informality. Halliday moves from "your thinking becomes, for me, alarmingly opaque" (lines 7–8) to "you are so young, so young" (37) over the course of his poem; Browning moves from the formal niceties of a host — "Will't please you sit and look at her?" (5) — to a vivid description of jealousy and the implication, in "I gave commands" (45), of murder.

ONLINE RESOURCES (manual p. 333)

JUDY PAGE HEITZMAN, *The Schoolroom on the Second Floor of the Knitting Mill* (p. 446)

This small, quiet poem demonstrates the impact the words of adults can have on the young; the speaker, an adult, is still haunted by a teacher's judgment. In the first stanza the reader is led to believe that the speaker holds Mrs. Lawrence tenderly in her memory; seeing the cardinals makes the speaker miss her. However, the details given in the first stanza include only Mrs. Lawrence's classroom manicure and a blueprint of the building that housed her classroom. The image of the teacher as she "carved and cleaned her nails" (line 2) can be read most immediately as an indictment of her teaching technique, but it can also be seen as an implied metaphor that foreshadows the harm Mrs. Lawrence can do. The nails can be read as claws, the cleaning and carving the daily maintenance of her weapons.

Another image that conveys a sense of the teacher's physical and pedagogical characteristics is the simile at the conclusion of the poem: "Her arms hang down like sausages" (22). Here Mrs. Lawrence is a figure to be pitied, a tired, defeated person who is totally oblivious to the effects of her words. The carving and cleaning of nails, the hanging arms, the quiet statement about Judy's poor leadership — all are mundane images. Harm is present all the time, ready to inflict lasting damage at any moment. You might want to ask your students to consider other insidious sources of quiet but serious harm: Students are likely to have their own stories of how quickly words can hurt, regardless of the speaker's awareness or intent.

POSSIBLE CONNECTIONS TO OTHER SELECTIONS

Emily Dickinson, "From all the Jails the Boys and Girls" (question #1, following)

Philip Larkin, "This Be the Verse" (question #2, following)

CONNECTIONS QUESTIONS IN TEXT (p. 447) WITH ANSWERS

1. Compare the representations and meanings of being a schoolchild in this poem with those in Dickinson's "From all the Jails the Boys and Girls" (p. 442).

   Both Dickinson and Heitzman establish the frustration of rules and a sly discounting of them: Dickinson, in her acknowledgment that schools are prison-like, admits the concern, and then admits that the "Bliss" (line 6) the children personify on their release is likely to be frowned on by others still imprisoned in less clear boundaries. Heitzman refers to the random nature of the rules the teacher insists she enforce by stating flatly, "That would be dangerous" (14). Both speakers quietly roll their eyes at the arbitrary strictures placed on schoolchildren, while being very attentive to the reality those confines create for the children.

2. Discuss how the past impinges on the present in Heitzman's poem and in Larkin's "This Be the Verse" (p. 621).

   Both Larkin and Heitzman convey the sense of the ways our experiences in childhood change us as people. Larkin insists that parents "fuck you up" (1), compounding your plight by giving you all of their faults plus "some extras" (4); no mention is made of the virtues passed down from generation to generation. Heitzman refers to the way a single instance of verbal condemnation haunts her: "I hear her every time I fail" (23). Heitzman also creates a sense of tenderness and nostalgia for the experience of school in her first stanza. While he acknowledges that we are not solely to blame for the "misery" (9) we hand on to our children, Larkin reveals no such tenderness.

R. S. GWYNN, *The Classroom at the Mall* (p. 447)

This poem offers a vision of academia enmeshed in consumer culture. "The Church of Reason in the Stalls of Trade" (line 42) provides many opportunities for humor. The portrait of the mall, "Musak" (19), and "plate glass windows" (26) is in contrast to allusions to Chaucer (12) and "promises to keep" (61), lifted from Frost's "Stopping by Woods on a Snowy Evening" (p. 353). Another distinction is made between the speaker, aware of the strange circumstances of this class, and the students, who don't seem to think the mall a strange place to encounter "one thought per week" (24). The rhyme scheme contributes to the humor developed through these contrasts.

The speaker uses a casual, conversational tone, and both speaker and school are portrayed as pretty slack: the teacher refers to the "Dean of Something" (1), who is more concerned about "P. R." (2) than effective teaching. Students might benefit from looking through this poem to find the contrasts mentioned above and others that trouble our expectations of academia. Mentioning the cost of tuition could bring some passion to a discussion of the relationship between higher learning and the material world.

POSSIBLE CONNECTIONS TO OTHER SELECTIONS

Marilyn Hacker, "Groves of Academe" (question #1, following)
Kathy Mangan, "An Arithmetic" (text p. 149)

CONNECTION QUESTION IN TEXT (p. 449) WITH ANSWER

1. How do the students in this poem compare with those in Marilyn Hacker's "Groves of Academe" (p. 444)? Where would you rather be a student? Why?

   The students in Gwynn's poem are portrayed as a diverse group, described by their day jobs ("housewives" [line 7], "student nurses" [7], "a part-time private cop" [10]) or by their personal attributes: "Ms. Light — serious, heavy, and very dark" (8). Ms. Light is the only student whose remarks are recorded; she's concerned about grades (29) and sums up the class by saying, "They sure had thoughts, those old guys" (55). While the speaker concedes that he "couldn't put it better anyway" (58), the overall impression is one of a student population barely involved with the class material. Hacker's poem, on the other hand, presents a group of students who are not named or individualized: they are characterized only through their own remarks. These remarks reveal vain students, who believe that reading "breaks [their] concentration" (8) or might "influence [their] style" (9). Neither class is presented as especially enlightening; with luck, your students will report that they prefer to stay where they are.

RICHARD WAKEFIELD, *In a Poetry Workshop* (p. 449)

This poem provides a kind of in-joke for people who are familiar with "the basics of modern verse" (line 1), prosody, the structure of a poetry class, Marx, Plato, and Wordsworth. Students may need a little guidance to understand the humor here; while they are likely to pick up on the tone, they may not see what's going on. You may want to ask what students know about poetry workshops and the concept of bringing poems to read with a group, reading them aloud, and working on them together. The rhyme and meter, in a poem that warns against both, provide tension between the form and the content of the poem. This tension renders the tone less than serious.

Wakefield's verse provides a good beginning for students' study of poems. One quick lesson learned is the distinction between poet and speaker: Wakefield's speaker may take his or her position as leader of a poetry workshop seriously, but Wakefield himself does not take his speaker's advice. This poem gives students a chance to articulate what they value in a poem. Are meter and rhyme important to them? Do they want to learn about the historical perspective of a piece, how it fits into larger artistic movements? Do they want to understand how Wordsworth and others have affected modern verse? Through humor, this poem provides a productive introduction to these issues.

18

Biographies of Selected Poets

When students respond strongly to a poem they often begin to wonder about the poet's life. Chapter 18 provides biographical information on poets whose work is included in the textbook. Students might observe how different these lives are from one other. For example, Wallace Stevens's work as an insurance lawyer in Hartford, Connecticut, certainly sets him apart from Lord Byron, whose tumultuous life moved like a whirlwind across the European continent. The work of poetry requires no one life or lifestyle.

Examination of the poet's lives might lead to fruitful class discussion. How much do we need to know about a poet's life to appreciate the poem? Which poets are themselves more interested in biography? (Robert Lowell, for instance, the author of "Life Studies," might be compared to Stevens.) You might even want to facilitate debate in class. Modern critics of poetry constantly argue this issue; students may enjoy a chance to have their say.

This debate about the usefulness of biographical information might find its way into students' papers. You might encourage students to consider the pros and cons of reading biographically in class, and then ask them to address the issue in an essay. A good essay topic would be a comparison of how two poets use material from their own lives. How are, say, William Carlos Williams's anecdotes from his medical practice different from George Herbert's chronicle of his religious quest?

A COLLECTION
OF POEMS

MAYA ANGELOU, *Africa* (p. 589)

This poem describes the continent of Africa as a woman, emphasizing her history of oppression and predicting her triumph in the future. You might begin a conversation about this poem by pointing out the contrasts between the anthropomorphized female Africa in each of the three stanzas. In each stanza, the meaning of the entire section is reflected in the poet's repeated use of the word *lain*. For instance, in the first stanza, "lain" refers to a sensual, even sexual Africa in years of rich repose, while in the second stanza, "lain" refers to an Africa that is violated and beaten. In the final stanza, Africa is no longer lying; rather, she is now rising and striding with images of strength and determination.

This poem uses color to contrast geographic or emotional states of being — an observation that may make a good writing assignment. For instance, the first stanza ends its vision of a rich, ripe Africa with the lines "Thus has she lain / Black through the years" (lines 7–8). This dark richness is contrasted in the second stanza with images of whiteness, coldness, and bloodlessness — "rime white and cold" (10) — which convey the violence brought to the sons, daughters, and continent of Africa herself.

You may wish to ask students who Angelou believes brought this violence to Africa and her children. Which lines of the poem can they cite as evidence? What is the predominant tone of the poem?

POSSIBLE CONNECTIONS TO OTHER SELECTIONS

Langston Hughes, "The Negro Speaks of Rivers" (text p. 372)
Wole Soyinka, "Future Plans" (text p. 664)

AUDIOVISUAL AND ONLINE RESOURCES (manual pp. 291, 322)

ANONYMOUS, *Bonny Barbara Allan* (p. 589)

Ballads can provide a good introduction to poetry, for they demonstrate many devices of other poetic forms — such as rhyme, meter, and image — within a narrative framework. Ballads, however, often begin abruptly, and the reader must infer the details that preceded their action. They employ simple language, tell their story through narrated events and dialogue, and often use refrains. The folk ballad was at its height in England and Scotland in the sixteenth and seventeenth centuries. These ballads were not written down but were passed along through an oral tradition, with the original author remaining anonymous. Literary ballads are derivatives of the folk ballad tradition. Keats's "La Belle Dame sans Merci" (text p. 618) is an example.

Notice how often this ballad refers to a broken love relationship. What can you infer about the relationships of the people in this ballad? Is it always one sex or the other who suffers? Is there a relationship between this ballad and modern-day popular songs? "Scarborough Fair" (text p. 171) might provide the basis for a discussion of the romantic situations presented in this ballad and the durability of such old "songs." Despite the list of impossible tasks that the speaker presents to his former lover as the price of reconciliation, the refrain names garden herbs associated with female power. Thyme tradi-

tionally is thought to enhance courage, sage wisdom, and rosemary memory, and parsley was used to decorate tombs — but both sage and rosemary had the additional connotations of growing in gardens where women ruled the households. You might wish to
have your students speculate on how such "mixed messages" might have been incorporated into this ballad. Also, "Scarborough Fair" was the basis for an antiwar song by the
folk-rock duo Simon and Garfunkel in the 1960s. Your students might be interested in
hearing how this old folk song was adapted for twentieth-century purposes.

Despite their ostensible narrative directness, ballads can be highly suggestive (rather
than straightforward) in their presentation. Psychological motivation is often implied
rather than spelled out. To explore this point, you might request, for example, that students in a two-to-three-page essay examine the reasons for and effects of the vengeful
acts of Barbara Allan.

These ballads contain central characters whose awareness (and, hence, voice) comes
into full power near the moment of their death. Again, this observation seems to support the psychological realism and suggestive truth that ballads can convey.

TIP FROM THE FIELD

When teaching "Bonny Barbara Allen" and other ballads, I begin by reading the
selection aloud or playing a recording of it, followed by a recording of early blues music
from Mississippi (e.g., songs by Robert Johnson or Howlin' Wolf). In conjunction, I distribute the lyrics from the blues songs to the class. I then ask my students to compare
these two oral-based forms.

— TIMOTHY PETERS, *Boston University*

ANONYMOUS, *Scottsboro* (p. 590)

Ballads often speak the concerns of a culture, giving voice and hope to an oppressed
people by encouraging them to keep their spirit alive in harsh circumstances. The black
American folk tradition contains many examples of this kind of ballad. Written long
after the Civil War, "Scottsboro" addresses a particular political situation, the Scottsboro case. The poet draws on the tradition of black folk ballads, finding a way to speak
in a context where his words are not welcome.

POSSIBLE CONNECTION TO ANOTHER SELECTION

Langston Hughes, "Ballad of the Landlord" (text p. 387)

W. H. AUDEN, *The Unknown Citizen* (p. 591)

Clearly, the speaker of this poem is not Auden himself; and the distance between
what the speaker says and what we assume Auden feels makes for a sharply satiric poem
about this "unknown" yet statistically well-documented citizen. The important question
for the class is, at what point and in what way do they realize they are reading satire?
Focus first on the epitaph, its impersonal numbers and its precise rhymes. In the opening lines, consider how to reconcile "sainthood" with "One against whom there was no
official complaint." Students familiar with George Orwell's fiction will probably enjoy
this caricature of bureaucracy. You may want to explore the fine line that separates duty
and regard for civic law from blind obedience.

POSSIBLE CONNECTION TO ANOTHER SELECTION

James Merrill, "Casual Wear" (text p. 159)

AUDIOVISUAL AND ONLINE RESOURCES (manual pp. 292, 323)

MARGARET AVISON, *Tennis* (p. 592)

Avison's poem focuses and reflects on the sensory aspects of a seemingly rigid, methodical sport. Rather than allow the framework of the sonnet form to restrict her description of playing tennis, she explores the possibilities that lie in metric deviation. Avison writes about the physical exhilaration of the game, as well as its visual appeal, lending the whole sonnet a sweeping, lyrical quality that is uncommon in most traditional sonnets: "Dancing white galliardes at tape or net / Till point, on the wire's tip, or the long bum- / ing arc to nethercourt marks game and set." (lines 7, 8). Avison sees unrestricted possibility within the basic rules of tennis, and also relishes that same sense of possibility in the writing of her sonnet. The game of tennis is transformed into an insular, fantastical world where the opponents can become poets themselves and "Score liquid Euclids in foolscaps of air" (14).

There are many visual and metrical "surprises" in this poem, such as the breakup of the word *buming* at the end of the line 7. Also surprising is the appearance of the words *The albinos* in line 12. What are some other "surprises," metrical or otherwise, in this sonnet? Have your students explain how these devices contribute to the overall liberation of the form. At what point does the poem transform from a mere description of the action of the game to something more imaginative?

POSSIBLE CONNECTIONS TO OTHER SELECTIONS

Peter Meinke, "The ABC of Aerobics" (text p. 270)

David Solway, "Windsurfing" (text p. 92)

WILLIAM BLAKE, *The Garden of Love* (p. 592)

This brief lyric poses in customary Blakean fashion the natural, free-flowing, and childlike expression of love against the restrictive and repressive adult structures of organized religion. The dialogue between the two is effectively demonstrated in the closing two lines, with their internal rhyme patterns, in particular the rhyming of "briars" (of the priests) and "desires" (of the young boy). The process of growing into adulthood is costly, according to Blake; it requires the exchange of simple pleasures for conventional morality.

POSSIBLE CONNECTION TO ANOTHER SELECTION

Emily Dickinson, "From all the Jails the Boys and Girls" (text p. 442)

WILLIAM BLAKE, *Infant Sorrow* (p. 592)

This brief poem uses the voice of an infant to demonstrate distrust of "the dangerous world" (line 2). Arriving "Helpless naked" (3), "Struggling" (5), the baby is soon "Bound and weary" (7) and has little hope. The parental response is not encouraging: the pain and fear of childbirth preclude a proper greeting. Blake's speaker seems to have been aware of the dangers of the world before his arrival, knowing that the world into which he "leapt" (2) was "dangerous" (2). His first contact does not seem to dissuade him from this bias.

Comparing this poem with Philip Larkin's "This Be the Verse" (text p. 621) could make for a satisfying wallow in misanthropy and pessimism. Choosing a low-energy day for your class, perhaps mid-winter, or just before finals, could allow for some healthy release and vivid discussion.

POSSIBLE CONNECTIONS TO OTHER SELECTIONS

Anne Bradstreet, "Before the Birth of One of Her Children" (text p. 594)

Philip Larkin, "This Be the Verse" (text p. 621)
Sue Owen, "Zero" (text p. 123)

LOUISE BOGAN, *Women* (p. 593)

Louise Bogan's famous dry wit is evident in the tone of this poem. Some of the ironies in this poem exist simply because Bogan is a woman: if women "do not see cattle cropping red winter grass" (line 5), how is Bogan able to report on it? If the inability to think of "wood cleft by an axe" (14) is inherently feminine, how does Bogan know it is "clean" (14)? Your students may enjoy ferreting out Bogan's intention here. The final lines suggest that there was some scrap of "life" the speaker regrets letting in over her door-sill. Is this poem a joke, demonstrating the ridiculousness of stereotypes about women? Is Bogan's speaker bitter about some way in which her behavior corresponds with the stereotype? What do your students imagine Bogan refers to in her oblique reference to her regrets? Asking students to write an imagined journal entry from the perspective of Bogan's speaker could allow them to assess her perspective with greater clarity.

POSSIBLE CONNECTIONS TO OTHER SELECTIONS

Sharon Olds, "Poem for the Breasts" (text p. 127)
Patricia Smith, "What It's Like to Be a Black Girl (For Those of You Who Aren't)" (text p. 104)
Alice Walker, "a woman is not a potted plant" (text p. 37)

ROBERT BLY, *Snowfall in the Afternoon* (p. 5934)

In these four three-line stanzas, the speaker of this poem describes an almost hallucinatory winter scene. By the end of the poem the distant barn has fully transformed into a ship, emphasizing the speaker's transforming perception, influenced by the hypnotic falling snow. You might begin discussion by talking about the structure of this poem. Bly very deliberately separates the stanzas by giving them numbers, and you might ask students to consider how the poem might read differently if the stanzas were merely separated by space. Do the numbers provide a sense of progression or differentiation between the various stanzas? Ask students to consider also whether the structure of the poem reflects the poem's content.

Examine in class the contrasts that Bly sets up in the poem — between the images of snow and darkness in the first two stanzas and the images of moving away and moving toward in the third and fourth stanzas. Ask students to consider these images and describe how they affect the mood of the poem.

Have students examine the final line of the poem: "All the sailors on deck have been blind for many years" (line 12). Who are the sailors on deck, and why might they be blind?

POSSIBLE CONNECTIONS TO OTHER SELECTIONS

Robert Bly, "Snowbanks North of the House" (text p. 150)
Henry Wadsworth Longfellow, "Snow-Flakes" (text p. 622)

ROO BORSON, *Talk* (p. 594)

This poem is a minute discussion of character and conversation as it is engendered in both men and women of different generations. The poet's point of view is the view of the casual street observer who focuses in on the use of "talk" and offers the reader very revealing thumbnail sketches of gender relationships.

Some of the most interesting perspectives that the poet offers are the glimpses of the characters' thoughts as they are revealed through their mannerisms. "Sometimes, looking at a girl, it / almost occurs to them, but they can't make it out, / they go pawing toward it through the fog" (lines 3–5). You may want to discuss with your students how the placement of the line breaks in the poem reflect the distracted, disjointed nature of the elderly men.

Another item for discussion would be to carefully scrutinize the ways in which the poet has used her words sparingly but effectively, to create a concise and thought-provoking analysis of men and women of different generations. What, does it seem, have the old men lost as a result of time and age? How do the young women, characterized as confused, compare with the young men? The old men? Ask your students if they think that the young women are bound to turn out like the old women in the poem. Why is it important to "know the value of oranges" (11)?

Finally, is the poet somehow linking herself with the young men in the last two lines of the poem by finally admitting her artistic tinkering with the people she observes?

POSSIBLE CONNECTION TO ANOTHER SELECTION

A. E. Housman, "When I was one-and-twenty" (text p. 209)

ANNE BRADSTREET, *Before the Birth of One of Her Children* (p. 594)

Until Anne Bradstreet's brother-in-law took a collection of her poems to London and had it published in 1650, no resident of the New World had published a book of poetry. Bradstreet's work enjoyed popularity in England and America. She was born and grew up on the estate of the earl of Lincoln, whose affairs her father managed. Bradstreet's father was eager to provide his daughter with the best possible education. When she was seventeen she and her new husband, Simon Bradstreet, sailed for Massachusetts, where she lived the rest of her life.

As a child Bradstreet contracted rheumatic fever, and its lifelong effects compounded the dangers attending seventeenth-century childbirth. What may seem at first an overdramatized farewell to a loved one can be viewed in this context as a sober reflection on life's capriciousness and an understandable wish to maintain some influence on the living. Perhaps the most striking moment in the poem occurs in line 16, when the only inexact end rhyme ("grave") coincides with a crucial change in tone and purpose. What had been a summary of Puritan attitudes (deeply felt, to be sure) toward life and death and a gently serious offering of "best wishes" to the speaker's husband becomes, with that crack in the voice, a plea to be remembered well.

You might discuss the appropriateness of the poet's choosing heroic couplets for this subject: how does the symmetry of the lines affect our understanding of the subject? You might also consider the way the speaker constructs her audience, like someone writing a diary. Is this truly private verse? Or does the speaker sense that people other than her children will read the poem?

POSSIBLE CONNECTIONS TO OTHER SELECTIONS

Anne Bradstreet, "The Author to Her Book" (text p. 117)
John Donne, "A Valediction: Forbidding Mourning" (text p. 130)

GWENDOLYN BROOKS, *The Mother* (p. 594)

This poem discusses a controversial issue in very contradictory images. The difference between the title and the first word points out this contradiction immediately. Isn't an abortion about *not* being a mother? Students may tend to simplify this poem because abortion is a heated moral and ethical issue. Urge them to consider the way the poem talks about the experience. They might begin by noting the matter-of-factness of the first stanza: the perfect rhymed couplets, the direct statements. This directness breaks down in the second stanza, as "You" shifts to "I."

Ask students to compare the first and second stanzas. How, for example, does *sweet*, a word that appears in both stanzas, mean something different each time? The rhyme scheme changes in the second stanza. How does this change affect the speaker's attitude toward her experience? She speaks of "I" and "you" in the second stanza. Is this poem directed to her unborn children, or to herself? Why does she list the events of her children's lost lives in lines 15–20? How does this listing affect the reader? Does the speaker effectively separate herself from her lost children, or is she somewhat confused about their loss? She returns to the direct statement at the end of the stanza, perhaps trying to regain control over herself. In the third stanza, the speaker admits that she is unsure of how to describe her experience in order to say "the truth" (line 28). Ask students to identify possible meanings for this truth. Is it definable? Finally, you might consider why the last stanza is separated from the rest.

A writing assignment might ask students to discuss at length the form of the poem. How does the structure illustrate the speaker's feelings or change of feeling?

Possible Connection to Another Selection

Anne Bradstreet, "Before the Birth of One of Her Children" (text p. 594)

ROBERT BROWNING, *Home-Thoughts, from Abroad* (p. 596)

This poem's tone evokes a strong sense of nostalgia: Browning's speaker moves through the changes spring brings from "the lowest boughs" (line 5) to his own "blossomed pear-tree" (11). The speaker laments that those back home do not appreciate these pleasant changes and are "unaware" (4). The narrative, filled with the enthusiasm of multiple exclamation points, takes his audience on a kind of virtual tour of his homeland. New students may be able to identify all too easily with this intense homesickness, the detailed awareness of far-off occurrences. An imitation poem might be a good way to bring them closer to this material; asking them to choose a familiar but far-off location and mimic Browning's format might be helpful. Students who are not interested in indulging their homesickness could write poems imagining some activity they'd prefer to their homework — a road trip, a party, skiing — and moving through it step by step.

Possible Connections to Other Selections

Anonymous, "Western Wind" (text p. 26)
Robert Hayden, "Those Winter Sundays" (text p. 10)

ROBERT BROWNING, *Meeting at Night* and *Parting at Morning* (p. 597)

The titles of these two lyrics ask that they be taught together. Have students summarize in a writing assignment the poems' themes and suggest their complementarity. Here are portrayed the coexisting desires in human beings for the bonds of love and the freedom of adventure. Discuss with the class the use of natural imagery in each poem and the relative displacement of the sense of a speaker.

You might also ask students if we can still read these poems with the unhesitating acceptance of the divisions that Browning seems to take for granted, namely, that Eros and the night world are linked in the acceptance of the feminine, but that the day world of action and adventure is the exclusive realm of man.

GEORGE GORDON, LORD BYRON, *She Walks in Beauty* (p. 597)

In the nineteenth century, George Gordon, Lord Byron, was commonly considered the greatest of the Romantic poets. He spent his childhood with his mother in Aberdeen, Scotland, in deprived circumstances despite an aristocratic heritage. In *Childe Harold, Don Juan,* and much of his other work, Byron chronicled the adventures of one or another example of what came to be known as the "Byronic hero," a gloomy, lusty, guilt-ridden individualist. The poet died of fever while participating in the Greek fight for independence from Turkey.

The title and first line of "She Walks in Beauty" can be an excellent entrance to the poem's explication. Students might puzzle over what it means to walk *in* beauty: is the beauty like a wrap or a cloud? The simile "like the night" hinges on that image. You might ask students if the speaker makes nature subservient to the woman, or the reverse. You might point out "gaudy" (line 6), a strange adjective for describing the day, to draw attention to the speaker's attitude toward nature.

Note the mood of timeless adoration in the second stanza. There is really no movement, only an exclamation of wonder. The exclamation is even more direct in the final stanza, where the woman's visage becomes a reflection of her spotless character. Students might explore the images in all three stanzas, looking for shifts from natural to social. How does the speaker move from "like the night" (1) to "a mind" (17) and "a heart" (18)? Why would he want to describe a woman in these terms? What effect does this description have on our idea of her? Do we really know her by the end of the poem?

For discussion of Byron's poetry, consult *Byron: Wrath and Rhyme*, edited by Alan Bold (London: Vision, 1983); Frederick Garber's *Self, Text, and Romantic Irony: The Example of Byron* (Princeton: Princeton UP, 1988); and Peter Mannings's *Byron and His Fictions* (Detroit: Wayne State U, 1978).

POSSIBLE CONNECTION TO ANOTHER SELECTION

William Wordsworth, "The Solitary Reaper" (text p. 647)

AUDIOVISUAL AND ONLINE RESOURCES (manual pp. 295, 326)

SAMUEL TAYLOR COLERIDGE, *Sonnet to the River Otter* (p. 598)

This sonnet, a love poem to a river important in the speaker's youth, provides an opportunity to indulge in longing for "the sweet scenes of childhood" (line 6). The carefree days of childhood and the anatomy of the beloved river work together: both are detailed with loving attention.

The period that separates the speaker from the river of his youth is presented with ambivalence: while childhood appears as "sweet" (6) and "careless" (14), the years of adulthood are characterized as "various-fated" (2), both "happy" (3) and "mournful" (3). Asking your students to read this poem out loud could help them see the effectiveness of the sounds Coleridge uses. "Skimmed the smooth thin stone" (4) conveys a light, pleasurable, specific carelessness, while the "many various-fated years" (2) of "Lone manhood's cares" (13) are vague in content, heavy and complex in sound.

You may wish to ask your students to write an essay comparing this poem's perspective on childhood with those of other poems in this collection that are not as sunny in tone. Examples are included below.

POSSIBLE CONNECTIONS TO OTHER SELECTIONS

Margaret Atwood, "Bored" (text p. 72)

Regina Barreca, "Nighttime Fires" (text p. 26)

William Blake, "Infant Sorrow" (text p. 592)

Michael Collier, "The Barber" (text p. 98)

SAMUEL TAYLOR COLERIDGE, *Kubla Khan: or, a Vision in a Dream* (p. 598)

Samuel Taylor Coleridge was born in Ottery St. Mary, Devonshire, but was sent to school in London, where he impressed his teachers and classmates (among whom was Charles Lamb) as an extremely precocious child. He attended Cambridge without taking a degree, enlisted for a short tour of duty in the Light Dragoons (a cavalry unit), planned a utopian community in America with Robert Southey, and married Southey's sister-in-law. He met William Wordsworth in 1795 and published *Lyrical Ballads* with him three years later. Coleridge became an opium addict in 1800–1801 because of the heavy doses of laudanum he'd taken to relieve the pain of several ailments, principally rheumatism. For the last eighteen years of his life, he was under the care (and under the roof) of Dr. James Gillman, writing steadily but never able to sustain the concentration needed to complete the large projects he kept planning.

Reputedly, "Kubla Khan" came to Coleridge "as in a vision" after he took a pre-scribed anodyne and fell into a deep sleep. What Coleridge was able to write down upon waking is only a fragment of what he dreamed. Figures such as the "pleasure-dome" and "the sacred river" take on an allegorical cast and suggest the power that inspires the writing of poetry. Although phrases such as "sunless sea" and "lifeless ocean" appear gloomy, they could also suggest mystery and the atmosphere conducive to bringing forth poems.

For a reading of this poem, consult Humphrey House's "Kubla Khan, Christabel, and Dejection," in *Coleridge* (London: Hart-Davis, 1953), reprinted in *Romanticism and Consciousness*, edited by Harold Bloom (New York: Norton, 1970). Another good essay to turn to is "The Daemonic in 'Kubla Khan': Toward Interpretation" by Charles I. Patterson Jr., in *PMLA* 89 (October 1974): 1033–1042. Patterson points out, for example, that the river in the poem is "sacred" because it seems to be possessed by a god who infuses in the poet a vision of beauty. Likewise, he identifies the "deep delight" mentioned in line 44 as "a daemonic inspiration." In a writing assignment you might ask students to explore imagery and sound patterns in order to demonstrate how Coleridge uses words to embody and suggest the idea that poetry is truly a "pleasure-dome," visionary and demonically inspired.

You could initiate discussion by asking students to locate and discuss the way Coleridge employs unusual language to describe the scene and to shape our perceptions of it. What is the effect, for instance, of alliteration in line 25 ("Five miles meandering with a mazy motion")?

POSSIBLE CONNECTIONS TO OTHER SELECTIONS

John Keats, "Ode to a Nightingale" (text p. 196)

William Butler Yeats, "Sailing to Byzantium" (text p. 651)

AUDIOVISUAL AND ONLINE RESOURCES (manual pp. 296, 327)

PAM CROW, *Meat Science* (p. 600)

The story this speaker retells attempts to provide some meaning for the odd and difficult experience of a stranger. The "drunk senior" (line 4) establishes an instant intimacy with the unnamed "you" of the poem and monopolizes the conversation, taking the opportunity to reveal a great deal about himself. The monopoly appears to be complete, as far as the speaker is aware: there is no reference to "you" speaking during the exchange. Students may be frustrated by the absence of a clear theme or reading from this poem; pointing out that life provides circumstances similarly difficult to get a "hold" (44) on could prove helpful for discussion.

POSSIBLE CONNECTIONS TO OTHER SELECTIONS

Andrew Hudgins, "Seventeen" (text p. 156)
Jay Meek, "Swimmers" (text p. 254)

VICTOR HERNÁNDEZ CRUZ, *Anonymous* (p. 601)

Beginning *in medias res*, the speaker tells us how things would have been different if he had "lived in those olden times" (line 1), presumably in fifteenth- or sixteenth-century England rather than in contemporary Manhattan. He is playing with the conventions of being a poet, which, based on the title and on lines 2 and 3, has much to do with one's name. According to the speaker, the life of a poet of yore consisted of the constant search for rhyme and of the ability to use the words "*alas* and *hath*" (7). The poet uses these words, but their use is heavily ironic since the poet lives on the Lower East Side of Manhattan rather than in the English court during the Renaissance. The poet's exact intent is not immediately obvious. His poem is somewhat experimental, eschewing punctuation (for the most part) and including words whose meaning isn't immediately obvious from the context (such as "measurement termination surprise" in line 5 or "Within thou *mambo* of much more haste" in line 19).

Before students begin to dig into some of these more obscure lines, you might begin a discussion by considering the implication of the title. "Anonymous" is occasionally the way we designate the author of a poem, but it is rarely the title. What do the names of poets sometimes connote? Do we read a poem differently if we know it is by a famous poet such as Shakespeare, or Eliot, or Wordsworth? If you have time, you might even begin such a discussion by having students read and discuss two poems without knowing the names of the authors, perhaps one by a "famous" author and one by a lesser-known author. When you reveal the authors' names, does it make a difference?

POSSIBLE CONNECTION TO ANOTHER SELECTION

Julio Marzán, "Ethnic Poetry" (text p. 158)

ONLINE RESOURCES (manual p. 328)

COUNTEE CULLEN, *Yet Do I Marvel* (p. 601)

This speaker addresses some age-old questions about the mystery of God's works, but concludes the poem by adding his own situation as a black poet to this list of mysteries. The allusions to Tantalus and Sisyphus aren't accidental; Tantalus represents a dream just out of reach and Sisyphus represents eternal struggle. Both of these situations are relevant to the black poet of 1925, and relevant to larger questions of God's goodness. It is interesting to note that, whereas the speaker addresses God, the examples by which he questions God's benevolence stem from the "pagan" classical mythology, mirroring, perhaps, the alienation the speaker feels.

Students have to fill in quite a bit here, though; the situation of the black poet might be difficult, but why is his situation mysterious, or as the title and the penultimate line suggest, marvelous? What is the relationship between God and the speaker? Is this God indifferent, capricious, omniscient, cruel, or all of the above?

POSSIBLE CONNECTIONS TO OTHER SELECTIONS

Gerard Manley Hopkins, "God's Grandeur" (text p. 181)

Langston Hughes, "Negro" (text p. 377)

AUDIOVISUAL AND ONLINE RESOURCES (manual pp. 296, 328)

E. E. CUMMINGS, *Buffalo Bill 's* (p. 602)

An interesting few moments of class discussion could address whether Cummings is singing the praises of Buffalo Bill in this poem. How does the word *defunct* strike our ears, especially in the second line of the poem? What is the speaker's tone as he asks the concluding question? Is he sincere or contemptuous?

POSSIBLE CONNECTION TO ANOTHER SELECTION

Marilyn Nelson Waniek, "Emily Dickinson's Defunct" (text p. 261)

MARY DI MICHELE, *As in the Beginning* (p. 602)

In this poem, the author focuses upon her father's hands, and how their appearance reflects the hardships he has had to endure in life. She begins the poem by asserting the basic knowledge that "A man has two hands" (line 1), acknowledging this fact as if it were an inalienable right that all men have, and that has been denied her father because of his work. "$250 for each digit &/or $100 for a joint" (8) hardly seeming compensation enough for her father's loss.

Throughout this poem, there is a distinct sense of an even greater loss than the loss of her father's fingers — there is also the poet's loss of the person her father was when he was young, and still unmarked by hardships: "give me my father's hands still brown and uncallused, / beautiful hands that broke bread for us at table" (20-21). The poet presents the reader with an image of her father as he once was, almost as if she were trying to go back in time and physically reconstruct him. This is evident in the last four lines in the poem, with the appearance of the words "whole," open," and "warm" "as they were in the beginning" (25).

To begin a discussion of this poem with students, you might want to focus on the title. How does this biblical reference reflect the circumstances of the poem? You also might want to discuss the poet's role as writer in the poem (see 12–13). How does the act of writing help the poet come to terms with her father's condition? What is the intended effect of the poet directly addressing her readers in lines 14–15? Ask your students to determine who the poet is speaking to when she repeats the phrase "give me" in the second section of the poem.

POSSIBLE CONNECTION TO ANOTHER SELECTION

Andrew Hudgins, "Elegy for My Father, Who Is Not Dead" (text p. 242)

GREGORY DJANIKIAN, *When I First Saw Snow* (p. 603)

This is a poem of transformation — a moment that is much larger and more significant in the poet's life than the simple event it describes. Ask students to point to specific lines in the poem that describe in detail the feel of this moment. Students are likely to point out the red bows (line 13), the dusting of snow on the gray planks of the porch (17), the smell of the pine tree (6), the feel of the sticky sap on his fingers (5), and, most particularly, the sounds (the music, the sound of the Monopoly game in progress, his boot buckles, and the imagined whistling of the train).

These images are woven together to effectively recreate the speaker's first experience of snow, but they take on larger relevance within the context of the beginning and ending of the poem. After reading the poem in class, you may wish to ask students about the beginning and the end — what do they make of the "papers" the family is waiting for (3)? How does an understanding of that phrase affect an understanding of the final two lines of the poem?

POSSIBLE CONNECTION TO ANOTHER SELECTION

John Keats, "On First Looking into Chapman's Homer" (text p. 226)

ONLINE RESOURCES (manual p. 324)

JOHN DONNE, *The Apparition* (p. 603)

Donne's poem carries the Renaissance conceit of the lover, pining away at the mercy of a cruel and scornful mistress, one step further; after the lover has died from his mistress's neglect, he takes his revenge by coming back to haunt her. Ask students to notice the various means by which the speaker seeks to characterize his former love. He calls her a "murderess" in the very first line. How else does he attempt to cast her in a bad light? Students may need to be informed that quicksilver (line 12) — mercury — was a common treatment for venereal disease in Donne's day. Do your students trust the speaker's description of his former love? What are the implications of the fact that there are actually *two* ghosts, the speaker (4) and the woman (13), in this poem? Notice that Donne uses three different metrical lengths in the first four lines. What is the effect of this constant change of rhythm and of the rhyme between "dead" and "bed" in these lines?

POSSIBLE CONNECTION TO ANOTHER SELECTION

John Donne, "The Flea" (text p. 604)

JOHN DONNE, *Batter My Heart* (p. 604)

Christian and Romantic traditions come together in this sonnet. Employing Christian tradition, Donne here portrays the soul as a maiden with Christ as her bridegroom. Borrowing from Petrarchan materials, Donne images the reluctant woman as a castle and her lover as the invading army. Without alluding to any particular tradition, we can also observe in this poem two modes of male aggression, namely, the waging of war and the pursuit of romantic conquest, again blended into a strong and brilliantly rendered metaphysical conceit. Donne is imploring his "three-personed" God to take strong measures against the enemy, Satan. In a typical metaphysical paradox, Donne moreover asks God to save him from Satan by imprisoning him within God's grace.

Rhythm and sound work remarkably in this sonnet to enforce its meaning. Review the heavy-stressed opening line — which sounds like the pounding of a relentless fist and is followed by the strong reiterated plosives of "break, blow, burn."

POSSIBLE CONNECTION TO ANOTHER SELECTION

Mark Jarman, "Unholy Sonnet" (text p. 232)

JOHN DONNE, *The Flea* (p. 604)

An interesting discussion or writing topic could be organized around the tradition of the *carpe diem* poem and how this poem both accommodates and alters that tradition.

The wit here is ingenious, and after the individual sections of the poem are explained, more time might be needed to review the parts and give the class a sense of the total effect of the poem's operations.

The reason the speaker even bothers to comment on the flea stems from his belief that a commingling of blood during intercourse (here, admittedly, by the agency of the flea) may result in conception. Hence his belief that the lovers must be "yea more than" united and that the flea's body has become a kind of "marriage temple." For the woman to crush the flea (which she does) is a multiple crime because in so doing she commits murder, suicide, and sacrilege (of the temple) and figuratively destroys the possible progeny. The flea in its death, though, also stands as logical emblem for why this courtship should be consummated. The reasoning is that little if any innocence or honor is spent in killing the flea, then, likewise, neither of those commodities would be spent "when thou yield'st to me."

One way to begin discussion is to consider the poem as an exercise in the making of meaning: what does the flea represent to the speaker, and how does its meaning change as the poem progresses? What, in effect, is the relation between the flea and the poem?

POSSIBLE CONNECTIONS TO OTHER SELECTIONS

Sally Croft, "Home-Baked Bread" (text p. 107)

John Donne, "Song" (text p. 189)

DAVID DONNELL, *The Canadian Prairie's View of Literature* (p. 605)

Donnell has flipped the perspective of this poem around in order to shed some light on the ways in which subject matter can influence the very creation of a poem or piece of literature. Donnell takes us on a tour of the rural landscape of Canada, and allows each environment to speak for itself as to the ways in which it should be and has been represented in art.

It is important to note the sudden, ironic gestures that the poet lends to his subject matter. For example, you might want to discuss with your students the sometimes conversational tone that the poem adopts. For example, "towns are alright; Ontario towns are urban; French towns are European; / the action should take place on a farm between April and October; / nature is quiet during winter; when it snows, there's a lot of it" (lines 6–8). Each item in this list is representational, rather than concrete. Discuss with your students what these images point to, and where they can be found elsewhere in literature. Would it be justifiable to say that the author is indicating some probable, stereotypical locales in which Canadian literature generally takes place, such as in "beverage rooms and cheap hotels" (13–14)? What does the author intend by the sudden appearance of Indians and Metis (15)?

It will also be important to discuss how the poet uses the semicolon in this poem to create a pastiche of images that can be put together to create a whole picture. How does this type of punctuation contribute to the overall effect of the poem?

POSSIBLE CONNECTION TO ANOTHER SELECTION

Robert Morgan, "On the Shape of a Poem" (text p. 249)

GEORGE ELIOT [MARY ANN EVANS], *In a London Drawingroom* (p. 606)

This poem could more accurately be titled "*From* a London Drawingroom" since the speaker's gaze seems to be directed entirely outward, through a window that makes London (or even the world) seem like a prison. The colors are drab, the people are lifeless, the architecture monotonous. Despite the monotony of the landscape, everyone is in constant motion, which is part of the problem; "No figure lingering / Pauses to feed the hunger of the eye / Or rest a little on the lap of life" (lines 10–12). Ask students to unpack these lines; what do they imply about these people and their surroundings, or about the relationship between this speaker and the rest of the world? What is meant by the phrase "multiplied identity" (16)? And in the last two lines, what do students suppose "men" are being punished for? By whom? The relationship between humankind and nature is also worth pursuing; we have presumably created the "smoke" of the first line, and the "solid fog" of the fourth line; yet the punishment seems to come from elsewhere. This poem is a good example of how an outward-looking description really reflects inward psychology.

POSSIBLE CONNECTIONS TO OTHER SELECTIONS

Matthew Arnold, "Dover Beach" (text p. 95)
T. S. Eliot, "The Love Song of J. Alfred Prufrock" (text p. 405)
Robert Hass, "Happiness" (text p. 44)

THOMAS HARDY, *Hap* (p. 606)

Bad luck, pain, and sorrow seem so happenstance, Hardy says in this sonnet. Does the attitude of the speaker ring true? He claims that it would be easier to bear ill chance if some vengeful god would openly proclaim his malevolent designs. Discuss with the class why even the machinations of some divinity appear preferable to the silent, indeterminate (and inhuman) operations of caprice.

POSSIBLE CONNECTION TO ANOTHER SELECTION

Langston Hughes, "Lenox Avenue: Midnight" (text p. 383)

THOMAS HARDY, *In Time of "The Breaking of Nations"* (p. 607)

This poem, published shortly after the beginning of World War I, demonstrates the speaker's belief in the timelessness of domestic life. Nations may break into pieces, and kingdoms may be destroyed, as the footnote to this poem suggests, but life and love in the countryside "will go onward the same / Though Dynasties pass" (lines 7–8).

Students may see this as a naïve view of international politics, or they may find it comforting. A discussion of this poem could center on what they've learned in history classes: How has the history they've studied been ordered? How do they imagine the speaker of this poem would choose to organize a history of the world?

POSSIBLE CONNECTIONS TO OTHER SELECTIONS

David Barber, "A Colonial Epitaph Annotated" (text p. 220)
Dylan Thomas, "The Hand That Signed the Paper" (text p. 120)

JOY HARJO, *Fishing* (p. 607)

This is a very rich prose poem by Native American poet Joy Harjo. You may want to open a discussion of this poem by pointing out the difference between what students usually consider "poetry" and the prose form of this poem. Ask students what makes this piece a poem. One possible exercise is to have students rewrite the first few lines in more conventional poetic lines. What is the effect of these changes? Why might Harjo have chosen to use the prose poem format?

In the poem, the speaker describes a fishing trip she has promised to make with her friend, Louis. Later she admits that "This / is the only place I can keep that promise, inside a poem as familiar to him / as the banks of his favorite fishing place" (12–14). Ask students to interpret these lines. Possible responses include that the poet never really does go to Louis's favorite spot along the river, or that the poem is the only way she can fish *with Louis* anymore.

The speaker makes several connections between fishing and dying throughout the poem. In class examine lines 18–27. Although it is never stated directly, she hints that Louis is dead. Additional references to death include the fossils and ashes in line 15; the fish asking "When is that old Creek coming back?" (16), then going on to refer to Louis in the past tense; and the poet stating that "Last night I dreamed I tried to die, I was going to / look for Louis" (18–19). Near the end of the poem, the speaker says, "I know most fishers to be liars most of the time. Even Louis when it / came to fishing, or even dying" (26–27).

The content of this poem could be divided into several sections, and it may be interesting to ask students to identify where they see these sections occurring. The first section might be the opening lines that present fish as heroic survivors; the second section could include the lines that introduce Louis as a friend and a fisher; the third section could be the dream sequence; and the final section could be the ending, in which the speaker explores the connection between fishing, dying, and the mystery of life.

After discussing the poem, you may wish to have students write about the characters that appear. What do we know about Louis — both literally and figuratively — from the poem? What do we know about the narrator? What do we know about their relationship?

POSSIBLE CONNECTION TO ANOTHER SELECTION

Elizabeth Bishop, "The Fish" (text p. 20)

AUDIOVISUAL AND ONLINE RESOURCES (manual pp. 299, 333)

FRANCES E. W. HARPER, *Learning to Read* (p. 608)

This sonnet, written shortly after the end of the Civil War, eloquently praises the efforts of Yankees from the North who traveled to the South after the war to help teach slaves to read. Harper also recalls her own passion for learning how to read, despite the fact that she "was rising sixty" (line 35). Harper chooses not to characterize any one Yankee or "Reb," but rather focuses on people such as Uncle Caldwell and Chloe to personalize the poem. This technique shows the struggle to be free through the experiences of not only Harper but also those around her.

Students should be reminded of the relationship between the poet and the poem: Harper is writing about adjusting to life as a free woman, and about learning how to read; this poem is a product of that endeavor. It represents a switch from spoken language to written. Expand on this point with students, for the poem takes on more depth as this is fleshed out. Also alert students to what ultimately drove Harper to learn to read: her desire to read the Bible. Although she was "rising sixty," she "got a pair of glasses" (37) and "never stopped till [she] could read The hymns and Testament" (39–40). The Bible, and the ability to read it, becomes symbolic of Harper's freedom from slavery.

POSSIBLE CONNECTIONS TO OTHER SELECTIONS

Langston Hughes, "Theme for English B" (text p. 442)
Philip Larkin, "A Study of Reading Habits" (text p. 22)

ANTHONY HECHT, *The Dover Bitch* (p. 609)

The subtitle of this poem is "A Criticism of Life," and Hecht indirectly makes his criticism by having as a backdrop Arnold's "Dover Beach" (text p. 95). That poem too was a criticism of society, of declining religious values and the disappearance of a moral center. The tone of this poem is initially amusing; the young woman is not going to be treated "as a sort of mournful cosmic last resort." She desires a relationship more carnal than platonic. The speaker obliges her, and now, in what seems to be a continuing casual relationship, he occasionally brings her perfume, called *Nuit d'Amour.* At the edges of this poem we still hear the sound of Arnold's armies of the night, a reminiscence that doesn't make the current times seem so much worse but does make our moral comprehension of them so much more slight and haphazard.

POSSIBLE CONNECTIONS TO OTHER SELECTIONS

Matthew Arnold, "Dover Beach" (text p. 95)

Peter De Vries, "To His Importunate Mistress" (text p. 246)

GEORGE HERBERT, *The Collar* (p. 610)

Herbert's poems were published after his death. Many of them deal with the hesitancy of commitment he felt before becoming an Anglican priest.

The title "The Collar" echoes *choler* (anger) and suggests the work collar that binds horses in their traces as well as the clerical collar. Explore with the class how the speaker's situation, the stress he feels, and his particular argument gradually emerge. In his meditation, he tries to argue himself out of his position of submission. His life is free; he deserves more than thorns. He would like to have some of the world's secular awards. The speaker then admonishes himself to forget the feeble restrictions — his "rope of sands." But when all is said and done, he capitulates. You might observe how this poem demonstrates a strong measure of psychological insight.

As a writing assignment, you might ask the class to explore in a two- to three-page paper how rhythm reinforces the meaning in this poem.

POSSIBLE CONNECTION TO ANOTHER SELECTION

Sir Philip Sidney, "Loving in Truth, and Fain in Verse My Love to Show" (text p. 637)

AUDIOVISUAL AND ONLINE RESOURCES (manual pp. 300, 335)

LINDA HOGAN, *Song for My Name* (p. 611)

You might want to begin a discussion of this poem by reminding students that in Native American tradition, names carry great significance, often reflecting or defining some important characteristic about a person. In fact, some Native Americans are given two names — a public name, which is used, and a private name that is kept secret in order to preserve its power.

In this poem, the speaker explores the significance of her own name — a name that she sees as a point of connection to her Native American heritage. You might ask students to identify the contrast that Hogan sets up in the poem between the darkness of the old woman's hair (lines 2–3), the grandfather's dark hands (7), and the "women / with black hair / and men with eyes like night" (11–13) and the mother, who is described as a "white dove" (19). In the mother's "own land," images of whiteness abound (20–22).

Ask students to consider why the speaker's father is not mentioned in the poem. It is this contrast between her mother and what we can assume to be her father's family that is the focus of the poem. The name the speaker is given reflects her Native American heritage, but she feels caught between cultures — she is "a woman living / between the white moon / and the red sun" (30–32). On a number of occasions, the speaker refers to her name as an indication of hardship. She writes, "It means no money / tomorrow"

(14–15); "If you have a name like this, / there's never enough water" (24–25); and "There is too much heat" (26). Ask students why the speaker never actually tells us her name. Explore the implications of the speaker's Native American ancestry. Which world is she "waiting to leave" (32)?

Jimmy Santiago Baca, "Green Chile" (text p. 96)

Ben Jonson, "On My First Son" (text p. 616)

AUDIOVISUAL AND ONLINE RESOURCES (manual pp. 300, 336)

M. CARL HOLMAN, *Mr. Z* (p. 612)

Students will readily perceive the irony of this poem: the man who lived so that his racial identity was all but obliterated earned as his summary obituary the reductive, faint, and defaming praise "One of the most distinguished members of his race." His loss is a double loss, to be sure; not only did he fail finally to be judged according to white standards (those he aspired to) but in the process of living up to those standards he "flourish[ed] without [the] roots" of his own racial identity. Review the poem for its ironic phrases. You may have to explain that racial, religious, and ethnic differences were often suppressed in favor of assimilation and that the celebration of and return to these differences is a relatively recent tendency.

POSSIBLE CONNECTION TO ANOTHER SELECTION

Langston Hughes, "Cross" (text p. 382)

GERARD MANLEY HOPKINS, *Hurrahing in Harvest* (p. 612)

This Italian, or Petrarchan, sonnet begins with a vivid description of the glories of early autumn. The repetition of "these things" (line 11) creates an insistence that shifts the intent of the poem outside its boundaries. The "beholder" (11) of all this beauty realizes that it was here all along; it's the act of seeing that has been absent. The response of the speaker to this beauty, then, is transcendent, powerful, joyous: "The heart rears wings bold and bolder / And hurls for him, O half hurls for him off under his feet" (13–14).

The poem provides many examples of Hopkins's signature sound innovations. The pleasure of these rich phrases infiltrates the whole of the poem, establishing sound that is as rich as the harvest time discussed. The intense language mimics the scene that Hopkins's speaker paints for his reader: the description of "stooks" (1), "clouds" (3), and "azurous hung hills" (9) establishes a relationship between speaker and reader as the sight of them unites the speaker and "our Saviour" (6). The speaker characterizes "all that glory in the heavens" (6) as "a / Rapturous love's greeting" (8), again sharing the roles of natural grandeur and carefully crafted language.

Hopkins's work provides good opportunities for the study of sound and meter; asking students to identify alliteration in the poem could help them see its effectiveness, and helping them to scan the poem could make its detailed pleasures more accessible. To clarify the basic optimism of this poem, you might want to try comparing it to William Blake's "Infant Sorrow" (p. 592). Blake's speaker's natural pessimism contrasts nicely with the sublime joy Hopkins's speaker details.

POSSIBLE CONNECTIONS TO OTHER SELECTIONS

William Blake, "Infant Sorrow" (text p. 592)

Anne Bradstreet, "To My Dear and Loving Husband" (text p. 436)

GERARD MANLEY HOPKINS, *Pied Beauty* (p. 613)

It seems appropriate for Hopkins to have used so many innovations in style, structure, and diction in a poem that glorifies God — the only entity "whose beauty is past change" (line 10) — by observing the great variety present in the earth and sky. Ask students to point out examples of poetic innovation in this poem and to suggest their effects on the poem.

In form, "Pied Beauty" is what Hopkins termed a "curtal [that is, shortened] sonnet." Not only is it shortened, but it is shortened to exactly three-fourths of a traditional sonnet: the "octet" is six lines, the "sestet" four and a half. Having compressed the sonnet structure to ten and a half lines, Hopkins must make careful word choices to convey meaning in fewer words. Note the hyphenated words, which are his own creations; is it possible to understand the meanings of these made-up compounds? Compare Hopkins's practice of creating new words to that of Lewis Carroll in "Jabberwocky" (text p. 000).

Students will need to know what *pied* means (patchy in color; splotched). How do the many synonyms for *pied* in the first few lines emphasize the theme of the poem? How does the repetition of the *le* sound (dappled, couple, stipple, tackle, fickle, freckled, adazzle) add a sense of rhythm and unity to this poem's untraditional metrics?

POSSIBLE CONNECTION TO ANOTHER SELECTION

E. E. Cummings, "in Just-" (text p. 251)

GERARD MANLEY HOPKINS, *The Windhover* (p. 613)

At the midpoint of his poetic career, Hopkins considered this poem "the best thing I ever wrote" (*The Letters of Gerard Manley Hopkins to Robert Bridges*, edited by C. C. Abbott, rev. 1955 [New York: Oxford UP], 85). Regardless of the poem's quality, students should be forewarned that this is a difficult work by a difficult poet. It may help them to know that even literary specialists have had a difficult time agreeing on the poem's exact meaning. In fact, Tom Dunne's Hopkins bibliography (1976) lists nearly one hundred different readings of the poem before 1970. With this in mind, you might ask students to discuss the overall feeling conveyed by this lyric, rather than expecting them to be able to explicate it line by line. In general, the poem begins with the speaker's observation of a kestrel hawk in flight. The speaker is drawn from passive observation into passionate feeling for the "ecstasy" (line 5) of the bird's soaring freedom: "My heart in hiding / Stirred for a bird, — the achieve of, the mastery of the thing!" (7–8). It then occurs to the speaker that the bird's creator is "a billion / Times told lovelier, more dangerous" (10–11) than the creature, and his awe expands to consider an even greater power.

Have students note that the poem is addressed "To Christ our Lord." The speaker directly speaks to Christ as "my chevalier" in line 11. Realizing that the poem is addressed to Christ leads to an interpretation of the final lines as references to Christ's suffering and death. Despite Christ's earthly humility (the "blue-bleak embers" of line 13), his true glory — "gold-vermilion" (14) — is revealed when he falls, galls, and gashes himself (14).

One might approach "The Windhover" structurally by comparing it to the less complex poem that precedes it in the text. In "The Windhover," as in "Pied Beauty," Hopkins alters the sonnet form to suit his purposes. Discuss how "The Windhover" conforms to and deviates from traditional sonnet form. In particular, note its division into thirteen lines and the indication of the "turn" not at the beginning of the sestet but with the poet's emphasis on the word *and* in line 10. How do these deviations from the traditional sonnet form affect the poem's meaning?

Also worth discussing are the striking use of alliteration in the first long line and the poet's choices of unusual words, as seen in previous poems. Note that to the poet, a Jesuit priest, the "billion" in line 10 is not hyperbole; if anything, it is an understatement.

Fortunately, a number of glosses and extended critical interpretations of the works of this difficult poet are available. Among these are Graham Storey's *A Preface to Hopkins* (London and New York: Longman, 1981); Paul Mariani's *A Commentary on the Complete Poems of Gerard Manley Hopkins* (Ithaca: Cornell UP, 1969); *Hopkins: A Collection of Critical Essays*, edited by Geoffrey Hartman (Englewood Cliffs: Twentieth-Century Views/ Prentice-Hall, 1966); and J. Hillis Miller's *The Disappearance of God* (Cambridge: Harvard UP, 1963).

POSSIBLE CONNECTION TO ANOTHER SELECTION

Gerard Manley Hopkins, "God's Grandeur" (text p. 181)

A. E. HOUSMAN, *Is my team ploughing* (p. 614)

This poem is in ballad form, with a typical question-response exchange between the Shropshire lad who has died and a supposedly impersonal voice that answers his queries. The surprise comes, of course, with the introduction of the second "I," who has a decidedly vested interest in the earthly life of the deceased.

You might ask students to trace the development of the worldly objects the speaker is interested in: what is the effect of his beginning with his team of horses and ending with questions about his girl and his friend? Does the development say anything about his sense of priority, or is the effect meant only to heighten the poem's final irony?

POSSIBLE CONNECTION TO ANOTHER SELECTION

Emily Dickinson, "Because I could not stop for Death —" (text p. 308)

A. E. HOUSMAN, *To an Athlete Dying Young* (p. 614)

You might discuss this poem in relation to the *carpe diem* tradition. Is it perverse to imagine such a connection in a poem that treats youth and death? Many students will have read this poem in high school. They might enjoy picking out recurrent words and themes — such as "shoulder-high" in stanzas I and II, "shady" in stanza IV, and "shade" in stanza VI; the various thresholds and sills or doorways in the poem; and the image of both the laurel and the rose as evanescent tokens of glory and youth — and exploring their function in the poem.

POSSIBLE CONNECTION TO ANOTHER SELECTION

Seamus Heaney, "Mid-term Break" (text p. 241)

RODNEY JONES, *TV* (p. 615)

The speaker of this poem gives a firsthand account of one of the most important shifts in American culture. The first stanza opens with a statement difficult to believe in an age familiar with televangelism: "All the preachers claimed it was Satan" (line 1). Immediately afterward, the speaker flashes forward momentarily, to look at those feared boxes from a contemporary perspective. The speaker does not appear to agree with the preachers, but few positive attributes are presented in defense of television, beyond the secret delight (8) it provides. It is compared to "the bomb" (5), and phrases associated with it include "heretical" (6). It was feared that "it would destroy things" (10), and the changes it creates in the "talk" (17) of those who have a television are ambivalent and vague: "recentness/ and distance" (18–19). The conclusion of this poem predicts that the image of the television screen "would stay with us" (30) and offers an image of suburban solitude: "the silence, / Then everyone disappearing into the houses" (31-32).

You might want to use this poem to initiate a discussion among your students about the worth of television and other technologies that compete for their attention: Do they believe that television, or film, or recorded music, or the Internet has damaged their sense of community? Has it destroyed "standards / And the sacredness of words in books" (10-11)? Why are some technologies deemed more dangerous than others are? How does the age of the technology affect our understanding of the threat that it presents? And what positive attributes of technological change does Jones's speaker overlook?

POSSIBLE CONNECTIONS TO OTHER SELECTIONS

Lisa Parker, "Snapping Beans" (text p. 38)
Mona Van Duyn, "What the Motorcycle Said" (text p. 190)

BEN JONSON, *On My First Son* (p. 1102)

A father's deep grief for his lost child as expressed in this beautiful epitaph needs little explication. However, the poem contains several ideas worthy of class discussion. Why does the poet think that we should envy those who die at an early age? Do your students agree? Do they think the poet believes it himself? How can a child be considered a "best piece of poetry" (line 10)? Have students suggest paraphrases for the last two lines, which are confusing because of the convoluted grammatical construction. Do these lines mean that the poet has learned a lesson about not caring too much for earthly joys, a reading that the use of the word *lent* in line 3 supports? Is he proposing that his great attachment to the child had something to do with his death?

POSSIBLE CONNECTION TO ANOTHER SELECTION

Anne Bradstreet, "Before the Birth of One of Her Children" (text p. 594)

BEN JONSON, *To Celia* (p. 616)

This poem is a laudatory devotion to a lover in which the speaker moves through conceits of drinking in the first stanza and conceits of the tribute of a rose in the second. This poem is in fact a good opportunity to examine a Petrarchan conceit, or rather, two conceits. After students have worked through each stanza, you might ask them if there is a definite relationship between them. Does the poem read like two poems, or do the two stanzas depend upon each other in a fundamental way?

You may also want to discuss whether the poem seems to be a bit *too* devotional; students may find the speaker's praise for his lover to be a bit too much, a bit unbelievable. You may want to discuss how poetic conventions change over time. Jonson's Celia is an exaggerated lover (her name connotes heaven), but that type of love or devotion was the subject of poetry in seventeenth-century England. An interesting writing assignment might be to have students trace the way in which such devotion changes over time by selecting representative love poems from the seventeenth century through the present.

POSSIBLE CONNECTIONS TO OTHER SELECTIONS

Robert Herrick, "Upon Julia's Clothes" (text p. 225)
Christopher Marlowe, "The Passionate Shepherd to His Love" (text p. 434)
William Shakespeare, "Not marble, nor the gilded monuments" (text p. 435)

JOHN KEATS, *To One Who Has Been Long in City Pent* (p. 617)

This Petrarchan sonnet is a kind of love poem to the countryside. The speaker moves quickly away from the trap the city represents in the first line to focus instead on the pleasures of escaping it. The "blue firmament" (line 4), "wavy grass" (7), "notes of Philomel" (10), and "sailing cloudlet's bright career" (11) paint a portrait of a pastoral experience the city dweller longs for, one that slips by quick as "an angel's tear" (13). The absence of the city is a presence in the poem, and the vivid description of what the city lacks combines with the first line to depict it as a prison.

Discussion might center on how the speaker's pleasures reflect on the city. Students might enjoy doing a little freewrite from the perspective of one who has been long in classroom pent; what pleasant presences are absent from the classroom?

Possible Connections to Other Selections

Christopher Marlowe, "The Passionate Shepherd to His Love" (text p. 434)
Charles Simic, "Filthy Landscape" (text p. 116)

JOHN KEATS, *Written in Disgust of Vulgar Superstition* (p. 617)

The irreverent tone of this poem is perhaps most immediately apparent in the casual phrases "some other" (lines 2, 3) and "more" (3, 4). The poem provides an alternate understanding of the ritual of prayer and religious community.

You might ask your students to write an essay comparing the characterization of religious faith in this poem with that found in poems by Hopkins or Herbert. How do Keats's "fresh flowers" (13) compare to Hopkins's "dappled things" (1) in "Pied Beauty"? How does Keats's observations of "sighing and wailing" (12) compare to Herbert's refusal to "sigh and pine" (3)? What might Keats have in common with these other poets? How do they differ in tone and approach?

Possible Connections to Other Selections

George Herbert, "The Collar" (text p. 610)
Gerard Manley Hopkins, "Hurrahing in Harvest" (text p. 612)
——, "Pied Beauty" (text p. 613)

JOHN KEATS, *When I have fears that I may cease to be* (p. 618)

The fears described in this sonnet are increasingly human, mortal, and intimate. Keats fears first that death may cut short the writing of his imagined "high-piled books"; then that he may never trace the "shadows" of "huge cloudy symbols of a high romance"; and, finally, that he might not see his beloved again. In the couplet, love and fame sink to nothingness, but Keats confronts his fear and is deepened by the experience.

There is a subtle order to the presentation of Keats's objects of regret. In a writing assignment, you might ask the class to comment on how one item seems to lead to the next and how their arrangement lends form and substance to this sonnet.

Possible Connections to Other Selections

Emily Dickinson, "This was a Poet — It is That" (text p. 305)
William Shakespeare, "Not marble, nor the gilded monuments" (text p. 435)

JOHN KEATS, *La Belle Dame sans Merci* (p. 618)

You might read this ballad in connection with other ballads in this book. How is it that ballads have stood the test of time and continued to appeal to many generations of listeners and readers? Is this ballad any different from medieval ballads? Is it more suggestive, perhaps, of a state of mind?

The opening three stanzas hold a descriptive value for the reader, for they present the knight as pale, ill, possibly aging and dying. The stanzas possess a rhetorical value as well, for they whet our curiosity. Just why is the knight trapped in this withered landscape?

The femme fatale figure goes back at least to Homeric legend and the wiles of Circe. Note how the "belle dame" appeals here to several senses — with her appearance, her voice, the foods she offers, the physical comforts of sleep. Above all else, though, she seems otherworldly, and Keats here seems to insist on her elfin qualities, her wild eyes, and her strange language.

Words change meaning and grow in and out of popularity over generations (even decades). Contrast the way we might use *enthrall* today (with what subjects) and what Keats intends by "La Belle Dame sans Merci / Hath thee in Thrall!" (lines 39–40). Note how the shortened line of each quatrain gives both a sense of closure and the chill of an inescapable doom.

In his well-known essay on the poem, Earl R. Wasserman begins by remarking, "It would be difficult in any reading of Keats's ballad not to be enthralled by the haunting power of its rhythm, by its delicate intermingling of the fragile and the grotesque, the tender and the weird, and by the perfect economy with which these effects are achieved" (from "La Belle Dame sans Merci," in his *The Finer Tone: Keats's Major Poems* [Baltimore: Johns Hopkins UP, 1953, 1967], 65–83, and reprinted in *English Romantic Poets: Modern Essays in Criticism,* edited by M. H. Abrams [New York: Oxford UP, 1960], 365–380). In a writing assignment you might ask students to select any one of these elements and discuss it with several examples to show how it shapes the tone and mood of the poem.

Other studies of this poem include Jane Cohen's "Keats's Humor in 'La Belle Dame sans Merci,'" *Keats-Shelley Journal* 17 (1968): 10–13, and Bernice Slote's "The Climate of Keats's 'La Belle Dame sans Merci,'" *Modern Language Quarterly* 21 (1960): 195–207.

POSSIBLE CONNECTIONS TO OTHER SELECTIONS

Anonymous, "Bonny Barbara Allan" (text p. 589)
Emily Dickinson, "Because I could not stop for Death —" (text p. 308)

WILLYCE KIM, *In This Heat* (p. 619)

This poem presents a dangerous world of heat, "night half-swollen / with the whispers / of the day" (lines 12–14). The center of this slender, understated poem is the story of "a Chinese girl" (18) who commits suicide when "No one believed" (28) that she was raped. The poem recognizes only one escape from these treacherous surroundings: sleep.

This poem's brief lines can provide an opportunity for students to consider line breaks. One exercise could take the same poem and present it in several different formats: try longer lines, lines of around ten syllables each, lines that consist of syntactical units, or lines that follow any other rules you make up. Ask students to try to identify Kim's reasoning, to find line breaks that they think are effective, or to rewrite the poem with line breaks they prefer.

POSSIBLE CONNECTIONS TO OTHER SELECTIONS

William Blake, "Infant Sorrow" (text p. 592)
Edna St. Vincent Millay, "I, Being Born a Woman; and Distressed" (text p. 626)

ETHERIDGE KNIGHT, *A Watts Mother Mourns While Boiling Beans* (p. 620)

One of the most striking aspects of this poem is its sound patterns. Alliteration ("blooming," "born," "bold," "blood") and assonance ("blooming," "blood") project the mother's (speaker's) anxiety and apprehension. She cannot just grieve, for she must worry about her husband's dinner. Ask students to think about how the sound patterns influence their reading of this poem, both literally and figuratively. Does the poem *demand* to be read a certain way? How does this reading affect its meaning?

POSSIBLE CONNECTION TO ANOTHER SELECTION

Countee Cullen, "Yet Do I Marvel" (text p. 601)

AUDIOVISUAL AND ONLINE RESOURCES (manual pp. 302, 334)

PHILIP LARKIN, *This Be the Verse* (p. 621)

At once indicting and absolving parenthood for the faults and woes of the world, this poem's depth goes beyond the humor and unexpectedness of its blunt first line. Students are likely to find some humor here because, or in spite of, Larkin's particularly "non-poetic" diction. But this poem is more than a simple cynical witticism.

Larkin builds a funny tone by inverting the syntax of the first line (which places the shocking "fuck" as the poem's second word), by lightening the tone with mocking language such as "just for you" in line 4, and by using childish words like "mum and dad" (line 1). Furthermore, readers may not expect this kind of "talk" from a poet — especially one who is espousing as serious a point as "Man hands on misery to man" (9). The contrast in the speaker's two levels of diction is, itself, funny, but at the same time, calls greater attention to the more serious, if not beautiful lines: "It deepens like a coastal shelf" (10). The glib ending, in particular, both humorously undermines the more serious message and enhances it by contrast.

You may want to begin a discussion by trying to characterize the speaker. Apart from the techniques of the poet, why would this speaker be funny when there is such a sad message sitting there in the middle of his diatribe? Is the speaker sad?

POSSIBLE CONNECTION TO ANOTHER SELECTION

Judy Page Heitzman, "The Schoolroom on the Second Floor of the Knitting Mill" (text p. 446)

LI-YOUNG LEE, *Eating Together* (p. 621)

This poem describes in meticulous detail a family eating dinner and then shifts to a metaphorical consideration of the speaker's father. The description of the father suggests that he has died. Encourage students to notice the sensual images that Lee uses to describe the meal in the first 8 lines of this poem. Every detail of the meal is given in great detail — from the exact food eaten to the precise way the mother will hold the fish between her fingers. Consider what the effect is of sharing the intricate details of the meal. Why might the poet wish to re-create the scene so carefully?

Point out the shift in the poem that occurs in line 9, where the poet moves from language that is literal to language that is figurative and metaphoric. Ask students what actual event do they suppose the poet is describing in this section. Are the images the poet chooses effective? What do students make of the poem's final line, "without any travelers, and lonely for no one" (12)?

Lee titles this poem "Eating Together" and describes his family gathered around the table for lunch. Ask students whether it is symbolic that his mother "will / taste the sweetest meat of the head" (6) the way his father did "weeks ago" (9). Consider whether this is a possible foreshadowing, representing a shift in the family hierarchy. Or is it simply a point of familial connection?

POSSIBLE CONNECTIONS TO OTHER SELECTIONS

Indira Sant, "Household Fires" (text p. 663)
Dylan Thomas, "Do not go gentle into that good night" (text p. 233)

AUDIOVISUAL AND ONLINE RESOURCES (manual pp. 302, 339)

RACHEL LODEN, *We Are Sorry to Say* (p. 621)

The speakers of this poem, an editorial "we," develop a surreal vision out of a sentence that sounds plucked from a form rejection letter. The poem capitalizes on the first sentence's use of the passive voice and inherent refusal to take responsibility for "the decision" (line 1) it reports. The personification of "the decision" allows some absurdist humor to enter: "the decision scares us" (7) and "wears / a muscle shirt" (8–9). The "tender envelopes/ that bleed hysterically" (17–18) present a rationale for this editorial distance: the bleeding envelopes represent the touchy writers — including Loden herself — who respond with passion, anger, or mocking verse when rejected. Students may want to discuss the humor in the poem.

POSSIBLE CONNECTIONS TO OTHER SELECTIONS

Stephen Dunn, "John & Mary" (text p. 133)
Richard Wakefield, "In a Poetry Workshop" (text p. 449)

ROBERT LOWELL, *For Sale* (p. 623)

This poem's speaker presents the death of his father and grief of his mother through the impersonality of a real estate transaction. The speaker does not convey any of his own feeling overtly, choosing instead to aim his precise observations at the house "on the market the month he died" (line 5). The poem is in three sentences; the first two provide animated emotional clarity for the house itself, while avoiding any reference to the emotional state of father, mother, or son, outside the "prodigal animosity" (2) with which it was "organized" (2). The final sentence moves the focus away from the house to "Mother" (13), previously unmentioned. She remains silent, but the final image of her, "mooned in a window" (13) presents a haunting portrait of grief and solitude, backed up by the hollow nostalgia of a house for sale.

POSSIBLE CONNECTIONS TO OTHER SELECTIONS

Li-Young Lee, "Eating Together" (text p. 621)
Rennie McQuilkin, "The Lighters" (text p. 149)

AUDIOVISUAL AND ONLINE RESOURCES (manual pp. 303, 340)

HENRY WADSWORTH LONGFELLOW, *Snow-Flakes* (p. 622)

The snow, generally described in terms of emotions and falterings of the human spirit, is taken in this poem to reveal something about "the troubled sky" (line 11) and "our cloudy fancies" (7) at the same time. The air is personified; the speaker insists that the snow is this poem which reveals "the secret of despair, / Long in its cloudy bosom hoarded" (15–16).

A good place to begin discussion is with the question of the speaker, who removes himself from the scene as much as possible. The only time he alludes to himself at all is with the plural pronoun "our" in line 7. What type of person must he be? Do we assume that he is feeling troubled, that he is full of grief and despair? What is his relationship to the scene that he is witnessing?

POSSIBLE CONNECTIONS TO OTHER SELECTIONS

Robert Frost, "Stopping by Woods on a Snowy Evening" (text p. 353)
Percy Bysshe Shelley, "Ode to the West Wind" (text p. 243)

AUDIOVISUAL AND ONLINE RESOURCES (manual pp. 302, 340)

AUDRE LORDE, *Hanging Fire* (p. 622)

This poem should be accessible enough to your students, who probably remember all too clearly what life felt like at age fourteen. You might either as a writing assignment or in class discussion ask students to supply and talk about lines from this poem that seem to ring especially true to their own memories of adolescence. Consider, for example, the opening five lines, expressing bewilderment over a physical body that seems no longer one's own, accompanied by the awakenings and trials of first love directed toward someone whose own maturing processes seem at a standstill. Students might also want to comment on the range of emotional pitches the speaker feels, including the adolescent anxiety and imaginative investment in death.

The three stanzas share a refrain — made up of the most rhythmic lines in the poem: "and momma's in the bedroom / with the door closed." You may want to touch lightly on the similarities this poem shares with the ballad tradition and comment on how this refrain effects a sense of closure in a poem that composes itself primarily according to the cadences of speech rhythms and fairly spontaneous thought patterns. The repetition of this line also lends a certain poignance to the speaker's voice. By the end of the poem, we have a clear sense that she will not receive much help from the person who could be expected to help her while she is "hanging fire." You might ask how long one goes through life "hanging fire."

POSSIBLE CONNECTION TO ANOTHER SELECTION

Indira Sant, "Household Fires" (text p. 663)

AUDIOVISUAL AND ONLINE RESOURCES (manual pp. 303, 340)

ARCHIBALD MACLEISH, *Ars Poetica* (p. 624)

In the first eight lines of his poem, MacLeish poses what seems to be a paradox: he states that a poem, which is an arrangement of words on a page, should be "mute," "Dumb," "Silent," and "wordless." Note, however, that the word *as* follows each of these adjectives; this suggests that poetry accomplishes its purpose not through the words, but by means of the metaphorical images created by the words. Poetry addresses itself not to the intellect, but to deeper, more abstract, more emotional levels. You might have students examine some of the metaphors employed in this poem. To what senses are they directed? What emotions do the images evoke? In lines 19–22, MacLeish gives examples of emotions that can be conveyed by specific images. How well do these images evoke the specified emotions? Can your students suggest other images that evoke grief or love? What image might convey hate? Fear?

The final two lines of the poem create another paradox: the poet/speaker who has argued against prosaic forms in favor of metaphorical images suddenly states this thesis directly. Do your students think the speaker mistrusts the reader's ability to comprehend the poem without a prosaic thesis statement? Note that the speaker's previous reiterations that "A poem should," are consistently followed by metaphors, whereas the statement "A poem should not" is followed by a direct assertion. Is the speaker, having demonstrated what a poem should be, now showing us what a poem should not be? Can your students suggest another explanation for the unpoetic format of these last two lines?

AUDIOVISUAL AND ONLINE RESOURCES (manual pp. 303, 341)

CLEOPATRA MATHIS, *What to Tip the Boatman?* (p. 624)

This elliptical poem offers a portrait of a little girl. The speaker observes the way she moves her hands in games and "signing the air" (line 20), "as if the ballast / of her self-hood rested there" (5-6). In classical mythology, the boatman on the river Styx was named Charon: he required a tip of a coin to take the dead across to the other side. Greeks buried their dead with the required coin in their mouths or hands. This child's hands are characterized as "an offering" (35) in the final image of the poem.

You might begin discussion by making sure students are familiar with Charon, the River Styx, and the allusion Mathis builds with these references. Do your students think these foreshadow a death? How does the characterization of the "silenced house" (26) confirm or deny this idea?

POSSIBLE CONNECTIONS TO OTHER SELECTIONS

Regina Barreca, "Nighttime Fires" (text p. 26)
Diane Thiel, "The Minefield" (text p. 166)

W. S. MERWIN, *For the Anniversary of My Death* (p. 625)

The speaker of this poem turns to the one thing that he understands: someday he'll die. He has lived through this date, "the day / When the last fires will wave to me" (line 2), every year of his life. The absence present in death is depicted as "the silence" (3), a "Tireless traveller" (4), endless silent echoes stretching out from the moment when life ends.

This certainty is discussed without any particular sadness; the consternation appears when the speaker turns to the life he finds himself in, "a strange garment" (7). Life is here portrayed as stranger than the certainty of death. This perplexity at the wonders of life, "the love of one woman / and the shamelessness of men" (9-10), is characterized as the mystery of three days of rain and the end to that rain.

The Talking Heads song "Same as It Ever Was" depicts some of this amazement at the way life turns out, the sudden appearance of what one's life is made of, whether or not those accoutrements seem earned. The phrase repeated in this song contains a tone similar to the poem's sentiment: "And you may find yourself in a beautiful house, with a beautiful wife, and you may ask yourself, well, how did I get here?" Bringing in a recording might be a fun way to illustrate Merwin's depiction of finding himself in life "as in a strange garment" (7).

POSSIBLE CONNECTIONS TO OTHER SELECTIONS

Thomas Hardy, "The Convergence of the Twain" (text p. 73)
Dylan Thomas, "Do not go gentle into that good night" (text p. 233)

EDNA ST. VINCENT MILLAY, *I, Being Born a Woman and Distressed* (p. 626)

The humor of this poem is present in the contrast between tone and content; the formal tone belies the harsh sentiments it conveys. The speaker admits that she desires "your person" (line 4), but wants to make clear that this physical desire is "the poor trea-son / of my stout blood against my staggering brain" (9–10). The "treason" will be over-ridden once the body has its desires met; the sexual "frenzy" (13) initiated by "needs and notions" (2) and the "propinquity" (3) of "you" does not signify the beginning of a romance. On the contrary, the speaker wants to "make it plain" (12) that she doesn't plan to speak to the object of her desires once those desires have been met.

Students may initially resist the stuffy tone here, especially if they need to turn to the dictionary to look up "propinquity" (3). However, salacious detail can often encour-age even reluctant readers to scan a page more thoroughly. Focusing on the cool and cut-ting remarks hidden in the heightened language of this poem could help students with more challenging work.

POSSIBLE CONNECTIONS TO OTHER SELECTIONS

Robert Hass, "A Story About the Body" (text p. 264)

Sharon Olds, "Sex without Love" (text p. 76)

AUDIOVISUAL AND ONLINE RESOURCES (manual pp. 304, 343)

JOHN MILTON, *On the Late Massacre in Piedmont* (p. 626)

Born in London, Milton began writing poetry at the age of fifteen. He had a remark-able aptitude for languages, mastering Latin, Greek, Hebrew, and most modern European languages before he completed his education in 1637. After earning his mas-ter's degree from Christ's College, Cambridge University, in 1632, he disappointed expectations that he would become a minister and embarked instead on a six-year peri-od of carefully self-designed study in which he read everything he could. (The eyestrain caused by his voracious study eventually led to his blindness in 1651.)

Milton dedicated his literary talent to the causes of religious and civil freedom dur-ing the years 1640 to 1660, writing Puritan propaganda and numerous political and social tracts. Milton argued vociferously on many issues: "Of Reformation Touching Church Discipline in England" (1641) denounced the episcopacy; his troubled relation-ship with seventeen-year-old Mary Powell, who left him after one month of marriage, inspired him to support the legalization of divorce in "Doctrine and Discipline of Divorce" (1643); "Areopagitica," (1644), one of his most famous polemics, argued the necessity of a free press; and his defense of the murder of King Charles I in "The Tenure of Kings and Magistrates" (1649), although contributing to his appointment as the sec-retary for foreign languages in Cromwell's government, nearly got him executed when the monarchy was restored in 1660.

He was arrested, but friends and colleagues intervened on his behalf, and he was eventually released. Blind and unemployed, he returned to his poetry and a quiet life with his third wife, Elizabeth Minshull. It was during these last years of his life that Milton produced (by dictating to relatives, friends, and paid assistants) his most famous and substantial works: the epic poems *Paradise Lost* (1667) and *Paradise Regained* (1671) and the verse drama *Samson Agonistes* (1671).

"On the Late Massacre in Piedmont" is a sonnet of accountability — in an almost bookkeeper sense of the term. The basic premise is contractual. The Waldenses have pre-served piety and faith in God over four centuries; now God should avenge their mas-sacre. *Even,* as the first word of line 3, is an imperative verb form, as in *Even the score.* Scorekeeping, in fact, matters in this sonnet, and students might find it a good exercise in reading to identify and analyze the numerical images. Nature, moreover, is shown as sympathetic to the Waldenses, for it redoubles the sound of their lamentations. The pas-sage ends with the elliptical phrase "and they / To heaven." Syntax again provides the verb *redoubled* and says, in effect, that the hills echoed the moans to heaven. Milton expresses the wish that future generations of Waldenses will augment their number "a hundredfold" to offset the Pope's power.

You might ask students to write an analytical and persuasive essay proving that this is either a plea for vengeance or the expression of a hope that the Waldenses will receive God's protection and strength throughout history.

POSSIBLE CONNECTIONS TO OTHER SELECTIONS

Wilfred Owen, "Dulce et Decorum Est" (text p. 162)
Alfred, Lord Tennyson, "The Charge of the Light Brigade" (text p. 216)

AUDIOVISUAL AND ONLINE RESOURCES (manual pp. 304, 343)

JOHN MILTON, *When I consider how my light is spent* (p. 627)

This sonnet is sometimes mistakenly titled "On His Blindness." You might begin by asking just what the topic of Milton's meditation is. He seems to be at midlife, neither old nor young. If Milton's blindness comes to mind as the subject, does that idea accommodate itself to the description "And that one talent which is death to hide / Lodged with me useless"? It would take some ingenuity to make blindness the equivalent of "talent" here. Far better to let "talent" stand in its old (biblical) and new senses and refer to Milton's poetic capability. At any rate, a discussion of this sonnet should prove useful in developing students' ability to select or discard extraliterary details in connection with a poem.

POSSIBLE CONNECTIONS TO OTHER SELECTIONS

Anne Bradstreet, "To My Dear and Loving Husband" (text p. 436)
Ben Jonson, "On My First Son" (text p. 616)
John Keats, "When I have fears that I may cease to be" (text p. 618)

N. SCOTT MOMADAY, *Crows in a Winter Composition* (p. 627)

The speaker of this poem paints a portrait of a cold world in which "the hard nature of crows" (line 17) presents a vague threat. The "soft distances" (2) beyond the trees and "the several silences, / Imposed on one another" (7) are "unintelligible" (8). In this context, in which a Zen-like "Nothing appeared" (5), the crows provide an unwelcome "definite, composed" (15) certainty.

Students might enjoy drawing some of the contrasts between the disdain felt for crows in this poem and the awe developed in Gerard Manley Hopkins's "The Windhover." While both poems turn their attention to birds, their tones and conclusions provide satisfying contrasts.

POSSIBLE CONNECTIONS TO OTHER SELECTIONS

Gregory Djanikian, "When I First Saw Snow" (text p. 603)
Robert Frost, "Stopping by Woods on a Snowy Evening" (text p. 353)
Gerard Manley Hopkins, "The Windhover" (text p. 613)

AUDIOVISUAL AND ONLINE RESOURCES (manual pp. 304, 343)

MARIANNE MOORE, *Poetry* (p. 628)

Moore was editor of *The Dial,* a literary magazine, from 1925 until its demise in 1929, so if this poem at times sounds like a manifesto, it is probably because it shares in the self-consciousness of an American literary scene that was trying to establish its own identity and formulate a modernist aesthetic.

You might pair this poem with MacLeish's "Ars Poetica" (text p. 624). Would Mac-Leish have liked "Poetry," or would he have found it too discursive, too much like prose? What precisely does Moore find objectionable about some poetry — possibly its stilted expressions, its overworked compulsion toward ornamentation, its "prettiness"? What do you suppose she means by "the genuine," and what images does she use to suggest it? The material after a colon usually explains the material preceding it. Is this the case at the beginning of stanza IV? Would Moore endorse the idea that anything can be material for a poem? What, if any, provisos or exceptions would she make?

These questions should help students begin to see not only what Moore is saying but also how similar the process of analysis can be in extracting ideas from either prose or poetry.

POSSIBLE CONNECTIONS TO OTHER SELECTIONS

Langston Hughes, "Formula" (text p. 382)
Archibald MacLeish, "Ars Poetica" (text p. 624)

AUDIOVISUAL AND ONLINE RESOURCES (manual pp. 304, 344)

PAT MORA, *Another Brown Man* (p. 628)

This poem provides an examination of a stranger who is physically reminiscent of someone the speaker loves. The speaker happens upon the stranger and struggles with profound feelings of loss and love conjured by the similarities and differences he notes. The stranger and the beloved share similar "hands and humor" (line 10), and the brief encounter with the stranger recalls the sorrow for the beloved.

Although the beloved is not dead, the speaker implies that death is not far off: "Your body / solid as an álamo, / we can never trust again" (19). The departure of the stranger, who merely leaves "his spot" (28), provides a parallel to the changes, the almost-grieving, that illness has brought to the speaker's relationship with the beloved, "another brown man" (9). The speaker uses tropes familiar to his readers, images of grief that are closely entwined with "blood" (1) and "tears" (3), referring to the medical nature of his beloved's condition through the "pinprick" (2) that appears in the first stanza and is echoed in the fifth.

You're likely to have students who can provide a translation of the Spanish words and phrases in this poem: "Cuban music" (5) and "Hey, beautiful" (13) are fairly simple to recognize, but "álamo" (18) may be less familiar: it means "poplar." The poplar tree is known for its strength, longevity, and hardness: it may provide an entry for discussion of this poem. Why does the speaker compare the body of the beloved to a poplar tree? Is this a purely positive comparison? How is the association effective? How is it confusing or inappropriate?

POSSIBLE CONNECTIONS TO OTHER SELECTIONS

Andrew Hudgins, "Elegy for My Father, Who Is Not Dead" (text p. 242)
Bruce Springsteen, "Streets of Philadelphia" (text p. 32)
Dylan Thomas, "Do not go gentle into that good night" (text p. 233)

ONLINE RESOURCES (manual p. 344)

ROBERT MORGAN, *Wind from a Waterfall* (p. 629)

This poem provides a descriptive portrait of a waterfall, seen through the experience of approaching the "tons of milk and spray" (line 10). The two brief declarative sentences in the first four lines lead to the breathless, longer sentences of the rest of the poem. Internal rhymes — "pour" (4) and "roar" (4), "darts" (16) and "barks" (18) — add to the dense intensity of the language.

While most of the poem focuses on accurate, thorough description, the final three lines extend their reach beyond the physical attributes of the waterfall, to imagine an alternate source for the power and grandeur witnessed at the river's edge. "Families long lost" (19) conjures mysterious, haunting images. This section of the poem, the reunion "stirred up" (20) by the violent "atmospheres pushed down" (11), could be the focus of some provocative discussion in your classroom: How do students understand this section? Does it seem to fit in with the more straightforward description that precedes it? What, for your students, is the effect of this conclusive turn?

POSSIBLE CONNECTIONS TO OTHER SELECTIONS

Robert Frost, "Spring Pools" (text p. 355)

SARAH MORGAN BRYAN PIATT, *A New Thanksgiving* (p. 630)

Though Sarah Morgan Bryan Piatt was a prolific poet, her work is not widely studied today. Her style might seem archaic to students at first, but there is much that they can learn from this poem. Remind students that poets often respond to traditional poems or prayers — in this case, the traditional Thanksgiving prayer. Ask students to determine the rhythm and rhyme scheme of the poem (iambic pentameter with quatrains rhymed in an *abab* pattern). Does the poem's form contribute to or detract from its powerful message? Have them consider the poet's first-person plural perspective. Is it too presumptuous? Or do all of us secretly pray for horrible things that will serve our own ends? Ask students to examine Piatt's melodramatic personification of the ocean in line 5. How does it compare with the tone in other parts of the poem?

SYLVIA PLATH, *Daddy* (p. 630)

Read this poem aloud before you begin teaching it. That way the class will hear some of the insistent and bizarre nursery-rhyme repetitions of sound that hammer their way through it. The critic A. Alvarez describes "Daddy" as a love poem. That idea, given the tone and imagery, might surprise some students, but it can be related to Plath's own comment on her father's early death and her attempt to cut through the entanglements of a relationship that never had a chance to mature.

The person we need most to love but are unable to is the one most likely to be projected in an effigy of hatred. One wants to exorcise what one cannot embrace. The most memorable feature of this poem is the string of transformations Plath projects on the father. From the inorganic statue to the mythical vampire (killed by a stake "in" the heart), the transforming range could not be wider. In this imaginative process Plath begins to think that she is a Jew and that her father is with the German Luftwaffe and then with the armored tank division ("panzer-man"). She eventually connects him with Fascism and the sadomasochism of male aggression against women. The real picture of Otto Plath as teacher is suddenly rendered in Plath's mind as surreal — father as devil. The crescendo of memories and images reaches its peak when Plath recalls an earlier suicide attempt (one she described, in fact, in her novel *The Bell Jar*). She also seems to implicate her husband, the British poet Ted Hughes, in this memory, as she portrays him in the roles of torturer and vampire.

Plath is often described as a "confessional poet." Despite the highly idiosyncratic nature of this poem, what in it allows for a sharing of this personal experience with a wide and impersonal audience? What, if any, are the universal themes touched on here? You might develop one of these questions into a writing assignment.

POSSIBLE CONNECTIONS TO OTHER SELECTIONS

Philip Larkin, "This Be the Verse" (text p. 621)

Linda Pastan, "Marks" (text p. 132)

Dylan Thomas, "Do not go gentle into that good night" (text p. 233)

SIR WALTER RALEGH, *The Nymph's Reply to the Shepherd* (p. 632)

This poem's speaker makes a reply to the shepherd in Christopher Marlowe's well-known poem, *The Passionate Shepherd to His Love*. Ralegh's imagined nymph responds with a pragmatic realism, in contrast to Marlowe's shepherd's romantic idealism. The "pretty pleasures" (line 3) the shepherd offers to entice his beloved — "gowns," "shoes," and "beds of roses" (13) — can't compete with the truth: youth does not last, and love may not "still breed" (21) in its absence.

Discussion and assignments could examine this pragmatism closely: consider assigning a fictitious journal entry from the nymph as she considers what to say. Her reply doesn't focus on her feelings for the shepherd. Does she love him? Are her stated concerns merely the means by which she avoids telling him she doesn't feel romantic toward him? What kind of future might she imagine for herself in contrast to the one the shepherd offers?

POSSIBLE CONNECTIONS TO OTHER SELECTIONS

Christopher Marlowe, "The Passionate Shepherd to His Love" (text p. 434)

Patricia Smith, "What It's Like to Be a Black Girl (For Those of You Who Aren't)" (text p. 104)

Alice Walker, "a woman is not a potted plant" (text p. 37)

ADRIENNE RICH, *Living in Sin* (p. 633)

This poem describes the experience of a woman whose love affair is anything but romantic. She focuses on the details of the room in which she and her lover meet, and they reveal her profound discontentment with her situation. Students will enjoy the title and its ironic reversal in context with the poem. Rich was married at the time she wrote this, but her "sin" was to see through the myth of romantic bliss in a one-room flat to the harsh particulars of daytime reality. Compare the roles of the man and the woman here. What might be some of the "minor demons"?

The images in this poem are worth examining. In lines 4–6, for example, the romantic point of view becomes an artful still life, a painting by Renoir perhaps.

POSSIBLE CONNECTIONS TO OTHER SELECTIONS

Sir Walter Ralegh, "The Nymph's Reply to the Shepherd" (text p. 632)

Sharon Olds, "Sex without Love" (text p. 76)

AUDIOVISUAL AND ONLINE RESOURCES (manual pp. 306, 348)

CHRISTINA GEORGINA ROSSETTI, *Some Ladies Dress in Muslin Full and White* (p. 633)

The speaker of this poem transforms herself from a rather benign observer of fashion into a misanthrope who would selectively eliminate men and women based on what they are wearing. You might ask students to locate the precise moments where her attitude seems to shift: does anything cause it? You might first ask them what they think the poet's tone or intention is. Which words indicate that light humor is the intended tone, and which words make the poem seem a biting satire? The poem may allow you to discuss the aggressive nature of humor, the very fine line between comedy and tragedy. Do students know anyone, or can they think of examples of professional comedians, whose brand of humor reveals antisocial tendencies? What motivates these humorists? Would they put Rossetti's speaker in the same camp?

POSSIBLE CONNECTIONS TO OTHER SELECTIONS

Louise Bogan, "Women" (text p. 593)

Emily Dickinson, "The Soul Selects her own Society" (text p. 303)

ONLINE RESOURCES (manual p. 349)

CHRISTINA GEORGINA ROSSETTI, *Promises Like Pie-Crust* (p. 634)

This poem's speaker offers a straightforward, no-nonsense response to romantic possibility. Some students may find the crisp tone a pleasure, while others may find her cynicism unwarranted. Do students agree with the speaker's assessment of the risks of relationships? What might the speaker and her addressee be missing if they maintain their relationship as "the friends we were / Nothing more but nothing less" (lines 21–22)? You may find it productive to focus on that "more" and "less"; what do we have to gain in romantic relationships? What do we stand to lose? Asking students to write a journal entry to consider their own feelings on the matter may help make discussion more productive. An essay assignment could establish correlations between students' own beliefs about love and the pessimistic or optimistic views of romantic relationships found in poems in this collection. Some possibilities for comparison are included below.

POSSIBLE CONNECTIONS TO OTHER SELECTIONS

Helen Farries, "Magic of Love" (text p. 30)

Christopher Marlowe, "The Passionate Shepherd to His Love" (text p. 434)

Edna St. Vincent Millay, "I, Being Born Woman and Distressed" (text p. 626)

Sharon Olds, "Sex without Love" (text p. 76)

Sir Walter Ralegh, "The Nymph's Reply to the Shepherd" (text p. 632)

WILLIAM SHAKESPEARE (p. 635)

Shakespeare's sonnets have been widely discussed. Some books that may offer useful observations on them include *A Casebook of Shakespeare's Sonnets,* edited by Gerald Willen and Victor B. Reed; Edward Hubler's *The Sense of Shakespeare's Sonnets* (Westport: Greenwood, 1976); and *Shakespeare's Sonnets,* edited with commentary by Stephen Booth (New Haven: Yale UP, 1977). The two songs given in this section, "Spring" and "Winter," are discussed by Bertrand Bronson in *Modern Language Notes* 63 (1948) and by C. L. Barber in *Shakespeare's Festive Comedy* (Princeton: Princeton UP, 1972).

WILLIAM SHAKESPEARE, *That time of year thou mayst in me behold* (p. 635)

Images of death and decay predominate in this sonnet. Ask students to identify the different metaphors for death that are presented in the poem's three quatrains. The first quatrain evokes the approach of winter as dying leaves drift to the ground; the image of "bare ruined choirs" in line 4 would probably have reminded Shakespeare's contemporaries of the many monastery churches that had gone to ruin in the wake of Henry VIII's dissolution of the English monasteries in the 1530s. The second quatrain evokes images of falling night; the third, of a dying fire whose embers are being extinguished by its own ashes.

The tone of the poem's concluding couplet could be a topic for class debate. Do students find the grimness of the first three quatrains to be mitigated by the poem's last two lines? The speaker seems to be suggesting to his friend or lover that the inevitability of death should sharpen his or her appreciation of the speaker's affections. Ask students to compare the portrayal of love as an anodyne against the inevitability of death in this poem with that idea as expressed in Matthew Arnold's "Dover Beach" (text p. 95).

Possible Connections to Other Selections

Matthew Arnold, "Dover Beach" (text p. 95)

Anne Bradstreet, "To My Dear and Loving Husband" (text p. 436)

Robert Hass, "Happiness" (text p. 44)

Richard Wilbur, "A Late Aubade" (text p. 68)

WILLIAM SHAKESPEARE, *When forty winters shall besiege thy brow* (p. 635)

"When forty winters shall besiege thy brow" provides another excellent example of the form of an English, or Shakespearean, sonnet. The central concept of the poem is expressed through three complementary quatrains, and the rhyme scheme — *abab cdcd efef gg* — adheres to the traditional Shakespearean sonnet form. Students unfamiliar with sonnet form should be referred to Chapter 9, "Poetic Forms," for a fuller explanation of the genre. They should then be encouraged to consider how form and content complement each other in this sonnet.

It may be useful to suggest that the sonnet is a well-organized argument. Generally, Shakespeare marshals his rhetoric to convince his audience — both the person addressed in the sonnet and the poem's readers — of a specific truth. Here, the poet warns the youthful subject of the poem that age, like winter, offers no true sustenance, and that the best antidote to old age is children. The poet's powers of persuasion rest primarily on threats: in the first quatrain, he depicts the physical effects of "forty winters" (line 1) and predicts that "Thy youth's proud livery, so gazed on now / Will be a tattered weed" (3–4). The second quatrain extends this rhetorical approach: the beauty of youth and "the treasure of thy lusty days" (6) are reduced merely to "deep-sunken eyes" (7) and "all-eating shame and thriftless praise" (8). In the final quatrain, Shakespeare offers an alternative to what he has depicted as a wasteful life: instead of having nothing to show for youth, the addressee might instead say, "This fair child of mine / Shall sum my count and make my old excuse" (10–11). In addition, the beauty of the parent's youth will live on in the next generation. The couplet emphasizes the advantages of the alternative described by the third quatrain: "This were to be new made when thou art old, / And see thy blood warm when thou feel'st it cold" (13–14). The final line smoothly blends with the opening line, touching on the harsher aspects of "forty winters" and yet contrasting the potential emptiness with the warmth offered by the poet's suggested alternative.

Possible Connections to Other Selections

Anne Bradstreet, "Before the Birth of One of Her Children" (text p. 594)

Judith Ortiz Cofer, "Common Ground" (text p. 59)

WILLIAM SHAKESPEARE, *When, in disgrace with Fortune and men's eyes* (p. 635)

This sonnet posits a future scenario in which the speaker will be outcast because of his fortune. He claims that he will be comforted by remembering his idyllic time with his lover, which presumably occurs in the present. A good starting point for analysis of this poem is its diction, since it contains several words — *bootless, featured, scope* — whose meanings have changed. Another interesting point for discussion is the religious allusion in line 12. Students might be invited to entertain the possibility that the "thee" in line 10 and "thy" in line 13 refer not to the conventional Petrarchan lover, but to God.

The sonnet's structure also merits attention. Ask students to compare the arrangement of the quatrains and concluding couplet in this poem with that of the other Shakespearean sonnets in the text. In which of the poems is there a sharp logical break between the quatrains and the couplet, and in which does this break occur after the octave? Is there any obvious relation between structure and content?

POSSIBLE CONNECTIONS TO OTHER SELECTIONS

John Donne, "A Valediction: Forbidding Mourning" (text p. 130)
William Shakespeare, "That time of year thou mayst in me behold" (text p. 635)

PERCY BYSSHE SHELLEY, *Ozymandias* (p. 636)

Many students will have read this Petrarchan sonnet in high school. You might begin by asking whether in an unintentionally ironic way Ozymandias may have been right; although he is far from outdistancing the rest of humanity in possessions and power, his statue is a reminder that all things are subject to decay and is thus a source of despair. The sonnet, despite its familiarity, still surprises by the quality of its versification. Observe in line 6 the delayed placement of "well," which underscores the closing cautionary note. The final lines, moreover, with the alliterated "boundless and bare" and "lone and level," do suggest the infinite reaches of both the desert and time.

POSSIBLE CONNECTIONS TO OTHER SELECTIONS

John Keats, "Ode on a Grecian Urn" (text p. 79)
William Butler Yeats, "Sailing to Byzantium" (text p. 651)

PERCY BYSSHE SHELLEY, *Sonnet: Lift not the painted veil* (p. 636)

This sonnet cautions against separating oneself from the world's appearances. The story of someone whose "lost heart was tender" (line 8) is intended to urge the reader against looking too closely at the world, where we may see "Fear / And Hope" (4–5) behind the "unreal shapes" (2) and "colours idly spread" (4) that make up the world as we know it. This is a complex poem; reading it out loud and asking students to work on a line-by-line analysis may help them to grapple with it. Students may also benefit from a brief discussion of transcendentalism and a reading of Ecclesiastes 1:2, in which the "Preacher" (14) finds that "all is vanity."

POSSIBLE CONNECTIONS TO OTHER SELECTIONS

Elizabeth Bishop, "The Fish" (text p. 20)
Emily Dickinson, "The thought beneath so slight a film" (text p. 293)
Gerard Manley Hopkins, "God's Grandeur" (text p. 181)

SIR PHILIP SIDNEY, *Loving in Truth, and Fain in Verse My Love to Show* (p. 637)

This sonnet's irregular meter matches its speaker's labored attempt to write it. Ask students to scan its lines, looking for irregularities. For example, the trochees at the beginnings of lines 1, 3, 4, 13, and so on illustrate the forced style that the speaker is trying to avert, while the irregular meter in line 9 aptly illustrates "words . . . halting forth."

Ask students to think about the images the speaker uses to describe his struggle to find the perfect writing style. His "sunburnt brain" (8) and the pregnancy metaphor ("great with child to speak" [12]) evoke an overfull, overcooked speaker who has worked too hard and gained little. How does the final line affirm our suspicions that there may be an easier way to write? Of course, Sidney has constructed his poem to make us feel this affirmation in the end.

Studies of this sonnet are included in the following discussions of *Astrophel and Stella* ("Loving in Truth" is the first sonnet in that sequence): David Kalsone's *Sidney's Poetry* (New York: Norton, 1970); Richard Lanham's "Pure and Impure Persuasion," and Collin Williamson's "Structure and Syntax in *Astrophel and Stella*" (both in *Essential Articles for the Study of Sir Philip Sidney*, edited by Arthur Kinney [Hamden: Archon, 1986]).

POSSIBLE CONNECTION TO ANOTHER SELECTION

E. E. Cummings, "since feeling is first" (text p. 438)

ONLINE RESOURCES (manual p. 350)

GARY SOTO, *Black Hair* (p. 637)

The speaker of this poem, reflecting on his youth, recalls baseball games, specifically games involving his hero, Hector Moreno. Hector becomes a mythical figure in the speaker's mind, "Quick and hard with turned muscles" (line 8), but the speaker is also "brilliant with *[his]* body" (1, 21) as he sits in the bleachers. There is a connection between them, the player and the fan, which is not easily defined but which is crucial to an understanding of the poem. You might ask students to locate all references to the way the body is used in the poem. What does the speaker mean when he declares "I was brilliant with my body"? Does that meaning change as the poem progresses? You might have to pause to consider the tension between metaphor and descriptive language in the poem, which begins with the title. The speaker's identity is tied up not only with the way he uses his body but with physical aspects of his ethnicity: black hair and brown skin. If those aspects connect him with Hector Moreno, what inhibits his identity? What can we assume about his home life based on the cryptic description of his parents at the end of the first stanza?

POSSIBLE CONNECTIONS TO OTHER SELECTIONS

Martín Espada, "Coca-Cola and Coco Frío" (text p. 671)
Gary Soto, "Mexicans Begin Jogging" (text p. 271)
Robert Wallace, "The Double-Play" (text p. 641)

WALLACE STEVENS, *The Emperor of Ice-Cream* (p. 638)

Even more than a parting word to the old woman about to be buried, this poem is a celebration of her mourners, who could still touch imagination's fire despite their impoverished surroundings. By covering the woman in her own embroidered winding sheet ("fantails" here are fantail pigeons), transforming the cigar roller into ice-cream creator, and gathering together like extras in a film extravaganza, they celebrate and affirm the gaudy, bawdy vitality of their lives, together with their creative power to "Let be be finale of seem." As a note, "deal" is furniture made of cheap wood, lacquered over to look more expensive.

You may want to ask students why the emperor of ice-cream is an emperor. Is this an indication that he knows how to move people through the pleasure principle, perhaps?

E. E. Cummings, "Buffalo Bill 's" (text p. 602)

T. S. Eliot, "The Love Song of J. Alfred Prufrock" (text p. 405)

AUDIOVISUAL AND ONLINE RESOURCES (manual pp. 308, 352)

ALFRED, LORD TENNYSON, *Ulysses* (p. 639)

Tennyson was only twenty-four when he wrote this monologue, magnificently creating the thoughts that must have plagued this hero who had striven with the gods. The poem is written in blank verse and preserves a certain conversational eloquence through its use of parallelism. Consider the infinitives in "How dull it is to pause, to make an end, / To rust unburnished, not to shine in use!" (lines 22–23). Ulysses seems to be passing on his power and authority to his son Telemachus, who will, apparently, have a gentler, less warlike (though no less important) kind of work to do. You might ask the class what they suppose Ulysses has in mind when he says in the final stanza, "Some work of noble note, may yet be done." Could this poem bear some autobiographical reflection on the life of a poet? This question could prompt a brief research paper.

POSSIBLE CONNECTIONS TO OTHER SELECTIONS

Emily Dickinson, "This was a Poet — It is That" (text p. 305)

William Butler Yeats, "Sailing to Byzantium" (text p. 651)

ALFRED, LORD TENNYSON, *Tears, Idle Tears* (p. 640)

The nostalgic tone of this poem is immediately apparent in the first stanza. Although the speaker claims to "know not what [his tears] mean" (line 1), he is able to link them to "the days that are no more" (5). Paradoxes and ambivalence are present throughout the poem: Tears "Rise in the heart" (3) while the speaker gazes upon "happy Autumn-fields" (4); the bygone days are described as "fresh" (10); dawn rises, witnessed by "dying ears" and "dying eyes" (13).

This final paradox is also present in Emily Dickinson's "O Sumptuous moment." Students may benefit from a close reading of these poems in tandem, examining in detail this notion of the value of a moment. While Tennyson's poem looks back on "the days that are no more" (5, 10, 15, 20), Dickinson's poem looks forward to imagine how her speaker's present happiness will be remembered. Both offer a paradox that is centered on the idea of memory. How do they compare?

POSSIBLE CONNECTIONS TO OTHER SELECTIONS

Emily Dickinson, "O Sumptuous moment" (text p. 311)

———, "Water, is taught by thirst" (text p. 296)

Robert Frost, "Nothing Gold Can Stay" (text p. 354)

ROBERT WALLACE, *The Double-Play* (p. 641)

You might in teaching this poem ask the class the following questions: In the terms of the game, what literally happened? (Outs were made at second, then first base.) For what other reason is this poem called "The Double-Play"? (Words are object, then subject of the sentence or phrase; from their syntactic position, they demonstrate a double play.) For a clear example, examine how "the ball" is used in the second tercet. Does this syntactic double play serve any purpose? (It does, for it suggests the split-second fluidity of motion and the quick redirection of the ball necessary to make the double play.) Overall, the poem suggests analogically the relation of baseball to poetry — another sort of double play.

264 A Collection of Poems

POSSIBLE CONNECTION TO ANOTHER SELECTION

Robert Francis, "Catch" (text p. 14)

PHILLIS WHEATLEY, *On Being Brought from Africa to America* (p. 642)

Phillis Wheatley was born in West Africa, kidnapped in 1761, and brought to Boston as a slave. Her owners, John and Susannah Wheatley, were impressed with Phillis's intelligence and raised her with their own children, teaching them how to read and write in English, Latin, and Greek. Her only book, *Poems on Various Subjects,* received international acclaim. Though she died in poverty, her poems held significance for members of the abolition movement as well as aspiring African American writers. On a first reading of this poem, students might wonder about Wheatley's accommodating tone. Certainly, Wheatley refers to her native Africa as "pagan" and her "benighted" race as an unrefined one. Remind students of the time in which Wheatley wrote and the restrictions imposed upon her as a woman writer of color. Indeed, the poem offers a revealing look at early American attitudes — the necessity of faith and redemption, the inherent "evil" of dark skin, and the importance of the Cain and Abel story as an argument for the enslavement of African men, women, and children. Point students toward Wheatley's ambivalent stance—though she is challenging white attitudes, she is also embracing their religion, language, and literary style. After a close reading, it becomes clear that Wheatley's poem is an open indictment of racism as well as a request for understanding.

WALT WHITMAN, *One's-Self I Sing* (p. 642)

This poem opens *Leaves of Grass* and is a kind of bugle announcement of several of Whitman's fondly held themes: the individual as both separate and a member of the democratic community; the equality of the sexes; the importance of both body and soul; and the "divinity" of modern humanity, which is not subject to kingly law. Some students will probably hear echoes of the opening lines of a traditional epic poem. Whitman is inverting epic convention somewhat by not singing of arms and men with the requisite bowings to the gods, but hailing the individual self.

As a writing assignment, you might ask the class to describe how and why this brief poem is a good opening for a book of poems. You might also ask students to say what seems particularly American about the poem.

POSSIBLE CONNECTION TO ANOTHER SELECTION

Sue Owen, "Zero" (text p. 123)

WALT WHITMAN, *When I Heard the Learn'd Astronomer* (p. 642)

Whitman's poem sets forth in verse the often-debated argument over the relative values of art and science; true to the traditions of American romanticism, art is the winner in Whitman's view. You might ask your students to recall other instances in which they have seen this issue debated. Which side seemed to have the stronger argument in each case? Is this necessarily an either/or debate? That is, are art and science ever interconnected? What about stanzaic and metrical patterns, in which art depends on numbers? (You might ask students why a poet like Whitman might not be impressed with this particular example.) Can your students think of any poet whose use of imagery or structures depends on scientific principles? Does science owe anything to the power of the artist's imagination?

POSSIBLE CONNECTION TO ANOTHER SELECTION

Emily Dickinson, "Some keep the Sabbath going to Church —" (text p. 298)

RICHARD WILBUR, *Love Calls Us to the Things of This World* (p. 643)

You might begin a discussion of this poem by talking about how a poet controls and convinces us of the truth of metaphors. Wilbur spends some time describing the motions of the wind-tossed laundry in order for us to see the laundry as "angels," and thus offer his prayer (lines 21–23) for a heaven on Earth.

To live as soul in a mock heaven would be incomplete, to say the least. The soul, like someone trying to sleep a while longer, resists the "punctual rape" of the day, which calls the soul back into the world of business and reality. Only when the sun rises does the soul out of "bitter love" join with the waking body and take down the laundry, an image for heaven. As it dismantles heaven, it clothes this daily world, without moral consideration for who wears the laundry — itself an act of graciousness and love. The nuns "keeping their difficult balance" suggest both the literal act of walking and the spiritual act of mediating between things of this world and things of the next.

You might review in class discussion phrases such as "punctual rape" (19), "every blessed day" (19), and "bitter love" (26).

POSSIBLE CONNECTION TO ANOTHER SELECTION

Gerard Manley Hopkins, "God's Grandeur" (text p. 181)

C. K. WILLIAMS, *The Nail* (p. 643)

The concerns of this challenging poem are alternately grotesque and philosophical. The casual, conversational tone the speaker employs from the first line — "some dictator or other" (line 1) — helps to modulate the difficult content.

The speaker contrasts the reporting of fact in this poem with "myth," "stone, or paint" (8). Williams's speaker wishes the nail of the title were merely metaphor, an imagined means by which we express the horrors of torture, or the particular cruelty of the dictator, rather than horrible fact.

A discussion of metaphor might be appropriate here; while Williams uses "The Nail" as "a way to tell the truth that grief is limitless, a way to tell us . . . / it's we who do such things" (12–13), he is not grateful for the metaphor. "It should be an emblem of itself, not itself, something that would mean not really have to happen" (9). Taking a few minutes to allow students to find other metaphors that depict "the brutal human world" (14) could prove helpful for discussion; examples are present in the poems listed below.

POSSIBLE CONNECTIONS TO OTHER SELECTIONS

Emily Dickinson, "After great pain, a formal feeling comes" (text p. 306)
James Merrill, "Casual Wear" (text p. 159)
Robin Morgan, "Invocation" (text p. 60)
Dylan Thomas, "The Hand That Signed the Paper" (text p. 120)

ONLINE RESOURCES (manual p. 354)

MILLER WILLIAMS, *Thinking About Bill, Dead of AIDS* (p. 644)

Williams's poem is about the experience of watching a friend with AIDS deal with the world around him as he succumbs to the disease. In the first stanza, the speaker admits ignorance of the processes by which the body turns on itself. Ask students to point out the metaphors of battle or war that the speaker uses to describe the onslaught of AIDS: "blood surrenders" (line 2), "rescinding all its normal orders" (4), "defenders of flesh" (5), "betraying the head" (5), and "pulling its guards back from all its borders" (6).

The second stanza moves from describing what is happening in Bill's body to describing the responses of others to his disease. Students may find line 9 particularly evocative — "your eyes drained of any reprimand." In the last three stanzas, the speaker explains the response of the "we" of the poem. Ask students to consider who the "we" represents. You may wish to pay special attention to lines like "partly to persuade / both you and us ... that we were loving and were not afraid" (10–12), "stopping, though, to set our smiles at the door" (15), and "we didn't know what look would hurt you least" (18). What emotion is the speaker intending to convey? Ask students to identify the conflict that occurs in this part of the poem. Who experiences this tension? Discuss whether this underlying conflict is ever resolved.

POSSIBLE CONNECTIONS TO OTHER SELECTIONS

Donald Hall, "Letter with No Address" (text p. 673)

Robert Hayden, "Those Winter Sundays" (text p. 10)

Andrew Hudgins, "Elegy for My Father, Who Is Not Dead" (text p. 242)

AUDIOVISUAL AND ONLINE RESOURCES (manual pp. 310, 354)

WILLIAM CARLOS WILLIAMS, *Spring and All* (p. 645)

All sounds a good deal like *fall,* and indeed there is something autumnal about Williams's chill spring, with its "reddish/purplish" bushes and "dead, brown leaves." But these tokens of death actually bespeak a quickening life of the season that connotes rebirth. The images of human birth are not far from Williams's mind in this poem, as he talks about the nameless "They" who come into the world naked. Syntactically "They" (line 16) stands for the vegetation of grass, wild carrot leaf, and the rest (all), but we do not know this until after the pronoun appears. Williams can thus have it both ways and point to both a human and a nonhuman world.

Williams's spring, like so many of his subjects, is earth-rooted, literally. No surface change here; this profound "change" is "rooted" far down, so that life springs forth from its depths.

You might ask the class whether there is any significance in the setting of the poem — by the road to the contagious hospital.

POSSIBLE CONNECTION TO ANOTHER SELECTION

Margaret Atwood, "February" (text p. 124)

WILLIAM CARLOS WILLIAMS, *This Is Just to Say* (p. 645)

Three possible writing assignments can be organized around this poem: (1) an essay talking about line breaks, necessary brevity, and careful word choice that validates this seemingly conversational statement as poetry; (2) a found poem, using a scrap of conversation or some lines from a short story, to make a poem about the length of this one; (3) a parody of this poem.

POSSIBLE CONNECTIONS TO OTHER SELECTIONS

Helen Chasin, "The Word *Plum*" (text p. 195)

Donald Justice, "Order in the Streets" (text p. 272)

Ezra Pound, "In a Station of the Metro" (text p. 110)

WILLIAM WORDSWORTH, *Lines Written in Early Spring* (p. 646)

This poem's speaker acknowledges the pleasure he takes in nostalgia: the "mood when pleasant thoughts / Bring sad thoughts to the mind" (lines 3–4) is described as "sweet" (3). However, the speaker moves beyond a personal sense of nostalgia to a larger, more universal concern: "What man has made of man" (8). In contrast to the careful detail used to describe "primrose-tufts" (9), "every flower" (11), "birds" (13), and "budding twigs" (17), the lamentation over what man has made of man is stated only by its absence. While these wonders of nature seem to enjoy "the air" (12) and take pleasure in "the least motion" (15), man responds to these "pleasant thoughts" (3) with sad ones.

Although Wordsworth contrasts the apparent joy of nature with his speaker's tendency toward melancholy, Gerard Manley Hopkins's "God's Grandeur" contrasts the obvious presence of God in the natural world with mankind's refusal to obey God's will. Students may benefit from a writing assignment that asks them to compare the two poems' use of the natural world to provide support for the arguments of the speakers.

POSSIBLE CONNECTIONS TO OTHER SELECTIONS

Gerard Manley Hopkins, "God's Grandeur" (text p. 181)
Alfred, Lord Tennyson, "Tears, Idle Tears" (text p. 640)

WILLIAM WORDSWORTH, *I Wandered Lonely as a Cloud* (p. 646)

The speaker of this poem finds comfort for his loneliness in nature. His connection to daffodils comforts him even in memory. In his preface to *Lyrical Ballads,* Wordsworth describes poetry as "the spontaneous overflow of powerful feelings: it takes its origin from emotion recollected in tranquillity." To some extent, this quotation explains the "wealth" that Wordsworth alludes to in line 18, for while reclining on his couch he can recall the heightened sense of pleasure the daffodils first brought him. From his mood of loneliness, he moves to a state of gladness. What else characterizes how the daffodils appear to him? Seemingly, they are a token of cosmic splendor in their extensiveness and golden sparkle.

POSSIBLE CONNECTIONS TO OTHER SELECTIONS

Emily Dickinson, "A Bird came down the Walk —" (text p. 173)
Robert Hass, "Happiness" (text p. 44)

WILLIAM WORDSWORTH, *A Slumber Did My Spirit Seal* (p. 647)

This is one of Wordsworth's "Lucy poems," and the "she" in line 3 alludes to Lucy. Apparently, this poem marks a loss for which the poet was unprepared. He was asleep to the possibilities of aging and death, and Lucy now seems well beyond the province of earthly years and more the spirit of eternal time. Is there a paradox in this poem? Probably so. The speaker's dream, which he had had in a more pleasant period, when he felt that they were both beyond the effects of time, turns out to be for Lucy ironically accurate, for like the rocks and stones and trees, she is now unaffected by the passage of time.

POSSIBLE CONNECTIONS TO OTHER SELECTIONS

John Keats, "When I have fears that I may cease to be" (text p. 618)
Percy Bysshe Shelley, "Ozymandias" (text p. 636)

WILLIAM WORDSWORTH, *The Solitary Reaper* (p. 647)

This poem seems to spill over its limits as fit lyric to become a spontaneous overflow of powerful feeling. Ask the class to note how many boundaries are exceeded here. In stanza I, for example, the song overflows the vales. In the final stanza the song seems without end, and the hearer hears it long after he leaves the singer behind. Implied too in the second and third stanzas is the song's ability to transcend place and history. As with other poetic figures of Wordsworth, this solitary reaper and her song provide a way into perceiving an order of existence beneath the surface. You might ask the class if it matters at all that the singer is female.

William Blake, "The Chimney Sweeper" (text p. 166)
Langston Hughes, "The Weary Blues" (text p. 380)

WILLIAM WORDSWORTH, *Mutability* (p. 648)

This poem examines the inevitability of change and the ability to see it clearly. The "unimaginable touch of time" (line 14) proves everything to be temporary, even the "outward forms" of "Truth" (7). Truth itself "fails not" (7), but the awesome changes in our lives may have some of us fooled; those "who meddle not with crime / Nor avarice, nor over-anxious care" (5–6) can see change as it is, a non-threatening part of life.

Among the examples Wordsworth offers are nature and political order; which provide comparisons to the "outward forms" of truth. Frost melts, and "the tower sublime / Of yesterday" (10–11) is no longer so impressive today.

The language is especially dense in this poem, and students are likely to be unfamiliar with its terms. Reading it aloud and working together on a line-by-line analysis of its meaning may prove helpful. Students may glean much of the meaning through an exercise that includes rewriting or restating the poem in more contemporary terms.

POSSIBLE CONNECTIONS TO OTHER SELECTIONS

Robert Frost, "Spring Pools" (text p. 355)
William Shakespeare, "Not marble, nor the gilded monuments" (text p. 435)
Percy Bysshe Shelley, "Sonnet: Lift not the painted veil" (text p. 636)

BARON WORMSER, *Shoplifting* (p. 649)

This poem examines the visceral response of fear generated when a shoplifter is caught in the act. The tragic conclusion, in which it is indicated that the criminal act was unjustifiable — "You don't even own a camera" (line 24) — indicts the reader; the use of the second person draws the reader into the discussion, establishes a conversational tone that makes a contrast between the remembrance of the "playground" (6) and the "old people" (8) who are often found on the bench by the exit.

The presence of authority and its contrast to the speaker are central to the narrative. The manager's imagined "lecture about kids" (11) and the cop's calm assertion that "you'll have to go to court" (14) provide the source for a possible writing exercise. Ask students to focus on the ways in which the poem details the physical responses to the events. Examples include "Your stomach melts and your heart starts to beat" (5) and "your head's raw dough / One moment, light as a balloon the next" (17–18). Students may relate to the description more easily if they spend some time trying to detail their own experiences with this kind of fear. You might find it effective to ask students to write a journal entry that recalls a run-in with authority.

POSSIBLE CONNECTIONS TO OTHER SELECTIONS

Gwendolyn Brooks, "We Real Cool" (text p. 81)
Saundra Sharp, "It's the Law: A Rap Poem" (text p. 33)

MITSUYE YAMADA, *A Bedtime Story* (p. 649)

Irony is this poem's most striking feature. A father tells his child an ancient story from his culture (we presume), and his daughter, the speaker, is unable to understand the story's message. To figure out the speaker's inability to grasp this message, we must look into the way the story is framed. At the beginning of the poem, the time is non-specific; the father begins his story as many stories begin: "Once upon a time" (line 1). At the end of the story, the speaker describes where the story is told, "In the comfort of our / hilltop home in Seattle / overlooking the valley" (41–43). This tension between the timeless and the present indicate a gap between father and daughter that goes beyond a typical generation gap. The daughter cannot grasp the moral of her father's story because she is safe and comfortable, and, presumably, privileged. The irony is that she cannot identify with the woman in the story who is turned away from houses in town, identify-ing instead with the townspeople who turn the old woman away. The speaker can no more see the message of the story than the people in that town can see the beauty of the moon. As readers of the poem, we are put in a similar position: what are we to take away from the story, frame-tale and all? Do students identify with the daughter (who wants a fuller story with a more exciting plot), with the father (who wants to pass on a piece of his culture), with both, with neither, or with the woman in the story? One way to enter such a discussion is to ask students how they read the poem's tone; is it meant to be humorous or instructive? Compare the poem's tone with that of the legend recounted.

POSSIBLE CONNECTIONS TO OTHER SELECTIONS

Margaret Atwood, "Bored" (text p. 72)

Jimmy Santiago Baca, "Green Chile" (text p. 96)

WILLIAM BUTLER YEATS, *Crazy Jane Talks with the Bishop* (p. 650)

Tradition has it that the fool is the purveyor of truth, and Crazy Jane, whose retort to the bishop is that "fair needs foul," is no exception. The paradoxical mutualities that Crazy Jane endorses find other correspondences in the last stanza, where the romantic ideal of love, we are told, pitches its mansion in "the place of excrement." Puns on *sole* and *whole* also invite a commingling of the platonic with the blatantly physical. According to John Unterecker, the bishop in the poem was a divinity student turned down by Jane for Jack the Journeyman. The bishop banished Jack, but Jane remained true to him *(A Reader's Guide to William Butler Yeats* [New York: Noonday, 1959]).

POSSIBLE CONNECTION TO ANOTHER SELECTION

Pam Crow, "Meat Science" (text p. 600)

WILLIAM BUTLER YEATS, *Leda and the Swan* (p. 650)

Some references in this poem might require clarification: the offspring of Leda and Zeus (as swan) was Helen, the most beautiful of women, who married Menelaus but was later awarded to Paris. Paris took her to Troy with him, thus occasioning the Trojan War and the death of Agamemnon, the leader of the Greeks. Agamemnon was married to Clytemnestra, Helen's sister.

According to Yeats's view, this rape marks a turning point in history and the down-ward spiraling of the gyres. The moment is dark and fraught with the onset of much tragedy that Leda cannot possibly know, yet she does seem to take on a measure of Zeus's power and come closer to assuming a consciousness of the divine than is ordi-narily possible. One point to consider in class discussion is Yeats's use of the rhetorical question in this poem. Does the poem suggest any answers to these questions? What do they do to the tone of the poem?

POSSIBLE CONNECTION TO ANOTHER SELECTION

Pam Crow, "Meat Science" (text p. 600)

WILLIAM BUTLER YEATS, *Sailing to Byzantium* (p. 651)

Byzantium, in historical terms, was the capital of the Eastern Roman Empire and was the holy city of Greek Orthodoxy. Explore with the class what Byzantium symbolically represents, especially in terms of Yeats's career as a poet. In a note to the poem, Yeats commented, "I have read somewhere that in the Emperor's Palace at Byzantium was a tree made of gold and silver and artificial birds that sang" (*The Collected Poems of William Butler Yeats* [New York: Macmillan, 1972], 453). Increasingly in his later poems, Yeats turned to art rather than nature as a means of transcending time.

POSSIBLE CONNECTIONS TO OTHER SELECTIONS

John Keats, "Ode on a Grecian Urn" (text p. 79)
William Shakespeare, "Not marble, nor the gilded monuments" (text p. 435)

WILLIAM BUTLER YEATS, *The Second Coming* (p. 652)

The pattern here of the falcon circling around the falconer indicates the pattern of the gyre, now tracing its widest circle and thus least subject to the control of the falconer. "Mere anarchy" is loosed on a world troubled by recent wars (World War I and the Russian Revolution). Yeats later claimed he was describing the rise of Fascism in Europe. What kind of order will assume its place over the next two thousand years, if the nature of that world is imaged by a description of the annunciating beast as blank, pitiless, and rough?

POSSIBLE CONNECTIONS TO OTHER SELECTIONS

Robert Frost, "Fire and Ice" (text p. 353)
William Butler Yeats, "Leda and the Swan" (text p. 651)

WILLIAM BUTLER YEATS, *The Wild Swans at Coole* (p. 653)

The speaker of this pensive poem examines the changes in himself in the nineteen years since he first counted the swans of the title. The speaker's "heart is sore" (line 14) in contrast to the "unwearied" (19) swans; "all's changed" (15) for the speaker since his "first time on this shore" (16), but the swans remain "brilliant" (13), "mysterious, beautiful" (26).

Students may find it helpful to focus on the fourth stanza. How does the depiction of the swans, with their stable loves and number, serve as a possible contrast to the unstated concerns of the speaker? Does the speaker envy the swans?

POSSIBLE CONNECTIONS TO OTHER SELECTIONS

Robert Hayden, "Those Winter Sundays" (text p. 10)
William Wordsworth, "Mutability" (text p. 648)

DAVID ZIEROTH, *Time over Earth* (p. 654)

The speaker in this poem tries to come to terms with the sensation of flight and travel. He is led to contemplate the differences in time spent over earth and time spent on earth. The speaker is intent on comparing the actions of what is occurring in the plane with the other passengers and his own fears of being suspended above earth. While the plane glides over "bank after bank of cloud / and the sudden open hole for rock or snow" (lines 1, 2) the other passengers wrestle with newspapers and "offer comments" (10) and "fight ennui" (6). Items such as "foam seats" (20) seem trite in comparison with the detrimental nature of being in flight. Meanwhile, the speaker cannot help but dwell on the immensity of the darkness and the uncertainty of making it back down to earth.

In the second part of the poem, the speaker realizes that he is unchanged by his experiences in the air. That "beam" (22) he relied upon to get the plane safely to the ground is forgotten in the prospect of discovering a new place on earth, along with all the others who are just as much in a rush to discover it as he is. He is soon to discover that in sleep, his subconscious has recorded all he has seen and feared in the plane, and he is changed with the realization that his state of suspension and fear have left an impression on him and can just as easily be experienced in those last moments before sleep.

You might enter into a discussion of this poem by asking students to compare the speaker's state of mind when he is in the air with what he experiences before he goes to sleep. What information has he gleaned from being in the plane, and how has that affected his everyday perspective? What is the poet's intention when he focuses on the actions of the other passengers on the plane?

POSSIBLE CONNECTIONS TO OTHER SELECTIONS

Emily Dickinson, "Because I could not stop for Death —" (text p. 308)
Robert Frost, "Acquainted with the Night" (text p. 139)

AN ALBUM OF WORLD LITERATURE

The poems in this section give students an opportunity to experience over fifty years of world literature written from often contradictory perspectives. The poems range from general comments on modern sensibility to more specific pleas for relief from the political upheaval that has torn apart many of the countries represented. Although it is hardly necessary to teach them chronologically, the poems do present some of the major historic events of the twentieth century, including World War II and the revolutions that have racked Central and South American countries in the latter part of the century.

Students will read these poems not only for historical and geographical information but for new perspectives on their own lives as well. Your class will have to reassess the reading they have done in English courses throughout their scholastic careers. How many readings from cultures other than their own have they encountered? What might be the effect of this very limited education?

Questioning their own biases will lead students to open up the poems to the extent that they realize that world literature is not simply about some "Other"; it is about all of us, living in an ever-contracting world where we must think as much about our labels and notions of "the Other" as we do about ourselves.

ANNA AKHMATOVA, *Lot's Wife* (p. 655)

Students are likely to be familiar with the story of Lot's wife. You may want to ask a student to bring in the biblical text for comparison (the story can be found in Genesis 19:15–26). Akhmatova imagines the "wild grief" (line 3) felt by Lot's wife in much greater detail than is provided in the original text. While the moral of the story is generally understood to be that Lot's wife should not have looked back, Akhmatova re-examines the act and sees it as a kind of courage. The familiar story, then, is given a new and unexpected conclusion: In the speaker's heart "she will not be forgot / Who, for a single glance, gave up her life" (15–16). Students may see this as an opportunity for a creative writing exercise, in which they flesh out the inner life of another famous person.

POSSIBLE CONNECTIONS TO OTHER SELECTIONS

Margaret Atwood, "you fit into me" (text p. 116)
Wyatt Prunty, "Elderly Lady Crossing on Green" (text p. 39)

AUDIOVISUAL AND ONLINE RESOURCES (manual pp. 291, 321)

CLARIBEL ALEGRÍA, *I Am Mirror* (p. 656)

Born in Estelí, Nicaragua, Alegría moved to El Salvador six months later; she therefore considers herself more Salvadoran than Nicaraguan. She attended George Washington University, graduating in 1948, and is married to the American writer Darwin J. Flakoll. She received the Casa de las Americas prize of Cuba in 1978 for her book *Sobrevivo*. Alegría and her husband have lived in many foreign countries; they now divide their time between Majorca, Spain, and Managua, Nicaragua.

The speaker in this poem describes her attempts to feel again after she has been numbed by violence. She looks for her identity in the mirror, only to see herself as another person; note her use of third-person pronouns to refer to herself: "she also pricks herself" (line 11). In an ironic twist of Descartes's *Cogito ergo sum,* the speaker feels her arm, saying, "I hurt / therefore I exist" (32–33). Her attention continually turns to the horror around her as she alternates between scenes of violence and an attempt to keep her identity amid the turmoil. In a series of negations that begins in line 44, the speaker denies the violence, losing her self in the process. She cannot sustain an identity and survive, so she becomes an object: "I am a blank mirror" (48).

In a writing assignment, you might ask students to trace the two strands of images in this poem: the images the speaker uses to describe herself and the images of violence. They might construct an argument explaining the relationship between the two, discussing the effect of the images on the poem's tone and theme.

POSSIBLE CONNECTIONS TO OTHER SELECTIONS

William Blake, "London" (text p. 101)

Sylvia Plath, "Mirror" (question #1, following)

CONNECTION QUESTION IN TEXT (p. 658) WITH ANSWER

1. Compare the ways Alegría uses mirror images to reflect life in El Salvador with Plath's concerns in "Mirror" (p. 126).

   Plath's speaker is first mirror, then lake. In a reversal of Alegría's technique, in which the speaker becomes the mirror, Plath shows how the mirror absorbs the woman looking into it. Both poets play with the notion of women as objects, but Alegría does so to reflect the turmoil in war-torn El Salvador, whereas Plath considers the woman's aging process and approaching death.

AUDIOVISUAL AND ONLINE RESOURCES (manual pp. 291, 322)

YEHUDA AMICHAI, *Jerusalem, 1985* (p. 658)

This brief poem contrasts the "bits of crumpled, wadded paper" (line 3) that represent wishes made or granted in the Wailing Wall with the failed journey of one that only made it as far as the "old iron gate" "across the way" (4). The spare language and mysterious source of the last two lines could make for some inventive discussion: Do students think the note is addressed to God, or to someone else? What might have prevented the writer from reaching the Wailing Wall?

Students may benefit from a brief discussion of the Wailing Wall. If you have Internet access in your classroom, you may find it interesting to visit **www.kotelkam.com**. *Kotel* means "wall" in Hebrew; this Web site offers a history of the Wailing Wall, as well as live video of the wall itself.

POSSIBLE CONNECTIONS TO OTHER SELECTIONS

Emily Dickinson, "I know that He exists" (text p. 327)

William Wordsworth, "London, 1802" (text p. 128)

FAIZ AHMED FAIZ, *If You Look at the City from Here* (p. 658)

The poem, an extended analogy comparing a city to a prison, does not answer for us a crucial question: where is "here" (lines 1, 11)? The "concentric circles" of line 2 and the "distant lamps" of line 18 indicate that the speaker is probably at a distance from the city. The question then becomes, why does distance from the city cause the speaker to alter his perspective? How would the city be seen differently if the speaker were on the streets of the city? Why is everyone placed on the same level, without "dignity" (12), when one is not close to them? And who imprisons them: is it some unnamed governmental force, or the physical city, or is it the people themselves? The impression that Faiz creates is vivid, but quite open to interpretation.

Possible Connections to Other Selections

William Blake, "London" (question #1, following)

George Eliot, "In a London Drawingroom" (text p. 606)

Rainer Maria Rilke, "The Panther" (question #2, following)

Connections Questions in Text (p. 659) with Answers

1. Compare the treatment of the city in this poem and in Blake's "London" (p. 101).

   In Blake's "London," the manacles of imprisonment are clearly "mind-forged." That is to say, we have created them through limitations in our thinking. The source of the manacles in Faiz's poem is less defined. There are striking similarities in the two descriptions, such as blood running down walls; but in Blake, we sense the origin of social ills based on the professions of people in the city (Chimney-sweeper, Soldier, Harlot). In Faiz, we are given no such clues.

2. Write an essay on the meaning of confinement in Faiz's poem and in Rilke's "The Panther" (p. 105).

   A main difference between these two poems is that the perspective is radically different. In Rilke's poem, it is as if we are in the cage with the panther, and there does not seem to be any world outside. In Faiz's poem, we know that there is a world beyond the city because we are outside of it along with the speaker. Although it looks as though there is no way out of the city, there must be. In the case of the panther, there truly is no way out.

XU GANG, *Red Azalea on the Cliff* (p. 659)

"Red Azalea on the Cliff" is a poem of paradoxes. The smiling azalea of the first line makes the speaker's heart "shudder with fear" (line 3). Hidden within beauty is the threat of disaster (5) — an idea that is central to the poem. Likewise, the sweetness of the flower encloses slyness, and its intimacy embraces distance (21–22).

In light of these paradoxes, encourage students to discuss what the red azalea might represent. What seems to be the relationship between humans and nature in the poem? Discuss what the red flower has to do with love.

Ask students to consider the last two lines of the poem, in particular, their meaning in light of Xu Gang's role in the Cultural Revolution and his later disillusionment.

Possible Connection to Another Selection

John Keats, "La Belle Dame sans Merci" (text p. 618)

Online Resources (manual p. 331)

PABLO NERUDA, *Sweetness, Always* (p. 660)

In an essay on "impure poetry," Chilean-born Pablo Neruda defended the importance to the poet's craft of not-so-nice images and words. Neruda criticized American poets for ignoring politics to pursue their own, "loftier" pleasures. Art was life for Neruda; he believed that poetry must be kept near the bone, where it originates, and not elevated to irrelevancy. "Sweetness, Always" illustrates this point in delicious, sense-appealing imagery, which contrasts with the dullness of more abstract poetry. The speaker defends the poor, the politically oppressed, the mundane, and the earthy as the truly valuable subjects for poetry.

The poem appeals to the sense of taste, pointing out that even the builders of great monuments have to eat. Talking about the body makes Neruda's appeal appropriate for every man and woman. Poems do indeed feed the world, although clearly the poets Neruda distrusts claim that feeding is not their job: "We are not feeding the world." Working from the extremes of underground and sky, Neruda focuses on the earth — at the level of the people: "and the poor adults' also." He derides the typical monuments of human power in favor of the food that creates living monuments of joy and misery — human beings.

Neruda's poetry has been discussed in Manuel Duran and Margery Safir's *Earth Tones* (Bloomington: Indiana UP, 1980); Rene de Costa's *The Poetry of Pablo Neruda* (Cambridge: Harvard UP, 1979); and "Pablo Neruda, 1904–1973," *Modern Poetry Studies* 5.1 (1974).

Possible Connections to Other Selections

Helen Chasin, "The Word *Plum*" (question #2, following)
Robert Frost, "Birches" (question #1, following)
Galway Kinnell, "Blackberry Eating" (question #2, following)

Connections Questions in Text (p. 662) with Answers

1. Compare the view of life offered in this poem with that in Frost's "Birches" (p. 347).

   The speaker's call for "sweetness, always" in Neruda's poem asks us to avoid vanity and seek "Verses of pastry which melt / into milk and sugar in the mouth" (lines 12–13). The speaker in Frost's "Birches" wishes to "get away from earth awhile" (48) and then return and start over again. Although both speakers ask us to return to earthly things, Neruda's speaker asks us to return to the sweetness of existence, whereas Frost's urges first an escape from a life "like a pathless wood" (44) in order to return to earth.

2. Write an essay that discusses Kinnell's "Blackberry Eating" (p. 176) and Chasin's "The Word *Plum*" (p. 195) as the sort of "eatable" poetry the speaker calls for in this poem.

   In Kinnell's "Blackberry Eating" and Chasin's "The Word *Plum*," the fruits could easily represent the "sweetness" the speaker asks for in Neruda's poem. The plum and the blackberries invite listeners to experience the world through a single, sensuous image, without much concern for "deep, philosophical" issues.

Audiovisual and Online Resources (manual pp. 304, 344)

OCTAVIO PAZ, *The Street* (p. 662)

A Mexican poet of metamorphic surrealism, Octavio Paz has influenced many writers, including William Carlos Williams, Denise Levertov, and Muriel Rukeyser, each of whom has translated him. He has served the Mexican diplomatic service in Paris, New Delhi, and New York.

Students may let this poem too easily defeat them or too easily collapse into platitudes: "OK, a guy becomes his own shadow or he can't tell whether he's real or not." The poem's simple diction, pleasing (and very frequent) rhymes, and skillful alliteration work in opposition to its mournful tone and shadowy imagery, a tension that mirrors the speaker's situation: the everyday world of streets, leaves, stones, and people is not at all everyday. Nothing has definition on "The Street" (note the references to night, blindness, and awkwardness and to the unstated reasons for the pursuit), yet the urgent certainty of the "narrative" is almost palpable.

You might ask students to change all the verbs in the poem to the past tense and comment on the resulting differences in tone. Other questions that would yield productive discussion or writing include: How would the poem's effect be altered if it ended with line 11? How does the speaker know the street is "long" if he walks "in blackness"? How can stones be anything but "silent"? To what extent could the poem's logic be considered dream logic?

POSSIBLE CONNECTIONS TO OTHER SELECTIONS

Robert Frost, "Acquainted with the Night" (question #1, following)

Langston Hughes, "Lenox Avenue: Midnight" (question #2, following)

CONNECTIONS QUESTIONS IN TEXT (p. 663) WITH ANSWERS

1. How does the speaker's anxiety in this poem compare with that in Frost's "Acquainted with the Night" (p. 139)?

   Frost's speaker in "Acquainted with the Night" vacillates between himself and the outside world, alternating between images of light and darkness, good and evil. Paz's speaker begins and ends in darkness, in the solipsistic prison of his own mind. Whereas Frost's speaker seems indecisive and brooding, Paz's is forever fixed in darkness, without hope. Frost's speaker feels alone in a realistic night setting where he sees "one luminary clock against the sky." His poem conveys loneliness rather than anxiety. Paz's scene, in contrast, is the landscape of persecution and nightmare.

2. Write an essay comparing the tone of this poem and that of Hughes's "Lenox Avenue: Midnight" (p. 383).

   Both Paz and Hughes set their poems on particular streets, and the setting affects the tone of the poems. The tone of Hughes's poem is one of melancholy, shaped by the jazz "rhythm of life" (line 1). The image of the gods laughing at the "weary heart of pain" (6) is oppressive and hopeless. Likewise, Paz's speaker does not leave any room for hope or escape from his own consciousness; thus, the tone of both poems is dismal.

AUDIOVISUAL AND ONLINE RESOURCES (manual pp. 305, 346)

INDIRA SANT, *Household Fires* (p. 663)

This poem delineates the roles (or "jobs") of four children in an Indian household. The father's role is only suggested, but the poem's final focus is on the mother, who seems to be caving in as a result of the demands placed on her. You might explore in discussion the effect of the way this poem is arranged: where are our sympathies? And would they be different if the poem were ordered differently? The poem categorizes the roles of the children in terms of gender, but also in terms of age. Is there a clear-cut hierarchy based on these criteria? If there were a sixth stanza about the father's "job," what would it be like and where would it most effectively be placed?

POSSIBLE CONNECTIONS TO OTHER SELECTIONS

Chitra Banerjee Divakuruni, "Indian Movie, New Jersey" (question #2, following)

Elaine Magarrell, "The Joy of Cooking" (text p. 134)

Linda Pastan, "Marks" (text p. 132)

Sylvia Plath, "Daddy" (question #1, following)

1. Implicit in this poem is the father's presence. Compare the treatment of the father in "Household Fires" and Plath's "Daddy" (p. 630).

    The key word in this question is "implicit." The father is cleverly hidden in "Household Fires," whereas the father in "Daddy," whether or not he is taken as the speaker's actual father, is attacked directly. "Household Fires" also seems to be representative of a broader cultural pattern, whereas the father in "Daddy" is more individualized. Finally, the speaker's problem with "daddy" in Plath's poem is personal, between the two of them; in Sant's poem, the conflict does not exist between two people but amidst an entire family.

2. Write an essay that compares the life described in this poem with Divakuruni's "Indian Movie, New Jersey" (p. 162).

    The focus of Divakuruni's poem is a cultural divide that brings families closer together. Indian culture is held up for praise, and no one's "mind . . . gets burned" as the mother's mind does in Sant's poem (lines 33–34). Their excursion to the movies at least enables them to forget about the troubles within their families while bonding with other Indians. In Sant's poem, the outside world doesn't factor into the family strife. Yet both poems seem stifling, as though there is no real way out of this pattern.

WOLE SOYINKA, *Future Plans* (p. 664)

Students may be intimidated by the demands placed on the reader in this poem — a complete understanding of "Future Plans" requires a rather extensive familiarity with world history. Soyinka is highly specific in naming the leaders from around the world who have become notorious for their dishonesty, their ruthless annihilation of those who objected to their policies, and their disregard for basic human rights. He ruthlessly satirizes their behavior and suggests that the information the people are allowed access to is not always accurate. For instance, those leaders whom we might consider to be "enemies" may in fact be in league (or, as Soyinka suggests in his pairing of Meir and Arafat, in bed).

One means of opening up class discussion of the poem is to encourage students to research one or more of the names listed here and to briefly report in class on their findings. However, even without a specific understanding of the variety of atrocities practiced by the leaders referred to in "Future Plans," students might easily perceive the intensity of the poem's irony. The first stanza, with its reference to "Forgers, framers, / Fabricators Inter- / national" (lines 2–4), conveys Soyinka's attitude toward the leaders whose names follow. In line 20, he epitomizes the corruption that is the subject of his poem when he writes of "Contraceptives stacked beneath the papal bunk" — an image that contrasts sharply with the Catholic mandate that church leaders take vows of celibacy and chastity. The final line of the poem provides a means of better understanding the title: here, Soyinka ominously notes that there are "more to come" (21) in the line of oppressive, dishonest leaders. Soyinka's sharp criticisms are not limited to any particular region of the world; in "Future Plans," he asserts that corruption is common to all human societies.

POSSIBLE CONNECTIONS TO OTHER SELECTIONS

Kenneth Fearing, "AD" (question #1, following)

Dylan Thomas, "The Hand That Signed the Paper" (text p. 120)

CONNECTION QUESTION IN TEXT (p. 665) WITH ANSWER

1. Discuss the political satire in "Future Plans" and in Fearing's "AD" (p. 144).

    Soyinka and Fearing rely on an almost comic tone in establishing their satirical views; they also adapt familiar patterns as they organize their arguments. Soyinka rates his subjects according to the Mach scheme; he also arranges his observations according to the agenda of a business meeting, including a calling to order and an agenda for unfinished business — "Projects in view" (11). Fearing also converts an ordinary form — a want ad — into the ideal method of conveying his satire on the mentality of a warmonger. The structure of these poems parallels their content: both poets build their satires on an outrage that such unacceptable beliefs and behaviors are evident on a regular basis.

ONLINE RESOURCES (manual p. 351)

WISLAWA SZYMBORSKA, *Maybe All This* (p. 665)

The suggestion of a larger reality in this poem is crafted with elegance and humor. The idea of a higher power watching over us is not new, nor is the notion that God observes even the most minute changes in our lives. However, characterizing this higher power as "some lab" (line 2) establishes objective, scientific distance that coexists with a tremendous love for the world.

Students may not notice that the poem begins with a long series of questions. These establish the uncertainty of the speaker about the meaning of "all this" (1). The capitalization of "Boss" (33) is the first admission that the lab could be something holy. The speaker's notions of a "no interference" (12) philosophy, the whole of mankind as "experimental generations" (5), does not warrant this capitalization. Rather, the "Boss" (33) is called when the poem turns to the "darling little being / with its tiny heart beating inside it" (28–29). It is this tenderness that seems to satisfy the curiosity and hope of the speaker, concluding the poem.

POSSIBLE CONNECTIONS TO OTHER SELECTIONS

Stephen Crane, "A Man Said to the Universe" (text p. 146)
Robert Frost, "Design" (text p. 356)
Gerard Manley Hopkins, "God's Grandeur" (text p. 181)

ONLINE RESOURCES (manual p. 353)

TOMAS TRANSTROMER, *April and Silence* (p. 667)

Students may find their traditional romantic notions about the connotations of spring challenged by Transtromer's poem, in which "Spring lies desolate" (line 1). However, "April and Silence" is part of a tradition in which poets have expounded on the negative qualities of spring. For example, Transtromer's opening line recalls that of Eliot's "The Wasteland": the cruelest month. The speaker's depression manifests itself throughout the poem. He focuses almost solely on what he lacks, on what he cannot achieve, and on his own inability to gain control. As he notes, "I am carried in my shadow / like a violin / in its black box" (7–9). Perhaps because of the limitations of translation, the poem may seem flat to some readers — some students may argue that the speaker is merely suffering from light deprivation. You might ask students whether they are inspired to empathize with the speaker of the poem. Why or why not?

POSSIBLE CONNECTION TO ANOTHER SELECTION

William Carlos Williams, "Spring and All" (question #1, following)

CONNECTION QUESTION IN TEXT (p. 645) WITH ANSWER

1. Discuss the description of spring in this poem and in Williams's "Spring and All" (p. 645).

    By the time April rolls around, we are so desperate for warmth and new growth that if the weather remains wintery, our souls contract and we become pessimists. If spring comes early, we are somehow more optimistic. Transtromer's "April and Silence" is reminiscent of our thoughts while enduring a late spring, when all we can recognize is what we are unable to achieve. Williams's "Spring and All," in contrast, reminds us of the moment when winter turns to spring and the dormant plants awaken.

AUDIOVISUAL RESOURCES (manual p. 309)

AN ALBUM OF CONTEMPORARY POEMS

Both the difficulties and the rewards of contemporary poetry derive from the same characteristics; namely, there are no set principles for the construction of contemporary poetry or the range of its style. It can be structured in stanzas, or in open free-verse paragraphs, or even as an uninterrupted block of prose. Contemporary poetry is as likely to be rhymed as unrhymed. The level of diction can be lofty and elegant or it can be spiced with slang, as in Peter Meinke's "The ABC of Aerobics" (text p. 270). In short, the idea of decorum, if it exists at all in contemporary poetry, is open ended.

Thematically, the field for discovering material for poems is also more extensive than ever before. Some of the poems here take as their motive an area of public concern relevant not only to the country of the poet but to an area other than or far more inclusive than a specific nation. We are living in an age that has given new meaning to the word *global,* and North American poetry especially seems to reflect this broadened interest. Other poems, such as Donald Hall's "Letter with No Address," embody a more private concern and voice the particular anxieties and observations of the individual. One point, though, that students should grasp is that our age does not dictate either an introspective poetry bound to extol and explore nature and the human mind or a public poetry pitched for a celebration of reason, country, and the famous. We can, and do, address both public and private issues, and certain poems manage to merge the dialectic of *polis* and *poesis.*

Without question, contemporary poets write about the age-old issues of love and death and the pain of growing up, but these themes, seemingly so essential and enduring, are changed by recent history, technology, and our systems of belief and values. Knowledge of the casualness of death and one's consequent vulnerability, as well as the prospect of mass extinction, also influences the way poets today think and write about death. The world of the contemporary poet is violent and nonsensical, but it is also diverse and exotic.

The poetry included here exhibits a wide range of techniques and levels of diction. The tools for reading poetry learned in earlier chapters will find their fullest application here. On the whole, though, the poems are highly accessible and offer a fine occasion for you and your students to observe the events, vocabulary, and concerns of the day worked into a poetic context. Perhaps that context will enable all of us to articulate more clearly what we desire, value, and wish to protect in this world.

BILLY COLLINS, *Marginalia* (p. 667)

At one time or another, everyone has found the margins of a borrowed paperback or textbook filled with handwritten observations and responses. Collins's meditation elevates this common occurrence to a transformative experience. In Collins's eyes, the scribbles are attempts to participate in and possess the text, to seize "the white perimeter as our own" (line 34). While *marginalia* refers to the handwritten comments one would find in the margins of a book, it can also refer to the seemingly peripheral concerns of life. Collins's poem is deceptively humorous and informal as he comments on the many kinds of marginalia he has enjoyed. Notice how the speaker compares the marginalia to various locations — a battlefield, a shore, a football field. In doing so, he suggests that the page is the site of conquest, reflection, or enthusiasm, depending on whatever the reader brings with him or her. The speaker's realization at the end of the poem is heartbreaking as well as affirmative: some marginalia carry the most urgent of messages — in this case, the loneliness of a girl in love. When the speaker recounts this story, we realize the revelatory power of a few scribbled notes.

POSSIBLE CONNECTION TO ANOTHER SELECTION

Philip Larkin, "A Study of Reading Habits" (text p. 22)

ONLINE RESOURCES (manual p. 327)

CORNELIUS EADY, *The Supremes* (p. 670)

This savagely cynical poem describes the fatalism of schoolchildren, who are "born to be gray" (line 1) — to conform. The poem, which continues to rely on dull-toned colors to paint its picture, is all about a soul-killing conformity that causes children to point out and ridicule any differences that exist between themselves and others. A good place to begin discussion is with the "long scream" (5, 18) that exists in the back of the schoolchildren's minds. Is this a scream of protest? Of angst? Of outrage? Students are likely to have experienced or witnessed the type of divisiveness that exists between the students in this poem. Where does it come from? Where does Eady think it comes from? There are a few possible answers to this question: the parents who "shook their heads and waited" (13) for their children to conform, the sometimes mind-numbing institution of primary education, the children themselves, the undefined "they" of line 25, or something like fate. In what sense can the wigs, lipstick, and sequins of the final lines be considered "self-defense"? How do the last three lines change our understanding of the speaker, or his classmates?

POSSIBLE CONNECTIONS TO OTHER SELECTIONS

Emily Dickinson, "From all the Jails the Boys and Girls" (question #2, following)
Judy Page Heitzman, "The Schoolroom on the Second Floor of the Knitting Mill" (question #1, following)
Louis Simpson, "In the Suburbs" (text p. 84)

CONNECTIONS QUESTIONS IN TEXT (p. 670) WITH ANSWERS

1. Discuss the speakers' memories of school in "The Supremes" and in Judy Page Heitzman's "The Schoolroom on the Second Floor of the Knitting Mill" (p. 446).

    In Heitzman's poem, the schoolteacher, Mrs. Lawrence, is singled out for her cruelty to children. Her desire to keep children "in line" is institutionally sanctioned, but her criticism of the speaker's leadership skills is unthoughtful. There is no "Mrs. Lawrence" to blame in "The Supremes." The children are victimized as much by their own human nature as they are by any one teacher, or by elementary school more generally.

2. In an essay compare the themes of "The Supremes" and Dickinson's "From all the Jails the Boys and Girls" (p. 442).

    The "long scream" of Eady's poem is released and transformed into "Bliss" in Dickinson's poem, but only temporarily. In both cases, school seems to represent a kind of imprisonment; yet in Dickinson's poem, the imprisonment is literal, whereas the prisons in Eady's poem are at least partially psychological or sociological.

ONLINE RESOURCES (manual p. 331)

MARTÍN ESPADA, *Coca-Cola and Coco Frío* (p. 671)

The cultural dichotomy set up by this poem is implicit in the title; a child of Puerto Rican descent is surprised to find that Puerto Ricans are more likely to drink Coca-Cola than to drink coconut milk. The boy is ultimately confused as to why his culture has been overshadowed by one that seems to him shallow by comparison. The implication in the final line is that Puerto Rican culture — as shown through the metaphor of coconut milk — is ultimately more nourishing than the version of American culture that has overshadowed the island. Besides the obvious analogy between coconut milk and mother's milk in the final lines, what other evidence is there in the poem that the two beverages are not to be taken at face value but rather as symbolic of broader issues?

POSSIBLE CONNECTIONS TO OTHER SELECTIONS

Martín Espada, "Latin Night at the Pawnshop" (text p. 62)
Langston Hughes, "Theme for English B" (question #1, following)
Tato Laviera, "AmeRícan" (question #2, following)
Gary Soto, "Mexicans Begin Jogging" (text p. 271)

CONNECTIONS QUESTIONS IN TEXT (p. 671) WITH ANSWERS

1. Compare what the boy in this poem discovers about Puerto Rico with what the speaker learns in Hughes's "Theme for English B" (p. 442).

    In both poems, two cultures mingle, but not altogether comfortably. The boy in Espada's poem marvels at Puerto Rico's inattention to itself in favor of America. There is a judgment implicit in his marveling, though; something has certainly been lost (or wasted) in this process. The speaker of Hughes's poem acknowledges that, though differences and animosity might exist between himself and his white professor, that's the way things are. Their relationship is more symbiotic, as he sees it, than the relationship between the United States and Puerto Rico in Espada's poem, in which Puerto Rican identity is almost completely overshadowed by American consumer culture.

2. Write an essay discussing the images used to describe Puerto Rico and the United States in this poem and in Laviera's "AmeRícan" (p. 269).

    Although the tone of "AmeRícan" shifts throughout the poem, it can be said in general that it is a more positive poem than "Coca-Cola and Coco Frío" in terms of the way U.S. and Puerto Rican cultures mix. One particularly interesting point to contrast in the two poems is the use of music: Pedro Flores, plena-rhythms, and jíbaro in Laviera's poem as opposed to Coca-Cola jingles from World War II in Espada's. Furthermore, the new generation in "AmeRícan" seems much more vital than the "fat boy" of Espada's poem. Language is another way to compare the two poems as a way of examining their treatment of their subject; in Laviera's poem, rules of standard English are ignored and a new hybrid language ensues, whereas in Espada's poem women sing songs "in a language they did not speak" (25).

ONLINE RESOURCES (manual p. 331)

DEBORAH GARRISON, *The Boss* (p. 672)

This poem's speaker provides a portrait of her boss through description of his appearance, his home, and his behavior when she "cried / for twenty minutes straight" (lines 23–24). Students may not realize at first that this is a poem "of love revealed" (35); you might find it helpful to move through the stanzas with them to uncover the "hot, corrective / sting" (12–13) of the speaker's inability to express herself to this admired man.

Comparing this poem to more explicit poems of love or rejection might provide for some good close reading. Possible choices are listed below.

POSSIBLE CONNECTIONS TO OTHER SELECTIONS

Louise Bogan, "Women" (text p. 593)

Edna St. Vincent Millay, "I, Being Born a Woman and Distressed" (text p. 626)

Adrienne Rich, "Living in Sin" (text p. 633)

ONLINE RESOURCES (manual p. 332)

DONALD HALL, *Letter with No Address* (p. 673)

The speaker of this poem, grief-stricken over the death of his wife, writes her a letter in which he describes both the events of his day-to-day life and his lingering emotions over her death. It is a devastatingly honest poem, hiding nothing from the reader. Much of the real heartbreak comes from the speaker's need to share even the most mundane details of his life with his wife. This is not a highflown "poetic" love, but a very deep, real, everyday love. The truly heart-rending irony is that the speaker especially needs his wife now, after, and because of, her death. You might begin by asking how students feel when they read something so personal. It is, after all, a "letter with no address"; do they feel as though they have stumbled upon someone's mail or diary? Is the speaker's purpose in writing the poem part of the way he deals with grief, or does the poem also serve another purpose, perhaps to connect his soul with that of his wife? In either case, where does the reader fit in?

The poem is also noteworthy for its vivid imagery. Much of this imagery serves to connect the world of the living and the world of the dead, or to show how these two worlds overlap. One way of opening up discussion is to have students locate two images in the poem, one that defines the poem's overall tone and another that seems to clash with this tone, then to work through the poet's reasoning for including both images. (For example, how do students reconcile the opening image of dying daffodils with the final image of automobiles as a symbol of lewd sexuality?)

POSSIBLE CONNECTIONS TO OTHER SELECTIONS

Emily Dickinson, "The Bustle in a House" (question #1, following)

Robert Frost, "Home Burial" (question #2, following)

Andrew Hudgins, "Elegy for My Father, Who Is Not Dead" (text p. 242)

AUDIOVISUAL AND ONLINE RESOURCES (manual pp. 299, 333)

CONNECTIONS QUESTIONS IN TEXT (p. 675) WITH ANSWERS

1. Compare how the speaker copes with grief in "Letter with No Address" with the speaker in Dickinson's "The Bustle in a House" (p. 312).

   It might be said that the speaker in Hall's poem is "Sweeping up the heart / And putting Love away" (Dickinson lines 5–6), but it seems as if this process will continue indefinitely, whereas in Dickinson it seems to be a way to return to routine. The speaker in "Letter with No Address" also describes his routine, but this routine doesn't allow him to forget the past. It doesn't seem as though he will ever be able to, yet that fact doesn't seem to be the source of misery in his life. The ongoing presence of his wife is just as inevitable as her death was. Yet there is something "solemn" about his bustling through life just as the bustle in Dickinson's poem "Is solemnest of industries" (3). Is his writing of this poem akin to "The Sweeping up the Heart" in Dickinson's poem?

2. Write an essay on the tone of this poem and Frost's "Home Burial" (p. 343).

   There is nothing of the animosity between Frost's couple in Hall's poem. The tone of "Letter with No Address" is solemn, touching, the world seen clearly through watery eyes. The speakers of Frost's poem are in a different phase of grief. They lash out at one another in bitterness and anger. Two common ways of dealing with loss are to focus on it intensely and to return to routine as though it didn't happen. In Frost's poem, the man and woman cannot understand the way the other has reacted. In Hall's poem, the two ways are reconciled in one person, who relies on both in turn.

JANE HIRSHFIELD, *The Lives of the Heart* (p. 676)

Students may be overwhelmed by the riot of metaphors that make up this poem. It is virtually impossible to comprehend the poem as a whole or to paraphrase its "meaning"; discussion is best undertaken by examining the metaphors individually. Depending on the number of students in your class, you might choose to assign one or two lines to each student and to have the students explore them. As the discussion evolves, try to place these metaphors into categories: In what clusters do the images fall? Does a pattern form before the poem shifts in line 29? One recurrent motif has to do with the formation of the earth, but that motif doesn't necessarily present itself as dominant because it is just as fragmented as the rest of the motifs. Do any metaphors seem particularly incomprehensible? Do we have a clearer understanding of "the lives of the heart" by the end of the poem, or is part of its purpose to show us the difficulty in defining them?

POSSIBLE CONNECTIONS TO OTHER SELECTIONS

Alice Jones, "The Foot" (question #2, following)
Jim Stevens, "Schizophrenia" (question #1, following)

CONNECTIONS QUESTIONS IN TEXT (p. 677) WITH ANSWERS

1. Discuss the use of personification in this poem and Stevens's "Schizophrenia" (p. 129).

   "Schizophrenia" uses personification in a much more systematic way than does "The Lives of the Heart." In Stevens's poem, the house is the subject; it acts as a person throughout the poem. In Hirshfield's poem, personification is one of many ways with which the poet describes the lives of the heart. Its personified aspects don't necessarily stand out any more than its animal or mineral aspects. The lives of the heart seem passive as well as active; personification isn't necessarily more helpful than any other form of metaphor.

2. Write an essay that compares the diction and images of "The Lives of the Heart" and Alice Jones's "The Foot" (p. 208).

   "The Foot" is described largely in scientific terms, gradually moving away from scientific language and toward the final image that reduces the foot to a kind of claw. "The Lives of the Heart" are described partially in scientific terms ("ligneous" in line 1, "calcified" in line 4), but that is only part of the spectrum of imagery associated with them. Perhaps it is a function of the subject; feet seem more easily defined than hearts do because of the endless metaphorical possibilities of the latter. As a result, "The Foot" seems to consider all of the possibilities of feet whereas "The Lives of the Heart" seems to expand the sense of its subject to the point that we are likely to feel distant from the subject at the end of the poem.

LINDA HOGAN, *Hunger* (p. 677)

To begin a discussion of this poem, you may wish to introduce students to the concept of a series poem — that is, a poem that provides readers with some sort of list, including some variations in the list for the sake of interest. Ask students to recreate the list that provides the structure of this poem. Notice how several of the stanzas begin with the word "Hunger" followed by a verb in which hunger is personified, for example, "Hunger crosses" (line 1), "Hunger was" (10), "Hunger knows" (15), and "Hunger lives" (29).

As you talk further about these images of hunger, students may discover some common threads between the descriptions of hunger and the descriptions of men in this poem. Both are said to sit on the ship and cry (lines 3, 9, and 35), and the way both hunger and the men are sated is through female images, particularly images of dolphins who are "like women" taken from the sea so that the men can "have their way with them" (13–14, 44–45).

Although at times it seems that Hunger represents a hunger for food, there are moments in the poem where it becomes clear that Hunger is more than a physical need for nourishment or sustenance. Ask students what they think Hunger represents.

Finally, you may wish to spend some time talking about the final stanza. Consider the line, "the body that wants to live beyond itself" (39). Ask students to interpret this line. Does their understanding of this line help explain the kinds of hunger the poet has in mind? Examine also the imagery at the end of the poem: "wanting to be inside, / to drink / and be held in / the thin, clear milk of the gods" (46–49). What significance is assigned based on gender in this poem, and what ultimately satisfies Hunger and the men in the poem?

POSSIBLE CONNECTIONS TO OTHER SELECTIONS

Sally Croft, "Home-Baked Bread" (question #2, following)

Emily Dickinson, " 'Heaven' — is what I cannot reach!" (text p. 299)

CONNECTION QUESTION IN TEXT (p. 678) WITH ANSWER

2. Discuss the relation between love and hunger in this poem and in Croft's "Home-Baked Bread" (p. 107).

   In both "Hunger" and "Home-Baked Bread," food is viewed as more than food. Both poems see food as a source of comfort, and more important, as something sexual. In "Home-Baked Bread," the imagery is unabashedly sexual as the poet suggests that there is a "cunning triumph" involved in baking bread that metamorphoses into other more overtly sexual triumphs. In "Hunger," Hogan suggests that Hunger is in reality an unattainable longing and desire that can never be satisfied.

PHILIP LEVINE, *Reinventing America* (p. 679)

Students may find that they don't think about the title to this poem until the final lines: the "huge" (line 1) city consisted only of the "village life" (48) of Europe, "brought to America with pure fidelity" (50). The richness of the various villages is present in the litanies that describe the speaker's childhood neighborhood: "Germans, Wops, Polacks, Jews, wild Irish" (36) among "Six bakeries, four barber shops, a five and dime, / twenty beer gardens, a Catholic church with a *shul* / next door" (38–40).

This richness is also present in the adventure of daily living the speaker describes, present in the "animal hungers" (7), the "night workers" (9), the "beautiful young wives" (12) and the rich experience of the "half-blind uncle" (17). America is reinvented between "all the old hatreds" (41) and Uncle Nathan's more personal concerns for "his honor and his ass" (29). "Life was ample" (35) in the city of the speaker's youth, but Levine's keen attention could likely find ample life in many circumstances. Comparisons might help demonstrate Levine's particular angle on his subject: How is his view of the city different from John Keats's in "To One Who Has Been Long in City Pent"? How is his view of America different from that presented by E. E. Cummings, Walt Whitman, R. S. Gwynne in the poems listed below?

POSSIBLE CONNECTIONS TO OTHER SELECTIONS

E. E. Cummings, "next to of course god america I" (text p. 146)

R. S. Gwynn, "The Classroom at the Mall" (text p. 447)
John Keats, "To One Who Has Been Long in City Pent" (text p. 617)
Walt Whitman, From "Song of the Open Road" (text p. 202)

AUDIOVISUAL AND ONLINE RESOURCES (manual pp. 303, 340)

GAIL MAZUR, *Snake in the Grass* (p. 680)

The sudden interaction with a snake at the center of this poem begins a complex train of thought. The abrupt first line thrusts the reader into the narrative just as the speaker is jolted by the sudden slither. The narrative moves from the snake to memories of childhood summers, then to the speaker's fears (line 22–23) and to the larger issue of the conclusion: the speaker's inability to find a "comfortable place" (9) and her desire to love her "small bewildering part in this world" (48). The title of this poem is an expression that refers to a sneak, someone who can't be trusted; in a discussion, you may find it helpful to ask students how the speaker's trust and confidence are undermined by the snake and her reaction to it.

A writing assignment on this poem could provide an opportunity for some close reading; you might try comparing Mazur's treatment of the "silly woman" (39) with the "womanly squall" (30) in Deborah Garrison's "The Boss" and the definitions of womanhood in Louise Bogan's "Women."

POSSIBLE CONNECTIONS TO OTHER SELECTIONS

Louise Bogan, "Women" (text p. 593)
Emily Dickinson, "Much Madness is divinest Sense —" (text p. 304)
Deborah Garrison, "The Boss" (text p. 672)

ONLINE RESOURCES (manual p. 342)

ROBERT MORGAN, *Time's Music* (p. 682)

The sharp focus of this poem expands quickly from the minutiae of "insects in an August field" (line 1) to encompass the enormousness of "space" (3) and "stars" (12). Just as suddenly, the focus narrows to "atoms" (4) and the slow incremental decay suggested by "half-life" (14). The poem shows how the shifting scope of time is present in each of these realms. Time marches on with "tiny chisels" (6), "ticking / away the summer" (10–11). Your students might find it helpful to compare this poem on the passage of time with other poems that present the changes time forces on us with more personal concern, even grief. Examples are included below.

POSSIBLE CONNECTIONS TO OTHER SELECTIONS

Sophie Cabot Black, "August" (text p. 125)
Emily Dickinson, "Oh Sumptuous moment" (text p. 131)
Jonathan Holden, "Cutting Loose on an August Night" (text p. 260)
Charles Simic, "Filthy Landscape" (text p. 110)
Alfred, Lord Tennyson, "Tears, Idle Tears" (text p. 641)

JOAN MURRAY, *Play-By-Play* (p. 683)

This series of hypothetical questions makes us consider the effect of older women gazing at and admiring the bodies of young men. One way to begin discussion is to try to answer each of the questions, read exactly as it is written, as a way to try to determine the speaker's intent in raising the questions. That is, are there implicit answers to the questions? It is a very different thing to ask "I wonder how men would react if they knew that women occasionally scrutinized their bodies" than it is to phrase the questions as the speaker of this poem does, in careful detail with a definite setting. Consider the word "caress" (line 16). If discussion strays too far into general questions of the effect of the female gaze, you might need to bring students back to the specific nature of this poem. It is all about perception, as the final lines make clear. One possible assignment is to have students write a poem from the perspective of these young men, either how they see themselves or how they see the women who are gazing at them. Try to encourage students to recognize the fine line between appreciation of beauty and sexual desire in this poem; how might the poem be different if the poem did not take place at an artist's colony with "marble Naiads" (21) as part of the background?

POSSIBLE CONNECTIONS TO OTHER SELECTIONS

Diane Ackerman, "A Fine, a Private Place" (question #1, following)
Robert Herrick, "To the Virgins, to Make Much of Time" (text p. 64)
Timothy Steele, "An Aubade" (question #2, following)

CONNECTIONS QUESTIONS IN TEXT (p. 684) WITH ANSWERS

1. Compare the voice of the speaker in "Play-By-Play" with that of Ackerman's in "A Fine, a Private Place" (p. 69).

    The speaker of "A Fine, a Private Place" never enters the poem as a first-person subject, unlike the speaker of "Play-By-Play." On the other hand, the speaker of Murray's poem remains distant through her use of hypothetical questions, whereas the speaker of Ackerman's poem narrates not only a series of events but the emotions that attended them. In this sense, Ackerman's poem is more of a "play-by-play," whereas Murray's asks, "what if we were to play?"

2. Write an essay on the speaker's gaze in this poem and in Steele's "An Aubade" (p. 439).

    A primary difference is that the speaker of Steele's poem obviously knows the object of his gaze intimately. There is no sense of invasiveness since she is obviously aware of his gaze and doesn't seem to mind it. The objects of the gaze in Murray's poem, though, do not necessarily know that they are being watched. Of course, the question remains as to whether the women in this poem are watching the men for a kind of sexual gratification or if they are appreciating and discussing them aesthetically. In both cases, the objects of the gaze are rendered in terms of their inherent beauty, but in Murray's poem there is the nagging sense that the men on the softball field might feel violated since they haven't in any way consented to being watched.

ONLINE RESOURCES (manual p. 344)

MARY OLIVER, *Seven White Butterflies* (p. 684)

The long sentence of this poem uses the image of seven butterflies "delicate in a hurry" (line 2) to illustrate that "all eternity / is in the moment" (7–8). Students may find the syntax unfamiliar or difficult; reading aloud will help to clarify its meaning. The familiar literary trope of fleeting existence is exemplified here in brief lives lived fully, "willing / to deliver themselves unto / the universe" (19–21). The butterflies are not sad about the duration of their time on earth; they are still able to "banter / and riot and rise" (14–15). In a discussion, the class might enjoy comparing this poem with others that incorporate similar themes, including those listed below. Do students think the ideas are difficult? Why does Oliver need the butterflies to make it look "so easy" (26)?

Emily Dickinson, "Water, is taught by thirst" (text p. 296)

William Wordsworth, "Lines Written in Early Spring" (text p. 646)

ONLINE RESOURCES (manual p. 345)

RONALD WALLACE, *Dogs* (p. 685)

Discussing dogs, this speaker investigates his long-lasting guilt over accidentally hitting and subsequently killing a dog. He begins with the childhood memory of "hit[ting] one with / a baseball bat. An accident" (lines 1–2). The dog is put to sleep. From there he moves to a series of the most ignoble acts that dogs have inflicted on him, to the one act that gives him the most pain: those dogs "whose slow eyes gazed at me, in love" (14).

The basic form of the Petrarchan sonnet calls attention to the way in which emotion is presented in the poem. At what points does the poem's tone shift, and what is our emotional response when it does? For a speaker who's "been barked at, bitten, nipped, knocked flat, slobbered over, humped, sprayed, beshat" (9–10), it might seem unusual for the most painful act to have been being the recipient of love. But the speaker (presumably an adult looking back) has endured years of "the lasting wrath / of memory's flagellation" (5–6), which the couplet recalls from the octave. He feels guilty.

POSSIBLE CONNECTIONS TO OTHER SELECTIONS

Andrew Hudgins, "Seventeen" (text p. 156)

Jane Kenyon, "The Blue Bowl" (text p. 106)

William Shakespeare, "My mistress' eyes are nothing like the sun" (question #2, following)

John Updike, "Dog's Death" (question #1, following)

CONNECTIONS QUESTIONS IN TEXT (p. 686) WITH ANSWERS

1. Compare this poem's theme with that in John Updike's "Dog's Death" (p. 11).

    Both speakers try to act as if the death of a dog is simply accidental, but their lives (or deaths) resonate anyway, causing pain in the lives of the speakers. Dogs seem helpless in both poems, as though waiting expectantly for humans to do something that will end their lives. But the speaker of Updike's poem doesn't seem to suffer the same "flagellation" of memory that Wallace's speaker suffers. The speaker of "Dogs" suffers guilt; the speaker of "Dog's Death" suffers pity. What do we suffer as we read each poem?

2. In an essay discuss the strategies used in this sonnet and William Shakespeare's "My mistress' eyes are nothing like the sun" (p. 229) to create emotion in the reader.

    In both poems, the speaker relies on humor before expressing tenderness in the final two lines, but the effect is different. Shakespeare's sonnet is humorous throughout; there is no disturbing undercurrent like the one that taints the beginning of Wallace's poem. "Dogs," in a sense, manipulates our emotions more than Shakespeare's sonnet does because it drags us back and forth throughout the poem between deep, affecting pain and a light treatment of its subject.

Suggested Thematic Units for Discussion and Writing

The following thematic units offer a selected list of titles from *Poetry: An Introduction*. These selections are organized around a particular subject or theme and can be used to generate topics for discussion and writing. The lists are intended to be representative rather than exhaustive, suggestive rather than definitive. One or more of the thematic groupings might be useful for encouraging students to create additional thematic categories based on their readings. Students' own perceptions of how the works are linked may prove to be particularly revealing.

HOME AND FAMILY

Margaret Atwood, *Bored*, 72
Margaret Atwood, *February*, 124
Gwendolyn Brooks, *The Mother*, 595
Emily Dickinson, *The Bustle in a House*, 312
Robert Frost, *Home Burial*, 343
Rachel Hadas, *The Red Hat*, 210
Donald Hall, *Letter with No Address*, 673
Robert Hayden, *Those Winter Sundays*, 10
Andrew Hudgins, *Elegy for My Father, Who Is Not Dead*, 242
Galway Kinnell, *After Making Love We Hear Footsteps*, 255
Philip Larkin, *This Be the Verse*, 621
Sharon Olds, *Rite of Passage*, 265
Sylvia Plath, *Daddy*, 630
Theodore Roethke, *My Papa's Waltz*, 217

QUESTIONS FOR DISCUSSION AND WRITING

1. Choose any five works and discuss the treatment of children in them. To what extent are children at the center of the conflicts in the works?

2. Discuss the importance of family grief in "Elegy for My Father, Who Is Not Dead," "The Bustle in a House," and "Home Burial." How does grief reveal character in these works?

3. Compare the views of the young boys in "Rite of Passage" to any three fathers included in the list. How does Olds's assessment of the boys' futures square with their adult counterparts?

4. Compare the themes of "After Making Love We Hear Footsteps" and "The Mother." What accounts for the tone of these poems? Explain whether or not you think either one can be charged with being sentimental.

5. Compare the speakers' attitudes toward their fathers in "Daddy" and "My Papa's Waltz." What role does a sense of awe play in each poem?

6. How does point of view affect the tone of "The Mother" and "Daddy"?

7. How do the speakers of Hall's "Letter with No Address" and Atwood's "Bored" invoke a sense of family? How does loss affect each speaker?

8. Compare the diction of Atwood's "February" and Hayden's "Those Winter Sundays." How do the sounds of the words contribute to each poem's sense of home?

LOVE AND ITS COMPLICATIONS

QUESTIONS FOR DISCUSSION AND WRITING

1. Using Marvell's "To His Coy Mistress" and Ackerman's "A Fine, a Private Place," explore how men and women agree and differ in their expectations about love.

2. Discuss Cummings's "since feeling is first," Herrick's "To the Virgins, to Make Much of Time," and Wilbur's "A Late Aubade" as *carpe diem* poems. (This type of poem is defined on p. 64 of the text.) Pay particular attention to the speakers' tones in the poems. What do they have in common?

3. How might Keats's "La Belle Dame sans Merci" be used as a commentary on Olds's "Sex without Love"?

4. Explain why love fails in Eliot's "The Love Song of J. Alfred Prufrock" and in Olds's "Sex without Love."

5. Compare the humorous tone of Shakespeare's "My mistress' eyes are nothing like the sun" with that of Atwood's "you fit into me."

6. Compare the sensuousness and sensuality in Croft's "Home-Baked Bread" and Song's "The White Porch." What is the effect of the implicit — rather than the explicit — nature of the sexuality in each poem?

7. Consider Dickinson's "Wild Nights — Wild Nights!" and Olds's "Sex without Love" as commenting upon one another. What do these works suggest to you about sexuality and love?

8. Compare the speakers' attitudes toward their loved ones in "since feeling is first" and "My mistress' eyes are nothing like the sun." How does each speaker portray positive images through negatives?

9. Choose several works and discuss how and why you feel they provide useful perspectives on love.

THE NATURAL WORLD

Elizabeth Bishop, *The Fish*, 20
William Blake, *The Tyger*, 214
James Dickey, *Deer Among Cattle*, 104
Emily Dickinson, *A narrow Fellow in the Grass*, 2
Robert Frost, *Design*, 356
Gerard Manley Hopkins, *Pied Beauty*, 613
John Keats, *To Autumn*, 109
Galway Kinnell, *Blackberry Eating*, 176
Alden Nowlan, *The Bull Moose*, 157
William Stafford, *Traveling through the Dark*, 155
William Carlos Williams, *Spring and All*, 645

QUESTIONS FOR DISCUSSION AND WRITING

1. Choose two poems from among Bishop's "The Fish," and Blake's "The Tyger," and discuss the effectiveness of their imagery. To what extent do the poems' meanings go beyond the subjects they describe?

2. Compare Dickinson's "A narrow Fellow in the Grass" with Blake's "The Tyger." How does the speaker's attitude toward the animal in each poem develop and grow complicated? How does your own response to snakes and tigers affect your reading of these poems?

3. Compare the imagery and themes of Keats's "To Autumn" and Williams's "Spring and All." Which poem appeals to you more? Explain why.

4. Discuss Hopkins's attitude toward nature in "Pied Beauty" and Frost's in "Design." What connections does each poem make between nature and God?

5. Contrast the individual's relations to nature in Stafford's "Traveling through the Dark" and Bishop's "The Fish." What attitudes about society are implicitly expressed in each poem?

6. How is nature discussed in Nowlan's "Bull Moose" and Dickey's "Deer Among Cattle"?

7. How do the speakers of "Traveling through the Dark" and "Design" define themselves in terms of the wildlife in their poems?

8. What do "The Tyger" and "The Bull Moose" have in common, in the speakers' assessments?

OTHER CULTURES

Claribel Alegría, *I Am Mirror*, 656
Jimmy Santiago Baca, *Green Chile*, 96
Chitra Banerjee Divakaruni, *Indian Movie, New Jersey*, 162
Gregory Djanikian, *When I First Saw Snow*, 603
Martín Espada, *Coca-Cola and Coco Frío*, 671
Julio Marzán, *Ethnic Poetry*, 158
Pablo Neruda, *Sweetness, Always*, 660
Octavio Paz, *The Street*, 662
Tomas Transtromer, *April and Silence*, 667
Mitsuye Yamada, *A Bedtime Story*, 649

QUESTIONS FOR DISCUSSION AND WRITING

1. Choose a work from the list and explain how it causes you to adjust or reassess your own cultural assumptions in order to understand and appreciate the perspective offered in the work.

2. Compare Espada's treatment of American food with Baca's look at his native "Green Chile." How do these two treatments reflect the speakers' attitudes towards their own culture and American culture?

3. Discuss Baca's and Divakaruni's respective attitudes toward their own cultures in "Green Chile" and "Indian Movie, New Jersey."

4. How are the simplest experiences in Neruda's "Sweetness, Always" and Djanikian's "When I First Saw Snow" rendered significant? Why are they significant?

5. Discuss the tone of Paz's "The Street" and Transtromer's "April and Silence." Despite their brevity each evokes a depth of feeling. What feelings are evoked by the tone of each poem?

6. How do Marzán's "Ethnic Poetry" and Divakaruni's "Indian Movie, New Jersey" comment on American culture while seeking to avoid it?

7. How do generational differences account for the speakers' attitudes toward their cultures in Yamada's "A Bedtime Story" and Divakaruni's "Indian Movie, New Jersey"?

WORK AND BUSINESS

William Blake, *The Chimney Sweeper,* 166
Emily Dickinson, *Success is counted sweetest,* 294
Kenneth Fearing, *AD,* 144
Robert Frost, *After Apple-Picking,* 346
Marilyn Hacker, *Groves of Academe,* 444
M. Carl Holman, *Mr. Z,* 612
Maxine Hong Kingston, *Restaurant,* 193
Katharyn Howd Machan, *Hazel Tells LaVerne,* 61
Marge Piercy, *The Secretary Chant,* 9
Edwin Arlington Robinson, *Richard Cory,* 143

QUESTIONS FOR DISCUSSION AND WRITING

1. Consider attitudes toward success in Dickinson's "Success is counted sweetest" and Robinson's "Richard Cory." How is true success defined and measured in these works?

2. How is humor used to characterize the world of work in Machan's "Hazel Tells LaVerne" and Piercy's "The Secretary Chant"? What serious points are made about work through the use of humor in these selections?

3. Choose three works that, in your opinion, present the most severe judgment upon business as a dehumanizing process.

4. Discuss the significance of the images used in Piercy's "The Secretary Chant" and Blake's "The Chimney Sweeper." What attitudes toward work emerge from these images?

5. How are advertisements and commercialism used as a means to comment upon societal values in Fearing's "AD"?

6. Compare the use of symbolism in Piercy's "The Secretary Chant" and Frost's "After Apple-Picking." How and for what purpose is work symbolized in each poem?

7. Compare the tones of Machan's "Hazel Tells LaVerne" and Dickinson's "Success is counted sweetest." How does each poet use diction to illuminate the speaker's attitudes toward the work presented?

Film, Video, and Audiocassette Resources

The following list organizes resources alphabetically by author. Resources include films and videos, tapes of poets reading their own work, interviews with poets, and films and videos that provide biographical information on a poet or general information on a particular period. This list is not intended to be exhaustive; rather, it is meant to provide a number of exciting possibilities for supplementing and provoking class discussion.

Many of the films and videos in this list will be most readily available from a local retailer. If not, you may contact the distributor by using the addresses and phone numbers provided at the end of the list. The films and videos marked with an asterisk (*) are available for rental from member institutions of the Consortium of College and University Media Centers. For further information, consult *The Educational Film & Video Locater*, published by R. R. Bowker.

AI *[recording]*
1 cassette (29 min.), 1988.
AI reads from her book *Sin* and discusses her writing and mixed ethnicity.
Distributed by New Letters on the Air.

Anna Akhmatova: Selected Poems *[recording]*
1 cassette (60 min.).
Akhmatova reads her poems in Russian. Includes transcript.
Distributed by Interlingua VA.

The Anna Akhmatova File
65 min., color, 1989.
Beta, VHS.
Documentary of the Russian poet. Russian with English subtitles.
Distributed by Facets Multimedia, Inc.

Fear and the Muse: The Story of Anna Akhmatova *[video]*
Color, VHS (60 min.), 1995.
With voices of Claire Bloom and Christopher Reeve.
Distributed by Mystic Fire Video.

Claribel Alegría: Who Raised Up This Prison's Bars? *[recording]*
1 cassette (58 min.), 1988.

Alegría reads her poems in Spanish, with translations by Carolyn Forché.
Distributed by Watershed Tapes.

Claribel Alegría *[recording]*
1 cassette (29 min.), 1991.
The Nicaraguan poet and writer talks about her autobiographical novel *Luisa in Reality Land*.
Distributed by New Letters on the Air.

A. R. Ammons *[recording]*
1 cassette (29 min.), 1984.
Distributed by New Letters on the Air.

Maya Angelou
30 min., color, 1982.
Beta, VHS, 1/2" open reel (EIAJ), 3/4" U-matic cassette.
Robert Cromie talks with the poet. A two-part series.
Distributed by Nebraska Educational Television Network.

Maya Angelou *[recording]*
1 cassette (60 min.).
Angelou reads from "And Still I Rise." With Heywood Hale Broun.
Distributed by Audio-Forum.

291

Maya Angelou [recording]
1 cassette (30 min.).
The poet reads from her poetry, talks about her memoirs, and discusses her refusal to speak for three years as a child.
Distributed by Tapes for Readers.

Maya Angelou [recording]
2 cassettes (150 min.), 1993.
Angelou's biography.
Distributed by Chelsea House Publishers.

Maya Angelou: I Know Why the Caged Bird Sings [recording]
2 cassettes (179 min.).
Angelou's autobiography.
Distributed by Random Audiobooks.

Maya Angelou: Making Magic in the World [recording]
1 cassette (60 min.), 1988.
Presents a trip from the Deep South to the heart of Africa and back again.
Distributed by New Dimensions Radio.

Maya Angelou
See also **"Literature: The Synthesis of Poetry"** on manual p. 313.

Treasury of Matthew Arnold [recording]
1 cassette.
Distributed by Spoken Arts.

Matthew Arnold
See also **"Literature: The Synthesis of Poetry," "Palgrave's Golden Treasury of English Poetry,"** and **"Victorian Poetry"** (film and recording) on manual pp. 313–315.

John Ashbery [recording]
1 cassette (29 min.), 1986.
Distributed by New Letters on the Air.

The Poetry of John Ashbery [recording]
1 cassette (39 min.), 1967.
Part of the YM-YWHA Poetry Center Series.
Distributed by Audio-Forum.

John Ashbery: Songs We Know Best [recording]
1 cassette (60 min.), 1989.
Distributed by Watershed Tapes.

John Ashbery
See also **"The Poet's Voice," "Poets in Person, No. 5"** (recording), and **"Potpourri of Poetry"** on manual p. 314.

The Poetry and Voice of Margaret Atwood [recording]
1 cassette (59 min.), 1977.
Distributed by Caedmon/HarperAudio.

Margaret Atwood Reads [recording]

1 cassette (36 min.).
Distributed by Caedmon/Harper Audio

The Poetry of W. H. Auden, Part I [recording]
1 cassette (50 min.), 1953.
Part of the YM-YWHA Poetry Center Series.
Distributed by Audio-Forum.

The Poetry of W. H. Auden, Part II [recording]
1 cassette (59 min.), 1966.
Part of the YM-YWHA Poetry Center Series.
Distributed by Audio-Forum.

W. H. Auden [recording]
1 cassette (48 min.).
Read by the poet.
Distributed by Spoken Arts.

W. H. Auden and the Writers of the 1930s [recording]
1 cassette (59 min.), 1953.
Read by Stephen Spender.
Distributed by Audio-Forum.

W. H. Auden Reading [recording]
1 cassette.
The poet reads his work.
Distributed by Caedmon/HarperAudio.

W. H. Auden Remembered [recording]
1 cassette (56 min.).
Read by Heywood H. Broun and Stephen Spender. From the Broun Radio Series.
Distributed by Audio-Forum.

W. H. Auden
See also **"The Poet's Voice," "Caedmon Treasury of Modern Poets Reading Their Own Poetry"** and **"Twentieth-Century Poets Reading Their Work"** on manual pp. 312–315.

Jimmy Santiago Baca [recording]
1 cassette (29 min.), 1991.
Distributed by New Letters on the Air.

Amiri Baraka [recording]
1 cassette (29 min.), 1988.
Distributed by New Letters on the Air.

Le Roi Jones/Imamu Amiri Baraka [recording]
1 cassette, 1976.
Distributed by Everett/Edwards.

John Berryman
See **"The Poet's Voice"** on manual p. 314.

Delmore Schwartz, Richard Blackmur, Stephen Spender, and Elizabeth Bishop
1 cassette.
Distributed by the Library of Congress.

Elizabeth Bishop
See **"Voices and Vision"** on manual p. 315.

Essay on William Blake
52 min., color, 1969.
3/4″ U-matic cassette, 16-mm film, special order formats.
A profile of the poet.
Distributed by Indiana University Instructional Support Services.

The Poetry of William Blake *[recording]*
1 cassette.
Distributed by Caedmon/HarperAudio.

Poetry of William Blake *[recording]*
1 cassette.
Distributed by Spoken Arts.

****William Blake***
26 min., color, 1973.
16-mm film.
Hosted by Kenneth Clark. Focuses on Blake's drawings and engravings.
Distributed by Pyramid Film and Video.

William Blake
30 min.
VHS.
A dramatization of Blake's inner world.
Distributed by Insight Media.

William Blake
57 min., color, 1976.
Beta, VHS, 3/4″ U-matic cassette, special order formats.
A biographical portrait.
Distributed by Time-Life Video.

William Blake: The Book of Thel *[recording]*
1 cassette.
Distributed by Audio-Forum.

William Blake: Selected Poems *[recording]*
2 cassettes (180 min.), 1992.
Includes "Tyger! Tyger!" and "A Poison Tree."
Distributed by Blackstone Audio Books.

William Blake: The Marriage of Heaven and Hell
30 min., color, 1984.
3/4″ U-matic cassette.
Dramatizes the life of Blake and his wife Catherine. With Anne Baxter and George Rose.
Distributed by Modern Talking Picture Service.

William Blake: Something About Poetry *[recording]*
1 cassette (22 min.), 1969.
Distributed by Audio-Forum.

William Blake
See also **"Introduction to English Poetry"** and **"Romantic Pioneers"** on manual pp. 313–315.

****William Blake: Poems*** *[recording]*
1 cassette (80 min.).
Distributed by HighBridge.

The Poetry of Robert Bly *[recording]*
1 cassette (38 min.), 1966.
Part of the YM-YWHA Poetry Series.
Distributed by Audio-Forum.

Robert Bly I & II *[recording]*
1 cassette (60 min.), 1979, 1991.
Distributed by New Letters on the Air.

Robert Bly: Booth and Bly, Poets
30 min., color, 1978.
1/2″ open reel (EIAJ), 3/4″ U-matic cassette.
A four-part series of workshops and readings by the poets.
Distributed by Nebraska Educational Television Network.

Robert Bly: An Evening of Poetry *[recording]*
2 cassettes.
Distributed by Sound Horizons.

Robert Bly: Fairy Tales for Men and Women *[recording]*
90 min., 1987.
Bly applies psychoanalytical analysis to poetry.
Distributed by Ally Press.

Robert Bly: For the Stomach — Selected Poems, 1974 *[recording]*
64 min.
Bly reads his poetry.
Distributed by Watershed Tapes.

Robert Bly: The Human Shadow *[recording]*
2 cassettes.
Distributed by Mystic Fire.

Robert Bly: A Man Writes to a Part of Himself
57 min., color, 1978.
3/4″ U-matic cassette, special order formats.
Poetry and conversation with the writer.
Distributed by Intermedia Arts of Minnesota.

Robert Bly: Poetry East and West *[recording]*
140 min., 1983.
Bly gives a poetry lecture, accompanied by the dulcimer.
Distributed by Dolphin Tapes.

Robert Bly: Poetry in Motion
30 min., color, 1981.
Beta, VHS, 3/4″ U-matic cassette.
Video biographies of three poets: Robert Bly, Frederick Marfred, and Thomas McGrath.
Distributed by Intermedia Arts of Minnesota.

Robert Bly: Poetry Reading — An Ancient Tradition [recording]
2 cassettes (150 min.), 1983.
Bly talks about the oral tradition in poetry.
Distributed by Dolphin Tapes.

Robert Bly — A Home in the Dark Grass: Poems & Meditations on Solitudes, Families, Disciplines [recording]
2 cassettes (131 min.), 1991.
Distributed by Ally Press Audio.

Robert Bly: Poems of Kabir [recording]
2 cassettes (1 hour, 59 min.), 1977, 1995.
Distributed by Audio Literature.

Robert Bly: Poems of Kabir [recording]
1 cassette.
Distributed by Ally Press.

Robert Bly: Selected Poems [recording]
2 cassettes (131 min.), 1987.
Distributed by Ally Press.

Robert Bly: The Six Powers of Poetry [recording]
1 cassette (90 min.), 1983.
A lecture from the San Jose Poetry Center.
Distributed by Dolphin Tapes.

Robert Bly
See also **"Moyers: The Power of the Word"** on manual p. 314.

Anne Bradstreet [recording]
1 cassette, 1976.
Distributed by Everett/Edwards.

Joseph Brodsky: A Maddening Space [video]
Color, VHS (60 min.), 1989.
Center for Visual History in association with Channel 4. Produced by Sasha Alpert, directed/written by Lawrence Pitkethly, narrated by Jason Robards. Distributed by Mystic Fire Video.

Joseph Brodsky Reads His Poetry [recording]
1 cassette (30 min.), 1988.
Distributed by Caedmon/HarperAudio.

Joseph Brodsky: Winter [recording]
1 cassette. (64 min.). In Russian and English.
Distributed by Watershed Tapes.

*Gwendolyn Brooks
30 min., b/w, 1966.
3/4″ U-matic cassette, 16-mm film, special order formats.
Brooks talks about her life and poetry.
Distributed by Indiana University Instructional Support Services.

Gwendolyn Brooks I & II [recording]
1 cassette (60 min.), 1988, 1989.
Distributed by New Letters on the Air.

Gwendolyn Brooks Reading Her Poetry [recording]
1 cassette.
Distributed by Caedmon/HarperAudio.

Gwendolyn Brooks
See also **"The Harlem Renaissance and Beyond"** on manual p. 313.

Elizabeth Barrett Browning: Sonnets from the Portuguese [recording]
1 cassette.
Performed by Katherine Cornell and Anthony Quayle.
Distributed by Caedmon/HarperAudio.

Elizabeth Barrett Browning: Sonnets from the Portuguese [recording]
1 cassette.
Read by Penelope Lee.
Distributed by Spoken Arts.

Elizabeth Barrett Browning
See also **"Victorian Poetry"** (film and recording) on manual p. 315.

Robert Browning: "My Last Duchess" & Other Poems [recording]
1 cassette.
Distributed by Caedmon/HarperAudio.

Robert Browning: Selected Poems [recording]
4 cassettes (360 min.).
Read by Frederick Davidson.
Distributed by Blackstone Audio Books.

The Poetry of Browning [recording]
1 cassette.
Distributed by Caedmon/HarperAudio.

*Robert Browning — His Life and Poetry
21 min., color, 1972.
Beta, VHS, 3/4″ U-matic cassette, 16-mm film, special order format.
A dramatization of Browning's life and several of his poems, including **"My Last Duchess."**
Distributed by International Film Bureau.

Treasury of Robert Browning [recording]
1 cassette.
Distributed by Spoken Arts.

Robert Browning
See also **"Victorian Poetry"** (recording) on manual p. 315.

Joseph Bruchac [recording]
1 cassette (29 min.), 1983.
Distributed by New Letters on the Air.

Joseph Bruchac Two [recording]
1 cassette (29 min.), 1993.
Distributed by New Letters on the Air.

Robert Burns: Love and Liberty
38 min., color, 1985.
Beta, VHS, 3/4″ U-matic cassette.
Burns's lyrics are sung and read aloud.
Distributed by Films for the Humanities and
Sciences.

Robert Burns: Love Songs *[recording]*
1 cassette.
Distributed by Spoken Arts.

Robert Burns: The Poetry of Robert Burns &
Border Ballads *[recording]*
1 cassette.
Distributed by Caedmon/HarperAudio.

Robert Burns
See also **"Palgrave's Golden Treasury of**
English Poetry" on manual p. 314.

Lord Byron: Selected Poems *[recording]*
2 cassettes (180 min.).
Read by Frederick Davidson.
Distributed by Blackstone Audio Books.

The Essential Byron *[recording]*
1 cassette.
Unabridged edition.
Distributed by Listening Library.

The Poetry of Byron *[recording]*
1 cassette.
Distributed by Caedmon/HarperAudio.

Treasury of George Gordon, Lord Byron
[recording]
1 cassette.
Distributed by Spoken Arts.

George Gordon, Lord Byron
See also **"English Literature: Romantic**
Period," "English Romantic Poetry,"
"Palgrave's Golden Treasury of
English Poetry," and **"The Young**
Romantics" on manual pp. 312–316.

Treasury of Lewis Carroll *[recording]*
1 cassette.
Distributed by Spoken Arts.

Lewis Carroll
See also **"Victorian Poetry"** (recording) on
manual p. 315.

As If: Poems Selected and Read by John Ciardi
[recording]
1 cassette, 1955.
Distributed by Smithsonian/Folkways Recordings.

Hans Juergensen & John Ciardi: World War II
[recording]
1 cassette (29 min.).
Distributed by New Letters on the Air.

The Poetry of John Ciardi *[recording]*
1 cassette (56 min.), 1964.
Distributed by Audio-Forum.

John Ciardi *[recording]*
1 cassette, 1991.
Distributed by Audio-Forum.

John Ciardi, I & II *[recording]*
1 cassette (60 min.), 1983, 1984.
The author reads poems about war, Italy,
and aging.
Distributed by New Letters on the Air.

John Ciardi: Twentieth-Century Poets in
English: Recordings of Poets Reading
Their Own Poetry, No. 27 *[recording]*
Distributed by the Library of Congress.

John Ciardi: You Read to Me, I'll Read to You
[recording]
1 cassette, 1992.
Distributed by Spoken Arts.

Amy Clampitt: The Dahlia Gardens *[recording]*
1 cassette (56 min.), 1986.
Distributed by Watershed Tapes.

Lucille Clifton *[recording]*
1 cassette (29 min.), 1989.
Distributed by New Letters on the Air.

Lucille Clifton: The Place for Keeping *[recording]*
1 cassette (45 min.).
Distributed by Watershed Tapes.

Judith Ortiz Cofer
See also **"Birthright: Growing Up His-**
panic" on manual p. 312.

Samuel Taylor Coleridge: The Fountain and
the Cave
57 min., color, 1974.
Beta, VHS, 3/4″ U-matic cassette.
A biography of the poet, filmed on location.
Narrated by Paul Scofield.
Distributed by Pyramid Film and Video.

The Poetry of Coleridge *[recording]*
1 cassette.
Distributed by Caedmon/HarperAudio.

Samuel Taylor Coleridge: The Rime of the
Ancient Mariner & Other Poems
[recording]
1 cassette.
Distributed by Spoken Arts.

Samuel Taylor Coleridge: The Rime of the
Ancient Mariner & Other Great Poems
[recording]
2 cassettes.
From the Cassette Bookshelf Series.
Distributed by Listening Library.

Samuel Taylor Coleridge
See also **"English Romantic Poetry," "Palgrave's Golden Treasury of English Poetry,"** and **"Romantic Pioneers"** on manual pp. 312–315.

The Poetry of Countee Cullen [recording]
1 cassette.
Distributed by Caedmon/HarperAudio.

Countee Cullen
See also **"The Harlem Renaissance and Beyond"** and **"Modern American Poetry"** on manual p. 313.

Countee Cullen: The Lost Zoo [recording]
1 cassette.
Distributed by Caedmon/HarperAudio.

E. E. Cummings Reading His Poetry [recording]
1 cassette.
Distributed by Caedmon/HarperAudio.

E. E. Cummings Reads [recording]
1 cassette (60 min.), 1987.
From The Poet Anniversary Series.
Distributed by Caedmon/HarperAudio.

E. E. Cummings Reads His Collected Poetry, 1920–1940, & Prose [recording]
2 cassettes (79 min.).
Distributed by Caedmon/HarperAudio.

E. E. Cummings Reads His Collected Poetry, 1943–1958 [recording]
2 cassettes.
Distributed by Caedmon/HarperAudio.

*E. E. Cummings: The Making of a Poet
24 min., 1978.
Beta, VHS, 3/4″ U-matic cassette.
A profile of Cummings told in his own words.
Distributed by Films for the Humanities and Sciences.

E. E. Cummings: Nonlectures [recordings]
6 cassettes.
(1) I & My Parents; (2) I & Their Son; (3) I & Self-discovery; (4) I & You & Is; (5) I & Now & Him; (6) I & Am & Santa Claus.
Distributed by Caedmon/HarperAudio.

Poems of E. E. Cummings [recording]
1 cassette (60 min.), 1981.
Part of the Poetic Heritage Series.
Distributed by Summer Stream.

E. E. Cummings: Twentieth-Century Poetry in English: Recordings of Poets Reading Their Own Poetry, No. 5 [recording]
Distributed by the Library of Congress.

E. E. Cummings
See also **"Poetry for People Who Hate Poetry," "Inner Ear, Parts 5 and 6,"** and **"Caedmon Treasury of Modern Poets Reading Their Own Poetry"** on manual pp. 312–314.

James Dickey [video]
Color, VHS (30 min.), 1989.
A production of the University of South Carolina and the South Carolina ETV Network.
Distributed by PBS Video.

James Dickey [recording]
1 cassette (29 min.), 1987.
Distributed by New Letters on the Air.

James Dickey [recording]
1 cassette, 1976.
Distributed by Tapes for Readers.

James Dickey Reads His Poetry & Prose [recording]
1 cassette, 1972.
Distributed by Caedmon/HarperAudio.

The Poems of James Dickey [recording]
1 cassette (52 min.), 1967.
Distributed by Spoken Arts.

Emily Dickinson: A Brighter Garden [recording]
1 cassette (15 min.).
Distributed by Spoken Arts.

Emily Dickinson: A Self-Portrait [recording]
2 cassettes (90 min.).
Distributed by Caedmon/HarperAudio, Filmic Archives.

Fifty Poems of Emily Dickinson [recording]
1 cassette (45 min.).
Distributed by Dove Audio.

Emily Dickinson: Seventy-Five Poems [recording]
2 cassettes (2 hours, 15 min.), 1990.
Distributed by Recorded Books.

*Emily Dickinson: The Belle of Amherst
90 min., color, 1980.
Beta, VHS, 3/4″ U-matic cassette.
With Julie Harris.
Distributed by Cifex Corporation.

*Emily Dickinson: A Certain Slant of Light
29 min., color, 1978.
Beta, VHS, 3/4″ U-matic cassette, 16-mm film.
Explores Dickinson's life and environment. Narrated by Julie Harris.
Distributed by Pyramid Film and Video.

*Emily Dickinson: Magic Prison — A Dialogue
    Set to Music*
35 min., color, 1969.
Beta, VHS, 3/4″ U-matic cassette, 16-mm
    film.
Dramatizes the letters between Dickinson
    and Colonel T. W. Higginson. With an
    introduction by Archibald MacLeish
    and music by Ezra Laderman.
Distributed by Britannica Films.

Emily Dickinson: Poems and Letters
    [recording]
2 cassettes.
Distributed by Recorded Books.

Emily Dickinson: Selected Poems [recording]
4 cassettes (360 min.), 1993.
Read by Mary Woods.
Distributed by Blackstone Audio Books.

Poems and Letters of Emily Dickinson
    [recording]
1 cassette.
Distributed by Caedmon/HarperAudio.

*Emily Dickinson
22 min., color, 1978.
Beta, VHS, 3/4″ U-matic cassette.
A film about the poet and her poems. Part of
    the "Authors" series.
Distributed by Journal Films Inc.

Emily Dickinson [recording]
1 cassette.
Distributed by Recorded Books.

Emily Dickinson Recalled in Song [recording]
1 cassette (30 min.).
Distributed by Audio-Forum.

Poems by Emily Dickinson [recording]
2 cassettes (236 min.), 1986.
Distributed by Audio Book Contractors.

Poems of Emily Dickinson [recording]
1 cassette.
Distributed by Spoken Arts.

*Poems of Emily Dickinson & Lizette
    Woodworth Reese [recording]*
1 cassette (60 min.), 1981.
Unabridged edition. Part of the "Poetic
    Heritage Series."
Distributed by Summer Stream.

Emily Dickinson
See also **"Inner Ear, Parts 3 and 4,"
    "Introduction to English Poetry,"
    "Voices and Vision," and "With a
    Feminine Touch"** on manual pp.
    313–316.

Essential Donne [recording]
From the Essential Poets Series.
Distributed by the Listening Library.

John Donne
40 min., color.
VHS.
Discusses the poet's life and works.
Distributed by Insight Media.

John Donne: Love Poems [recording]
1 cassette.
Distributed by Recorded Books.

John Donne: Selected Poems [recording]
2 cassettes (180 min.), 1992.
Read by Frederick Davidson.
Distributed by Blackstone Audio Books.

The Love Poems of John Donne [recording]
1 cassette.
Distributed by Caedmon/HarperAudio.

Treasury of John Donne [recording]
1 cassette.
Distributed by Spoken Arts.

John Donne
See also **"Metaphysical and Devotional
    Poetry"** and **"Palgrave's Golden
    Treasury of English Poetry"** on manu-
    al pp. 313–314.

H. D. [Hilda Doolittle]: Helen in Egypt
    [recording]
1 cassette (39 min.).
Part of the Archive Series.
Distributed by Watershed Tapes.

Michael Drayton
See **"Medieval and Elizabethan Poetry"** on
    manual p. 313.

*Paul Laurence Dunbar: American Poet
14 min., color, 1966.
Beta, VHS, 3/4″ U-matic cassette, 16-mm
    film, open-captioned.
A biographical sketch of the poet.
Distributed by Phoenix/BFA Films.

*Paul Laurence Dunbar
22 min., color, 1973.
Beta, VHS, 3/4″ U-matic cassette.
A biographical tribute to the poet. Directed
    by Carlton Moss.
Distributed by Pyramid Film and Video.

*The Mysterious Mr. Eliot
62 min., color, 1973.
Beta, VHS, 3/4″ U-matic cassette, 16-mm
    film.
A biographical film about the poet.
Distributed by Insight Media and CRM
    Films.

T. S. Eliot: Selected Poems *[recording]*
1 cassette (49 min.), 1971.
The author reads his poetry, including "The Waste Land."
Distributed by Caedmon/HarperAudio.

T. S. Eliot: Four Quartets *[recording]*
1 cassette.
Distributed by Caedmon/HarperAudio.

T. S. Eliot: Twentieth-Century Poetry in English: Recordings of Poets Reading Their Own Poetry, No. 3 *[recording]*
Distributed by the Library of Congress.

T. S. Eliot and George Orwell *[recording]*
1 cassette (41 min.), 1953.
Read by Stephen Spender.
Distributed by Caedmon/HarperAudio.

T. S. Eliot Reading "The Love Song of J. Alfred Prufrock" *[recording]*
1 cassette.
Distributed by Caedmon/HarperAudio.

T. S. Eliot Reading "The Waste Land" & Other Poems
1 cassette.
Distributed by Caedmon/HarperAudio.

T. S. Eliot
See also **"Modern American Poetry," "The Poet's Voice," "Voices and Vision,"** and **"Caedmon Treasury of Modern Poets Reading Their Own Poetry"** on manual pp. 312–315.

Carolyn Forché *[recording]*
1 cassette (29 min.), 1989.
Distributed by New Letters on the Air.

Carolyn Forché: Ourselves or Nothing *[recording]*
1 cassette (58 min.), 1983.
Distributed by Watershed Tapes.

Afterglow: A Tribute to Robert Frost
35 min., color, 1989.
Beta, VHS, 3/4″ U-matic cassette.
Starring and directed by Burgess Meredith.
Distributed by Pyramid Film and Video.

Robert Frost *[recording]*
1 cassette, 1981.
Includes "The Pasture" and "Stopping by Woods on a Snowy Evening."
Distributed by the Library of Congress

*Robert Frost: A First Acquaintance
16 min., color, 1974.
Beta, VHS, 3/4″ U-matic cassette, 16-mm film.
An examination of Frost's life through his poems.
Distributed by Films for the Humanities and Sciences.

Frost and Whitman
30 min., b/w, 1963.
Beta, VHS, 1/2″ open reel (EIAJ), 3/4″ U-matic cassette, 2″ quadraplex open reel.
Will Geer performs excerpts from the two poets' works.
Distributed by New York State Education Department.

An Interview with Robert Frost
30 min., b/w, 1952.
Beta, VHS, 3/4″ U-matic cassette.
Bela Kornitzer interviews Frost, who reads from his poetry.
Distributed by Social Studies School Service.

*Robert Frost: A Lover's Quarrel with the World
40 min., b/w, 1970.
Beta, VHS, 3/4″ U-matic cassette, 16-mm film.
A documentary film on Frost's philosophic and artistic ideas.
Distributed by Phoenix/BFA Films.

*Robert Frost
10 min., color, 1972.
Beta, VHS, 3/4″ U-matic cassette, 16-mm film.
A biographical sketch of the poet.
Distributed by AIMS Media Inc.

Robert Frost in Recital *[recording]*
1 cassette.
Distributed by Caedmon/HarperAudio.

Robert Frost Reads *[recording]*
1 cassette (60 min.), 1987.
From The Poet Anniversary Series.
Distributed by Caedmon/HarperAudio.

Robert Frost Reads His Poems *[recording]*
1 cassette (55 min.), 1965.
Distributed by Audio-Forum.

Robert Frost Reads His Poetry *[recording]*
1 cassette (48 min.).
Distributed by Recorded Books.

Robert Frost Reads "The Road Not Taken" & Other Poems *[recording]*
1 cassette.
Distributed by Caedmon/HarperAudio.

*Robert Frost's New England
22 min., color, 1976.
Beta, VHS, 3/4″ U-matic cassette, 16-mm film, special order formats. Ancillary materials available.
Explores some of Frost's poetry relating to New England and its seasons.
Distributed by Churchill Media.

*Robert Frost: Twentieth-Century Poetry in
  English: Recordings of Poets Reading
  Their Own Poetry, No. 6 [recording]*
Distributed by the Library of Congress.

Robert Frost
See also **"Literature: The Synthesis of
  Poetry," "Modern American Poetry,"
  "Poetry by Americans," "The Poet's
  Voice," "Voices and Vision,"** and
  **"Caedmon Treasury of Modern Poets
  Reading Their Own Poetry"** on manu-
  al pp. 312–315.

Alice Fulton [recording]
1 cassette (29 min.).
Distributed by New Letters on the Air.

Allen Ginsberg [recording]
1 cassette (29 min.), 1988.
The author talks about the Beat movement
  and his ongoing battle against censorship.
Distributed by New Letters on the Air.

Allen Ginsberg: First Blues [recording]
Recorded in the 1970s, these songs represent
  Ginsberg's earliest experiments combin-
  ing improvised text with music.
Distributed by Poet's Audio Center.

Allen Ginsberg [video]
Color, Beta, VHS, 3/4″ U-matic cassette (50
  min.), Writers on Writing Series.
Distributed by The Roland Collection.

Allen Ginsberg: When the Muse Calls, Answer!
  [video]
Color, VHS (30 min.).
Distributed by Filmic Archives.

*Allen Ginsberg: Potpourri of Poetry —
  Summer, Nineteen Seventy-Five
  [recording]*
1 cassette.
Distributed by Caedmon/HarperAudio.

The Life and Times of Allen Ginsberg
83 min., color, 1993.
VHS.
Chronicles the life of the poet with commen-
  tary from Abbie Hoffman, Ken Kesey,
  Jack Kerouac, Joan Baez, and others.
Distributed by First Run/Icarus Films.

Allen Ginsberg
See also **"Fried Shoes, Cooked Diamonds,"
  "The Poet's Voice," "Potpourri of
  Poetry," "A Movable Feast," "Spoken
  Arts Treasury of American Jewish
  Poets Reading Their Poems, Vol. VI,"**
  and **"Poets in Person"** on manual pp.
  312–315.

*Marilyn Hacker: The Poetry and Voice of
  Marilyn Hacker [recording]*
1 cassette.
Distributed by Caedmon/HarperAudio.

Donald Hall: Prose and Poetry [recording]
2 cassettes (93 hrs.), 1997.
Distributed by Audio Bookshelf.

Donald Hall [recording]
1 cassette (29 min.), 1987.
Distributed by New Letters on the Air.

Donald Hall [recording]
1 cassette (29 min.), 1987.
Distributed by Spoken Arts.

*Donald Hall and Jane Kenyon: A Life
  Together*
60 min., color.
VHS.
Bill Moyers interviews these husband-and-
  wife poets at their home in New
  Hampshire.
Distributed by Films for the Humanities and
  Sciences.

Donald Hall: Names of Horses [recording]
1 cassette (53 min.), 1986.
Distributed by Watershed Tapes.

The Poetry of Donald Hall [recording]
1 cassette (26 min.), 1964.
Part of the YM-YWHA Poetry Center Series.
Distributed by Audio-Forum.

The Poetry of Thomas Hardy [recording]
1 cassette.
Distributed by Caedmon/HarperAudio.

Thomas Hardy
See also **"Introduction to English Poetry,"
  "Romantics and Realists,"** and
  "Victorian Poetry" (recording) on
  manual pp. 313–315.

Joy Harjo [recording]
1 cassette (29 min.), 1991.
The author plays the saxophone and reads
  from her work.
Distributed by New Letters on the Air.

Joy Harjo & Barney Bush [recording]
1 cassette (29 min.), 1983.
Native American poets Harjo and Bush read
  from their work.
Distributed by New Letters on the Air.

Joy Harjo: Furious Light [recording]
1 cassette (56 min.), 1986.
Selected poems with musical accompani-
  ment.
Distributed by Watershed Tapes.

Michael S. Harper: Hear Where Coltrane Is
   [recording]
1 cassette (60 min.), 1971, 1984. Poems
   accompanied by music.
Distributed by Watershed Tapes.

Robert Hass: A Story About the Body
   [recording]
1 cassette, 1988.
Distributed by Watershed Tapes.

William Hathaway [recording]
1 cassette (29 min.), 1984.
Distributed by New Letters on the Air.

Seamus Heaney [recording]
2 cassettes, 1990.
Heaney reads his own work and a personal
   selection of classic poems by
   Shakespeare, Marvell, Hardy, Yeats,
   Blake, and others.
Distributed by Poet's Audio Center.

Seamus Heaney: Stepping Stones [recording]
1 cassette (72 min.), 1996.
Distributed by Penguin Audiobooks.

*Seamus Heaney: Poet in Limboland
29 min., color, 1972.
Beta, VHS, 3/4″ U-matic cassette, 16-mm
   film.
Heaney discusses his poetry and political
   problems in Ireland.
Distributed by Films for the Humanities and
   Sciences.

Anthony Hecht I & II [recording]
1 cassette (60 min.), 1985, 1988.
Distributed by New Letters on the Air.

George Herbert
See "**Introduction to English Poetry**" and
   "**Metaphysical and Devotional
   Poetry**" on manual p. 313.

Robert Herrick
See "**Palgrave's Golden Treasury of
   English Poetry**" on manual p. 314.

Linda Hogan [recording]
1 cassette (29 min.), 1990.
Distributed by New Letters on the Air.

Poetry of John Hollander [recording]
1 cassette, (29 min.), 1967.
Part of the YM-YWHA Poetry Center Series.
Distributed by Audio-Forum.

John Hollander
See also "**Spoken Arts Treasury of
   American Jewish Poets Reading Their
   Poems, Vol. VII**" (recording) on manu-
   al p. 315.

The Poetry of Gerard Manley Hopkins
   [recording]
1 cassette.
Distributed by Caedmon/HarperAudio.

*Gerard Manley Hopkins: The Wreck of the
   Deutschland [recording]*
1 cassette.
Distributed by Audio-Forum.

Gerard Manley Hopkins
See also "**Romantics and Realists**" and
   "**Victorian Poetry**" (recording) on
   manual p. 315.

*A. E. Housman: "A Shropshire Lad" & Other
   Poetry [recording]*
1 cassette.
Distributed by Caedmon/HarperAudio.

A. E. Housman
See also "**Romantics and Realists**" and
   "**Victorian Poetry**" (recording) on
   manual p. 315.

*Langston Hughes
24 min., color, 1971.
Beta, VHS, 3/4″ U-matic cassette, 16-mm
   film.
A biographical sketch of the poet.
Distributed by Carousel Film & Video.

Langston Hughes: The Dream Keeper [video]
Color, VHS (60 min.), 1988.
Distributed by the Annenberg/CPB Collec-
   tion.

*Langston Hughes: Looking for Langston
   [video]*
Color, VHS (45 min.), 1992. Produced by
   Isaac Julien.
Distributed by Water Bearer Films.

Langston Hughes Reads [recording]
1 cassette (50 min.).
Distributed by Caedmon/HarperAudio,
   Filmic Archives.

*Langston Hughes Reads and Talks about His
   Poems [recording]*
1 cassette (42 min.).
Distributed by Dove Audio.

*Langston Hughes: Dream Keeper and Other
   Poems [recording]*
1 cassette, 1955.
Distributed by Smithsonian/Folkways Recordings.

*Langston Hughes: The Making of a Poet
   [recording]*
1 cassette (30 min.).
Read by the poet.
Distributed by National Public Radio.

Langston Hughes: Poetry & Reflections
[recording]
1 cassette.
Performed by the author.
Distributed by Caedmon/HarperAudio.

Langston Hughes Reads and Talks about His Poems [recording]
1 cassette.
Includes "The Negro Speaks of Rivers" and "Dream Boogie."
Distributed by Spoken Arts.

The Poetry of Langston Hughes [recording]
2 cassettes.
Performed by Ruby Dee and Ossie Davis.
Distributed by Caedmon/HarperAudio.

The Voice of Langston Hughes: Selected Poetry and Prose [recording]
1 cassette or CD (38 min.).
Selections from the years 1925–1932. The author reads poetry from *The Dream Keeper and Other Poems* and *Simple Speaks His Mind,* and he narrates his text from *The Story of Jazz, Rhythms of the World,* and *The Glory of Negro History.*
Distributed by Smithsonian/Folkways Recordings.

Langston Hughes: Simple Stories [recording]
1 cassette.
Performed by Ossie Davis.
Distributed by Caedmon/HarperAudio.

Langston Hughes
See also **"Harlem Renaissance: The Black Poets," "The Harlem Renaissance and Beyond," "Modern American Poetry,"** and **"Voices and Vision"** and **"Twentieth-Century Poets Reading Their Work"** on manual pp. 313–315.

Ted Hughes: Selections from Crow and Wodwo [recording]
1 cassette (47 min.), 1979.
Distributed by Caedmon/HarperAudio.

Five Poems by Ted Hughes
20 min., color.
VHS.
Read and introduced by the author.
Distributed by Films for the Humanities and Sciences.

Randall Jarrell: The Bat Poet [recording]
1 cassette.
Distributed by Caedmon/HarperAudio.

The Poetry of Randall Jarrell [recording]
1 cassette (67 min.), 1963.
Part of the YM-YWHA Poetry Center Series.
Distributed by Audio-Forum.

Randall Jarrell Reads and Discusses His Poems against War [recording]
1 cassette.
Distributed by Caedmon/HarperAudio.

Randall Jarrell
See also **"The Poet's Voice"** on manual p. 314.

Ben Jonson
Poetry of the Early Seventeenth Century [recording]
1 cassette.
Distributed by Spoken Arts.

Donald Justice: "Childhood" & Other Poems [recording]
1 cassette (55 min.), 1985.
Distributed by Watershed Tapes.

Donald Justice I & II [recording]
1 cassette (60 min.), 1984, 1989.
Distributed by New Letters on the Air.

*John Keats — His Life and Death
55 min., color, 1973.
Beta, VHS, 3/4″ U-matic cassette, 16-mm film.
Extended version of **"John Keats — Poet"** (see below). Explores the poet's affair with Fanny Browne and the events surrounding his death. Written by Archibald MacLeish.
Distributed by Britannica Films.

*John Keats — Poet
31 min., color, 1973.
Beta, VHS, 3/4″ U-matic cassette, 16-mm film.
A biography of the poet, with excerpts from his letters and poems. Written by Archibald MacLeish.
Distributed by Britannica Films.

John Keats: Selected Poems [recording]
2 cassettes (180 min.), 1993.
Read by Frederick Davidson.
Distributed by Blackstone Audio Books.

John Keats: Odes [recording]
1 cassette.
Distributed by Audio-Forum.

The Poetry of Keats [recording]
1 cassette.
Distributed by Caedmon/HarperAudio.

Treasury of John Keats [recording]
1 cassette.
Distributed by Spoken Arts.

John Keats
See also **"English Literature: Romantic Period," "Palgrave's Golden Treasury**

of English Poetry," and **"The Young Romantics"** on manual pp. 312–316.

X. J. Kennedy: Is Seeing Believing?[recording]
1 cassette (60 min.), 1985.
Distributed by Watershed Tapes.

Jane Kenyon [recording]
1 cassette, 1987.
Distributed by New Letters on the Air.

Maxine Hong Kingston[recording]
1 cassette, 1986.
Interview.
Distributed by American Audio Prose Library.

The Stories of Maxine Hong Kingston
54 min., color, 1990.
VHS.
Kingston discusses her perspective of the "Great American Melting Pot."
Distributed by University of Washington Educational Media Collection.

Galway Kinnell I & II [recording]
1 cassette (60 min.), 1982, 1991.
Distributed by New Letters on the Air.

The Poetry of Galway Kinnell [recording]
1 cassette (33 min.), 1965.
Part of the YM-YWHA Poetry Center Series.
Distributed by Audio-Forum.

The Poetry & Voice of Galway Kinnell [recording]
1 cassette.
Distributed by Caedmon/HarperAudio.

Galway Kinnell
See also **"Moyers: The Power of the Word"** on manual p. 314.

Carolyn Kizer: An Ear to the Earth [recording]
1 cassette (63 min.), 1977.
Distributed by Watershed Tapes.

Carolyn Kizer [recording]
1 cassette (29 min.), 1985.
Distributed by New Letters on the Air.

Carolyn Kizer: Reading Her Poetry [recording]
1 cassette.
Distributed by Sound Photosynthesis.

Carolyn Kizer: Selected Poems [recording]
1 cassette (63 min.), 1977.
Distributed by Watershed Tapes.

Etheridge Knight I [recording]
1 cassette (29 min.), 1986.
Distributed by New Letters on the Air.

Etheridge Knight II [recording]
1 cassette (29 min.), 1989.
Distributed by New Letters on the Air.

Etheridge Knight: So My Soul Can Sing [recording]
1 cassette (50 min.).
Distributed by Watershed Tapes.

Ted Kooser [recording]
1 cassette (29 min.), 1984.
Distributed by New Letters on the Air.

Maxine Kumin: Progress Report [recording]
1 cassette (42 min.), 1976.
Distributed by Watershed Tapes.

Maxine Kumin I & II [recording]
1 cassette (60 min.), 1980, 1987.
Distributed by New Letters on the Air.

Maxine Kumin
See also **"Poets in Person, No. 2"** (recording) on manual p. 314.

Poems of D. H. Lawrence [recording]
1 cassette (36 min.).
Distributed by Spoken Arts.

Li-Young Lee: The City in Which I Love You [recording]
1 cassette (29 min.), 1990.
Reads from his book which was the year's Lamont Poetry Selection.
Distributed by New Letters on the Air.

Li-Young Lee
See also **"A Movable Feast"** on manual p. 313.

Denise Levertov [recording]
1 cassette (29 min.), 1983.
The author reads her poems and discusses political activism and the responsibility of a writer.
Distributed by New Letters on the Air.

Denise Levertov: The Acolyte [recording]
1 cassette (63 min.), 1985.
Distributed by Watershed Tapes.

Poetry: Denise Levertov and Charles Olson
30 min., b/w, 1966.
3/4″ U-matic cassette, 16-mm film, special order formats.
An introduction to the two poets' work.
Distributed by Indiana University Instructional Support Services.

The Poetry of Denise Levertov [recording]
1 cassette (37 min.), 1965.
Part of the YM-YWHA Poetry Center Series.
Distributed by Audio-Forum.

Denise Levertov
See also **"Spoken Arts Treasury of American Jewish Poets Reading Their Poems, Vol. V"** (recording) on manual p. 315.

Philip Levine [recording]
1 cassette (29 min.), 1986.
Distributed by New Letters on the Air.

Philip Levine: Hear Me [recording]
1 cassette (62 min.), 1977.
Features selected poems.
Distributed by Watershed Tapes, Audio-Forum.

The Poetry and Voice of Philip Levine
[recording]
1 cassette.
Distributed by Caedmon/HarperAudio.

Philip Levine
See also **"Spoken Arts Treasury of American Poets Reading Their Poems, Vol. II"** (recording) on manual p. 315.

Henry Wadsworth Longfellow: The Best-Loved Poems of Longfellow [recording]
1 cassette (55 min.), 1996. Read by Hal Holbrook.
Distributed by Caedmon/HarperAudio.

Henry Wadsworth Longfellow: Songs of Hiawatha and More Poems
[recording]
3 cassettes (3 hrs., 9 min.).
Distributed by Audio Book Contractors.

Treasury of Henry Wadsworth Longfellow
[recording]
1 cassette (54 min.), 1986.
Distributed by Spoken Arts.

Audre Lorde [recording]
1 cassette (29 min.), 1979.
The author reads her poetry and discusses her ideas about poetry and her experiences in West Africa.
Distributed by New Letters on the Air.

Audre Lorde: Shorelines [recording]
1 cassette (53 min.), 1985.
Distributed by Watershed Tapes.

*Poetry — Richard Wilbur and Robert Lowell
30 min., b/w, 1966.
3/4″ U-matic cassette, 16-mm film, special order formats.
Interviews with the two poets.
Distributed by Indiana University Instructional Support Services.

The Poetry of Robert Lowell [recording]
1 cassette (28 min.), 1968.
Part of the YM-YWHA Poetry Center Series.
Distributed by Audio-Forum.

Robert Lowell: Twentieth-Century Poetry in English: Recordings of Poets Reading

Their Own Poetry, Nos. 11 and 32–33
[recording]
Distributed by the Library of Congress.

Robert Lowell
"Voices and Vision" on manual p. 000.

Archibald MacLeish Reads His Poetry
[recording]
1 cassette.
Distributed by Caedmon/HarperAudio.

Archibald MacLeish: Twentieth-Century Poetry in English: Recordings of Poets Reading Their Own Poetry: Nine Pulitzer Prize Poets, No. 29 [recording]
Distributed by the Library of Congress.

Archibald MacLeish
See also **"Caedmon Treasury of Modern Poets Reading Their Own Poetry"** on manual p. 312.

Christopher Marlowe: Elizabethan Love Poems
[recording]
1 cassette (50 min.).
Unabridged edition.
Distributed by Spoken Arts.

Christopher Marlowe
See also **"Medieval and Elizabethan Poetry"** and **"Palgrave's Golden Treasury of English Poetry"** on manual pp. 313–314.

Andrew Marvell: Ralph Richardson Reads Andrew Marvell [recording]
1 cassette.
Distributed by Audio-Forum.

Andrew Marvell
See also **"Metaphysical and Devotional Poetry"** on manual p. 313.

James Merrill: Reflected Houses
[recording]
1 cassette (60 min.), 1988.
Distributed by Watershed Tapes.

James Merrill: Voices from Sandover
116 min., color.
A dramatic adaptation of Merrill's "The Changing Light at Sandover" and a summation of the poetic thought of this influential American poet. The cassette concludes with an interview of Merrill by Helen Vendler.
Distributed by Films for the Humanities and Sciences.

James Merrill
See also **"Poets in Person, No. 4"** on manual p. 314.

Edna St. Vincent Millay: Renascence
60 min., color.
A biography of the poet.
Distributed by Films for the Humanities and
    Sciences.

Poems of Edna St. Vincent Millay *[recording]*
1 cassette (60 min.), 1981.
Part of the Poetic Heritage Series.
Distributed by Summer Stream.

Poetry of Edna St. Vincent Millay *[recording]*
1 cassette.
Distributed by Caedmon/HarperAudio.

Edna St. Vincent Millay
See also **"With a Feminine Touch"** on man-
    ual p. 316.

*Milton
28 min., color, 1989.
Beta, VHS, 3/4″ U-matic cassette.
Looks at Milton's sonnets to his wife
    Katherine and "Paradise Lost."
Distributed by Films for the Humanities and
    Sciences.

*Milton and 17th Century Poetry
35 min., color, 1989.
Beta, VHS, 3/4″ U-matic cassette.
A study of Milton and other metaphysical
    poets.
Distributed by Films for the Humanities and
    Sciences.

Milton by Himself
27 min., color, 1989.
Beta, VHS, 3/4″ U-matic cassette.
A biography constructed from Milton's
    autobiographical writings.
Distributed by Films for the Humanities and
    Sciences.

Milton the Puritan: Portrait of a Mind
    [recording]
10 cassettes (900 min.).
Distributed by Books on Tape.

The Poetry of John Milton *[recording]*
1 cassette.
Distributed by Caedmon/HarperAudio.

Treasury of John Milton *[recording]*
1 cassette.
Distributed by Spoken Arts.

John Milton
See also **"Introduction to English Poetry"**
    and **"Palgrave's Golden Treasury of
    English Poetry"** on manual pp.
    313–314.

N. Scott Momaday
50 min., color.

The author discusses the creative sources of
    his work.
Distributed by Films for the Humanities and
    Sciences.

N. Scott Momaday: House Made of Dawn
    [recording]
1 cassette (39 min.).
Momaday reads excerpts from his stories.
Distributed by the American Audio Prose
    Library.

N. Scott Momaday: House Made of Dawn
    [recording]
7 cassettes (7 hours).
Distributed by Books on Tape.

N. Scott Momaday Reading *[recording]*
2 cassettes (109 min.), 1983.
Distributed by American Audio Prose
    Library.

**Marianne Moore Reading Her Poems &
    Fables from La Fontaine** *[recording]*
1 cassette.
Distributed by Caedmon/HarperAudio.

Marianne Moore Reads Her Poetry *[recording]*
1 cassette (22 min.), 1965.
Distributed by Audio-Forum.

Marianne Moore
See also **"Inner Ear, Parts 3 and 4,"
    "Modern American Poetry," "The
    Poet's Voice," "Voices and Vision,"
    and "Caedmon Treasury of Modern
    Poets Reading Their Own Poetry"** on
    manual pp. 312–315.

Pablo Neruda: Poet
30 min., b/w, 1972.
Beta, VHS, 3/4″ U-matic cassette.
A profile of the poet.
Distributed by Cinema Guild.

Pablo Neruda: Selected Poems
    [recording]
1 cassette.
In Spanish.
Distributed by Applause Productions.

*Yo Soy Pablo Neruda
29 min., b/w, 1967.
Beta, VHS, 3/4″ U-matic, 16-mm film.
A profile of the poet. Narrated by Sir
    Anthony Quayle.
Distributed by Films for the Humanities and
    Sciences.

John Frederick Nims *[recording]*
1 cassette (29 min.), 1986.
A reading by the Chicago poet.
Distributed by New Letters on the Air.

Sharon Olds *[recording]*
1 cassette (29 min.), 1992.
Distributed by New Letters on the Air.

Sharon Olds: Coming Back to Life *[recording]*
1 cassette (60 min.).
Distributed by Audio-Forum.

Michael O'Brien & Sharon Olds *[recording]*
1 cassette (29 min.).
Distributed by New Letters on the Air.

Sharon Olds
See also **"Moyers: The Power of the Word"** on manual p. 314.

Wilfred Owen: War Requiem *[video]*
Color & b/w, VHS (92 min.), 1988.
Written and directed by Derek Jarman, music by Benjamin Britten.
Distributed by Mystic Fire Video.

Wilfred Owen: War Requiem *[recording]*
2 compact discs, 1993.
Distributed by Deutsche Grammophone.

The Pity of War: From the Works of Wilfred Owen *[recording]*
58 min., color, 1987.
Beta, VHS, 3/4″ U-matic cassette.
A documentary drawn from Owen's poems, diaries, and letters.
Distributed by Films for the Humanities and Sciences.

Dorothy Parker *[recording]*
2 cassettes.
Read by Mary M. Lewis.
Distributed by Cassette Works.

An Informal Hour with Dorothy Parker *[recording]*
1 cassette.
The author reads her short story "Horsie" as well as twenty-six poems.
Distributed by Spoken Arts.

Dorothy Parker
See also **"Spoken Arts Treasury of American Jewish Poets Reading Their Poems, Vol. 1"** (recording) on manual p. 315.

Linda Pastan *[recording]*
1 cassette (29 min.).
Distributed by New Letters on the Air.

Linda Pastan: Mosaic *[recording]*
1 cassette (51 min.), 1988.
Distributed by Watershed Tapes.

*Octavio Paz: An Uncommon Poet
28 min., color, 198?.
Beta, VHS, 3/4″ U-matic cassette, 16-mm film.

The poet talks about the distinctions between his two careers: poet and political activist.
Distributed by Films for the Humanities and Sciences.

Octavio Paz
See also **"Moyers: The Power of the Word"** on manual p. 314.

Marge Piercy: At the Core *[recording]*
1 cassette (58 min.), 1977.
Distributed by Watershed Tapes.

Sylvia Plath: The Bell Jar
113 min., color, 1979.
Beta, VHS.
Based on Plath's semi-autobiographical novel.
See local retailer.

Sylvia Plath *[video]*
Color, VHS (1988).
Distributed by Annenberg/CPB Collection and Mystic Fire.

Sylvia Plath
4 programs (30 min. each), color, 1974.
VHS, 1/2″ open reel (EIAJ), 3/4″ U-matic cassette, 2″ quadraplex open reel.
A biographical examination of the poet and her work.
Distributed by New York State Education Department.

Sylvia Plath *[recording]*
1 cassette (48 min.), 1962.
A historic reading of fifteen poems recorded the month before the poet's suicide.
Distributed by Poet's Audio Center.

Sylvia Plath: Letters Home
90 min., color, 1985.
Beta, VHS, 3/4″ U-matic cassette.
Staged version of Plath's letters to her mother.
Distributed by Films for the Humanities and Sciences.

Sylvia Plath, Part I: The Struggle
30 min., color, 1974.
Beta, VHS, 1/2″ open reel (EIAJ), 3/4″ U-matic cassette, 2″ quadraplex open reel.
A dramatization of Plath's poetry by The Royal Shakespeare Company.
Distributed by New York State Education Department.

Sylvia Plath, Part II: Getting There
30 min., color, 1974.
Beta, VHS, 1/2″ open reel (EIAJ), 3/4″ U-matic cassette, 2″ quadraplex open reel.
Plath's poems are set to music by Elizabeth

Swados and performed by Michele Collison.

Distributed by New York State Education Department.

Sylvia Plath Reading Her Poetry [recording]
1 cassette.
Distributed by Caedmon/HarperAudio.

Sylvia Plath Reads [recording]
1 cassette (60 min.), 1987.
From The Poet Anniversary Series.
Distributed by Caedmon/HarperAudio.

Sylvia Plath
See also **"The Poet's Voice," "Voices and Vision,"** and **"With a Feminine Touch"** on manual pp. 314–316.

Edgar Allan Poe: "The Raven," "The Bells", and Other Poems [recording]
1 cassette.
Distributed by Spoken Arts.

Edgar Allan Poe [recording]
2 cassettes (2 hours).
Distributed by Dove Audio.

Edgar Allan Poe
See also **"Poetry by Americans"** on manual p. 314.

Treasury of Alexander Pope [recording]
1 cassette.
Distributed by Spoken Arts.

Alexander Pope
See also **"English Literature: Eighteenth Century"** and **"Restoration and Augustan Poetry"** on manual pp. 312 and 314.

Ezra Pound Reading "Cantico Del Sole," "Canto Ninety-Nine" & Other Poems [recording]
2 cassettes.
Distributed by Caedmon/HarperAudio.

*Ezra Pound: Poet's Poet
29 min., b/w, 1970.
Beta, VHS, 3/4″ U-matic cassette, 16-mm film.
A profile of Pound and his influence on later poets.
Distributed by Films for the Humanities and Sciences.

Ezra Pound
See also **"Modern American Poetry," "The Poet's Voice," "Voices and Vision,"** and **"Caedmon Treasury of Modern Poets Reading Their Own Poetry"** on manual pp. 312–315.

Walter Ralegh
See **"Medieval and Elizabethan Poetry"** on manual p. 313.

Adrienne Rich: Planetarium: A Retrospective 1950 to 1980 [recording]
1 cassette (63 min.), 1986.
Part of the YM-YWHA Poetry Center Series.
Distributed by Watershed Tapes.

The Poetry of Adrienne Rich [recording]
1 cassette (36 min.), 1968.
Part of the YM-YWHA Poetry Center Series.
Distributed by Audio-Forum.

Adrienne Rich: Tracking the Contradictions: Poems 1981–1985 [recording]
1 cassette (53 min.), 1986.
Distributed by Watershed Tapes.

Adrienne Rich
See also **"Poets in Person, No. 4"** (recording) on manual p. 314.

The Poetry of Rainer Maria Rilke [recording]
1 cassette.
In German.
Distributed by Caedmon/HarperAudio.

Rainer Maria Rilke: Selected Poems [recording]
2 cassettes (118 min.), 1988.
From the Spiritual Classics on Cassette Series.
Distributed by Audio Literature.

Alberto A. Ríos: Reading His Poetry [recording]
1 cassette.
Distributed by Sound Photosynthesis.

Alberto Ríos
See also **"Birthright: Growing Up Hispanic"** on manual p. 312.

The Poetry of Theodore Roethke [recording]
1 cassette (36 min.).
Part of the YM-YWHA Poetry Center Series.
Distributed by Audio-Forum.

Theodore Roethke [recording]
1 cassette (48 min.), 1972.
A posthumous collection of Roethke reading his poetry.
Distributed by Caedmon/HarperAudio.

Theodore Roethke: Twentieth-Century Poetry in English: Recordings of Poets Reading Their Own Poetry, No. 10 [recording]
Distributed by the Library of Congress.

Words for the Wind: Read by Theodore Roethke [recording]
1 cassette, 1962.
Distributed by Smithsonian/Folkways Recordings.

Theodore Roethke
See **"The Poet's Voice"** on manual p. 314.

Anne Sexton Reads Her Poetry [recording]
1 cassette.
Distributed by Caedmon/HarperAudio.

The Poetry of Anne Sexton [recording]
1 cassette (35 min.), 1964.
Part of the YM-YWHA Poetry Center Series.
Distributed by Audio-Forum.

**William Shakespeare: Poetry and Hidden
Poetry*
53 min., color, 1984.
A micro-examination of Shakespeare's poetry and its hidden meanings. Produced by the Royal Shakespeare Company.
Distributed by Films for the Humanities and Sciences.

Selected Sonnets by Shakespeare
40 min., color, 1984.
Beta, VHS, 3/4″ U-matic cassette.
Features readings by Ben Kingsley and Jane Lapotaire.
Distributed by Films for the Humanities and Sciences.

Selected Sonnets of Shakespeare [recording]
1 cassette.
Distributed by Spoken Arts.

William Shakespeare: The Sonnets [recording]
1 cassette.
Distributed by Recorded Books.

William Shakespeare Sonnets [recording]
2 cassettes (120 min.).
Distributed by Caedmon/HarperAudio.

William Shakespeare's Sonnets
150 min., color, 1984.
Beta, VHS, 3/4″ U-matic cassette.
An in-depth look at fifteen of Shakespeare's sonnets. With Ben Kingsley, Roger Reese, Claire Bloom, Jane Lapotaire, A. L. Rowse, and Stephen Spender.
Distributed by Films for the Humanities and Sciences.

William Shakespeare
See also **"Poetry for People Who Hate Poetry," "England: Background of Literature," "Introduction to English Poetry," "Medieval and Elizabethan Poetry,"** and **"Palgrave's Golden Treasury of English Poetry"** on manual pp. 312–314.

The Poetry of Shelley [recording]
1 cassette.
Distributed by Caedmon/HarperAudio.

Treasury of Percy Bysshe Shelley [recording]
1 cassette.
Distributed by Spoken Arts.

Percy Bysshe Shelley
See also **"English Literature: Romantic Period," "English Romantic Poetry," "Introduction to English Poetry,"** and **"Palgrave's Golden Treasury of English Poetry"** on manual pp. 312–314.

Louis Simpson [recording]
1 cassette (29 min.), 1983.
Distributed by New Letters on the Air.

Louis Simpson: Physical Universe [recording]
1 cassette (57 min.), 1985.
Distributed by Watershed Tapes.

*W. D. Snodgrass: Calling from the Wood's Edge
[recording]*
1 cassette (58 min.), 1986.
Distributed by Watershed Tapes.

**Gary Snyder: Poetry — Phillip Whalen and
Gary Snyder*
30 min., b/w, 1966.
3/4″ U-matic cassette, 16-mm film, special order formats.
Interviews with the two poets.
Distributed by Indiana University Instructional Support Services.

Gary Snyder: This Is Our Body [recording]
1 cassette (61 min.), 1989.
Distributed by Watershed Tapes.

Gary Snyder: Poetry for an Island [recording]
1 cassette, 1974.
Gary Snyder and Nanao Sakaki read their own and others' poems.
Distributed by University of California Extension Media Center.

*Gary Snyder: Turtle Island [recording]
1 cassette (1 hour, 10 min.).
Distributed by Chelsea Green Pub.

Gary Snyder
See also **"Inner Ear, Parts 5 and 6"** on manual p. 313.

*Delmore Schwartz, Richard Blackmur,
Stephen Spender, and Elizabeth Bishop
[recording]*
1 cassette.
Distributed by the Library of Congress.

Gary Soto I & II [recording]
1 cassette (60 min.), 1982, 1992.
The author reads his work and talks about the recent rise of Chicano literature.
Distributed by New Letters on the Air.

Gary Soto
See also **"Poets in Person, No. 7"** (recording) on manual p. 314.

Bruce Springsteen's Greatest Hits *[recording]*
1 CD.
Contains Springsteen's hit single "Streets of Philadelphia."
Distributed by Columbia Records.

Philadelphia
125 min., color, 1994.
VHS.
Film starring Tom Hanks and Denzel Washington and featuring Bruce Springsteen's hit single "Streets of Philadelphia."
See local retailer.

William Stafford I & II *[recording]*
1 cassette (60 min.), 1983, 1984.
The author reads his poetry and discusses politics, poetry, and the writing process.
Distributed by New Letters on the Air.

William Stafford: Troubleshooting *[recording]*
1 cassette (50 min.), 1984.
Distributed by Watershed Tapes.

William Stafford
See also **"Moyers: The Power of the Word"** on manual p. 314.

Wallace Stevens Reads *[recording]*
1 cassette (60 min.), 1987.
Part of The Poet Anniversary Series.
Distributed by Caedmon/HarperAudio.

Wallace Stevens Reading His Poems *[recording]*
1 cassette.
Distributed by Caedmon/HarperAudio.

Wallace Stevens
See also **"Inner Ear, Parts 3 and 4," "Modern American Poetry," "The Poet's Voice," "Voices and Vision,"** and **"Caedmon Treasury of Modern Poets Reading Their Own Poetry"** on manual pp. 312–315.

Mark Strand: The Untelling *[recording]*
1 cassette (56 min.).
Distributed by Watershed Tapes.

The Poetry of May Swenson *[recording]*
1 cassette (32 min.), 1963.
Part of the YM-YWHA Poetry Center Series.
Distributed by Audio-Forum.

The Poetry and Voice of May Swenson *[recording]*
1 cassette.
Distributed by Caedmon/HarperAudio.

Treasury of Alfred, Lord Tennyson *[recording]*
1 cassette.
Read by Robert Speaight.
Includes "Ulysses," "The Lotus Eaters," and "The Charge of the Light Brigade."
Distributed by Spoken Arts.

The Poetry of Tennyson *[recording]*
1 cassette.
Distributed by Caedmon/HarperAudio.

Alfred, Lord Tennyson: Portrait of a Poet *[recording]*
1 cassette (53 min.).
Distributed by Watershed Tapes.

Alfred, Lord Tennyson
See also **"England: Background of Literature," "Palgrave's Golden Treasury of English Poetry,"** and **"Victorian Poetry"** (film and recording) on manual pp. 312–315.

*****The Days of Dylan Thomas**
21 min., b/w, 1965.
Beta, VHS, 3/4″ U-matic cassette, 16-mm film.
A biography of the poet.
Distributed by CRM Films.

Dylan Thomas *[recording]*
4 cassettes.
Distributed by Caedmon/HarperAudio.

Dylan Thomas
25 min., color, 1982.
Beta, VHS, 3/4″ U-matic cassette.
A portrait of the poet.
Distributed by Films, Inc.

*****A Dylan Thomas Memoir**
28 min., color, 1972.
Beta, VHS, 3/4″ U-matic cassette, 16-mm film.
A character study of the poet.
Distributed by Pyramid Film and Video.

Dylan Thomas Soundbook *[recording]*
4 cassettes.
Read by the author.
Distributed by Caedmon/HarperAudio.

Dylan Thomas Reading "And Death Shall Have No Dominion" & Other Poems *[recording]*
1 cassette.
Distributed by Caedmon/HarperAudio.

Dylan Thomas Reading His Poetry *[recording]*
2 cassettes.
Distributed by Caedmon/HarperAudio.

Dylan Thomas Reading "Quite Early One Morning" & Other Poems *[recording]*

1 cassette.
Distributed by Caedmon/HarperAudio.

***Dylan Thomas Reading "Over Sir John's Hill"
& Other Poems*** *[recording]*
1 cassette.
Distributed by Caedmon/HarperAudio.

Dylan Thomas Reads a Personal Anthology
[recording]
1 cassette.
Distributed by Caedmon/HarperAudio.

An Evening with Dylan Thomas *[recording]*
1 cassette.
Distributed by Caedmon/HarperAudio.

***Dylan Thomas: In Country Heaven — The
Evolution of a Poem*** *[recording]*
1 cassette.
Distributed by Caedmon/HarperAudio.

Dylan Thomas: A Portrait
26 min., color, 1989.
Beta, VHS, 3/4″ U-matic cassette.
A biographical film.
Distributed by Films for the Humanities and
Sciences.

Dylan Thomas: An Appreciation *[recording]*
1 cassette.
Distributed by Audio-Forum.

Dylan Thomas: Under Milkwood *[recording]*
2 cassettes (90 min.).
Distributed by S & S Audio.

The Wales of Dylan Thomas
Color, 1989.
Images of Wales in Thomas's poetry, prose,
and drama.
Distributed by Films for the Humanities and
Sciences.

Dylan Thomas
See also **"Caedmon Treasury of Modern
Poets Reading Their Own Poetry"** on
manual p. 312.

Tomas Transtromer: The Blue House
[recording]
1 cassette (58 min.), 1986.
Distributed by Watershed Tapes.

John Updike, I and II *[recording]*
2 cassettes (58 min.), 1987.
Distributed by New Letters on the Air.

The Poetry of John Updike *[recording]*
1 cassette (47 min.), 1967.
Part of the YM-YWHA Poetry Center Series.
Distributed by Audio-Forum.

Diane Wakoski I & II *[recording]*
1 cassette (60 min.), 1977, 1984.

Distributed by New Letters on the Air.

Derek Walcott
Bill Moyer's A World of Ideas: Derek Walcott
[video]
Color, VHS (29 min.), 1989.
Distributed by PBS Video.

Derek Walcott Reads *[recording]*
1 cassette (90 min.).
Distributed by Caedmon/HarperAudio.

Omeros *[recording]*
1 cassette (29 min.), 1990.
Distributed by New Letters on the Air.

*Walcott on Poetry *[recording]*
1 cassette.
Distributed by the Center for National
Humanities.

Alice Walker: Interview with Kay Bonetti
[recording]
2 cassettes (82 min.), 1988.
Distributed by American Audio Prose
Library.

Edmund Waller
See **"Palgrave's Golden Treasury of
English Poetry"** on manual p. 314.

***Walt Whitman: "Crossing Brooklyn Ferry" &
Other Poems*** *[recording]*
1 cassette.
Distributed by Caedmon/HarperAudio.

Walt Whitman: American Poet, 1819–1892
[recording]
Color, VHS (30 min.), 1994
Distributed by Kultur.

The Democratic Vistas of Walt Whitman
[recording]
1 cassette (22 min.), 1968.
By Louis Untermeyer. Part of the Makers of
the Modern World Series.
Distributed by Audio-Forum.

*Walt Whitman: Endlessly Rocking
21 min., color, 1986.
Beta, VHS, 3/4″ U-matic cassette.
Shows a teacher's unsuccessful attempts to
interest her students in Whitman.
Distributed by Centre Communications.

Walt Whitman: Frost and Whitman
30 min., b/w, 1963.
Beta, VHS, 1/2″open reel (EIAJ), 3/4″ U-matic
cassette, 2″ quadraplex open reel.
Will Geer performs excerpts from the two
poets' works.
Distributed by New York State Education
Department.

Walt Whitman: Galway Kinnell Reads Walt Whitman [recording]
1 cassette (59 min.).
Kinnell reads excerpts from "Song of Myself," "I Sing the Body Electric," and several shorter poems.
Distributed by Sound Rx.

Walt Whitman: The Living Tradition
20 min., color, 1983.
Beta, VHS, 3/4″ U-matic cassette.
Allen Ginsberg reads Whitman's poetry.
Distributed by Centre Communications.

Walt Whitman: Memoranda During the War: From Specimen Days [recording]
240 min.
Distributed by Recorded Books.

Walt Whitman: Orson Welles Reads "Song of Myself" [recording]
1 cassette.
Distributed by Audio-Forum.

*Walt Whitman: Poet for a New Age
29 min., color, 1972.
Beta, VHS, 3/4″ U-matic cassette, 16-mm film.
A study of the poet.
Distributed by Britannica Films.

Readings of Walt Whitman [recording]
1 cassette, 1957.
Distributed by Smithsonian/Folkways Recordings.

Treasury of Walt Whitman: Leaves of Grass, I & II [recording]
2 cassettes (92 min.).
Unabridged edition.
Distributed by Spoken Arts.

Walt Whitman: Twentieth-Century Poetry in English, Nos. 13–17 [recording]
From the Leaves of Grass Centennial Series.
Distributed by the Library of Congress.

*Walt Whitman
10 min., color, 1972.
Beta, VHS, 3/4″ U-matic cassette, 16-mm film, open captioned.
Readings and a discussion of Whitman's life. Hosted by Efrem Zimbalist, Jr.
Distributed by AIMS Media Inc.

Walt Whitman
12 min., color, 1989.
Beta, VHS, 3/4″ U-matic cassette.
Examines Whitman's poetic language.
Distributed by Films for the Humanities and Sciences.

*Walt Whitman's Civil War
15 min., color, 1988.
Beta, VHS, 3/4″ U-matic cassette.
Discusses Whitman's perspective on the war.
Distributed by Churchill Media.

Walt Whitman
See also **"Poetry by Americans"** and **"Voices and Vision"** on manual pp. 314 and 315.

Richard Wilbur [recording]
1 cassette (29 min.), 1990.
The author reads his poems and talks about early influences and censorship.
Distributed by New Letters on the Air.

Poems of Richard Wilbur [recording]
1 cassette.
Distributed by Spoken Arts.

*Poetry — Richard Wilbur and Robert Lowell
30 min., b/w, 1966.
3/4″ U-matic cassette, 16-mm film, special order formats.
Interviews with the two poets.
Distributed by Indiana University Instructional Support Services.

Richard Wilbur Reading His Poetry [recording]
1 cassette.
Distributed by Caedmon/HarperAudio.

Richard Wilbur
See also **"Caedmon Treasury of Modern Poets Reading Their Own Poetry"** and **"Twentieth-Century Poets Reading Their Work"** on manual pp. 312 and 315.

Miller Williams [recording]
1 cassette (29 min.), 1985.
Distributed by New Letters on the Air.

Miller Williams [recording]
1 cassette (29 min.), 1985.
Distributed by New Letters on the Air.

Poems of Miller Williams [recording]
1 cassette.
Read by the author.
Distributed by Spoken Arts.

The Poetry of Miller Williams [recording]
1 cassette (26 min.), 1969.
Part of the YM-YWHA Poetry Center Series.
Distributed by Audio-Forum.

William Carlos Williams Reads His Poetry [recording]
1 cassette.
Distributed by Caedmon/HarperAudio.

William Carlos Williams: People and the Stones: Selected Poems[recording]
1 cassette (60 min.).
Distributed by Watershed Tapes.

William Carlos Williams
See also **"Inner Ear, Part 1," "The Poet's Voice," "Voices and Vision,"** and **"Caedmon Treasury of Modern Poets Reading Their Own Poetry"** on manual pp. 312–315.

William Wordsworth: Selected Poems [recording]
2 cassettes (180 min.).
Read by Frederick Davidson.
Distributed by Blackstone Audio Books.

The Poetry of Wordsworth [recording]
1 cassette.
Distributed by Caedmon/HarperAudio.

Treasury of William Wordsworth [recording]
1 cassette.
Distributed by Spoken Arts.

William Wordsworth: William and Dorothy
52 min., color, 1989.
Beta, VHS, 3/4″ U-matic cassette.
Explores Wordsworth's poetry and his troubled relationship with his sister. Directed by Ken Russell.
Distributed by Films for the Humanities and Sciences.

*William Wordsworth
28 min., color, 1989.
Beta, VHS, 3/4″ U-matic cassette.
An examination of the poet's work set against the Lake District, subject for many of the poems.
Distributed by Films for the Humanities and Sciences.

William Wordsworth and the English Lakes
15 min., color, 1989.
Beta, VHS, 3/4″ U-matic cassette.
Looks at Wordsworth's use of language.
Distributed by Films for the Humanities and Sciences.

William Wordsworth
See also **"English Literature: Romantic Period," "English Romantic Poetry," "Introduction to English Poetry," "Palgrave's Golden Treasury of English Poetry," "Romantic Pioneers,"** and **"The Young Romantics"** on manual pp. 312–316.

The Poetry & Voice of James Wright [recording]
1 cassette.
Distributed by Caedmon/HarperAudio.

Thomas Wyatt
See **"Medieval and Elizabethan Poetry"** and **"Palgrave's Golden Treasury of English Poetry"** on manual pp. 313–314.

Dylan Thomas Reads the Poetry of W. B. Yeats & Others [recording]
1 cassette.
Includes readings of Yeats, Louis MacNeice, George Barker, Walter de la Mare, W. H. Davies, D. H. Lawrence, and W. H. Auden.
Distributed by Caedmon/HarperAudio.

The Love Poems of William Butler Yeats
30 min., b/w, 1967.
Beta, VHS, 1/2″ open reel (EIAJ), 3/4″ U-matic cassette, 2″ quadraplex open reel.
Selections from the poet's works.
Distributed by New York State Education Department.

Poems by W. B. Yeats and Poems for Several Voices
1 cassette, 1973.
Includes "Sailing to Byzantium" and features poems by Thomas Hardy, Robert Graves, and Gerard Manley Hopkins.
Read by V. C. Clinton-Baddeley, Jill Balcon, and M. Westbury.
Distributed by Smithsonian/Folkways Recordings.

Poems of William Butler Yeats [recording]
1 cassette.
Distributed by Spoken Arts.

The Poetry of William Butler Yeats [recording]
1 cassette.
Distributed by Caedmon/HarperAudio.

William Butler Yeats, et al.: Treasury of Irish Verse, Folk Tales, & Ballads [recording]
6 cassettes (294 min.), 1986.
Distributed by Spoken Arts.

William Butler Yeats: Twentieth-Century Poets Read Their Works [recording]
6 cassettes (270 min.), 1986.
Distributed by Spoken Arts.

W. B. Yeats [recording]
1 cassette (49 min.), 1953.
Read by Stephen Spender.
Distributed by Audio-Forum.

*Yeats Country
19 min., color, 1965.
VHS, 3/4″ U-matic cassette, 16-mm film.
Juxtaposes Yeats's poetry with scenes of the Ireland he wrote about.
Distributed by International Film Bureau.

Yeats Remembered
30 min.
VHS.
Biographical film using period photographs and interviews with the poet and his family.
Distributed by Insight Media.

William Butler Yeats
See also **"Introduction to English Poetry," "Caedmon Treasury of Modern Poets Reading Their Own Poetry"** and **"Twentieth-Century Poets Reading Their Work"** on manual pp. 312–315.

GENERAL RESOURCES

Anthology of Contemporary American Poetry [recording]
1 cassette, 1961.
Includes poems by John Ciardi, Richard Ebhardt, Theodore Roethke, Howard Nemerov, Galway Kinnell, Donald Justice, May Swenson, Richard Wilbur, Karl Shapiro, and others.
Distributed by Smithsonian/Folkways Recordings.

Anthology of Negro Poets [recording]
1 cassette, 1954.
Includes the poetry of Langston Hughes, Sterling Brown, Claude McKay, Countee Cullen, Margaret Walter, and Gwendolyn Brooks.
Distributed by Smithsonian/Folkways Recordings.

Anthology of Nineteenth Century American Poets [recording]
1 cassette.
Includes Longfellow, Holmes, Whittier, Lowell, Emerson, Poe, and Whitman.
Distributed by Spoken Arts.

Archive of Recorded Poetry and Literature
Library of Congress

Birthright: Growing Up Hispanic
59 min., color, 1989.
VHS, Beta, 3/4″ U-matic cassette.
Focuses on the achievements of Hispanic American writers. Includes the work of Alberto Ríos and Judith Ortiz Cofer.
Distributed by Cinema Guild.

Caedmon Treasury of Modern Poets Reading Their Own Poetry [recording]
2 cassettes (95 min.).
Includes T. S. Eliot, W. B. Yeats, W. H. Auden, Edith Sitwell, Dylan Thomas, Robert Graves, Gertrude Stein, Archibald MacLeish, E. E. Cummings, Marianne Moore, Stephen Spender, Conrad Aiken, Robert Frost, William Carlos Williams, Wallace Stevens, Ezra Pound, Richard Wilbur, and others.
Distributed by Caedmon/HarperCollins.

Conversation Pieces: Short Poems by Thomas, Hardy, Housman, Auden, Keats, and Others
1 cassette, 1964.
Distributed by Smithsonian/Folkways Recordings.

*England: Background of Literature
11 min., color, 1962.
Beta, VHS, 3/4″ U-matic cassette, 16-mm film, special order formats.
Presents the works of English writers against the backgrounds that inspired them: Shakespeare, Dickens, and Tennyson.
Distributed by Coronet/MTI Film & Video.

*English Literature: Eighteenth Century
14 min., color, 1958.
Beta, VHS, 3/4″ U-matic cassette, 16-mm film, special order formats.
Treats the work of Addison and Steele, Pope, Swift, and others.
Distributed by Coronet/MTI Film & Video.

*English Literature: Romantic Period
13 min., color, 1957.
Beta, VHS, 3/4″ U-matic cassette, 16-mm film, special order formats.
Includes selections from Wordsworth, Byron, Shelley, Keats, and others.
Distributed by Coronet/MTI Film & Video.

*English Literature: Seventeenth Century
13 min., color, 1958.
Beta, VHS, 3/4″ U-matic cassette, 16-mm film, special order formats.
Examines works by Jonson, Pepys, and others.
Distributed by Coronet/MTI Film & Video.

English Romantic Poetry: Coleridge, Shelley, Byron, Wordsworth [recording]
3 cassettes.
Distributed by Recorded Books.

*Fried Shoes, Cooked Diamonds
55 min., color, 1982.
Beta, VHS, 3/4″ U-matic cassette.
Documents a summer at the Jack Kerouac School of Poetics at the Naropa Institute in Boulder, Colorado. Features such poets from the Beat generation as Allen Ginsberg, Gregory Corso, William S. Burroughs, Peter Orlovsky, and Timothy Leary.
Distributed by Centre Communications, Inc. and Mystic Fire.

Great Poets of the Romantic Age *[recording]*
6 cassettes (270 min.), 1986.
Distributed by Spoken Arts.

Haiku
19 min., color, 1974.
Beta, VHS, 3/4″ U-matic cassette, 16-mm film.
An overview of this poetic form.
Distributed by AIMS Media Inc.

Harlem Renaissance: The Black Poets
20 min., color, 198?.
Beta, VHS, 3/4″ U-matic cassette, 16-mm film.
Discusses this era, including an examination of Georgia Douglas Johnson, Fenton Johnson, W. E. B. Du Bois, and Langston Hughes.
Distributed by Carousel Film & Video.

The Harlem Renaissance and Beyond
31 min., 1989.
VHS.
A still-image program with excerpts from Countee Cullen, Langston Hughes, Claude McKay, Gwendolyn Brooks, Alice Walker, and Richard Wright.
Distributed by Insight Media.

Inner Ear, Part 1 *[recording]*
1 cassette (60 min.).
Includes the poetry of Carl Sandburg and William Carlos Williams.
Distributed by National Public Radio.

Inner Ear, Parts 3 and 4 *[recording]*
1 cassette (60 min.).
Emily Dickinson, Marianne Moore, and Wallace Stevens.
Distributed by National Public Radio.

Inner Ear, Parts 5 and 6 *[recording]*
1 cassette (60 min.).
E. E. Cummings and Gary Snyder.
Distributed by National Public Radio.

In Their Own Voices: A Century of Recorded Poetry *[recording]*
4 compact discs.
Distributed by Rhino Records.

Introduction to English Poetry
28 min., color, 1989.
Beta, VHS, 3/4″ U-matic cassette.
Introduces students to English verse, with readings from Chaucer, Shakespeare, Herbert, Milton, Swift, Blake, Wordsworth, Shelley, Emily Brontë, Dickinson, Hardy, Yeats, and Ted Hughes.
Distributed by Films for the Humanities and Sciences.

Lannan Literary Series *[video]*
26 cassettes (1 hour each), color, VHS, 1989–1991.
Carolyn Forché, Allen Ginsberg, Louise Glück, Galway Kinnell, W. S. Merwin, Lucille Clifton, Czeslaw Milosz, Octavio Paz, Yehuda Amichai, Joy Harjo, Victor Hernandez Cruz, Kay Boyle, Alice Walker, Ishmael Reed, Richard Wilbur, Carlos Fuentes, Robert Creeley, Larry Heinemann, Sonya Sanchez, Andrei Voznesensky, Ernesto Cardenal, Anne Waldman, Sharon Olds, Amiri Baraka, Gary Snyder.
Distributed by The Lannan Foundation/ Metropolitan Pictures/EZTV.

Literature: The Synthesis of Poetry
30 min.
VHS.
Hosted by Maya Angelou, who reads some of her own work, as well as the poetry of Frost, Sandburg, and Arnold.
Distributed by Insight Media.

Medieval and Elizabethan Poetry
28 min., color, 1989.
Beta, VHS, 3/4″ U-matic cassette.
Examines trends of the period, focusing on John Skelton, Thomas Wyatt, Tichborne, Nashe, Walter Ralegh, Marlowe, Drayton, and Shakespeare.
Distributed by Films for the Humanities and Sciences.

Metaphysical and Devotional Poetry
28 min., color, 1989.
Beta, VHS, 3/4″ U-matic cassette.
Looks at the works of John Donne, George Herbert, and Andrew Marvell.
Distributed by Films for the Humanities and Sciences.

Modern American Poetry
45 min., 1989.
VHS.
Hosted by Helen Vendler. Deals with poets from between the World Wars: Eliot, Pound, Stevens, Cullen, Hughes, Frost, Moore, and Crane. Focuses on development of an American, as distinct from European, voice.
Distributed by Insight Media.

A Movable Feast
8 programs (30 min. each), color, 1991.
VHS.
Hosted by Tom Vitale. Profiles eight contemporary writers: (1) Allen Ginsberg; (2) Joyce Carol Oates; (3) Li-Young Lee; (4) Sonia Sanchez; (5) T. Coraghessan

Boyle; (6) T. R. Pearson; (7) Trey Ellis; (8) W. S. Merwin.

Distributed by Acorn Media.

Moyers: The Power of the Word

6 programs (60 min. each), color, 1989.

Beta, VHS, 3/4″ U-matic cassette.

Bill Moyers talks with modern poets: James Autry, Quincy Troupe, Joy Harjo, Mary Tallmountain, Gerald Stern, Li-Young Lee, Stanley Kunitz, Sharon Olds, William Stafford, W. S. Merwin, Galway Kinnell, Robert Bly, and Octavio Paz.

Distributed by PBS Video.

Palgrave's Golden Treasury of English Poetry [recording]

2 cassettes.

Includes Marlowe, Shakespeare, Barnefield, Wyatt, Lyly, Donne, Herrick, Dryden, Waller, Lovelace, Milton, Gray, Rogers, Burns, Goldsmith, Keats, Wordsworth, Byron, Shelley, Coleridge, Tennyson, Arnold, and Crashaw.

Distributed by Caedmon/HarperAudio.

Poems from Black Africa [recording]

1 cassette.

Many poets and poems from Africa, including oral traditions from various parts of the continent (Nigeria, South Africa, Ghana, and others).

Distributed by Caedmon/HarperAudio.

Poetic Forms [recording]

5 cassettes (300 min.), 1988.

Includes the list poem, the ode, the prose poem, the sonnet, the haiku, the blues poem, the villanelle, the ballad, the acrostic, and free verse.

Distributed by Teachers & Writers Collaborative.

*Poetry: A Beginner's Guide

26 min., color, 1986.

Beta, VHS, 3/4″ U-matic cassette.

Interviews contemporary poets and examines the tools they use.

Distributed by Coronet/MTI Film & Video.

*Poetry by Americans

4 programs (10 min. each), color, 1988.

Beta, VHS, 3/4″ U-matic cassette, 16-mm film.

Robert Frost, Edgar Allan Poe, James Weldon Johnson, and Walt Whitman. Narrated by Leonard Nimoy, Lorne Greene, Raymond St. Jacques, and Efrem Zimbalist, Jr.

Distributed by AIMS Media Inc.

*Poetry for People Who Hate Poetry

3 programs (15 min. each), color, 1980.

Beta, VHS, 3/4″ U-matic cassette, special order formats.

Roger Steffens makes poetry accessible to students. Three programs: (1) About words; (2) E. E. Cummings; (3) Shakespeare.

Distributed by Churchill Media.

Poetry in Motion

90 min., color, 1982.

Laser optical videodisc.

A performance anthology of 24 North American poets, including Ntozake Shange, Amiri Baraka, Anne Waldman, William Burroughs, Ted Berrigan, John Cage, Tom Waits, and others. Performed by Ntozake Shange, Amiri Baraka, and Anne Waldman.

Distributed by Voyager Company.

Poets in Person: A Series on American Poets & Their Art [recording]

7 programs (30 min. each), 1991.

Thirteen poets in conversation, reading their poems, discussing their lives, work, and the changing styles in contemporary American poetry: (1) Allen Ginsberg; (2) Karl Shapiro, Maxine Kumin; (3) W. S. Merwin, Gwendolyn Brooks; (4) James Merrill, Adrienne Rich; (5) John Ashbery, Sharon Olds; (6) Charles Wright, Rita Dove; (7) Gary Soto, A. R. Ammons.

Distributed by Modern Poetry.

The Poet's Voice [recording]

6 cassettes.

From the tape archive of the Poetry Room, Harvard University. Includes John Ashbery, W. H. Auden, John Berryman, T. S. Eliot, Robert Frost, Allen Ginsberg, Randall Jarrell, Robinson Jeffers, Marianne Moore, Sylvia Plath, Ezra Pound, Theodore Roethke, Wallace Stevens, and William Carlos Williams.

Distributed by Watershed Tapes.

Potpourri of Poetry — from the Jack Kerouac School of Disembodied Poetics, Summer 1975 [recording]

1 cassette (60 min.), 1975.

Allen Ginsberg, Dianne DiPrima, John Ashbery, Ted Berrigan, Philip Whalen, and others.

Distributed by Watershed Tapes.

*Restoration and Augustan Poetry

28 min., color, 1989.

Beta, VHS, 3/4″ U-matic cassette.

Discusses the age of satire in England, including the Earl of Rochester, John

Dryden, Jonathan Swift, and Alexander Pope.
Distributed by Films for the Humanities and Sciences.

Romantic Pioneers
28 min., color, 1989.
Beta, VHS, 3/4″ U-matic cassette.
Readings of poems by Christopher Smart, William Blake, William Wordsworth, and Samuel Taylor Coleridge.
Distributed by Films for the Humanities and Sciences.

Romantics and Realists
28 min., color, 1989.
Beta, VHS, 3/4″ U-matic cassette.
Discusses Thomas Hardy, Gerard Manley Hopkins, A. E. Housman, and Rudyard Kipling.
Distributed by Films for the Humanities and Sciences.

Serenade: Poets of New York [recording]
1 cassette, 1957.
Read by Aaron Kramer, Maxwell Maxwell, and Bodenheim.
Distributed by Smithsonian/Folkways Recordings.

Spoken Arts Treasury of American Jewish Poets Reading Their Poems [recording]
7 cassettes.
Includes the work of Dorothy Parker, Phillip Levine, Anthony Hecht, Denise Levertov, Allen Ginsberg, and John Hollander.
Distributed by Spoken Arts.

The Spoken Arts Treasury of 100 Modern American Poets Reading Their Poems [recording].
1985.
Distributed by Spoken Arts.

A Survey of English and American Poetry
16 programs (28 min. each), color, 1987.
Beta, VHS, 3/4″ U-matic cassette.
A history and anthology of English-language poetry. Programs include: (1) Intro-duction to English Poetry; (2) Old English Poetry; (3) Chaucer; (4) Medieval to Elizabethan Poetry; (5) The Maturing Shakespeare; (6) Metaphysical and Devotional Poetry; (7) Milton; (8) Restoration and Augustan Poetry; (9) Romantic Pioneers; (10) William Words-worth; (11) The Younger Romantics; (12) Victorian Poetry; (13) American Pioneers; (14) Romantics and Realists;

(15) The Earlier Twentieth Century; (16) The Later Twentieth Century.
Distributed by Films for the Humanities and Sciences.

Teaching Poetry
30 min., color, 1990.
VHS.
A new approach to teaching poetry. Includes discussion questions and homework assignments.
Distributed by Video Aided Instruction.

Twentieth-Century Poets in English: Recordings of Poets Reading Their Own Poetry [recording]
33 volumes.
Distributed by the Library of Congress.

Twentieth-Century Poets Reading Their Work [recording]
6 cassettes.
Includes William Butler Yeats, Stephen Spender, Langston Hughes, W. H. Auden, Richard Wilbur, and James Dickey.
Distributed by Spoken Arts.

Victorian Poetry
28 min., color, 1989.
Beta, VHS, 3/4″ U-matic cassette.
An examination of works by Alfred Tennyson, Emily Brontë, Christina Rossetti, Elizabeth Barrett Browning, Matthew Arnold, and Algernon Swinburne.
Distributed by Films for the Humanities and Sciences.

Victorian Poetry [recording]
3 cassettes.
Includes John Henry; E. B. Browning; Edward Fitzgerald; Alfred, Lord Tennyson; W. M. Thackeray; Robert Browning; Edward Lear; Charlotte Brontë; Emily Brontë; A. H. Clough; Charles Kingsley; George Eliot; Matthew Arnold; George Meredith; Dante Gabriel Rossetti; Christina Rossetti; Lewis Carroll; James Thomson; Algernon Charles Swinburne; Thomas Hardy; Gerard Manley Hopkins; Coventry Patmore; Robert Bridges; William Ernest Henley; R. L. Stevenson; Oscar Wilde; A. E. Housman; Francis Thompson; George Santayana; Arthur Symons; and Rudyard Kipling.
Distributed by Caedmon/HarperAudio.

Voices and Vision
13 programs (60 min. each), color, 1988.

Beta, VHS, 3/4″ U-matic cassette.

A series exploring the lives of some of America's best poets. Hosted by Joseph Brodsky, Mary McCarthy, James Baldwin, and Adrienne Rich. Programs include: (1) Elizabeth Bishop; (2) Hart Crane; (3) Emily Dickinson; (4) T. S. Eliot; (5) Robert Frost; (6) Langston Hughes; (7) Robert Lowell; (8) Marianne Moore; (9) Sylvia Plath; (10) Ezra Pound; (11) Wallace Stevens; (12) Walt Whitman; (13) William Carlos Williams. Distributed by the Annenberg/CPB Collection.

With a Feminine Touch
45 min., color, 1990.
VHS.

Readings from Emily Dickinson, Anne Brontë, Charlotte Brontë, Emily Brontë, Sylvia Plath, and Edna St. Vincent Millay. Read by Valerie Harper and Claire Bloom.
Distributed by Monterey Home Video.

The Young Romantics
28 min., color, 1989.
Beta, VHS, 3/4″ U-matic cassette.
Features the work of John Keats, William Wordsworth, and Lord Byron.
Distributed by Films for the Humanities and Sciences.
1.
Part of the Poetic Heritage Series.
Distributed by Summer Stream.

DIRECTORY OF DISTRIBUTORS

Acorn Media
7910 Woodmont Avenue
Suite 350
Bethesda, MD 20814
(301) 907-0030
(800) 999-0212

AIMS Media Inc.
9710 DeSoto Ave.
Chatsworth, CA 91311-9409
(818) 773-4300
(800) 367-2467

Ally Press
524 Orleans St.
St. Paul, MN 55107
(612) 291-2652

American Audio Prose Library
P.O. Box 842
Columbia, MO 65205
(314) 443-0361
(800) 447-2275

Annenberg/CPB Collection
P.O. Box 2345
South Burlington, VT 05407-2345

Applause Productions
85-A Fernwood Lane
Roslyn, NY 11576
(516) 365-1259
(800) 253-5351

Audio Book Contractors
P.O. Box 40115
Washington, DC 20016
(202) 363-3429

Audio Bookshelf
174 Prescott Hill Road
Northport, ME 04849
(800) 234-1713

Audio Brandon Films
See *Films, Inc.*

Audio-Forum
Jeffrey Norton Publishers
96 Broad St.
Guilford, CT 06437
(203) 453-9794
(800) 243-1234

Audio Literature
P.O. Box 7123
Berkeley, CA 94707
(800) 841-2665

Barr Entertainment
12801 Schabarum Ave.
P.O. Box 7878
Irwindale, CA 91706
(818) 338-7878

Blackstone Audio Books
P.O. Box 969
Ashland, OR 97520
(503) 776-5179
(800) 729-2665

Books in Motion
E. 9212 Montgomery
Suite 501
Spokane, WA 99206
(509) 922-1646
(800) 752-3199

Books on Tape
P.O. Box 7900
Newport Beach, CA 92658
(714) 548-5525
(800) 626-3333

Britannica Films
310 South Michigan Ave.
Chicago, IL 60604
(800) 621-3900

Caedmon/HarperAudio
P.O. Box 588
Dunmore, PA 18512
(717) 343-4761
(800) 242-7737
(800) 982-4377 (in Pennsylvania)

Carousel Film & Video
260 Fifth Ave.
Suite 405
New York, NY 10001
(212) 683-1660
(800) 683-1660

Cassette Works
125 North Aspen
Azusa, CA 91702
(818) 969-6699
(800) 423-8273

Center for Humanities, Inc.
Box 1000
Mount Kisco, NY 10549
(914) 666-4100
(800) 431-1242

Centre Communications
1800 30th St.
Suite 207
Boulder, CO 80301
(303) 444-1166
(800) 886-1166

Chelsea House Publishers
Division of Main Line Book Co.
P.O. Box 914
Brommall, PA 19008
(610) 353-5166
(800) 848-2665

Churchill Media
6901 Woodley Ave.
Van Nuys, CA 91406-4844
(818) 778-1978
(800) 334-7830

Cifex Corporation
1 Teconic Hills Center
Southampton, NY 11968
(516) 283-4795

Cinema Guild
1697 Broadway
Suite 506
New York, NY 10019
(212) 246-5522
(800) 723-5522

Columbia Records
550 Madison Avenue
New York, NY 10022-3211
(212) 833-8000

Coronet/MTI Film & Video
P.O. Box 2649
Columbus, OH 43216
(614) 876-0371
(800) 321-3106

CRM Films
2215 Faraday Ave.
Carlsbad, CA 92008-7295
(619) 431-9800
(800) 421-0833

Crown Publishers
See **Random Audiobooks**

Direct Cinema Limited, Inc.
P.O. Box 10003
Santa Monica, CA 90410
(310) 396-4774
(800) 345-6748

Dolphin Tapes
P.O. Box 71
Esalen Hot Springs
Big Sur, CA 93920
(408) 667-2252

Dove Audio
301 North Canon Drive
Beverly Hills, CA 90210

Facets Multimedia, Inc.
1517 W. Fullerton Ave.
Chicago, IL 60614
(800) 331-6197

**Films for the Humanities
and Sciences**
12 Cerrine Road
Monmouth Junction, NJ 08852
(609) 275-1400
(800) 257-5126

Films, Inc.
5547 North Ravenswood Ave.
Chicago, IL 60640-1199
(312) 878-2600
(800) 323-4222

First Run/Icarus Films
153 Waverly Place
New York, NY 10014
(212) 727-1711
(800) 876-1710

**Indiana University Instructional
    Support Services**
Franklin Hall, Room 0001
Bloomington, IN 47405-5901
(812) 855-2853

Insight Media
2162 Broadway
New York, NY 10024
(212) 721-6316
(800) 233-9910

Interlingua VA
2615 Columbia Pike
P.O. Box 4132
Arlington, VA 22204
(703) 920-6644

Intermedia Arts of Minnesota
425 Ontario St. SE
Minneapolis, MN 55414
(612) 627-4444

International Film Bureau
332 S. Michigan Ave.
Suite 450
Chicago, IL 60604-4382
(312) 427-4545
(800) 432-2241

Kultur
195 Highway #36
West Long Branch, NJ 07764
(908) 229-2343
(800) 458-5887

Learning Corporation of America
See **Coronet/MTI Film & Video**

Library of Congress
orders to:
Superintendent of Documents
P.O. Box 371954
Pittsburgh, PA 15250-7954
(202) 783-3238

Listening Library
1 Park Ave.
Old Greenwich, CT 06870
(203) 637-3616
(800) 243-4504

Maryland Public Television
11767 Owings Mills Blvd.
Owings Mills, MD 21117
(410) 356-5600

Media Concepts Press
331 North Broad St.
Philadelphia, PA 19107
(215) 923-2545

Media Guild
11722 Sorrento Valley Rd., Suite E
San Diego, CA 92121
(619) 755-9191
(800) 886-9191

Modern Poetry
60 W. Walton Street
Chicago, IL 60610
(312) 255-3703

Modern Talking Picture Service
4707 140th Avenue North
Suite 105
Clearwater, FL 34622
(813) 541-7571
(800) 243-6877

Monterey Home Video
28038 Dorothy Drive
Suite 1
Agoura Hills, CA 91301
(818) 597-0047
(800) 424-2593

Mystic Fire
P.O. Box 9323
South Burlington, VT 05407
(800) 292-9001

National Broadcasting Company
30 Rockefeller Plaza
New York, NY 10112
(212) 664-4444

National Public Radio
Audience Services
635 Massachusetts Avenue NW
Washington, DC 20001
(202) 414-3232

Nebraska Educational Television Network
Public Affairs Unit
1800 N. 33 St.
Lincoln, NE 68583
(402) 472-3611

New Dimensions Radio
P.O. Box 569
Ukiah, CA 95482
(707) 468-5215
(800) 935-8273

New Letters on the Air
University of Missouri at Kansas City
5100 Rockhill Rd.
Kansas City, MO 64110
(816) 235-1168

New York State Education Department
Media Distribution Network
Room C-7, Concourse Level
Cultural Education Center
Albany, NY 12230
(518) 474-1265

PBS Video
1320 Braddock Place
Alexandria, VA 22314-1698
(703) 739-5380

Phoenix/BFA Films
2349 Chaffee Drive
St. Louis, MO 63146
(314) 569-0211
(800) 221-1274

Poet's Audio Center
P.O. Box 50145
Washington, DC 20091-0145
(202) 722-9105

Random Audiobooks
400 Hahn Rd.
Westminster, MD 21157
(800) 733-3000

Recorded Books
270 Skipjack Rd.
Prince Frederick, MD 20678
(301) 535-5590
(800) 638-1304

Rhino Records
10635 Santa Monica Boulevard
Los Angeles, CA 90025-4900

The Roland Collection
22D Hollywood Avenue
Hohokus, NJ 07423
(201) 251-8200

S & S Audio
795 Abbot Blvd.
Fort Lee, NJ 07024
(201) 224-3100
(800) 734-4758

Smithsonian/Folkways Recordings
Office of Folklife Programs
955 L'Enfant Plaza, Suite 2600
Smithsonian Institution
Washington, DC 20560
(202) 287-3262

Sound Horizons
250 W. 57th St.
Suite 1517
New York, NY 10107
(212) 956-6235
(800) 524-8355

Sound Photosynthesis
P.O. Box 2111
Mill Valley, CA 94942-2111
(415) 383-6712

Spoken Arts
801 94th Ave. N.
St. Petersburg, FL 33702
(813) 578-7600
(800) 726-8090

Summer Stream
P.O. Box 6056
Santa Barbara, CA 93160
(805) 962-6540

Tapes for Readers
4410 Lingan Road
Washington, DC 20007
(202) 338-1215

Teachers & Writers Collaborative
5 Union Square W.
New York, NY 10003
(212) 691-6590

Time-Life Video
Customer Service
1450 East Parham Rd.
Richmond, VA 23280
(800) 621-7026

*University of California Extension
    Media Center*
2000 Center Street
Suite 400
Berkeley, CA 94704
(510) 642-0460

*University of Washington Educational
    Media Collection*
Kane Hall, DG-10
Seattle, WA 98195
(206) 543-9909

Video Aided Instruction
P.O. Box 332
Roslyn Heights, NY 11577
(800) 238-1512

Voyager Company
1 Bridge Street
Irvington, NY 10533
(914) 591-5500
(800) 446-2001

Water Bearer Films
205 West End Ave.
Suite 24H
New York, NY 10023
(212) 580-8185
(800) 551-8304

Watershed Tapes
Dist. by Inland Book Co.
P.O. Box 120261
East Haven, CT 06512
(203) 467-4257
(800) 243-0138

WNET/Thirteen Non-Broadcast
356 West 58th St.
New York, NY 10019
(212) 560-2000
(800) 367-2467

Online Resources

The following list organizes Internet resources alphabetically according to author. As with the Film, Video, and Audiocassette Resource list, this list is not intended to be exhaustive; the Internet provides countless possibilities for research, and these sites should be taken as suggestions and starting points for more in-depth research.

DIANE ACKERMAN

Mystery of the Senses with Diane Ackerman
<http://www.weta.org/weta/education/teachers/itv/mos/>
The Mystery of the Senses is a five-part *Nova* documentary based on Ackerman's *A Natural History of the Senses*. This site gives biographical and bibliographical information.

Creative Quotations from Diane Ackerman
<http://www.bemorecreative.com/one/285.htm>
This site has collected salient quotations from Ackerman's books. The quotations refer to the creative process and to the process of reading poetry.

VIRGINIA HAMILTON ADAIR

Online News Hour
<http://www.pbs.org/newshour/bb/entertainment/september96/adair_9-4.html>
This site provides an interview of Adair by commentator Elizabeth Farnsworth. The interview is given in text and in RealAudio.

Rattle Magazine
<http://www.rattle.com/rattle7/70000073.htm>
This site has an interview with Adair by Alan Fox. Adair discusses her writing process and her past.

The Richmond Review
<http://www.richmondreview.co.uk/books/ants.html>
This site provides an informative book review of Adair's *Ants on the Melon*.

ANNA AHKMATOVA

The Ahkmatova Project
<http://www.akhmatovaproject.com/page4.html>
This excellent Web site provides biographical and bibliographic information on the Russian poet. Individual poems and photographs of Ahkmatova are also given.

Poems of Anna Ahkmatova
<http://www.az.com/˜katrinat/np/akhma.htm>
This site has collected Ahkmatova's poetry. The selection is helpful and concise.

<http://webserver.rcds.rye.ny.us/id/Poetry/lisa's%20page>
This site is dedicated to biographical information on Akhmatova. It also has links to Web pages with Ahkmatova's poetry.

Claribel Alegría

Latin American Women Writers
<http://www.anselm.edu/homepage/tmfaith/lawomenwriters.html>
This Web page gives links to Alegría's poetry. It also provides links to the work of other Latin American women writers.

Paula Gunn Allen

Native Authors
<http://nativeauthors.com/search/bio/biogunnallen.html>
This Web site is dedicated to the work of Native American writers. The site provides biographical information on Allen and a list of her works.

Native American Authors
<http://www.library.arizona.edu/library/teams/fah/subpathpages/allen.htm>
This page provides extensive bibliographical information on Paula Gunn Allen.

Julia Alvarez

<http://www.middlebury.edu/~english/facpub/Alv-autobio.html>
<http://www.middlebury.edu/~english/facpub/JAlvarez.html>
The detailed biography on the first of these two Middlebury College sites extensively quotes Alvarez herself. On the second site she lists a comprehensive bibliography of her essays, articles, poetry, and fiction.

Julia Alvarez Profile
<http://www.lasmujeres.com/Alvarez'%20profile.htm>
This page gives a biographical profile of Alvarez. This is a good place to get basic background information.

Yehuda Amichai

The Academy of American Poets — Yehuda Amichai
<http://www.poets.org/poets/poets.cfm?prmID=126>
This page contains good biographical information on the Israeli poet. The page also prints Amichai's poem "Memorial for the War Dead."

The Jewish Student On-Line Resource Center
<http://www.us-israel.org/jsource/biography/amichai.html>
This site gives a helpful biographical profile. The profile considers "Amichai's conviction that a modern poetry must confront and reflect contemporary issues."

A. R. Ammons

The A. R. Ammons Home Page
<http://www.wilmington.org/poets/ammons.html>
This site gives a short biographical sketch and excerpts from Ammons's work. Of particular interest is a sound clip of Ammons reading his poem "Eyesight."

The Academy of American Poets
<http://www.poets.org/poets/poets.cfm?prmID=49>
This site posts an extensive biographical sketch and three of Ammons's poems. The site also contains links to more Ammons-related material on the Web.

Readings in Contemporary Poetry
<http://www.diacenter.org/prg/poetry/94_95/amhecht.html>
The Dia Center is an arts foundation in New York City. This site gives their brief biographical sketch of Ammons and the text of his poem "An Improvisation for Angular Momentum."

MAYA ANGELOU

The Academy of American Poets
<http://www.poets.org/poets/poets.cfm?prmID=88>
The Maya Angelou page on this site provides a biographical sketch and three poems of Angelou's. Additional links make this a valuable site.

Maya Angelou
<http://www.cwrl.utexas.edu/~mmaynard/Maya/maya5.html>
This page posts a short biography and an extensive bibliography. The audio and video clips on the page should be especially useful to students.

Maya Angelou, Links and Resources
<http://ucaswww.mcm.uc.edu/worldfest/about.html>
This page is a good place to start Web research on Angelou. In addition to providing biographical and bibliographical information, the site contains numerous links to Angelou-related material on the Web.

Visions: Maya Angelou
<http://bsd.mojones.com/mother_jones/MJ95/kelley.html>
The magazine *Mother Jones* has posted this extensive interview with Angelou. The poet issues her "call to arms to the nation's artists."

MATTHEW ARNOLD

The Academy of American Poets
<http://www.poets.org>
This page provides a comprehensive biographical sketch of the English poet. The page also gives a number of helpful links.

The Matthew Arnold Discussion Port
<http://federalistnavy.com/poetry/MATTHEWARNOLD1822-1888hall/wwwboard.html>
This discussion site posts messages related to Matthew Arnold. This page is an ideal place to get viewpoints from other contemporary readers of Arnold's poetry and prose.

The Matthew Arnold Page
<http://www.accd.edu/sac/english/bailey/arnold.htm>
The Matthew Arnold page contains a concise bibliographical summary.

MARGARET ATWOOD

Margaret Atwood's Poetry
<http://www.interpole.com/atwood/front.htm>
This site is the ideal place to start Web research on Atwood. In addition to providing critical analysis and biographical information, the Web page also contains links to more Atwood material on the Web.

W. H. AUDEN

The Academy of American Poets
<http://www.poets.org/poets/poets.cfm?prmID=121>
This site provides a biographical sketch, a bibliography, poems by Auden, and many helpful links. Especially interesting is a sound clip of Auden reading his poem "On the Circuit."

W. H. Auden 1907–73
<http://www.lit.kobe-u.ac.jp/~hishika/auden.htm>
This page posts bibliographical information, poems by Auden, and valuable links to other sites.

W. H. Auden
<http://longman.awl.com/kennedy/auden/biography.html>
This site provides a comprehensive biographical sketch of the British poet. The profile is valuable for tracing the development of Auden's career.

JIMMY SANTIAGO BACA

The Official Home Page
<http://www.swcp.com/~baca/>
This page is a good place to start research on Baca. The site posts a biographical sketch, poems, audio clips, and interviews.

DAVID BARBER

The Atlantic Monthly Poetry Pages
<http://www.theatlantic.com/unbound/poetry/poetry.htm>
This is the poetry page from "Atlantic Unbound." The site contains text and audio clips of Barber's poems and an essay of Barber's on the poet Stanley Kunitz.

MATSUO BASHŌ

Bashō's Life
<http://darkwing.uoregon.edu/~kohl/basho/b_life.html>
This page contains an extensive biographical profile of the seventeenth-century poet. The site is a good place to learn about the context of Bashō's poetry.

Grand Inspirators
<http://www.globaldialog.com/~thefko/tom/gi_basho.html>
The "Grand Inspirators" page collects links to numerous Bashō-related sites on the Web. They also print short excerpts of Bashō's haiku.

History of Haiku
<http://www.big.or.jp/~loupe/links/ehisto/ebasho.shtml>
This page provides a useful synopsis of Bashō's life and work. Excerpts from Bashō's haikus are also given.

The Poetry of Bashō
<http://members.aol.com/markabird/basho.html>
"The Poetry of Bashō" has excerpted six haikus by Bashō. The poems are approriately presented alongside a Japanese hanging scroll.

ELIZABETH BISHOP

The Academy of American Poets — Elizabeth Bishop
<http://www.poets.org/poets/poets.cfm?prmID=7>
The Academy of American Poets' page on Bishop contains a useful biographical profile and several poems by Bishop. Links to other relevant pages are also provided.

Elizabeth Bishop, 1911–1979
<http://www.english.uiuc.edu/maps/poets/a_f/bishop/bishop.htm>
This is the page on Bishop provided by the Modern American Poetry site. The page includes poems by Bishop, excerpts from the poet's correspondence with Marriane Moore and links to other Web sites.

Elizabeth Bishop, American Poet
<http://iberia.vassar.edu/bishop/>
This page on Bishop is maintained by Vassar College, the poet's alma mater. Biographical information and excerpts from Bishop's work are provided. A number of critical essays on the poet make this page particularly valuable.

SOPHIE CABOT BLACK

The Artemis Project
<http://www.artemisproject.com/>
The Artemis project is a Web site dedicated to the work of American women artists. They provide a short biographical sketch of Black, reviews of her work, and two new poems by Black.

"Sophie Cabot Black, The Dia Center"
<http://diacenter.org/prg/poetry/94_95/bitblack.html>
This site is presented by The Dia Center, an arts foundation in Manhattan. A short biographical profile and Black's poem "Higher Ground" are given on this page.

WILLIAM BLAKE

The Blake Digital Text Project
<http://virtual.park.uga.edu/~wblake/home1.html>
The Blake Digital Text project contains poems and engravings by Blake. Most useful, however, is the online concordance to Blake's work provided by the site.

The William Blake Archive
<http://jefferson.village.virginia.edu/blake/main.html>
This site is a hypermedia archive sponsored by the Library of Congress and The Getty Center. The extensive material on this site, including links to other relevant pages, makes it a good place to start research on Blake.

A View on William Blake
<http://world.std.com/~albright/blake.html> .
This site clearly presents background information on the English poet. The suggested bibliography on this site should be useful to anyone researching Blake.

ROBERT BLY

<http://www.encyclopedia.com>
Encyclopedia.com's page on Robert Bly offers a short biographical sketch of the poet. The links to numerous articles related to Bly, however, are particularly useful.

LOUISE BOGAN

The Academy of American Poets — Louise Bogan
<http://www.poets.org>
The academy's page on Bogan includes biographical and bibliographical information and useful links. The texts of several poems by Bogan are posted on this page.

Louise Bogan 1897–1970
<http://www.english.uiuc.edu/maps/poets/a_f/bogan/bogan.htm>
This is the Modern American Poetry Site's page on Bogan. It contains several insightful essays on Bogan poems.

ANNE BRADSTREET

Anne Bradstreet 1612–1672
<http://www.gonzaga.edu/faculty/campbell/enl310/bradstreet.htm>
This site offers bibliographical information and a selection of poems. It also contains useful links.

Selected Poetry of Anne Bradstreet
<http://www.library.utoronto.ca/utel/rp/authors/abrad.html>
This page is maintained by the University of Toronto Libraries. It offers a representative selection of poems by Bradstreet.

Index to the Poetry of Anne Bradstreet
<http://www.puritansermons.com/poetry/anneindx.htm>
This page is maintained by the "Puritan Sermons Site." It is a good place to find background information on Bradstreet. It also offers a selection of poems by Bradstreet.

GWENDOLYN BROOKS

The Acadmy of American Poets — Gwendolyn Brooks
<http://www.poets.org>
The academy's page on Brooks provides biographical and bibliographical information, as well as links. It has posted the text of several of Brooks's poems.

Voices from The Gap, Women Writers of Color
<http://voices.cla.umn.edu/authors/GwendolynBrooks.html>
This site offers biographical and bibliographical information. It also provides an excerpt from Brooks's poem "Corners on the Curving Sky."

The Gwendolyn Brooks Page
<http://www.accd.edu/sac/english/bailey/brooksg.htm>
"The Gwendolyn Brooks Page" is sponsored by San Antonio College. It contains bibliographical information, relevant links, and Brooks's poem "We Real Cool."

ELIZABETH BARRETT BROWNING

The Academy of American Poets — Elizabeth Barrett Browning
<http://www.poets.org/poets/poets.cfm?prmID=153>
The academy's page on Browning provides biographical and bibliographical information as well as links. It also posts the texts of poems by Browning.

The Browning Pages
<http://www.public.asu.edu/~jolmatt/browning/>
This page is dedicated to Robert and E. B. Browning. The "Regarding Elizabeth" section offers a helpful biographical sketch and links.

Gale's Poetry Resource Center
<http://www.gale.com/freresrc/poets_cn/brwnebio.htm>
This page on Browning is maintained by the Gale Group. It provides a detailed biographical profile and links.

Women's Studies Database Reading Room
<http://www.inform.umd.edu/EdRes/Topic/WomensStudies/ReadingRoom/Poetry/Barrett
Browning/SonnetsFromThePortuguese/>
This site is maintained by The University of Maryland, College Park. It offers the text to Browning's "Sonnets from the Portuguese."

ROBERT BROWNING

The Academy of American Poets — Robert Browning
<http://www.poets.org/poets/poets.cfm?prmID=185>
The academy's Browning page provides biographical and bibliographical information, as well as links. It also offers the texts of selected poems by Browning.

The Browning Pages
<http://www.public.asu.edu/~jolmatt/browning/>
"The Browning Pages" offers a selection of poetry by Browning. The biographical sketch and links, however, are especially valuable.

Robert Browning, 1812–1889
<http://ccis09.baylor.edu/WWWproviders/Library/LibDepts/ABL/RB.html>
This site is maintained by the Baylor University Libraries. It offers a concise biographical sketch.

LORD BYRON

The Lord Byron Home Page
<http://www.geocities.com/Athens/Acropolis/8916/byron.html>
This site offers bibliographical information, excerpts from poems by Byron, and links. The "Byron chat" on this page, however, makes it especially lively.

Lord Byron Pages
<http://www.jamm.com/byron/index.html>
This page offers good biographical and bibliographical information. It also has a helpful list of key quotations by Byron.

The San Antonio College Lord Byron Page
<http://www.accd.edu/sac/english/bailey/byron.htm>
This page is maintained by the San Antonio College LitWeb. It provides bibliographical information and links.

LEWIS CARROLL

The Academy of American Poets — Lewis Carroll
<http://www.poets.org/poets/poets.cfm?prmID=79>
The academy's page on Carroll provides a concise biographical sketch. It also offers the text to Carroll's poem "Jabberwocky."

Lewis Carroll Home Page
<http://www.lewiscarroll.org/carroll.html>
This site offers valuable resources and critical perspectives. It is maintained by the Lewis Carroll Society of North America.

ROSARIO CASTELLANOS

Pages of Mexican Poetry
<http://www.columbia.edu/~gmo9/poetry/rosario/rosario2.html>
"Pages of Mexican Poetry" offers this page on Castellanos. The page provides a good biographical sketch, and valuable links.

KELLY CHERRY

The Atlantic Poetry Pages
<http://www.theatlantic.com/unbound/poetry/antholog/cherry/field.htm>
The Atlantic Poetry Pages has posted Cherry's poem "Field Notes." A RealAudio file of Cherry reading the poem is also provided.

JUDITH ORTIZ COFER

Judith Ortiz Cofer Page
<http://parallel.park.uga.edu/~jcofer/>
This page offers helpful bibliographical information and criticism. It also has posted Cofer's poem "First Job."

SAMUEL TAYLOR COLERIDGE

The Samuel Taylor Coleridge Archive
<http://etext.lib.virginia.edu/stc/Coleridge/stc.html>
This site offers extensive material on Coleridge. Resources include poems, criticism, and links.

Samuel Taylor Coleridge 1772–1834
<http://netpoets.com/classic/016000.htm>
This site offers a helpful biographical sketch of Coleridge and a selection of his poems.

The Romantics Page
<http://www.unm.edu/~garyh/romantic/romantic.html>
This site is dedicated to romantic literature of the early nineteenth century. It has good resources on Coleridge and valuable links to his contemporaries.

MICHAEL COLLIER

Poetry Net
<http://members.aol.com/poetrynet/month/archive/collier/intro.html>
This site provides a short biographical profile of Collier.

BILLY COLLINS

Billy Collins
<http://www.bigsnap.com/billy.html>
This is Billy Collins's own official Web site. It offers poems by Collins, interviews, and dates of upcoming readings.

Poetry Daily
<http://www.cstone.net/~poems/artdrown.htm>
Poetry Daily is a Web site that posts a new contemporary poem each day. This page provides Collins's poem "Dear Reader," along with a biographical profile and short reviews.

Poetry Magazine
<http://www.poetrymagazine.org/featured_poet_040300.html>
This is the Web site of *Poetry Magazine*, one of the nation's oldest, most respected poetry periodicals. It has posted Collins's poem "Today."

STEPHEN CRANE

Stephen Crane
<http://www.it.cc.mn.us/literature/scrane.htm>
This site offers excerpts from Crane's work and good background information. Crane's novels, as well as his poetry, are discussed on this page.

VICTOR HERNANDEZ CRUZ

<http://www.wnet.org/archive/lol/cruz.html>
This page is dedicated entirely to Cruz's poetry. It has posted poems such as "Today is a day of great joy" and short biographical sketch.

COUNTEE CULLEN

The Academy of American Poets — Countee Cullen
<http://www.poets.org>
The academy's page on Cullen offers biographical and bibliographical information as well as links. It has also posted poems by Cullen.

Black Media Foundation
<http://www.bmf.net/history/cullen.htm>
The Black Media Foundation has posted articles from its *Harlem Youth Newspaper* on the Web. This page provides a good profile of Cullen from that newspaper.

Countee Cullen, 1903–1946
<http://www.english.uiuc.edu/maps/poets/a_f/cullen/cullen.htm>
This is the Modern American Poetry Site's page on Cullen. It offers helpful biographical and critical essays on the Harlem Renaissance poet.

Countee Cullen Teacher Research File
<http://falcon.jmu.edu/~ramseyil/cullen.htm>
The Countee Cullen Teacher Research File has posted biographical and bibliographical information and links. As its name suggests, this page is geared toward teachers who teach Cullen.

E. E. CUMMINGS

The Academy of American Poets — E. E. Cummings
<http://www.poets.org/poets/poets.cfm?prmID=157>
The academy's page on Cummings offers a biographical sketch, a bibliography, and links. It has also posted poems by Cummings.

E. E. Cummings 1894–1962
<http://www.english.uiuc.edu/maps/poets/a_f/cummings/cummings.htm>
This is the Modern American Poetry Site's page on Cummings. It has posted numerous critical perspectives on individual poems.

Spring: The Journal of the cummings Society
<http://www.gvsu.edu/english/Cummings/Index.htm>
This site is the perfect place for Cummings fanatics. It offers extensive critical, biographical, and bibliographical information.

JAMES DICKEY

James Dickey 1923–1997
<http://www.english.uiuc.edu/maps/poets/a_f/dickey/dickey.htm>
This site includes a RealAudio file of Dickey reading from his work.

James Dickey Newsletter and James Dickey Society
<http://www.jamesdickey.org/>
The James Dickey Newsletter site offers an extensive bibliography. It also provides study topics that might be useful to those teaching poems by Dickey.

In Memory of James Dickey
<http://www.pbs.org/newshour/bb/remember/1997/dickey_1-20.html>
This page is part of PBS's "On Line News Hour" site. It provides the transcript of a discussion, in memory of Dickey, with Elizabeth Farnsworth and Stanley Plumly. Plumly reads Dickey's "Deer Among Cattle."

EMILY DICKINSON

The Academy of American Poets — Emily Dickinson
<http://www.poets.org>
The academy's site on Dickinson provides biographical and bibliographical information, as well as numerous links. It has also posts poems by Dickinson.

The Atlantic Poetry Pages, Soundings
<http://www.theatlantic.com/unbound/poetry/soundings/dickinson.htm>
This page is part of the Atlantic's Poetry Pages site. It presents sound files of contemporary poets Luice Brock-Broido, Steven Cramer, and Mary Jo Salter reading "I cannot live with you."

Emily Dickinson (1830–1886)
<http://www.gale.com/freresrc/poets_cn/dicknbio.htm>
This page is part of the Gale Group's site. It gives a concise yet detailed biographical profile.

Reckless Genius
<http://www.salonmagazine.com/feature/1997/11/cov_03kinnell.html>
Salon magazine has posted this page. It offers the contemporary poet Galway Kinnell's tribute to Dickinson.

CHITRA BANERJEE DIVAKARUNI

<http://www.bookradio.com/interviews/divakaruni/html/divakaruni02.html>
"Book radio.com" provides an interview with the Indian poet. The interview is available on a RealAudio file.

GREGORY DJANIKIAN

The Cortland Review
<http://www.cortlandreview.com/features/holiday98/greg.htm>
The *Cortland Review* has posted Djanikian's poem "When I First Saw Snow," about immigrating to America with his family from Egypt. The poem is available on RealAudio.

JOHN DONNE

The Academy of American Poets — John Donne
<http://www.poets.org/poets/poets.cfm?prmID=247>
The academy's page on Donne offers biographical and bibliographical information, as well as links. It has also posted the text to such poems by Donne as "The Baite" and "Valediction: Forbidding Mourning."

Luminarium
<http://www.luminarium.org>
"Luminarium" is an excellent poetry site dedicated to medieval, Renaissance, and seventeenth-century English poetry. Its page on Donne offers extensive selections from Donne's work, in addition to essays on Donne.

Selected Poetry of John Donne (1572–1631)
<http://www.library.utoronto.ca/utel/rp/authors/donne.html>
This site is maintained by the University of Toronto. It provides selected poems by Donne.

H.D.

The Academy of American Poets — H.D.
<http://www.poets.org/poets/poets.cfm?prmID=238>
The academy's page on H.D. provides biographical and bibliographical information, as well as links. It has also posted such H.D. poems as "At Baia" and "Helen."

H. D. (Hilda Doolittle) 1886–1961
<http://www.english.uiuc.edu/maps/poets/g_l/hd/hd.htm>
This is the Modern American Poetry Site's page on H. D. It provides critical perspectives on the poet, including essays on classical mythology in H. D.'s poems.

The H. D. Home Page
<http://www.well.com/user/heddy/>
This site is dedicated entirely to H. D. It provides valuable articles, including "Teaching H. D."

Hilda Doolittle's Home Page
<http://www.cichone.com/jlc/hd/hd.html>
This page offers helpful links and a biographical sketch of H. D.

MARK DOTY

The Academy of American Poets — Mark Doty
<http://www.poets.org/poets/poets.cfm?prmID=92>
The academy's page on Doty gives biographical and bibliographical information, in addition to links. It also has posted poems by Doty, such as "Broadway" and "The Embrace."

The Cortland Review
<http://www.cortlandreview.com/features/dec98/>
The *Cortland Review* ran this interview with Doty in its December 1998 issue. The interview is available in text and in RealAudio.

PAUL LAURENCE DUNBAR

Paul Laurence Dunbar 1872–1906
<http://www.traverse.com/people/dot/dunbar.html>
The biographical profile on this page should be particularly helpful. This page should be a good place to learn the literary-historical context of Dunbar's work.

The Paul Laurence Dunbar Collection
<http://www.dayton.lib.oh.us/~ads_elli/dunbar.htm>
This site is maintained by the Dayton, Ohio Public Library. It offers extensive biographical and bibliographical information, criticism, and poems.

STEPHEN DUNN

The Cortland Review
<http://www.cortlandreview.com/features/00/03/index.html>
Stephen Dunn was the March 2000 "Feature Poet" on the *Cortland Review* site. This page offers an interview with Dunn, available in text and in RealAudio.

MONA VAN DUYN

The Academy of American Poets — Mona Van Duyn
<http://www.poets.org/poets/poets.cfm?prmID=171>
The academy's page on Van Duyn offers biographical and bibliographical information, as well as links. It gives the text of Van Duyn's poem "Letters from a Father."

CORNELIUS EADY

The Academy of American Poets — Cornelius Eady
<http://www.poets.org/poets/poets.cfm?prmID=57>
The academy's page on Eady offers biographical and bibliographical information on Eady, as well as links. It has posted the text of Eady's poem "I'm a Fool to Love You."

Poets Chat
<http://www.writenet.org/poetschat/poetschat_ceady.html>
This site provides the text of an interview with Eady. It also prints his poem "Thelonius Monk."

T. S. ELIOT

The Academy of American Poets — T. S. Eliot
<http://www.poets.org/poets/poets.cfm?prmID=18>
The academy's page on Eliot offers biographical and bibliographical information, as well as links. The page has also posted poems by Eliot.

Thomas Stearns Eliot 1888–1965
<http://www.english.uiuc.edu/maps/poets/a_f/eliot/eliot.htm>
This is the Modern American Poetry Site's page on Eliot. It provides essays on Eliot, poems, and a biographical sketch by Stephen Spender.

tseliot campfire chat
<http://killdevilhill.com/tseliotchat/wwwboard.html>
This site offers a good profile of Eliot and excerpts from his work. The chat on this page, however, makes it particularly lively.

What the Thunder Said
<http://www.deathclock.com/thunder/>
This site is dedicated entirely to the modernist poet. It offers excerpts from Eliot's prose, a timeline, and critical essays on Eliot.

MARTÍN ESPADA

Martín Espada (1957–)
<http://www.english.uiuc.edu/maps/poets/a_f/espada/espada.htm>
The Modern American Poetry Site's page on Espada offers critical essays on his work. The discussions of thematic content should be especially valuable.

FAIZ AHMED FAIZ

Faiz Ahmed Faiz
<http://www.griffe.com/projects/worldlit/pakistan/faiz.html>
This page offers a brief biographical sketch of Faiz. The poems this page has posted, "August, 1952" and "Ghazal," make it particularly helpful.

KENNETH FEARING

Kenneth Fearing (1902–1961)
<http://www.english.uiuc.edu/maps/poets/a_f/fearing/fearing.htm>
This is the Modern American Poetry Site's page on Fearing. It offers a good bibliography and essays on Fearing's work.

ROBERT FROST

The Academy of American Poets — Robert Frost
<http://www.poets.org/poets/poets.cfm?prmID=196>
The academy's page on Frost provides a biographical sketch, bibliographical information, and numerous links. The page has also posted poems by Frost.

The Atlantic Unbound, Soundings
<http://www.theatlantic.com/unbound/poetry/soundings/frost.htm>
This page is part of the Atlantic Poetry Pages site. It offers one sound file of the contemporary poets Peter Davison, Donald Hall, and Maxine Kumin reading "The Wood Pile." A helpful introduction by Davison is provided.

The Gale Group, Robert Frost (1874–1963)
<http://www.gale.com/freresrc/poets_cn/frostbio.htm>
This page offers helpful biographical information on Frost. It should be a good place to learn about the context of Frost's work.

Robert Frost (1874–1963)
<http://www.english.uiuc.edu/maps/poets/a_f/frost/frost.htm>
This is the Modern American Poetry Site's page on Frost. It offers critical essays on specific poems by Frost. An overview by the critic William Pritchard is particularly valuable.

The Robert Frost Web Page
<http://www.pro-net.co.uk/home/catalyst/RF/body.html>
The Robert Frost Web Page provides biographical and bibliographical information, as well as poems. It also contains excerpts from interviews and audio files of Frost reading.

DEBORAH GARRISON

Up All Night with Deborah Garrison
<http://www.randomhouse.com/atrandom/deborahgarrison/index.html>
"At Random" magazine has a number of pages dedicated to poetry. This one offers an interview with Garrison.

SANDRA GILBERT

UCD English Department
<http://wwwenglish.ucdavis.edu/Faculty/gilbert/gilbert.htm>
The U.C. Davis faculty page provides good biographical and bibliographical information on Gilbert.

ALLEN GINSBERG

The Academy of American Poets — Allen Ginsberg
<http://www.poets.org/poets/poets.cfm?prmID=8>
The academy's page on Ginsberg provides biographical and bibliographical information as well as links. It has also posted Ginsberg's poem "Supermarket in California."

Allen Ginsberg, Ashes and Blues
<http://www.levity.com/corduroy/ginsberg/home.htm>
This site is dedicated entirely to Ginsberg. It offers a biographical sketch, interviews, and helpful links.

Shadow Changes into Bone
<http://www.ginzy.com/>
"Shadow Changes into Bone" is the page for true Ginsberg fans. It provides poems, interviews, and even an extensive collection of photos.

NIKKI GIOVANNI

The Academy of American Poets — Nikki Giovanni
<http://www.poets.org/poets/poets.cfm?prmID=176>
The academy's page on Giovanni provides biographical and bibliographical information , as well as links. It has posted the texts of poems by Giovanni.

Nikki Giovanni
<http://ucl.broward.cc.fl.us/writers/giovanni.htm>
The Broward Community College Library maintains this page. It offers links, interviews, and poems by Giovanni.

RACHEL HADAS

The Academy of American Poets — Rachel Hadas
<http://www.poets.org/poets/poets.cfm?prmID=199>
The academy's page on Hadas provides biographical and bibliographical information, as well as links.

Sunset
<http://bostonreview.mit.edu/BR20.2/Hadas.html>
Boston Review has extensive poetry resources. On this page you can read Hadas's poems "Sunset" and "Orange."

DONALD HALL

An Audible Anthology
<http://www.theatlantic.com/unbound/poetry/antholog/aaindx.htm>
This page is part of the Atlantic Poetry Pages site. It contains Hall's poem "Distressed Haiku" and others, available in text and in RealAudio.

Life at Eagle Pond: The Poetry of Jane Kenyon and Donald Hall
<http://www.izaak.unh.edu/specoll/exhibits/kenhall.htm>
This site offers excerpts from Hall's poetry, a biographical sketch of Hall, links, and even drafts of some of Hall's poems. The page also provides information on Hall's late wife Jane Kenyon.

MARK HALLIDAY

Mark Halliday Reads
<http://www.tcom.ohiou.edu/books/poetry/halliday/mark_halliday.htm>
This page is maintained by Ohio University. It provides three poems by Halliday in RealAudio.

THOMAS HARDY

The Academy of American Poets — Thomas Hardy
<http://www.poets.org/poets/poets.cfm?prmID=111>
The academy's page on Hardy provides biographical and bibliographical information, as well as links. It has also posted the texts of such Hardy poems as "Afterwards."

Atlantic Poetry Pages, Soundings
<http://www.theatlantic.com/unbound/poetry/soundings/hardy.htm>
This page is part of the Atlantic Poetry Pages site. It provides sound files of Hardy's "During Wind and Rain" read by Philip Levine, Donald Hall, and Rosanna Warren. Levine writes an introduction.

The Poetry Archives, Thomas Hardy
<http://www.emule.com/poetry/works.cgi?author=6>
This page is provided by emule.com. It offers a comprehensive selection of Hardy poems.

Thomas Hardy
<http://pages.ripco.net/~mws/hardy.html>
This is a page dedicated entirely to Thomas Hardy. It provides poems, a biographical sketch, and links.

JOY HARJO

The Academy of American Poets — Joy Harjo
<http://www.poets.org/poets/poets.cfm?prmID=61>
The academy's page on Harjo offers biographical and bibliographical information on the poet, as well as links. It has posted Harjo's poem "Deer Dancer."

Joy Harjo
<http://www.hanksville.org/storytellers/joy/>
This is "A Joy Harjo home page." It offers extensive biographical information and links.

JEFFREY HARRISON

<http://www.sewanee.edu/sreview/Harrison104.2.198.html>
This page is part of the *Sewannee Review*'s poetry site. It prints Harrison's poem "Double Exposure."

ROBERT HASS

The Academy of American Poets — Robert Hass
<http://www.poets.org/poets/poets.cfm?prmID=198>
The academy's page on Hass offers extensive biographical and bibliographical information and links. It has also posted the texts of poems by Hass.

Readings in Contemporary Poetry
<http://www.diacenter.org/prg/poetry/95_96/intrhass.html>
This page is part of the Dia Center's poetry site. It offers excerpts from Hass's work and an introduction to a reading Hass gave by Brighde Mullins.

White House Millennium Evening
<http://www.whitehouse.gov/Initiatives/Millennium/mill_eve3.html>
This page provides the transcript to an evening Hass and fellow poets Robert Pinsky and Rita Dove hosted at the White House. President and Mrs. Clinton also participated in the presentation.

ROBERT HAYDEN

The Academy of American Poets — Robert Hayden
<http://www.poets.org/poets/poets.cfm?prmID=200>
The academy's page on Hayden offers biographical and bibliographical information, as well as links. It has posted the texts of Hayden poems such as "Frederick Douglass" and "Full Moon."

Brittanica.com
<http://www.britannica.com/bcom/magazine/article/0,5744,245481,00.html>
Brittanica.com's page on Hayden offers a particularly valuable exchange between the poets Harryette Mullen and Stephen Yenser on Hayden. This exchange was originally printed in the *Antioch Review*.

SEAMUS HEANEY

Loud and Clear
<http://www.the-times.co.uk/news/pages/tim/99/03/27/timbooboo02001.html?1603026>
This page offers the *London Times* profile of Heaney by Nigel Williamson. Heaney's poem "Carlo" is also posted.

Poetic Giant with his Feet on the Ground
<http://www.the-times.co.uk/news/pages/tim/98/09/11/timfeafea02002.html?1603026>
This page offers a helpful profile of Heaney. It also prints his poem "Afterwards."

Readings in Contemporary Poetry
<http://www.diacenter.org/prg/poetry/87_88/heaneybio.html>
This page is part of the Dia Center's poetry site. It contains a RealAudio file of Heaney reading "Anahorish."

Seamus Heaney
<http://metalab.unc.edu/dykki/poetry/heaney/heaney-cov.html>
This site is maintained by the University of North Carolina, Chapel Hill. It offers recordings of whole poetry readings given by poets. This page provides one by Heaney.

ANTHONY HECHT

The Academy of American Poets — Anthony Hecht
<http://www.poets.org/poets/poets.cfm?prmID=47>
The academy's page on Hecht offers a good biographical profile. It also gives the texts of such poems by Hecht as "The Transparent Man."

GEORGE HERBERT

George Herbert
<http://www.cs.wm.edu/~hallyn/herbert.html>
This site offers a helpful yet short profile of Herbert. It also has posted a selection of poems.

The George Herbert Page
<http://www.accd.edu/sac/english/bailey/herbert.htm>
This page is part of the San Antonio College LitWeb. It offers good background information and links.

The Works of George Herbert
<http://www.luminarium.org/sevenlit/herbert/herbbib.htm>
This is Luminarium's page on Herbert. It offers an extensive sample from his poetry, and essays on his work.

ROBERT HERRICK

The Academy of American Poets — Robert Herrick
<http://www.poets.org/poets/poets.cfm?prmID=201>
The academy's page on Herrick offers biographical information and links. It also contains the texts of poems by Herrick.

Dead Poet's Society: Robert Herrick
<http://www.presgroup.com/poets/herrick.html>
The Dead Poets Society's page on Herrick offers a good selection of poems. Herrick's epigrams are particularly well represented here.

Robert Herrick (1591–1674)
<http://www.luminarium.org/sevenlit/herrick/>
This is Luminarium's page on Herrick. It offers an extensive sample of Herrick's poetry, and essays on his work.

WILLIAM HEYEN

<http://www.english.upenn.edu/~afilreis/88/heyen-bib.html>
This page is maintained by the University of Pennsylvania. It offers a brief biographical sketch of the contemporary poet, as well as links.

Sycamore and Ash
<http://www.poems.com/sycamhey.htm>
This page is offered by Poetry Daily. It contains Heyen's prose poem "Sycamore and Ash."

EDWARD HIRSCH

The Academy of American Poets — Edward Hirsch
<http://www.poets.org/poets/poets.cfm?prmID=158>
The academy's page on Hirsch offers good biographical and bibliographical information on Hirsch, as well as links. It also provides the text of Hirsch's "In Memoriam Paul Celan."

Poetry Forum
<http://www.poetryforum.org/aud_MAY1.htm>
"Poetry Forum" has posted Hirsch's poem "Wild Gratitude." It is available in text and in RealAudio.

JANE HIRSCHFIELD

Jane Hirschfield
<http://www.salcomm.com/joe/hirschfield1.htm>
This page is offered by Salon.com. It contains the text of Hirschfield's poem "Cycladic Figure: The Harp Player."

LI HO

Index of Poems
<http://www.cs.uiowa.edu/~yhe/poetry/li_ho_index.html>
This site is maintained by the University of Iowa. It provides a selection of poems by Li Ho.

Li Ho
<http://mockingbird.creighton.edu/worldlit/lit/liho.html>
Creighton University maintains this page. It offers excerpts from Li Ho's work.

LINDA HOGAN

Linda Hogan
<http://www.hanksville.org/storytellers/linda/>
This page offers biographical information. It also provides helpful links.

Linda Hogan — Writing the Southwest
<http://www.unm.edu/~wrtgsw/hogan.html>
This page gives good background information on the poet. It also provides an audio file on Hogan.

Native Authors
<http://nativeauthors.com/search/bio/biohogan.html>
This is the Native Authors site, providing biographical information on Hogan.

GERARD MANLEY HOPKINS

Literature of the Victorian Period
<http://www.accd.edu/sac/english/bailey/victoria.htm>
This is the San Antonio College Libraries' page on Hopkins. It provides poems by Hopkins and his contemporaries.

The Victorian Web
<http://landow.stg.brown.edu/victorian/hopkins/gmhov.html>
The Victorian Web page on Hopkins should be valuable for those who want background information. It contains essays on themes in Hopkins's work and on his poetic structure.

Web Concordance — Gerard Manley Hopkins
<http://www.dundee.ac.uk/english/wics/gmh/framconc.htm>
This site is an interactive Web concordance to Hopkins's work. It also posts the poems.

A. E. HOUSMAN

A. E. Housman
<http://www.hearts-ease.org/library/housman/bio.html>
This page provides a useful though brief biographical sketch. It also offers a selection of poems.

Encyclopedia.com
<http://www.encyclopedia.com/articles/06044.html>
This site offers short biographies and useful articles on Housman.

Project Bartleby
<http://www.bartleby.com/index.html>
This site is Columbia's "Bartleby Project." It contains work by Housman, including all of "A Shropshire Lad."

ANDREW HUDGINS

The Atlantic Poetry Pages
<http://www.theatlantic.com/unbound/poetry/antholog/hudgins/dragon.htm>
This site is part of the Atlantic Poetry Pages site. It offers Hudgins's poem "Dragonfly 97.07" in RealAudio.

Image: A Journal of the Arts and Religion
<http://www.imagejournal.org/hudgins.html>
This page is maintained by *Image*. It gives the text of Hudgins's poem "Blur."

LANGSTON HUGHES

The Academy of American Poets — Langston Hughes
<http://www.poets.org>
The academy's page on Hughes offers extensive biographical and bibliographical information on Hughes as well as links. It also provides the texts of several poems by Hughes.

Langston Hughes (1902–1967)
<http://www.english.uiuc.edu/maps/poets/g_l/hughes/hughes.htm>
This is the Modern American Poetry Site's page on Hughes. It offers a particularly valuable essay on Hughes's life and career by Arnold Rampersand, in addition to essays on specific poems and themes.

Teacher Resource File
<http://falcon.jmu.edu/~ramseyil/hughes.htm>
This site offers a good biographical profile of Hughes. As its name suggests, however, the site should be especially valuable to teachers looking for lesson plans related to Hughes.

MARK JARMAN

The Academy of American Poets — Mark Jarman
<http://www.poets.org/poets/poets.cfm?prmID=94>
The academy's page on Jarman offers biographical and bibliographical information on Jarman, as well as links. It has also posted the text of his poem "The Black Riviera."

Atlantic Poetry Pages
<http://www.theatlantic.com/unbound/poetry/antholog/jarman/psalm.htm>
This page is part of the Atlantic Poetry Pages site. It offers Jarman's poem "Psalm" in RealAudio.

The Cortland Review
<http://www.cortlandreview.com/features/99/01/>
The *Cortland Review* has posted poems by Jarman. It also offers an interview with the poet.

Poet Talks about Experiences with Literature
<http://www.spub.ksu.edu/issues/v101/fa/n029/aande/a.e-jarman-reading-beebe.html>
This page is provided by the Kansas State University Collegian. It gives a good profile of Jarman.

RANDALL JARRELL

The Academy of American Poets — Randall Jarrell
<http://www.poets.org/poets/poets.cfm?prmID=9>
The academy's page on Jarrell provides biographical and bibliographical information on Jarrell. It has also posted poems such as "The Death of the Ball Turret Gunner" and "Next Day."

Randall Jarrell (1914–1965)
<http://www.english.uiuc.edu/maps/poets/g_l/jarrell/jarrell.htm>
This is the Modern American Poetry Site's page on Jarrell. It provides essays on Jarrell and excerpts from letters describing army life.

BEN JONSON

Ben Jonson (1572–1637)
<http://www.luminarium.org/sevenlit/jonson/index.html>
This is Luminarium's page on Jonson. It offers an extensive sample of Jonson's poetry, as well as essays on the work.

Ben (Origin Unknown) Jonson
<http://www.incompetech.com/authors/jonson/>
This site offers a good biographical sketch of Jonson. The sketch is informed by some of Jonson's own quick-witted humor.

Cygnus Web Design
<http://www.cygnuswebdesign.com/writings/wr-jonso.html>
This site offers a good biographical profile. The links provided by this site are particularly helpful.

DONALD JUSTICE

The Academy of American Poets — Donald Justice
<http://www.poets.org/poets/poets.cfm?prmID=40>
This site offers good biographical information on Justice. It has also posted the text of his poem "Ode to a Dressmaker's Dummy." The poem is available in RealAudio as well.

JOHN KEATS

The Academy of American Poets — John Keats
<http://www.poets.org/poets/poets.cfm?prmID=67>
The academy's page on Keats provides helpful biographical and bibliographical information, as well as links. It has posted the texts of such Keats poems as "La Belle Dame Sans Merci."

John Keats, Romantic Poet
<http://www.etsu.edu/english/muse/musepage.htm>
This is the Digital Muse Center's page on Keats. It offers biographical information, poems, and links. It is a particularly well-designed page.

Project Bartleby
<http://www.bartleby.com/index.html>
This is Columbia's Bartleby Project. It offers a collection of Keats's poetry.

JANE KENYON

Atlantic Poetry Pages
<http://www.theatlantic.com/unbound/poetry/antholog/kenyon/whyweep.htm>
This page is part of the Atlantic Poetry Pages site. It offers Kenyon's "Woman, Why Are You Weeping" and other poems, read by Donald Hall, in RealAudio.

N.E.A. Writers' Corner
<http://arts.endow.gov/explore/Writers/Kenyon.html>
The N.E.A. has good resources on poets. This page contains Kenyon's poem "Otherwise" and biographical information on the poet.

MAXINE HONG KINGSTON

Maxine Hong Kingston — Teacher's Resource Guide
<http://falcon.jmu.edu/~ramseyil/kingston.htm>
This page offers critical essays and a biographical sketch of Kingston. The lesson plans on this page, however, are particularly helpful.

Voices from the Gap — Maxine Hong Kingston
<http://voices.cla.umn.edu/authors/MaxineHongKingston.html>
"Voices from the Gap" is a site dedicated to women writers of color. This page offers good critical and biographical perspectives on Kingston's work.

GALWAY KINNELL

Amy Munno's Galway Kinnell Page
<http://www.webspan.net/~amunno/galway.html>
This page offers biographical and bibliographical information, as well as poems like "Blackberry Eating." The Web master's personal anecdote about Kinnell is a particularly nice touch.

Atlantic Poetry Pages
<http://www.theatlantic.com/unbound/poetry/soundings/whitman.htm>
This page is part of the Atlantic Poetry Pages site. It offers a sound file of Kinnell reading Whitman's "As I Ebb'd with the Ocean of Life." Poets Frank Bidart and Marie Howe also read.

RUDYARD KIPLING

Encyclopedia.com
<http://www.encyclopedia.com/articles/06988.html>
This site provides a brief biographical sketch of Kipling. The articles on this site should be especially helpful.

Malaspina.com
<http://www.mala.bc.ca/~mcneil/kipling.htm>
This site offers a concise biographical sketch of Kipling. Its links, however, are especially useful.

The Nobel Foundation
<http://www.nobel.se/laureates/literature-1907-1-bio.html>
This is the Nobel Foundation's site. It provides good information on Kipling, who won the Nobel Prize in Literature in 1907.

Rudyard Kipling: An Overview
<http://landow.stg.brown.edu/victorian/kipling/kiplingov.html>
This is the Victorian Web's page on Kipling. It offers valuable critical essays.

CAROLYN KIZER

The Academy of American Poets — Carolyn Kizer
<http://www.poets.org/poets/poets.cfm?prmID=58>
The academy's page on Kizer provides a good biographical sketch. It also offers two poems: "On a Line from Valery (The Gulf War)" and "Parent's Pantoum."

ETHERIDGE KNIGHT

The Academy of American Poets — Etheridge Knight
<http://www.poets.org/poets/poets.cfm?prmID=159>
The academy's page on Knight gives a good profile of the poet. It also posts his poem "The Idea of Ancestry."

PHILIP LARKIN

The Academy of American Poets — Philip Larkin
<http://www.poets.org>
The academy's page on Larkin offers good biographical and bibliographical information on the poet. It also has posted an essay "High Talk: Influences from the British Isles."

Days
<http://can.dpmms.cam.ac.uk/~gjm11/poems/days.html>
This page displays Larkin's poem "Days."

TATO LAVIERA

Tato Laviera — Born 1951
<http://college.hmco.com/english/heath/syllabuild/iguide/laviera.html>
This page offers a good biographical sketch of Laviera. The "classroom issues" section, however, should be of particular interest to instructors.

Li-Young Lee

Lee, Li-Young: The Gift
<http://endeavor.med.nyu.edu/lit-med/lit-med-db/webdocs/webdescrips/lee1454-des-.html>
This page is maintained by New York University. It provides a summary of and commentary on "The Gift."

Leaning House Poetry
<http://www.leaninghouse.com/library/lee.html>
This site provides a concise biographical sketch and bibliography. Lee's poem "The Weight of Sweetness" is also presented here.

Philip Levine

The Academy of American Poets — Philip Levine
<http://www.poets.org/poets/poets.cfm?prmID=19>
The academy's page on Levine offers good biographical and bibliographical information, in addition to links. It also posts the text of Levine's poem "Coming Close."

Atlantic Poetry Pages
<http://www.theatlantic.com/unbound/poetry/levine.htm>
This site has posted an interview with Levine by Wen Stephenson. It also offers Levine poems in RealAudio.

Philip Levine (1928–)
<http://www.english.uiuc.edu/maps/poets/g_l/levine/levine.htm>
This is the Modern American Poetry Site's page on Levine. It provides essays on Levine and a bibliography.

J. Patrick Lewis

J. Patrick Lewis Home Page
<http://www.otterbein.edu/home/fac/JPLWS/>
This site provides a biographical sketch and a bibliography. It even offers the author's e-mail address, should students or instructors wish to correspond.

Henry Wadsworth Longfellow

The Atlantic Poetry Pages
<http://www.theatlantic.com/unbound/poetry/longfel/hwlindex.htm>
This page is part of the Atlantic Poetry Pages site. It offers works by Longfellow printed in the *Atlantic*.

Henry Wadsworth Longfellow
<http://EclecticEsoterica.com/longfellow.html>
This page offers a good biographical sketch. The selection of poems on this page is particularly helpful.

Henry Wadsworth Longfellow: American Poet
<http://www2.ucsc.edu/~varese/long.htm>
A description of Longfellow's meeting with Dickens makes this page interesting. A photograph of Longfellow is also posted on this page.

Audre Lorde

<http://www.math.buffalo.edu/~sww/poetry/lorde_audre.html>
This is "Snally Gaster's African American Phat Library" site. It offers Lord's "Coal" and other poems.

Robert Lowell

The Academy of American Poets — Robert Lowell
<http://www.poets.org/poets/poets.cfm?prmID=10>
The academy's page on Lowell offers good biographical and bibliographical information, as well as links. Lowell's poem "The Public Garden" is available here in RealAudio.

My Poet Pages
<http://www.lit.kobe-u.ac.jp/~hishika/lowell.htm>
This page is maintained by the University of Kobe in Japan. It posts Lowell's poem "Father's Bedroom" and a good bibliography.

Robert Lowell (1917–1977)
<http://www.english.uiuc.edu/maps/poets/g_l/lowell/lowell.htm>
This is the Modern American Poetry Site's page on Lowell. It offers numerous critical perspectives on the poet.

Robert Lowell — For the Union Dead
<http://urc1.cc.kuleuven.ac.be/~m9607356/Robert_Lowell.html>
"Robert Lowell — For the Union Dead" provides a helpful biographical sketch. The page also contains a discussion of Lowell's craft, and an excellent list of links.

Robert Lowell
<http://www.it.cc.mn.us/literature/lowell.htm>
Itasca Community College maintains this site. It offers poems by Lowell, a bibliography, and links.

ARCHIBALD MACLEISH

The Academy of American Poets — Archibald MacLeish
<http://www.poets.org/poets/poets.cfm?prmID=48>
This site gives a concise biographical sketch, a bibliography, links, and the text of two of MacLeish's poems.

Archibald MacLeish 1892–1982 Port
<http://federalistnavy.com/poetry/ARCHIBALDMacLEISH1892-1982hall/wwwboard.html>
This site is a particularly lively one. It provides the text of an ongoing discussion of MacLeish's poems.

Did You Know? Background on Archibald MacLeish
<http://rothpoem.com/duk_am.html>
Roth Publishing's PoemFinder maintains this site. It offers good background information on MacLeish.

CHRISTOPHER MARLOWE

<http://www.incompetech.com/authors/kitmarlowe/>
This site offers a good biographical sketch of the poet.

Christopher Marlowe (1564–1593)
<http://www.luminarium.org/renlit/marlowe.htm>
This is Luminarium's page on Marlowe. It provides works by Marlowe and essays on the works.

The Complete Works of Christopher Marlowe
<http://www.perseus.tufts.edu/Texts/Marlowe.html>
The Perseus Project at Tufts offers this page. It contains Marlowe's complete works.

San Antonio College LitWeb — Christopher Marlowe Page
<http://www.accd.edu/sac/english/bailey/marlowe.htm>
This page is part of the San Antonio College's Renaissance site. It provides bibliographical information and good links.

ANDREW MARVELL

Andrew Marvell (1621–1678)
<http://www.luminarium.org/sevenlit/marvell/index.html>
This is Luminarium's page on Marvell. It offers an extensive selection from Marvell's works and essays on the work.

Miscellaneous Poems

<http://etext.lib.virginia.edu/etcbin/browse-mixed-new?id=MarPoem&tag=public&images=
images/modeng&data=/texts/english/modeng/parsed>
The University of Virginia Library maintains this site. It provides the complete text of
Marvell's "Miscellaneous Poems."

The Bartleby Project
<http://www.bartleby.org/105/144.html>
This page is part of Columbia's "Bartleby Project." It prints Marvell's poem "On a Drop of
Dew."

GAIL MAZUR

The Atlantic Poetry Pages
<http://theatlantic.com/unbound/poetry/antholog/mazur/theycant.htm>
This page is part of the Atlantic Poetry Pages site. It offers Mazur's poem "They Can't Take
That Away From Me" in RealAudio.

Housebook: Gail Beckwith Mazur
<http://elsa.photo.net/housebook/house_nf22.html>
This page is offered by the photographer Elsa Dorfman. It provides a photo of the poet and
an interesting profile.

Young Apple Tree, December
<http://www3.theatlanticmonthly.com/unbound/poetry/antholog/mazur/9912appletree.htm>
This page is part of the Atlantic Poetry Pages site. It provides Mazur's poem "Young Apple
Tree, December" in RealAudio.

MICHAEL McFEE

The Blue Moon Review
<http://www.thebluemoon.com/4/sum98poemcfee.html>
This page is part of the *Blue Moon Review*'s site. It offers three poems by McFee.

RENNIE McQUILKIN

Poetry Daily
<http://www.cstone.net/~poems/gettymcq.htm>
This page is offered by Poetry Daily. It contains McQuilkin's poem "Learning the Angels."

JAMES MERRILL

Poets in Person
<http://www.wilmington.org/poets/merrill.html>
This page is part of the Poets in Person site. It contains a concise biographical profile and a
RealAudio clip of Merrill reading from "The Ballroom at Sandover."

Featured Poet James Merrill
<http://www.randomhouse.com/knopf/poetry/features/19990415/>
This page gives a short profile and sound clips of Merrill reading "The School Play" and "The
Kimono."

W. S. MERWIN

The Academy of American Poets — W.S. Merwin
<http://www.poets.org/poets/poets.cfm?prmID=124>
The academy's page on Merwin offers provides good biographical and bibliographical information on the poet. It also posts his poems "My Friends" and "Yesterday."

W.S. Merwin (1927–)
<http://www.english.uiuc.edu/maps/poets/m_r/merwin/merwin.htm>
This is the Modern American Poetry Site's page on Merwin. It provides numerous critical perspectives on the poet's work.

Swimming Up Into Poetry

<http://www.theatlantic.com/unbound/poetry/antholog/merwin/pdmerwin.htm>
This site is part of the Atlantic Poetry Pages site. It contains an essay by the poet Peter Davison on Merwin.

EDNA ST. VINCENT MILLAY

The Academy of American Poets — Edna St. Vincent Millay

<http://www.poets.org/poets/poets.cfm?prmID=161>
The academy's page on Millay offers a good biographical profile, as well as links. It also posts the poem "Witch-Wife."

Edna St. Vincent Millay (1892–1950)

<http://www.english.uiuc.edu/maps/poets/m_r/millay/millay.htm>
This is the Modern American Poetry Site's page on Millay. It offers helpful essays on the poet.

Women's Studies Database

<http://www.inform.umd.edu/EdRes/Topic/WomensStudies/ReadingRoom/Poetry/Millay/>
The University of Maryland, College Park, maintains this page. It gives a good selection of poems by Millay.

JOHN MILTON

The Classic Text: John Milton

<http://www.uwm.edu/Dept/Library/special/exhibits/clastext/clspg117.htm>
This site has posted information on *Paradise Lost*. The site also offers links to pages on other great epics.

John Milton (1608–1674)

<http://www.luminarium.org>
This is Luminarium's page on Milton. It offers generous excerpts from Milton's works, as well as essays on Milton.

John Milton Reading Room

<http://www.dartmouth.edu/~milton/reading_room/index.html>
This site is maintained by Dartmouth College. It offers excerpts from Milton's poetry and prose, as well as superb student essays on Milton.

The Milton-L Home Page

<http://www.urich.edu/~creamer/milton/audio.html>
This site offers sections of *Paradise Lost* on audio files. It also provides texts of Milton's poetry and prose, and even a list of upcoming events related to Milton.

JANICE MIRIKITANI

An Analysis of the Poetry of Janice Mirikitani

<http://www.oxy.edu/~kareem/Janice.htm>
This page is offered by *Amerasia Journal*. It provides a good analysis of Janice Mirikitani's work.

Poetry — Janice Mirikitani

<http://members.spree.com/sip/beyondmarty/poets/mirikitani.htm>
This site offers a concise biographical sketch of the poet. It also posts her poem "Suicide Note."

N. SCOTT MOMADAY

<http://nativeauthors.com/search/bio/biomomaday.html>
The Native Authors site maintains this page. It provides a good biographical sketch, and helpful links.

JANICE TOWNLEY MOORE

ReadersNdex
<http://www.readersndex.com/imprint/0000027/00002qw/author.html>
This page provides a good biographical sketch of Moore. It also contains an interview with Moore on writing about food.

MARIANNE MOORE

The Academy of American Poets — Marianne Moore
<http://www.poets.org/poets/poets>
The academy's page on Moore provides biographical and bibliographical information, as well as links. It also posts the texts of poems by Moore.

Kenneth Burke and His Circles
<http://www.la.psu.edu/~jselzer/burke/table2.htm>
This site offers four papers on Moore. It also posts Moore's poem "Marriage."

Marianne Moore (1897–1972)
<http://www.cwrl.utexas.edu/~slatin/20c_poetry/projects/lives/mm.html>
The University of Texas's "Imagist Women" site maintains this page. It contains poems by Moore. "PAL: Marianne Moore"

Voices and Visions
<http://www.learner.org/catalog/literature/vvseries/vvspot/Moore.html>
This page is part of the "Voices and Visions" site. It offers a video presentation of Moore's poem "The Fish."

PAT MORA

<http://www.patmora.com/>
This is the official Pat Mora Home Page. It provides poetry by Mora, author information, and even a schedule of events.

PAUL MULDOON

New York State Writers Institute
<http://www.albany.edu/writers-inst/muldoon.html>
The New York State Writers Institute, where Muldoon has taught, offers this page. It provides a biographical sketch and short reviews of Muldoon's work.

Paul Muldoon Pages
<http://www.uni-leipzig.de/~angl/muldoon/muldoon.htm>
The University of Leipzig's English program maintains this page. It gives biographical information and links to Muldoon's poetry on the Web.

JOAN MURRAY

New York State Writers Institute
<http://www.albany.edu/writers-inst/murray.html>
The New York State Writers Institute, where Murray has taught, maintains this page. It offers a biographical sketch and short reviews of Murray's work.

PABLO NERUDA

The Nobel Prize Internet Archive
<http://www.almaz.com/nobel/literature/1971a.html>
This page is maintained by the Nobel Foundation. It gives biographical information on and poems by the 1971 winner of the Nobel Prize in Literature.

Pablo Neruda, 1904–1973
<http://www.kirjasto.sci.fi/neruda.htm>
This page provides extensive biographical and background information. It also has valuable links.

Pablo Neruda Poems
<http://www.lone-star.net/literature/pablo/index.html>
This site posts poems by Neruda translated by Nathaniel Tarn. The poems include Neruda's "Ode to the Book."

JOHN FREDERICK NIMS

John Frederick Nims 1913–1999
<http://www.poetrymagazine.org/nims_obit.html>
Poetry Magazine offers this page. It contains an obituary of Nims.

ALDEN NOWLAN

The Alden Nowlan Interviews
<http://www.unb.ca/qwerte/nowlan/>
This site contains extensive interviews of Nowlan. It also posts excerpts from his poetry.

SHARON OLDS

The Academy of American Poets — Sharon Olds
<http://www.poets.org/poets/poets>
The academy's page on Olds offers biographical and bibliographical information, as well as links. It also contains the texts of poems by Olds.

Poetry Daily
<http://www.poems.com/try-oold.htm>
This page is offered by Poetry Daily. It gives Olds's poem "The Try-Outs."

Sharon Olds (1942–)
<http://www.english.uiuc.edu/maps/poets/m_r/olds/olds.htm>
This is the Modern American Poetry Site's page on Olds. It gives critical perspectives on the poet's work, as well as an interview.

MARY OLIVER

Faculty — Mary Oliver
<http://www.bennington.edu/bencol2/faculty/oliver.html>
This site is maintained by Bennington College. It provides useful biographical and bibliographical information.

The Mary Oliver Page
<http://ppl.nhmccd.edu/~dcox/ohenry/oliver.html>
This is the offical Mary Oliver Home Page. It provides poems by Oliver and essays on the poet.

WILFRED OWEN

The Poems of Wilfred Owen
<http://www3.pitt.edu/~novosel/owen.html>
This page offers good biographical and bibliographical information. It also contains helpful links.

Wilfred Owen (1893–1918)
<http://www.cc.emory.edu/ENGLISH/LostPoets/Owen2.html>
Emory University maintains this page on Owen. It offers poems, as well as information on the poet and links.

The Wilfred Owen Association
<http://www.wilfred.owen.association.mcmail.com/>
This site includes excerpts from Owen's work, as well as essays on Owen. It also provides extensive Web links.

The Wilfred Owen Multimedia Digital Archive
<http://www.hcu.ox.ac.uk/jtap/>
The Owen archive contains extensive excerpts from Owen's work, as well background information. This site even offers film clips of WWI's western front.

LINDA PASTAN

Positively Poets: Linda Pastan
<http://www.91.cyberhost.net/alittlep/pastan.html>
This site provides a short profile of Pastan. It also posts her poem "Meditation by the Stove."

The Atlantic Poetry Pages
<http://www.theatlantic.com/unbound/poetry/antholog/pastan/deer.htm>
This page is part of the Atlantic Poetry Pages site. It give Pastan's poem "Deer" in text and in RealAudio.

OCTAVIO PAZ

Encyclopedia.com
<http://www.encyclopedia.com/articles/09933.html>
This page is Encylopedia.com's entry for Paz. It includes links to many relevant articles.

MOLLY PEACOCK

Poetry Society of America
<http://www.poetrysociety.org/officers.html>
This is the Poetry Society of America's site. Molly Peacock is a co-president of the society.

MARGE PIERCY

Marge Piercy Home Page
<http://www.capecod.net/~tmpiercy/>
This site provides helpful excerpts from Piercy's work. It also contains interviews, essays, and a schedule of readings.

Poems by Marge Piercy
<http://www.tear.com/poems/piercy/>
This site posts several poems by Piercy. Her poem "Bridging" should be of special interest.

SYLVIA PLATH

The Academy of American Poets — Sylvia Plath
<http://www.poets.org/poets/poets.cfm?prmID=11>
The academy's page on Plath gives good biographical and bibliographical information on Plath, as well as links. It also posts the texts of such poems as "Daddy" and "Lady Lazarus."

Rory's Sylvia Plath Page
<http://victorian.fortunecity.com/plath/500/main.htm>
This page offers poems by Plath and criticism of her work. It also provides good links.

Sylvia Plath (1932–1963)
<http://dte6.educ.ualberta.ca/nethowto_support/examples/j_welz/>
The University of Alberta maintains this page. It contains biographical information, poems, essays on Plath, and links.

Voices and Visions
<http://www.learner.org/catalog/literature/vvseries/vvspot/Plath.html>
This page is provided by the Voices and Visions site. It contains a video presentation of Plath's "Daddy," as well as extensive links.

Sylvia Plath (1932–1963)
<http://www.english.uiuc.edu/maps/poets/m_r/plath/plath.htm>
This is the Modern American Poetry Site's page on Plath. It contains many critiques of individual Plath poems.

EDGAR ALLAN POE

The Folio Club
<http://www.watershed.winnipeg.mb.ca/poefolio.html>
This is a page dedicated entirely to Poe. It gives a biographical sketch, excerpts from Poe's work, and student responses.

ALEXANDER POPE

<http://freemasonry.bc.ca/biography/pope_alex/alex_pope.html>
This site gives a short biographical sketch, excerpts from Pope's work in poetry and prose, and famous Pope quotations too.

Garden Visit
<http://www.gardenvisit.com/b/pope1.htm>
"Garden Visit" discusses Pope's influence on eighteenth-century English garden design. The page refers students to Pope's "Epistle to Lord Burlington."

San Antonio College LitWeb
<http://www.accd.edu/sac/english/bailey/18thcent.htm>
This is the Restoration and Eighteenth-Century English page from the LitWeb site. It contains selections from Pope's works. This page should be good for learning about the context of Pope's work.

EZRA POUND

The Academy of American Poets — Ezra Pound
<http://www.poets.org/poets/poets.cfm?prmID=162>
The academy's page on Pound provides good biographical and bibliographical information on the poet. It also posts numerous poems and links.

Electronic Poetry Center
<http://wings.buffalo.edu/epc/authors/pound/>
The Electronic Poetry Center at Buffalo University maintains this page on Pound. The page offers extensive links.

Kybernekia
<http://www.uncg.edu/eng/pound/canto.htm>
This page is offered by the University of North Carolina, Greensboro. It contains a Hypertext version of Pound's eighty-first canto.

Ezra Pound (1885–1972)
<http://www.lit.kobe-u.ac.jp/~hishika/pound.htm>
This site is maintained by Kobe University in Japan. It provides truly voluminous resources.

Voices and Visions
<http://www.learner.org/catalog/literature/vvseries/vvspot/Pound.html>
This page is part of the Voices and Visions site. It offers a video presentation of the eighty-first canto.

WYATT PRUNTY

Sewanee Review
<http://cloud9.sewanee.edu/sreview/Prunty101.1.39.html>
This page is part of the *Sewannee Review*'s site. It contains Prunty's poem "Blood."

Wyatt Prunty (June 1998)
<http://members.aol.com/poetrynet/month/archive/prunty/intro.html>
This page provides a helpful profile of Prunty. Topics include his childhood and his poetic technique.

ADRIENNE RICH

The Academy of American Poets — Adrienne Rich
<http://www.poets.org/poets/poets.cfm?prmID=50>
The academy's page on Rich offers good biographical and bibliographical information on the poet. It also contains poems and links.

Adrienne Rich (1929–)
<http://www.english.uiuc.edu/maps/poets/m_r/rich/rich.htm>
This is the Modern American Poetry Site's page on Rich. It offers valuable critical essays on the poet's work.

Adrienne Rich Home Page
<http://www.wilmington.org/poets/rich1.html>
This page is part of the Poets in Person series by Joseph Parisi. It provides a short biographical sketch and excerpts from Rich's work.

RAINER MARIA RILKE

Encyclopedia.com
<http://www.encyclopedia.com/articles/10995.html>
This page offers a brief biographical sketch of the German poet. The links to many helpful articles, however, are particularly valuable.

Rainer Maria Rilke
<http://cmgm.stanford.edu/~ahmad/rilke.html>
Stanford University maintains this site. It offers short Rilke poems translated by Stephen Mitchell.

Rainer Maria Rilke Web Site
<http://www.mtsu.edu/~dlavery/rmrind.htm>
This site offers quotations from Rilke, a photo gallery, and an essay on Rilke's poetics by David Lavery.

ALBERTO RÍOS

The Academy of American Poets — Alberto Ríos
<http://www.poets.org/poets/poets.cfm?prmID=51>
The academy's page on Ríos provides good biographical information, as well as links. It also posts his poem "The Cities Inside Us."

Discovering The Alphabet of Life
<http://researchmag.asu.edu/articles/alphabet.html>
Arizona State University has posted this article on Ríos by Sheilah Britton.

EDWIN ARLINGTON ROBINSON

Edward Arlington Robinson (1869–1935)
<http://www.okcom.net/~ggao/NorthAm/America/robinson1.html>
This site is dedicated to the American poet Edward Arlington Robinson. It posts Robinson's poem "Richard Cory."

LitWeb
<http://www.accd.edu/sac/english/bailey/amerlit2.http>
This page is the San Antonio College Litweb's American Literature index. The index provides work by Robinson and his contemporaries. This is a good site for getting contextual information on Robinson.

THEODORE ROETHKE

Ken Hope's Home Page
<http://www.northshore.net/homepages/hope/engRoethke.html>
This is a Web page dedicated to modern poetry. Three Roethke poems are posted here.

Theodore Roethke

<http://gawow.com/roethke/index.html>

This page provides excerpts from Roethke's work, as well as biographical information. Links to other relevant sites are also given.

The Academy of American Poets — Theodore Roethke

<http://www.poets.org/poets/poets.cfm?prmID=13>

The academy's page on Roethke gives a helpful biographical sketch, the text of several Roethke poems, and a bibliography. Useful links are posted at the bottom of the page.

CHRISTINA GEORGINA ROSSETTI

LitWeb

<http://www.accd.edu/sac/english/bailey/rossettc.htm>

This page is part of the San Antonio College's LitWeb. The page gives a helpful bibliography.

The Victorian Web

<http://landow.stg.brown.edu/victorian/crossetti/crov.html>

The Victorian Web is a good place to start research on Rossetti. This site provides essays on selected themes in Rossetti's work.

Sonnet Central

<http://www.sonnets.org/rossettc.htm>

This is a Web site devoted to the sonnet. Rossetti sonnets are posted here. Links to other sites are also given.

CARL SANDBURG

<http://www.poets.org/poets/poets.cfm?prmID=29>

The academy's page on Sandburg gives a biographical sketch, a bibliography, and helpful links. Sandburg poems such as "Fog" are also provided.

Carl Sandburg (1878–1967)

<http://www.english.uiuc.edu/maps/poets/s_z/sandburg/sandburg.htm>

This is the Modern American Poetry Site's page on Sandburg. The page posts essays on Sandburg and a useful bibliography.

SAPPHO

<http://cmgm.stanford.edu/~ahmad/sappho.html>

Stanford University oversees this site. They have posted Sappho poems in versions by various translators.

Sappho ca. 625 B.C.

<http://www.mala.bc.ca/~mcneil/sappho.htm>

This is the Malaspina Great Books Site's page on Sappho. This page provides numerous links and excerpts from Sappho's work.

Sappho Page

<http://www.temple.edu/classics/sappho.html>

"Sappho Page" is maintained by the Temple University Classics Department. Articles on Greek history and poetry make this a useful place to find background information on Sappho.

WILLIAM SHAKESPEARE

The Academy of American Poets — William Shakespeare

<http://www.poets.org/poets/poets.cfm?prmID=123>

The academy's Shakespeare page has posted biographical and bibliographical information, along with the text of several Shakespeare poems. This page's links make it a good place to start research on this most famous of poets.

The Atlantic Poetry Pages

<http://www.theatlantic.com/unbound/poetry/soundings/shakespeare.htm>
The Atlantic's Poetry Pages site provides, as part of its "Soundings" project, RealAudio clips of four contemporary poets (Mark Doty, Linda Gregorson, W. S. Merwin, and Lloyd Schwartz) reading Shakespeare's Sonnet 116. Gregorson writes an insightful introduction.

William Shakespeare (1554–1616)

<http://www.imagi-nation.com/moonstruck/clsc12.htm>
This site provides a concise biographical sketch and bibliographical information. Links to other relevant sites make this page particularly helpful.

The Stratford on Avon Guide to William Shakespeare

<http://www.stratford.co.uk/bard1.html>
This site provides biographical and historical context. The site is particularly interesting, however, for its information on Shakespeare-related events going on today.

The Life and Times of Mr. William Shakespeare

<http://www.gprc.ab.ca/courses_and_programs/en1010/shakespeare/>
This site gives excerpts from Shakespeare's work, and a synopsis of historical background relating to him. It also has posted a quiz to "test your Shakespeare I.Q."

PERCY BYSSHE SHELLEY

The Academy of American Poets — Percy Bysshe Shelley

<http://www.poets.org/poets/poets.cfm?prmID=182>
The academy's page provides biographical information, a bibliography, and useful links. The texts of Shelly poems such as "Ozymandias" are also given.

Project Bartleby

<http://www.bartleby.com/index.html>
This is Columbia University's Project Bartleby. It provides the complete works of Shelley online.

The Shelley Home Page

<http://www.geocities.com/Athens/Acropolis/8916/shelley.html>
The Shelley Home Page is dedicated to Percy Bysshe Shelley, Mary Shelly, and Mary Wollstonecraft. The site has posted works by Shelley, a bibliography, and links.

Percy Bysshe Shelley

<http://members.aol.com/ericblomqu/shelley.htm>
This page is maintained by Sonnet Central. It has posted several of Shelley's sonnets.

SIR PHILIP SIDNEY

<http://www.luminarium.org/renlit/sidney.htm>
This is Luminarium's Sidney page. The page provides poetry by Sidney, a biography, and articles on Sidney's poetry.

Bartleby.com

<http://www.bartleby.com/99/128.html>
This page is provided by Columbia University's Bartleby project. It has posted famous quotations by Philip Sidney.

CHARLES SIMIC

The Academy of American Poets — Charles Simic

<http://www.poets.org/poets/poets.cfm?prmID=28>
The academy's page on Simic gives a short biographical sketch, a bibliography, and plenty of helpful links. It also posts the texts of Simic poems such as "The White Room."

The Cortland Review

<http://www.cortlandreview.com/issuefour/>
The *Cortland Review*'s fourth issue contains an interview with Simic. Poems by Simic are also posted on this Web page.

An Interview with Charles Simic
<http://student-www.uchicago.edu/orgs/literary-review/106/Pages-10-11.16.html>
The University of Chicago has posted this informative interview with Charles Simic. Nicolas Patterson is the interviewer.

LOUIS SIMPSON

<http://www.poets.org/poets/poets.cfm?prmID=87>
The academy's page on Simpson gives a biographical sketch, a bibliography, and links to other relevant places. The texts of such Simpson poems as "Honeymoon" are also provided.

Two Poems
<http://www.cortlandreview.com/issue/9/simpson9.htm>
The *Cortland Review* has posted both the French version of François Villon's "Ballade des Dames de Temps Jadis" and Simpson's translation of it. The page provides RealAudio clips of Simpson reading both the French and the English.

DAVID R. SLAVITT

The Cortland Review
<http://www.cortlandreview.com/issue/7/slavitt7.htm>
The *Cortland Review*'s seventh issue contains Slavitt's poem "Readers." A RealAudio clip of Slavitt reading the poem is also available.

ERNEST SLYMAN

The Poet Watch
<http://www.geocities.com/SoHo/7514/>
This is Ernest Slyman's own home page. The page provides numerous links to other poetry-related sites.

CATHY SONG

<http://www.geocities.com/SoHo/7514/>
This page is provided by Baylor University's Beall Poetry Festival Site. It gives a concise biographical sketch of Cathy Song.

GARY SOTO

The Academy of American Poets — Gary Soto
<http://www.poets.org/poets/poets.cfm?prmID=234>
The academy's Gary Soto page gives a biographical sketch, a bibliography, and links. It also provides the text of Soto's poem "Mission Tire Factory, 1969."

Gary Soto Home Page
<http://www.wilmington.org/poets/soto.html>
This page is a part of "Poets in Person," edited by Joseph Parisi. The site is valuable for the sound clip it provides of Soto reading from his work.

ROBERT SOUTHEY

The Robert Southey Page
<http://www.accd.edu/sac/english/bailey/southey.htm>
Maintained by the San Antonio College's LitWeb, this page gives a comprehensive bibliography of Southey's works and a selection of excerpts. The page also contains relevant links.

WOLE SOYINKA

Biography of Wole Soyinka
<http://www.nobel.se/laureates/literature-1986-1-bio.html>
This site is maintained by the Nobel Foundation. It gives a valuable biographical sketch of Soyinka, who won the Nobel Prize for Literature in 1986.

Conversation with Wole Soyinka
<http://globetrotter.berkeley.edu/Elberg/Soyinka/soyinka-con0.html>
This page, from the University of California, Berkeley, has posted informative interviews with Soyinka. The interviews are available in text and in RealAudio.

Wole Soyinka: An Overview
<http://landow.stg.brown.edu/post/soyinka/soyinkaov.html>
This page, maintained by Brown University, provides extensive critical material on Soyinka. Topics include African history and religion. A bibliography is also given.

WILLIAM STAFFORD

News from Nowhere
<http://www.newsfromnowhere.com/whenbilldied.html>
This page is provided by the "news from nowhere" site. It posts a poem by Robert Bly that elegizes Stafford.

Plains Poet, William Stafford
<http://www.uakron.edu/english/palmer/staff.html>
This site is maintained by the University of Akron. It gives a brief biographical sketch of Stafford and links to his poems.

TIMOTHY STEELE

About Timothy Steele
<http://curriculum.calstatela.edu/faculty/tsteele/TSpage4/page4.html>
This site provides helpful biographical and bibliographical information on Steele. It also posts some of Steele's poems and articles about the poet.

In the Spotlight
<http://www.calstatela.edu/academic/al/spotlight.html>
This site is maintained by California State University, Los Angeles. It gives a helpful biographical sketch of Timothy Steele and also posts one of his poems.

WALLACE STEVENS

The Academy of American Poets — Wallace Stevens
<http://www.poets.org/poets/poets.cfm?prmID=125>
The academy's Stevens page gives biographical and bibliographical information, as well as helpful links. The page also posts the texts of several of Stevens's poems.

The Poetry of Wallace Stevens
<http://roderickscott.tripod.com/wally/index.html>
This page posts biographical information on Stevens and a selection of his poems. The index provides an especially useful bibliography.

Wallace Stevens
<http://www.english.upenn.edu/~afilreis/Stevens/home.html>
This page provides the text of several poems by Stevens and concise biographical information. Excerpts from letters, obituaries, and friends' anecdotes make this page especially valuable.

Wallace Stevens (1879–1955)
<http://www.english.uiuc.edu/maps/poets/s_z/stevens/stevens.htm>
This is the Modern American Poetry Site's page on Stevens. The page posts numerous critiques on Stevens's poems and excerpts from his letters.

MAY SWENSON

The Academy of American Poets — May Swenson
<http://www.poets.org/poets/poets.cfm?prmID=170>
The academy's page offers biographical and bibliographical information on Swenson, as well as relevant links. The page also posts the text to Swenson's poem "Blue."

Washington Post
<http://www.washingtonpost.com/wp-srv/style/books/features/19980913.htm>
This page is provided by the *Washington Post*'s "Poet's Choice" site. It contains a discussion of May Swenson's poem "Question" by the poet Robert Hass, as well as the poem itself.

WISLAWA SZYMBORSKA

Wislawa Szymborska's Home Page
<http://www.polishworld.com/wsz/>
This page on Szymborska is provided by Polish World. It contains poems by Szymborska, biographical information, and useful articles about the poet.

ALFRED, LORD TENNYSON

<http://www.clarkeweb.com/tennyson/>
This site is maintained by Joe Clarke. It contains poems by Tennyson, biographical information, and useful links.

Alfred, Lord Tennyson: An Overview
<http://landow.stg.brown.edu/victorian/tennyson/tennyov.html>
This is the Victorian Web's page on Tennyson. It contains helpful essays on themes in Tennyson's work. This site should be particularly valuable for finding background information on Tennyson.

The Alfred, Lord Tennyson Page
<http://www.accd.edu/sac/english/bailey/tennyson.htm>
This is the page on Tennyson provided by the San Antonio College's LitWeb. The page has posted a bibliography and links to relevant Web sites.

DYLAN THOMAS

The Academy of American Poets — Dylan Thomas
<http://www.poets.org/poets/poets>
The academy's page gives biographical and bibliographical information on Thomas. The site also posts valuable links and the texts of many of Thomas's poems.

The Craft and Art of Dylan Thomas
<http://www.geocities.com/SoHo/Studios/6433/BoatHouse.html>
This page posts a number of poems by Thomas, as well as biographical information. Helpful links are also provided.

The Craft and Sullen Art of Dylan Thomas
<http://pcug.org.au/~wwhatman/DylanThomas/dylan.html>
This site gives a large proportion of Thomas's work, as well as biographical and bibliographical information. The site is particularly helpful for the sound clips of Thomas reading his work.

ALICE WALKER

<http://www.cwrl.utexas.edu/~mmaynard/Walker/walker.htm>
This page is maintained by the University of Texas. It gives a good biographical sketch of Walker, a bibliography, and links to other relevant sites.

Creative Quotations from Alice Walker
<http://www.bemorecreative.com/one/301.htm>
This page is maintained by the "Be More Creative" site. It collects quotations from Walker's work.

Encyclopedia.com
<http://www.encyclopedia.com/articles/13597.html>
This is Encyclopedia.com's page on Alice Walker. It contains a brief biographical sketch and a number of helpful articles.

WALT WHITMAN

The Academy of American Poets — Walt Whitman
<http://www.poets.org/poets/poets.cfm?prmID=127>
The academy's Whitman page provides biographical and bibliographical information and many valuable links. The page also posts the texts of several poems by Whitman.

As I Ebb'd with the Ocean of Life
<http://www.theatlantic.com/unbound/poetry/soundings/whitman.htm>
This page is provided by the Atlantic Monthly's Poetry Pages. It gives RealAudio files of Whitman's poem as read by the poets Frank Bidart, Marie Howe, and Galway Kinnell. The poet Steven Cramer's introduction is particularly informative.

Poet at Work
<http://lcweb2.loc.gov/ammem/wwhome.html>
This page is maintained by the Library of Congress. It contains the text of rare Whitman documents from the Thomas Biggs Harned Walt Whitman Collection.

Reminiscences of Walt Whitman
<http://www.theatlantic.com/unbound/poetry/whitman/walt.htm>
This page is provided by the Atlantic Monthly's Poetry Pages. It gives the text of an article by John Townsend Trowbridge originally published by the *Atlantic* in 1902. Trowbridge remembers his meetings with Whitman.

The Walt Whitman Hypertext Archive
<http://jefferson.village.Virginia.EDU/whitman/>
This page provides biographical and bibliographical information on Whitman. The main feature of the page, however, is a hypertext presentation of Whitman's work that compares different drafts of the same poems. This page should be valuable to anyone doing research on Whitman.

RICHARD WILBUR

The Academy of American Poets — Richard Wilbur
<http://www.poets.org/poets/poets.cfm?prmID=206>
The academy's site gives useful biographical and bibliographical information on Wilbur. It also provides helpful links and the texts of several poems by Wilbur.

C. K. WILLIAMS

Grief
<http://mchip00.nyu.edu/lit-med/lit-med-db/webdocs/webdescrips/williams1144-des-.html>
This page is maintained by New York University. It provides a concise summary and discussion of Williams' poem "Grief."

Online NewsHour
<http://www.pbs.org/newshour/bb/entertainment/jan-june00/williams_4-19.html>
This page is offered by Online NewsHour. The page contains an interview with Williams conducted by Elizabeth Farnsworth. Williams discusses the development of his work and his having won the Pulitzer Prize.

MILLER WILLIAMS

Online NewsHour
<http://www.pbs.org/newshour/bb/entertainment/jan-june97/williams_1-16.html>
This page is offered by Online NewsHour. The page contains an interview with Miller Williams conducted before he read his inaugural poem. The interview is available in RealAudio.

WILLIAM CARLOS WILLIAMS

Amy Munno's William Carlos Williams Page
<http://www.webspan.net/~amunno/wcw.html>
This page presents selected poems by Williams that were inspired by paintings. The page also offers images of the paintings.

The Academy of American Poets — William Carlos Williams
<http://www.poets.org/poets/poets.cfm?prmID=120>
The academy's Williams page contains biographical and bibliographical information and many valuable links. Texts of poems by Williams are also provided.

Voices and Visions
<http://www.learner.org/catalog/literature/vvseries/vvspot/Williams.html>
This page is offered by the Voices and Visions site. On this page you can view a video based on Williams's poem "The Great Figure."

Williams Carlos Williams
<http://www.gale.com/freresrc/poets_cn/wilmsbio.htm>
This page is provided by the Gale Group. The page gives a good biographical sketch of Williams and is particularly useful for posting links to sites on other poets in Williams's circle.

William Carlos Williams (1883–1963)
<http://www.english.uiuc.edu/maps/poets/s_z/williams/williams.htm>
This page is provided by the Modern American Poetry site. It contains numerous critiques of individual poems by Williams and aspects of his work.

WILLIAM WORDSWORTH

Project Bartleby
<http://www.bartleby.com/index.html>
This site is Project Bartleby, a vast literature archive provided by Columbia University. It has posted the "Complete Poetical Works" of Wordsworth.

The Romantics Page
<http://www.unm.edu/~garyh/romantic/romantic.html>
The Romantics Page is maintained by the University of New Mexico. It provides a number of resources related to William Wordsworth.

William Wordsworth
<http://www.kirjasto.sci.fi/wordswor.htm>
This page has posted a good biographical profile of Wordsworth. The bibliography and links on this page should also be helpful.

William Wordsworth 1770–1850
<http://citd.scar.utoronto.ca/English/ENGB02Y/Wordsworth.html>
This page is offered by the University of Toronto. It gives a short biographical sketch, a selection of poems, and a discussion of Wordsworth's poetics.

The William Wordsworth Page
<http://www.accd.edu/sac/english/bailey/wordswor.htm>
The William Wordsworth Page is part of the San Antonio College's LitWeb. It gives an extensive bibliography and useful links.

WILLIAM BUTLER YEATS

The Academy of American Poets — W. B. Yeats
<http://www.poets.org/poets/poets>
This is the Academy of American Poets' page on Yeats. It contains biographical and bibliographical information, links, and the texts of several poems by Yeats.

The Nobel Prize Internet Archive
<http://nobelprizes.com/nobel/literature/1923a.html>
This site is offered by the Nobel Foundation. It contains an informative biographical profile and numerous links.

Soundings — Easter 1916
<http://www.theatlantic.com/unbound/poetry/soundings/yeats.htm>
This page is part of the Atlantic's Poetry Pages. It provides audio clips of three American poets (Peter Davison, Philip Levine, and Richard Wilbur) reading Yeats's poem "Easter 1916." A concise introduction is written by the poet David Barber.

William Butler Yeats
<http://www.gale.com/freresrc/poets_cn/yeatsbio.htm>
This page is provided by the Gale Group. It gives a helpful biographical sketch of Yeats that describes themes in his poetry.

William Butler Yeats — Louise Bogan
<http://www.theatlantic.com/unbound/poetry/yeats/bogan.htm>
This page has posted an obituary of Yeats written by the poet Louise Bogan and originally printed in 1938. The obituary provides useful information on Yeats's life and work.

Literature Aloud

Literature Aloud — available as either a cassette or a CD — features the work of poets treated in depth (Dickinson, Frost, and Hughes); poems that serve as excellent examples of the elements of poetry discussed in the text (sound, imagery, rhythm, form, and so on); and, finally, a rich selection of classic and contemporary poems.

Regina Barreca, *Nighttime Fires* (Chapter 1, p. 26)
Elizabeth Bishop, *The Fish* (Chapter 1, p. 20)
Robert Bly, *Snowbanks North of the House* (Chapter 6, p. 150)
Gwendolyn Brooks, *The Mother* (Collection of Poems, p. 595)
Gwendolyn Brooks, *We Real Cool* (Chapter 3, p. 81)
E. E. Cummings, *next to of course god america i* (Chapter 6, p. 146)
Emily Dickinson, *I heard a Fly buzz — when I died —* (Chapter 12, p. 307)
Emily Dickinson, *Presentiment — is that long Shadow — on the lawn —* (Chapter 5, p. 116)
Emily Dickinson, *There's a certain Slant of light* (Chapter 20, p. 538)
Emily Dickinson, *What Soft — Cherubic Creatures —* (Chapter 12, p. 302)
Emily Dickinson, *Wild Nights — Wild Nights!* (Chapter 12, p. 300)
John Donne, *The Flea* (Collection of Poems, p. 605)
John Donne, *The Sun Rising* (Chapter 1, p. 42)
T. S. Eliot, *The Love Song of J. Alfred Prufrock* (Chapter 15, p. 405)
Robert Frost, *Acquainted with the Night* (Chapter 6, p. 139)
Robert Frost, *After Apple-Picking* (Chapter 13, p. 346)
Robert Frost, *Birches* (Chapter 13, p. 347)
Robert Frost, *Mending Wall* (Chapter 13, p. 342)
Donald Hall, *Letter with No Address* (Collection of Poems, p. 673)
Anthony Hecht, *The Dover Bitch* (Collection of Poems, p. 609)
Langston Hughes, *Dream Variations* (Chapter 14, p. 380)
Langston Hughes, *Harlem* (Chapter 14, p. 391)
Langston Hughes, *Negro* (Chapter 14, p. 377)
Langston Hughes, *The Negro Speaks of Rivers* (Chapter 14, p. 372)
Langston Hughes, *The Weary Blues* (Chapter 14, p. 380)
John Keats, *La Belle Dame sans Merci* (Collection of Poems, p. 618)
Aron Keesbury, *Song to a Waitress* (Chapter 8, p. 218)
X. J. Kennedy, *A Visit from St. Sigmund* (Chapter 9, p. 247)
Jane Kenyon, *The Blue Bowl* (Chapter 4, p. 106)
Galway Kinnell, *After Making Love We Hear Footsteps* (Chapter 10, p. 255)
Galway Kinnell, *Blackberry Eating* (Chapter 7, p. 176)
Etheridge Knight, *A Watts Mother Mourns while Boiling Beans* (Collection of Poems, p. 620)
Kathryn Howd Machan, *Hazel Tells LaVerne* (Chapter 3, p. 61)
Sharon Olds, *Rite of Passage* (Chapter 10, p. 265)
Linda Pastan, *Marks* (Chapter 5, p. 132)
Theodore Roethke, *My Papa's Waltz* (Chapter 8, p. 217)

William Shakespeare, *My mistress' eyes are nothing like the sun* (Chapter 9, p. 229)
William Shakespeare, *Shall I compare thee to a summer's day?* (Chapter 9, p. 228)
William Shakespeare, *When forty winters shall besiege thy brow* (Collection of Poems, p. 636)
Gary Soto, *Black Hair* (Collection of Poems, p. 637)
Dylan Thomas, *Do not go gentle into that good night* (Chapter 9, p. 233)
Richard Wilbur, *Love Calls Us to the Things of This World* (Collection of Poems, p. 643)
William Carlos Williams, *The Red Wheelbarrow* (Chapter 10, p. 257)
William Butler Yeats, *That the Night Come* (Chapter 8, p. 207)

ORDERING INFORMATION

Literature Aloud is available to adopters of *Poetry: An Introduction,* Third Edition. To obtain a copy, please contact your local Bedford/St. Martin's sales representative or call 1-800-446-8923.

Index